Exploring Norms and Family Laws across the Globe

Exploring Norms and Family Laws across the Globe

Edited by
Melissa L. Breger

LEXINGTON BOOKS
Lanham • Boulder • New York • London

Published by Lexington Books
An imprint of The Rowman & Littlefield Publishing Group, Inc.
4501 Forbes Boulevard, Suite 200, Lanham, Maryland 20706
www.rowman.com

86-90 Paul Street, London EC2A 4NE, United Kingdom

British Library Cataloguing in Publication Information Available

Library of Congress Cataloging-in-Publication Data Available

ISBN 9781793618351 (cloth) | ISBN 9781793618368 (electronic)

This book is dedicated to my own family

Contents

Acknowledgments

I am tremendously grateful to the 20 contributors who helped create and launch this book on comparative family law. Each chapter provides a window into the world of a particular issue in different jurisdictions. It has been a joy and a labor of love to work alongside these scholars over the past two years plus. I have so enjoyed collaborating with them and learning from them. When I first envisioned this book in 2019, I had no idea how much I would treasure the work and the connections to these scholars along the way. I am already planning future collaborations.

Thank you so much to Rowman & Littlefield and Lexington Books, particularly Becca Rohde Beurer, managing editor and associate acquisitions editor. I thank you for accepting my book proposal so quickly and with such encouragement. Thank you also to Carter Moran, acquisitions assistant, for your support and feedback on finalizing the manuscript. Thank you both for guiding me through my first edited collection—an often Byzantine and complicated route indeed.

A special thank you to my amazing research assistants from Albany Law School, who helped mold this book throughout its evolving process, most notably Madison Forsander, Elizabeth Getz, and Daniel Schmidt. My appreciation to Sherri Anne Meyer for her endless charts, organizational skills, and formatting help. Thank you so much to our Schaffer Law Library director at Albany Law School, Professor David Walker. And a heartfelt thank you to Albany Law School itself for granting me a sabbatical so that I could complete this book project with the time and attention it required.

A thank you is owed to my dear husband (Tom) and two children (Kalyn and Bezyn) who patiently accommodated my need to focus so much of my energy into this work. I owe gratitude to my loving parents, siblings, and friends who have steadfastly supported my work and my scholarly endeavors for decades.

Most importantly, I will always hold dear the countless beautiful children and women I represented in the courtroom. Each client has greatly inspired and validated my lifelong dedication to the many issues of family and juvenile law. It is because of you that I hope to contribute further to the field of family law, where it all began.

Introduction

Melissa L. Breger

Family law. Global norms. Society.

The law of the family.

Tying these concepts together has been a fascinating journey and a labor of love.

Family law is by its nature extremely broad and expansive. Few areas of the law reach both the breadths and the depths of family law, while simultaneously touching upon such truly fundamental and deeply personal issues.

This book is a compilation of significant topics in global and modern family law. Each chapter delves into topics integral to family law jurisprudence and serves as a novel examination into a deep slice of family law. Together, the 4 parts and 16 chapters create a melodious and intriguing examination of groundbreaking and cutting-edge areas of law in the realm of the family.

The chapters can be read individually as stand-alone works, as each is centered around a different theme of family law. The chapters can also be read as parts, which consist of a group of four related chapters. Or the book can enjoyably be read cover to cover.

The four parts primarily focus upon a major family law topic with the authors examining the laws across jurisdictions, cross-nationally, or in some cases intra-jurisdictionally. It is through this comparative lens that we see how family law concepts are woven into the fabric of overall society around the globe.

Contemporary global family law questions linger: What makes up the composition of a family under the law? Should its dissolution or intended disentanglement be a function of the law? What about the children intertwined in such families? What is the law's role in assigning and dissolving parental rights? How does the legal system influence family structures and behavior? The authors will seek to answer these questions and more.

In this book, I endeavor to distill family law down to its essence and core, addressing how families are formed, then dissolved, and at times re-created. Thus, it makes tremendous sense to begin the discussion of family law with an exploration of the union of two adult individuals in some kind of intimate relationship (e.g., marriage, civil union, domestic partnership, dating, cohabitating). It then seems that we could imagine such a relationship bearing children through some form (e.g., birth, adoption, assisted reproduction) and begin to address the issue of parenting. We would then naturally flow to focusing upon those children, along with their rights and needs. After which, we would sum up with overarching ideas of family law systems and culture.

Therefore, part I talks about adult intimate relationships that may or may not bear children, but ought to be recognized regardless of gender, sexuality, gender preferences, identity, composition, household, or the like. Countries across the globe do not universally agree on whether and how courts should view functional families, often leaning toward more formalistic definitions. This part has four brilliant chapters exploring the law, its consequences, and the social norms of adult intimate relationships across the globe.

Part II then delves into parenting norms, and how the law can and should play a role. Whether it is through the child welfare system or the regulation of homeschooling, how the courts govern parenting through a gender-focused prism, or by analyzing laws within the realm of adoption, the authors explore the issues deeply. This part has four exceptional chapters for readers to learn about the tensions and balances in family law which regulate the area of parenthood.

Part III then addresses the children themselves. What are children's rights to be free of violence, whether family violence or structural violence? What about their special educational and medical needs? What about having their voices truly heard in the courtroom and beyond? Another four excellent chapters form this part and situate children in the legal setting.

Finally, part IV and its fascinating four chapters cover the overarching premises and the underlying themes of family law. When should the law begin to regulate a "child" and would that include gametes? What about transgender families? How do some countries, such as Ethiopia, approach family law? What can we learn from the post-apartheid systems and the anti-carceral systems regarding the right to parent a child without the law severing that relationship? This part conveys concepts of culture and norms and legal systems to bring the whole weight of family law into focus.

Notably, parts II and III are intertwined and intrinsically related, as they both focus upon the intersection of governments, parenting, and children. In fact, it was often a challenge to determine which chapter should be placed in which part. So many of the chapters, including my own, easily spanned several categories. The parts are there to organize the 16 chapters for the reader, but by no means should they be seen as silos. There are overlaps and synergies that do not lend themselves to being placed squarely into the four parts. Those synergies reflect the complex interconnectedness of the themes in the book. As just one example, the chapters written by Professor Kennedy, Bartholet, Gupta-Kagan, Seymore, and others could have just as easily fit in part III, as they fit in II or IV.

This book delves deeply into core basics of family law, while interweaving the concept of social norms as a prevalent common thread. In terms of family law, it is especially instructive to observe and learn about families and norms globally, because family law is constantly evolving. This area of the law changes as society itself changes. As leading comparative family law scholar Harry Krause notes:

> For all their very real differences, nations around the world find themselves facing fundamentally similar dilemmas in defining and regulating the modern family. Accordingly, it makes sense to take stock of what has been tried and what has—or has not—worked elsewhere.[1]

While exploring family laws across the globe, the book stays rooted in the concepts of social norms. Social norms are the attitudes and rules and behavioral expectations within society about what ought to be done and what ought not to be done. The idea that law reflects normative social attitudes, and then social attitudes reflect law, braids throughout the chapters as a common theoretical thread. Laws are created to reflect new norms, and new norms influence courts and legislation, particularly in the field of family law. By utilizing socio-legal principles such as social norms as theoretical underpinnings, the authors offer novel perspectives on ways that norms within family law may be changed over time. Societal norms inform family law, and in turn, family law informs societal norms.

This book includes chapters from some of the world's leading family law scholars, as well as from some bright and emerging scholars, all of whom are endeavoring to answer the above questions and beyond.

More specifically, part I looks into the international norms and laws that govern intimate relationships. Here, we explore what it means to be in a relationship that is sanctified (or not) by the national laws. What are the tensions between how the government tries to regulate some relationships, as well as those relationships it chooses not to acknowledge? Through expert analysis of various states and countries, the authors in part I explore whether or not marriage should be the ultimate goal, and how the law should support options outside of marriage.

As Dr. Wells-Greco questions in chapter 3:

> Should the law perhaps instead look to the reality of lived relationships rather than whether or not a particular set of formalities have been followed (whether in accordance with civil or religious norms)? Arguably protection from exploitation or unjust disadvantage would be better served by the law looking in most cases to the relationship not the ceremony. The purpose of family law is to determine the responsibilities of individuals to each other and the responsibilities of families and the state and the community to each other and those responsibilities lie primarily within the family unit. . . . The law has a very specific and concrete role to play. While the law is only one tool, it is a critical one as it signals to society at large what is and is not acceptable within the law.

Professors Naomi Cahn and June Carbone start off our journey in chapter 1 by exploring the legal regulation of unmarried relationships. They recognize that nonmarital cohabitation has become so widespread in North America and Europe over the last half century that it has changed from a once legally stigmatized status to a now legally accepted status. Chapter 1 notes factors that often contribute to the legal treatment of nonmarital cohabitation including religion, education, and social norms. Cahn and Carbone outline four approaches that countries have applied to intimate couples' relationships: (1) formal marriage, (2) marriage by imposition, (3) legally recognized marriage, and (4) an ad hoc approach. Cahn and Carbone examine how changing demographics of nonmarital cohabitation are affecting the United States and its states' varying responses to the economic rights of such cohabitants, while providing the reader with comparative information about other countries, such as the Canadian provinces and France. Often, the law of cohabitation is simultaneously in dialogue and in tension with the laws of marriage. As Cahn and Carbone expertly examine patterns in the United States and in European countries and Canada, they lay the groundwork for the next three chapters in the part and provide us with a sense of the landscape of the laws governing intimate relationships.

Our second chapter on intimate relationships is written by Dr. Andy Hayward. In chapter 2, Hayward explores how liberal a variety of countries are when granting legal protections to nonmarital families. These protections include offerings such as registered partnerships and alternatives, or functional equivalents to marriage for couples, including same-sex couples. Hayward questions if these nonmarital offerings broaden the social concept of marriage and embrace broader conceptions of family recognition, or just problematically replicate and reinforce marital norms. These nonmarital labels are often implicitly grounded in marriage and are judicially interpreted through a marital lens. Hayward draws upon the nonmarital regimes in England and Wales and questions whether there are dangers associated with viewing registered partnerships as capable of facilitating broader relationship recognition. Chapter 2 posits that potential exists for creativity and greater distinctiveness by demonstrating the experience of England and Wales as an interesting example of how civil partnerships are not static and can evolve over time. Ultimately, the recognition of a plurality of interpersonal relationships is ideal.

This segues perfectly to chapter 3 by Dr. Michael Wells-Greco, who also situates his writing in England and Wales and focuses upon the dangers of their law's non-recognition of certain relationships. He raises concerns about English law not legitimizing certain types of marriages, such as *nikah*, proxy, non-age, polygamous, and consanguineous relationships. He analyzes the legal position of foreign Islamic marriages under English law, the surrounding public policy considerations, and the impact of European human-rights standards upon the law's recognition and non-recognition of relationships. Wells-Greco focuses on the societal importance of families and the law surrounding families, and how non-recognition impacts family matters. Chapter 3 considers where the balance lies in upholding marriages entered into in good faith and upon personal and religious beliefs versus the law declaring such relationships as nonexistent for judicial purposes. Wells-Greco further considers the extent to which family law can inform societal norms regarding marriage.

This leads us seamlessly into chapter 4, which focuses specifically on the formation of the matrimonial bond and how it is established in the family laws in the country of Algeria. We learn from Professor Nahas Mahieddin's chapter about the sociocultural and historical Islamic influences in Algeria. In Algeria, the concepts of family and marriage have been based on Islam for over 10 centuries, before and after French colonization. He explains how colonization impacted the Algerian identity and the laws, while Algerian family law still maintained connections to the Arab and Muslim culture. In particular, Mahieddin explores the idea of consent to marriage and the conditions necessary for marriage, as well as matrimonial guardianship in Algeria. Chapter 4 presents the evolution of family laws, specifically marriage, in Algeria over multiple decades.

After reading part I, which truly delves into the nuances of intimate partnerships in myriad forms, we then move to part II. Part II imagines that at least some of these intimate partnerships have resulted in children, and analyzes how the law now regulates that parentage.

We hear first from Josh Gupta-Kagan in chapter 5. Professor Gupta-Kagan contrasts the U.S. child welfare laws and policies with the laws and policies of Nordic countries regarding foster care and adoption. He posits that, despite the United States offering stronger legal protection for parental rights, a focus on quickly arriving at a permanent legal resolution to problematic family situations has resulted in significantly more frequent termination of parental rights and state-mandated adoption. While Nordic countries lack the strong legal protections of parental rights present in the United States, their focus on providing the child stability rather than a permanent legal resolution results in more long-term foster care and less frequent severing of parental rights. Gupta-Kagan's well-researched chapter points out how the United States' adversarial and coercive system differs from the Nordic countries strong safety net for parents, which rarely results in termination of parental rights even when the parents and children cannot reunify. Gupta-Kagan then compares new developments in the United States and in Nordic countries and posits that the two are converging to some degree. Furthermore, chapter 5 tackles pertinent issues of racial diversity as it relates to parental rights—an historically fraught issue in the United States and a relatively new and growing one in the Nordic countries. We revisit some of these issues again in our final chapter, chapter 16.

In chapter 6, Professor Malinda Seymore urges us to imagine adoption as an addition to a family, not an erasure. Chapter 6 contrasts United States' policy with cultural norms and laws around the world, exploring adoption in indigenous cultures in the South Pacific, the practice of raising children outside the home in a particular tribe in Benin, Africa, Muslim laws and norms, and the history of and evolving trends in French law. France practices two forms of legal adoption: plenary adoption, which subtracts the biological family and replaces them with the adoptive family, and simple adoption, which preserves the biological family's rights while adding legal rights to the adoptive family. Traditional adoption in the United States has thus far focused upon the former, yet it is in flux, encouraging increased openness. By applying the language and standards of international agreements like the United Nations Convention on the Rights of the Child (CRC) and the Hague Convention on Intercountry Adoption, and by considering the conclusions of the relevant social science literature, Seymore strongly argues that adoption should be seen as addition instead of erasure, allowing continuing contact between birth parents and adoptive families. A growing body of empirical research shows that openness in adoption benefits adopted persons, and in the case of transracial adoption, openness facilitates racial identity formation.

The next chapter is written by Professor Daphna Hacker. Chapter 7 challenges the problematic discourse of father's rights groups who are seeking to change the family laws in Israel. The chapter shines a light on the gap between what the law states in terms of child custody and child support, contrasted with what social workers, judges, and lawyers promote in terms of joint physical custody and shared child support duty. Hacker explains that fake news and discursive violence promoted by Israeli fathers' groups portray fathers as the victims of the family legal system. Chapter 7 opens up new and important questions regarding the formation of legal norms when rational discussion is too often compromised by lies and threats. She persuasively argues that empirical evidence demonstrates how in reality, Israeli judicial activism is extreme in comparison to other jurisdictions, both in its push toward equal parental time and economic responsibility, and in the gap between the actual gender labor division among Israeli families.

We finish part II with an intriguing exposé into the world of homeschooling, which is surprisingly unregulated in the United States. Without regulations there are a number of concerns such as total parental power, child maltreatment, harmful parental ideologies, and lack of children's rights. In chapter 8, Professor Elizabeth Bartholet asserts that parents who homeschool are largely free to abuse their children, free from the eyes of teachers and others mandated to report suspected maltreatment to child protection services. Bartholet contrasts the United States' model with other countries, some of which ban homeschooling altogether. Those countries which do allow homeschooling regulate it relatively strictly to ensure that children receive education comparable to those provided in the public schools. Bartholet posits that this contrast is in part because other countries have a stronger tradition of children's rights and accord less deference to parental power to determine their children's lives and futures. This powerful chapter argues for a transformation in the understanding of child rights in the United States and a related transformation in the legal regime surrounding homeschooling. Bartholet proposes solutions, restrictions, and laws for the United States to consider adopting.

The exploration into the CRC in part II then perfectly flows into part III of our book, which explores how the child is situated within the larger legal system. This part offers an even deeper dive into the CRC. While in the past paternalism and parental control characterized how society and the law constructed the parent-child relationship, more recently we have seen a much stronger focus on child rights discourse, child autonomy, and child empowerment. Exploring key modern disputes in this context, part III explores how to find the correct balance between the competing, and sometimes irreconcilable, interests of parents, children, and the state. Notably, many have surmised that the way a government treats its children is a useful indicator of its fortitude. Even in the face of international treaties and court cases bestowing upon children a panoply of rights, many child rights remain unrecognized globally.

Chapter 9, our first chapter in part III, is my own cowritten chapter penned with my amazing coauthors Professors Lucy Sorensen, Victor Asal, and Charmaine Willis. This interdisciplinary chapter investigates theories of re-norming and the social norms approach, pertaining specifically to corporal punishment of children by parents in the home, with original empirical cross-national data. We meticulously examine 200 country's CRC reports, along with other reporting, and we note patterns of global norms pertaining to corporal punishment against children in the home. We suggest that a norm cascade—a rapid shift toward a new social norm—may have occurred once Sweden abolished corporal punishment in the home, and then neighboring countries followed suit. A basic premise of chapter 9 is that corporal punishment by parental figures is physically and psychologically traumatic for children. It presents ideas about how to change social norms in countries where it is still prevalent.

In chapter 10, Dr. Jessica Corsi similarly relies upon the CRC in a thought-provoking way. Corsi invites us to view systemic issues, such as poverty, as violence to children due to the harm it causes them ("structural violence"). Data from social science literature notes that structural violence, such as poverty, is a driver of interpersonal violence against children (VAC). The law regarding VAC, however, often emphasizes individual and familial factors, ignoring links to the structure. Utilizing the CRC and English law as examples, Corsi analyzes the ways in which legal approaches to VAC are disconnected from evidence that poverty is linked to VAC. Corsi displays the link between poverty and violence against children and exposes how legal approaches to VAC have failed to recognize this connection. She ultimately suggests that legal approaches could offer greater legal protection against VAC through a novel Rights-Poverty-Violence framework that reimagines current legal approaches. Rather than having the law address the child protection and poverty alleviation fields separately, the framework she designed can offer greater legal protection by addressing these issues jointly.

Chapter 11 is written by Dr. Michelle Fernando, who additionally explores the CRC. This chapter compares the laws, practices, and attitudes relating to children's participation in contested child custody proceedings in Australia, the United Kingdom, New Zealand, and Canada. It critiques the methods by which children's views are heard in the courtroom, through the lens of international law obligations under the CRC, which recognizes that children have a right to express their views and be heard in any proceedings affecting them. Fernando poses the question of what role judges may play in influencing how children and their voices are viewed in proceedings, and whether writing judgments from a child's rights perspective may change the social norms about children's autonomy and how children's rights are respected. Fernando aptly points out the importance of listening to what children have to say, because their opinions are a significant element in how the court determines the child's best interests, and ultimately this may change the social norms surrounding children's autonomy.

Part III is then closed by Professor Mark Henaghan in chapter 12. Again referencing the CRC, with a specific look at disability and education, Henaghan calls upon both the CRC and the 2006 Convention on the Rights of Persons with Disabilities to analyze similarities and differences between the policies and legislation surrounding the education of disabled children in Australia, Canada, the United Kingdom, the United States, and New Zealand. Henaghan argues that laws need to shift in understanding about disability from viewing disability as an individual deficit that must be cured or overcome individually to seeing it as a social problem that society must overcome. Central to the endeavor are children with disabilities and their parents actively participating in shaping their educational experience, as well as actually implementing meaningful and effective policies in schools which move beyond mere aspiration. The theme of chapter 12 is that while it is important to have norms which set the targets that states must meet, it is even more crucial to be eternally vigilant in how these norms are being interpreted and implemented if disabled children are to receive opportunities for education equal with other children. Henaghan examines the gap between the lofty rhetoric of relatively developed nations and the reality revealed by data within those nations. Chapter 12 is a perfect conclusion to part III as it emphasizes what earlier chapters in the part denote, that at all times the voices of the children at issue must be given prominence and adhered to as much as possible.

Then part IV, our final part, brings together many of the themes from above and looks to the future of the family around the world. This part explores critical issues, such as addressing normative and descriptive aspirations of global family law, as well as its intersectional implications for gender equality, racism, and indigenous rights. It addresses rights for transgender individuals under the law and explores several countries' focus upon family law. It also raises fascinating questions about when gamete donors and the donor-conceived children have rights under the law.

As Professor Fiona Kelly notes in chapter 13:

> While the regulation of donor linking may not be understood as falling within the traditional parameters of family law, the concept requires one to grapple with many of the more contentious themes of modern family law: definitions of kinship and the process of kin-making, recognition of non-normative families, and the relative significance of genetic and social ties to defining family and parentage.

In this timely chapter, Kelly explains that a growing number of donor-conceived people have asserted the right to know their genetic origins, including the identity of their sperm and/or egg donor. Though the global trend is moving toward ending donor anonymity, approaches to the release of information to donor-conceived people, often referred to as "donor-linking," vary dramatically. There are some poignant overlaps between the analysis in chapter

13 and that of chapter 6 about open and closed adoptions. Through a review of the regulation of donor-linking in Europe, North America and Australia, Kelly identifies three donor-linking approaches and then analyzes them, arguing that each approach reflects the legal, historical, and cultural norms of the relevant jurisdiction. The overall tension is between the competing rights of donor anonymity and donor child's right to identity and psychological health. Kelly asserts that the social norms around donor-linking are often changing faster than the laws.

Then in chapter 14, Dr. Yeshwant Jairam Naik analyzes the failure of legal regimes to recognize the gender with which transgender persons identify and how that erasure puts the individuals at risk and infringes upon their fundamental rights. Having official documents that either misgender them, or that reflect the change in their officially recognized gender, exposes transgender people to discrimination and harassment. This chapter examines the treatment of transgender persons within legal regimes throughout Europe and Asia, providing a comparative analysis of social and legal attitudes, as well as family law and jurisprudence. It finds that while there is some variability across the globe, transgender people are generally inadequately protected by the law and face inordinate hurdles to accessing their fundamental rights. On the positive side, the chapter notes a widespread trend growing toward greater recognition, protection, and empowerment for transgender people around the world. Naik provides a country-by-country explanation of legal standards for changing genders, gender markers, and transgender people's right to marriage and divorce. Overall, this chapter highlights the shared social and legal attitudes toward transgender individuals in the East and West.

Leading us to an in-depth examination of Ethiopian family law is Dr. Sileshi Bedasie Hirko in chapter 15. In multinational states such as Ethiopia, normative pluralism—the idea that multiple sets of norms can exist in the same place—and its implications are critical for the development of robust and inclusive family laws. In particular, international norms such as human rights and local societal norms inform and shape the various aspects of family laws. In Ethiopia, the corpus of the multinational family laws—consisting of several states' family laws—has undergone a substantial transformation over the last two decades. Before diving into the transformation of the last two decades, he provides an encompassing historical background of the government and its laws to situate the reader in their understanding of the transformation. The extent to which the normative pluralism underpins, guides, transforms, and shapes the development of multinational family laws in Ethiopia remains unexplored. Hence, this chapter examines the place of normative pluralism and its implications for the development of family laws in Ethiopia.

We then close with Professor Deseriee Kennedy in chapter 16 with a thought-provoking chapter outlining how U.S. child welfare policies, poverty, and a racially biased criminal justice system reinforce each other to control families that live on society's margins. Policies regarding family preservation and child welfare differ across the globe; while most nations profess to act in a child's best interests, there are significant variations in how countries implement that principle. When these issues arise, economic resources, race, racism, class, and classism, gender, and sexism often intersect. However, reliance on family separation as a means of resolving cases of neglect may be ineffective in helping resolve the underlying issues that precipitate state involvement and may do significant harm to children and their families. Interventionist and punitive child welfare policies intersect with poverty and a criminal justice system that disproportionately punishes the poor and people of color, splitting families apart. This chapter analyzes the intersection of child welfare and mass incarceration in the United States with Post-Apartheid South Africa. This matching analysis demonstrates Kennedy's point that both South Africa and the United States share a history of racism that reflects in legislation involving children. Such a comparison provides an opportunity to caution against child welfare and criminal justice policies that rely on child removal and fail to respect family unity. Kennedy concludes by restating the importance of considering the true best interests of the child when dealing with the family.

In sum, the 16 chapters that follow bring forward novel questions and analyses into the field of family law. A deep examination of the laws can be especially enlightening when cross-pollinating ideas across countries and allowing for new societal norms and laws to emerge.

The contributors of this book have worked together in a number of ways since 2019. We routinely collaborated to discuss various themes in our chapters in order to bring in strands from each other's works to create an overarching composite framework and cohesive synthesized narrative. While we had hoped to unite in person in Albany, New York, in May 2020, the pandemic had its own plan. We instead met on a half-day Zoom conference, and it was quite productive, nonetheless. As the ongoing process unfolded, we discovered many synergies and connections throughout our work, which we continued to discuss over email for the years to follow.

Many of us presented together at the Law and Society Association (LSA) Annual Meeting in 2021. We will do so again in Lisbon, Portugal, in July 2022. We present our research on panels that we develop through the newly created Global Family Law International Research Collaboration (IRC-13). I imagined the IRC after observing that there was not yet a cohesive, established group of global family law scholars in the international and interdisciplinary space of LSA.

I owe a tremendous thank you to the contributors of this book. In the end, our collaborations have been a treasure. The thoughts in this book are extremely pertinent to current family law debates and offer invaluable perspective on so many critical issues.

I hope the readers of this book find it to be timely and a book that adds to the current dialogue surrounding this vital area of the law, family law. It should stimulate further thought—serving as both a basis for discussion and an inspiration for future works and collaborations. I sincerely hope you enjoy reading and learning from this book, as much as I enjoyed creating it. It is my wish that as soon as you finish one chapter, you cannot wait to read the next.

NOTES

1. Henry Krause, "Comparative Family Law-Past Traditions Battle Future Trends and Vice Versa" in *The Oxford Handbook of Comparative Law*, eds. Reiman and Zimmerman (Oxford University Press, 2006), 1101.

Part I

INTIMATE RELATIONSHIPS

EXAMINING THE LAWS AND NORMS OF ADULT RELATIONSHIPS ACROSS THE GLOBE

Chapter 1

Nonmarital Norms

Naomi Cahn and June Carbone

INTRODUCTION

What happens when family law and family norms move apart—and do so in different ways for different parts of the population? Nonmarital cohabitation has become so widespread in North America and Europe over the past half-century that it has changed from a legally stigmatized to a legally accepted status. Despite this, the development and institutionalization of marital versus nonmarital norms continue to vary by country. While legal standards have traditionally reinforced mainstream understandings of marriage, neither legal norms nor societal mores shape unmarried relationships to the same degree. Instead, unmarried relationships remain far more varied than married ones, and the legal standards that govern them do not necessarily correspond to the parties' expectations as completely as they do within modern marriages. This disconnect happened in part because unmarried relationships reflect differing attitudes toward marriage in different counties and in part because the reasons couple do not marry vary within different communities, even within the same country. These differences complicate the legal regulation of unmarried relationships.

At the national level, the legal approach to nonmarriage often reflects the attitudes of opinion-shaping elites. In countries such as France, the movement away from marriage corresponds, in part, to a strong secular tradition, particularly among the well-educated.[1] These couples establish marriage-like relationships outside of marriage and they have supported the extension of the legal and financial advantages of marriage to the unmarried. France has joined a number of European countries that either allow unmarried couples to opt into an alternative status or impose legal obligations on the basis of the nature of the relationships.[2] Where elites lead the movement away from marriage, they may also lead in the determination of the normative content of alternative statuses.

In countries like the United States, on the other hand, the growth of nonmarriage is more closely associated with economic and racial inequality, with poor minority communities leading the move away from marriage. These couples may not necessarily benefit from the legal obligations associated with marriage and are less likely to opt into status-based or contractual alternatives if they are available. In both groups of countries, the solutions that work for the highly educated may not necessarily serve the interests of others.

These differences have important consequences for the legal design of regimes governing intimate relationships. Countries have developed four distinct approaches to intimate couples' relationships: formal marriage, marriage by imposition, legally recognized marriage-like obligations by choice, and an ad hoc approach which may, or may not, recognize contractual solutions. These approaches define nonmarriage by reference to marriage. Yet, marriage and marriage-like benefits by choice involve intentional interactions with the law, while marriage by imposition and the ad hoc approach may involve conflicting intents. This chapter examines the United States in the context of patterns found in other high-income countries including European countries and Canada. It finds that the extension of marriage-like benefits to the unmarried often assists the sophisticated, without necessarily leading to shared understandings for others or guidance in the construction of new legal provisions.

DEMOGRAPHY

The United States has long been thought of as distinctive among developed nations because of its continuing religiosity. In looking at relationship formation, many attribute the continuing importance of marriage to that religiosity.[3] That is, they assume that those who are religious continue to marry while secularists lead the movement into other relationships. This analysis, however, which has some truth in European countries like France,[4] is in many ways misleading when applied to the United States. In the United States, the increase in cohabitation is not necessarily driven by a rejection of religious marriage. Instead, it reflects multiple different factors. First, in the religious parts of the country, the average age of marriage and first birth remains relatively young, and that contributes to relationship instability. Yes, marriage rates are higher in these areas of the country, but divorce and re-partnering rates are higher as well, contributing to cohabitation at later ages.[5] Second, the better educated, particularly among the most secular, increasingly cohabit before marriage. These "trial marriages" are part of a more general shift toward deferred family formation and lower overall fertility. Finally, those who have children without marrying tend overwhelming to be poorer, less educated and more likely to be members of minority communities. These groups are not moving away from religiously defined relationship norms. Instead, they lack the prerequisites, such as financial stability, trust, and mutual respect, that make unqualified commitment to their current partners appropriate. For none of these groups does cohabitation reflect a rejection of marriage per se, and thus the needs—and relationship norms—of these groups differ from those who seek legal alternatives because they object to traditional marriage.

In the United States generally, nonmarital cohabitation has become so common that the share of adults who have lived with a romantic partner at some point in their lives "is now higher than the share who have ever been married."[6] Popular acceptance has also increased to the point where 69% of Americans view cohabitation as acceptable even if it does not lead to marriage. For those under the age of 30, the number approving rises to 78%.[7] Yet, the meaning of cohabitation may vary for different groups, complicating the demographic picture of cohabitation in the United States.

First, religion does play a role. As we explained in *Red Families v. Blue Families*, perhaps the most important role of religion is in keeping the age for first marriage low in the more religious parts of the country such as Mormon Utah and the Bible Belt South.[8] Observant couples, embedded in religious communities, who attend religious services together, have lower divorce rates than the nonobservant.[9] Yet, religious areas of the country tend to have higher rates of divorce and teen births, partly as a result of the opposition to public support for contraception and abortion[10] and partly because early marriage and pregnancies hindering further education and limiting economic opportunities increase relationship instability.[11] This greater instability contributes to re-partnering later in life. Sociologist Andrew Cherlin found that, given this dynamic, American marriages generally tend to be less stable than European cohabitations.[12] He also found that white women with a high school but not a college degree tend to have the largest number of cohabiting partners over the course of their lives, including both married and unmarried relationships.[13] Those who marry young, have children, divorce, and live with new partners often have different expectations for their subsequent relationships than they did for their marriages. Accordingly, while religious observation generally tends to reduce cohabitation, it does not eliminate it, and it contributes to somewhat different patterns in intimate relationships in more religious parts of the country.

Second, the college-educated elites have dramatically increased their rates of cohabitation without abandoning the relationship between marriage and childrearing. For example, most studies of American cohabitation find that women with less education are more likely to cohabit and less likely to marry than women with college degrees. Yet, the differences in those currently cohabitating have narrowed substantially across educational lines; the much bigger differences are in marriage rates and in the percentages of cohabitants who later marry their nonmarital partners.[14]

For college graduates, greater cohabitation is part of a more general delay in family formation and childbearing, and it frequently leads to marriage. For college graduates, 65% of cohabiting unions become marriages compared to 31% for high school grads.[15] Moreover, while cohabitation before marriage once correlated with higher divorce rates, this is no longer true. As the more highly educated have become more likely to cohabit, the relationship between cohabitation and divorce has declined.[16]

Third, in the United States, to a greater degree than many countries, declining marriage rates reflect greater economic and racial inequality. For African Americans, one factor in these declining rates has been the fact that women outnumber men due to higher male death rates and mass incarceration of black men. However, the gap in wealth accumulation between blacks and whites is likely even more significant, as economic stability has become a key factor in a couple choosing to marry.[17] Black women are slightly less likely than white women or Latina women to have ever cohabited, and are also less likely to convert their cohabiting relationships into marriage,[18] and they are not only less likely to marry than other groups, but they are more likely to be raising a child on their own without a cohabiting partner.[19]

In addition, less-educated women generally find that their cohabitations do not last as long as those of their wealthier peers. The couples are less likely to marry[20] and the women are more likely to engage in serial cohabitations with multiple partners.[21] Given these developments, cohabitation has not simply taken the place of marriage. The most basic difference is that marriage is still a relationship shaped by shared norms. Central to those norms is the fidelity of the couple to each other and the relationship; married couples have higher levels of trust and are more likely to believe that their partners will act in their best interests.[22] Cohabitation, in contrast, does not necessarily mean the same thing for different groups. Many cohabitants, for example, report that they are not financially ready for marriage.[23] For some couples, this means that they do not believe that their partners can ever make enough of a contribution to make marriage worthwhile. For others, it may mean that they are still in school and not ready to assume the responsibilities that come with marriage.[24] With older couples, the reasons may be different. Susan Brown notes that cohabiting allows married partners to protect financial assets and prevents them from the potential of losing Social Security or pension benefits based on a former spouse.[25] Overall, greater relationship instability has accompanied greater economic instability.[26]

Comparative Demography: The Rate of Cohabitation Is Increasing Globally

In Canada, "common law couples" (couples cohabiting without marriage) constitute one-fifth of all couples, a tripling since 1981. [27] In many European countries, there are similar trends, albeit with variation by country.[28] For example, the proportion of the population that has been married is higher in countries in southern Europe than in northern European countries; in contrast, the reverse is true with respect to unmarried cohabitation.[29] Within individual countries, the practices have varied over time. Sweden, which has long led the Northern European move away from marriage, saw an increase in marriage rates after 1998.[30] On the other hand, in France, the number of couples choosing a formalized "PAC" (pacte civil de solidarité, or domestic partnership, discussed further *infra*) over marriage increased during the same time period, and, as in the United States, those choosing formal commitment through either a PAC or marriage have a higher education and income than other cohabiting couples.[31]

A major difference, however, is that, in contrast to the views of U.S. cohabiters, those in Europe are more likely to view cohabitation as a stable alternative to marriage.[32] That's because, in the United States, the better off have remained more likely to marry and cohabitating relationships are "much less marriage-like," and "remain less stable and of shorter duration and are less likely to segue into marriage than in Europe."[33]

Changing Norms

The content of unmarried relationships is often defined in contrast with married ones. Marriage was once identified by patriarchal norms, leading some opposed to such norms not to marry. Today, marriage, particularly in the United States, has been redefined to promote formal equality. These new norms emphasize interdependent finances and shared parenting, again persuading some who do not see their relationships in such terms not to marry.[34] This dynamic, however, creates a challenge for legal regulation of these relationships.

The norms attending traditional marriage were designed to "channel"[35] intimate relationships into marriage in order to address women's vulnerability from the risk of pregnancy and marshal the resources needed for childrearing. These norms, which stemmed from the male monopoly on the major sources of income and wealth, subordinated women to their husbands during marriage, as husbands controlled the family's resources and women were expected to defer to (or love, honor, and obey) their husbands.

Neither marriage nor unmarried relationships are still thought of in such terms. With the availability of reliable contraception and abortion, women are better able to control their fertility. In addition, women are no longer either economically dependent because of gender or childbearing per se, nor necessarily the lower-earning spouse in intimate relationships. And unmarried relationships may not necessarily be about childbearing at all or, even if there are children in the household, the two partners may not necessarily share equal responsibility for them. This changes the relationship between married and unmarried arrangements. When women were viewed as intrinsically unequal to men, marriage institutionalized norms that saw men as having an obligation to marry as the price of sexual access and women as subject to inequality within marriage as the price of financial security. Today, instead, marriage embodies norms of reciprocal exchange, shared decision-making, economic partnership, and mutual respect. Many opt out of marriage because of community norms that suggest that marriage is inappropriate with a partner unlikely to be able to be capable of equal contributions or shared decision-making that advances the couples' mutual interests.

This leads to a central irony in the regulation of unmarried relationships. Those who champion the imposition of greater responsibilities on unmarried partners are most concerned about traditionally gendered unions, with higher-earning partners in a relationship with a lower earner who contributes more domestically.[36] In these cases, the men may not marry precisely because they do not want to assume a long-term commitment to a partner they do not view as an equal. But the same thing is true for many women, particularly low-income women paired with blue-collar men who no longer enjoy better economic opportunities than their partners simply because they are men. Among marriages in the bottom income quintile, the wife earns more than the husband in almost 70% of the unions in comparison with under 30% of wives in families with incomes in the top quintile.[37] And lower income women report concern about a commitment to a financially unreliable man; these women fear that such commitments may threaten the resources on which they depend to take care of themselves and their children.[38] In short, when marriage was a union premised on formal inequality, men who did not marry the dependent women they impregnated were "cads"; the norms of the day tied the obligation to marry to male privilege.[39] Today, women who do not marry the dependent men with whom they are living are often viewed as wise. Community norms suggest that a commitment to a man who cannot carry his own weight in a relationship is foolish.[40]

Legal Standards

Legal decisions, whether they impose or reject obligations, influence community expectations. They make cohabitation—and the practices associated with it—more visible. This increased visibility encourages couples to make more conscious choices about their relationships, further contributing to the development of community norms. In some cases, the community norms lead to shared expectations, such as the expectation that cohabitation without marriage involves no obligation to share an inheritance, while at other times, it leads to more carefully framed choices, such as the need for unmarried couples to consider whether to title their shared residence as a joint tenancy in or a tenancy in common. And the evolving community standards may in turn influence the law. Of course, while legal regulation may help systematize emerging norms for family behavior, it cannot fundamentally alter the forces that produce the shifting norms. Moreover, the forces that produce these changes—the long-term shift in women's roles, the erosion of highly paid manufacturing jobs for relatively unskilled men, greater societal inequality, the sexual revolution, and women's greater control over their own reproduction, are themselves complex and controversial.

Full legal recognition of nonmarriage accordingly requires engaging in the process of norm systemization. Yet, it is difficult to do justice to the variety of nonmarital cohabitations; one size does not fit all. Existing legal regimes occur on a continuum from complete nonrecognition, which has become increasingly rare in developed countries, to recognition of contractual agreements to opt-in situations in which couples choose a particular status to an opt-out regime, with status imposed. The most basic issue, in the United States and internationally, is whether to facilitate couples' ability to opt into a preordained status such as PACS in France or domestic partnerships in some American states or whether to impose obligations on the basis of the relationship itself. The classic example of the latter is common law marriage; a decreasing number of states treat couples who live together and hold themselves out as married as indistinguishable from those who enter into formal marriage.[41] Underlying these different regimes is a fundamental normative question: should a couple's decision to live together and commingle their lives give rise to obligations that survive the relationships or should the couple be seen as having no obligations to each other except for those they specifically embrace?

In the United States, the 50 states differ considerably in their legal approach to family law, but most now permit explicit contracting, even if they do not always enforce such contracts.[42] While some states also imply obligations on the basis of cohabitation alone, most have backed away from such rulings, requiring either an explicit showing of intent or financial intermingling more akin to a business relationship. This leaves open the possibility of legislatively crafted opt-in statuses in the future.

The case that thrust legal recognition of cohabitation into public consciousness was *Marvin v. Marvin*, a case involving a famous actor at the height of his career and a Hollywood starlet.[43] Before *Marvin*, courts typically rejected claims for support between cohabitants; a woman who lived with a man without a ring on her finger was both stigmatized and pitied as a fool, who should have known better than to rely on a man's promises.

In *Marvin*, the California Supreme Court held that contracts between unmarried couples would henceforth be enforceable. The courts would no longer presume that contracts for support necessarily involved sex as the consideration; instead, the courts would treat such contracts as enforceable absent a showing that sex was the express purpose of the agreement. *Marvin* and its progeny helped ratify recognition of nonmarriage as a distinct relationship and remove some of the stigma associated with nonmarital sexuality.

But *Marvin*, and the cases that followed, also raised a potentially more radical claim; they suggested not only that parties could enter into contractual relationships, but also that continuing financial obligations could be presumed from the nature of the relationship. That is, if a couple entered into an arrangement in which the party with the higher income provided support while the other party attended to the couple's household needs, the higher earning party would be presumed to have agreed to support the other party for a period beyond the end of the relationship. This latter allegation, couched in the language of implied-in-law contract, assumes a moral obligation.

The cases following *Marvin*, however, drew back from the idea of implied contract, finding that the mere fact of a traditional relationship between a higher-earning partner and one who gave up other opportunities to contribute to household management did not give rise to a duty to provide compensation.

Where courts have imposed obligations on nonmarital partners in the absence of a contract, they have done so by extending unjust enrichment claims to property ownership. These cases typically involve relatively sophisticated parties, who, in the context of longer-term relationships, commingle their financial assets. Courts have recognized the need to oversee the division of assets at the termination of the relationship, without becoming involved in the relationship terms themselves, though not all states grant such relief to unmarried couples. The Illinois Supreme Court in 2016, for example, rejected calls to extend farther-reaching obligations on unmarried couples. In *Blumenthal v. Brewer*,[44] the Illinois Court of Appeals had addressed a relationship between two women, a doctor and a lawyer, who had lived together for 26 years and raised three children together. Throughout most of the period, the couple could not marry; yet, they had a relationship essentially indistinguishable from a fully committed, financially interdependent marriage.

Nonetheless, the Illinois Supreme Court, while agreeing that the courts could oversee the untangling of the parties' contributions to joint assets such as their house, rejected claims that arose from the nature of the relationship. The case generated controversy with its emphasis on the state's continuing interest in distinguishing between marital and nonmarital relationships, and the importance of preventing "marriage from becoming in effect a private contract terminable at will, by disfavoring the grant of mutually enforceable property rights to knowingly unmarried cohabitants." Yet, its refusal to recognize claims arising from the intimate relationship itself is consistent with cases from other jurisdictions.

The most ambitious effort to recognize broad obligations among cohabitants came from the American Law Institute's *Principles of Family Dissolution* (ALI *Principles*).[45] The ALI *Principles* effectively extend the marital remedies of equitable distribution of property and alimony to cohabitants, but its approach has not been fully adopted by any state. And some states remain reluctant to recognize actions by unmarried couples against each other at all, not because of a refusal to recognize the relationship, but due to a wariness of becoming entangled in the substance of the claims without a clear legal or normative basis on which to resolve them.

Court rulings instead reflect studies of the couples' own attitudes toward nonmarriage.[46] Unmarried couples are less likely to combine their finances than married couples, with a substantially smaller percentage opening joint bank accounts or titling property jointly.[47] Indeed, a major reason for parties' unwillingness to marry is often an unwillingness to make a financial commitment to a partner who is seen as more of a liability than an asset. The parties in reported opinions are not necessarily representative of the group; they typically have more committed relationships—and often more money and a greater sense of betrayal—than the average cohabitant.[48]

Courts often sympathize with the parties who feel cheated. And, as with the ALI *Principles*, there are some who, in the name of dismantling the distinctions between marriage and nonmarriage, would apply marital principles to these parties, arguing that, regardless of intent, the law should impose marital-type norms. But both the courts and the general public have come to accept that many couples regard an unequal relationship as a reason not to marry rather than a justification for imposing marriage-like obligations. Greater acceptance has moved toward recognition of nonmarriage as a different status than marriage.

OTHER RELATIONSHIP RIGHTS

Jurisdictions also continue to treat nonmarital relationships differently from marital ones in numerous ways, ranging from parenthood to tort claims to employment discrimination.[49] Parenthood and custody rights are particularly complicated. On the one hand, the states increasingly recognize two (and in some states more) parents outside of marriage.[50] This recognition has increased as unmarried mothers have become more likely than they were a half-century ago to live with the fathers of their children. On the other hand, unmarried mothers are more likely than married mothers to assume primary responsibility for their children and they are also more likely than married mothers to end the relationship with the father because of domestic violence or other conflicts that make shared parental rights inappropriate.[51]

In accordance with these developments, the process of acquiring legal parenthood continues to differ for marital and nonmarital parents. For married parents, the marital presumption assumes that both spouses are the parents of any child born into the marriage; it accordingly functions as an "opt-out" system. In contrast, while all states recognize the woman who gives birth as a parent, a nonmarital partner who does not give birth to the child must take affirmative steps to establish parenthood. This functions as an "opt-in" system for the second parent.

Custodial rights, in contrast, do not necessarily vary with the parents' marital status, although they do vary in practice. In divorce actions, the courts routinely award shared custody, absent a strong showing that such custody is inappropriate. In contrast, when unmarried couples split, there is no automatic event that will produce such an order, and unmarried parents, who tend to be poorer than married ones, are less likely to have the resources or the will to engage in litigation. Accordingly, married parents are much more likely than unmarried partners to obtain joint custodial rights following a break-up.[52]

Moreover, while family members are often the only ones who can presumptively sue for certain torts, like intentional infliction of emotional distress or loss of consortium, those torts are not available to nonmarital cohabitants. The gravamen of these torts stems from the emotional harm the law is willing to recognize in some relationships but not others. Family status allows one to sue for the loss of one's spouse even though one cannot sue for the loss of a nonmarital partner.[53]

On the other hand, certain types of legal protections applicable to marital partners or family members also apply to nonmarital cohabitants. For example, the domestic abuse statutes of many states generally include unmarried persons who reside together or who have a child in common (even if they are not living together) as among the "family or household members" who may seek a civil protection order against abuse. Some states also include persons in a dating relationship.[54]

In addition, premarital cohabitation may be relevant to property distribution upon divorce.[55]

Statutory Approaches to Nonmarriage

While much of cohabitation law is common law, some states have enacted statutes that either require contracts to be in writing or that allow for an opt-in status with many of the same rights of marriage.

Contracts

A few states regulate contracts between nonmarital cohabitants through their statute of frauds, including Minnesota, New Jersey, and Texas.[56] For example, New Jersey requires a writing, "signed by the party to be charged therewith," in order to enforce a support obligation between cohabitants.[57] These states do not otherwise include legislative regulation of the procedure or substance of the contracts.

Opt-in

In response to the needs of same-sex couples who could not marry, some jurisdictions developed various models that allow couples to opt into marital-type obligations;[58] these statuses are not, however, widely used by couples for whom marriage is an option, which now includes same-sex couples (unlike the French PACS). One of the earliest examples was the state of Hawaii, which developed the status of reciprocal beneficiaries.[59] Those who register are subject to state-prescribed rights and responsibilities, permitting unmarried adults who are not eligible for marriage to register their reciprocal beneficiary relationship with the state director of health.[60]

Reciprocal beneficiaries receive rights relating to health insurance, hospital visitation, healthcare decision-making, suits for wrongful death, time off for bereavement, and some property rights, including the ability to hold property in a tenancy by the entirety. A reciprocal beneficiary is treated as a spouse for purposes of intestacy, the elective share, and a premarital will.[61] The status does not impose post-relationship responsibilities if the relationship is voluntarily terminated.[62]

Colorado established the status of "designated beneficiary" in 2009.[63] It is an opt-in status, with individuals allowed to specify which responsibilities attach to their relationship. The status is available to any two unmarried people over the age of 18 who are not in a civil union or marriage or another designated beneficiary relationship.[64] That means it is available to intimate partners as well as any other two individuals who choose the status. The agreement must be properly recorded to be valid.

The individuals can each choose to include or to exclude any of the 16 rights and protections including jointly owning property, inheriting through intestacy, making healthcare decisions, suing for wrongful death, and benefiting from workers' compensation.[65] The status does not impose post-relationship responsibilities if the relationship is voluntarily terminated.

Civil unions generally offer the same rights as marriage, and, while some are limited to same-sex couples, others include opposite-sex couples as well. Vermont was the first state to recognize civil unions, although, as of 2009, they are no longer available there.[66] Civil unions are currently available in Colorado, Hawaii, Illinois, and New Jersey.[67]

Domestic partnerships carry a variety of benefits, depending on the jurisdiction. The following jurisdictions allow domestic partnerships: California, the District of Columbia, Maine, Nevada, New Jersey, Oregon, Washington, and Wisconsin. Many employers and municipalities also recognize domestic partnerships.[68] As an example, California only allows couples of the same sex or those over the age of 62 to enter domestic partnerships.[69] The benefits, rights, and responsibilities are the same as marriage.[70]

As a final note, a minority of states recognizes common law marriages.[71] The requirements for a common law marriage typically include the following: (1) the parties must be eligible for marriage; (2) they must cohabit; (3) they must hold themselves out as married; and (4) they must have the mutual intent to be married. While the status truly is common law in most of the states that recognize it, a few have enacted statutes legitimating common law marriage.[72] Some states also recognize *putative spousehood*,[73] an equitable doctrine that accords relief to a cohabitant who was married, believing in good faith there was no impediment to the marriage (although one existed).

RESPONSES OUTSIDE OF THE UNITED STATES

Legal approaches to cohabitation in other countries range from piecemeal to statutory. For example, in Poland, "general legal principles," such as unjust enrichment, apply at the end of a cohabiting relationship.[74] England and Spain have similarly taken a "piecemeal" approach.[75] In contrast, other countries offer "opt-in" or "opt-out" forms of legal recognition for cohabitants. Countries such as the Netherlands and France have implemented an opt-in approach, which entitles partners to specific rights, such as joint income tax and inheritance, with separation much easier than divorce.[76]

France, which has experienced a declining marriage rate for the past half-century,[77] has simultaneously seen a growing number of cohabitants as well as increasing recognition of same-sex relationships.[78] In 1999, France adopted PACS to address the legal status of same-sex couples.[79] PACS set out various rights and duties for cohabitants; a PACS begins upon registration of a written agreement with the appropriate civil official.[80] Once registered, the couple receives many of the benefits of marriage, including income, estate, and gift-tax benefits, and they are also jointly responsible for each other's debts.

PACS have become increasingly popular, although it is not clear whether they reflect changes in norms, or have caused those changes.[81]

Some countries, for example, Sweden and Norway, have extended many of the same rights and responsibilities available in marriage to cohabiting couples, assuming they meet certain preconditions, such as living together for a specific period of time or having children together.[82]

In Canada, all of the provinces (except Quebec) have established an opt-out system for cohabitants.[83] After either having a child together or living together for a certain period of time, the couple is considered common law married and is entitled to many of the same rights as marital partners.[84]

The province of Alberta, for example, adopted its Adult Interdependent Relationships Act in 2002. The status as an adult interdependent partner can be conferred by contractual agreement, living together in an interdependent relationship for three years, or living in such a relationship and having a child in common, so it is both an opt-in and opt-out regime.[85] It confers many of the same rights, obligations, and benefits as does marriage, including division of property at termination,[86] and spousal support.[87] Moreover, if one partner dies intestate, then the surviving partner has rights comparable to those of a surviving spouse. Similar systems are in place in other Anglophile jurisdictions, including Australia.[88]

There is some evidence that laws do have an impact on behavior. For example, there is "a sharp distinction between high levels of nonmarital fertility in France and low levels in neighboring Switzerland, despite sharing a similar language and employees who commute daily"; the differing levels may be "due to strict Swiss policies for unmarried fathers, who were not allowed to pass down their surname if they were not married to the mother of their child."[89]

CONCLUSION

Determining the legal recognition appropriate for unmarried couples requires determining the purpose of legal regulation. We have argued elsewhere that the purpose of recognizing such relationships is autonomy; that is, support for the ability of intimate couples to enter into relationships on terms of their choosing without being forced into a one-size-fits-all version of marriage. The concept of autonomy, by itself, however, cannot provide a comprehensive explanation because unmarried couples often do not agree on the terms that govern their relationships. So the choice of default provisions, whether the provisions involve obligations similar to marriage, or no obligations at all, involves a choice of norms that will necessarily favor some parties at the expense of others.

We suggest that legal regulations should promote two concepts. First, legal regulations should provide notice as to the nature of the obligations couples incur when entering into a relationship, and, second, the idea of notice should depend not just on formalities such as registration or contract, but on the extent to which default obligations correspond to community norms about responsibility for dependent partners. These concepts of notice and consonance with community norms may include public policy concerns about protecting the vulnerable, but only to the extent they involve accepted community norms that put couples on notice of the obligations they are undertaking. Otherwise, the regulation of nonmarriage risks simply replicating marriage as the consequence of cohabitation.

NOTES

1. See, e.g., Scott Sayare and Maïa de la Baume, "In France, Civil Unions Gain Favor Over Marriage," *New York Times*, December 15, 2010. https://www.nytimes.com/2010/12/16/world/europe/16france.html (observing that in France, marriage is still viewed "as a 'heavy and invasive' institution with deep ties to Christianity.").

2. Sayare, "Civil Unions"; *see also* Wilfried Rault and Krystyna Horko, "The Intimate Orientations of the First 'PACS' Couples in France," *Population (English Edition, 2002-)* 66, no. 2 (April–June 2011): 304, http://www.jstor.com/stable/41488603

3. Andrew J. Cherlin, *The Marriage-Go-Round: The State of Marriage and the Family in America Today* (New York: Vintage Books, 2010), 113–114. *See also* David Masci and Claire Gecewicz, "Share of Married Adults Varies Widely Across U.S. Religious Groups," *Pew Research Center*, March 19, 2018, http://pewrsr.ch/2u8PzCP

4. See, e.g., Sayare, "Civil Unions."

5. Cherlin, *Marriage-Go-Round*, 14–15.

6. Susan L. Brown, *Families in America* (University of California Press, 2017), 53; Karen Guzzo, "Trends in Cohabitation Outcomes: Compositional Changes and Engagement Among Never-Married Young Adults," *Journal of Marriage and Family,* 76(4) (August 2014): 824, https://www.ncbi.nlm.nih.gov/pmc/articles/PMC4712741/

7. Nikki Graf, "Key Findings on Marriage and Cohabitation in the U.S.," Pew Research Center, November 6, 2019, https://pewrsr.ch/2NnfuOJ

8. Naomi Cahn and June Carbone, *Red Families v. Blue Families: Legal Polarization and the Creation of Culture* (New York: Oxford University Press, 2010).

9. W. Bradford Wilcox and Nicholas H. Wolfinger, *Soul Mates: Religion, Sex, Love, and Marriage Among African Americans and Latinos* (New York: Oxford University Press, 2016), 143.

10. Cahn and Carbone, *Red Families v. Blue Families*, 22–24.

11. Jennifer Glass and Philip Levchak, "Red States, Blue States, and Divorce: Understanding the Impact of Conservative Protestantism on Regional Variation in Divorce Rates," *American Journal of Sociology* 119, no. 4 (January 2014): 1002–1046, www.jstor.org/stable/10.1086/674703

12. Cherlin, *Marriage-Go*-Round, 17.

13. Andrew J. Cherlin, "Between Poor and Prosperous: Do the Family Patterns of Moderately-Educated Americans Deserve a Closer Look?" in *Social Class and Changing Families in an Unequal America*, eds. Marcia J. Carlson and Paula England (Stanford University Press, 2011), 68–84.

14. Graf, "Key Findings."

15. Esther O. Lamidi, "Are Cohabiting Unions Lasting Longer? Two Decades of Change in the Duration of Cohabitation (1980–2004)," 10, Tbl. 3 (2015), http://paa2015.princeton.edu/papers/153280

16. Alicia G. VanOrman and Paola Scommegna, "Understanding the Dynamics of Family Change in the United States" (July 2016): 13, http://www.prb.org/pdf16/prb-population-bulletin-71.1-complex-families-2016.pdf

17. Alicia G. VanOrman and Paola Scommegna, "Understanding the Dynamics of Family Change in the United States" (July 2016): 6–7, http://www.prb.org/pdf16/prb-population-bulletin-71.1-complex-families-2016.pdf; Wendy D. Manning and Bart Stykes, "Twenty-Five Years of Change in Cohabitation in the U.S., 1987–2013," National Center for Family and Marriage Research Family Profile FP-15-01 (2015).

18. VanOrman and Scommegna, *Dynamics of Family Change,* 8–9 & Fig. 7.

19. Andrew Golub and Megan Reid, "Cohabitation and Repartnering among Low-Income Black Mothers," *Journal of Black Sexuality and Relationships* 1, no. 3 (Winter 2015): 61. doi: 10.1353/bsr.2015.0006

20. Lamidi, "Cohabiting Unions," 10, Tbl. 3.

21. Lamidi, "Cohabiting Unions," 10, Tbl. 3.

22. Graf, "Key Findings."

23. Graf, "Key Findings," table 6.

24. Graf, "Key Findings," table 6 (44% cite not being far enough along in their careers as a major or minor reason not to marry).

25. Susan L. Brown, *Families in America* (University of California Press, 2017), 50–51.

26. In *Labor's Love Lost*, Cherlin documents the correlations between the decline in well-paying male blue-collar jobs and the decline in marriage. Andrew J. Cherlin, *Labor's Love Lost: the Rise and Fall of the Working Class Family in America* (Russell Sage Foundation, 2014).

27. Families, households and marital status: Key results from the 2016 Census, Statistics Canada (August 2017).

https://www150.statcan.gc.ca/n1/daily-quotidien/170802/dq170802a-eng.html

28. Brienna Perelli-Harris and Mark Lyons-Amos, *Changes in Partnership Patterns Across the Life Course: An Examination of 14 Countries in Europe and the United States*, https://www.demographic-research.org/volumes/vol33/6

29. Brienna Perelli-Harris and Mark Lyons-Amos, "Partnership Patterns in the United States and across Europe: The Role of Education and Country Context," *Social Forces* 95, no. 1 (September 2016). doi: 10.1093/sf/sow054

30. Sofi Ohlsson-Wijk, "Sweden's Marriage Revival: An Analysis of the New-Millennium Switch from Long-Term Decline to Increasing Popularity," *Population Studies* 65, no. 2 (2011), www.jstor.org/stable/23056741

31. "French Cohabiting Unmarried Couples Are 'More Equal,'" The Connexion, Nov. 17, 2017, https://www.connexionfrance.com/French-news/French-cohabiting-unmarried-couples-are-more-equal

32. Sharon Sassler and Daniel T. Lichter, "Cohabitation and Marriage: Complexity and Diversity in Union-Formation Patterns," *Journal of Marriage and Family* 82 (2020), doi.org/10.1111/jomf.12617

33. Sassler, "Cohabitation and Marriage," 39.

34. June Carbone and Naomi Cahn, "Nonmarriage," *Maryland Law Review* 76, no. 1 (2016): 91–92.

35. *See* Carl E. Schneider, "The Channelling Function in Family Law," *Hofstra Law Review* 20 (Spring 1992).

36. Albertina Antognini, "The Law of Nonmarriage," *Boston College Law Review* 58, no.1 (January 2017): 62–64.

37. Sarah Jane Glynn, Breadwinning Mothers Continue to Be the U.S. Norm fig. 3 (May 10, 2019), https://www.americanprogress.org/issues/women/reports/2019/05/10/469739/breadwinning-mothers-continue-u-s-norm/ (2017 statistics)

38. Cynthia G. Bowman, "Social Science and Legal Policy: The Case of Heterosexual Cohabitation," *Cornell Journal of Law and Family Studies* 9, no. 1 (2007): 11. *See also*, Amber Lapp, "How Class Influences Pregnancy Ambivalence," Institute for Family Studies (April 27, 2015), http://family-studies.org/how-class-influences-pregnancy-ambivalence/

39. George A. Akerlof, Janet L. Yellen, and Michael L. Katz, "An Analysis of Out-of-Wedlock Childbearing in the United States," *The Quarterly Journal of Economics* 111, no. 2 (May 1996): 277–317.

40. William Julius Wilson, *When Work Disappears: The World of the New Urban Poor* (New York: Vintage Books, 1996), 105.

41. Kaiponanea T. Matsumura, "Choosing Marriage," *U.C. Davis Law Review* 50, no. 5 (June 2017): 1999–2066 (listing Colorado, Iowa, Kansas, Montana, New Hampshire, Rhode Island, South Carolina, Texas, Utah, and the District of Columbia).

42. See Albertina Antognini, "Nonmarital Contracts," *Stanford Law Review* 73, no. 1 (January 2021): 67–154.

43. *Marvin v. Marvin*, 557 P.2d 106 (Cal. 1976).

44. 69 N.E.3d 834 (Ill. 2016).

45. American Law Institute, *Principles of the Law of Family Dissolution: Analysis and Recommendations* (2000).

46. E.g., Daniel T. Lichter, Sharon Sassler, and Richard N. Turner, "Cohabitation, Post-Conception Unions, and the Rise in Nonmarital Fertility," *Social Science Research* 47 (2014): 134; Sharon Sassler and Amanda J. Miller, "Class Differences in Cohabitation Processes," *Family Relationships* 60 (2011): 163.

47. Fenaba R. Addo and Sharon Sassler, "Financial Arrangements and Relationship Quality in Low-Income Couples," *Family Relationships* 59, no. 4 (October 2010): 408, 411 (finding that married couples are more likely to pool income).

48. See, e.g., Marsha Garrison, "Nonmarital Cohabitation: Social Revolution and Legal Regulation," *Family Law Quarterly* 42, no. 3 (Fall 2008): 309, 315–22 (summarizing the studies and cases). Women with less education are more likely to cohabit, and their relationships are less likely to transition to marriage. See Casey E. Copen et al., "First Premarital Cohabitation in the United States: 2006–2010 National Survey of Family Growth," *National Health Statistics Report* (April 2013): 4–6, figs. 1–3, http://www.cdc.gov/nchs/data/nhsr/nhsr064.pdf

49. See Courtney G. Joslin, "Marital Status Discrimination 2.0," *Boston University Law Review* 95, no. 3 (May 2015): 805.

50. Naomi Cahn and June Carbone, "Parents, Babies and More Parents," *Chicago-Kent Law Review* 92, no. 1 (July 2017).

51. Carbone and Cahn, "Nonmarriage."

52. June Carbone and Naomi Cahn, "The Triple System of Family Law," *Michigan State Law Review* (2013): 1221–22.

53. Of course, plaintiffs have sought to recover for loss of consortium in the absence of a formal, legally recognized family relationship. E.g., *Fitzsimmons v. Mini Coach of Boston, Inc.*, 799 N.E.2d 1256, 1257 (Mass. 2003); *see also Milberger v. KBHL, LLC*, 486 F. Supp. 2d 1156, 1160–65 (D. Haw. 2007) (applying Hawaii law).

54. See, e.g., Mass. Gen. Laws, ch. 209A, § 1 (2019).

55. In *Matter of Munson and Beal*, 146 A.3d 153, 158 (N.H. 2016); *Collins v. Wassell*, 323 P.3d 1216, 1225–26 (Haw. 2014).

56. *See* Minn. Stat. Ann. § 513.075 (West 1980) ("Cohabitation; property and financial agreements"). The Texas statute of frauds covers agreements made "on consideration of marriage or [] of nonmarital conjugal cohabitation." Tex. Bus. & Com. Code Ann. § 26.01(b)(3) (West 2005).

57. N.J. Stat. Ann. § 25:1-5(h) (West 2010).

58. For an overview of many of the different statuses, see "Marriage, Domestic Partnerships, and Civil Unions: Same-Sex Couples Within the United States," *National Center. for Lesbian Rights* (2017), http://www.nclrights.org/wp-content/uploads/2013/07/Relationship_Recognition.pdf

59. Haw. Rev. Stat. Ann. § 572C-1 et seq. (West 2017).

60. Haw. Rev. Stat. Ann. § 572C-5 (West 2017).

61. Haw. Rev. Stat. Ann. § 560:2-102 (West 2017) (intestacy); § 560:2-202 ("Elective share"); § 560:2-301 (premarital will). It appears when adopting the UPC, Hawaii added "or reciprocal beneficiary" after the word "spouse." Haw. Rev. Stat. Ann. § 560:2-402 (West 2017) ("Homestead allowance").

62. Haw. Rev. Stat. Ann. § 572C-7 (West 2012) (no mention of death in the statute); *see* "About Reciprocal Beneficiary Relationships," Hawaii Department of

Health, accessed October 13, 2017, http://health.hawaii.gov/vitalrecords/about-reciprocal-beneficiary-relationships/#register (providing the forms and links for registering and terminating the reciprocal beneficiary relationship).

63. Colo. Rev. Stat. Ann. §§ 15-22-101; 15-22-112 (West 2009).

64. Colo. Rev. Stat. Ann. § 15-22-104 (West 2013) ("Requirements for a valid designated beneficiary agreement").

65. Colo. Rev. Stat. Ann. § 15-22-105 (West 2017).

66. The legalization of same-sex marriage resulted in other states withdrawing the option of civil unions, "Civil Unions & Domestic Partnership Statutes," National Conference of State Legislatures (last updated March 10, 2020), http://www.ncsl.org/research/human-services/civil-unions-and-domestic-partnership-statutes.aspx

67. Colo. Rev. Stat. Ann. §§ 14-15-107; 14-15-117 (West 2017); D.C. Code Ann. §§32-701; 32-710 (West 2016) (passed as B18-0010, 2009-2010 Council, 18th Period (D.C. 2009)); Haw. Rev. Stat. Ann. §§ 572B-1 et seq. (West 2012); 750 Ill. Comp. Stat. Ann. 75/1 (West 2011); N.J. Stat. Ann. §§ 37:1-28; 37:1-36 (West 2007), *invalidated by Garden State Equal. v. Dow*, 79 A.3d 1036 (N.J. 2013).

68. National Conference of State Legislatures, "Civil Unions."

69. Cal. Fam. Code § 297 (West 2012) (note that there are additional criteria, such as mental capacity, but that same-sex couples remain able to access the status regardless of whether they are under the age of 62, as of Oct. 14, 2017).

70. Cal. Fam. Code § 297.5 (West 2007).

71. Matsumura, "Choosing Marriage," 2066 (listing Colorado, Iowa, Kansas, Montana, New Hampshire, Rhode Island, South Carolina, Texas, Utah, and the District of Columbia).

72. *See* Mont. Code Ann. § 40-1-403 (West 2017) (pending legislation under S.B. 375, 65th Leg., 2017 Sess., (Mont. 2017)); Tex. Fam. Code Ann. § 2.401 (West 2005), *invalidated by Ranolls v. Dewling*, 223 F. Supp. 3d 613, 623 (E.D. Tex. 2016) (pending legislation in H.B. 573, 85th Leg. (Tex. 2017)); Utah Code Ann. § 30-1-4.5 (West 2011); N.H. Rev. Stat. Ann. § 457:39 (West 2017). Colorado establishes eligibility requirements. Colo. Rev. Stat. Ann. § 14-2-109.5 (West 2006).

73. E.g., Unif. Marriage and Divorce Act § 209 (Unif. Law Comm'n 1973).

74. Margaret Ryznar and Anna Stępień-Sporek, "Cohabitation Worldwide Today," *Georgia State University Law Review* 35, no. 2 (Winter 2019): 299–328.

75. Brienna Perelli-Harris, "Universal or Unique? Understanding Differences in Partnership Experiences across Europe," in *Unequal Family Lives: Causes and Consequences in Europe and the Americas*, eds. Naomi R. Cahn, et al. (Cambridge University Press: July 2018): 83–104, https://www.cambridge.org/core/books/unequal-family-lives/universal-or-unique-understanding-diversity-in-partnership-experiences-across-europe/AC49D5C35AA804D96E095B0CD93195C9/core-reader

76. Perelli-Harris, "Universal or Unique."

77. Ji Hyun Kim, Scott A. Oliver, and Margaret Ryznar, "The Rise of PACS: A New Type of Commitment from the City of Love," *Washburn Law Journal* 56, no. 1 (Winter 2017): 69, 82; Claude Martin and Irène Théry, "The PACS and Marriage and Cohabitation in France," *International Journal of Law, Policy and the Family* 15, no. 1 (April 2001): 135–158.

78. Martin and Thery, "PACS and Marriage," 9.

79. *See, e.g.*, Consulate General of France in New York, *Civil Union (PACS)* (2013), https://newyork.consulfrance.org/Civil-Union-PACS; Sayare, "Civil Unions."

80. *See* "Pacs: en Mairie à Partir du 1er Novembre 2017," Française Service-Public (May 16, 2017), https://www.servicepublic.fr/particuliers/actualites/A11143

81. Sayare, "Civil Unions."

82. Perelli-Harris, "Universal or Unique."

83. See Robert Leckey, "Cohabitation, Law Reform, and the Litigants," *International. Journal of Law, Policy, and the Family* 31, no. 2 (August 2017): 131–146.

84. Amanda Kazia, "4 Myths About Common-Law Relationships," *CBC News* (March 20, 2013, 1:18 PM), http://www.cbc.ca/news/canada/4-myths-about-common-law-relationships-1.1315129; Leckey, "Cohabitation, Law Reform," 132–135.

85. "Adult Interdependent Relationships," Canadian Legal FAQs, accessed July 8, 2020, https://www.law-faqs.org/alberta-faqs/family-law/adult-interdependent-relationships/

86. "Dividing Property Between Unmarried Partners," Alberta.ca, accessed July 8, 2020, www.alberta.ca/dividing-property-between-unmarried-partners.aspx; Family Property Act Sec. 7 (2020), http://www.qp.alberta.ca/documents/Acts/F04P7.pdf

87. Alberta Government, "Resolution Services: Spousal/Partner Support" (January 2017), https://www.alberta.ca/assets/documents/rcas-general-information-spousal-and-partner-support.pdf

88. Lawrence W. Waggoner, "Marriage Is on the Decline and Cohabitation Is on the Rise: At What Point, If Ever, Should Unmarried Partners Acquire Marital Rights?," *Family Law Quarterly* 50, no. 2 (Summer 2016): 215–246.

89. Perelli-Harris, "Universal or Unique."

Chapter 2

New Models of Registered Partnership Reform

Embracing Family Recognition Beyond Marriage?

Andy Hayward

INTRODUCTION

Across the Western world, countries are grappling with the rise in relationships taking place outside of marriage. Statistics indicate an exponential rise in cohabitation,[1] and, for some jurisdictions, the cohabiting family has now become the fastest growing relationship type.[2] While some couples are choosing to reject marriage, others, such as same-sex couples, may find that choice denied to them. At present only 29 countries permit the celebration of same-sex marriage forcing same-sex couples in other countries to cohabit and thus be exposed to ordinarily fewer and, in some instances, no legal protections. This picture is complicated further through jurisdictions introducing relationship registration regimes, sometimes in a bid to recognize both types of couple, thereby creating a tiered framework of formalized relationships.[3]

Civil partnerships, also known as registered partnerships or civil unions, exist in multiple forms and may be used by mixed-sex couples as an alternative to marriage or by same-sex couples as a functional equivalent to marriage, often at a time when introducing same-sex marriage would be too politically controversial. These forms reveal jurisdictions having to confront family recognition *beyond* marriage and determine what shape that regulation should take. More specifically, they evidence the creation of a second formalized status that, depending on the jurisdiction, may have a complementary or antagonistic relationship with the more established and, for some, revered status of marriage.

With a view to discerning emerging norms in family law, this chapter interrogates the evolution of civil partnerships both in terms of their initial inception and once established in a particular jurisdiction. Noting shifting patterns as to their use, it questions how far civil partnerships can evidence meaningful recognition and respect by a state for nonmarital families. The core focus will be on so-called "opt-in" registration regimes rather than "opt-out" regimes, although it should be noted that some jurisdictions operate both simultaneously.[4] Whereas the former involves couples voluntarily assuming protections through an act of registration, the latter sees eligible couples automatically obtaining legal protections but in a manner that falls short of conferring upon them a status and often subject to an ability to disapply the default regime.

This chapter is divided into three parts. The first part sketches the original impetus behind civil partnerships and isolates specific reform models. Identifying new reform models, the second part explores the unique position of England and Wales that, as an example of a novel approach, forces us to evaluate the value of civil partnerships once same-sex marriage is introduced. The third part questions whether the proliferation of civil partnership regimes truly evidences family recognition beyond marriage. It will be argued that although civil partnerships are often underpinned by liberal values of inclusivity and protection for the vulnerable, their current use largely evidences replication of marital norms, as opposed to real innovation in family recognition. Indeed, established reform patterns evidence a cascading of marriage onto civil partners rather than a genuine conversation as to how a plurality of interpersonal relationships in society can be recognized. If a state wishes to truly embrace family recognition beyond marriage and harness the potential and creativity of civil partnerships as an artificial state-construct in that endeavor, reform must arise from first principles and in a manner that resists the magnetism of marriage.

TRADITIONAL MODELS OF CIVIL PARTNERSHIP REFORM

For centuries marriage has been central in our understanding of the family, and indeed the creation of family law.[5] While unmarried cohabitation is certainly not a modern phenomenon, it is apparent that the law's response has only taken shape relatively recently. Stephen Cretney is accurate when observing that "for much of the 20th century, family law was able simply to ignore the family outside marriage."[6] Prior to the mid-20th century, cohabitation between mixed-sex cohabitants was stigmatized by society and received limited, if any, legal protections. In England and Wales, the remark that such couples were "living in sin" was used by Asquith LJ in the Court of Appeal as late as 1950,[7] which echoes the use in 1954 of the pejorative term "concubine" by Vallee J in the California Court of Appeal.[8] Even much later that disapproving judicial discourse can be observed in other jurisdictions—the British Columbia Court of Appeal used the term "mistress" as late as 1994.[9] Same-sex cohabitants were subjected to even harsher legal treatment and it is only toward the end of the 20th century and after the decriminalization of sexual activity between consenting homosexual adults that some jurisdictions would even accept those relationships as capable of constituting a family.[10]

Change in the societal perceptions of both unmarried mixed- and same-sex couples materialized through a variety of different factors. These included the removal of discrimination on the basis of illegitimacy, a gradually declining marriage rate, and a greater appreciation of functionality, as opposed to formalism, when recognizing the family. Indeed, in the English Court of Appeal, Waite LJ observed in *Fitzpatrick and Sterling Housing Association* that:

> The question is more what a family does than what a family is. A family unit is a social organisation which functions through its linking of members closely together. The functions may be procreative, sexual, sociable, economic, emotional.[11]

By noting that unmarried couples were often functioning in a manner identical to spouses, the continued denial of any form of legal recognition required reappraisal. This disparity was particularly noticeable upon relationship breakdown where spouses were often protected through equitable redistribution frameworks or community of property regimes, yet cohabitants had to rely on property law or contract law principles that were not devised with interpersonal relationships in mind. The rise of contractualization in family law and greater use of marital agreements also meant that pressure for change came from the opposite direction.[12] Spouses themselves were also trying to reform marriage and its consequences from within thereby rejecting that status as "an unyielding over-protective fence surrounding the couple."[13] Clearly the marriage-centric approach to family law was under attack.

Crucially for this chapter, the introduction of civil partnerships and thus extension of the protective reach of family law to a wider range of couples is one strategy for tackling this problem. Another method, which is outside the scope of this chapter, is creating a framework of "opt-out" protections that would apply to all couples after the satisfaction of requirements such as a cohabitation for a specific number of years or the presence of a child. While couples might be able to disapply such scheme, the nature and extent of legal protections can vary considerably. For example, the Scottish[14] and Irish[15] regimes offer relatively weak protections and see the courts making relatively small financial awards on breakdown whereas, and provided qualifying requirements have been met, the New Zealand[16] and Australia "de facto" regimes grant courts the same powers as in proceedings between spouses upon divorce.[17]

The introduction of a second formalized status can be justified using a variety of different reasons. One justification for their use is to offer protections for same-sex couples, who at a particular time were unable to marry. The vanguard in this movement is Denmark, which was the first country in the world to introduce a Registered Partnership Act exclusively for same-sex couples in 1989.[18] The regime, and gradual amendments to it, largely created legal equivalence between registered partners and spouses. It produced a relationship status similar to marriage but without the right to marry in a Church of Denmark ceremony, jointly adopt or have joint custody of children. Put differently, it was a copy of marriage with the politically controversial elements present at that time excised. In spite of these omissions, the Act was lauded as a landmark step in the recognition of LGBT+ families and, as noted by Nielsen, had the important effect of changing public perceptions of same-sex relationships.[19] Other liberal, progressive jurisdictions followed Denmark and similar registered partnership regimes were introduced in Norway (1993), Sweden (1995), Greenland (1996), and Iceland (1996).

Different strategies were adopted elsewhere. In Belgium, for example, the Belgian Parliament introduced a relationship status of legal cohabitation in 1998 which was a "new minimalist status" offering marginally increased protections to those cohabiting.[20] The significance of this move, however, lies in the fact that the regime was open to mixed-sex couples (who did not want to marry), same-sex couples (who, prior to 2003, could not marry) and, more interestingly, close relatives and friends. This reform was controversial, but a key strategy adopted, common with many same-sex only civil partnership reforms, was to differentiate the regime and underline that it was in no way competing with the privileged status of marriage. The French *pacte civil de solidarité* (PACS) can be viewed as a variant of this model, although it should be noted that it confers upon the parties much greater protections than the Belgian regime and is limited to intimate mixed or same-sex relationships. These early innovations reveal a degree of creativity in terms of the modes for protecting the family beyond marriage but a divergence in opinion as to effectiveness. The strong, robust protections seen in the Scandinavian countries were largely welcomed but, while they offered LGBT+ couples protections, they were clearly a concession by a state unwilling at that time to introduce marriage equality. They similarly did nothing to protect mixed-sex couples with objections to marriage. At the other end of the spectrum, the Belgium model was viewed as "excessively broad but insufficiently deep" in terms of the extent of legal protections.[21]

A key moment when delineating reform patterns is the introduction of same-sex marriage. The arrival of marriage equality is often met with celebrations among the LGBT+ community, but it does prompt difficult questions as to the enduring value of civil partnerships. The Netherlands led the way by being the first country in the world to introduce same-sex marriage in 2001, with a comparatively small number of countries following suit through legislation, appellate court rulings, and even referenda.[22] Two models can be discerned here. Where a jurisdiction introduced civil partnerships exclusively for same-sex couples and then subsequently introduced same-sex marriage, it is likely that the partnership regime is phased out. The explanation here is that because the civil partnership regime was originally conceptualized as a functional equivalent to marriage, at a time when same-sex marriage was politically too controversial, that need has now gone. Indeed, Scherpe notes, where a partnership scheme is more or less the identical copy of marriage, once the original is made available, there is "no need to keep the copy."[23] This approach also aligns with the general pattern adopted by countries when incrementally protecting in law the interests of LGBT+ people.[24] Examples of countries that phased out their regimes following marriage equality include Norway, Iceland, Sweden, Denmark, Finland, Ireland, and Germany. Even in these jurisdictions, civil partnerships do serve a limited purpose as that status will still exist for those in pre-existing unions, but no new partnerships can be registered.

Conversely, an alternative model can be discerned where a jurisdiction has introduced a civil partnership regime for both mixed- and same-sex couples, and then subsequently legislated for marriage equality. Here, it is likely that the earlier partnership regime is retained. The rationale for keeping this scheme is that the partnership regime from its inception operated as an alternative to marriage or offered something substantively different in terms of legal protections. The need for a different method of formalization endures in spite of the availability of marriage for all couples. There is variation here. Some jurisdictions like the Netherlands have retained civil partnerships and they confer largely identical rights upon the parties as marriage. In contrast, France and Belgium also kept their earlier regimes but, as stated above, it should be noted that the legal rights are not as far-reaching.

When reflecting on what these approaches mean for relationship recognition beyond marriage, it is clear that their futures are inextricably linked to the availability of same-sex marriage and can only be understood with reference to that particular status. Kees Waaldijk exemplifies this approach through classifying civil partnership regimes as "marriage," "quasi marriage," and "semi-marriage."[25] With the Scandinavian or "Nordic Model," there was a clear duplication of marriage norms and transferral onto same-sex couples. In many ways this could be viewed as a positive development, particularly as it enabled the argument to be made in the ensuing same-sex marriage debates that same-sex marriage would be a linguistic or symbolic change as opposed to a substantive one because couples already had the benefits of marriage protections. Similarly through bolstering public acceptance of same-sex relationships it was able to convey "same-sex commitment" as something no different to that expressed in a mixed-sex marriage.[26] But it did mean that same-sex couples were required to emulate relationship patterns that they may not feel truly reflected the lived realities of their relationship or that what they were originally given was merely a stepping stone toward marriage, which is widely conceptualized as the "final stop for 'full equality' for lesbian and gay men."[27] It was for some couples in same-sex partnerships an acknowledgment that their relationship was, in the words of Harding, "marriage-lite" offering the "same great taste, half the respect of regular marriage."[28] Therefore the decision to phase out this status might appear logical and, indeed, was not met in those jurisdictions with considerable resistance or controversy.

In contrast, the Dutch model of retention of registered partnership regimes post-marriage equality appears, at face value, to offer greater potential to recognize the family beyond marriage. By operating two formalized statuses in tandem it might appear that couples with ideological objections to marriage may have an alternative method for formalization. But here, the introduction of same-sex marriage stimulated a key debate that has featured prominently in equality and anti-discrimination jurisprudence as to the meaning of difference.[29] Put differently, can it be said that couples have a choice as to two genuinely distinct relationship forms?

To determine how far relationship plurality is indeed recognized, a closer examination of the countries that retained civil partnership regimes must be undertaken. At one extreme, the Dutch regime largely emulates marriage and any initial substantive legal distinctions have over time been removed. Conversely, at the other end, the Belgian and to a lesser extent French regime provide evidence of greater respect for relationships that do not wish to conform to a historical or even revised gender-neutral vision of marriage. The difficulty, however, lies in the detail. The availability of legal cohabitation to nonconjugal relationships in Belgium was introduced to differentiate that reform from marriage but has been criticized.[30] As Swennen notes, "in specific statutes substantial legal consequences of registered partnership are aimed at, or even conditioned on, it being sexual," which has the effect of undercutting the progressive, nonconjugal appeal of the regime.[31] While legal cohabitation in Belgium is popular, it has been questioned by academics and policy-makers whether eligibility should now be narrowed and legal consequences intensified so that, in effect, the only difference between that status and marriage would be the name.[32] Similarly, the French *pacte civil de solidarité*, at face value, appears distinct from marriage in that it was conceived and legally defined in the French Civil Code as a contract entered into by two individuals to organize their life in common. But since its introduction it has undergone what Fulchiron has termed "matrimonialisation" whereby the courts, notably the Conseil constitutionnel, have closed the gap between the regimes in terms of debarring PACS couples from contracting out of specific rules.[33] Here, we see the alternatives to marriage looking decidedly marriage-like.

Regardless of the model adopted, the early flirtation of jurisdictions with civil partnerships reveals, whether explicitly or implicitly, a clear engagement with marriage. For same-sex couples this trend is perhaps understandable in light of same-sex marriage often being seen as the ultimate prize in LGBT+ activism. Similarly, as marriage has a long history and is structurally engrained within the legal understanding of interpersonal relationships, it is hardly surprising that it may be used as a starting point when discussing broader family recognition. Nevertheless, this methodology still reveals channeling of individuals *towards* marriage and, as exemplified by comments made by the majority in the United States Supreme Court decision in *Obergefell v. Hodges,* a modern eulogization of marriage as the gold standard for all couples.[34] The next section analyzes the recent contribution of England and Wales to this debate as a jurisdiction that fundamentally departed from the aforementioned Nordic and Dutch models to civil partnership reform.

THE EMERGENCE OF A NEW REFORM PATTERN IN ENGLAND AND WALES

Civil partnerships were introduced in England and Wales through the Civil Partnership Act 2004. They are an opt-in relationship status and, until very recently, were limited to same-sex couples. The justification behind initially excluding mixed-sex couples was that they had long been able to access religious and civil forms of marriage and, as same-sex marriage was not permitted in 2004, there needed to be a mechanism that granted same-sex couples some legal recognition of their relationship.[35] The registration regime was essentially "marriage in all but name."[36] With a few key exceptions, civil partnership and civil marriage are very similar in terms of the formalities for creation, legal consequences upon registration, and dissolution. Those wishing to register a civil partnership must not be within the prohibited degrees, must be over the age of 16 and cannot already be married or in a pre-existing civil partnership. This indicates that the motivations to introduce civil partnerships mapped onto those equally present in the Nordic countries, discussed above. The regime created a functional equivalent to marriage and, for those hoping for same-sex marriage, a "painful compromise between genuine equality and no rights at all."[37] In a bid to allay fears that the regime might be seen to undermine marriage, Parliament even went so far as to introduce an elaborate new vocabulary for civil partnerships to create differentiation.

Civil partnerships were highly popular among the LGBT+ community, particularly when first introduced. In the first three days of the Act coming into force in December 2005 there were 1,227 registrations with 1,857 concluded by the end of that year. The following year saw 14,943 registrations. In subsequent years the total number of civil partnerships registered gradually decreased to around 6,000. However, calls to introduce same-sex marriage intensified. In 2012 a consultation exercise was undertaken, and the government stated its commitment to introduce same-sex marriage.[38] The exercise produced the highest number of responses to a public consultation and exposed the controversial nature of same-sex marriage for some individuals. Crucially, there was clear support for the retention of civil partnerships and, more importantly, 61% of the respondents supported extension of the regime to mixed-sex couples.[39] Many respondents in favor of extending civil partnerships were motivated by an objection to same-sex marriage, but this does reveal considerable support for a method of formalization that had only been recently introduced. The Marriage (Same Sex Couples) Act 2013 was enacted with the first ceremonies taking place in March 2014.

The moment the first same-sex ceremonies took place, England and Wales had effectively departed from the aforementioned Nordic and Dutch models. As civil partnerships largely mimicked civil marriage in terms of the conferral of rights and were a same-sex only construct, there was a strong case for phasing out the regime post-marriage equality. But through refusing to phase out the regime England and Wales (alongside Scotland that followed suit one year later) became the first jurisdiction in the world to offer greater protections to same-sex couples than mixed-sex couples. Same-sex couples had the option of two formalized statuses, whereas mixed-sex couples were limited to one. Significantly for this chapter the logic and legitimacy of this approach prompted a public conversation as to the meaning of relationship formalization. This was facilitated by Section 15 of the Marriage (Same Sex Couples) Act 2013 that mandated the Secretary of State to conduct a review of the future of civil partnerships. This inconclusive review, conducted in 2014 by the Department for Culture, Media and Sport, generated considerably fewer responses than the earlier Equal Civil Marriage consultation.[40] Fifty-five percent of respondents were against the phasing out of civil partnerships, while only 22% were in favor of extending them to different-sex couples. Absent a "united call for change," the government chose to take no further action.[41]

There was a concerted campaign to open up civil partnerships to mixed-sex couples wishing to access an alternative status to marriage. A key element that raised awareness of the asymmetrical and discriminatory position was a legal challenge by a mixed-sex couple seeking a civil partnership.[42] In *R (on the application of Steinfeld and Keidan) v Secretary of State for International Development*, the Supreme Court ruled that the ban on mixed-sex civil partnerships constituted discrimination under Articles 8 (right to respect for private and family life) and 14 (prohibition of discrimination) of the European Convention on Human Rights.[43] Motivated by the Supreme Court ruling and supported by the Equal Civil Partnerships campaign, several Private Members Bills were introduced into Parliament seeking the extension of the regime. Ultimately the Civil Partnerships, Marriages and Deaths (Registration etc) Act 2019 was passed. This paved the way for the Civil Partnership (Opposite Sex Couple) Regulations 2019, which came into force at the end of December 2019, enabling mixed-sex couples to access civil partnerships in the same manner as same-sex couples.

What does this development tell us about family recognition beyond marriage? Two observations can be made. First, the reform campaign prompted an important discussion as to the precise difference between marriage and civil partnership. The *Steinfeld* litigation was brought by a couple who possessed strong ideological objections to marriage believing it to be a patriarchal institution. They believed that civil partnerships were much more egalitarian, secular and neutral in nature, and did not suffer from the same historical baggage of marriage. These arguments advanced in the litigation received extensive scrutiny in the mainstream media and academic community. There was considerable support for a status that was perceived to be different to marriage. LGBT+ charities, in particular, believed that retention of the regime and extension to mixed-sex couples would be positive in buttressing civil partnerships as a now established status and converting it into an institution that plays an important role in people's lives. One high-profile campaigner, Peter Tatchell, argued that phasing out the regime would "provoke an almighty backlash" and inflict "catastrophic damage" on relations between the government and the LGBT+ community. Yet, at the same time, the *Steinfeld* couple were subject to robust criticism. Indeed, when referring to the litigants, one tabloid journalist advised: "this exhibitionist couple, and anyone else with a fake grievance . . . to stop being so silly—and thank their lucky stars that, in this cruel and unjust world, they've suffered nothing more serious to make a fuss about."[44] This view was echoed by a respondent in a study of LGBT+ couples by Jowett and Peel who believed the extension of civil partnerships was "insulting" in light of the fact that mixed-sex couples had not experienced the same systematic, structural oppression experienced by LGBT+ couples.[45] This division of opinion is important because it reveals a fundamental dispute as to both the substantive and symbolic differences between marriage and civil partnership. Furthermore, like the experience of jurisdictions discussed above, it also shows marital norms operating in the background.

As to substantive differences, the litigation and later Parliamentary debates revealed extensive confusion as to rights and entitlements of civil partners. For example, it was argued that civil partnerships offered a lighter form of legal commitment or the ability for couples to "effectively grant each other greater rights."[46] Yet closer examination of the provisions reveal civil partnerships are not a more malleable status than marriage, nor can they be modified by the parties themselves like the French PACS. Even that capacity in France has been restricted in a manner to suggest greater alignment between the PACS and marriage. Similarly, it was observed in the Parliamentary debates that civil partnerships provided "an option for people who want to have a legal relationship but not necessarily a religious one."[47] This overlooks the fact that since December 2011, civil partnerships can be celebrated on religious premises provided the organization opts in and the act of registration remains secular.

If it is accepted that civil partnerships emulate a marital model in terms of offering a high level of substantive legal protection, then it follows that the key differentiation between the regimes must be symbolism. It should be noted here that, while an ephemeral quality, symbolism and the formal, outward expression of a relationship clearly matters to couples. For example, in the context of Italy's refusal to offer same-sex couples any mechanism for formalizing relationships, the European Court of Human Rights ruled that civil partnerships possessed "an intrinsic value . . . irrespective of the legal effects, however narrow or extensive, that they would introduce."[48] Thus, it is understandable why couples might want the public signaling of a relationship offered by civil partnerships. It appears that this aspect played a particularly significant role in the campaign for equal civil partnerships in England and Wales. Access to civic benefits was not the sole motivating force behind equal civil partnerships but operated alongside an anxiety as to the absence of a status or, viewed differently, the perceived invisibility of unmarried couples. As a jurisdiction, England and Wales provide limited protection to cohabitants and no dedicated regime applicable upon relationship breakdown. Thus, unlike other jurisdictions offering a safety net to these couples when relationships end, there is a stark disparity in legal treatment dependent on status. This need to acknowledge the commitment of couples was a key narrative noticeable in the campaign for civil partnership reform but, yet again, led the discourse back to the value of formalization and what Van Acker has termed a "conception of the desirable."[49] With marriage representing the archetypal respected relationship, it was particularly striking how couples ideologically opposed to marriage sought legal recognition through framing their case by reference to marital norms. Indeed, references were made as to the stability offered by formalization thereby juxtaposing the strength of possessing a marriage-like status with the fragility of cohabitation.

A second observation can be made. Although comparisons to marriage featured in the academic discourse, a new approach has emerged in relation to civil partnership reform that is different from the Nordic and Dutch models. By extending a regime to mixed-sex couples that was originally designed for same-sex couples, England and Wales evidenced a novel repurposing of civil partnerships. Of itself, this move offers interesting insights into how a changing societal attitude as to formalization can prompt an evolution of a status and hints at potential for more dynamic relationship recognition beyond marriage. Moreover, examples are now emerging of other jurisdictions in Europe approaching civil partnership reform creatively.[50] Austria, for example, introduced marriage equality on January 1, 2019, and simultaneously opened up to mixed-sex couples their originally same-sex only civil partnership regime, first introduced in 2010.[51] Interestingly, like England and Wales, the refusal to permit mixed-sex civil partnerships was also challenged in the courts in Austria, albeit with an unsuccessful application taken to the European Court of Human Rights in *Ratzenböck and Seydl v Austria*.[52] While discrimination experienced by mixed-sex couples can be resolved through phasing out or extending civil partnership regimes, where strategic litigation has occurred there now is greater likelihood that a regime is extended. Cumulatively, what these experiences suggest is that the inevitability of the retention or phasing out of civil partnerships, premised on the Dutch or Nordic models is no longer certain and an increase, rather than decrease, in the use of civil partnerships is taking place. But, crucially for this chapter, can it be said that these recent trends evidence a genuine engagement with recognizing the diversity of relationship structures?

EMBRACING FAMILY RECOGNITION BEYOND MARRIAGE

To date, jurisdictions grappling with second formalized statuses have introduced reforms that whether directly or indirectly replicate and reinforce marital norms through creating statuses that are conjugal and dyadic. In some ways, this is understandable because marriage has always been the definitive model for couple regulation and to create something new might be unrealistically aspirational. Similarly, family law policymakers are responding to what they consider the most pressing needs and thus narrow marriage-lite regimes could be viewed as both politically and pragmatically sensible rather than more theoretically informed root-and-branch reforms. But it is argued that this current approach to second formalized statuses presents multiple problems.

First, by absorbing marital norms, civil partnerships often facilitate mimicry of marriage. The functionality-based arguments made by mixed-sex couples seeking a civil partnership provide ample evidence of that process at play. Although civil partnerships can be viewed as a "construct of statute" and thus may offer something different to the legacy-laden concept of marriage, at present the space for creativity, personalization, and departure from marriage-like legal obligations is limited.[53] Even the more dynamic contract-based regimes like the French PACS prevent parties from truly imprinting their values onto that particular status.

Second, the development of civil partnerships often tells us more about the types of desirable families that the state wishes to support than the lived plurality of different forms. Attempts to incorporate into civil partnership regimes alternative relationships of care and dependency, such as between nonconjugal carers and siblings, have often been used disingenuously to further extend coverage so as to dilute a particular proposal or serve as a wrecking amendment. In many jurisdictions civil partnership debates have seen attempts to include siblings within the schemes, but with limited exceptions, these have been resisted.[54] But these attempts, particularly in relation to preexisting regimes, reveal how marriage-centric conjugal ideas create barriers for recognition. For example, including siblings within the civil partnership regime in England and Wales would shoe-horn such relationships into a status conceived for intimate relationships. If implemented it would envisage one sibling "divorcing" their other sibling.[55] Even with schemes that do permit family members forming a status, deficiencies arise suggesting that they are not fully effective or equipped to recognize relationship plurality. In Belgium, while a parent and child can create a status of legal cohabitation, it can only be with one child at a time, which creates an obvious issue if that parent has more than one child. Here we see the dyadic approach to relationship recognition dominating and the structure of regimes suppressing alternative forms.[56]

Third, introducing civil partnerships can sometimes stymie broader family law reform that could meaningfully embrace a diverse range of relationships. For example, while there is a pressing need for opt-out cohabitation protections in England and Wales, the current government's pro-formalization stance that underpinned the extension of the regime to mixed-sex couples, means that such reform is, at present, unlikely. When announcing the recent reform the government positioned mixed-sex civil partnerships as a *solution* to cohabitation stating that they were to be introduced to "give long-term, cohabiting, opposite-sex couples who do not want to marry the opportunity to gain rights, protections and recognition, encouraging stable family relationships."[57] The effect of this narrative creates a problematic hierarchy of relationship forms and a dichotomy of "insiders" and "outsiders." Craig Lind identified this trend in the context of greater protection of same-sex couples noting that their recognition, through a process of "normalization," has shown that "alternative ways of living domestic lives are being marginalized."[58] Resonating with the issues associated with modern family recognition through formalization, Lind further noted:

> People who are unsuited to these lifestyles remain outsiders in society. And the question we must ask ourselves is whether or not we have really progressed when we have managed to enlarge the group of the privileged and retain our prejudices in relation to others.[59]

Thus, the issue becomes how to better recognize families beyond marriage. One method is to acknowledge explicitly the continued dominance of marital norms in the construction of civil partnerships (despite claims to the contrary) and to explore whether marriage should be the starting point for family recognition, particularly in light of declining marriage rates. That questioning has already begun with the publication of several academic critiques exploring the continued prioritization of marriage in law.[60] More recent scholarship has intensified the interrogation of why marriage remains so privileged[61] and whether it should be welcomed by feminists and members of the LGBT+ community.[62] But it is unfortunate that in spite of this discourse civil partnerships have often been presented as something new, when upon closer inspection, they generally offer a recycling of existing norms conceived for a conjugal, domestic relationship performed exclusively between two people.

Another strategy is to avoid consciously the homogenization of nonmarital families and accept that a diversity of relationship forms necessitates a plurality of legal responses. This acceptance should envisage a constellation of formalized statuses and preferably a registration regime that offers something fundamentally different to marriage so as to provide opportunities to express different types of family. Equally protections not dependent on formalization are necessary too in that they may better reflect the changing, potentially fluctuating, nature of commitment within a relationship over time.[63] To achieve this end, policymakers must engage with the couples themselves so as to avoid the top-down cascading of marital norms that we have seen in civil partnership reform. As Carbone and Cahn persuasively argue, although writing in the cohabitation context, mimicry of marriage or extension of marriage norms to the infinitely diverse nonmarital family is not a viable reform solution because, paradoxically, "imposing equality fosters inequality."[64]

CONCLUSION

This chapter does not deny that civil partnerships have made a profoundly important contribution to the lives of many couples. Without a doubt they played a key role in stimulating greater public acceptance and legal recognition for LGBT+ couples and continue to operate as a valued institution for same-sex couples unable to marry or choosing not to do so. It is thus indisputable that civil partnerships have facilitated greater opportunities for formalization. But whether they act as a means for truly embracing family recognition beyond marriage still remains questionable.

That position, however, may be changing when it is recalled that it is only relatively recently that some states have operated systems of two formalized statuses and accordingly a period of time is required for marriage and civil partnerships to coexist and mature separately. Contexts are also changing too. It should be remembered that civil partnerships were often conceived as a mechanism to offer protection to same-sex couples and were developed incrementally through political compromise. As we have seen, it was often the case that elements in proposals perceived to be more radical such as non-conjugal relationships were removed. Today Western democracies, which have introduced same-sex marriage and are now turning to cohabitation, are presented with a fundamentally different legal landscape. In France, for example, the "matrimonialisation" process of the PACS originally began when same-sex couples tried to make it more marriage-like at a time when marriage was denied to them. Now the option of same-sex marriage is permitted in France, a space is created for couples to shape the PACS, without reference to marriage, and in a manner motivated by different imperatives. Similarly, the unique approach of England and Wales not only evidences a departure from the Nordic and Dutch models of civil partnership reform but also provides insights into how a status might evolve and over time be recalibrated to the needs of a different group of couples.

While many civil partnership regimes still mimic marriage, it is hoped that continued engagement with the status by a new wave of mixed- and same-sex couples will create differing ideologies, norms, and even ceremonial rites. That process is already happening as, despite the availability of equal marriage in a significant minority of countries, couples are still registering partnerships. As a result, albeit with differing levels of success, couples are beginning to sculpt frameworks for their joint lives and over time this process may gradually disrupt the magnetic influence of marriage. It is here that lies the real potential for family recognition beyond marriage.

NOTES

1. See e.g. Nikki Graf, "Key Findings on Marriage and Cohabitation in the U.S.," Pew Research Center, November 6, 2019, https://pewrsr.ch/2NnfuOJ, Statistics Canada, *Portrait of Families and Living Arrangements in Canada—Families, Households and Marital Status, 2011 Census of Population,* September 2012, https://

www12.statcan.gc.ca/census-recensement/2011/as-sa/98-312-x/98-312-x2011001-eng.pdf, Australian Bureau of Statistics, *Marriages and Divorces, Australia 2018*, November 27, 2019, https://www.abs.gov.au/statistics/people/people-and-communities/marriages-and-divorces-australia/latest-release

2. See Office for National Statistics, *Families and Households in the UK*. November 15, 2019, https://www.ons.gov.uk/releases/familiesandhouseholdsintheuk2019

3. For comparative survey see Jens M Scherpe and Andy Hayward, *The Future of Registered Partnerships—Family Recognition Beyond Marriage?* (Cambridge: Intersentia, 2017). See also Erez Aloni, "Registering Relationships," *Tulane Law Review* 87, no. 3 (2013): 573.

4. See, for example, New Zealand that has adopted a tiered system of marriage, civil union *and* protection for non-registered or de facto couples.

5. Alan Brown, *What is The Family of Law?: The Influence of the Nuclear Family* (Hart Publishing, 2019).

6. Stephen Cretney, *Family Law in the Twentieth Century: A History* (Oxford: Oxford University Press, 2003), 517.

7. *Gammans v. Ekins* [1950] 2 All ER 140, 141.

8. *Hill v. Estate of Westbrook* 95 Cal App 2d 599, 603, 213 P.2d 727 (1950).

9. *Crick v. Ludwig* (1994) 11 7 DLR (4th) 228.

10. See Stephen Cretney, *Same Sex Relationships: From "Odious Crime" to "Gay Marriage"* (Oxford: Oxford University Press, 2006).

11. *Fitzpatrick v. Sterling Housing Association Ltd* [1998] Ch. 304, 339.

12. Jens M Scherpe and Brian Sloan, "Contractualisation of Family Law in England & Wales: Autonomy vs Judicial Discretion" in *Contractualisation of Family Law—Global Perspectives,* ed. Frederik Swennen (Springer, 2015), 165–191.

13. Laurence Francoz-Terminal, "Registered Partnerships in France," in Scherpe and Hayward, *The Future of Registered Partnerships,* 184.

14. See Frankie McCarthy, "Cohabitation: Lessons from North of the Border?," *Child and Family Law Quarterly* 23, no. 3 (September 2011): 277 and Joanna Miles et al., "Cohabitation: Lessons from Research North of the Border?," *Child and Family Law Quarterly* 23, no. 3 (September 2011): 302.

15. See Brian Tobin, "The Regulation of Cohabitation in Ireland: Achieving Equilibrium Between Protection and Paternalism?," *Journal of Social Welfare and Family Law* 35 no. 3 (June 2013): 279 and John Mee, "Cohabitation Law Reform in Ireland," *Child and Family Law Quarterly* 23, no. 3 (September 2011): 323.

16. See William R Atkin, "'De Facto Relationships' in New Zealand—A Largely Unified Law," *Family Law Quarterly* 50, no. 2 (Summer, 2016): 303.

17. See Patrick Parkinson, "Family Property Division and the Principle of Judicial Restraint," *UNSW Law Journal* 41, no. 2 (June 2018): 380.

18. See Ingrid Lund-Andersen, "The Danish Registered Partnership Act, 1989: Has the Act Meant a Change in Attitudes?," in *Legal Recognition of Same-Sex Partnerships: A Study of National, European and International Law,* ed. Robert Wintemute and Mads Andenaes, (Hart Publishing, 2001).

19. Linda Nielsen, "Family Rights and the Registered Partnership in Denmark," *International Journal of Family Law* 4, no. 3 (1990): 297.

20. Geoffrey Willems, "Registered Partnerships in Belgium," in Scherpe and Hayward, *The Future of Registered Partnerships,* 385.

21. Geoffrey Willems, "Registered Partnerships in Belgium," 385.

22. See Brian Tobin, "Marriage Equality in Australia and Ireland: Separate Jurisdictions, Similar Politics," *Australian Journal of Family Law* 32, no. 3 (September 2019): 294.

23. Jens M. Scherpe, "The Past, Present and Future of Civil Partnerships," in Scherpe and Hayward, *The Future of Registered Partnerships,* 577.

24. See e.g. *M v. Secretary of State for Work and Pensions* [2006] UKHL 11 [93] (Baroness Hale) and Brenda Hale, "Homosexual Rights," *Child and Family Law Quarterly* 16, no. 2 (June 2004): 125.

25. Kees Waaldijk, "Others May Follow: The Introduction of Marriage Quasi-Marriage, and Semi-Marriage for Same-Sex Couples in European Countries," *New England Law Review* 38, no. 3 (2003–2004): 569, 583.

26. *Wilkinson v. Kitzinger (No 2)* [2006] EWHC 2022 (Fam) [121] (Sir Mark Potter P).

27. Nicola Barker, *Not the Marrying Kind: A Feminist Critique of Same-Sex Marriage* (Palgrave Macmillan, 2012) 2. See also Kenneth McK Norrie, "Marriage Is for Heterosexuals—May the Rest of Us Be Saved from It," *Child and Family Law Quarterly* 12, no. 4 (December 2000): 363.

28. Rosie Harding, "'Dogs are "Registered", People Shouldn't Be': Legal Consciousness and Lesbian and Gay Rights," *Social and Legal Studies* 15, no. 4 (December 2006): 511, 524.

29. Nicholas Bamforth, "The Benefits of Marriage in All But Name? Same-Sex Couples and the Civil Partnership Act 2004," *Child and Family Law Quarterly* 19, no. 2 (June 2007): 133.

30. See Olivier de Schutter and Kees Waaldijk, "Major Legal Consequences of Marriage, Cohabitation and Registered Partnership for Different-Sex and Same-Sex Partners in Belgium," in *More or Less Together: Levels of Legal Consequences of Marriage, Cohabitation and Registered Partnership for Different-Sex and Same-Sex Partners. A Comparative Study of Nine European Countries*, ed. Kees Waaldijk (Leiden University, December 2005), https://openaccess.leidenuniv.nl/handle/1887/12585

31. Frederik Swennen, "Un-Coupling Family Law: The Legal Recognition and Protection of Adult Unions Outside of Conjugal Coupledom," *Feminist Legal Studies* 28, no. 1 (March 2020): 39, 41.

32. See Alain-Charles Van Gysel, "La cohabitation légale: *quo vadis?*," *Revue trimestrielle de droit familial* (2015): 39–40.

33. Hugues Fulchiron, "Le mariage est-il soluble dans le partenariat (et réciproquement)?," in *Mélanges en l'honneur de Jean Hauser* (LexisNexis/Dalloz, 2012), 125.

34. *Obergefell v. Hodges*, 576 U.S. 644, 135 S Ct 2584 (2015).

35. See Department of Trade and Industry, *Civil Partnership: A Framework for the Legal Recognition of Same-Sex Couples* (London, 2003), 13.

36. *Wilkinson v. Kitzinger (No 2)* [2006] EWHC 2022 (Fam) [88].

37. Sue Wilkinson and Celia Kitzinger, "In Support of Equal Marriage: Why Civil Partnership Is Not Enough," *Psychology of Women Review* 8, no. 1 (Spring 2006): 54.

38. HM Government, *Equal Marriage: The Government's Response* (London, 2012).

39. HM Government, *Equal Marriage*, 42.

40. Department for Culture, Media and Sport, *Civil Partnership Review (England and Wales): A Consultation* (London, 2014).

41. Department for Culture, Media and Sport, *Civil Partnership Review*, 4.

42. See Helen Fenwick and Andy Hayward, "Rejecting Asymmetry of Access to Formal Relationship Statuses for Same- and Different-Sex Couples at Strasbourg and Domestically," *European Human Rights Law Review*, no. 6 (December 2017): 544.

43. [2018] UKSC 32. See Andy Hayward, "Equal Civil Partnerships, Discrimination and the Indulgence of Time," *Modern Law Review* 82, no. 5 (September 2019): 922–35.

44. Tom Utley, "A Straight Couple Whining Because They Can't Have a Civil Partnership? Give Me Strength!," *The Daily Mail*, December 5, 2014.

45. Adam Jowett and Elizabeth Peel, "'A Question of Equality and Choice': Same-Sex Couples' Attitudes towards Civil Partnership after the Introduction of Same-Sex Marriage," *Psychology and Sexuality* 8, nos. 1–2 (April 2017): 69, 75.

46. A point made by Kevin Hollinrake MP: Hansard, HC Deb, vol 656, col 682 (15 March 2019).

47. Hansard, HC Deb, vol 656, col 685 (15 March 2019) (Kevin Foster MP).

48. (2015) 65 EHRR 957, [174]. See Andy Hayward, "Same-sex Registered Partnerships—A Right to be Recognised?," *Cambridge Law Journal,* 75, no. 1 (January 2016): 27–30.

49. Elizabeth van Acker, "Disconnected Relationship Values and Marriage Policies in England," *Journal of Social Welfare and Family Law* 38, no. 1 (January 2016): 36–37.

50. See also the Isle of Man, Gibraltar, the Falkland Islands. Note Greece introduced mixed-sex only civil partnerships in 2008 but later made them gender-neutral in 2015 in light of that position being found to breach the European Convention on Human Rights in *Vallianatos v. Greece* (2014) 59 E.H.R.R. 12.

51. Austrian Constitutional Court Judgment: G 258/2017, 4 December 2017. See also the expansion of the Californian Domestic Partnership law to all couples introduced in January 2020.

52. [2017] ECHR 947.

53. *R v. Bala and others* [2016] EWCA Crim 560 [38] (Davies LJ).

54. See e.g. The Netherlands discussed in Kees Waaldijk, "Small Change: How the Road to Same-Sex Marriage Got Paved in the Netherlands," in Wintemute and Andenaes, *Legal Recognition of Same-Sex Partnerships*, 436, 444.

55. In England and Wales, civil partners technically do not divorce, they dissolve their partnership.

56. Geoffrey Willems, "Registered Partnerships in Belgium," in Scherpe and Hayward, *The Future of Registered Partnerships* 382, 387.

57. Government Equalities Office, *Implementing Opposite-Sex Civil Partnerships: Next Steps,* July 2019, 5. See Andy Hayward, "The *Steinfeld* Effect: Equal Civil Partnerships and the Construction of the Cohabitant," *Child and Family Law Quarterly* 31, no. 4 (December 2019): 283.

58. Craig Lind, "Sexuality and Same-Sex Relationships in Law," in *Sexually Repositioned: Diversity and the Law,* eds. Belinda Brooks-Gordon, Lorraine Gelsthorpe, Martin Johnson and Andrew Bainham (Hart Publishing, 2004), 126.

59. Lind, "Sexuality," 126.

60. Martha Albertson Fineman, "Why Marriage?," *Virginia Journal of Social Policy and the Law* 9, no. 1 (2001): 239–71.

61. Sheila Jeffreys, "The Need to Abolish Marriage," *Feminism & Psychology,* 14, no. 2 (May 2004): 327 and Claire Chambers, *Against Marriage: An Egalitarian Defence of the Marriage-Free State* (Oxford: Oxford University Press, 2017).

62. Nicola Barker, *Not the Marrying Kind: A Feminist Critique of Same-Sex Marriage* (Palgrave Macmillan, 2012).

63. Anne Barlow and Janet Smithson, "Legal Assumptions, Cohabitants' Talk and the Rocky Road to Reform," *Child and Family Law Quarterly* 22, no. 3 (September 2010): 328.

64. June Carbone and Naomi Cahn, "Nonmarriage," *Maryland Law Review* 76, no. 1 (2016): 55, 59. See also June Carbone and Naomi Cahn, "Blackstonian Marriage, Gender, and Cohabitation," *Arizona State Law Journal* 51, no. 4 (December 2019): 1247.

Chapter 3

Recognition of Islamic Marriages in the UK

Continuity of Marriage Status or Nonexistent Marriages?

Michael Wells-Greco

INTRODUCTION

The family unit is one of the most important private spheres, yet it is an area of life which faces both societal and legal expectations. It is this confrontation which gives rise to public debate about allocating responsibility for financial and care responsibility, individual and collective self-determination, and, more broadly, what societal norms should be promoted by legal recognition. The composition of family units is becoming more varied in many countries. The reasons why people may wish (not) to marry are equally varied. Nevertheless, marriage is weaved into the fabric of society nationally and internationally. Despite its pervasiveness, there is no one holistic definition of marriage. As the European Court of Human Rights (ECtHR) has put it: "Marriage has deep-rooted social and cultural connotations which may differ largely from one society to another."[1]

The adherence of members of religious communities around the world to religious family laws or the persistence of religion as a—or the—governing source of family obligations to members of that community has raised much research interest.[2] Migration from Islamic countries to the United Kingdom—and to many other countries in Europe—has added to this pluralization.[3] Questions of Islamic (family) law[4] are important for non-Muslim states, which have had to consider the legal status to be offered to religious marriages and the recognition of foreign marriages within their legal frameworks.[5] Even though persons resident in England are subject to English family law[6] (including rules of recognition), the day-to-day family lives of many Muslims can be, in practice, determined by Islamic law.[7] A 2018 "Independent Review into the application of Sharia law in England and Wales" found that a significant number of Muslim couples do not register their religious marriage as a civil marriage.[8] Regarding the number of polygamous marriages, one estimate suggests that there are up to 20,000 de facto polygamous marriages in the UK.[9] An apparent proliferation of unrecognized[10]—so-called "nikah-only"[11]—marriages in England has been observed, and the English courts have been charged with considering the extent to which a foreign marriage (including a polygamous marriage) lawfully celebrated abroad should be recognized in England. A report published by Cardiff University highlighted a main area of concern as being unregistered marriages,[12] in other words Muslim women who had no option in conformity with their religion but to use a Sharia council[13] when their relationships broke down because they had a religious but not a legal marriage. Research continues to show that unregistered marriages remain prelevant.[14] In the past decade, there have been six reported court cases in England of unregistered Muslim marriages involving British Muslims.[15]

The challenge posed to English law and legal institutions within the UK (and in other states) is the manner—and the extent—in which English law can accommodate individual choice in matters of religion while at the same time upholding fundamental principles. This chapter explores instances and the implications of the (non-) recognition of certain marriages—nikah, proxy, non-age, polygamous, and consanguineous—in England and Wales. The legal position of foreign Islamic marriages under English law, the surrounding public policy considerations and the impact of European human-rights standards in the context of Islamic marriages are also discussed. This chapter considers where the balance lies in upholding noncompliant marriages (from an English law perspective) entered into in good faith versus declaring such relationships as nonexistent for judicial purposes. It also considers the extent to which family law can inform societal norms regarding marriage.

THE POSITION OF ISLAMIC MARRIAGES UNDER ENGLISH LAW

In order to be recognized as legally valid, all marriages which take place in the UK must be monogamous and must be carried out in accordance with the requirements of the relevant legislation. A marriage will not be recongized if certain formalities as to the ceremony have not been complied with. For example, a marriage must take place in a registered venue and there must be present a registrar of marriages or authorized person. There are several routes into legal marriage in England and Wales with different options based upon whether a religious or civil ceremony is chosen. In England and Wales, pursuant to the Marriage Act 1949 (as amended), there are four main categories of marriage ceremony: civil marriage ceremonies; marriages contracted according to the rites of the Church of England or Wales; marriages contracted according to Quaker and Jewish traditions; and marriages conducted in other non-Anglican religious ceremonies. Different religions are therefore treated differently. For those Muslims in the UK who have an Islamic religious marriage ceremony and do not have an additional civil ceremony in the UK, their marriage will not be recognized as being legally valid. The consequences of this are particularly significant as a non-qualifying marriage in England and Wales is likely to be considered "nonexistent."[16]

Countries applying Islamic law to marriages tend to apply fewer formalities compared with English law. As mentioned above, private unregistered ceremonies may give rise to a valid marriage under local law and proxy ceremonies (conducted in the absence of one of the parties) may be accepted.[17] The substantive conditions of marriage may also be different.[18] English law insists on monogamy, while an interpretation of Islamic law permits polygamy[19] and allows men to have up to four wives. In traditional Islamic law, there is no minimum age for marriage, while English law sets a minimum age of 18 years (albeit, at the time of writing, the law allows marriage at the age of 16 provided there is parental consent[20]). Consent requirements can also differ.

The differences between Islamic and English conceptions of marriage can therefore result in Islamic marriages celebrated abroad not being recognized in England. In some instances, this will be relatively uncontroversial. For example, child marriage represents a violation of the fundamental human rights of children, predominantly girls, and results in a range of serious related issues for the child. Shia "muta" (temporary) marriages will not be considered sufficiently analogous to English conceptions of marriage for lack of a permanent marital commitment as understood under English law. In other instances, a foreign marriage which may be far removed from the normal meaning of marriage and does not satisfy English requirements for a marriage—for example, monogamy—may, in certain circumstances, be recognized.

Any interpretation of Islamic (or any foreign) law which marginalizes women is objectionable from the perspective of English gender-equality social norms and in law. However, Islamic law is not a single monolithic entity.[21] Traditional standards have been modified by statute and custom in many countries applying Islamic law—and in some specific cases, the applicable rules will match (or go further than[22]) English domestic requirements.[23] Comparative research shows that there are diverse and plural lived experiences of how Muslim marriages are entered into.[24] The result is a plurality of marital relationship norms which speaks against the idea of one holistic concept of "Muslim marriage."[25]

(NON-)RECOGNITION OF FOREIGN ISLAMIC MARRIAGES UNDER ENGLISH LAW

English law allows for recognition of a foreign marriage if: the foreign institution is sufficiently analogous to English conceptions of marriage as to be capable of being characterized as a "marriage" under English law (the "characterization" test); there is nothing in the laws of either person's country of domicile at the time of the marriage which prevents the marriage being recognized ("dual domicile" test for essential validity)[26]; any previous marriage of the couple have broken down permanently;[27] and that a marriage which takes place outside of England and Wales in accordance with foreign law is valid in England if it is valid according to the law of the jurisdiction where it was celebrated[28]—*lex loci celebrationis*.[29]

Even if the foreign marriage satisfies the *lex loci celebrationis* rule, the recognition of certain foreign Islamic marriages may be affected by the public policy doctrine. This doctrine can have a validating or an invalidating effect: in other words, it may serve to invalidate a marriage which is formally and essentially valid—or may validate a foreign marriage which fails to satisfy one of those requirements (where one of the foreign invalidating restrictions is considered highly objectionable). The more radical the divergences in domestic standards, the more likely it is that public policy will come into play—and, as the case law suggests—Islamic marriage recognition is vulnerable to public policy considerations.

In addition to constituting, in effect, a societal judgment on the moral status of a marriage, the non-recognition of a foreign marriage results in a limping legal relationship status (*rapports juridiques boiteuses*). A "limping legal relation" is a legal relationship that exists in one legal system but not in another, or when valid in both, it has different legal effects in each of them. This entails negative consequences concerning, for example, maintenance, succession, and paternity, which may well result in a child being ultimately given less protection in law.

Whether the marriage is void or "non-qualifying" under English law has significant ramifications in terms of financial responsibilities within the family unit. If the marriage is considered void, it is deemed invalid in English law, yet, in the event of a breakdown of the relationship, financial remedy claims can still be made. Such remedies include all the usual financial orders available to divorcing couples that have a valid marriage, for example, annual payments, including lump sums, property and pension sharing. If there is a declaration of non-marriage[30], short for "nonexistent marriage" (or more recently, "non-qualifying marriage"[31]), financial remedy claims are not available.

Some couples may be able to regularize their status through a marriage ceremony in England. Such partners will then be required to obtain a dissolution of their marriage prior to marrying in England. This may be entirely impractical if the stay in England is for a limited period. Even in the event of a longer-term move to England, the need for a prior dissolution of the partnership necessarily entails a disruption of status and the grant of such dissolution may be contingent on a resumption of residence in the country where the marriage was registered (there being no dissolution mechanism available in England given that the marriage is not recognized).

Having discussed the more general impact of the English law approach to recognition, consideration now turns to consider specific aspects of certain Islamic marriage and their accommodation within the English legal order in order to identify the public policy considerations.

SPECIFIC CASES

"Nikah-Only" Marriages

In *Akhter v. Khan*[32] the Court of Appeal in 2020 overturned a decision of a lower court which held that *nikah* ceremony could be classified as a void marriage giving rise to financial remedies. The Court of Appeal unanimously found that no marriage ceremony took place under English law. By way of brief summary (with the parties referred to as "husband" and "wife" for convenience), the wife issued a petition for divorce from the husband on November 4, 2016, claiming they had been married in 1998. The husband defended the divorce on the basis that the parties had not entered a valid marriage according to English law but had instead undergone a nikah. A very strong argument by the wife on human-rights grounds prompted the English court to consider the European Convention on Human Rights (ECHR) and consider the best interests of the children. The Court of Appeal found that the nikah conducted in this case did not create a void marriage because it was a "non-qualifying" ceremony. It also found that while the petitioner's right to respect to family life was undoubtedly engaged, the failure of the state to recognize the nikah as a legal marriage was not in breach of those rights.

Proxy Marriages

Concerns arise with respect to the recognition of foreign proxy marriages. English law requires the presence of the spouses at a domestic marriage ceremony.[33] The 1962 UN Convention on Consent to Marriage insists on party presence save "where the circumstances are exceptional."[34] Proxy and absentee marriage forms are susceptible to abuse in contracting marriages of convenience and the circumvention of immigration restrictions.

The English court held in *Apt v. Apt*[35] that foreign proxy marriages can be recognized even if the absent party was domiciled and residing in England at the time of the foreign ceremony. It has been confirmed that the doctrine laid down in *Apt v. Apt* can apply to non-Christian proxy marriage ceremonies.[36] A proxy marriage is (for English law purposes) therefore classified as a method of giving consent, as distinct from the consent itself. Consequently, a proxy marriage is a matter of the form of the ceremony or proceeding under English law and is determined based on the *lexi loci celebrationis*. The Court noted in *Apt v. Apt* that there is no doctrine of public policy which invalidates under English law a proxy marriage provided that the form of the ceremony or proceeding is valid in that country and is performed strictly in accordance with the laws of that country and contains nothing abhorrent to Christian ideas.

Non-Age

The lack of marital age falls under the test for capacity to marry in England. Under English law the minimum age is regulated in the Marriage Act 1949, in Section 2, where it is stated that "a marriage solemnized between persons either of whom is under the age of sixteen shall be void." For foreign marriages, the dual domicile test allows (at least in principle) for the recognition of foreign marriages involving young teenagers and children—and in England in the late 1960s, the marriage in Nigeria of a 26-year-old man and a 13-year-old girl, both domiciled in Nigeria, where the marriage was valid, was held to be entitled to recognition when they arrived in London shortly after the ceremony (*Mohamed v. Knott*[37]). The dual domicile test has been replaced by a statutory rule which requires non-recognition of a foreign marriage where either party was less than 18 years[38] and where either was resident in England at the time of the marriage. With an increased human-rights emphasis on non-age and on the criminalization of child marriage,[39] a marriage similar to that in *Mohamed v. Knott* would very likely be refused recognition as a matter of public policy.[40]

Polygamy

Polygamous marriages seem to form a distinct category under the English law. Even if a foreign marriage was both formally and essentially valid according to the laws to be applied under English private international law, the marriage could be assessed as being invalid if the marriage was (actually or potentially[41]) polygamous. If neither of the parties is domiciled in England at the time of the celebration of the marriage, the concept of the potentially polygamous marriages is still relevant. In *R v. Immigration Appeal Tribunal ex parte Jan*,[42] the English court did not recognize the polygamous (second) marriage of a Pakistani man with a Pakistani woman on the basis that the man had an English domicile at the time of the second marriage.

Marriages which are in reality monogamous but are celebrated under a law which permits polygamy are regarded as valid.[43] All potentially polygamous marriages, which are actually monogamous, are therefore valid under English law.

Examining the general English case law on polygamous marriages, the degree of recognition of polygamous marriages differs. The recognition of a polygamous marriage is a "limited recognition": the scope of the recognition depends on the specific case of each polygamous marriage. For example, the recognition of a polygamous marriage does not necessarily lead, for example, to a direct assumption of entitlement to a state pension, to which the partners in a monogamous marriage would be entitled to. Yet, in the event of a breakdown of the relationship, financial remedy claims can still be made.[44]

THEMES EMERGING FROM THE CASE LAW

Although in an increasingly globalized world cultural traditions and concepts as well as religious beliefs and legal norms have to be taken into account, the safeguarding of the freedom to marry, as well as the recognition and protection of a potentially existing family life, including children already born out of the relationship, is at stake. The case law presented here emphasizes the continued importance of English norms of essential validity in controlling the formation of a marriage and, where possible, upholding the status of marriage. An obvious concern is that any judgment on the status of a marriage leads to moral suspicion.

The financial impact upon parties and their family, who enter into religious marriages only in England or their foreign marriage is not recognized can be significant. In place of the wide range of financial claims available under English law, the parties are treated as if they are cohabitants.[45]

What this (brief) overview also shows is that there are several public policy considerations: the equality principle (equality between the sexes); inviolability of the person; the protection of and respect for family life; and the freedom of religion (if the informal marriage has been established by entering into a religious marriage).[46] These public policy considerations are understood and framed by the UK's human-rights undertakings. Particular reference is given to the ECHR.[47]

IMPACT OF THE ECHR ON ISLAMIC MARRIAGES IN EUROPE

The UK is a contracting state party to the ECHR.[48] The ECHR is an international treaty drawn up within the Council of Europe, which was established in Strasbourg in 1949. The ECHR sets out a list of human rights and fundamental freedoms. It establishes a regional mechanism that allows individuals to hold governments and their agents to account and creates an independent supranational court. It is a fundamental feature of the European machinery of human-rights protection established by the ECHR that it is subsidiary to the national systems safeguarding human rights. It is first and foremost the duty of states—through their governments, legislatures, and courts—to protect human rights. The limits of the supervisory role of the ECtHR are defined by the doctrine of the "margin of appreciation," which recognizes that national authorities are in the best place to decide how human rights should be applied in practice. It is not the ECtHR's task to take the place of national courts, but rather to review the decisions they deliver in the exercise of their domestic authority.

It emerges from the English case law that the public policy of the UK cannot be understood as being made exclusively of national principles and values. Rather, public policy represents a focus point where national values and supranational imperatives including the international human-rights undertakings interconnect[49]: public policy, in order to properly play a role in respect of the recognition of foreign judgments or civil status documents in matters of personal status and family relationships, should, as commented by Franzina, be treated

> as the result of a dynamic process of osmosis between local and regional policies [. . .] i.e. a perspective where the point of view of the forum is no longer a merely national one, but embodies that state's international undertakings concerning, inter alia, the protection of human rights.[50]

That being so, what, then, are the public policy considerations in the context of Islamic marriages as identified by the ECtHR?

Non-recognition of a Foreign Marriage

Mary Green and Ajad Farhat v. Malta[51] arose out of the Maltese authorities' refusal to recognize the validity of a marriage in Libya of a Maltese citizen, Ms. Green. The problem was that Ms. Green was already married in Malta to Mr. X, a citizen of Malta. At the time, divorce was unknown in Maltese law.[52] As a result, Ms. Green had gone to Libya, converted to Islam by means of a declaration—which had the added benefit of automatically dissolving her marriage to a Christian, according to precepts of Islamic law and in conformity with Libyan law—and had married Mr. Farhat. The spouses then established their matrimonial domicile in Libya. The fact remains that when, after some 20 years of residence in Libya, Ms. Green and her new husband applied to have their marriage registered in Malta, the director of the Public Registry refused to do so. The director claimed that Ms. Green had not proven that her first marriage had been dissolved and that her second marriage had not been polygamous, and therefore, the marriage in Libya could not be recognized as it was contrary to Maltese public policy. The Maltese courts upheld this determination. The ECtHR found that the national authorities had not exceeded their margin of appreciation either in imposing the requirements or in applying them in the applicants' case. For the Court:

> [the] requirements [of a valid foreign marriage] fall within the sphere of the respondent State's public policy [. . .]. In view of the interests of the community in ensuring monogamous marriages, and those of the third party directly involved, namely the first applicant's first husband, the Court cannot find that, in the circumstances of the case the domestic courts failed to strike a fair balance between the conflicting interests. Thus, the situation complained of can be regarded as necessary in a democratic society for the prevention of disorder and the protection of the rights of others.[53]

Non-recognition of a Foreign Child Marriage

The ECtHR has also considered the extent of a contracting state's compliance with the ECHR in the context of the recognition of a foreign child marriage. In *Z.H. & R.H. v. Switzerland*,[54] the two applicants—ZH and RH—were Afghan nationals who had married in a religious ceremony in September 2010 in Iran where they were residing illegally. At the time, ZH was 14 years old and RH was 18 years old. Their marriage was not registered. In September 2011, the applicants applied for asylum in Switzerland. The Swiss authorities refused asylum because the applicants had already been granted asylum in Italy. The refusal also noted that the applicants had failed to provide evidence of marriage and that their alleged marriage could not be validly recognized in Switzerland because it was illegal under the relevant provision of the Afghan law, which contained an absolute prohibition on marriage for women under 15 years of age, as well as manifestly incompatible with Swiss law, since sexual intercourse with a child under the age of 16 was a crime under the Swiss Criminal Code. The applicants complained to the ECtHR of Switzerland's failure to grant RH a residence permit in order to allow the two applicants to exercise their right to respect for family life. The ECtHR found that there was no violation. Given the importance to be attached to the protection of children and the fostering of secure family environments, the court ruled that Article 8 ECHR cannot be interpreted as imposing on any state party to the ECHR an obligation to recognize a marriage, religious or otherwise, contracted by a 14-year-old child. Switzerland was, for the court, entitled not to recognize the marriage resulting from what is perceived under law as an exploitative and abusive situation.

Non-recognition of a Religious Marriage

The ECtHR has also examined the non-recognition of a (domestic) religious marriage. *Şerife Yeğit v. Turkey*[55] concerned a man and woman entered into a religious Islamic marriage in Turkey in 1976. Six children were born within this marriage. The husband died in 2002. The wife asked for the registration of her marriage in the Turkish register and for the registration of the children as being the children of the deceased husband. The registration of the children was accepted, but the registration of the marriage was refused. The wife requested her deceased husband's pension and health benefits both after and up until the refusal to register the marriage. Those claims were also refused. The wife argued that the refusal of those benefits constituted a violation of, or at least a lack of respect for, her right to respect for family life. The court considered that there was a de facto existing family life that fell within the protection of Article 8 ECHR. However, the claim of the wife was eventually dismissed. The court took the position that civil marriages are available to all people in the state without distinction and therefore no breach of Article 12 ECHR right to marry (nor Article 14's prohibition of discrimination) had occurred when the respective states failed to recognize the informal marriage of the applicants.[56] The ECtHR follows the Turkish authorities in the assessment of the legitimate aim, that the aim pursued by the Turkish legislator is the protection of women. Yet, ironically the complete denial of the—monogamous—marriage of Şerife Yiğit, exactly had as its consequence that a woman was left financially unprotected.

THEMES EMERGING FROM THE ECTHR

The case law presented here also raises several public policy considerations: the equality principle (equality between the sexes); the protection of and respect for private and family life; and the freedom of religion (if the informal marriage has been established by entering into a religious marriage). The ECHR has not been successfully invoked to give rise to civil effects to an informal religious marriage. However, the question whether informal marriages should nevertheless be characterized as a marriage for certain (financial) purposes requires a more nuanced answer and, as the case law in England shows, is very relevant to assigning financial responsibility in the event of a breakdown of a relationship.

The ECtHR has found that a state's refusal, on principle, to recognize a marriage resulting from what is perceived under law as an exploitative and abusive situation is entirely proportionate even where in respect of the facts of the case this result might be to reduce potential protections, be it family law rights that would otherwise arise as in *Şerife Yiğit* or immigration-type rights as in *Z.H. & R.H. v. Switzerland.* As seen in *Şerife Yiğit* (and from the English case law review), states are to a large extent free to restrict such legal protection to formally valid marriages. For the UK authorities, as discussed above, legal certainty, as well as the possibility to exercise control over marriages, constitute important elements to enhance a restrictive policy.

We can also identify from the case law that the mere fact that the parties' expectations to have a marriage recognized and being entitled to protection does not mean that such expectations can never be disturbed where there are legitimate reasons to do so. But such reasons for disturbing their expectations must be assessed against the parties' interests in the stability of their family status, in light of the principle of proportionality, which requires the state to balance the interest of the community and the individuals concerned. As concluded above, that a similar status could not have been acquired under the recognizing forum's own system of law will not, in itself, be enough.

CONCLUSION

For many British Muslims the traditional form of religious marriage is essential for the parties, their families, and their community.[57] While some couples may knowingly choose to enter only into a religious Muslim marriage, concerns surround the potential for Muslim "spouses" to unknowingly be party to a marriage with no legal status under English law. As recommended by an independent inquiry in the UK in 2018,[58] legislative changes in the UK are needed to ensure that civil marriages are conducted before or at the same time as the Islamic marriage ceremony, bringing Islamic marriage in line with Christian and Jewish marriage.[59] Such a change would ensure that a greater number of spouses will have the full protection afforded to them in family law. For any proposed changes to marriage laws to be effective, the issue of what is meaningful to all those involved must be taken into account. However, as Sardar Ali questions,

> are nikah-only ceremonies, with the full knowledge that they do not carry official recognition, based on free and full consent of both parties to the marriage, an informed, conscious iteration of Muslim family law in England?[60]

From that perspective, the extent to which the state should interfere where parties have knowingly chosen to enter into a relationship that does not have the legal implications of "marriage" for the purposes of English law is open to debate.

The case law presented emphasizes the significance in law of a marriage ceremony. Should the law perhaps instead look to the reality of lived relationships rather than whether or not a particular set of formalities have been followed (whether in accordance with civil or religious norms)? Arguably protection from exploitation or unjust disadvantage would be better served by the law looking in most cases to the relationship not the ceremony. The purpose of family law is to determine the responsibilities of individuals to each other and the responsibilities of families and the state and the community to each other[61] and those responsibilities lie primarily within the family unit. A central tension that seems to come out of the cases is the inherent public policy difficulty between on the one hand recognizing marriages in order to allow the law and the courts to do justice between parties in the event of a breakdown (and this author would suggest, in other areas of the law e.g. succession) while on the other not recognizing marriages where to do so would approve of a relationship that is objectionable to the recognizing state's norms (e.g., bans on child/non-age marriage, polygamous marriages) even if the result of this is lack of protection in family law terms.

This overview has shown that the public policy considerations in the UK are understood and framed by the UK's human-rights undertakings. The law has a very specific and concrete role to play. While the law is only one tool, it is a critical one as it signals to society at large what is and is not acceptable within the law. At the same time, the discourse of accommodation of cultural and religious identity in family law often focuses on the question of violation of gender equality through religious law.[62] Thinking in such terms, however, ignores the importance of understanding the relationship between national law and religion(s) in the UK, which is valuable considering the real lives of the UK's diverse and multicultural population.

NOTES

1. *Schalk and Kopf v. Austria* [2010] ECHR 995, para. 62.
2. See, for example, Mouez Khalfaoui and Justin Jones, "Islamic Family Law in Europe and Islamic World: Current Situation and Challenges," *Electronic Journal*

of Islamic and Middle Eastern Law 8, no. 1 (2020), accessed October 1, 2021, https://www.zora.uzh.ch/id/eprint/186936/1/EJIMEL_SpecialIssue81.pdf; Rajnaara C. Akhtar, Rebecca Probert and Annelies Moors, "Informal Muslim Marriages: Regulations and Contestations" *Oxford Journal of Law and Religion* 7, no. 3 (October 2018): 367–375; Shaheen Sardar Ali, *Modern Challenges to Islamic Law* (London: Cambridge University Press, 2016); Andrea Büchler, "Islamic Family Law in Europe? From Dichotomies to Discourse - or: Beyond Cultural and Religious Identity in Family Law," *International Journal of Law in Context* 8, no. 2 (2012): 196–210.

3. For a discussion in other countries see, Marie Ní Shúilleabháin, "Overseas Marriage and Divorce in Islamic Form: A Critical Perspective on the Development of Irish Private International Law," in *Minority Religions Under Irish Law Islam in National and International Context*, eds. Kathryn O' Sullivan et al. (Brill, 2019), 31, Chapter 7; Kaiser Chaudhary, *Pakistani Marriages and the Private International Laws of Germany and England* (Oisterwijk, The Netherlands: Wolf Legal Publishers, 2014); J. Macfarlane, *Understanding Trends in American Muslim Divorce and Marriage: A Discussion Guide for Families and Communities* (ISPU, 2012), accessed October 1, 2021, https://www.ispu.org/wp-content/uploads/2016/08/ISPU-Report_Marriage-II_Macfarlane_WEB.pdf

4. Islamic family law is a major component of the body of stipulations, commands, and ethical guidance that collectively make up the Sharia, often referred to as Islamic law.

5. England and Wales is a legal jurisdiction covering England and Wales, two of the four constituent countries of the UK. Both Scotland and Northern Ireland have their own separate systems of family law.

6. Although the UK is a unified jurisdiction for many purposes, this is not the case for family law.

7. See, among others, "The independent review into the application of Sharia law in England and Wales Presented to Parliament by the Secretary of State for the Home Department by Command of Her Majesty," CM9560, February 2018, accessed October 1, 2021, https://assets.publishing.service.gov.uk/government/uploads/system/uploads/attachment_data/file/678478/6.4152_HO_CPFG_Report_into_Sharia_Law_in_the_UK_WEB.pdf; Rajnaara Akhtar, "Unregistered Muslim Marriages in the UK, Examining Normative Influences Shaping Choice of Legal Protection," in *Personal Autonomy in Plural Societies, A Principle and its Paradoxes*, eds. Marie-Claire Foblets et al. (London and New York: Routledge, 2018), 140–155.

8. "The independent review into the application of Sharia law in England and Wales Presented to Parliament by the Secretary of State for the Home Department by Command of Her Majesty," February 2018, accessed October 1, 2021, https://assets.publishing.service.gov.uk/government/uploads/system/uploads/attachment_data/file/678478/6.4152_HO_CPFG_Report_into_Sharia_Law_in_the_UK_WEB.pdf

9. John Bingham, "Mass Polygamy in UK Muslim Community—Claim," The Telegraph, December 10, 2014, http://www.telegraph.co.uk/news/religion/11284421/Mass-polygamy-in-UK-Muslim-community-claim. html

10. Rajnaara Akhtar, "Unregistered Muslim Marriages in the UK, Examining Normative Influences Shaping Choice of Legal Protection," in *Personal Autonomy*

in Plural Societies, A Principle and its Paradoxes, eds. Marie-Claire Foblets et al. (London and New York: Routledge, 2018), 140–155.

11. A Nikah ceromny is a Muslim marriage ceremony.

12. Gillian Douglas et al., "Social Cohesion and Religious Law: Marriage, Divorce and Religious Courts," *Cardiff Law School* (2011), accessed October 1, 2021, https://orca.cardiff.ac.uk/26308/

13. A UK Ministry of Justice had initiated research into mapping of Sharia Councils in England and Wales led by S. Bano: "An Exploratory Study of Sharīʿah Councils in England with Respect to Family Law," 2012, accessed October 1, 2021, http://www.reading.ac.uk/web/FILES/law/An_exploratory_study_of_Sharīʿah_councils_in_England_with_respect_to_family_law_.pdf

14. Vishal Vora, "The Continuing Muslim Marriage Conundrum: The Law of England and Wales on Religious Marriage and Non-Marriage in the United Kingdom," *Journal of Muslim Minority Affairs* 40, no. 1 (2020): 148–162.

15. *MA v. JA and the Attorney General* [2012] EWHC 2219 (Fam); *Sharbatly v. Shagroon* [2012] EWCA Civ 1507; *Dukali v. Lamrani (Attorney General Intervening)* [2012] EWHC 1748 (Fam); *Al-Saedy v. Musawi (Presumption of Marriage)* [2010] EWCA 3293 (Fam); *El Gamal v. Al Maktoum* [2011] EWHC 3763 (Fam); *Akhter v. Khan* (2018) 54 EWFC and, upon appeal, *Akhter v. Khan* [2020] EWCA Civ 122.

16. See Kathryn O'Sullivan and Layla Jackson, "Muslim Marriage (Non)-Recognition: Implications and Possible Solutions," *Journal of Social Welfare and Family Law* 39, no. 1 (February 2017): 22–41.

17. Prakash Shah, "Inconvenient Marriages, or What Happens When Ethnic Minorities Marry Trans-jurisdictionally," *Utrecht Law Review* 6, no. 2 (2010): 24–25.

18. Amira Mashhour, "Islamic Law and Gender Equality—Could There be a Common Ground?: A Study of Divorce and Polygamy in Sharia Law and Contemporary Legislation in Tunisia and Egypt," *Human Rights Quarterly* 27, no. 2 (2005): 562.

19. See Prakash Shah, "Attitudes to Polygamy in English Law," *International and Comparative Law Quarterly* 52 (2003): 369 and Prakash Shah, "Inconvenient Marriages, or What Happens When Ethnic Minorities Marry Trans-jurisdictionally," *Utrecht Law Review* 6, no. 2 (2010): 17.

20. Note that there is a bill pending before the UK Parliament to revoke parental or judicial consent which permits the marriage or civil partnership of a child and to criminalize child marriage or civil partnership under the age of 18; and for connected purposes, Marriage and Civil Partnership (Minimum Age) (No.2) Bill, Session 2019–2021 (UK).

21. It is also important to acknowledge that there are discrete "schools" of Sharia, and differing interpretations of the Quran relevant to marriage.

22. Under the Marriage Act 1949, there are various relationships which are not allowed. First cousins is about the closest which is permitted.

23. See, e.g., regarding Pakistan, Kaiser Chaudhary, *Pakistani Marriages and the Private International Laws of Germany and England* (Oisterwijk, The Netherlands: Wolf Legal Publishers, 2014), Chapter 5.

24. Rajnaara C. Akhtar, Rebecca Probert and Annelies Moors, "Informal Muslim Marriages: Regulations and Contestations," *Oxford Journal of Law and Religion* 7, no. 3 (October 2018): 367–375; Akhtar Rajnaara, "Unregistered Muslim Marriages: An Emerging Culture of Celebrating Rites and Compromising Rights," in *Marriage Rites and Rights*, eds. Joanna Miles (Oxford: Hart, 2015), 167–192.

25. Vishal Vora, "The Continuing Muslim Marriage Conundrum: The Law of England and Wales on Religious Marriage and Non-Marriage in the United Kingdom," *Journal of Muslim Minority Affairs* 40, no. 1 (2020): 148–162.

26. Rule 73 of *The Conflicts of Laws*, Dicey, Morris & Collins (15th edition).

27. Home Office, "Family Policy: Partners, Divorce and Dissolution," May 29, 2019, accessed on October 1, 2021, https://assets.publishing.service.gov.uk/government/uploads/system/uploads/attachment_data/file/835362/Partner_divorce_and_dissolution_guidance_v.1.0ext.pdf

28. In a 2014 case, Mrs. Justice Roberts considered whether a specific marriage which had taken place abroad should be recognized in England and Wales. The judge quoted as authority on this subject a 1930 case where the Privy Council held: ". . . *If a marriage is good by the laws of the country where it is effected, it is good all over the world. . . . If the so-called marriage is no marriage in the place where it is celebrated, there is no marriage anywhere* . . ." *K v. A* [2014] EWHC 3850 (Fam), para. 44, quoting from *Berthiaume v. Dastous* [1930] AC 79.

29. The two statutory exceptions arc provided in the Foreign Marriage Act of 1892 and apply for consular marriages and for marriages of members of the British forces serving abroad. The common law exception applies if a marriage is celebrated in accordance with the requirements of English common law, where the use of the local form is impossible.

30. This is a court-developed concept; there is no mention of such a status in statute.

31. See the discussion in *Akhter v. Khan* [2020] EWCA Civ 122.

32. [2020] EWCA Civ 122.

33. According Section 44(3) Marriage Act 1949 both parties to the marriage are obliged to be present at the marriage ceremony.

34. Convention on Consent to Marriage, Minimum Age for Marriage and Registration of Marriages, 1962, 521 U.N.T.S 231, Art. 1(2).

35. [1948] P 83.

36. See, e.g. *Awuku v. Secretary of State for the Home Dept* [2017] EWCA Civ 178 dealing with recognition of a Ghanaian customary ceremony and Kareem [2014] UKUT 00024 (IAC).

37. [1969] 1 Q.B. 1.

38. Note that the Marriage Act 1949 includes exceptions that allow marriage from the age of 16 years.

39. A number of laws operate to criminalize child marriage in the UK. In 2014, the Anti-Social Behaviour and Policing Act established the criminal offense of forced marriage, which by definition includes child marriage. In addition, the Serious Crime Act 2015 established the offense of controlling or coercing intimate or family relationships.

40. See, infra, the discussion on *Z.H. & R.H. v. Switzerland* [2015] ECHR 1075.

41. A marriage is considered to be potentially polygamous if a spouse is actually not married to more than one other spouse, but the national law where the marriage was concluded allows that person marry more than one spouse.

42. *R v. Immigration Appeal Tribunal ex parte Asfar Jan* [1995] Imm AR 440.

43. Private International Law (Miscellaneous Provisions) Act 1995.

44. Section 47 Matrimonial Causes Act 1973.

45. Thus the only financial protection upon the breakdown of the relationship is under the Trust of Land and Appointment of Trustees Act 1996—declarations and order relating to land or property held in the parties names and, if there are children, an application under Schedule 1 of the Children Act 1989.

46. See Susan Rutten, "Protection of Spouses in Informal Marriages by Human Rights," *Utrecht Law Review* 6, no. 2 (June 2010): 77–79.

47. The Council of Europe, not to be mistaken with the European Union, counts 47 Member states. The European Court of Human Rights is one of its organs.

48. The Human Rights Act 1998 gives effect in domestic law in the UK to the ECHR.

49. Pietro Franzina, "Some remarks on the Relevance of Article 8 of the ECHR to the Recognition of Family Status Judicially Created Abroad," *Diritti Umani e Diritto Internazionale* 5, no. 3 (2011). See also Mathias Forteau, "L'ordre public 'transnational' ou 'réellement international': l'order public international face à l'enchevêtrement croissant du droit international privé et du droit international public," *Journal du droit international* (2011).

50. Pietro Franzina, "Some remarks on the Relevance of Article 8 of the ECHR to the Recognition of Family Status Judicially Created Abroad," *Diritti Umani e Diritto Internazionale* 5, no. 3 (2011).

51. [2010] ECHR 1223.

52. Following a referendum in Malta on May 28, 2011, the law on divorce came into force on October 1, 2011 and is now regulated by the Maltese Civil Code.

53. [2010] ECHR 1223.

54. [2015] ECHR 1075.

55. [2010] ECHR 1672.

56. Approach followed in *Muñoz Díaz v. Spain,* [2009] ECHR 2017.

57. See, for example, Vishal Vora, "The Continuing Muslim Marriage Conundrum: The Law of England and Wales on Religious Marriage and Non-Marriage in the United Kingdom," *Journal of Muslim Minority Affairs* 40, no. 1 (2020): 148–162; Mouez Khalfaoui and Justin Jones, "Islamic Family Law in Europe and Islamic World: Current Situation and Challenges," *Electronic Journal of Islamic and Middle Eastern Law* 8, no. 1 (2020), accessed October 1, 2021, https://www.zora.uzh.ch/id/eprint/186936/1/EJIMEL_SpecialIssue81.pdf

58. "The independent review into the application of Sharia law in England and Wales Presented to Parliament by the Secretary of State for the Home Department by Command of Her Majesty," February 2018, accessed October 1, 2021, https://assets.publishing.service.gov.uk/government/uploads/system/uploads/attachment_data/file/678478/6.4152_HO_CPFG_Report_into_Sharia_Law_in_the_UK_WEB.pdf

59. In January 2019, the Parliamentary Assembly of the Council of Europe passed a resolution which raised concerns about the operation of Sharia councils in the UK, highlighting marital issues and Islamic divorce proceedings. The resolution called on the UK to make it a legal requirement for Muslim couples to register their marriages civilly before or at the same time as their religious ceremony, and to ensure that Sharia councils operate within the law. See Resolution 2253 (2019), January 22, 2019, accessed October 1, 2021, http://assembly.coe.int/nw/xml/XRef/Xref-XML2HTML-en.asp?fileid=25353

60. See Shaheen Sardar Ali, "Blurred Boundaries; Muddied Waters or Multiculturalism Gone Astray? Some Reflections on 'The Independent Review into the Application of Sharia Law in England and Wales,'" *Islamic Law Blog*, March 19, 2018, accessed October 1, 2021, https://islamiclaw.blog/2018/03/19/symposium-on-the-independent-review-into-the-application-of-sharia-law-in-england-and-wales-by-the-uk-home-office/; Shaheen Sardar Ali, *Modern Challenges to Islamic Law* (Cambridge University Press, 2016).

61. See, for example, Alison Diduck, "Family Law's Instincts and the Relational Subject," in *Embracing Vulnerability The Challenges and Implications for Law,* eds. Daniel Bedford and Jonathan Herring (London: Routledge, 2020), Part 1; and Alison Diduck, "Family Law and Family Responsibility," in *Responsibility, Law and the Family*, eds. Jo Bridgeman et al. (London: Routelage, 2008), Chapter 13.

62. See the discussion of Andrea Büchler, "Islamic Family Law in Europe? From Dichotomies to Discourse—or: Beyond Cultural and Religious Identity in Family Law," *International Journal of Law in Context* 8, no. 2 (2012): 196–210.

Chapter 4

Norms of Muslim Marriage and Divorce

The Evolution of Algerian Family Law through the Examples of Matrimonial Guardianship and Consent to Marriage

Nahas Mahieddin

The century and the needs of man
give rise to unforeseen circumstances by law.
The legislature must therefore combine this necessity
and always find the application of these laws in his wisdom.
Hamdan ben Othman Khoja[1]

INTRODUCTION

Algerian family law is considered to be affiliated with Muslim law. This statement is true but must be relativized. Indeed, the original rules of this law are internalized in the consciousness to such an extent that they are considered as constitutive of the Algerian identity. But family law in Algeria has undergone the evolution of history and it is no longer possible today to think of its normative content as the Muslim jurists of the past did. It remains that the contemporary national law is elaborated according to a conception, a logic, and a methodology taken from the European legal thought while continuing to be inspired by the former law built according to a method and a logic specific to the casuistic law. This results in a paradox particularly visible in family law which does not escape, moreover, the evolutions of the societal behaviors and the commitments taken in the framework of the international conventions to which Algeria adhered.

It is this evolution at the normative level that I will try to expose through the study of the rules relating to the formation of the matrimonial bond both before colonization and from 1830 to the present day.

MATRIMONIAL GUARDIANSHIP IN MUSLIM LAW AND ITS APPLICATION IN ALGERIA BEFORE COLONIZATION

Before colonization and for several centuries, the populations of North Africa and its center, which would become present-day Algeria, were mostly of the Muslim faith and, as such, were subject to the provisions of Muslim law.[2]

According to Muslim jurists, marriage is the foundation of the legitimacy of family life. The regularity of this union is thus conditioned by the respect of a certain number of rules considered as constitutive (arkân) of the marriage contract. In Maliki Muslim law (dominant in Algeria), these conditions are the intervention of a matrimonial guardian (wali al-zawâdj), the payment of a dowry to the wife (sadâq), the legal capacity to marry required of each of the two suitors (mahall) as well as the formulation of the marriage proposal and its acceptance (sigha) considered as the expression of the consent to the envisaged marital union. The presence of witnesses at the time of the conclusion of the marriage contract or at the latest, but imperatively, at the time of its consummation, is also a condition of validity, on pain of its dissolution.[3]

The dowry, as well as the legal capacity required of each of the candidates for marriage and the presence of witnesses are the subject of interesting developments reported in the classical legal literature.[4] The moment when the request for marriage is formulated and its acceptance, which is considered the expression of the consent to the marriage, constitute an interesting and particularly complex problem. This issue has been the subject of debate and controversy for centuries. The main reason for this situation is the question of matrimonial guardianship which intervenes during this process and which conditions the validity of the consent to marriage and thus the marriage itself. It is the examination of this last subject where I will limit this chapter because it symbolizes in a significant way the evolution of family law in Algeria.

Indeed a 15th-century jurist wrote about matrimonial guardianship that "it is both accepted by all, but also the most controversial. . . ." In fact, the debates and opinions on this subject already appear in the texts of the commentators of the Traditions of the Prophet, who specify that it is a practice known in the Arab society long before the appearance of Islam. It is not, therefore, an institution created ex nihilo by Muslim jurists, some of whom justify its foundation a posteriori in at least one verse of the Koran (II, 231–232)[5] (without agreeing on the answer to the question of who this injunction is addressed to[6]) and in statements attributed to the Prophet from which the rule "no marriage without a matrimonial guardian" is said to derive.[7] The diversity of opinions on this subject since the 7th century shows that there were no precise rules in this matter and the divergences will appear in the doctrine elaborated by the fuqahâ' (jurists)—institutionalizing this guardianship according to the socio-cultural context within which each of them evolves. It is appropriate to add that Ibn al-Qasam,[8] a direct disciple of the founding master of Maliki Muslim law, did not hesitate to state that the matrimonial guardian is more a custom (sunna) than a legal obligation (fardh).[9] Ibn Rushd (Averroes of Cordoba) himself did not hesitate to qualify the arguments put forward by each party as being based on interpretations that he called "plausible" (muhtamala) because of the diversity of meanings that can be attributed to the terms of the texts used.[10] Finally, a contemporary theologian has summarized this situation well by noting that "it is the consequence of an ancient but constant interaction between doctrine, tradition and custom, all of which agree that the woman should not be allowed to contract a marriage directly."[11]

Beyond the doctrinal debates and limiting ourselves to the theoretically applicable Maliki law,[12] the presence and the consent expressed by the matrimonial guardian (walî) condition the validity of the marriage. This guardianship is exercised in priority by the father[13] over his children who can impose the marriage on them and especially on the daughter (if she has never been married before -bikr-). In the absence of a father, matrimonial guardianship is exercised by the closest relative among the agnates (ᶜasab) according to an order on which Muslim jurists have divergent opinions.[14] This right of constraint (djebr) can also be exercised by the testamentary guardian (wasî) chosen by the father if the latter has previously designated the future husband of his daughter. Moreover, it should be specified that the guardian appointed by the judge has no right of matrimonial constraint on his wards.[15]

A woman can be a guardian under certain conditions and exercise the rights inherent to this function but must delegate a man to represent her in the conclusion of the marriage of her own daughters or wards.

In summary, in Muslim law, the theory teaches that marriage is always concluded by the matrimonial guardian and that the woman's consent is never expressed personally and directly by her.[16]

It is now appropriate to examine the practical application of these rules by the judicial authorities in Algeria before 1830 in order to better appreciate the evolution of the law on the issue of matrimonial guardianship from the 19th century to the present day.

In Algeria, it is traditional for jurists to compile cases (nawâzil) and opinions (fatwâ) (intended for individuals and judges[17]). The currently known works date back to the 14th century and extend to the beginning of the 20th century. It is interesting to note that they emanate from several regions of

Algeria[18] and thus allow us to have an overview of the jurisprudence in family matters over a rather long period.

First of all, these collections confirm the attachment of their authors to Maliki law by multiplying the doctrinal references[19] without ignoring the isolated points of view expressed within this school. In matters of matrimonial guardianship as well as consent to marriage, it appears that they are the subject of numerous disputes, not only because of ignorance of the rules applicable in the matter, but also because of abuses committed by the guardians.[20] Finally, there is a certain willingness not to oppose local customs head-on.

In general, it is also interesting to observe from a selection of the cases that some jurists make a distinction between legal rules in the strict sense and those with a moral connotation, even if they are part of the *corpus juris* in its classical orthodox conception. Thus, some do not hesitate to suggest that moral provisions should not be applied, in order to avoid "the annulment of most marriages concluded[.]"[21]

An examination of the cases recorded in these collections shows a certain variability in the application of the law which reflects a different appreciation of similar facts. For example, the marriage of a *thayyib* woman (widow or divorcee) contracted by her father was declared valid on the grounds that he had power of attorney for his daughter, where she claimed that the power of attorney had been forced upon her under threat. On the contrary, in a similar case, the marriage contracted by the wife's brother is being investigated because the wife stated that she gave her consent under duress. It is questionable whether in the first case the validity of the marriage is recognized despite the lack of consent of the wife and whether the argument of the power of attorney is not an expression of the desire not to challenge the paternal authority despite the statements of the wife, while it is more acceptable to challenge that of a brother.[22]

This indecision in the application of fiqh rules can also be observed with regard to the validity of a marriage concluded by a testamentary guardian (wasî appointed by the father) without the consent of the daughter. Three solutions are reported for the resolution of this case. Two of them consider that the delegation of the right of constraint by the father is valid as long as he has expressly declared to the person he has chosen as guardian to "act towards his daughter as he would towards his own daughter[.]"[23] The marriage thus is valid as long as it has been formally ratified by the cadi (Muslim judge). But a third solution is added by the author of the review who notes that "if the majority of jurists recognize the validity of the delegation of the matrimonial guardianship of the father to the testamentary guardian," it is nevertheless necessary to specify that Malikite authors like al-Siyyûrî (died in 1070) or al-Lakhmî (died in 1085) specify that "The father does not have any more this legal power of constraint as soon as his daughter reaches the puberty and a fortiori the wasi, who cannot in his quality, exercice the matrimonial guardianship on his pupil."[24]

But it also happens that social reasons justify the rejection by the judge of a request for annulment of a marriage concluded by the woman without the intervention of a matrimonial guardian. Thus, the judicial archives of the city of Médéa dating from the beginning of the 19th century, preserve a judgment of the Sharᶜî (Court that applies Muslim law) Court which rejects such a request introduced by a cousin of the wife. The magistrate, after having recalled that "if (such) action is founded in law and that [if] the practice of marriage without a matrimonial guardian is unfortunate, declares nevertheless that in the case in question, the union thus concluded remains legally valid since it has allowed the woman to get out of a situation of extreme indigence[.]"[25]

These few examples of rulings or opinions of jurisconsults concerning disputes in matters of matrimonial guardianship and consent to marriage in Algeria before 1830 show a diversity of opinions as to the interpretation of the same basic rules and the numerous answers given to similar cases give the image of a confused legislative system criticized for several centuries by some like Ibn al Muqaffaᶜ (died in 757) in his Epistle "Risala fî al-Sahâba" because it can lead to an inequality of treatment of litigants,[26] but appreciated by others like Abû Djaʿfar al-Qommî (died 991).[27] In fact, this situation reflects what Muslim law is, namely an ideal law made up of basic principles that the judge must implement using reasoning techniques to solve the cases submitted to him. In addition to a higher doctrinal and theoretical law, there is at a lower level an intellectual approach proper to the practitioner called upon to solve cases arising from real social activity.[28]

These collections are an almost perfect illustration. It was the result of a conception of social and legal norms specific to Muslim society that colonization was to upset, but which did not disappear completely. The fact remains that the eruption of European legal thought into Algerian society lead to a break in the legal logic around which Muslim law evolved and continues to disrupt the Algerian legal system and which the national legislature seems powerless to correct.

THE EVOLUTION OF THE LAW ON MATRIMONIAL GUARDIANSHIP FROM THE SECOND HALF OF THE 19TH CENTURY TO THE PRESENT DAY

At the beginning of the colonial period, the French authorities did not have a precise knowledge of the content of local law and had kept in force the rules of fiqh for disputes between Muslims. But very quickly, a series of texts were progressively adopted to integrate the courts into the colonial jurisdictional order while limiting the jurisdictional competence of Algerian magistrates who would apply Muslim law under the control of French magistrates.[29]

In order to apply Muslim law in accordance with the commitments made by the French authorities (the first text enshrining this commitment in law is a decree of October 22, 1830[30]) and to overcome the difficulties encountered in its knowledge, the treatise of Khalil ibn Ishaq (Mukhtasar) was translated into French by Nicolas Perron and published in Paris between 1848 and 1854 and made available to magistrates. This translation, which appears as a simple "technical" operation (although scientifically debatable),[31] has in fact the practical consequence of presenting the local normative system according to the French conception of law. Khalil's text became for the magistrates practicing in Algeria the first reference in Muslim law, just as the French Civil Code of 1804 was for French law.

If the maintenance in force of Muslim law in Algeria is debated by the doctrine,[32] it is legally applied as soon as it is inserted in the French legal order by the legislature who limits it progressively to the sole personal status.[33] Its apprehension is however the object of a new approach which ends up giving it a new face progressively shaped by the jurisprudence of the courts and which the doctrine, elaborated by the masters of thought of the University of Algiers, theorizes and entitles "Algerian Moslem law."[34]

One can distinguish two stages carried out in parallel in this process. The first, dictated by logic, aims at the knowledge of Muslim law and the translations into French of its main texts "secularize" its expression. The second, carried out both by legislative or regulatory means and by judicial activity, aims to detach the rules of personal status from other provisions of Muslim law. Family law is thus autonomized, which makes it possible to intervene on its content, which is analyzed with the help of categories and legal methods specific to Romano-Germanic legal thought.

A study of the jurisprudence of the French courts and of the doctrine on personal status shows, on the one hand, that Muslim law is considered to be customary law and, on the other hand, that they express two opposing tendencies, "one seeking to excessively favor everything that goes in the direction of assimilation to French law, the other striving, on the contrary, to safeguard the full autonomy of local statutes."[35]

In general the reform of Muslim law by the colonial judge was also done through the use of the notion of "public order" or "moral considerations" as they were conceived at the time in European culture.[36] But more specifically, in matters of matrimonial guardianship and consent to marriage, the courts continue to apply Muslim law, recognizing the father's right to compel marriage, while reaffirming that it must not be exercised contrary to the child's interest and excluding it when the woman is no longer under paternal power or has already been married.

Without opposing the spirit of classical fiqh, jurisprudence sometimes intervenes to put an end to the doctrinal controversies of Muslim jurists by refusing, for example, to annul a marriage concluded by a guardian other than the one provided for according to the order established by some ancient Muslim jurisconsults,[37] or to confirm that the interest of the child must be taken into consideration before the rights of the father.[38] But it also happens that some French judges overturn the decisions of some Muslim judges, such as the Cadi of Guerfa (City in the east of Algeria), who ruled that the age of nubility was 18 years, thus allowing the daughter to validly consent to her marriage only from that age. The cassation was based on the idea "that it was not the custom of the 'natives' to marry their daughters so late,"[39] whereas this Cadi was applying a provision proposed by Khalil in his Mukhtasar.[40]

The French legislature therefore let the courts apply Muslim law in family matters and make occasional "corrections" without directly intervening on its content. It is only in 1930 that a text was adopted to prohibit marriages before the age of 15 years under penalty of nullity and penal sanctions for the offenders. This provision was only applicable to Algerians from Kabylia.[41]

It was not until 1959 that marriage contracted by persons of local civil status (Algerian Muslims not having the status of citizens subject to the French Civil Code) was regulated by an ordinance dated February 4 of that same year.[42] This text is also discriminatory since it does not apply to unions concluded according to Ibadite law.[43] Although it does not affect all the rules of Muslim law in matters of marriage, this ordinance brings provisions which have, at least in theory, an effect on the question of consent as well as on matrimonial guardianship. Indeed, it states more clearly than the classical Muslim jurists do that marriage is formed by the consent of both spouses. It is added that this consent is expressed verbally, publicly and in person.[44] Thus, any third party is prevented from intervening in the formation of the marriage and the guardian is no longer considered as a participant in the conclusion of the marriage contract.

Thus, matrimonial guardianship and the title of matrimonial guardian no longer have any legal existence in positive law. The law thus completes what the judges have progressively built through a long process of neutralization of the law of matrimonial constraint initiated, at this date, for more than two decades.[45]

At independence, Algeria took over this legal heritage by adopting a law renewing the legislation in force on December 31, 1962.[46] This text only expresses as reservations to the application of the legislation adopted before this date "the provisions contrary to national sovereignty or of a colonialist or discriminatory nature"[47] without adding the principles or rules of Muslim law. If this silence does not seem to be an oversight on the part of the national legislature, it must be interpreted as an acceptance of the application of the texts promulgated by the French legislature before independence in matters of personal status, in particular those relating to guardianship and marriage[48] in spite of the strong criticisms emitted by the Algerian nationalists during their adoption.[49]

The main 1959 text on marriage thus remained in force, but the judges who formally referred to it[50] recalled at the same time that in matters of personal status, it was Muslim law that should be applied.[51] Thus, from 1962 onward, the law inherited from the colonial period was "corrected" by the reintroduction of the rules of Muslim law and in particular the institution of the matrimonial guardian. This situation persisted until the promulgation of a Family Code in 1984,[52] with the exception of a law raising the minimum age for marriage[53] and a few provisions adopted to respond to particular situations.

The current situation can be presented by distinguishing two periods. The first begins in 1962 with the independence of Algeria and ends in 1984 with the adoption of a Family Code. The second is divided into two stages. The one initiated by the 1984 Code followed by the one that starts in 2005 with the modifications that were made to this text.

Before the promulgation of the Family Code, the courts, and in particular the Supreme Court, applied Muslim law literally, sometimes disregarding positive law texts.[54] But the validity of marriages concluded under the 1959 texts is not questioned although some of the conditions provided for by the Muslim law have not been met. The legal effects of a legally concluded marriage therefore remain acquired. It is nevertheless curious that the Algerian magistrates continue to qualify the conjugal unions not transcribed in the civil status as "customary marriages" (zawâdj ᶜurfî) thus taking up the vocabulary and the terminology of the colonial law to designate the marriages celebrated according to the rules of the Muslim law.

In 1984, the Family Code tries to reconcile a certain fidelity to Muslim law without however rejecting all the provisions introduced by the pre-1962 legislation, while introducing some innovations that take into account the evolution of society's mores. If we limit ourselves to the rules relating to matrimonial guardianship and consent to marriage, it is recalled on the one hand that "marriage is celebrated by the consent of the two spouses" but "in the presence of the woman's guardian"[55] who "concludes" the union for her.[56] On the other hand, it is specified that "the matrimonial guardian, whether he is the father or not, is not authorized to force the person under his guardianship to marry"[57] except that the "father has the possibility of opposing the marriage of his 'bikr' daughter (i.e., 'never married') if it is in her 'interest[.]'"[58] This possibility is also granted to the guardian if he considers that it is not "profitable" to his ward without specifying whether it is an interest of a moral and/or material nature, nor what is meant by "profitable" (aslah),[59] nor how to prove it. Thus, it appears that the law recognizes that the father and the matrimonial guardian have a right to control the marriage of the daughter, which, without going as far as coercion, is exercised by the implicit granting of a marriage authorization. Moreover, the reading of the text allows us to add that if the judge can be seized to authorize the marriage of the woman when the impediment comes from her guardian, it does not seem that such a recourse is accepted when the opposition comes from the father.

The right of constraint is thus formally abrogated, but the wording of the text relating to it does not allow one to conclude that the woman can marry by expressing her consent personally,[60] especially since it is permitted to be represented at the conclusion of the marriage.[61] The structuring of the text and its wording, as well as the possibility for the spouses to be represented, can thus allow the father or the guardian to exercise indirectly the matrimonial constraint.[62]

The 2005 amendments to the Family Code correct this situation.[63] First of all, the legal age of marriageability is set at 19 years for both sexes. Before this age, the exemption can only be granted by the judge referred by the legal representative of the minor who is heard by the judge in order to ensure that the aptitude (physiological and psychological) of the person concerned for marriage is established.[64] The judge rules by an order that is not subject to appeal.[65] A distinction is thus made between legal guardianship exercised over a minor, whatever his or her gender, and matrimonial guardianship, which cannot be exercised over a minor who must personally consent to his or her marriage.[66]

Moreover, with regard to consent to marriage, it is stipulated that "marriage is a contract" concluded by the exchange of the consent of the two spouses. In addition, and in order to ensure that the consent is expressed personally by each of the spouses, their representation by a third party (even with a power of attorney) is no longer authorized.[67] The exercise of matrimonial guardianship through a misuse of the law is therefore no longer possible.

It remains that if the matrimonial guardianship has no more legal existence, the guardian does not disappear from the Algerian legal lexicon and the character is present at the time of the formation of the marriage contract. It is thus appropriate to question his place and his role in this procedure. It follows from the combined reading of Articles 9 and 11 in their new version that "the adult woman concludes her marriage contract" and not her guardian as in the 1984 Code. Moreover and contrary to the Malikite Muslim law which considers the function of walî as a basic condition for the validity of the marriage, the latter does not intervene any more as principal actor in its conclusion. Finally, the order of the persons who can act as walî according to the Muslim law is no longer taken into account and the woman has the possibility to choose him even outside her family although the father or a close relative remain privileged persons. The presence of the guardian is now only a condition of form without consequence on the validity of the marriage. The wali is only a witness, a symbolic figure of the traditional marriage. Nevertheless, he is still present in his traditional role of representative of the spouses during the ceremony of blessing of the marriage (called "Fâtiha") officiated by a man of religion, a ceremony which is only authorized if the interested parties present a marriage certificate issued by a civil registrar.[68]

CONCLUSION

In summary, it appears that the issue of matrimonial guardianship and consent to marriage has undergone a significant evolution by being totally dissociated in positive law. This evolution is bound to continue provided that the history of Muslim law is interpreted more objectively in order to pursue family law in a less discriminatory and more egalitarian sense.

From a more general point of view, it can be seen that the sacredness attributed to Muslim law is no longer a decisive argument for refusing the necessary reforms, since several of its rules are no longer part of the positive law in force, and some provisions of the current law even prove to be contrary to classical Maliki fiqh. Moreover, a legislative policy, without denying the legal heritage bequeathed by the ancient jurisconsults, would rely on a stricter understanding of this past in order to build a body of law governed by a single legal logic.

The difficulties of interpreting the law and the contradictions that sometimes appear would thus be avoided or at least limited. Indeed, the legal dualism that characterizes the legislative systems of which a part remains affiliated to Muslim law is a source of difficulty because of the double logic to which some of its rules are subjected. Thus, some are subject to constitutional public policy while others, notably those of family law, are subject to Muslim public policy. However, the provisions of the family law in force are themselves disrupted in their application since its provisions are extracted from their original context to be promulgated in a disparate manner while associating them with provisions foreign to Muslim law. Thus, family law, which continues to be presented as remaining faithful to Muslim law, is in reality a disparate body of law that obeys neither the logic of classical fiqh nor that of current legislative systems, while sometimes being in contradiction with constitutional principles.

The legislature must therefore start from the Muslim law, but then go beyond this law, to build a more coherent normative set while responding to the realities of history but also to the expectations of the contemporary Algerian society.

NOTES

1. Sidy Hamdan ben Othman Khoja, *Aperçu historique et statistique sur la Régence d'Alger, intitulé en arabe Le Miroir*, transl. in French by Hassuna Deghis, edited by Goetschy & Cie, Paris, 1833, p. 105. Hamdan ben Othman Khoja was born in Algiers in 1773. He was a law teacher then a senior official in the administration of the Regency of Algiers before colonization. He was also the author of several books. He died in Istanbul in 1842.

2. For the process of Islamization and Arabization of North Africa, see among other studies Allaoua Amara, *L'islamisation du Maghreb central (VIIe–XI e siècle)*, in Dominique Valérian (ed.), *Islamisation et arabisation de l'Occident musulman médiéval (VIIe–XIe siècle)*, Sorbonne Publications, Paris, 2011, p. 103.

3. Khalîl ibn Ishâq (died in 1365), *Mukhtasar fî fiqh al-Imâm Mâlik*, ed. Dâr al-Basâ'ir, Algiers, 1st ed., 2012, p. 89.

4. For more developments on these issues, see Wahba al-Zahîlî, *al-Fiqh al-islâmî wa adillatuhu*, ed. Dâr al-Fikr, Damascus, 1st ed., 1984, Tome 7, p. 48 and following. Ibn al-Hammâm (hanafi jurist died in 1457), Sharh Fath al-Qadîr, ed. Dâr al-Kutub al-'ilmiyya, Beirut, 1st ed., 2003, vol. 3, p. 246.

5. Hamza Boubakeur, *Le Coran. Traduction et commentaire*, ed. ENAG, Algiers, 1994, vol. 1, pp. 246–247.

6. The Qur'an expressly condemns the practice of the husband opposing the remarriage of his wife after having repudiated her, as well as that of the matrimonial guardian when the repudiated wife agrees to return to her former husband.

7. Bukhari, *Sahih*, cAlam al Kutub edition, Beirut (no date of edition), vol. 7, p. 26 and following.

8. ʿAbdur-Rahmān Ibn al-Qāsim (745–813) was a student of Imam Malik founder of the school that bears his name.

9. Muhammad ibn Rushd (d. 1199), *Bidâyat al-Mujtahid wa Nihâyat al-Muqtasid*, ed. Dâr al-Maʿrifa, Beirut, 9th ed., 1988, vol. 2, pp. 8 ff.

10. Muhammad ibn Rushd (d. 1199), *Bidâyat al-Mujtahid wa Nihâyat al-Muqtasid*, ed. Dâr al-Maʿrifa, Beirut, 9th ed., 1988, vol. 2, pp. 8 ff.

11. H. Boubakeur, *Le Coran.* op. cit., vol. 1, p. 249.

12. We voluntarily neglect the ibadite doctrine (followed in Algeria by a part of the population, notably in the Mzab region) as well as the Hanafi doctrine. For the Hanafi doctrine see mainly Ibn ʿÂbidîn (died in 1836), *Radd al-Mukhtâr*, ed. Dâr ʿÂlam al-Kutub, Riyâdh, Special edition, 2003, vol. 4, p. 153 ff; for the ibadite law, see Muhammad Ben Yûsuf al-Tfiyesh (died in 1914), *Kitâb Sharh al-Nîl*, ed. Dâr al-Fath, Beirut, 2d. edition, 1972, vol. 6, especially from page 100. As regards customary rights relating to marriage and more specifically to matrimonial guardianship, see Ramon Basagana and Ali Sayad, *Habitat traditionnel et structures familiales en Kabylie*, Publications of the *Centre de recherches anthropologiques, préhistoriques et ethnographiques,* Algiers, no. XXIII, 1974, p. 87 and the bibliography cited therein.

13. The *wali* must be male, of puberty age and of Muslim faith. Muslim jurists have different views on whether the matrimonial guardian should be a legally emancipated person (*rushd*) or not (Ibn Rushd, *Bidâya*, op. cit., vol. 2, p. 12).

14. Ibn Djuzayy (died 1341), *al-Qawânîn al-fiqhiyya fî talkhîs madhab al-Mâlikiyya*, Dâr Ibn Hazm ed., Beirut, 1st ed., 2013, p. 345; For more developments on this question, see Ibn Rushd, *Bidâya*, op. cit. vol. 2, p. 13.

15. Ibn Djuzayy, *al-Qawânîn al-fiqhiyya,* op. cit., p. 345.

16. These are the provisions taught in theory on matrimonial guardianship and consent to marriage by the main Malekite jurists such as Ibn Abî Zad al-Qayrawânî (died in 923), author of the *Risâla* (Epistle) (See Léon Bercher, *La Risâla ou Epître sur les éléments du dogme et de la loi de l'Islam selon le rite mâlikite* [Arabic text and French translation with notes], Editions Populaires de l'Armée, 5th edition., Algiers, 1968), or Khalil ibn Ishâq (died in 1366), author of the famous *Mukhtasar* (Précis) (See the last French translation of the entire text of the Khalil's *Mukhtasar* was done by Georges-Henri Bousquet, published by La Maison des Livres (Alger) & A. Maisonneuve (Paris), 4 vols, 1956–1962), or Ibn ʿÂsam (died in 1456), author of the *Tuhfat* (Masterpiece) (See Octave Houdas & Félix Martel, *Traité de Droit musulman. La Tohfat d'Ebn Acem.* Translation, commentary, and notes, ed. Gavault Saint Lager, Algiers, 1882) traditionally studied in Algeria.

17. Ismail Warscheid, *Nawâzil de l'Ouest saharien (XVIIè–XXè siècles) : une tradition jurisprudentielle africaine*, in *Encyclopédie des historiographies Afriques, Amériques, Asies*, ed. Livre Presses of INALCO, Paris, 2020, vol. 1- Tome 2, p. 1273.

18. Among the known collections, we can quote in chronological order and for the North of Algeria "*al-Durar al-Maknûna fî Nawâzil Mazûna*" written by Abû Zakariya' al-Maghîlî al-Mâzûnî (died in 1478) (Mazûna is a medium-sized but historically and culturally important city located in the West of Algeria); "*Nawâzil Qusantina*" by Muhammad ben cAbd al-Karîm al-Faggûn (died in 1702) (Constantine is also a historically and culturally important city located in eastern Algeria).

For the South, these collections are more numerous because they are better preserved. We can cite "*Nawâzil al-Djantûrî*" written by ʿAbd al-Rahmân al-Djantûrî (died in 1747); "*Nawâzil al-Zadjlâwî*" by Muhammad ben Ahmidân al-Zadjlâwî (died in 1798); "*Ghunyat al-muqtasid al-sâ'il fîmâ waqca fî Tuwât min-al-qadâyâ wa-l masâ'il*" written by Muhammad cAbd al-cAzîz al-Balbâlî (died in 1845) who listed the decisions and opinions of the jurist (and judge) ʿAbd al Haqq ben al-Bakri (died in 1796) This enumeration is not exhaustive and several of the collections of the Algerian South are still in manuscript and are the subject of published studies in various forms.

19. M'Barek Djacfrî, *Aʿlâm al-Fatwâ wa al-Nawâzil fî Mantiqat Tuwât bi-l Djanûb al-Gharbî al-Djazâ'irî bayn al-Qarnayn 12 wa 14 al-Hijtiyayn*, in *Madjallat al-Buhûth wa al-Dirâsât*, University of El-Oued (Algeria), no. 15, 2013, p. 334; Ibrâhim Balbâlî, *Nawâzil Mantiqat Tuwât wa Dawruhâ fî Khadmati al-Madhab al-Mâlikî "Dirâsa Tatbîqiyya calâ Nawâzil al-Zadjlâwî,*" in *al-Manhal*, Institute of Islamic Sciences, University of el-Oued, no. 3, 2016, p.71. This observation is valid for all the collections whatever their geographical origin (North -East and West- or South) with the exception of the Mzab region where the ibadite law is dominant.

20. It is indeed significant that the questions of matrimonial guardianship and the consent of the woman to marriage are relatively numerous and are exposed at the beginning of the chapter devoted to the conjugal union. This is the case for the

collection of case studies compiled in the 15th century by Abû Zakariyâ' (died in 1478) (22 case studies dealing with the problems of matrimonial guardianship and consent out of nearly 40 cases on marriage) and the one compiled at the end of the 17th century by ʿAbd al-Karîm Lafgûn (died in 1702) (four case studies dealing with the questions of guardianship and consent out of nine cases relating to marriage).

21. Abû Zakariyâ' (died 1478), *al-Durar al-maknûna fî nawâzil Mazûna*, Text prepared and annotated by al-Karîf Muhammad Redâ, PhD thesis, Faculty of Humanities and Islamic Sciences, University of Oran 1, 2016, p. 97.

22. Abû Zakariyâ', *al-Durar al-maknûna*, op. cit., p. 91.

23. Abû Zakariyâ' (died 1478), *al-Durar al-maknûna fî nawâzil Mazûna*, Text prepared and annotated by al-Karîf Muhammad Redâ, PhD thesis, Faculty of Humanities and Islamic Sciences, University of Oran 1, 2016, p. 97.

24. Abû Zakariyâ', *al-Durar al-maknûna*, op. cit., p. 104. Another example of marriage concluded without the consent of the daughter and against her will is reported in a collection of cases written at the end of the 17th century by a Constantinian jurist. The author writes "This marriage must be annulled because it was concluded against the wife's will and without her consent." See Muhammad ʿAbd al-Karîm Lafggûn (died 1702), *Nawâzil Qusantina*. Text prepared, introduced and annotated by Houari Touati and Aïcha Belabid, Zaytûn Editions, Oran, 2018, p. 63.

25. A. Sacd-Allah, *Daftar Mahkamat al-M'diya (al-Djazâ'ir) awâkhir al-ʿahd al-ʿuthmânî (1821–1839)*, in *La vie économique des provinces arabes et leurs sources documentaires à l'époque ottomane*, Etudes réunies et présentées par Abdeljelil Temimi, Centre d'Etudes et de Recherches sur les Provinces Arabes à l'Epoque Ottomane, Zaghouan (Tunisie), 1986, vol. 1, Tome 1, p. 142.

26. Ibn al-Muqaffaʿ, *Risâla fî al-Sahâba*, in Muhammad Kurd cAlî, *Rasâ'il al-Bulaghâ'*, ed. Dâr al-Kutub al-cArabiyya al-Kubrâ, Cairo, 1913, p. 120; This text has been edited and translated into French by Charles Pellat, *Ibn a-Muqaffaʿ (mort vers 140-757), "conseilleur" du calife*, in the collection "Publications du Département d'Islamologie de l'Université de Paris-Sorbonne," Paris, 1976.

27. Abû Djacfar al-Qommî (died 991), *ʿIlal al-Sharâ'iʿ*, ed. Dâr al-Murtadâ, Beirut, 1st ed., 2006, tome 1, p. 88.

28. Ibn khaldûn, *al- Muqaddima*, ed. Där al Kitâb al-Lunânî , Beirut, vol. 1, 2nd ed., p. 798 and p. 812, 1979.

29. Muslim jurisdictions were maintained but organized differently before and after 1870 according to the principles of autonomy implemented under the policy of the Second Empire in France, followed by the assimilationist policy after the establishment of the Third Republic. The ordinance of September 26, 1842, limited the powers of the Muslim judge (*Cadi*). The judgments of the *Cadi* could be appealed to the Court of Appeal, which was composed of French magistrates. A decree of August 20, 1848, placed Muslim justice under the authority of the minister of war and thus of the governor general and not under the authority of the French minister of justice. Muslim judges were under the supervision of the Attorney General (decree of December 31, 1859). An *option of jurisdiction* is possible for Algerian Muslim litigants who can therefore request the application of French civil law to judge their family disputes. A decree of August 29, 1874, instituted in Kabylia the "judge of the

peace" (*Juge de Paix*) in place of the *Cadi*. A Muslim Revision Chamber (*Chambre de Révisison Musulmane*) near the Court of Appeal of Algiers was created which played the role of a *Court of Cassation* in matters of personal status (see *La justice en Algérie 1830-1962*, ed. La documentation française, Paris, 2005).

30. See the texts on the organization of Justice in Algeria after colonization in M. P. de Ménerville, *Dictionnaire de la législation algérienne*, vol. 1, 1830–1860, 2nd edition, Bastid (Algiers) and Durand (Paris), 1867, p. 410 and following.

31. François Cadoz, *Droit musulman. Examen critique de la traduction qu'a faite M. Perron du livre de Khalil*, ed. Challamel Ainé, Paris, 1870.

32. Frédéric Godin, *De l'application du Droit musulman en Algérie*, Adolphe Jourdan, Alger, 1900.

33. Jules Roussier, *L'application du Chrac au Maghreb en 1959*, in Die Welt des Islams, éd. Brill, vol. 6, no. 1/2, 1959, p. 25.

34. See Claude Bontems, *Le droit musulman algérien à l'époque colonial. De l'invention à la codification*, ed. Slatkine Erudition, Geneva, 2014.

35. Maurice Borrmans, *Statut personnel et famille au Maghreb de 1940 à nos jours*, ed. Mouton, Paris-La Haye, 1977, p. 441.

36. See the developments on the application of Muslim law in relation to French public order in M. Morand, *Introduction à l'étude du droit musulman algérien*, ed. Jules Carbonel, Algiers, 1921, p. 21.

37. Judgment of the Chamber of Muslim Appeals of the Court of Appeal of Algiers, March 26, 1927, in *Revue algérienne, tunisienne et marocaine de législation et de jurisprudence*, Algiers, 1930, 2nd part, p. 131.

38. Muslim Review Chamber of the Court of Appeal of Algiers, April 11, 1922, in *Journal de Robe, Algiers*, 1923, p. 35 and in *Revue Algérienne, tunisienne et marocaine de législation et de jurisprudence*, Algiers, 1923, 2nd part, p. 183.

39. Decision of November 4, 1862, cited in Sautayra and Cherbonneau, *Droit musulman. Du statut personnel et des successions*, tome 1, ed. Maisonneuve et Cie, Paris, 1873, p. 76.

40. Khalîl ibn Ishâq (died in 1365), *Mukhtasar fî fiqh al-Imâm Mâlik*, ed. Dâr al-Basâ'ir, Algiers, First ed., 2012, p.164.

41. Law of May 2, 1930, *concerning the declaration of engagement and the age of marriage of the Kabyles*, in *Journal officiel de la République française*, no. 107 of May 4, 1930, p. 5002.

42. Ordinance no. 59-274 of February 4, 1959, relating to marriage contracted in the departments of Algeria, the Oasis and the Saoura by persons of local civil status, in *Journal officiel de la République française* of February 11, 1959, p. 1860.

43. Article 10 of the aforementioned Ordinance of February 4, 1959.

44. Paragraphs 1 and 2 of the Article 2 of this same 1959 ordinance.

45. Jules Roussier-Théaux, *La neutralisation du droit de djebr*, in *Revue africaine* (African Review, Publication of the Algerian Historical Society), Algiers, vol. 81, 1938, p. 161.

46. Law no. 62–157 of December 31, 1962, *tending to renew until further notice the legislation in force on December 31, 1962*, in *Journal officiel de la République algérienne*, no. 2, of January 11, 1963, p. 18.

47. Article 2 of the aforementioned law of December 31, 1962.

48. Nahas M. Mahieddin, *Le droit algérien de la famille. Une double succession sous bénéfice d'inventaire*, in *Algérie, 50 ans après. La part du Droit* (Collective work under the direction of Professor Walid Laggoune), ed. AJED, Algiers, 2013, p. 304.

49. These criticisms were published in the newspaper of the Front de Libération Nationale (National Liberation Front (FLN)), *el-Moudjahid*, dated July 6, 1959, during the Algerian War of Independence. For an opposing viewpoint among Algerians, see an article by Ahmed Djebbour in the newspaper, *L'Echo d'Alger*, quoted by Diane Sambron, *L'évolution du statut juridique de la femme musulmane à l'époque coloniale*, in *La Justice en Algérie 1830–1962*, ed. La Documentation française, Paris, 2005, p. 140.

50. Supreme Court, Chamber of Private Law, Judgment of December 23, 1964, in *Revue algérienne des sciences juridiques, économiques et politiques*, Faculty of Law of Algiers, no. 2, 1965, p. 86; Judgment of February 10, 1965, in this same Journal, no. 2, 1965, p. 89; Judgment of February 1, 1965, in this same Journal, no. 3, 1966, p. 872.

51. Supreme Court, Chamber of Private Law, Judgment of December 29, 1965, in *Revue algérienne des sciences juridiques, économiques et politiques*, 1966, no. 1, p. 112.

52. Law no. 84-11 of June 9, 1984, on the *Family Code*, in *Journal officiel de la République algérienne*, no. 24 of June 12, 1984, p. 612.

53. Law no. 63-224 of June 29, 1963, *fixing the minimum age for marriage*, in *Journal officiel de la République algérienne,* no. 44 of July 2, 1963, p. 681.

54. Supreme Court, Decision of November 22, 1982, in Journal *Nashrat al-Qudât*, 1986, no. 2, p. 32; Supreme Court, Decision of December 23, 1968, in Journal *Nashretal-Qudât*, 1969, no. 5, p. 61.

55. Article 9 of the Family Code.

56. Article 11 of the Family Code.

57. Article 13 of the Family Code.

58. Article 12 of the Family Code.

59. Paragraph 1 of article 12 of the Family Code.

60. Paragraph 1 of Article 10 of the Family Code states that "*consent derives from the request of one of the two parties and the acceptance of the other.*" We note that the legislature uses the word "*derives*" and does not use the words "*the consent is expressed.*"

61. Article 20 of the Family Code.

62. Al-Ghawtî Benmelha, *Qânûn al-usra calâ daw' al-fiqh wa-l-qadâ'*, ed. OPU, Alger, 3rd ed., 2015, p. 32.

63. Ordinance of February 27, 2005 *modifying and completing the law of 9 June on the Family Code*, in *Journal officiel de la République algérienne*, no. 15 of February 27, 2007, p. 17.

64. New Article 7 of the Family Code.

65. The Arabic version of Article 13 explicitly refers to the minor daughter (*qâsira*) as well as it should be clarified that in this version, the term *muwâfaqa* is officially translated as *consent* when it literally means *agreement.*

66. Paragraph 2 of the new Article 11 of the Family Code. New Article 13 of the Family Code. The Arabic official version of Article 13 is more precise than the translation made in French (although published in the Official Journal) and expressly mentions *the minor daughter* (*qâsira*).

67. Article 18 of the Ordinance of February 27, 2007 *modifying and completing the law of 9 June on the Family Code*, in *Journal officiel de la république algérienne*, no. 15 du 27 février 2005, p. 17

68. This procedure was instituted by a circular issued by the Algerian Ministry of Religious Affairs instructing imams of mosques not to perform the ceremony of *Fatiha* if the interested parties do not present a marriage certificate drawn up by the civil registrar.

Part II

PARENTS

ANALYZING GLOBAL NORMS OF PARENTING AND THEIR INTERSECTION WITH CHILD RIGHTS

Chapter 5

Establishing New Permanent Family Relationships in United States and Nordic Child Protection Systems

Josh Gupta-Kagan

INTRODUCTION

Gaps between the liberal United States and social welfare-oriented Nordic nations[1] have historically extended to child protection systems. American policies have featured more coercive and adversarial state intervention—mandatory investigations of child abuse or neglect allegations, involuntary removals of children from parents deemed unfit, and strict timelines for those parents to reunify followed by terminating the parent-child relationship and creating a new relationship via adoption. Nordic policies have long featured a stronger safety net provided to all families and voluntary services offered to families identified by child welfare agencies.[2] Even when children were removed, forced terminations of parental rights and adoptions have been rare, with ongoing parent-child relationships protected through long-term foster-care placements.

Some scholars have observed, however, that in recent years, the systems have "begun to converge."[3] The American system has developed more voluntary services and reduced the number of mandatory investigations. In Nordic nations, legal reforms have mandated more coercive steps (such as mandated reporting of abuse allegations to police), and out-of-home placement rates have increased (though different definitions make international comparisons difficult).[4]

This chapter focuses on the comparative creation of new parent and parent-like relationships across U.S. and Nordic child protection systems when authorities determine that parents and children cannot reunify. Creating new families and permanently ending others can represent the most drastic and emotionally fraught elements of state intervention in families, and one would expect the historic differences between the two nations to impact this area. Indeed, U.S. systems continue to use terminations of parental rights and involuntary adoptions far more frequently than Nordic countries. But the overall legal trends, and potential future developments, are more complex.

Trends in the United States and Nordic nations regarding permanency provide evidence of a modest convergence. In the United States, terminations of parental rights remain common, but other forms of permanency, especially guardianship, which grants permanent legal custody of foster children to a new family while maintaining children's legal relationship with their parents, have grown in usage. In Nordic nations, terminations and adoptions remain rare, but nations have begun to question the number of placement disruptions in long-term foster care and call for more permanency for foster children by permitting more adoptions.

In one area, U.S. law may even provide a model for Nordic nations' increasing focus on permanency for foster children. U.S. law has developed a spectrum of permanency options when parent-child reunification is ruled out, providing alternatives to terminations of parental rights. In contrast, most Nordic countries have focused on adoption as the alternative to long-term foster care when reunification is ruled out. In this way, the Nordic trend to consider adoption more frequently presents a "puzzle."[5] The historic focus on maintaining relationships between children in out-of-home care and their parents should lead to openness to permanency options that challenge the exclusivity of parenthood—options such as guardianship, as well as post-adoption contact agreements. This option is evident in one Nordic country, Sweden, which has no statutory mechanism for adoption but does provide for the equivalent of guardianship. The option is not prevalent in other Nordic countries—but developing it could provide an appropriate balance for their child protection systems' historic commitment to respecting family bonds and newer focus on providing permanency.

Finally, comparing the two categories of child protection systems reveals that child protection law is only one of several factors relevant to how child protection legal systems create new family arrangements. In the United States, legal protections against terminations of parental rights are comparatively strong compared to those in many Nordic nations, yet the United States has significantly more terminations. That curious relationship suggests that factors other than specific legal provisions shape the actions of child protection systems in each category.

UNITED STATES

In most international comparative studies, the United States is a leading exemplar of "liberal" welfare systems, meaning a relatively less generous welfare state, and, in the context of child welfare, low funding of programs to prevent child maltreatment and a focus on "detection" of child maltreatment "and coercive measures to separate the child from his or family."[6] Once children are in foster care, the American child protection system emphasizes "the philosophy of permanency planning."[7] That philosophy demands that child protection agencies and courts move with urgency to help children leave foster care—seen as temporary and by definition insecure—to some kind of legally permanent relationship—reunification with a parent, or the creation of new caregiver-child legal bonds intended to be permanent.

This section explores the United States' approach to permanency for foster children when reunification is ruled out—including both continuing common use of involuntary terminations of parental rights and adoptions, and the 21st-century trend toward the use of a wider spectrum of permanency options, including those which do not depend on involuntary terminations.

A Priority for Permanency

When children cannot reunify with parents, American child protection law and legal systems seek to move children out of foster care and into new permanent families. Failure to do so is viewed as a significant systemic failure, depriving children of new permanent family relationships. American law reflects its emphasis on legal permanency in multiple ways. First, it treats remaining in foster care as a negative outcome to be avoided whenever possible. Keeping a child in foster care without working toward some form of legal permanency requires setting a permanency plan of "another planned permanent living arrangement."[8] But American family courts and child protection agencies can only select that permanency plan in narrow circumstances, when other options have been ruled out.[9] Indeed, it has become axiomatic that permanency is generally preferred to remaining in foster care, which is often seen as synonymous with impermanency and instability. Accordingly, permanency has been a pillar of American child protection case management and law since at least the 1980s.[10] This view builds on empirical research showing particularly bad outcomes for children who grow up in foster care—poor educational and employment outcomes, and a strong correlation with adult homelessness and incarceration.[11]

Second, American law establishes timelines and court procedures intended to drive cases to some kind of permanent resolution without children spending multiple years in foster care. Once a child has been in foster care for 12 months, authorities must hold review hearings at least every six months and focus on each child's permanency options.[12] When a child has remained in foster care for 15 months (technically, 15 of the previous 22 months), states must generally file to terminate parental rights, though several exceptions exist.[13]

This legal structure has resulted in a steadily large number of children whose legal relationship with their parents is severed through termination of parental rights orders—1,300 in fiscal year 2018.[14] And it leads to the creation of a large number of new family units, with 61,900 children adopted from foster care and 26,084 foster children placed with permanent legal guardians in fiscal year 2018.[15] It can also lead to the creation of "legal orphans"[16]—children whose legal ties to their parents are severed, but for whom the state fails to create new families, which those statistics suggest occurs to 8,400 children each year.

A Growing Spectrum of Permanency Options

The United States' concept of permanency has evolved over time. A generation ago, when children could not reunify with parents, terminating parental rights and finding adoptive parents for the children was seen as the primary option. But through the early 21st century, a spectrum of permanency options has developed. In addition to traditional adoption—in which the legal relationship between biological parents and children is extinguished and a new parent-child relationship is created—American permanency options now include at least[17] two other options—adoption with post-adoption contact agreements, and legal guardianship.

These options have changed the permanency landscape. In fiscal year 2003, less than 11,000 children left foster care to live with permanent guardians, accounting for 17% of all new permanent families created for foster children.[18] Subsequently, the number of guardianships has more than doubled, to more than 26,000 in fiscal year 2018, accounting for nearly 30% of all new permanent families created for foster children.[19] This shift was aided by a 2008 expansion of federal financial support for subsidies paid to kinship guardians.[20] (Federal data does not distinguish traditional adoptions from those with post-adoption contact agreements, so it is difficult to offer similar statistics regarding the latter.)

The availability of various permanency options requires determining which option is best when children cannot reunify with their parents. These decisions, in turn, have significant impacts on the extent of state intervention to create new permanent families, especially the frequency with which state authorities terminate parent-child legal relationships.

Legally, a clear hierarchy exists—adoption is preferred over guardianship. States must rule out adoption before considering guardianship (or, more precisely, before the state child protection agency may obtain federal support for a kinship guardianship subsidy).[21] Implementing that hierarchy varies significantly. Some state courts suggest that a relative's desire to pursue guardianship rather than adoption suffices to rule out adoption.[22] As a matter of practice, significant variations exist—even in whether foster parents are informed if guardianship is an option.[23]

That legal hierarchy and inconsistent practice have given rise to criticism. A strong argument exists for treating guardianship as equal, or even preferred, to adoption. Studies of the American child protection system show that offering guardianship increases the number of children who leave foster care to reside with permanent families, reduces litigation over termination of parental rights and thus maintains both children's legal and social relationships with parents, avoids the risk of creating legal orphans, and provides just as much stability as adoption.[24] In particular, guardianships last just as long and do not disrupt (that is, children do not leave a guardian's custody) with any more frequency than adoptions do.[25]

Within the spectrum of permanency options, empirical studies are clear that no single option provides a guarantee of stability. Most children who are the subjects of adoptions or guardianships have stable family lives, but some adoptive families do break up, as do "pre-adoptive" placements (foster homes intended to become adoptive families), and guardianships. One study tracked such children for 10 years or until they turned 18 and found that 13% had some long-term interruption in their caregiving arrangements.[26]

Connection with Kinship Care

The growth of guardianship in the United States coincided with an increasing reliance on kinship caregivers for foster children. Kinship caregivers had physical custody of about 18% of foster children in the early 1980s, and that number increased significantly as foster-care rolls expanded later that decade and into the 1990s.[27] By the early 2000s, nearly a quarter of all American foster children lived with kinship caregivers, and that proportion increased to nearly a third by 2016.[28] Some data reports even higher figures—36%.[29]

American law and child protection systems often see guardianship as particularly appropriate for kinship caregivers. Historically, kinship caregivers were expected to be more hesitant to pursue the termination of a relative's parental rights, and they and the child might see each other as child and grandparent (or aunt, uncle, etc.) rather than parent and child. Parents were also presumed to be more willing to agree to guardianship than to adoption, and to any new permanent family arrangement involving a trusted family member than a stranger. Guardianship was thus most easily understood in this context, and federal subsidies are only available for kinship guardians.[30] Leading advocates for guardianship even describe it as "legal guardianship by kin."[31] It is important to note, however, that guardianship is not limited to kin; anyone (even a non-kinship foster parent) can become a guardian under state laws. And many American states (though not a majority) even use their own funds to subsidize such guardianships.[32]

Racial Disparities

Given the United States' long and troubled history regarding race, it is no surprise that significant racial disparities exist in the American child protection system, along with long-running debates regarding the causes of those disparities.[33] These disparities continue through permanency decisions, and the particular weight of such decisions—especially adoptions and terminations of parental rights—can make such decisions even more fraught.

Concerns about the overrepresentation of children of color in foster care and termination of parental rights cases have contributed to the growth of guardianship as an alternative to adoption. Native Americans and African American families have long histories of preferring kinship care without terminating parental rights, so guardianship is often seen as a means to avoid terminations.[34]

Legal Structure

In order to terminate parental rights and adopt children over parents' objections, American law requires state authorities to prove both that the parents are unfit and that the termination and adoption are in the child's best interest. In addition, states must meet an elevated standard of proof—clear and convincing evidence—to support a termination.[35] Parents do not enjoy a constitutional right to counsel in termination cases, but the vast majority of states provide counsel as a matter of state law.[36]

Establishing guardianships generally come with a somewhat less significant set of legal protections for parents. Because the state infringes on the parent-child relationship less severely, legal protections can be lessened—though this has been criticized given equivalent permanency of adoptions and guardianships.[37]

NORDIC NATIONS

Nordic nations—Denmark, Finland, Iceland, Norway, and Sweden—are generally seen as following a social democratic welfare state model.[38] In Nordic child protection systems, this model translates to an emphasis on voluntary services to families and using the least amount of state coercion possible—in particular, reserving involuntary child removals to foster care for the most severe cases. When it comes to permanency for foster children,

Nordic nations reflect a deep reluctance to sever permanently parent-child relationships.[39]

More Long-Term Foster Care, Rare Adoptions

Very few Nordic foster children leave foster care to adoption, and Nordic nations have instead relied on long-term foster care.[40] One illustrative study reflected a strong cultural aversion to adoption over parents' objections among Nordic child protection professionals. Researchers surveyed case workers in the United States, Great Britain, and Norway regarding what they would recommend in an identical fact pattern: A child who lived since infancy and for two and a half years with a foster family, and the child's parents continue to have substance abuse problems and have visited the child, but the child's mother opposes a potential adoption by the foster parents. Nearly all (96% or more) of American and British case workers indicated they would support adoption in this case. Significantly fewer—only 59%—of Norwegian workers supported adoption, with the remainder supporting continued foster care. Those opposing adoption focused on the mother's objections, and sought more time for the parents to rehabilitate.[41] That a significant percentage of Nordic case workers resisted adoption, even with parents who remained unfit and unlikely to become fit and who had no relationship with the child, reflects the strong aversion to forced terminations and adoption.

That deep-seated aversion to involuntary adoptions is born out in the low numbers of adoptions. In Norway, for instance, foster-care adoptions ranged from single digits to 65 based on the year and precise counting method.[42] In contrast, two American states with similar populations to Norway had 580 or more foster-child adoptions each.[43]

Some legal barriers to adoption exist as well. In Sweden, the law does not even provide a mechanism for foster children to be adopted.[44] Finland was historically slow to enact any adoption statute; no adoption law of any kind existed there until 1925, and that law focused on private adoptions, not foster-care adoptions.[45]

A result of this Nordic aversion to involuntary adoption is a focus on foster placement stability more than permanence for children.[46] Indeed, Nordic nations feature significant use of long-term foster care—maintaining children's legal relationships with their parents and the possibility of reunification, without taking steps to permanently change the child's legal family relationships.

Concerns with the Status Quo—And Modest Reform Trends

Some voices have raised concerns about Nordic systems' reliance on long-term foster care, echoing concerns raised in the United States. In particular, some have criticized long-term foster care as inherently impermanent, and often leading to high rates of placement disruptions,[47] although studies reach inconsistent results regarding the extent of placement disruptions.[48] Others note that compared with some kind of legal permanency, long-term foster care can leave children not knowing how long they can or will stay in a particular foster home, a feeling that can undermine children's sense of stability and belonging,[49] and lead to a range of negative outcomes.[50] The de-emphasis of legal permanency has been called the "blind spot of the Norwegian system."[51]

These concerns led to calls for reforms that would make Nordic systems slightly more like their American counterparts—emphasize permanency more, with a particular focus on adoption.[52] Those calls appear to have gained some modest traction. The same observers identify a trend across Denmark, Finland, and Norway "to be more adoption-friendly to achieve the goal about permanency for children."[53] That view is supported by calls in these countries to revise adoption laws to make involuntary adoptions of foster children easier.[54]

Kinship Care

Historically, kinship care was used relatively infrequently in Nordic countries,[55] but more recently this area has been one of convergence.[56] While international comparisons show Nordic kinship foster-care rates to be somewhat lower than American rates, they are still significant—22.6% in Norway, and 30.0% in Sweden, compared to 36.0% in the United States.[57] Moreover, in at least some Nordic nations, the proportion of kinship care is growing; for instance, increasing in Norway from 10.8% in 2000 to 22.6% in 2010, and an estimated 12% increase in Sweden in the same time period.[58]

Commentators have suggested that increasing Nordic kinship care rates could affect permanency decisions by increasing parental support for permanent placements with kin.[59] However, a strong connection between the growth of kinship care and permanency outcomes has not yet developed within Nordic nations.

Expanding Racial and Ethnic Diversity

While the United States remains significantly more racially and ethnically diverse than Nordic nations, increasing immigration to Nordic nations has led to more diverse populations. And Nordic child welfare systems have begun to reflect ethnic disproportionalities, with children of immigrants overrepresented in foster care.[60] The relative newness of this issue to Nordic systems is reflected in the literature, with frequent statements acknowledging the need for more study and understanding of the issue.[61]

Contrasting Examples—Norway and Sweden

An exploration of two examples illustrates the status quo, the trend toward greater emphasis on permanency, and the impact of law on these issues.

Norway

One might expect Norwegian law to impose significant barriers to adoptions. However, Norwegian law is relatively open to adoption, providing that foster children may be adopted when

> it must be regarded as probable that the parents will be permanently unable to provide the child with proper care *or* the child has become so attached to persons and the environment where he or she is living that, on the basis of an overall assessment, removing the child may lead to serious problems for him or her.[62]

Notably, in contrast to the United States, this statute does *not* require the government to prove that a parent is unfit at the time of the adoption and, instead, permits adoptions to proceed based only on the child's strong attachments to foster parents, even if a parent has rehabilitated. This emphasis on foster parent-foster child relationships is consistent with other provisions of Norwegian law making it difficult to reunify parents and children "if the child has become so attached to the persons and the environment where he or she is living that . . . removing the child may lead to serious problems for him or her."[63] Commentators have described Norway's law as not "set[ting] particular strict restrictions and high thresholds for the use of adoptions."[64]

While those statutory provisions suggest legal support for adoptions, a leading European Court for Human Rights case pushes somewhat in the opposite direction. *Johansen v. Norway* involved a child removed from her mother, Adele Johansen, "shortly after birth" with "very little contact" between mother and child in the years which followed; the Norwegian court described Ms. Johansen as essentially a "stranger" to her child.[65] That fact resulted, however, from a questionable decision to prohibit any contact between Ms. Johansen and her child within months of her placement in foster care—even when an older child was reunifying with her.[66] That court relied upon a psychologist who opined that removing the child from her foster parents could cause significant damage because of her relatively young age and the foster parents' role as her only stable long-term caregivers.[67] Norwegian authorities based the adoption on these facts and the child's bonds with her foster parents—not Ms. Johansen's unfitness. Indeed, Ms. Johansen appeared fit; about one year after the child's initial removal and while the case was still pending, Ms. Johansen's situation improved "to the point where she would have been able to provide her daughter with a satisfactory upbringing."[68]

The crux of the *Johansen* ruling focused on the relatively quick action by Norwegian authorities to cut-off contact between Ms. Johansen and her daughter and move toward adoption. That action, the European Court for Human Rights ruled, required "a stricter scrutiny" than placing the child in foster care temporarily;[69] it "totally deprived the applicant of her family life with the child" and should occur only in "exceptional circumstances . . . justified if they were motivated by an overriding requirement pertaining to the child's best interests."[70]

Johansen is cited for limiting numbers of foster-care adoptions in Norway by suggesting that the law will prohibit such adoptions.[71] Nonetheless, this court decision did not go as far as U.S. law does in requiring proof of present unfitness, and it involved hopefully uncommon actions of cutting a child off from her mother extremely early in life.

One subsequent Norwegian legal reform seeks to make adoption easier without violating *Johansen*. Norwegian authorities may now order post-adoption contact between biological parents and their adopted children.[72] This reform makes adoptions more defensible to some legal challenges when they do not cut-off all contact between biological parents and children—a central concern of *Johansen*. The number of adoptions from foster care have increased in recent years; they averaged 32 annually between 2006 and 2011, and 60 annually between 2014 and 2018. Nonetheless, these figures remain dramatically low compared to the United States and adoption remains controversial in Norway.[73] Norway has not engaged in legal reforms to utilize guardianship as an alternative to adoption.

Sweden

Sweden exhibits a similar aversion to adoption as Norway, but through a more straightforward legal mechanism—Swedish law contains no provision for adoption without parents' consent.[74]

Swedish law does, however, provide for permanent custody to be granted to foster parents without terminating parental rights and creating a new parent-child relationship. Foster parents can become "specially appointed custodians" of foster children,[75] and in such cases, children and parents have an ongoing right to some kind of contact.[76] This status is roughly similar to guardianship in American law. Sweden uses this permanency option with apparently increasing frequency—246 times in 2012, up from 125 in 2005 and 64 in 2003[77]—and, since 2012, has incentivized foster parents to seek this status by continuing to provide financial and other supports to them after becoming specially appointed custodians.[78] While increasing, these figures still reflect a small percentage of Swedish children who remain in long-term foster care.[79]

DISCUSSION: A COMPARATIVE ANALYSIS AND LESSONS EACH CATEGORY CAN TAKE FROM THE OTHER

Differences in the law and practice of finding foster children permanent homes remain significant between American and Nordic child protection systems. Involuntary adoptions and terminations of parental rights remain an essential part of the American child protection system, and remarkably rare in Nordic nations. The American system features a stronger imperative to move toward some kind of legal permanency than Nordic systems, which reflect greater acceptance of long-term foster care.

Nonetheless, as in other areas, the two types of child protection systems' permanency practices are converging, however modestly. In the United States, the trend has been to expand the number of permanency options other than traditional closed adoptions—including both adoption with contact agreements and guardianship. In Nordic nations, the trend is toward an increased concern about children in long-term foster care and thus a somewhat greater push to create permanent family ties for foster children unlikely to reunify with parents. Some Nordic nations are loosening adoption laws, while Sweden has made somewhat greater use of a legal relationship akin to guardianship.

The contrasts between the two categories of child protection systems and the tentative steps toward a convergence between them, raise the possibility that each could learn from the other. The Nordic systems demonstrate that functioning child protection systems need not heavily depend on adoptions and terminations of parental rights. The American system demonstrates that a variety of permanent legal statuses can provide foster children with permanency without necessarily terminating their entire legal relationship with parents.

A range of more specific points may be gleaned from this comparison. First, legal standards which make adoptions or terminations of parental rights harder or easier is only one issue among many in understanding what actually happens in foster-care cases. Both categories of systems start with a recognition of a special and protected status for relationships between parents and children. The American system, however, features laws which more clearly protect those relationships against state intervention—an involuntary adoption requires the state to prove parental unfitness by clear and convincing evidence. Several Nordic systems, in contrast, permit the state to rely instead on children's bonding with foster parents, and even limiting European Court for Human Rights decisions do not prohibit that reliance. Intriguingly, the different levels of legal protections against terminations of parental rights and adoptions have an inverse relationship with the frequency with which those invasions of the parent-child relationship take effect. They occur much more frequently in the United States, the nation with stronger legal protections, than in Nordic nations with comparatively weaker protections. The law must be considered in the context of broader cultural norms and the actual practice of permanency decisions by child protection agencies and courts.

Second, Nordic nations should be primed to expand their use of permanency options like guardianship. Nordic nations have a long-standing aversion to traditional involuntary adoption, which is now being balanced by an increasing concern about long-term foster care and thus a step toward the American emphasis on legal permanency. A legal status which provides a permanent legal caregiving relationship for the child with a custodian, but which does not sever parental rights, seems like an attractive compromise. The American experience with guardianship demonstrates that such a legal status can achieve those goals. Indeed, growing acceptance of adoption with contact agreements in Norway and Denmark suggest an increasing openness to a related compromise. Yet only one Nordic nation, Sweden, has used a legal status akin to guardianship with any significant numbers. Such legal statuses warrant greater attention in Nordic nations.

Indeed, using guardianship more frequently in Nordic nations may avoid one key difficulty faced in the United States. The American child protection system remains conflicted regarding any preferences between adoption and guardianship. The law creates a preference for adoption, but data showing that guardianship is just as permanent, and practice in some states making it easy to overcome a presumption for adoption suggests that, at least in some U.S. jurisdictions, guardianship and adoptions are more equal. Nordic nations' greater aversion to forced terminations and adoptions could make this legal landscape easier; a hierarchy placing guardianship over adoption is more likely there.

Third, both systems have lessons for each other regarding the connection between kinship caregivers and the creation of new permanent families. The availability of non-kinship guardianship in the United States makes clear that this option can be effectively used for non-kinship caregivers who make up the bulk of Nordic long-term foster parents; to the extent Nordic nations are primed to expand their use of guardianship, that phenomenon should apply equally to kinship and non-kinship foster homes. On the flip side, the particular success of guardianship in the United States with kinship caregivers indicates that this permanency option could be particularly appealing for kinship foster parents in Nordic nations and should be explored. The United States could learn from Sweden that guardianship can provide a useful alternative to adoption and terminating parental rights for any long-term foster parent, not only kin. More particularly, states within the United States that do not frequently use non-kinship guardianship could consider doing so.

Relatedly, guardianship has often been presented in America as particularly appealing to racial minorities, especially groups with traditions of extended family caregiving. Guardianship has proven a useful tool in the United States for children and families of all backgrounds, so such statements should not be exaggerated. That said, there is a potential that the growing diversity of Nordic populations—with ethnic minorities overrepresented in foster care—could indicate that a variety of permanency options could help find the best choice for an individual child and family.

Fourth, the American experience also provides notes of caution for Nordic nations seeking to improve permanency for children unlikely to reunify with parents. Creating legally permanent relationships does not guarantee that those relationships will remain through adulthood. In particular, a growing amount of research in America demonstrates that legally permanent relationships of all types do, in fact, disrupt.[80] Reunified children return to foster care and adoptions and guardianships disrupt. Accordingly, Nordic systems should anticipate providing voluntary support services to families of former foster children to help them stay together, and should not view an increased emphasis on permanency as a panacea for placement disruptions.

CONCLUSION

The "convergence" observed by Gilbert between the United States and Nordic child protection system exists regarding the formation of new family relationships for foster children unlikely to reunify with parents: in the United States, options other than termination of parental rights and involuntary adoptions are increasingly used, while in Nordic nations, a greater focus on legal permanency is developing. Significant differences remain—in particular, the United States continues to use adoptions and terminations dramatically more frequently than Nordic nations. Respective experiences in the two categories provide a host of potential lessons that they may take from each other—especially the potential to provide legal permanency that respects the ongoing importance of parent-child legal relationships.

NOTES

1. Such comparisons are common in contrasting approaches to public support for families. See, e.g., Eichner, Maxine. *The Free-Market Family: How the Market*

Crushed the American Dream (and How It Can Be Restored) (Oxford: Oxford Scholarship Online, 2020): 21–27, 37–40 (comparing United States and Finland).

2. *See, e.g.* Gilbert, Neil, Nigel Parton, & Marik Skivenes, "Introduction," in *Child Protection Systems: International Trends and Orientations,* eds. Neil Gilbert, Nigel Parton, & Marik Skivenes (2011): 3–11 (describing distinguishing nations with child protection and family service orientations, and placing United States and Nordic systems in separate categories for comparison).

3. Gilbert, Neil. "A Comparative Study of Child Welfare Systems: Abstract Orientations and Concrete Results," *Children and Youth Services Review* 34, no. 3 (March 2012): 532–536.

4. Gilbert (2011): 533. Pösö, Tarja, Marit Skivenes & Anne-Dorthe Hestbæk. "Child Protection Systems within the Danish, Finnish and Norwegian Welfare States—Time for a Child Centric Approach?" *European Journal of Social Work* 17 (2013): 475, 481.

5. Pösö, Skivenes, and Hestbæk (2013) refer to "the puzzle of the Nordic child protection systems and outcomes." *Id.* at 482.

6. del Valle, Jorge F. & Amaia Bravo. "Current Trends, Figures and Challenges in Out of Home Child Care: An International Comparative Analysis," *Psychosocial Intervention* 22 (2013): 251, 252.

7. *Id.* at 255.

8. 42 U.S.C. § 675(5)(B)-(C).

9. 42 U.S.C. § 675a(a).

10. § 675(5)(C)(i) (2011)).

4 For a brief history of the "permanency planning" movement leading to this codification, *see* , Mark F. "New Permanency Strategies for Children in Foster Care," in *Child Welfare Research: Advances for Practice and Policy*, ed. Duncan Lindsey & Aron Shlonsky (New York: Oxford University Press, 2008): 108, 111–12; Hardin, Mark. "Child Protection Cases in a Unified Family Court," *Family Law Quarterly* 32, no. 1 (Spring 1998): 147, 151–52.

11. *See, e.g.* Mangold, Susan Vivian. "Extending Non-Exclusive Parenting and the Right to Protection for Older Foster Children: Creating Third Options in Permanency Planning," *The Buffalo Law Review* 48 (2000): 835, 864–65 (collecting research).

12. 42 U.S.C. § 675(5).

13. 42 U.S.C. § 675(5)(C).

14. U.S. Dept of Health & Human Services, Administration for Children & Families, Children's Bureau, *Trends in Foster Care and Adoption FY 2009–FY 2018* (2019), https://www.acf.hhs.gov/sites/default/files/cb/trends_fostercare_adoption_09thru18.pdf

15. U.S. Dept of Health & Human Services, Administration for Children & Families, Children's Bureau, *The AFCARS Report: Preliminary FY 2018 Estimates as of August 22, 2019 – No. 26*, at 3 (2019), https://www.acf.hhs.gov/sites/default/files/cb/afcarsreport26.pdf

16. Martin Guggenheim coined this term. Martin Guggenheim, "The Effects of Recent Trends to Accelerate the Termination of Parental Rights of Children in Foster

Care—An Empirical Analysis in Two States," *Family Law Quarterly* 29 (1995): 121, 122.

17. Other state-specific options exist, such as adoption without terminating parental rights when the biological and adoptive parents agree. Calif. Fam. Code § 8617; Gupta-Kagan, Josh. "Non-Exclusive Adoption and Child Welfare," *Alabama Law Review* 66, no. 4 (2015): 715–65.

18. U.S. Dept of Health & Human Services, Administration for Children & Families, Children's Bureau, *The AFCARS Report: Interim FY 2003 Estimates as of June 2006*, at 4 (2006), https://www.acf.hhs.gov/sites/default/files/cb/afcarsreport26.pdf. The percentage reported is calculated by dividing the number of guardianships by the sum of all adoptions and guardianships.

19. AFCARS, *supra* note 13, at 3. The percentage reported is calculated by dividing the number of guardianships by the sum of the total number of adoptions and guardianships.

20. Fostering Connections to Success and Increasing Adoptions Act of 2008, Pub. L. 110–351, § 101, *codified at* 42 U.S.C. §§ 671(a)(28) & 673(d).

21. 42 U.S.C. § 673(d)(3)(A)(ii).

22. *E.g. N.J. Div. of Youth & Fam. Servs. v. P.P.*, 852 A.2d 1093, 1105 (N.J. 2004) (trial courts may consider guardianship rather than adoption when potential adoptive parents "decline to adopt").

23. Children's Defense Fund, Child Trends, American Bar Association Center on Children and the Law, Case Family Programs, Child Focus, and Generations United, *Making it Work: Using the Guardianship Assistance Program (GAP) to Close the Permanency Gap for Children in Foster Care* (2012); U.S. Dept of Health and Human Servs., Admin. For Children and Families, Admin. On Children, Youth and Families, Children's Bureau, *Synthesis of Findings: Subsidized Guardianship Child Welfare Waiver Demonstrations* 28(2011).

24. *See* Gupta-Kagan, Josh. "The New Permanency," *U.C. Davis Journal of Juvenile Law & Policy* 19, no. 1 (Winter 2015): 1–83 (summarizing arguments and collecting studies).

25. U.S. Dept of Health and Human Servs., Admin. for Children and Families, Admin. on Children, Youth and Families, Children's Bureau, *Synthesis of Findings: Subsidized Guardianship Child Welfare Waiver Demonstrations*, 18–20 (2011), *available at* http://www.acf.hhs.gov/sites/default/files/cb/subsidized_0.pdf

26. Rolock, Nancy. "Post-Permanency Continuity: What Happens After Adoption and Guardianship from Foster Care?" *Journal of Public Child Welfare* 9 (2015): 153–73.

27. Testa, Mark F. & Jennifer Miller. "Evolution of Private Guardianship as a Child Welfare Resource," in *Child Welfare for the 21st Century: A Handbook of Practies, Policies, and Programs*, eds. Gerald P. Mallon & Meg McCartt Hess (New York: Columbia University Press, 2005): 405, 410–411.

28. U.S. Department of Health and Human Services, Administration for Children and Families, Administration on Children, Youth and Families, Children's Bureau, Foster Care Statistics 2017, 4 (2019), https://www.childwelfare.gov/pubPDFs/foster.pdf

29. del Valle & Bravo (2013): 255.

30. 42 U.S.C. § 673(d)

31. Testa, Mark F. "The Quality of Permanence—Lasting or Binding? Subsidized Guardianship and Kinship Foster Care as Alternatives to Adoption," *Virginia Journal of Social Policy and Law* 12 (2005): 499, 538.

32. Patten, Eliza. "The Subordination of Subsidized Guardianship in Child Welfare Proceedings," *N.Y.U. Review of Law and Social Change* 29 (2004): 237–76.

33. For a discussion of relevant data and debates, see Cooper, Tanya A. "Racial Bias in American Foster Care: The National Debate," *Marquette Law Review* 97 (2013): 2015. del Valle, Jorge F. & Amaia Bravo. "Current Trends, Figures and Challenges in Out of Home Child Care: An International Comparative Analysis," *Psychosocial Intervention* 22 (2013): 251.

34. *E.g.* Godsoe, Cynthia. "The Permanency Puzzle," *Michigan State Law Review* 2013 (2013): 1113.

35. *Santosky v. Kramer*, 455 U.S. 745 (1982).

36. *Lassiter v. Department of Social Services*, 452 U.S. 18 (1981).

37. *E.g.* Gupta-Kagan (2015).

38. *E.g.* del Valle & Bravo (2013): 251.

39. *Id.* at 255.

40. Gilbert (2011): 535.

41. Skivenes, Marit & Øyvind Samnøy Tefre. "Adoption in the Child Welfare System—A Cross-Country Analysis of Child Welfare Workers' Recommendations for or Against Adoption," *Children & Youth Services Review* 34 (2012): 2220–8.

42. Statistisk sentralbyrå: adoptions, https://www.ssb.no/en/adopsjon; Skivenes, Marit & June Thoburn. "Pathways to Permanence in England and Norway: A Critical Analysis of Documents and Data," *Children & Youth Services Review* 67 (2016): 152, 155 (reporting 36 "adoptions of children in the child welfare system"); Backe-Hansen, Elizabeth, Ingrid Højer, Yvonne Sjöblom, and Jan Storø. "Out of Home Care in Norway and Sweden—Similar and Different," *Psychosocial Intervention* 22 (December 2013): 193–202 (after accounting for step-parent adoptions, finding "less than ten adoptions per year . . . effected as a child welfare measure").

43. This data refer to Minnesota and South Carolina. U.S. Department of Health and Human Services, Administration for Children and Families, Administration on Children, Youth and Families, Children's Bureau, Age at Adoption Finalization: October 1, 2010 to September 30, 2011 (FY 2011), https://www.acf.hhs.gov/sites/default/files/cb/final_age2011.pdf. Data collection and definitional differences make international empirical comparisons difficult; the point here is simply that foster-care adoptions occur significantly more frequently in the United States than in Nordic countries.

44. Sweden, Children & Parents Code; del Valle & Bravo (2013): 255.

45. Pylkkänen, Anu. "Substitute Children and Adoption in Finnish Legal History," *Scandinavian Journal of History* 20 (1995): 129–40.

46. Holtan, Amy, Bjørn Helge Handegård, Renee Thørnblad, Svein Arild Vis. "Placement Disruption in Long-Term Kinship and Nonkinship Foster Care," *Children & Youth Services Review* 35, no. 7 (July 2013): 1087, 1088.

47. Pösö, Skivenes & Hestbæk (2013): 484.
48. Holtan, *et al.* (2013): 1092–93.
49. Skivenes & Tefre (2012): 2221.
50. Skivenes & Thoburn (2016): 157.
51. *Id.*
52. *E.g.* Pösö, *et al.* (2013): 485.
53. *Id.* at 481.
54. *Denmark Could Ease Laws on Forced Adoption*, The Local dk, February 26, 2019, https://www.thelocal.dk/20190226/denmark-could-ease-laws-on-forced-adoption
55. Holtan, Amy, *et al.* "A Comparison of Mental Health Problems in Kinship and Nonkinship Foster Care," *European Journal of Child and Adolescent Psychiatry* 14, no. 4 (July 2005): 200–7.
56. *See, e.g.*, oltan, Amy & Renee Thørnblad. "Kinship Foster Parenting; Gender, Class and Labour-Force Participation," *European Journal of Social Work* 12 (2009): 465, 466.
57. del valle & Bravo (2013): 255.
58. Backe-Hansen, *et al.* (2013): 195, 199.
59. Holtan, *et al.* (2005): 203–204.
60. Backe-Hansen, *et al.* (2013): 197.
61. *See, e.g. id.* ("However, we know very little about how to design good services for these groups or of possible differential effects of the services.").
62. Norwegian Child Welfare Act § 4-20 (emphasis added).
63. Norwegian Child Welfare Act § 4-21.
64. Skivenes & Tefre (2012): 2222.
65. *Johansen v. Norway*, 23 Eur. Ct. H.R. 33, 44 (1996).
66. *Id.* at 42.
67. *Id.* at 44–45.
68. *Id.*at 74.
69. *Id.* at 68.
70. *Id.* at 73.
71. *See* Skivenes & Thoburn (2016): 153 (describing adoptions in Norway as "rarely" occurring since *Johansen*).
72. Norwegian Child Welfare Act § 4-20a.
73. Skivenes & Thoburn (2016): 158.
74. Backe-Hansen, *et al.* (2013): 198.
75. Sweden Children and Parents Code, Chapter 6, § 8.
76. *Id.* at § 15.
77. Backe-Hansen, *et al.* (2013): 199; Wisso, Therese & Helena Johansson, "Transferring Custody from Birth Parents to Foster Parents—An Ambiguous Matter," *Journal of Social Welfare and Family Law* 40 (2018): 321, 327.
78. *Id.*
79. *Id.*
80. *Supra* note 26.

Chapter 6

Separation and Connectedness

Global Norms of Open vs. Closed Adoption

Malinda L. Seymore

INTRODUCTION

In modern American adoption law, adoption begins with erasure—a child's biological parents are legally erased and replaced with adoptive parents. That erasure was further enforced traditionally with secrecy about the birth parents. American adoption law does not recognize any legal rights in birth parents to continue contact with the child, except in limited circumstances and generally only when the adoptive parents agree.[1] This notion of erasure and secrecy is not, however, universal. In other cultures norms of connection and openness exist together with adoption. And there are arguments that international agreements like the Convention on the Rights of the Child and the Hague Convention on International Adoption support increased openness in adoption. This chapter explores these norms.

TRADITIONAL ADOPTION IN THE UNITED STATES

Secrecy has long been a hallmark of American adoption, though, before World War II, most children adopted were older and knew the identity and whereabouts of their biological parents.[2] Often, biological parents and adoptive parents made the adoption arrangements on their own, without an intermediary, and thus knew each other's identity and whereabouts.[3] Secrecy was introduced by progressive reformers in order to keep birth parents away from their children placed for adoption.[4] Reformers seeking to "save" children from poverty were concerned that birth parents would look to reunite with their children and would, thereby, undo all the good work of saving the children.[5] "Progressive Era social workers began to include in relinquishment forms signed by birth parents promises not to seek out the child, to learn the child's location, or to interfere in any way with the child or adoptive parents."[6]

It was not long after the Progressive period that "disappearing" the birth parents became a standard practice in American adoption; in 1938, the influential Child Welfare League of America formalized the requirement that "the identity of the adopting parents should be kept from the natural parents."[7] By 1948, a majority of states had legislation sealing adoption records.[8] Birth parents were further erased as states began to provide "amended birth certificates" to adoptive parents, where the birth parents names would be removed from the child's birth certificate and replaced with the names of the adoptive parents.[9] "By the mid-1960s, the confidentiality regime had transmogrified into a secrecy regime, with birth parents denied information about the adoptive parents and the child's whereabouts, with adoption records sealed to all, and with records of original birth certificates also sealed."[10]

Secrecy was seen as the perfect solution; it allowed adopted children to be "treated as if they had been born into the adoptive family."[11] The practice of secrecy created an "alternative family," where it was "as if the birth mother had never borne this child, as if the adoptive mother herself had."[12] The erasure of the birth family allowed for "the perfect and complete substitute for creating a family through childbirth."[13] As Professor Annette Appell puts it, "the adoption paradigm became one of fictive birth that substituted the adoptive parents for the birth parents."[14]

Much of the notion of secrecy and separation rely on the idea that birth parents are generally benefited by that approach, that a complete break benefits bonding of adoptees to their new families, and that adoptive parents need a clean slate opportunity to create a new family without being concerned with birth family influence. There is little in the psychosocial literature to support this.

While a majority of birth parents are generally satisfied with their adoption decision, a significant portion experience negative psychological symptoms that can be long-term.[15] In one study comparing adolescents who chose to parent and those who chose to relinquish for adoption, those who relinquished were less comfortable with their decision than those who parented.[16] In the first two years following relinquishment birth mothers experience "a powerful sense of loss and isolation,"[17] and even two years after relinquishment some birth mothers continue to experience effects of adoption relinquishment on their emotional well-being.[18] While some researchers report feelings of satisfaction by birth mothers four years after birth, most also experience continuing grief and loss,[19] ongoing depression, shame, and negative self-image.[20] In one study, the majority of birth mothers reported "no decrease in feelings of sadness, anger, and guilt since their relinquishment up to 30 years [before]."[21]

Although there are few studies of birth fathers, in one study birth fathers described the adoption as producing deep and long-lasting feelings, reporting that the adoption placement "'looms large' in their lives many years later."[22] Some reported that as long as five years post-adoption they still experienced significant distress relating to the adoption placement.[23] Most of the men in that study reported hopes for contact with the child placed for adoption in the future.[24] In one study 72% of birth fathers expressed current negative feelings about placing their child for adoption, with those who felt pressured to place a child for adoption five times as likely to harbor current negative feelings.[25]

Adoptees may not experience adoption as the unconditionally happy event adoptive parents and society ascribe to it but as a fraught and ambivalent experience.[26] Some adoptees experience adoption as a profound loss,[27] experiencing fear of abandonment, rejection, and struggling with trust and attachment issues that can affect future relationships.[28] Adoptees face stigma associated with being adopted in a bio-centric world.[29] Many adoptees struggle with adoption identity, which may explain high levels of behavior problems observed in adopted children and adolescents.[30] While adoptees represent less than 2% of the childhood population in the United States, they represent 10–15% of those in mental healthcare facilities.[31]

Adoptive parents have not been well-studied in the psychosocial literature.[32] But it is generally understood that in addition to the same parenting challenges all parents face, adoptive parents "also negotiate a number of additional tasks unique to the adoption process."[33] Adoption usually follows years of infertility and attempts and failure at conception, leading to grief and stress.[34] Adoptive parents who experienced infertility may have experienced the loss of the biological child they wanted to have.[35] If adoption "is used unconsciously as a way of avoiding the issue" of infertility, an individual may experience "general anxiety, depression, a devalued self-image, resentment of one partner for another, disruptions in marital communication, and so on."[36] Uncertainty surrounding the process—a timing that might be shorter or longer than pregnancy, the anxiety-producing home study, "mutual adaptation [that] may not be as smooth as with a newborn infant"[37]—adds to typical transition-to-parenthood stress.[38] What one study calls "adoptive strains," defined as "more enduring, chronic or recurrent problems and conflicts that adoptive parents face on a routine basis that can result in increased feelings of distress," including concerns about bonding and instant parenthood, potential for future developmental or mental health issues in the adopted child, fears about birth parents, and concerns about how and when to disclose the adoption to the child.[39] These issues may be exacerbated if the adoption involves an older,[40] institutionalized,[41] or special-needs child.[42]

Openness and continuing contact improve the relationship between adoptees and their adoptive parents, increase adoptees' self-esteem and confidence, and help in racial identity formation in transracial adoptees.[43] Adoptive parents feel more certain about the permanency of the adoption as they feel less fear about the birth parents.[44] Birth mothers experience less grief when they know that their children are happy in their adoptive homes.[45] Birth fathers feel more positively about the adoption when they are involved in the process.[46] In all, an adoption process that encourages continuing relationships is better for all involved.

ADOPTION NORMS IN OTHER CULTURES

The American notion of erase-and-replace adoption is not the exclusive way adoption is practiced throughout the world. Sharing children between families exists in each culture, but the contours of that sharing differ. As Isabelle Leblic puts it, "There is a great diversity of adoption situations in the world, and we can say without much risk that the circulation of children is an almost universal phenomenon."[47] In some Polynesian cultures, children are seen as belonging to the larger society rather than to individual parents, so children are not placed for adoption through any legal process, but may still be moved around from family to family for a variety of purposes.[48] As Leblic notes in her study of traditional adoption in French Polynesia and New Caledonia:

> One of the most important features of traditional adoption in Polynesia, as more generally in Oceania, is that birth parents and adoptive parents choose each other and, in the majority of cases, stay in touch (there is no secret about adoption). As a consequence, the children add together the rights and obligations of their two kin groups (birth and adoption).[49]

In traditional Maori culture, children were freely shared among families, with the children retaining family and tribal ties with their original family.[50] In Samoa, as many as 40% of children in a village survey were not living with biological families but were being raised in loose adoption or fostering relationships. In one island of Papua New Guinea, as many as half of the inhabitants of some villages are adopted while maintaining connections with birth families.[51]

In one tribe in Benin, Africa, 30% of children are raised outside their natal home by foster parents but often maintain relationships with natal family.[52] In one ethnographic study of the tribe where 150 people were interviewed in the 1990s, only 2 had lived exclusively with their biological parents.[53] Riley & Van Vleet note:

> In this area of western Africa, both birth parents and foster parents are part of a broad kinship system. Birth relationships are recognized and used to determine who has a claim to the child. Because patrilineality, or tracing relationships through the father's male ancestors, is the guiding principle that separates people into different social groups, a child is seen as belonging to his or her biological father's patrilineal clan—and this association is maintained throughout life. But in addition to this kin relationship, others are usually established as well, and fostering is particularly important in this kinship system. Indeed, fosterage is emphasized as the best way to raise children, and it is this belief that results in the relatively high rates of fostering among the Baatombu.[54]

Because children of the Baatombu are not seen as belonging exclusively to the biological parents, but rather belonging to the broader clan, the biological parents are not supposed to be acknowledged in public. Nonetheless, Alber observed that the connections were maintained despite the public separation:

> Many people told me very emotional stories about how and when they came to learn the names and identities of their biological parents. I was told numerous stories about little gestures or little gifts offered secretly by biological parents to their children. Away from the watching public, hidden in their houses or when nobody is present, biological parents do take an interest in their children. They offer them food, give them presents of money or clothes, and take care of them from a distance. Such practices are not only shared knowledge, but are actually expected from biological parents, especially from the mother.[55]

Alber sums up his findings, saying, "Biological parenthood—despite of all these norms and practices that deny it—is seen as something especially valuable among the Baatombu. Possibly this is so exactly *because* one has to deny it in public."[56]

In much of the Muslim world, adoption as practiced in the West does not exist. Traditional Islamic law generally holds that adoption as practiced in the West is religiously prohibited.[57] As Faisal Kutty explains:

> The prohibition is traced to the Qur'ān and Prophetic traditions. As Mohamed Fadel notes the primary sources negate the idea that someone other than the biological parents can fictitiously became a parent in the same position as a biological parent. He points out that the Qur'ān 58:2 states "their mothers are only those who have given birth to them."[58]

Preserving a child's relationships to biological family is considered a moral imperative and many Islamic scholars viewed the erase-and-replace method of adoption as "a complete 'erasure of natal identity.'"[59] There is, however, a form of sponsorship or fosterage in Islam called *kafala*:

> With *kafala* comes the responsibility of upbringing the adopted child as your own. It tries to achieve a balance between raising the child as your own all the while ensuring the adopted child's identity is not absorbed into the identity of the adoptive family. Negation of the biological identity would be considered *haram* or forbidden.[60]

This cultural understanding of adoption is reflected in law in various Muslim countries, including Egyptian law banning Western-style adoption.[61] In some Muslim countries, including Iran and Lebanon, legal adoption is available, and attitudes have shifted to more acceptance of adoption and in vitro fertilization.[62]

France has a centuries-old history of adoption as addition, not subtraction.[63] Since 1804, France has recognized *adoption simple*, a form of "additive filiation," where a person is made legally a member of one family without cutting off ties from the biological family.[64] *Adoption simple* at first was restricted to the adoption of adults, but in 1923 *adoption simple* was reformed to make minors adoptable as well.[65] *Adoption simple* was "no longer only a matter of finding an heir for a family, but also a child to be raised."[66] By 1939, France had also created another form of adoption—"plenary adoption"—that severed completely the ties between biological family and adopted child.[67] But France preserved *adoption simple* as an alternative as well.[68] Beginning in the 1970s, with considerable growth in divorce in France, there was a spike in *adoption simple* attributable to a growth in step-parent adoption.[69] As one sociologist states, "Overall, it appears that simple adoption is more common today that it has ever been."[70]

INCREASED OPENNESS IN U.S. ADOPTION

As these brief examples illustrate, traditional adoption in the United States, patterned as severing all previous family ties, and replacing that now-erased family with a new, permanent, and legal family, is not an exclusive global norm. And that pattern is changing in the United States as well. After its long history of secrecy in domestic adoption, there is a robust trend toward openness.[71] In 1964, sociologist H. David Kirk first proposed what we call open adoption today, suggesting that birth mothers and adoptive parents meet before the adoption and exchange reports and pictures throughout the child's life.[72] Open adoption grew in practice, and by the mid-1980s, "agencies increasingly provided pictures of the placed child to birthparents, let birthparents select adoptive parents for the child, arranged meetings between birthparents and adoptive parents without sharing identifying information, and offered ongoing contact between parties."[73]

Despite the wide availability of promised openness by agencies, there are still significant problems with ensuring openness in American domestic adoptions. Once a birth parent's legal rights as a parent have been terminated to make way for the adoption, there is no legal right for continuing contact.[74] In many states, open adoption agreements are not legally enforceable.[75] In those states where open adoption agreements are enforceable, they are only enforceable when the intricacies of the effective statutes are followed,[76] or in only some adoptions or between only some parties.[77] It is still common practice in states without enforceable open-adoption agreements, however, for agencies and adoptive parents to enter into such unenforceable "agreements."[78]

ADOPTION ACROSS BORDERS: WHEN NORMS COLLIDE

Different cultural understandings of adoption can cause conflicts with the global transfer of children across borders. Jini Roby's and Stephanie Matsumora's study of adoption from the Marshall Islands illustrates the problem with the evocative title *If I Give You My Child, Aren't We Family?*[79] In the Marshall Islands, adoption is completely open and the parental rights of birth parents are not terminated:

> The Marshallese viewed adoption as an expansion of jural rights and an extension of family boundaries. The adopted child serves as a link between two families creating a relation of kinship for support and expanded rights. Children are viewed as property of the family and may be given as gifts. Walsh documented the Marshallese belief that all adoptions are "open" and that their child can return home to the Marshall Islands, as customary in traditional Marshallese adoptions.[80]

Roby and Matsumora found that an astounding 82.2% of women who relinquished children to international adoption to the United States did so under the mistaken belief that "their children would later return to the RMI [Marshall Islands] at the age of 18 with a good education and material wealth."[81] The women had eventually concluded that they were not likely to be reunited with their children because the promised letters, pictures, and monetary gifts were never received or had stopped after the adoptions.[82] The mistaken understanding of the Western meaning of adoption induced the women into relinquishment; 87.7% said, "if they had known at the time of placement that they would never see or hear from the child again, they would not have made the decision to relinquish."[83]

In cultures that view adoption as addition of family, rather than subtraction of family, international adoption to Western countries with different understandings has the potential to defraud and coerce birth parents. International instruments like the Hague Convention on Intercountry Adoption and the Convention on the Rights of the Child are designed to protect children's rights to family connections, though lax enforcement makes them less effective than hoped.

INTERNATIONAL ADOPTION NORMS AS EXPRESSED IN TREATIES AND INTERNATIONAL AGREEMENTS

Global norms are often reflected in international conventions regarding human rights. International human rights law came late to the regulation of international adoption, however.[84] The first draft of the Convention on the Rights of the Child (CRC), submitted to the UN Commission on Human Rights, did not have any provisions directly addressing adoption.[85] Barbados and Colombia first mentioned that adoption should be addressed in the CRC, and their comments served as the origins of Article 21 of the CRC, which first proposed requirements for international adoption.[86] The CRC was not adopted by the UN General Assembly until 1989.[87] Private international law entered the regulatory field with the Hague Convention on Protection of Children and Co-operation in Respect of Intercountry Adoption, promulgated in 1993. As one scholar describes it, the Hague Convention "took the lofty ideals of the U.N. Convention [on the Rights of the Child] into the arena of nitty gritty detail relevant to States 'sending' and 'receiving' children in this multicultural exchange of human beings."[88] The CRC and the Hague Convention have, together, created the regulatory framework for international adoption, though the provisions of the CRC apply to domestic adoption as well.

The CRC "is the first human rights treaty expressly to recognize a right to identity."[89] Article 7 of the CRC provides for a child's identity rights—the right to a name, registration, and nationality at birth, and "the right to know and be cared for by his or her parents."[90] Article 8 further focuses on identity, providing that "States Parties undertake to respect the right of the child to preserve his or her identity, including nationality, name and family relations as recognized by law without unlawful interference."[91]

Article 9 of the CRC addresses separation of parent and child. In addition to providing that such separation should not happen against the will of the child and parent, and setting out safeguards for separation because of abuse or neglect, Article 9 also provides: "States Parties shall respect the right of the child who is separated from one or both parents to maintain personal relations and direct contact with both parents on a regular basis, except if it is contrary to the child's best interests."[92] If "parents" in Article 7 include biological parents in cases of adoption, then we must give "parents" the same meaning in Article 9. When Articles 7 and 9 are taken together, the rights of the child go beyond merely knowing who one's parents are as a matter of identity but encompasses ongoing contact—what we commonly call open adoption. But despite these provisions, international adoption as currently practiced utilizes the Western norm of erase-and-replace adoption rather than adoption with ongoing connections.

CONCLUSION

In the book *Roots*, author Alex Haley wrote, "In all of us there is a hunger, marrow-deep, to know our heritage—to know who we are and where we have come from. Without this enriching knowledge, there is a hollow yearning. No matter what our attainments in life, there is still a vacuum, an emptiness, and the most disquieting loneliness."[93] In fiction, he recognized a truth that the law of adoption as currently practiced in the West ignores, but that psychosocial research has found salient in adoption. Law's conception of adoption ignores that psychosocial literature, that marrow-deep hunger.

Different cultural understandings of adoption across the world have resulted in different legal frameworks for adoption, and viewing adoption as addition rather than subtraction may well be in the best interest of children. A growing body of empirical research shows that openness in adoption benefits adopted persons. Continuing contact with the birth family is correlated to improved self-esteem, better relationships with adoptive family, and fewer externalizing negative behaviors. In transracial adoption, openness facilitates racial identity formation.

American adoption law's tradition of erase-and-replace is not inevitable in adoption, as is evidenced by the variety of adoption forms across the globe. American law's insistence that a child can have no more than two parents is a barrier to expanding legal families to include birth parents and adoptive parents together, but that limitation may be changing. California has recently passed legislation to make clear that a child can have more than two legal parents.[94] Effective in 2016, the Maine Parentage Act allows courts to recognize that a child has more than two parents.[95] New York case law has recognized tri-parent custody in some cases, though the law stops short of mandating three legal parents.[96] The New York model starts with parenting agreements that delineate the rights and responsibilities of the parents, which can address the most frequently expressed concern of more than two parents, that the more parents there are, the more disagreement there will be over child-rearing responsibilities. There may also be great promise in collaborative lawyering to address these concerns.[97]

More states should follow the lead of states that accept that children can have more than two parents. Western regimes of adoption should consider worldwide norms of child-sharing that conceive of adoption as addition rather than subtraction of parents and families. While adoption is often about creating a family where no biological ties exist, adoption has long insisted on mimicking biology with careful matching of child and adoptive parents on multiple axes: race, religion, ancestral origins, intelligence and social class; as well as minutia like skin tone, hair and eye color, and hair texture.[98] But adoption today makes little attempt to create a family that looks as if created by biology. Transracial adoption[99] and same-sex adoption[100] are but two examples of families by design that make no pretense of natural conception over legal creation. The paradigm of only two legal parents should also give way to the realities of complex family life as lived experience dictates.

With the growth of the Internet[101] and the availability of DNA testing,[102] there is little secrecy possible in adoption anymore. The predominant Western model of erasing birth parents by extinguishing parental rights and then replacing those parents with the adoptive parents is giving way to more openness and continuing contact. Nonetheless, the legal model of adoption still maintains the primacy of the biological model of the nuclear family, with birth family cut off from adoptive family. The psychosocial literature confirms that continuing contact between birth and adoptive families can be positive for all members of the adoption triad, refuting the necessity for the erase-and-replace model. While maintaining connections, especially legally enforceable connections, may be more complicated than cutting those connections, more complex family relationships are proliferating in this age of growing divorce and remarriage. Expanding definitions of family in adoption can be informed by an understanding of various norms of adoption across the globe, some of which recognize the enduring importance of family connection.

NOTES

1. Child Welfare Information Gateway, *Postadoption Contact Agreements Between Birth and Adoptive Families* (Washington, DC: U.S. Department of Health and Human Services, Children's Bureau, 2019), 2, https://www.childwelfare.gov/topics/systemwide/laws-policies/statutes/cooperative/ ("Approximately 29 States and the District of Columbia currently have statutes that allow written and enforceable agreements.").

2. Malinda L. Seymore, "Openness in International Adoption." *Columbia Human Rights Law Review* 46, no. 3 (2015): 168–69; E. Wayne Carp, *Family Matters: Secrecy and Disclosure in the History of Adoption* (Cambridge, MA: Harvard University Press, 1998), 73 & 88; Deborah H. Siegel & Susan Livingston Smith, *Openness in Adoption: From Secrecy and Stigma to Knowledge and Connections* (Evan B. Donaldson Adoption Institute, 2012), 10.

3. Seymore, "Openness in International Adoption," 168–69.

4. E. Wayne Carp, *Family Matters*, 103.

5. Ibid. Naomi Cahn, "Birthing Relationships," *Wisconsin Women's Law Journal* 17, no. 2 (2002): 173; Elizabeth J. Samuels, "Surrender and Subordination: Birth Mothers and Adoption Law Reform," *Michigan Journal of Gender & Law* 20, no. 1 (2013): 53.

6. Seymore, "Openness in International Adoption," 168–69, citing E. Wayne Carp, *Adoption Politics: Bastard Nation & Ballot Initiative 58* (Lawrence: University of Kansas Press, 2004), 7; Carp, *Family Matters,* 104; Samuels, "Surrender and Subordination," 53–54.

7. Janine M. Baer, *Growing in the Dark: Adoption Secrecy and its Consequences* (Xlibris, 2004), 72.

8. Carp, *Adoption Politics*, 9.

9. Elizabeth J. Samuels, "The Idea of Adoption: An Inquiry into the History of Adult Adoptee Access to Birth Records," *Rutgers Law Review* 53, no. 2 (2001): 374–75.

10. Seymore, "Openness in International Adoption," 168–69.

11. Elinor B. Rosenberg, *The Adoption Life Cycle: The Children and Their Families Through the Years* (New York: The Free Press, 1992), 10.

12. Ibid.

13. Samuels, "The Idea of Adoption," 406–407.

14. Annette R. Appell, "The Endurance of Biological Connection: Heteronormativity, Same-Sex Parenting and the Lessons of Adoption," *Brigham Young University Journal of Public Law* 22, no. 2 (2008): 289–325.

15. Mary O. Wiley & Amanda Baden, "Birth Parents in Adoption: Research, Practice, and Counseling Psychology," *The Counseling Psychologist* 33, no. 1 (2005): 15; Carole Smith & Janette Logan, *After Adoption: Direct Contact and Relationships* (London: Routledge, 2004), 115.

16. Debra Kalmuss, Pearila B. Namerow & Ursula Bauer, "Short-term Consequences of Parenting Versus Adoption Among Young Unmarried Women," *Journal of Marriage and the Family.* 54, no. 1 (February 1992): 80. But see Steven D. McLaughlin, Susan Pearce, Diane L. Manninen & Linda D. Winges, "To Parent or Relinquish: Consequences For Adolescent Mothers," *Social Work.* 33, no. 4 (1988): 320 (no significant difference in psychological outcomes for adolescents who placed and adolescents who parented).

17. Wiley & Baden, "Birth Parents in Adoption," 26.

18. Ibid., 30.

19. Ibid., 29.

20. George M. Burnell & Mary A. Norfleet, "Women Who Place Their Infants Up for Adoption: A Pilot Study," *Patient Counseling & Health Education*, 1, no.

4 (1979): 169; Robin Winkler & Margaret Van Keppel, *Relinquishing Mothers in Adoption: Their Long-Term Adjustment* (Melbourne, Australia: Institute of Family Studies, 1984).

21. Wiley & Baden, "Birth Parents in Adoption," 30.

22. Gary Clapton, *Birth Fathers and their Adoption Experiences* (London: Jessica Kingsley Publishers, 2008), 67. See also Smith & Logan, *After Adoption,* 115.

23. Clapton, *Birth Fathers*, 111–12.

24. Ibid., 155.

25. Eva Y. Deykin, Patricia Patti & Jon Ryan, "Fathers of Adopted Children: A Study of the Impact of Child Surrender on Birthfathers," *American Journal of Orthopsychiatry* 58, no. 2 (1988): 246.

26. David M. Brodzinsky, "Long-Term Outcomes in Adoption," *Future of Children* 3, no. 1 (2003): 153; Penny C. Partridge, "The Particular Challenges of Being Adopted," *Smith College Studies in Social Work* 61, no. 2 (1991): 199; Joana Soares, et al., "Adoption-Related Gains, Losses and Difficulties: The Adopted Child's Perspective," *Child & Adolescent Social Work Journal* 36, no. 3 (2019): 259.

27. Partridge, "Particular Challenges of Being Adopted," 199.

28. Michael F. McGinn, "Developmental Challenges for Adoptees across the Life Cycle," in *Handbook of Adoption: Implications of Researchers, Practitioners and Families* (Thousand Oaks, CA: Sage Publications, 2007), 65.

29. James G. Dwyer, "First Parents: Reconceptualizing Newborn Adoption," *Capital University Law Review* 37, no. 2 (2008): 295–96; A. Baden, "'Do You Know Your *Real* Parents?' and Other Adoption Microaggressions," *Adoption Quarterly* 19, no. 1 (February 2016): 1–25.

30. David M. Brodzinsky, Leslie M. Singer & Anne Braff, "Children's Understanding of Adoption," *Child Development* 55, no. 3 (June 1984): 869; David M. Brodzinsky, Marshall D. Schecter & Robin Marantz Henig, *Being Adopted: The Lifelong Search for Self* (New York: Anchor Books, 1992); Daniel W. Smith & David M. Brodzinsky, "Stress and Coping in Adopted Children: A Developmental Study," *Journal of Clinical Child Psychology* 23, no. 1 (1994): 91; Femmie Juffer, "Children's Awareness of Adoption and Their Problem Behavior in Families with 7-year-old Internationally Adopted Children," *Adoption Quarterly.* 9, no. 2–3 (2006): 1.

31. David M. Brodzinsky, "A Stress and Coping Model of Adoption Adjustment," in *The Psychology of Adoption* (Oxford: Oxford University Press, 1990), 3. See also Michael Wierzbicki, "Psychological Adjustment of Adoptees: A Meta-Analysis," *Journal of Clinical Child Psychology* 22, no. 4 (1993): 447 (adoptees significantly overrepresented in clinical populations). It is possible that the overrepresentation of adoptees in clinical populations is not because of increased incidences of psychological problems, but because of increased rates of referrals by adoptive parents and professionals who are aware of issues relating to adoption and, therefore, might be more inclined to refer. Brodzinsky, "Long-Term Outcomes," 154.

32. Jesus Palacios & Yolanda Sanchez-Sandoval, "Stress in Parents of Adopted Children," *International Journal of Behavioral Development* 30, no. 6 (2006): 481; Smith & Logan, *After Adoption*, 87.

33. Palacios & Sanchez-Sandoval, "Stress in Parents," 481; Gloria W. Bird, Rick Peterson & Stephanie H. Miller, "Factors Associated with Distress among Support-Seeking Adoptive Parents," *Family Relations* 51, no. 3 (July 2002): 215.

34. Palacios & Sanchez-Sandoval, "Stress in Parents," 481; Judith C. Daniluk & Joss Hurtig-Mitchell, "Themes of Hope and Healing: Infertile Couples' Experiences of Adoption," *Journal of Counseling & Development.* 81, no. 4 (2003): 389

35. David M. Brodzinsky, "Adjustment to Adoption: A Psychosocial Perspective," 7 *Clinical Psychology Review* 7 (1987): 25–47 (infertility complicates transition to adoptive parenthood).

36. Ibid., 31.

37. Palacios & Sanchez-Sandoval, "Stress in Parents," 481.

38. Ibid.

39. G.W. Gloria W. Bird et al., "Support-Seeking Adoptive Parents," 215.

40. David M. Brodzinsky & Marshall D. Schechter, *The Psychology of Adoption* (Oxford: Oxford University Press, 1990).

41. Henry Mainemer, Lorraine Gilman & Elinor Ames, "Parenting Stress in Families Adopting Children from Romanian Orphanages," *Journal of Family Issues* 19, no. 2 (1998): 164; Sharon Judge, "The Impact of Early Institutionalization on Child and Family Outcomes," *Adoption Quarterly* 7, no. 3 (2004): 31.

42. Katalina McGlone et al., "Psychological Stress in Adoptive Parents of Special-Needs Children," *Child Welfare* 81, no. 2 (2002): 151.

43. David M. Brodzinsky, "Family Structural Openness and Communication Openness as Predictors in the Adjustment of Adopted Children," *Adoption Quarterly* 9, no. 4 (2006): 10; Marianne Berry, "Adoptive Parents' Perceptions of, and Comfort with, Open Adoption," *Child Welfare* 72, no. 3 (May 1993): 246; Margaret Sykes, "Adoption with Contact: A Study of Adoptive Parents and the Impact of Continuing Contact with Families of Origin," *Adoption & Fostering* 24, no. 4 (2000): 25; Haley K. Horstman, Colleen W. Colaner & Christine E. Rittenour, "Contributing Factors of Adult Adoptees' Identity Work and Self-Esteem: Family Communication Patterns and Adoption-Specific Communication," *Journal of Family Communication* 16, no. 3 (2016): 263; A. Baden et al., "Delaying Adoption Disclosure: A Survey of Late Discovery Adoptees," *Journal of Family Issues* 40, no. 9 (2019): 1172.

44. Harold D. Grotevant & Ruth G. McRoy, *Openness in Adoption: Exploring Family Connections* (Thousand Oaks, CA: Sage Publications, 1998), 90–92; Deborah H. Siegel, "Open Adoption of Infants: Adoptive Parents' Feelings Seven Years Later," *Social Work* 48, no. 3 (2003): 417; X. Ge et al., "Bridging the Divide: Openness in Adoption and Postadoption Psychosocial Adjustment Among Birth and Adoptive Parents," *Journal of Family Psychology* 22, no. 4 (2008): 529.

45. Ge et al., "Bridging the Divide," 529; Ruth G. McRoy et al., "Open Adoptions: Longitudinal Outcomes for the Adoption Triad," in *Handbook of Adoption*, 180; Cinda L. Christian et al., "Grief Resolution of Birthmothers in Confidential, Time-Limited Mediated, Ongoing Mediated, and Fully Disclosed Adoptions," *Adoption Quarterly* 1, no. 2 (December 1997): 52.

46. Deykin et al., "Fathers of Adopted Children," 243.

47. Isabelle Leblic, "From French Polynesia to France: The Legacy of Fa'a'amu Traditional Adoption in 'International' Adoption," *Anthropologica* 56, no. 2 (2014): 453.

48. Ibid.

49. Ibid., 450.

50. George Graham, "Whangai Tamariki: The Custom Pertaining to the Adoption of Children in Accordance with Ancient Maori Custom," *Journal of Polynesian Society* 57, no. 3 (1948): 268.

51. Astrid Anderson, "Adoption and Belonging in Wogeo, Papua New Guinea," in *Cross-Cultural Approaches to Adoption* (Oxfordshire: Routledge Press, 2004), 135.

52. Nancy E. Riley & Krista E. Van Vleet, *Making Families Through Adoption* (Thousand Oaks, CA: Sage Publications, 2012), 17–18.

53. Ibid., 18.

54. Ibid.

55. Erdemute Alber, "'The Real Parents are the Foster Parents:' Social Parenthood among the Baatombu in Northern Benin," in *Cross-cultural Approaches to Adoption*, 42.

56. Ibid.

57. Faisal Kutty, "Islamic Law and Adoptions," in *The Intercountry Adoption Debate: Dialogues Across Disciplines* (Newcastle upon Tyne: Cambridge Scholars Press, 2015), 526.

58. Ibid.

59. Ibid.

60. Ibid.

61. Andrea Buchler & Eveline S. Kayasseh, "Fostering and Adoption in Islamic Law—Under Consideration of the Laws of Morocco, Egypt, and the United Arab Emirates," *Electronic Journal of Islamic & Middle Eastern Law* 6 (2018): 31–55, https://www.researchgate.net/publication/328757350_Fostering_and_Adoption_in_Islamic_Law_-_Under_Consideration_of_the_Laws_of_Morocco_Egypt_and_the_United_Arab_Emirates

62. Marcia C. Inhorn, "'He Won't Be My Son': Middle Eastern Muslim Men's Discourses of Adoption and Gamete Donation," *Medical Anthropology Quarterly* 20, no. 1 (March 2006): 94.

63. Laura J. Schwartz, "Models for Parenthood in Adoption Law: The French Conception," *Vanderbilt Journal of Transnational Law* 28, no. 5 (1995): 1090.

64. Kristin Elizabeth Gager, *Blood Ties and Fictive Ties: Adoption and Family Life in Early Modern France* (Princeton: Princeton University Press, 1996); Jean-Francois Mignot, "'Simple' Adoption in France: Revival of an Old Institution (1804–2007)," *Revue Francaise de Sociologie* 56 (2015): 525–60 .

65. Mignot, "'Simple' Adoption," 367; Pierre Verdier, "'Limited adoption' in France," *Adoption & Fostering* 12, no. 1 (1988): 42 (noting that simple adoption is "possible at any age.").

66. Mignot, "'Simple' Adoption," 367.

67. Ibid., 368.

68. Ibid.

69. Ibid., 371. ("The opportunities for step-parents to adopt their step-children are increasing, so much so that the number of simple adoptees has crossed a second threshold: it has gone up from about 1,500 to about 10,000 per year.")

70. Ann Hartman & Joan Laird, "Family Treatment After Adoption: Common Themes," in *The Psychology of Adoption*, 221.

71. Susan M. Wolfgram, "Openness in Adoption: What We Know So Far—A Critical Review of the Literature," *Social Work* 53, no. 2 (2008): 136 ("The term open adoption refers to a continuum of options that enables birth parents and adoptive parents to have information about and communication with one another before or after placement of the child or at both times."); Siegel & Smith, *Openness in Adoption*, 10. The continuing contact in open adoption can vary from mediated exchange of information and photos throughout the child's life to continuing in-person contact between the birth family, the adoptive family. and the child. Ibid.

72. Carp, *Family Matters*, 198; Susan M. Henney et al., "The Impact of Openness on Adoption Agency Practices: A Longitudinal Perspective," *Adoption Quarterly* 6, no. 3 (2003): 323.

73. Grotevant & McRoy, *Openness in Adoption*, 34.

74. Malinda L. Seymore, "Sixteen and Pregnant: Minors' Consent in Abortion and Adoption," *Yale Journal of Law & Feminism* 25, no. 1 (2013): 153.

75. Child Welfare Information Gateway, *Postadoption Contact Agreements*, 2. *See also* Annette R. Appell, "Blending Families through Adoption: Implications for Collaborative Adoption Law and Practice," *Boston University Law Review* 75, no. 4 (1995): 997; Annette R. Appell, "Reflections on the Movement Toward a More Child-Centered Adoption," *Western New England Law Review* 32, no. 1 (May 2010): 1; Cynthia E. Cordle, "Open Adoption: The Need for Legislative Action," *Virginia Journal of Social Policy & Law* 2, no. 2 (1995): 275; Amy L. Doherty, "Foster Care and Adoption: A Look at Open Adoption," *Journal of Contemporary Legal Issues* 11, no. 1 (1997): 591; Leigh Gaddie, "Open Adoption," *Journal of the American Academy of Matrimonial Lawyers* 22, no. 2 (2009): 499.

76. Seymore, "Sixteen and Pregnant," 153.

77. Ibid., 158.

78. Ibid.

79. Jini L. Roby & Stephanie Matsumura, "If I Give You My Child, Aren't We Family? A Study of Birthmothers Participating in Marshall Islands–U.S. Adoptions," *Adoption Quarterly* 5, no. 4 (2002): 7.

80. Ibid., 11.

81. Ibid., 22.

82. Ibid.

83. Ibid., 25.

84. Trevor Buck, *International Child Law* (2nd ed., Routledge, 2011), 244, noting the slow growth of international human rights law and the even slower recognition of international children's rights law as hampering the development of international law on intercountry adoption. See also Sonja Starr & Lea Brilmayer, "Family Separation as a Violation of International Law," *Berkeley Journal of International*

Law 21, no. 2 (2003): 216–18, noting that consideration of family rights of any kind in international law was a late development.

85. Sylvain Vite & Herve Boechat, *A Commentary on the United States Convention on the Rights of the Child: Article 21 Adoption* (Boston: Martinus Nijhoff Publishers, 2008), 3.

86. Ibid.

87. Ursula Kilkelly, "Using the Convention of the Rights of the Child in Law and Policy: Two Ways to Improve Compliance," in *The Human Rights of Children: From Vision to Implementation* (UK: Ashgate Publishing Limited, 2011), 178.

88. Alexandra Maravel, "The U.N. Convention on the Rights of the Child and the Hague Conference on Private International Law: The Dynamics of Children's Rights through Legal Strata," *Transnational Law & Contemporary Problems* 6, no. 2 (1996): 319.

89. Michael Freeman, "The New Birth Right? Identity and the Child of Reproduction Revolution," *International Journal of Children's Rights*. 4, no. 3 (1996): 273–297.

90. UN General Assembly, Convention on the Rights of the Child, November 20, 1989, United Nations, Treaty Series, vol. 1577, p. 3, Art. 7, available at: https://www.refworld.org/docid/3ae6b38f0.html [accessed 1 December 2020].

91. Ibid., Art. 8(1).

92. Ibid., Art. 9(3). Jaap E. Doek, "What Does the Children's Convention Require," *Emory International Law Review*. 20, no. 1 (2006): 203.

93. Alex Haley, *Roots* (New York: Doubleday, 1976).

94. Calfornia Family Code § 7601(c) (2014) (Defining parent-child relationship "does not preclude a finding that a child has a parent and child relationship with more than two parents.").

95. Maine Revised. Statutes § 1891(5) (2016) (recognition of a "de facto parent" "does not disestablish the parentage of any other parent.").

96. Matter of *David S. v. Samantha G.* 59 Misc. 3d 960 (N.Y. Fam. Ct. 2018); *Dawn M. v. Michael M.*, 55 Misc. 3d 865 (N.Y. Sup. Ct. 2017); but see Matter of *Tomeka N.H. v. Jesus R.*, 183 A.D.3d 106 (N.Y. Sup. Ct. App. Div. 2020) (rejecting tri-parent custody on the basis of the statute language that "either parent" may have a standing to seek custody, with the word "either" implying only two parents).

97. Malinda L. Seymore, "Ethical Lawyering in Adoption: Centering the Child in Adoption Law," *Adoption Quarterly* (2020). doi: 10.1080/10926755.2020.1834041

98. Naomi Cahn, "Perfect Substitutes or the Real Thing?," *Duke Law Journal* 52, no. 6 (2003): 1149.

99. Elisha Marr, "U.S. Transracial Adoption Trends in the 21st Century," *Adoption Quarterly* 20, no. 3 (2017): 234 (transracial adoptions represented 21–24% of adoptions between 2000 and 2012); Nicholas Zill, "The Changing Face of Adoption in the United States," *Institute of Family Studies* (blog), August 8, 2017, https://ifstudies.org/blog/the-changing-face-of-adoption-in-the-united-states (analysis of data from the Early Childhood Longitudinal Studies of the Kindergarten Class of 2010–2011 and the Kindergarten Class of 1998–1999 from the National Center for Education Statistics of the U.S. Department of Education shows that "90% of Asian

adoptees, 64% of multiracial adoptees, 62% of Hispanic adoptees, and 55% of black adoptees" were being raised in transracial placements in 2011).

100. Suzanne M. Johnson & Elizabeth O'Connor, *The Gay Baby Boom: The Psychology of Gay Parenthood* (New York: NYU Press, 2002) (between 6 and 14 million children in the United States are being raised by at least one parent who is gay); Cynthia Godsoe, "Adopting the Gay Family," *Tulane Law Review* 90, no. 2 (2015): 311 (noting that though there is likely a problem of undercounting, at least "65,000 children have been adopted from state care by openly LGB individuals"); *Obergefell v. Hodges*, 576 U.S. 644, 135 S. Ct. 2071 (2015) (in recognizing gay marriage, the Supreme Court acknowledged the role of gay families in adopting children).

101. Child Welfare Information Gateway, *Searching for Birth Relatives* (Washington, DC: U.S. Department of Health and Human Services, Children's Bureau, May 2018), 5 (focusing on using social media to find relatives), https://www.childwelfare.gov/pubpdfs/f_search.pdf

102. Stephanie Pappas, "Genetic Testing and Family Secrets," *Monitor on Psychology*, June 2018, 44.

Chapter 7

Post-Divorce Parental Norms in the Age of Fake News and Discursive Violence

The Israeli Case in a Comparative Context

Daphna Hacker

INTRODUCTION

Toward the end of the second millennium, many countries implemented dramatic changes within their child custody and support laws that (a) left behind presumptions that prefer mothers as the physical custodian,[1] and (b) weakened fathers' economic responsibility for their children.[2] These changes were allegedly based on new norms of gender equality within the family and the market.[3] However, both the family and the market are still deeply gendered social institutions. Hence, as several feminist critics have observed, such legal reforms within child custody and support are problematic insofar as they do not acknowledge how parental care is actually provided and as a consequence harm children and their primary care-givers.[4]

As this chapter will demonstrate, Israel has joined this legal-reform trend relatively recently, but in an unusual way that is even more problematic than in most other countries. While the law-in-the-books still holds the "tender years' presumption" and imposes an absolute and enhanced paternal duty to provide financial child support, in practice, judges vigorously promote joint physical custody and shared child support duty. This extreme judicial activism reflects a normative shift among professionals and the general public characterized by *apparent* gender neutrality regarding fatherhood and motherhood. However, not only is this normative change evolving only in relation to post-divorce parenthood, and not pre-divorce, but it also does not reflect an actual empirical social change in the labor division within Israeli families or in the Israeli labor market, which is even more deeply gendered than that of many other developed countries. Moreover, this empirically unfounded new judicial activism leaves the legal field that governs families in a chaotic state, and ignores the many ways in which Israeli family law, which is based on religious law, still discriminates against women.

In what follows, I will argue that, as in several other countries,[5] the changes introduced to the legal understanding and formation of child custody and support laws in Israel, as well as the norms that back them up, cannot be understood detached from the emergence of fathers' groups and their battle to change the field of family law in favor of men. This battle is being fought using deeply harmful tactics including fake news and discursive violence that replace rational discussion with fear and bullying, all of which is detrimental to mothers and children. The Israeli case, notwithstanding its unique characteristics, is an alarming warning sign regarding this battle, its strategies, and its outcomes. It also opens up, more generally, new and important questions regarding the formation of legal norms in the era of fake news and uncontrolled, violent virtual discourse.

In the first part of this chapter, I will map the dramatic changes to the law-in-action that have taken place in Israel in recent years in relation to post-divorce parental duties and rights and the norms on which they are based. Such changes are radical, relative to comparable changes in other parts of the world. I will further provide data demonstrating that these changes and norms cannot be explained by actual changes in the gendered labor division within Israeli families. In the second part, I will set out the argument that, just as in several other countries, the dramatic changes in court decisions vis-à-vis child custody and support are, rather, directly affected by the discourse promoted by fathers' groups. In the case of Israel, such groups falsely portray fathers as the victims of a vicious legal system, while employing lies, shaming, and threats—amounting to fake news and violent discourse—to build this narrative. The Conclusion will discuss the lessons that other jurisdictions might learn from the Israeli case study regarding the formation of current familial norms, their translation into law, and their social ramifications.

RADICAL LAW-IN-ACTION RELATED TO CHILD CUSTODY AND SUPPORT

When one opens the Israeli law books, one might get the impression that nothing has changed in the last six decades in relation to post-divorce parental rights and duties. Regarding child custody, the Capacity and Guardianship Law, 1962, determines both parents to be the legal custodians of their children, regardless of their marital status, yet still incorporates the tender years presumption, which guides courts to rule that "children up to the age of six shall be with their mother unless there are special reasons for instructing otherwise."[6] For many years, this presumption, together with judicial rulings that promoted the same custody arrangement for all siblings, regardless of age—and that objected to changes after the child reached the age of six unless circumstances other than older age justified it—led to the domination of maternal sole physical custody, both within court decisions and in arrangements reached by the parents in the shadow of the law.[7]

Regarding child support, the 1959 Israeli law states that "a person owes his and his spouse's minor children's maintenance according to the personal law abiding him."[8] "Personal law" means religious law, which has a profound impact on Israeli family law.[9] The two major religious groups in Israel are Jews (75%) and Muslims (18%),[10] and, under both Jewish and Islamic laws, the father has greater responsibility than the mother to support the child financially. Generally, the father has an absolute sole duty to cover the costs of his children's basic needs, for as long as they are dependent and regardless of his economic means.[11] According to Jewish law, above the stage of dependency (set at 15 by the Israeli Rabbinical Authority) and for needs that exceed the basic necessities, the father has a special duty to provide, but here the amount is dependent on his actual economic means and the ability of the child to support himself ("specific charity duty"). The mother has a much weaker duty. According to religious law, she has a "general charity duty" toward *all* those in need, particularly family members. In practice, the mother's duty translates into an obligation to share, with the father, the costs related to her children beyond their basic needs until they are 15 years old, and the costs of all their needs after the age of 15.[12]

Both the tender years presumption and the religious child support duty adopted by civil law discriminate against men, as they are treated as the primary breadwinner and secondary caregiver, regardless of the actual parental role they (and the mother) played in their children's lives prior to their divorce or separation. Notwithstanding, women are also harshly discriminated-against within Israeli family law. As there is only *religious* marriage and divorce in Israel, these realms are governed by the jurisdiction of religious courts.[13] This means that women are subordinated to patriarchal courts,[14] in which there are only male judges,[15] and a woman's testimony is deemed less valid than a man's.[16] It also means that women are subjected to patriarchal religious laws that judge their moral behavior more severely than men's,[17] that allow a man whose wife refuses to divorce him to establish a second new family in circumstances that are not permitted for women, and that give men much greater negotiating power over the conditions of the separation.[18]

However, while the legal aspects that discriminate against women within Israeli family law are perceived by the public and policymakers as part of the state and religion status quo that would not change in the foreseeable future by the Israeli parliament, in recent years, mostly due to powerful activism by fathers' groups,[19] the legal aspects that discriminate against fathers have attracted much attention from politicians, civil society organizations, professionals in the legal field, journalists, and the public as a whole. This attention has led to the current state of affairs in which the laws governing child custody and support are no more than dying letters in the law books, replaced by dramatically different judicial law-in-action.

The first serious attempt to weaken the legal tender years presumption was pursued by the Tel Aviv District Court in July 2000. In a case concerned with divorced parents, which generated significant public interest,[20] Judge Porat—a leading legal expert in family law—ordered that the physical custody of a four-year-old boy be shifted from the mother to the father, following her request to relocate abroad with the child, in the face of the father's objection. Judge Porat justified his ruling based on an alleged new norm that recognizes "the centrality and importance of the father for the child, especially at a tender age."[21] However, this attempt failed when the Supreme Court overruled the District Court decision and allowed the mother to relocate with the child, re-establishing the norm on which the tender years presumption is based, that "usually the attachment between tender years children and their mother is stronger than their attachment to their father."[22]

It took seven more years for the process of the erosion of the tender years presumption to take hold, starting with the mid-term recommendations of a government committee on post-divorce parental responsibility (the Shnit Committee), published in 2008[23] and re-adopted in the final report of the committee in 2011.[24] The Shnit Committee recommended that the concepts of "custody" and "visitation" be replaced with the concepts of "parental responsibility" and a "parental plan," that the tender years presumption be abolished, and that a set of criteria be established to guide judges when determining the best interest of the child and the parental plan that would best serve the child. These proposed criteria include the needs and wishes of the child, the right of the child to significant, personal, direct, and regular contact with both her parents, the willingness of each parent to cooperate with the other, the skills that each of them has and that are needed to fulfill their parental responsibility, the care that was provided by each parent to the child before the separation, and the child's right to contact with the extended family. The committee also recommended that if, applied together, these criteria were insufficient in helping the judge to determine the time allocated to each parent within the parental plan, then a "crucial weight" should be given to preserving the "stability in the child's life and the way and the extent the child was cared for by each parent during his life and until the decision, without that harming the consideration of preserving the contact of the child with both his parents."[25] In its recommendations, the committee also refused to allow any legal recognition of a parent as the primary caregiver after separation, even in cases in which the parental plan obviously demonstrates that one of the parents would perform that role.

A decade has passed since the publication of the Shnit Committee recommendations, and while the Israeli parliament discussed them several times, they have not yet been adopted. Moreover, the committee did *not* recommend joint physical custody arrangements, clarifying that "joint parental responsibility does not necessarily mean equal dwelling time of the child with each of the parents."[26] Yet, during this time, the notion of joint physical custody, previously considered by all professionals in the family law field as an exception suitable only in rare cases,[27] has become a mainstream norm in Israel. This shift, first fiercely lobbied-for by fathers' groups,[28] was then adopted by leading politicians[29] and journalists,[30] and was soon assimilated by social workers reporting to the court and by Family Court judges.[31]

Indeed, my study, conducted in the late 1990s,[32] looked into the legal arrangements surrounding parental divorce, and the perceptions of motherhood and fatherhood on which they were based, and found a high degree of suspicion toward joint physical custody arrangements among therapeutic and legal professionals. The rate of sole maternal custody as part of divorce arrangements (n = 360) at that time stood at more than 90%. Moreover, the Israeli Supreme Court repeatedly reminds the lower courts that the tender years presumption is still in the law books and should be obeyed.[33] Yet, findings from the recent study by Orit Jeckman-Ladani reveal that Family Court judges basically stopped waiting for the legislator to change the law and stopped obeying the Supreme Court. This dramatic judicial activism by lower court judges has irrevocably changed the landscape of child custody rulings in Israel. Examining all published 153 Family Court decisions handed-down between 2008 and 2018, Jeckman-Ladani found that the most common parental plan shaped by the judges (42%), including in cases of families with children younger than six, is one in which the children spend at least six nights every fortnight at each of the parent's homes. This constitutes de facto joint physical custody, although it is not always referred to as such by the judge: at times, it is camouflaged behind a formal title of *maternal* sole physical custody. Actual sole maternal custody, in which the children spend more than nine nights at the mother's home every fortnight, was found in only 40% of the cases, while paternal sole custody was awarded in 17% of the sample cases.[34]

The qualitative part of Jeckman-Ladani's study reveals the normative shift within the perceptions of the Family Court judges that explain the quantitative findings. For example, analyzing the published rulings of Judge Varda Ben Shahar, Jeckman-Ladani found that in 2009 this judge handed down two decisions involving children under the age of six. In both cases, she ruled in favor of sole maternal custody, without even mentioning the option of joint physical custody. The justification presented for the preference given to the mother was very brief in both cases. In one, the tender years presumption was mentioned,[35] and, in the other, the judge acknowledged that the "children are also attached to their father," but nevertheless stated: "Taking into consideration the age of the minors, I set the custody of the minors with their mother."[36] However, since 2010, the published rulings of this judge have favored joint physical custody, including in cases involving very young children. For example, in her decision to order joint physical custody for twins aged two years and nine months (with eight nights spent at the mother's home and six at the father's), Judge Ben Shahar explained: "Granting priority to one parent over the other by setting that parent as the custodian grants that parent advantages in the ability to influence the children [. . .] to the point of alienating the children from the other parent."[37]

Indeed, the erosion of the tender years presumption has been so dramatic in recent years that, when I lecture on it to lay audiences, many argue that it is no longer in the law books, when in fact it *is* still there. Likewise, family lawyers' websites no longer mention the tender years presumption, but rather describe the different custody options that can be shaped when parents separate, including the option of joint physical custody of children of all ages.[38]

This chronicle, of a shift from the tender years doctrine in the law books to mainstream joint physical custody within court decisions, is echoed in the chronicle of change in child support law. Soon after the Shnit Committee published its final report on parental responsibility, another government committee, which was devoted to child support (the Shifman Committee), published its recommendations. These were also revolutionary, calling for a new child support law that would be detached from religious law and that would split the financial burden between the parents according to their relative earnings, with some weight granted also to the amount of time the child spends at each parent's home.[39]

While these two principles initially appear reasonable and fair, a closer look reveals the shortcomings of this committee's recommendations. As Halperin-Kaddari and her colleagues demonstrate, the mathematical formula suggested by the committee to calculate the child maintenance rate was based on an unrealistic understanding of how much it actually costs to raise a child. The proposed formula also made an over-optimistic assumption that, if a child spends a significant amount of time with both parents, then the economic needs of the child are adequately covered by them both, even if no child support sum is legally set and paid by one parent to the other.[40] In fact, if the Shifman Committee's recommendations and its suggested formula had been adopted by the legislator, the economic security of children of divorced parents would have been severely compromised.[41] Luckily, they were not. Nevertheless, the paternal absolute and enhanced duty to support the children established by the law is now being visibly eroded by the judiciary—although this process began almost imperceptibly, decades ago.

As early as the 1980s, the Israeli Supreme Court ruled that the child's minimal needs (food, housing, clothing), which the law dictates as being the sole responsibility of the father until the age of 15, should be interpreted narrowly, so that the rest of the child's needs would be covered by both parents, according to their relative means.[42] Next, in the early 2000s, the Israeli Supreme Court paved the way for integrating the mother's income into the calculation of the amount of child support the father has to pay. In doing so, it imposed part of the child support duty on the mother, entirely disregarding the (religious) weaker maternal duty to support the child adopted by the legislator. The Supreme Court did not provide any explanation for this major normative shift.[43]

This erosion of the paternal absolute duty to provide financial support to children in cases of parental separation has continued more dramatically after the publication of the Shifman Committee's recommendations. In particular, Family Court judges have started to reduce the sums the father is ordered to pay in cases of joint physical custody. This varies significantly from judge to judge, ranging from a 25% reduction in the father's child support obligation to a 100% reduction, compared to the sums the father would have paid in the case of sole maternal physical custody. District Court judges have attempted to establish some order in the rules of child support in cases of joint physical custody, but no unified formula has emerged on a national scale.[44]

In July 2017, the Supreme Court ruled, in a decision that attracted much attention,[45] that, in cases of joint physical custody of children above the age of six, the father does not have an absolute and enhanced duty to support them, but rather both parents should support their children according to their relative income from all sources. However, the Supreme Court judges were not very clear as to how the sums should be calculated, and disputes soon followed. There are also conflicting interpretations of the relevance of this ruling to cases of sole physical custody, to cases in which there is a substantial difference in the parents' incomes, and to cases that were already concluded before this decision was handed down.[46] Notwithstanding these ambiguities, the relatively clear message from the Supreme Court was that the norm of gender equality between parents should rule the issue of child support. Judge Fogelman, who delivered the main ruling that was supported by the other six judges, declared: "The differentiation between women and men, which is based on stereotypical reasoning, as opposed to a relevant difference, is wrong discrimination that cannot be tolerated, even if it holds a 'benefit' for women, who are the main group protected by the prohibition on sex-based discrimination."[47]

The vague guidelines provided by the Supreme Court on how to set a gender-neutral case-by-case child support rate have only added to the existing chaos caused by the disparity in lower courts' judgments. Indeed, as Jeckman-Ladani's study demonstrates, the child support rates dictated by judges may vary enormously, even in similar familial and economic circumstances. Moreover, Jeckman-Ladani demonstrates the overall impact of the new joint physical custody norm on the amount of child support dictated by the courts, including for children younger than six. On average, fathers in a joint-custody arrangement are ordered by the court to pay about two-thirds of what they would have paid, had the mother been the sole physical custodian. Moreover, Jeckman-Ladani also documents a drop over the past decade in the sums fathers have been ordered to pay, even in cases of maternal custody and, in particular, when the children are under the age of six where fathers are ordered today to pay about $100 less than 10 years ago.[48] What is truly astounding (and central to my argument) is not the proportion of fathers' versus mothers' financial contributions per se, but that these changes have been possible at all, given that they are not the outcome of legislative reform and contradict the paternal duty to support set by the law.

It is important to stress that the erosion of the two key legal guidelines to parental separation—the tender years presumption and fathers' absolute and sole duty to provide for their children's basic needs—affects not only court rulings but also the more common scenario of the divorce being concluded by an arrangement reached by negotiation or mediation. Although the guidelines are still present in the law books, the actual legal state of affairs has shifted so dramatically and has become so chaotic that there is no longer a clear "shadow of the law," and responsible lawyers cannot guide their clients on risk management if the negotiation is to fail and the case would reach the court.[49] This new reality places mothers in a more vulnerable negotiation position than in the past, without the protection they were granted by the legislature, in an already discriminatory legal arena shaped by religious law, and in a socioeconomic reality that makes it harder for them to endure long and expensive litigation.[50]

While in all Western jurisdictions the tender years doctrine as well as the paternal absolute duty to support the children financially are no longer in the law books, it seems that the Israeli case is extreme in driving toward joint physical custody with decreased child support paid by fathers. Joint physical custody is extremely rare as a legal presumption and most jurisdictions would still expect the court to rule on one parent as the sole physical custodian or primary caregiver, or on one of the parent's homes as the primary home of the children. Moreover, many jurisdictions are careful to order joint physical custody in cases of parental conflict; and, unlike the Israeli case, even joint legal custody is not ordered in all cases.[51] For example, in Canada, only 20% of all reported child custody court decisions in 2015 ordered joint physical custody (defined as at least 40% of the time living with each parent), while the mother was the sole physical custodian or her home was the primary residence in 58% of the cases. Mothers were also the sole *legal* custodians in 20% of the cases.[52] Likewise, in Australia, considered one of the pioneering jurisdictions in promoting joint physical custody, this is the arrangement within only 16% of post-divorce families, rarely enforced by courts.[53] Indeed, a survey of custody arrangements of children aged 11, 13, and 15, in 37 countries (n = 92,886), found that the average rate of joint physical custody is only 5.7%.[54] Finally, while child support laws are drafted these days in gender-neutral language, there are jurisdictions that are nevertheless careful, when awarding joint physical custody, to avoid automatically setting substantially diminished sums to be paid by the higher-earning parent to the other parent, so as to secure a similar standard of living for the children at both their parents' homes.[55] Moreover, unlike in Israel,[56] many jurisdictions establish special mechanisms to ensure clear and fast collection of child support, usually paid by the father.[57]

The new Israeli legal activism regarding child custody and support—apparently in the name of gender equality—also looks extreme when the actual gendered labor division within families is taken into consideration within a comparative context. Unlike in many Western countries, Israel is not witnessing a decline in birth rates; Israeli women have, on average, three children—by far the highest rate among developed countries.[58] Moreover, in most Israeli families, the mother is the primary caregiver, investing, on average 50.5 hours per week in childcare and housework, compared to 21.3 hours that the father invests.[59] The government does not encourage active fatherhood,[60] and the only major attempt to do so—by allowing paternal leave—failed, with less than 1% of fathers entitled to stay at home with their newborn seizing the opportunity.[61]

The predominance of women in the unpaid labor force has a devastating impact on Israeli women's ability to participate on par with men in the salaried market. While Israeli women's participation rate in the labor force is relatively high, they are overly represented in the part-time sector,[62] concentrated in just a few female-dominated professions,[63] and underrepresented in managerial positions.[64] The outcome most relevant to our discussion is that Israel is rated very low compared to other developed countries in the World Bank's gender wage-gap index.[65] Israeli women's average monthly salary is just 68% of men's, and there is a 16% gap in the hourly payment in favor of men.[66] Not surprisingly, in most Israeli families, the father earns more than the mother.[67]

Hence, the dramatic law-in action shift, described above, cannot be explained by an actual social change. Unfortunately, the law-in-the-books is the law that still reflects the gendered labor division in most Israeli families. The exceptional stagnation on the part of the Israeli parliament (which, unlike other national legislators, has not reformed child custody and support laws) has undoubtedly contributed to this judicial activism in Israel. However, as I argue in the next part of this chapter, the radical content of the law-in-action shift toward alleged gender-neutral child custody and support—which grants too little recognition to the actual primary caregiver prior to the separation and to the gendered inequality within the labor force—cannot be explained detached from the impact of Israeli fathers' groups and their illegitimate *modi operandi*. I contend that this shift was born out of unfounded moral panic fueled by a false narrative planted by fathers' groups through a deliberately orchestrated intimidation campaign.

THE ILLEGITIMATE DISCOURSE OF ISRAELI FATHERS' GROUPS

In several countries, fathers' groups have played a major role in driving forward legislative reforms related to child custody and support.[68] While it is easier to prove the impact of a certain discourse on parliament than on the judiciary, as there are parliamentary records that can point to effective lobbying, I nevertheless argue that the discourse led by Israeli fathers' groups has contributed significantly to the radical judicial activism described in the first part of the chapter. My position is based on the aforementioned lack of actual social change in Israeli gendered familial labor division, together with the time proximity between fathers' group activism and the change in custody and child support law-in-action. As I will demonstrate, the alarming feature of fathers' group activism is that part of it relies on propagating fake news and discursive violence aimed at establishing the narrative of divorced fathers' "victimization" in order to change public opinion and judicial policy related to parental conflicts upon divorce.

As I have detailed elsewhere,[69] the beginning of the third millennium witnessed the establishment of about ten fathers' organizations in Israel. While the membership of most of these organizations is not large, they are characterized by very devoted activists and effective networking. Their main goal is to change family law in Israel, by replacing the tender years presumption with the vague "best interest of the child" standard or by a joint physical custody presumption,[70] and by minimizing fathers' child support duty.[71] As in other countries,[72] recently, they have also sought to promote the notion that women routinely falsely accuse men of domestic violence[73] and that there is a widespread phenomenon of mothers alienating their children from their fathers.[74] While some of the fathers involved in these organizations are undoubtedly motivated by love for their children, and might have been mistreated by the imperfect welfare or legal systems, the misogynist and anti-feminist discourse promoted by these organizations,[75] as well as the illegitimate tactics they are using, which I detail next, point to their being part of the global backlash movement of men striving to push back feminist achievements, including within family law and divorce procedures.[76]

The Israeli fathers' groups promote their agenda in a variety of ways, including parliamentary lobbying, demonstrations, media appearances, and the creation of websites providing divorce-related information and commentary. While much of this activism is legal and legitimate, some is absolutely not, and includes lies, threats, and violence against those whom they perceive as objecting to their ideology and goals.

I wish to concentrate here on one of the many false "facts" that can be found in the discourse promoted by Israeli fathers' groups. Time and time again, they argue that *hundreds* of divorced fathers commit suicide each year because of the discrimination they face during the divorce procedure. While in fact, the yearly average number (2010–2014) of divorced fathers of minor children who commit suicide is 21,[77] and there is *no* available data on the motive or its relation to the divorce procedure. Moreover, there is no difference in the suicide rate between divorced men who fathered children under the age of 21, and other divorced men.[78] Indeed, the spread of false "statistics" of suicide rates among divorced fathers, I will briefly detail here, provide an interesting example of the evolution of fake news aimed at changing family law and its successful penetration into mainstream public discourse.

The shocking alleged numbers of fathers committing suicide due to the horrible treatment and discrimination they experience at the hands of the welfare and legal systems during the divorce procedure, as the narrative goes, first appeared in Israeli public discourse in April 2008, in an online article published by the chairman of one of the fathers' organizations. He argued that "if you are a man and in divorce procedures all the systems hold the assumption that you are violent, bothersome, miserly, a thief, an extortionist, and even a pedophile." He also "revealed" what he claimed to be "one of the best-kept secrets in the country," citing a statistic allegedly derived from a report by the Ministry of Health, according to which "hundreds of men and fathers commit suicide, and to be exact 300 a year."[79]

As we have seen, these numbers have no correlation to reality—they are an outright lie. Yet, this is the tip of the iceberg. Since 2010, Israeli activist divorced fathers have not hesitated to use fabricated statistics when transnationally suing Israeli government ministers, judges, social workers, and psychologists over alleged gross violations of Israeli divorced men's human rights, their emotional torment, and the egregious gender discrimination they claim to suffer at the hands of the Israeli welfare and legal systems. Strikingly, they have abused the invitation that was extended by the United States to foreigners who are tortured or suffer from gross violation of human rights by their governments,[80] with the intention of maximizing embarrassment to the Israeli government and intimidating professionals who are involved in divorce procedures and who do not satisfy these fathers' wishes. Among the many lies detailed in their baseless lawsuits,[81] is that the suicide rate of divorced fathers in Israel is 1 in 72, and that the risk for fathers in Israel of dying as an outcome of their divorce procedure is 14 times higher than for people becoming addicted to cocaine in New York.[82]

The campaign of the Israeli fathers' groups is ambitious in scope; they did not hesitate, for example, to report these lies to the United Nations (UN). In 2011, they submitted a shadow report to the UN Committee on Economic, Social and Cultural Rights. According to the report—which included no reference or source for the claim—in Israel: "Bias against men in the Judiciary, Administrative and enforcement arms of the Government has created the most distorted, cruel and unconscionable family law system in the Western World. Men are ignored, ridiculed, impoverished, jailed and disengaged from their children on a daily basis." Included among the many false arguments in the report was the statistic that 200 Israeli men commit suicide each year due to the discrimination they experience in divorce procedures.[83]

Similar "statistics" of suicide rates among divorced fathers in Israel continued to show up from time to time in the virtual sphere,[84] and mainstream media. For example, in one of Israel's largest newspapers, an article was published in 2012 under the title "Trapped Men," which stated that "Out of the 400 men who commit suicide [each year], 200 are divorced men with children."[85]

While the Ministry of Health published its statistics on suicide rates with specific segmentation of divorced fathers with children under the age of 18 only in 2017, I received the raw data from the Ministry already in 2012 and was able to report to the Parliamentary Committee on the Promotion of Women's Status that, contrary to the fathers' groups claims, in the period 2000–2009, on average, each year, 15 divorced men (fathers and not-fathers) aged 25–44 committed suicide, and 20 aged 45–64 did so (which is an age category less relevant to divorce disputes). The Head of the Committee endorsed my report and stated during the meeting to the fathers' groups' representatives that "all the statistics you bring on the issue of men's suicide—these statistics are unfounded, they have no base."[86] However, the representatives were unmoved by the facts, arguing that "200 divorced fathers kill themselves each year."[87]

The ongoing attempt of the fathers' groups to stir up moral panic regarding the apparent suicide rate among divorced fathers and to connect it to reforms in family law is evident in the discourse promoted by MP Kish, who is very active in recent years in promoting divorced fathers' interests in parliament. For example, in April 2016, one of his Facebook posts also published as a column in the media, said:

> In the last few days, two divorced fathers killed themselves. . . . They went through suffering and torment that are hard to understand and that must stop. . . . The only tool I have is legislation. . . . I am doing all that I can to promote the two main laws: the abolishment of the tender years presumption and changing the child support laws.[88]

While this and other MPs' attempts to change these laws have so far failed, the judiciary *has* changed them in this same spirit, as discussed earlier in this chapter.

Spreading fake news is not the only illegitimate strategy employed by Israeli fathers' groups. Their discourse also includes online threats and cyber bullying that create fear. I cannot elaborate on all the components of this violent discourse, and will only mention two vital collectives targeted and threatened by the fathers' groups: social workers and judges.

Social workers are on the front line, dealing directly with divorcing fathers as part of their role providing child custody recommendations to the courts. In a 2014 media interview, the head of the government department responsible for the social workers who make recommendations to the courts dealing with child custody, described some of the threats she and other social workers receive. She stated: "The attacks on social workers come from fathers and from mothers, the essential difference being that the fathers are organized and the mothers not so much. The fathers' groups are more ferocious and they also know how to conduct effective lobbying." After describing the aforementioned lawsuits in the United States (in which she was one of the defendants), as well as cases of online shaming and violations of privacy targeted at specific social workers by angry fathers, she claimed:

> There is no doubt that physical violence is harder because it risks lives, but emotional virtual violence leaves you with no control, you cannot stop it, and you cannot control who is exposed to it, nor its future consequences.[89]

The intense exposure to fathers' demands, in a threatening climate created by the fathers' groups, explains, I would argue, the fact that the social workers (most of whom are women) were the first to advance the norm of joint physical custody. Between 2008 and 2010, the number of recommendations for this arrangement doubled from 309 to 778.[90] The fact that some of these recommendations include the title "joint custody," even though the parental plan recommended by the social worker clearly positions the mother as the primary caregiver,[91] hints at the possibility that, in some cases, the social worker is trying to maneuver between the demands of the father and the best interest of the child as she perceives it. Moreover, as someone professionally involved in the field of family law for more than two decades, I can testify to the silencing process that contributed to the current reality in which it is very hard to find a professional from the therapeutic fields (social workers, psychologists, and so on) who is willing to publicly argue in favor of preserving the role of the primary caregiver post-divorce, although, in private conversations, many social workers still hold the position that the parental plan should reflect the special attachment created between the primary caregiving parent and the children. This echoes the account provided by the former Chairwoman of the Parliamentary Committee on the Right of the Child, who stated in 2013 that social workers (and divorced mothers) refuse to participate in the committee's discussion related to family law, in fear of divorced fathers. She also described how she, and other parliament members, were threatened by fathers' groups, which, for example, sent them WhatsApp messages with a picture of a gun, or bouquets of flowers to their children's kindergartens so as to signal that they know who and where the children are.[92]

Likewise, judges are targeted by the fathers' groups on a personal level—so much so, that in 2012 they asked the Courts Management Office to act against the shaming and threats they were experiencing on the Internet.[93] While we can presume that most judges hold to their professional integrity and rule on child custody and support as they understand serves the best interest of the child in question, some might be influenced by the moral panic promoted by the fathers' groups as well as by fear for their career and personal safety. Indeed, one Family Court judge admitted to me in a private conversation that his fear for his and his family's safety, created by the fathers' groups, does indeed affect his decisions. Likewise, I am told off the record by several judges that they are worried by the reforms promoted by their colleagues described in the first part. These judges perceive joint physical custody as a complicated arrangement not suited to, for example, families in high conflict; and they also worry that children's economic needs are harmed by the lower child support sums fathers are ordered to pay the mother.

Indeed, while the appropriate custody criteria and child support formula that should be adopted by the law are heatedly debated from time to time in parliament, such debates seem like poor attempts to shut the stable door after the horse has bolted. The legal reality has radically changed, with the tender years doctrine and the paternal absolute and enhanced duty to support the children no longer guiding the legal field governing divorce. As demonstrated in this chapter, this change is not the outcome of a social change in familial gendered labor division or of a normative shift based on a rational discussion or a political consensus. It is, first and foremost, the outcome of activism on the part of lower courts, shaped in the shadow of deliberately orchestrated fake news and discursive violence promoted by fathers' groups.

CONCLUSION

The relatively new phenomena of fake news and virtual discursive violence are attracting the attention of researchers[94] and policymakers,[95] yet their impact on norm-creation and the law is still to be further studied empirically and discussed theoretically. The Israeli case study is an alarming warning sign, pointing to the challenges that responsible players in the legal field must overcome in an era in which even leaders of great states do not hesitate to use these two tactics.

In Israel and indeed worldwide, I hold that legislators must take upon themselves the task of creating a platform for rational discussions, including by refraining from inviting guest speakers who are known to spread fake news or use discursive violence; judges and state social workers must be protected by the state—threats and defamation must be removed from the Internet and people who threaten judges and social workers must be identified and prosecuted; associations of private therapeutic professionals who take part in legal proceedings, as well as associations of mediators and of lawyers, must speak up strongly against fake news and discursive violence, and must protect their members, including by funding private suits against identified individuals and organizations that use threats, defamation, or violation of privacy among their strategies; researchers must fight back against fake news by seeking reliable data and making it accessible to the public, and must be brave in the face of attempts to silence them; and feminist and other liberal and responsible activists must find new ways to influence public opinion without surrendering to the misleading and violent tactics used by misogynist, racist, and nationalist activists.

Returning to the field of family law, I believe the key to addressing the challenges created by illegitimate tactics used by fathers' groups is to center on children's rights, interests, needs, and wishes. While the gender power relations between parents must be addressed by the law and its carriers, parental duties and rights must be shaped, first and foremost, through a child-centered lens. While this is a recognized core value of modern family law, it is not always implemented,[96] and it is additionally marginalized by the victimization discourse promoted, so vociferously, by fathers' groups.[97] Among the tragedies of the Israeli case study is the fact that there is only one significant and relevant child advocacy NGO, and that, while it voiced its concerns regarding the impact of the abolishment of the tender years doctrine on children, during the Shnit Committee discussions,[98] it has remained silent over the law-in-action reforms in child custody and support ever since. All responsible professional actors engaged with family law must bring children back into the foreground by studying the impact of legal reforms on their well-being,[99] and by insisting on hearing children during divorce proceedings.[100] They must also prevent irresponsible fathers (and mothers) from using their children as part of their private and public divorce battles.[101] The unpalatable alternative, if we fail to address the challenges of fake news and discursive violence in family law, is to abandon children to the power of liars and bullies.

NOTES

1. Carol Smart and Selma Sevenhuijsen, eds., *Child Custody and the Politics of Gender* (London: Routledge, 1989).

2. Lenore J. Weitzman, *The Divorce Revolution: The Unexpected Social and Economic Consequences for Women and Children in America* (New York: Free Press, 1987), 39.

3. Smart and Sevenhuijsen, *Child Custody*; Daniel R. Meyer et al., "Child Support Reform: Lessons from Wisconsin," *Family Relations* 45, no. 1 (January 1996): 11–18; Kay Cook and Kristin Natalier, "The Gendered Framing of Australia's Child Support Reforms," *International Journal of Law, Policy and the Family* 27, no. 1 (April 2013): 28–50. doi: 10.1093/lawfam/ebs013

4. For example, Susan B. Boyd, "Autonomy for Mothers? Relational Theory and Parenting Apart," *Feminist Legal Studies* 18, no. 2 (August 2010): 137–58. doi: 10.1007/s10691-010-9152-3. Reg Graycar, "Family Law Reform in Australia, or Frozen Chooks Revisited Again?" *Theoretical Inquiries in Law* 13, no. 1 (2012): 241–69; Susan B. Boyd, "Backlash Against Feminism: Canadian Custody and Access Reform Debates of the Late 20th Century," *CJWL* 16, no. 2 (2004): 255–90; Kay Cook and Kristin Natalier, "Gender and Evidence in Family Law Reform: A Case Study of Quantification and Anecdote in Framing and Legitimising the 'Problems' with Child Support in Australia," *Feminist Legal Studies* 24, no. 2 (July 2016): 147–67. doi:10.1007/s10691-016-9317-9; Cook and Natalier, "The Gendered," 28–50; Meyer et al., "Child Support Reform," 11–18; Smart and Sevenhuijsen, *Child Custody*.

5. Richard Collier and Sally Sheldon, eds., *Fathers' Rights Activism and Legal Reform in Comparative Perspective* (Oxford and Portland: Hart Publications, 2006).

6. *Capacity and Guardianship Law, 1962*, § 25 [all translations from Hebrew are the author's].

7. Daphna Hacker, *Parenthood in the Law: Behind the Scene of Custody and Visitation upon Divorce* (Tel Aviv: Hakibbutz Hameuchad Publishing House Ltd, 2008). [Hebrew]

8. The Family Amendment (Maintenance) Law § 3(a). Hebrew is a highly gendered language and the law is written in the male form, while usually (as in this case) applying to both men and women.

9. Ruth Halperin-Kaddari, *Women in Israel: A State of Their Own* (Philadelphia: University of Pennsylvania Press, 2004); Eliav Shochetman, "Women's Status in Marriage and Divorce Law," in *Women's Status in Israeli Law and Society*, eds. Frances Raday, Carmel Shalev and Michal Liban-Kobi (Jerusalem: Shocken, 1995), 380–436. [Hebrew]

10. The rest are Christians or have no religious affiliation. See Israeli Central Bureau of Statistics Media Release, *Religion and Self-Definition of Extent of Religiosity: Selected Data from the Society In Israel Report*, no. 10 (June 2018), http://www.cbs.gov.il/he/ mediarelease/DocLib/2018/195/32_18_195b.pdf. [Hebrew]

11. Shava Menashe, "Maintenance of Minor Children in Jewish Law and in Positive Law," (part 1 & 2) *Tel Aviv Law Review* 7, no. 2 & 3 (1979–1980): 316–44, 583–617 [Hebrew]; Badruddin Hj Ibrahim and Azizah Mohd, "The Child's Right to Maintenance: The Extent of the Family's Responsibilities in Islamic Law and According to the Family Law Provisions of Muslim Countries," *Arab Law Quarterly* 25, no. 4 (January 2011): 401–22.

12. FC (Jerusalem) 1886/04 *A.L, R.L, B.L, S.L, v. D.L* (2006).

13. Religious courts in Israel have sole jurisdiction over the acts of marriage and divorce, and, under certain conditions, parallel jurisdiction in matters related to divorce, including child custody and support. See Daphna Hacker, "Religious Tribunals in Democratic States: Lessons from the Israeli Rabbinical Courts," *Journal of Law and Religion* 27, no. 1 (2012): 59–81.

14. Eliezer Hadad, On the Status of Women in Rabbinical Courts (The Israeli Democracy Institute, 2013). [Hebrew]

15. In 2017, the first female religious judge was appointed to the Sharia Courts. However, no such nominations are admitted for the Rabbinical Courts.

16. http://www.daat.ac.il/encyclopedia/value.asp?id1=3589

17. Hanoch Dagan and Daphna Hacker, "The Doctrine of Specific Shared Ownership Toward the Fourth Act in HCJ 4602/13," *Law Studies* 32, no. 1 (2019): 519–44. [Hebrew]

18. Ruth Halperin-Kaddari, *Women in Israel*, 235–41.

19. Daphna Hacker, "Men's Groups as a New Challenge to the Israeli Feminist Movement: Lessons from the Ongoing Gender War over the Tender Years Presumption," *Israel Studies* 18, no. 3 (2013): 29–40.

20. Daphna Hacker and Ronen Shamir, "Concepts of Motherhood, Fatherhood and Family in Israeli Courts: A Case Study," *Israeli Sociology* 5, no. 2 (2003): 311–40 [Hebrew].

21. DA 1125/99 *K.Z v. D.L* 5 (2000).

22. CAA 4575/00 *Row v. Dow* 323 (2001).

23. Governmental Committee on Aspects of Parental Responsibility upon Divorce (The Shnit Committee), *Interim Report*, April 2008.

24. Governmental Committee on Aspects of Parental Responsibility upon Divorce (The Shnit Committee), *Final Report*, December 2011.

25. The Shnit Committee, *Final Report*, 7.

26. Id.

27. Hacker, *Parenthood in the Law,* 259.

28. For example, Shared Parenting Equals Children's Interests, accessed December 15, 2019, https://shared-parenting.co.il/joint-custody/; The Coalition for Children and Family in Israel, accessed December 15, 2019, http://ccfisrael.org/israel_fathers_rights_news/; D is for Dad, accessed December 15, 2019, https://www.facebook.com/zedekhevraati. [All, Hebrew]

29. For example, PM Yoav Kish and PM Gila Gamliel submitted a law proposal supporting joint physical custody, https://bit.ly/2SKiNT9.

30. For example, Lanski Naama, "Dad's Voice," *Israel Hayom*, June 10, 2016, https://www.israelhayom.co.il/article/388213. [Hebrew]

31. Daphna Hacker and Ruth Halperin-Kaddari, "The Ruling Rules in Custody Disputers: On the Dangers of the Parental Sameness Illusion in a Gendered Reality," *Mishpat and Mimshal* 15, no. 1–2 (2013): 91–170. [Hebrew]

32. Hacker, *Parenthood in the Law.*

33. For example, FAR 1858-14 *Roe v. Doe* (2014).

34. Orit Jeckman-Ladani, *Legal Activism in Israeli Family Law* (MA Thesis, Tel Aviv University, Israel, 2020). [Hebrew]

35. FC (Reshon Letzion) 37671/09 *S.M v. A.M* (2009).

36. DCR (Reshon Letzion) 207/09 *N.M, N.H, N.l, N.Y v. N.M* (2009).

37. FC 28951/09 (Reshon Letzion) A.G.G, *M.G, A.G v. T.G* (2010).

38. For example, "What is Joint Custody?" Rotenberg Law Firm, accessed December 30, 2019, https://rotenberglaw.co.il/What-Is-Joint-Custody?; "Shared Custody," Eleanor Leibovitch Law Firm, accessed December 30, 2019, https://bit.ly/2V6RWlj. [All, Hebrew]

39. *The Shifman Committee Report* (The Israeli Department of Justice, 2012).

40. Ruth Halperin-Kaddari, Keren Horovitz, and Shay Zilberberg "The Chaos in Child Support Judgements," *Law and Business Journal* (IDC Law Review) 19, no. 3 (December 2016): 1235–69. [Hebrew]

41. Id., 1266.

42. Id., 1238.

43. Hacker and Halperin-Kaddari, "The Ruling Rules," 157; FAR 2433/04 G.T *v.* D.T (2005); FAR 5750/03 *Ohana v. Ohana* (2003).

44. Halperin-Kaddari, Horovitz, and Zilberberg, "The Chaos"; FAR 5750/03 *Ohana v. Ohana* 2 (2003); FAR 2433/04 G.T v. D.T (2005).

45. For example, Anat Lifshitz and Shahar Lifshitz, "Support of Children Aged 6 to 15 Following FAR 5750/03," *Bar-Ilan Law Studies* 32 (2020): 545–633. [Hebrew]

46. The Ruth and Emanuel Rackman Center for the Advancement of Women's Status, *The Ruling in DAR 919/15 Roe v. Doe: Presentation and Analysis*, September 2017, https://bit.ly/2FceQhZ. [Hebrew]

47. FAR 919/ 15 *Row v. Dow*, Judge Fogelman §107.

48. Orit Jeckman-Ladani, "Legal Activism."

49. Daphna Hacker, "Legal Activism in Family Law," *ICON-S-Il* (Blog), May 1, 2018, https://bit.ly/39rQ9Mx. [Hebrew]

50. This is so due to their lower economic status, detailed next, as well as their fertility biological clock and spousal relations social clock.

51. Hacker and Halperin-Kaddari, "The Ruling Rules," 91–170.

52. Nicholas Bala et al., "Shared Parenting in Canada: Increasing Use But Continued Controversy," *Family Court Review: An Interdisciplinary Journal* (special issue: International Demographics of Joint Custody) 55, no. 4 (October 2017): 513–30. doi: 10.1111/fcre.12301

53. Bruce M. Smyth, Jennifer E. McIntosh, Robert E. Emery & Shelby L. Higgs Howarth, "Shared-Time Parenting: Evaluating the Evidence of Risks and Benefits to Children," in *Parenting Plan Evaluations: Applied Research for the Family Court*, eds. Lesley Drozd, Michael Saini & Nancy Olesen (Oxford: Oxford University Press, 2016), 118–69, at 119, 121.

54. Anja Steinbach, Lara Augustijn & Gerrit Corkadi, "Joint Physical Custody and Adolescents' Life Satisfaction in 37 North American and European Countries," *Family Processes* (2020), 1–17, at 4. doi: 10.1111/famp.12536. The survey is based on data from 2002, 2006 and 2010.

55. *The Shifman Committee Report*, 33–53.

56. Divorced Israeli fathers owe millions of dollars to the social security system due to their failure to pay child support. See Natnaela Berkley, Women Receiving Child Support From The National Insurance Institute of Israel-2017 (Jerusalem: The National Insurance Institute of Israel, 2018), https://www.btl.gov.il/Publications/survey/Pages/seker_297.aspx. [Hebrew]

57. *The Shifman Committee Report*, 33–53.

58. Alex Weinreb, Dov Chernichovsky, and Aviv Brill, "Israel's Exceptional Fertility," in State of the Nation Report 2018, Taub Center for Social Policy Studies in Israel, December 2018, http://taubcenter.org.il/wp-content/files_mf/exceptionalfertilityeng.pdf

59. Amit Kaplan, *Invisible Work: Work Time and Gender Information and Policy Principles* (Jerusalem: The Van Leer Jerusalem Institute, 2012). [Hebrew]

60. Daphna Hacker and Michal Frenkel, "Active Parenthood and Employment Equal Opportunities: The Need to Change the Characteristics of the Labor Force," *Labor, Society and Law* 11 (2005): 275–303. [Hebrew]

61. Yaara Maan, *The Right to Active Fatherhood: Recommendations for changing the maternity leave policy in Israel* (Tel Aviv, Israel: The Israel Women's Network, February 2018). [Hebrew]

62. CBS, Central Bureau of Statistics, *Employed Persons Usually Working Part-Time, by Reason for Part-Time Work, Population Group and Sex*, August 2018, https://old.cbs.gov.il/reader/shnaton/templ_shnaton.html?num_tab=st12_21&CYear=2018. [Hebrew]

63. The Van Leer Jerusalem Institute, *Gender Inequalities in Employment, Gender Index 2018: Gendered inequality in Israel*, accessed March 12, 2020, https://bit.ly/2Fcz3o0. [Hebrew]

64. Hagar Tzameret, et al., *Gender Index 2018: Gendered inequality in Israel* (Jerusalem, Israel: The Van Leer Jerusalem Institute, 2018),4 accessed March 12, 2020, https://bit.ly/2IS4k1e. [Hebrew]

65. World Bank, *Women, Business and the Law 2019: A decade of Reform*, 2019, https://openknowledge.worldbank.org/bitstream/handle/10986/31327/WBL2019.pdf?sequence=4&isAllowed=y

66. Noga Dagan Buzaglo and Yael Hasson, *Gender Wage Gap in Israel: 2020* (Tel Aviv, Israel: Adva Center, 2020), https://adva.org/wp-content/uploads/2020/03/Gender-Gaps-2020.pdf. [Hebrew]

67. Israeli Central Bureau of Statistics, Media Release, *Data Collection for the International Women's Day*, March 2019, https://www.cbs.gov.il/he/mediarelease/DocLib/2019/075/11_19_075b.pdf. [Hebrew] An exception to the rule are Ultra-Orthodox families, in which, in many cases, the woman participates in the paid labor force while the man studies in a religious institute. See Rivka Neriya Ben-Shahar, "To Be the Wife of a *Talmid Hacham* [Torah Scholar]: How Ultra-Orthodox Women Perceive the Socio-Economic Reality of the 'Learners' Society," *The Study of the Ultra-Orthodox Society* 2 (2015): 169–92. [Hebrew]

68. For the Canadian case, see Susan B. Boyd, "Demonizing Mothers: Fathers' Rights Discourses in Child Custody Law Reform Processes," *Journal of the Motherhood Initiative for Research and Community Involvement* 6, no. 1 (2004): 52–74. For the U.S. case, see Leora N. Rosen, Molly Dragiewicz, and Jennifer C. Gibbs, "Fathers' Rights Groups: Demographic Correlates and Impact on Custody Policy," *Violence Against Women* 15, no. 5 (May 2009): 513–31. For Australia, see Helen Rhoades, "Yearning for the Law: Fathers' Groups and Family Law Reform in Australia," in *Fathers' Rights Activism and Legal Reform in Comparative Perspective*, eds. Richard Collier and Sally Sheldon (Oxford and Portland: Hart Publications, 2006).

69. Daphna Hacker, "Men's Groups," 29–40.

70. See, for example, "Equal Parenting Equals Child Interest," accessed March 12, 2020, https://bit.ly/37oFzUr; "Coalition for Children and Family in Israel," http://ccfisrael.org/; "Alef is for Abba," accessed March 12, 2020, https://www.facebook.com/zedekhevraati; "Equal Parenting: For Equal Parenting After Divorce," accessed March 12, 2020, https://www.facebook.com/parental.equality.israel1/. [All, Hebrew]

71. See, for example, https://shared-parenting.co.il/, accessed March 12, 2020. [Hebrew]

72. Michael Flood, "'Fathers' Rights' and the Defense of Paternal Authority in Australia," *Violence Against Women* 16, no. 3 (2010): 328–47; Molly Dragiewicz, "Patriarchy Reasserted: Fathers' Rights and Anti-VAWA Activism," *Feminist Criminology* 3, no. 2 (April 2008): 121–44; Miranda Kaye and Julia Tolmie, "Discoursing Dads: The Rhetorical Devices of Fathers' Rights Groups," *Melbourne University Law Review* 22, no. 1 (1998): 162–94; Michele A. Adams, "Framing Contests in Child Custody Disputes: Parental Alienation Syndrome, Child Abuse, Gender, and Fathers' Rights," *Family Law Quarterly* 40, no. 2 (Summer 2016): 315–38.

73. Yoav Mazeh, *False Allegation of Sexual Abuse and Domestic Violence*, KPF, March 2016, https://bit.ly/367rURB. [Hebrew]

74. "Parental Alienation Syndrome—Whether a Syndrome or Not—Is Destructive to the Whole Family System," *Shared Parenting*, accessed January 3, 2020, https://shared-parenting.co.il/wp-content/uploads/2014/03/רדמס-תינור.pdf;

"Parental Alienation Syndrome," Equal Parenting Equals Child Interest, accessed January 3,2020, https://shared-parenting.co.il/parental-alienation/. [All, Hebrew]

75. One example of this discourse is the term "feminazi," used by Israeli fathers' activists, as well as by fathers' groups in other countries. Toril Moi, "'I Am Not a Feminist, but . . .': How Feminism Became the F-Word," *PMLA* 121, no. 5 (October 2006): 1735–41; Bethany M. Coston and Michael Kimmel, "White Men as the New Victims: Reverse Discrimination Cases and the Men's Rights Movement," *Nevada Law Journal* 13, no. 2 (2013): 386; Noam Barkan, "Not Surrendering," *Yedeot Aharonot*, January 14, 2018, https://www.yediot.co.il/articles/0,7340,L-5070955,00.html [Hebrew]; Noga Cohen, "The Discourse About False Accusations Covers Women's Hatred," *Haaretz*, April 16, 2016, https://www.haaretz.co.il/blogs/nogacohen/BLOG-1.2909463. [Hebrew]

76. Susan Faludi, *Backlash: The Undeclared War Against American Women* (New York: Doubleday, 1992); Molly Dragiewicz, *Equality with a Vengenace: Men's Right Groups, Battered Women, and Antifeminist Backlash* (Boston: Northeastern University Press, 2011); Robert Menzies, "Virtual Backlash: Representations of Men's 'Rights' and Feminist 'Wrongs' in Cyberspace," in *Reaction and Resistance: Feminism, Law, and Social Change*, eds. Dorothy E. Chunn, Susan B. Boyd and Hester Lessard (Vancouver: UBC Press, 2007): 65.

77. Ziona Hacklay, Nehama Goldberger and Miriam Aburaba, "Suicide in Israel," Ministry of Health 2017, PP presentation, slide no. 15.

78. Jiska Monnickendam-Givon and Rada Haisesi, "Data on Suicide rates among Adults according to Familial Status," Research and Information Center, Israeli Parliament, May 22, 2017, p. 8.

79. Yair Tibon, "Every Son That is Born You Must Throw into the Nile," *News1: First Class*, April 15, 2008, http://www.news1.co.il/Archive/003-D-29038-00.html. [Hebrew]

80. *The Torture Victims Protection Act (TVPA)*, Pub.L. 102-256, 106 Stat. 73 (1992); *Racketeer Influenced and Corrupt Organizations Act (RICO)*, 18 U.S.C., Chapter 96, §1961–68.

81. Daphna Hacker, "Divorced Israeli Men's Abuse of Transnational Human Rights Law," *Canadian Journal of Women and the Law* 28, no. 1 (April 2016): 91–115.

82. *Weisskopf v. Jewish Agency for Israel, Inc.*, No 12-6844 (SDNY 2013) [on file with author].

83. "Report of the Israeli NGOs for Fathers' Rights by the Coalition for the Children and Family, www.ccfisrael.org, to the 47th Session of the Committee on Economic, Social, and Cultural Rights (to be held on November 14–December 2, 2011) Regarding Implementation of the International Covenant on Economic, Social and Cultural Rights—ICESCR in Israel," http://ccfisrael.org/wp-content/uploads/2011/07/CCFISRAEL-REPORT-TO-UN-7-7-2011.pdf

84. Eli Daniel, "Divorced Men Are Committing Suicide and the Feminist Inquisition is Celebrating," *Men and Fathers* (Blog); November 18, 2011, http://saloona.co.il/fathers/?p=41 [Hebrew]; Yaacon Ben Issaschar, "The Holocaust of the Divorced Fathers: 150 Are Killed Every Year," *News1: First Class*, December 4, 2011, http://www.news1.co.il/Archive/003-D-66620-00.html. [All, Hebrew]

85. Dana Spector, "Men in A Trap," *Yediot Aharonot*, January 27, 2012 [Hebrew].

86. Israeli Parliament, *Protocol of the Joint Committee of the Rights of the Child and the Committee of the Advancement of Women's Status* (February 7, 2012): 28–29.

87. Id., 41.

88. M.P. Yuav Kish, "Enough is Enough", Channel 7, April 6, 2016, https://www.inn.co.il/news/520732. [Hebrew]

89. Naomi Darom, "Divorce in Israel: The Dark Side of the Custody Battles," *Haaretz*, September 9, 2014, https://www.haaretz.co.il/magazine/.premium-1.2436824. [Hebrew]

90. Hacker and Halperin-Kaddari, "The Ruling Rules," 238.

91. Id., 287.

92. Jonathan Lis, "MPs: Fathers Harass Us because We Are against the Abolishing of the Tender Years Presumption," Haaretz, December 25, 2013, https://www.haaretz.co.il/news/politi/1.2199053. [Hebrew]

93. Zarhin Tomer, "Family Judges Complain of Growing Threats from Parents," *Haaretz*, August 29, 2012, https://www.haaretz.co.il/news/law/1.1811594. [Hebrew]

94. David M.J. Lazer et al., "The Science of Fake News: Addressing Fake News Requires a Multidisciplinary Effort," *Science* 359, no. 6380 (March 2018): 1094–96. doi: 10.1126/science.aao2998; Natalija Bitiukova et al., *Disinformation and Propaganda: Impact on the Functioning of the Rule of Law in the EU and Its Member States* (European Parliament's Policy Department for Citizens' Rights and Constitutional Affairs, 2018). http://www.europarl.europa.eu/RegData/etudes/STUD/2019/608864/IPOL_STU(2019)608864_EN.pdf; Björnstjern Baade, "Fake News and International Law," *The European Journal of International Law* 29, no. 4 (2018): 1357–76. doi: 10.1093/ejil/chy071 2019

95. For soft law of Internet service providers, see Natalie Alkiviadou, "Hate Speech on Social Media Networks: Towards a Regulatory Framework?" *Information and Communications Technology Law*, 28, no. 1 (2018): 19–35. doi: 10.1080/13600834.2018.1494417; David O. Klein, and Joshua R. Wueller, "Fake News: A Legal Perspective," *Journal of Internet Law* 20, no. 10 (2017): 1–13. Natalija Bitiukova et al., *Disinformation and Propaganda.*

96. For example, Daphna Hacker, "Children's Exclusion from Divorce Proceedings," *College of Management Law Review* 22 (2006): 63–72. [Hebrew]

97. See, also, Elizabeth S. Scott & Robert E. Emery, "Gender Politics and Child Custody: The Puzzling Persistence of the Best-Interests Standard," *Law and Contemporary Problems*, 77 (2014): 69–108; Laura Bernardi & Dimitri Mortelmans, "Advances in Research on Shared Physical Custody by Interdisciplinary Approaches," in *Shared Physical Custody*, eds. Laura Bernardi & Dimitri Mortelmans (Springer, 2021), 5–21.

98. *Israel National Council for the Child, Divorce and Children: Recommendation to the Shnit Committee*, on file with author. [Hebrew]

99. A recent alarming study found that the rate of divorce among the lower socioeconomic third in Israel is double that of the upper third. See Amit Kaplan and Anat Herbst, "Stratified Patterns of Divorce: Earnings, Education, and Gender,"

Demographic Research, 32 (2015): 949–82. No study is available on the impact of the recent shift toward joint physical custody and less child support paid by the father to the mother on poor children.

100. A recent legal reform encouraging divorce mediation in Israel is threatening to diminish children's participation in the process of shaping their family's post-divorce arrangement, as children are often excluded from mediation sessions.

101. While I have seen divorced fathers expose their children by, for example, bringing them to Parliamentary discussions, I hear of many mothers who refuse to do the same, preferring to protect their children's privacy and well-being.

Chapter 8

Homeschooling*

Elizabeth Bartholet

INTRODUCTION

The legal status of homeschooling in the United States stands in significant contrast to its status in the rest of the world. In the United States, there are virtually no meaningful restrictions governing homeschooling. It is a world of parental rights absolutism. In contrast, most other countries place significant restrictions on homeschooling. Some ban it altogether while others regulate to ensure that parents are qualified to teach and that they provide their children an adequate education. Relatedly, other countries place a much higher priority on child rights.

Homeschooling in the United States has grown rapidly, with now 3–4% of children homeschooled. Some think that the school shutdowns resulting from the COVID-19 pandemic may create a new population of homeschoolers after schools open up. A much smaller percentage of children are homeschooled in other countries, but the homeschooling movement here has been promoting elimination of restrictive regulations and expansion of homeschooling abroad.

This chapter focuses on the nature of the unregulated homeschooling regime here in the United States. It opens with a discussion of how the current approach abroad might serve as a model for regulatory reform here.

The homeschooling movement's aggressive advocacy in the United States has created a regime posing significant dangers to children and society. Parents can keep their children at home free from any real scrutiny as to

 This chapter relies substantially on Elizabeth Bartholet, "Homeschooling: Parent Rights Absolutism vs. Child Rights to Education & Protection," *Arizona Law Review* Vol. 62, No. 1 (2020). Many of the claims made here are discussed and documented in more detail there. Publications related to some of the issues in this chapter appear at https://bartholet.wpengine.com/child-welfare-issues/#homeschooling.

whether or how they are educating their children. Many homeschooling parents have legitimate reasons to educate their children at home. Many provide their children with high-quality education, comparable in scope to public education, and ensure that they engage with their peers and the larger society. But a significant subset homeschool because they want to isolate their children from society and shield them from ideas and values central to our democracy. Some provide an extremely narrow and limited form of education, or none at all. Some engage in abuse and neglect, free from the risk that teachers will report them to child protection services (CPS). This chapter calls for a radical transformation in the homeschooling regime in the United States, and a related rethinking of child rights.

Homeschooling here is a realm of near-absolute parental power. This power is inconsistent with important rights supposedly guaranteed to children under state constitutions and state legislation throughout the land. It is inconsistent with the human rights of children.

Children are at serious risk for ongoing abuse and neglect in the isolated families that constitute a significant part of the homeschooling world. Mandated reporters are key to child protection, and compulsory education has served to protect many children against maltreatment. Teachers and other education personnel have long been responsible for a significant percentage of all reports to CPS, larger than any other group. Parents have no obligation apart from compulsory education to get their children out of the home, where they can be observed by others and reported for obvious signs of maltreatment. Parents don't have to take their children to doctors. And unlike parents in many of our peer countries, they don't have to allow health practitioners into their homes during their children's infancy.

Homeschooling proponents make two primary arguments in defense of the current regime, one factual and one legal. The factual claim is that homeschooled children do as well as or better than public school children academically. The legal claim is that parent rights are and ought to be absolute.

The factual claim is largely based on flawed advocacy research that is not true social science.[1] We have no way of identifying the total group of homeschoolers, and thus no way of knowing how homeschoolers do on average. We do know that the great majority don't take the SAT or ACT or attend selective colleges and universities.[2] The research indicates that even the atypically successful subset of homeschoolers who attend college have some significant problems as compared to non-homeschoolers.[3]

But the homeschooling advocates' factual claim is also beside the point. Even if many homeschooled children did do acceptably on some academic measures, this would say nothing about significant subsets of homeschooled children we should be concerned about. These subsets include those whose parents are either uninterested in or incapable of educating their children and those whose parents subject them to serious abuse and neglect.

Also, academic success says nothing about success in terms of preparing students for civic engagement. Many homeschooled children miss out on exposure to others with different experiences and values. Most all miss out on extracurricular activities like student government and team sports. A large percentage of homeschooling parents are ideologically committed to isolating their children from the majority culture and indoctrinating them in views and values in conflict with that culture. Some believe that women should be subservient to men; others believe that race stamps some people as inferior. Many don't believe in the scientific method, looking to the Bible instead as their source for understanding.

The legal claim made in defense of the current homeschooling regime is based on dangerous ideas about parent rights—that those with enormous power over infants and children should be subject to virtually no check on that power. That parents should have monopoly control over children's lives, development, and experience. That parents are entitled to raise their children in isolation, so that they will replicate the parents' views and lifestyle choices.

This legal claim is inconsistent with children's right to what has been called an "open future"—the right to grow up to exercise meaningful choice about their own future views, religions, work, and lifestyles.

It is inconsistent with our legal and cultural history. From early on, our law recognized that the state has a role to play in child-rearing and that parents have responsibilities and not just rights.[4] Over the decades, law has played an increasingly active role guaranteeing children important rights, including rights to be free from labor and from unfair criminal punishment, along child rights to education and to protection against maltreatment.

The legal claim is also inconsistent with an idea central to compulsory education—that the state has a powerful interest in educating children in ways that enable positive participation in the larger society.

Finally, the legal claim stands in contrast with human-rights treaties and with the constitutional law of most other nations. These laws recognize that children have powerful rights both to education and to protection against maltreatment, and that nations have duties to protect those rights. They recognize the importance of an education exposing children to societal values and preparing them for civic engagement.

Current thinking about homeschooling issues in the United States is skewed by assumptions that *parents* have powerfully protected rights in the education and protection arenas, while *children* do not. Parents are said to have rights to raise and control their children, while children have no reciprocal rights to appropriate parental care. States are said to have rights to regulate education and to protect children if they choose to, but not *duties*. This way of thinking relates to the traditional understanding of our Federal Constitution as providing negative but not positive rights—rights to protection against state intervention but not rights to positive help from the state. This constitutional understanding leaves states free not to protect children if they choose not to.

The current homeschooling regime exists not because our society through its elected representatives has decided it *should*. It exists because homeschooling advocacy groups have become an overwhelming political force.

It seems obvious that any appropriate weighing of the interests at stake would result in significant reform legislation designed to guarantee children adequate education and protection. The question is whether we can move beyond current power politics to achieve such reform.

INTERNATIONAL LAW AS A MODEL FOR THE UNITED STATES

The U.S. Constitution with its negative rights structure is an anomaly, outdated and inadequate by the standards of the rest of the world. Negative rights—rights to be free from state intervention—are particularly inadequate for children, most of whom are incapable by virtue of their youth of the kind of autonomy that negative rights protect. The key rights for children are positive rights—rights to be provided for and protected by government so that they can grow up to enjoy autonomy and other adult rights.

The U.S. Constitution's focus on negative rights represents an older western constitutional tradition, "increasingly out of step with emerging constitutional norms . . . in the rest of the world."[5] Almost all other countries' constitutions provide positive rights, as do human-rights treaties. Other countries' legislative law provides significant restrictions on homeschooling, consistent with their constitutions and their treaty obligations.

Human Rights Treaties

The Convention on the Rights of the Child demands that nations honor child human rights equally with adult human rights.[6] It imposes a *duty* on nations to provide education and protection against maltreatment. Article 28(1) provides that nation states shall recognize the child's right to education, and Article 29(1) makes clear that this includes the right to be educated in ways that enable the child to respect societal values and to participate fully in society. Article 29(2) specifies that private schools must conform to minimum state standards. Article 19(1) provides that nation states "shall take all appropriate . . . measures to protect the child from all forms of physical or mental violence, injury or abuse, neglect or negligent treatment, maltreatment or exploitation."

Other human-rights treaties also provide children significant rights to education and protection. The International Covenant on Economic, Social and Cultural Rights provides a wide range of positive rights and requires that nation states ensure their full realization. It recognizes a broad right to education that includes the right to full development and the right to participate meaningfully in society with appreciation of societal values.[7] It specifies that private education must conform to minimum state standards.

The International Covenant on Civil and Political Rights provides extensive positive rights and imposes related duties on states, including by adopting legislative or other measures necessary. These rights include protection against private violence and private deprivation of liberty.[8]

Other Nations' Domestic Laws

Child rights to education and to protection against maltreatment are two of the four most popular positive social and economic rights in other countries' constitutions. A full two-thirds of all countries' constitutions include these rights.[9]

Most other countries impose far more restrictions on homeschooling than we do.[10] Many ban homeschooling altogether, others fail to legally recognize it, and many that allow homeschooling impose significant requirements, often including required home visits and annual testing.

European regulation ranges from restrictive to relatively permissive. On the restrictive end, several countries, including Bulgaria, Germany, the Netherlands, Sweden, and Spain, virtually or completely prohibit homeschooling. Germany's Federal Constitutional Court upheld the ban based partly on "the general interest . . . in avoiding the emergence of parallel societies based on separate philosophical convictions and the importance of integrating minorities," as well as the importance of exposing children to those with different backgrounds and beliefs.[11] The court noted that even if homeschooling could meet children's academic needs, the social integration required for a tolerant society could only be achieved through attendance at school. Sweden allows homeschooling only in "special circumstances"—religious or philosophical convictions do not qualify as valid reasons for homeschooling.

Many countries that allow homeschooling, such as Norway, Australia, and New Zealand, and a number of post-Communist countries, have strict regulation and very limited numbers of homeschoolers. China prohibits homeschooling.

European countries on the permissive end generally have far more restrictions than exist in the United States. They require registration and have some monitoring system, typically through annual school-administered tests, and sometimes also through home visits. Most require parents to follow the standard school curriculum. France permits homeschooling but requires notice and home visits, which include interviewing the child and reviewing the educational plan. It prescribes the subjects to be taught and requires that children attain the same standard by age 16 as those educated in school. The UK is unusual in having very little regulation.

South Africa allows homeschooling but has many requirements, including that parents "not instill unfair discrimination, racism or religious intolerance," and that the "values of the constitution of the Republic of South Africa prevail in the education."[12]

Israel allows homeschooling only under significant restrictions: parents must demonstrate they will provide an adequate education, will enable the child to interact with peers, that the child "will develop values relating to life in society," and that there will be adequate evaluation of learning success. Approval is conditioned on a home visit confirming that the child will receive a proper education, and parents must reapply every two years for an extension.[13] In Brazil there is no legislation authorizing homeschooling, and the highest court ruled recently that homeschooling was not lawful.

Regulation in other countries is not moving systematically in the direction of deregulation, as is the case in the United States. Many countries have instead been increasing restrictions including Canada, Australia, and a number of European countries.

HOMESCHOOLING IN THE UNITED STATES

The Facts

The Varied Nature of the Homeschooling Population

Parents choose to homeschool for a wide variety of reasons. Many have good reason to pursue an alternative to public school. Some feel that their children will be discriminated against in the public schools, denied disability accommodations, or bullied. Some want their children free to pursue demanding commitments in dance, sports, or theater, and others live in remote areas with no nearby schools, all falling into a category characterized as "practical" or "convenience" homeschooling. Some want to avoid the flaws they see in traditional education, such as an overemphasis on rote learning and testing, and others are concerned with the low quality of their local schools.

The majority of homeschooling parents are conservative Christians, with many motivated significantly by religious reasons.[14] Many reject mainstream, democratic values and want to ensure that their children adopt their parents' religious and social views. Many belong to fundamentalist religious groups, groups that Michael Rebell describes in his book, *Flunking Democracy*, as believing "that exposing their children to ideas such as secularism, atheism, feminism, and value relativism is inconsistent with the values they espouse and undermines their ability to inculcate in their children their beliefs in the sacred, absolute truth of the Bible."[15] Many use alternative textbooks that teach creationism instead of evolution. Many seek to create for their children a system of total socialization aimed at negating other influences.

Many religious homeschoolers object in principle to some core goals of public education:

> They reject the value of independent thinking about values and aims in life, they oppose instruction in scientific methodologies. . . . To the extent parents in this group do value secular learning, they treat it—even basic literacy—as of little importance compared to unflinching acceptance of religious doctrine and reactionary political views.[16]

Many homeschoolers raise their children in ways at odds with ideas about the importance of autonomy central to our liberal tradition:

> The children in some of these homes are being schooled quite intentionally for lives of submission to authority, not for autonomy. . . . They are discouraged from developing either the will or the skills to break those bonds.[17]

Some homeschooling parents are extreme religious ideologues who live in near-total isolation and hold views in serious conflict with core democratic values. Some believe that women should be totally subservient to men and educated in ways that promote such subservience.

Some engage in homeschooling to promote racist ideologies. A recent book describes a young leader of the white nationalist movement, Derek Black.[18] Pulled out of school because his parents wanted to avoid the Haitians and Hispanics in West Palm Beach's school system, he grew up totally immersed in the culture of white supremacy, encountering little in the way of diverse perspectives. His homeschooling education included building a children's website for Stormfront, the largest racist community on the Internet.

Many homeschooling parents have such limited education themselves that their ability to teach advanced academic subject matter is doubtful. Fifteen percent have less than a high-school degree; another 16% have no more than that. In 11% of homeschooling families neither parent speaks English.[19]

Many homeschooling parents are simply not interested in educating their children. Some remove their children from school to avoid truancy or child maltreatment charges, as discussed below.

An increasing number of parents are deciding to homeschool in order to avoid vaccination requirements as public authorities move to tighten up such requirements in order to address public health concerns.[20] Some parents choose to educate their children only in extraordinarily narrow skills—one father, for example, has focused his son's entire education on preparation for competitive video gaming.[21]

The Child Maltreatment Piece of the Homeschooling Picture

Child abuse and neglect characterize a subset of homeschooling families. Many parents choose homeschooling precisely because it enables them to escape the attention of CPS, since teachers and other school personnel are "mandated reporters" required by law to report suspected child maltreatment. Some parents take their children out of school when teachers report them for suspected violation of child protection laws.

In addition, the very isolation of so many homeschooling families puts children at risk. Child maltreatment takes place disproportionately in families cut off from the larger community.

There is no way now to determine the exact scope of the child maltreatment problem because, given the absence of regulation, we simply don't know all those who are in the homeschooling population. But we know enough to know that homeschooling in its current unregulated form poses serious risks of abuse and neglect. Many experts have voiced concern based on their research and experience.[22]

One telling study is a systematic analysis of all students withdrawn from school, allegedly for homeschooling, in six Connecticut school districts over a several-year period.[23] It found that of the 380 students withdrawn, more than one-third lived in families with at least one prior accepted report to CPS of child maltreatment and one-fourth lived in families with multiple prior reports.[24]

Child abuse pediatricians have found a very high percentage of home-schooled children represented in samples of extremely serious abuse cases. One study focused on a sample of cases involving horrific child torture.[25] Out of the school-age children, 76% were either never allowed to go to school or were withdrawn for homeschooling.

Homeschooling graduates have formed several organizations to voice their concerns with the risks homeschooling poses to children, including the risk of maltreatment. The leading organization, Coalition for Responsible Home Education (CRHE), has published research documenting evidence of the significant connection between child maltreatment and homeschooling.[26]

The Law

The U.S. Supreme Court and the state and lower federal courts have made it clear that states are free to establish a range of restrictions on homeschooling designed to ensure that children receive an adequate education. Few courts have indicated that strict scrutiny should be applied in assessing constitutionality, and few restrictions on homeschooling have been struck down.[27]

However, state law today imposes almost no restrictions. The homeschooling movement has been overwhelmingly successful in state legislatures over the past several decades, first legitimizing homeschooling in all states, next removing from the books almost all meaningful restrictions, and finally fighting off attempts to introduce new restrictions.

Homeschooling went from being illegal in many states in 1980 to being legal in all states today. Homeschooling requirements that had been common are now rare: for example, requirements that parents have some educational credentials such as high-school degrees, that they submit planned curricula, and that students be objectively tested for learning progress. The pace of this transformation has been breathtaking.

"Homeschooling now exists in a virtual legal void; parents have near-total authority over what their children learn and how they are disciplined."[28] Jeffrey Shulman recently conducted a 50-state survey on state regulation.[29] His research supports the above claim:

> Perhaps most egregious is the degree to which states allow children to fall off the regulatory radar altogether. About twelve states fail to impose any notification requirement on homeschoolers, effectively eliminating the need for contact with education officials. In about ten states requiring some form of notice, the requirement is limited to one-time notification, eliminating the need for any form of continuing outside contact. The notification requirement may be as simple as a mere statement of intent to homeschool, without further curricular detail or continuing assessment, and acceptance is almost always automatic. In some states, parents may escape a notification requirement altogether by homeschooling under the supervision of an "umbrella" private school itself free from attendance reporting requirements (usually because it is church-affiliated).
>
> Only about ten states require homeschooling instructors to have teaching qualifications, generally a high school diploma or its equivalence. But even this minimal guarantee of teacher competency may be bypassed by affiliation with an umbrella school, in response to religious objection, or at the discretion of local education officials.
>
> In at least fourteen states there are no curricular requirements. . . . Where pre-approval of a homeschooling curriculum is mandated, approval may be at the complete discretion of local education officials.
>
> In only about nine states are there relatively rigorous assessment requirements. Several states with assessment requirements do not require homeschoolers to submit testing results or impose minimal testing scores. In other states, parents may submit student portfolios in lieu of more objective test scores.

Homeschooling laws and regulations often provide special exemptions for religious homeschoolers, providing additional immunity from restrictions.

Even when restrictions exist on paper, they are often meaningless in reality, as typically there is little to no enforcement. Some states that set requirements for credentials, subjects taught, or instructional hours fail to require that parents submit the requisite information; others fail to review, or check the accuracy of information submitted. Parents may simply have to submit a letter saying they will teach certain subjects, and then they are free to do whatever they want. Assessment requirements are characterized by similarly lax enforcement. Dwyer and Peters' recent comprehensive study of homeschooling concludes that enforcement problems result in effectively no restrictions.[30]

The effective law of homeschooling is that parents are free to subject their children to abuse and neglect. Only a few states have legislation providing any protection at all to homeschooled children identified as at high risk for abuse and neglect. And the protection in those states is extremely limited. Pennsylvania bans homeschooling if any person in the household has been convicted of crimes in the past five years that would disqualify them from teaching in public school. But it relies on homeschooling parents to provide accurate information rather than conducting an independent background check. Arkansas bans homeschooling if a registered sex offender lives in the household but, rather than mandating a background check, relies on local school districts to take the initiative. Georgia recently passed a very limited law in response to the horrific torture and murder of two homeschooled students, providing only that child protective services be notified of homeschooling parents who fail to fill out a required declaration of intent to homeschool.

No state has a system requiring that homeschooling families be screened or monitored based on past or present CPS involvement and related evidence of maltreatment. Thus parents with extensive records of serious child maltreatment documented by CPS, parents who have had children removed to foster care or had their parental rights to children terminated based on prior maltreatment, can take children currently in their custody out of school for purposes of alleged homeschooling without any questions being raised.

When scandals have erupted involving horrific abuse suffered by children supposedly being homeschooled, the homeschooling movement has successfully fought off attempts to impose protective regulation. Examples abound of legislators proposing modest protective regulation only to be overwhelmed by the movement's lobbying force.[31]

The Politics

Ideological Nature and Political Dominance of the Homeschooling Movement

It is the religious ideologues who dominate the homeschooling movement. They founded the extraordinarily powerful Homeschooling Legal Defense

Association (HSLDA), which has played the leading role fighting against regulation. The different political strains and variety of populations represented within the homeschooling population are not reflected in the political leadership of the HSLDA.

Founded in 1983, the HSLDA grew at a phenomenal pace as it established leadership in the homeschooling advocacy world. Its advocacy efforts are backed by local homeschooling organizations in every state. It has branches in several other countries and encourages them to rally opposition to restrictive regulation abroad.

There is a wide range of critics of homeschooling, but none of them exercise real political power or have significant influence in shaping policy. Many who grew up homeschooled have spoken out about problems related both to education and to maltreatment. CRHE constitutes their main advocacy organization and is active in both documenting abuses and promoting legislative reform. However, it has not to date had a significant impact on law.

Professional educators are critical of homeschooling. The National Education Association (NEA), the nation's largest teachers' union, is against homeschooling being permitted at all,[32] and says that *if* permitted, licensing, curriculum, and testing requirements should apply. However, the NEA has not embraced this cause with anything resembling the passion and resources of the homeschooling movement.

Many serious academics have leveled severe criticism at the current homeschooling regime. Lawyers and other professionals with child maltreatment expertise have noted the risks to children in homeschooling. Researchers have worked internationally to critique the policy advocacy research put out by the homeschooling movement and to promote methodologically sound research.[33]

But it is the conservative religious homeschoolers that engage aggressively in the courts and legislatures. They overwhelmingly dominate policy advocacy. They are well-financed, well-organized, and passionately motivated to push their particular cause. As a result, like the gun lobby, they wield political power vastly disproportionate to their numbers.

So while there are many critics of homeschooling, they have to date proven powerless on the advocacy battlefield.

Positions and Tactics of the Homeschooling Movement

The homeschooling movement takes the position that parents have, and should have, absolute power over the education of their children. It relies on both natural law and on constitutional theory. The constitutional claim looks to cases recognizing parent rights as part of the liberty guaranteed by substantive due process, and to religious freedom guarantees.

Movement advocates generally contend that any restrictions on homeschooling violate parent rights, even such minimal requirements as registration.

The movement also opposes other restrictions on parent power including in the area of child maltreatment. To this end, HSLDA created a new organization, ParentalRights.org (PRO). PRO advocates amending the Federal Constitution to further expand and entrench parental power.[34] Its proposed amendment would effectively establish a strict scrutiny standard governing all state intervention in the family on behalf of children. The extremes of its position are illustrated by the stated limit: "this article shall not be construed to apply to a parental action or decision that would end life." [35]

The homeschooling movement has opposed U.S. ratification of the Convention on the Rights of the Child (CRC). Ratified by every other country in the world, the CRC gives child rights equal status with adult rights. It gives children affirmative rights to be educated and protected against maltreatment, imposing related duties on nations. The movement considers this vindication of child human rights a wrongful threat to parental power.

PRO has a companion organization called the Parental Rights Foundation. It engages in advocacy challenging CPS efforts to protect children.[36]

The homeschooling movement has been both strategic and brutal in its tactics. The HSLDA has built its membership to impressive numbers, providing a significant base of financial support and a large list of potential lobbyists. It now has over 80,000 families, a full-time staff of dozens, and annual revenue of well over $11 million.

Membership benefits include a guarantee of legal representation in any situation where homeschooling parents are threatened with restrictions related to education or child protection. Members are promised a 24/7 emergency hotline, and legal representation by an experienced litigation team.

HSLDA founded a Political Action Committee in 2003, dedicated to supporting pro-homeschooling candidates for federal office. HSLDA maintains a Legislative Action Center and encourages its members to get involved in lobbying locally and nationally.

HSLDA has demonstrated its lobbying power in numerous recent cases where it has successfully beaten back proposed regulatory reform introduced in response to homeschooling scandals.[37]

A recent comprehensive book on homeschooling credits HSLDA's legislative success to its "ability to foment outrage among homeschoolers . . . causing any legislator who supports . . . regulation to become the victim of a relentless barrage of hostile communications—occasionally including death threats—by mail, email, and office visits."[38] A recent article quotes a state legislative aide: "I've never seen a lobby more powerful and scary."[39]

HSLDA uses these tactics not just to bully legislators, but to shut down all discussion, as I have recently experienced. In March 2020, I published a law review article on homeschooling, and engaged in related media interviews. With others I have been planning a homeschooling conference to discuss concerns and possible reform initiatives. These initiatives have triggered a barrage of hostile attacks, including more than one thousand emails, tweets, and telephone messages. Many are hate-filled, obscenity-laced, personal attacks. Many wish me a prolonged, torturous death. Some contain veiled or not so veiled threats—one warns, for example, that people who say the kinds of thing I do have been murdered. The goal is clearly to silence me and shut down our planned conference.[40]

These attacks are telling not just in terms of the tactics used by the homeschooling movement, but also its political power. Secretary of State Mike Pompeo and Senator Ted Cruz have tweeted repeated personal attacks on me. Right-wing radio personality Rush Limbaugh has used his shows to go after me, claiming that I personify the problems with liberalism, and making sure to spell my name repeatedly so that all can know whom to target. Many dozens of right-wing media articles have condemned me. The attacks are also telling in terms of the values expressed. Many talk of their God-given right to total control over their child, free from any intervention by the state whatsoever. One says that my thinking illustrates why women shouldn't be allowed to open their mouths without first taking an IQ test.

Similar tactics have been used to silence other academic critics. One leading intellectual had a project some years ago analyzing the constitutional issues surrounding homeschooling. Online publication of an excerpt triggered such an onslaught of hostility that the project was dropped.

THE WAY FORWARD

The current homeschooling regime gives parents free rein to educate their children or not, free rein to commit egregious child abuse, and free rein to isolate their children entirely from society.

The homeschooling movement relies on adult autonomy rights to oppose all homeschooling regulation. But such rights should not trump child rights to an education allowing them to exercise autonomy rights in their future lives, including rights to make career and lifestyle choices. The movement relies on adult religious freedom rights to oppose regulation. But such rights should not trump child rights to exposure to alternative views, enabling them to exercise future choice about their own religion.

We need a new legal regime designed to ensure that all children actually enjoy the rights to an adequate education and to adequate protection against child maltreatment that appear to be guaranteed by law.

But given the current politics of homeschooling, legislatures are not likely to enact significant reform on their own initiative. Accordingly, to move forward, we need a change in the culture surrounding child rights generally and their rights to education and protection in particular. We need a new understanding of children's constitutional and human rights, and related political and litigation campaigns.

Constitutional doctrine should recognize that children have enforceable *rights* to an appropriate education and to protection against maltreatment. This would mean that legislatures could be *required* to enact legislation protecting those rights.

DEVELOPING A CONSTITUTIONAL DUTY TO EDUCATE AND PROTECT CHILDREN IN THE UNITED STATES

The building blocks already exist in the United States for developing appropriate constitutional doctrine guaranteeing children's affirmative rights to education and protection against maltreatment.[41]

There are bases in current law for concluding that the Federal Constitution provides children with positive rights to education and protection. One lies in substantive due process and the other in equal protection doctrine.[42] Lawyers have recognized the potential for using the Constitution to achieve educational reform, mounting challenges in different federal courts with the goal of getting the Supreme Court to find that schools that fail to provide a minimally adequate education violate child rights.[43] A similar campaign could be mounted challenging the current homeschooling regime.

However, while it is easy to argue for the direction that the Court *should* move in interpreting the Constitution, it does not seem likely that the current court *will* so move in any near future. The current majority is not enthusiastic about expanding individual rights. The Court's *DeShaney* case is a significant barrier, with the majority finding that the child had no constitutional right to state action providing protection against the father's brutal abuse.[44] Another barrier is the Court's general interpretation of the Constitution as providing negative rather than positive rights. The best hope now for any litigation strategy lies in the state courts.

State constitutions have a powerful positive rights tradition. Emily Zackin documents in her book, *Looking for Rights in All the Wrong Places*, how state constitutions have established extensive positive rights in the areas of education, labor, and the environment.[45] Some state constitutions also recognize positive rights to health and welfare. Jeffrey Sutton's book, *51 Imperfect Solutions*, makes a convincing case that state constitutions may provide the most promising source of rights in education and other arenas.[46]

All states provide in their constitutions support for children's rights to education.[47] Litigation in state courts based on these provisions has been very successful, both in challenging inequitable funding systems and in challenging substantive educational inadequacy. Michael Rebell points out that in recent education adequacy cases, many state courts have given teeth to the right to an adequate education, specifying that it includes important academic and vocational capacities, and includes civic understanding and preparation "to function productively as civil participants."[48] Courts in almost half the states have held that their constitutions' educational provisions guarantee the right to an adequate education, and that a primary purpose of education is to prepare students for civic participation, including employment. Zackin discusses the rationale for these constitutional provisions as follows:

> It is important to realize that public education in America has long been, and continues to be, understood not only as a means of elevating the individual and preparing him for the responsibilities of citizenship, but also of protecting the republic itself.[49]

These state constitutional provisions on education provide a strong basis for challenges to the homeschooling regime.

A variety of other existing state constitutional provisions provide an opportunity to expand child rights to protection. Two-thirds of state constitutions guarantee the right to pursue happiness, and some provide the right to safety.[50] Many state constitutional provisions provide rights related to care of the needy and protection of health. Some of these provide for "legal, social and economic justice," and "opportunity for the fullest development of the individual." Some provide rights for those of "immature age," and others "unable to provide or care for themselves."[51]

Positive rights have often been added to state constitutions over the years in response to the needs of groups with relatively limited political power—groups that have failed to achieve their goals in state legislatures. They have sought these constitutional amendments specifically to force the hand of recalcitrant legislators.

Child advocates might buttress a litigation campaign relying on current state constitutional provisions, with a strategy to strengthen protection through state constitutional amendments.

RECOMMENDED RESTRICTIONS

States should impose significant restrictions on homeschooling. Legislatures should ideally do this on their own initiative. But courts must make clear that the current regime violates children's constitutional rights, and that restrictions along the lines described below are *required.*

The new regime should place the burden on parents who want to homeschool to demonstrate that they have a legitimate need, and that they are capable of and committed to providing education comparable in scope to that provided in public schools. Parents should be screened by CPS and disqualified from homeschooling for any record of serious abuse or neglect. Homeschooled children should be tested for learning progress on an annual basis, at minimum, with tests administered by public authorities.

When homeschooling is allowed, children should still be required to attend some courses and extracurricular programs at school. This is important to ensure socialization, contact with mandated reporters, and exposure to alternative views and values. The goal is not to indoctrinate children in any orthodoxy but to expose them to a wide range of views. It is to prepare them to function as citizens. And it is to enable meaningful choices in their future lives about their own views, religions, work, and lifestyles.

CONCLUSION: A NEW POLITICAL AND LEGAL REALITY

Regulatory reform along the lines sketched above *should* be possible, if legislators made decisions based on weighing the interests at stake. But the reality is that such reform will not happen without a political sea change. Critics of homeschooling regularly express despair about the prospects for even modest regulatory reform.

There are many thoughtful critics of homeschooling who have called for significant reform. But they have wielded no power capable of countering the organized political force of the homeschooling movement.

And these critics have limited political potential. Academics don't generally get involved in policy advocacy beyond writing articles. Homeschooling graduates don't have the same kind of motivation that members of other groups often have to advocate for change. By definition, they have graduated out of homeschooler status. Even those who felt victimized by their homeschooling experience will for the most part want simply to move on with their lives. Other critics of homeschooling don't seem to have the motivation that homeschooling parents have to fight the regulatory battle.

What is needed is a true child rights movement. Yet creation of such a movement has always been a challenge. Children are by definition powerless, totally powerless in early childhood, and disenfranchised until adulthood.

The courts may be essential to move things forward. Constitutions are supposed to protect the rights of those with no potential for protecting themselves through political systems.[52] Children are the quintessential politically powerless group.

NOTES

1. On the research, see generally Bartholet, "Homeschooling," Subsection I.D; Robert Kunzman and Milton Gaither, "Homeschooling: An Updated Comprehensive Survey of the Research," *Other Education: The Journal of Educational Alternatives*, Vol. 9, No. 1 (2020).

2. Kunzman and Gaither, "Homeschooling," 21.

3. See Bartholet, "Homeschooling," section I.D.1.

4. Jeffrey Shulman, "Private School Regulation: Individual Rights and Educational Responsibilities," in *The Oxford Handbook of Children and The Law*, ed. James G. Dwyer (Oxford: Oxford University Press, 2020): 702.

5. Evan Rosevear, Ran Hirschl, and Courtney Jung, "Justiciable and Aspirational Economic and Social Rights in National Constitutions," in *The Future of Economic and Social Rights*, ed. Katharine G. Young (Cambridge: Cambridge University Press, 2019): 37–65.

6. United Nations, "United Nations Convention on the Rights of the Child," United Nations Treaty Series, Vol. 1577, p. 3 (New York: United Nations Treaty Collection, 1989).

7. United Nations, "United Nations International Covenant on Economic, Social and Cultural Rights (ICESCR)," United Nations Treaty Series, Vol. 999, p. 171 and Vol. 1057, p. 407 (New York: United Nations Treaty Collection, 1966) [hereinafter ICESCR].

8. United Nations, "United Nations International Covenant on Civil and Political Rights," United Nations Treaty Series Vol. 999, p. 171 and Vol. 1057, p. 407 (New York: United Nations Treaty Collection, 1966).

9. Katharine G. Young, "Introduction," in *The Future of Economic and Social Rights*, ed. Katharine G. Young (Cambridge: Cambridge University Press, 2019): 5.

10. Milton Gaither, *The Wiley Handbook of Home Education* (Hoboken: Wiley-Blackwell, 2016): see generally Chapters 12–20; Kunzman and Gaither, "Homeschooling," 40–48; Bartholet, "Homeschooling," section I.V.2.

11. Daniel Monk, "Home Education: A Human Right?" in *International Perspectives on Home Education: Do We Still Need Schools?* ed. Paula Rothermel (London: Palgrave Macmillan, 2015): 171–72.

12. Michael Olalekan Olatunji, "Contemporary Homeschooling and the Issue of Racism: The Case of South Africa," in *The Wiley Handbook* (Hoboken: Wiley-Blackwell, 2016): 497–98, 507.

13. Arnon Gutfeld and Yoram Rabin, "Homeschooling in the U.S. and Its Lesson for Israel," *Israel Yearbook on Human Rights*, Vol. 47 (October 2017): 215–17.

14. Estimates range widely, from a majority up to 90%. See Bartholet, "Homeschooling," footnote 33.

15. Michael A. Rebell, *Flunking Democracy: Schools, Courts, and Civic Participation* (Chicago: Chicago University Press, 2018): 86.

16. James G. Dwyer and Shawn F. Peters, *Homeschooling: The History and Philosophy of a Controversial Practice* (Chicago: Chicago University Press, 2019): 204.

17. Robin West, *Religious Rights as Protected Wrongs: The Case of Homeschooling* (unpublished manuscript: on file with author, 2013): 17.

18. Eli Saslow, *Rising out of Hatred: The Awakening of a Former White Nationalist* (New York: Doubleday, 2018).

19. Meghan McQuiggan and Mahi Megra, *Parent and Family Involvement in Education: Results from The National Household Education Surveys Program Of 2016: First Look* (Washington DC: U.S. Department of Education, 2017): 18.

20. This has been a huge issue in New York and California, for example, as discussed in Bartholet, "Homeschooling," footnote 65.

21. Dugan Arnett, "With Dad's Support, One Teen is Playing 'Fortnite' Instead of Going to High School," The Boston Globe, July 6, 2019, https://www.bostonglobe.com/metro/2019/07/06/father-son-all-teen-bid-for-esports-stardom/EhZCdGUDYouhT2DEkilhCL/story.html

22. See generally Bartholet, Homeschooling, section IC.

23. State of Connecticut: Office of the Child, "Advocate, Examining Connecticut's Safety Net for Children Withdrawn from School for the Purpose of Homeschooling—Supplemental Investigation to OCA's December 12, 2017 Report Regarding the Death of Matthew Tirado" (2018): 1–2, http://www.ct.gov/oca/lib/oca/OCA.Memo.Homeschooling.4.25.2018.pdf.

24. Emily Putnam-Hornstein, "Report of Maltreatment as a Risk Factor for Injury Death: A Prospective Birth Cohort Study," *Child Maltreatment,* Vol. 16, No. 3 (2011): 163, 171–72 (Prior reports are known to be the best predictors of maltreatment, regardless of whether those reports are substantiated. A "prior allegation to CPS" found "the strongest independent risk factor for injury mortality before the age of five").

25. Barbara Knox et al., "Child Torture as a Form of Child Abuse," *Journal of Child and Adolescent Trauma*, Vol. 7, No. 1 (2014): 7.

26. Coalition for Responsible Education (CRHE), "At-Risk Homeschooled Children: An Issue Brief" (2017): 2–4. https://www.responsiblehomeschooling.org/wp-content/uploads/2017/05/CRHE-At-Risk-Children-Brief.pdf; see also CRHE, "Some Preliminary Data on Homeschool Child Fatalities, Homeschooling's Invisible Children" (2016) ("Our preliminary research suggests that homeschooled children are at a greater risk of dying from child abuse than are traditionally schooled children"), NEE.

27. Bartholet, "Homeschooling," section II.A.

28. Kathryn Joyce, "The Homeschool Apostates," The American Prospect, February 9, 2014, http://prospect.org/article/homeschool-apostates.

29. Jeffrey Shulman, *50-State Survey: Home School Regulations: Notification, Certification, Curriculum and Assessment Requirements* (unpublished manuscript: on file with author, 2018).

30. Dwyer and Peters, *Homeschooling*, at 67–68, 70–72.

31. Bartholet, "Homeschooling," at III.C.2.b.

32. National Education Association, "2020–2021 NEA Resolutions" (2020): 37, https://www.nea.org/sites/default/files/2020-09/NEA%20Resolutions_2020-2021.pdf ("The National Education Association believes that homeschooling programs based on parental choice cannot provide the student with a comprehensive education experience").

33. See discussion of ICHER in Bartholet, "Homeschooling," Subsection I.D.2.

34. Christopher Lubienski, Tiffany Puckett, and T. Jameson Brewer, "Does Homeschooling 'Work'? A Critique of the Empirical Claims and Agenda of Advocacy Organizations," *Peabody Journal of Education*, Vol. 88, No. 3 (2013): 378, 389; "Protecting Children by Empowering Parents," *ParentalRights.org*, last visited September 22, 2020, https://parentalrights.org/.

35. "The Amendment," *ParentalRights.org*, last visited September 22, 2020, https://parentalrights.org/amendment/.

36. "About Us," *Parental Rights Foundation*, last visited September 22, 2020, https://parentalrights.org/about/.

37. See cases described in Bartholet, "Homeschooling," 53–56.

38. Dwyer and Peters, *Homeschooling*, 65.

39. Jessica Huseman, "Small Group Goes to Great Lengths to Block Homeschooling Regulation," ProPublica, August 27, 2015, https://www.propublica.org/ article/small-group-goes-great-lengths-to-block-homeschooling-regulation.

40. Liz Mineo, "A Warning on Homeschooling," *The Harvard Gazette*, May 15, 2020, https://news.harvard.edu/gazette/story/2020/05/law-school-professor-says-there-may-be-a-dark-side-of-homeschooling/; Bartholet et al., "No Need for Bullying in The Debate on Homeschooling," The Imprint, May 26, 2020, https://imprintnews.org/child-welfare-2/no-need-bullying-in-debate-homeschooling/43876.

41. See generally Rebell, *Flunking Democracy*, 124–74, 160–66; Dwyer and Peters, *Homeschooling*, 199, 227–28; Anne C. Dailey and Laura A. Rosenbury, "The New Law of the Child," *The Yale Law Review,* Vol. 127, No. 6 (April 2018): 1448–537; Jeffrey Shulman, "Toward Constitutional Parenthood," *The Constitutional Parent: Rights, Responsibilities, and the Enfranchisement of the Child* (New Haven: Yale University Press, 2014).

42. Bartholet, "Homeschooling," section IV.B.1.

43. See generally "Chapter 7: Advancing Civic Preparation Through the Federal Courts," in Rebell, *Flunking Democracy*, 151; Dana Goldstein, "Are Civics Lessons A Constitutional Right? This Student is Suing for Them," N.Y. Times, November 28, 2018, https://www.nytimes.com/2018/11/28/us/civics-rhode-island-schools.html?smtyp=cur&smid=tw-nytimes.

44. *DeShaney v. Winnebago County Department of Social Services*, 489 U.S. (1989): 189, 195, 197.

45. Emily J. Zackin, *Looking for Rights in All the Wrong Places: Why State Constitutions Contain America's Positive Rights* (Princeton: Princeton University Press, 2013): 1–17. Also see generally Chapters 5–7.

46. Jeffrey Sutton, *51 Imperfect Solutions: States and the Making of American Constitutional Law* (Oxford: Oxford University Press, 2018).

47. Michael A. Rebell, *Courts and Kids: Pursuing Educational Equity Through the State Courts* (Chicago: Chicago University Press, 2013): 17–18.

48. Michael A. Rebell, "The Right to Education in the American State Courts," in *The Future of Economic and Social Rights*, ed. Katharine G. Young (Cambridge: Cambridge University Press, 2019): 143–144.

49. Zackin, *Looking for Rights*, 74–75.

50. Carol N. Chodroff, "Children's Need for Safe Housing," *Children's Legal Rights Journal*, Vol. 24, No. 1 (2004): 3–4.

51. Sarah Ramsey and Daan Braveman, "Let Them Starve: Government's Obligation to Children in Poverty," *Temple Law Review*, Vol. 68, No. 1 (1995): 1623.

52. *United States v. Carolene Products Company*, 304 U.S. (1938): 144, 152.

Part III

CHILDREN

SITUATING THE CHILD WITHIN THE LEGAL SYSTEM AND GLOBAL NORMS

Chapter 9

Global Norms in the Context of Corporal Punishment against Children

Melissa L. Breger, Lucy Sorensen, Victor Asal, and Charmaine N. Willis

INTRODUCTION

For centuries, the law and its courts have shaped the parent-child relationship across the globe.[1] Rights have ebbed and flowed across the so-called "triad" of rights—the child, the parents, and the government. Rights have fluctuated from laws that favor the government's ability to regulate parenting—to laws that view parental rights as supreme—to laws that expressly validate children's individual rights.

Fundamentally, parents' rights to control and guide the upbringing of their children have enduring and deep roots in legal history. The legal system has routinely held parental rights in great deference, viewing the business of raising children as a "private" matter. In fact, early laws did not even reflect the concept of individual children's rights. Illustratively, older English laws and theories, such as "the chattel theory," viewed children as the actual physical property of their parents, specifically of their fathers.[2]

In recent decades across the globe, children's individual rights have begun to strengthen. Indeed, in certain contexts, children's rights have even been considered on par with parental rights, particularly in progressive child-centered countries in Scandinavia. Although there are still many nations that do not honor children as individuals possessing their own legal rights, increasingly, children's rights continue to be delineated and amplified in countries across the world.

The clearest example of an international evolution of child rights in a law or treaty is evident in the United Nations Convention on the Rights of the Child (CRC). Every nation worldwide, except the United States, has both signed and ratified this treaty; the United States has signed, but not yet ratified it.[3] At least theoretically, demonstrated by the groundswell of support for the treaty (the most ratified international treaty to date), children's individual human rights have been steadily advancing.

THE PSYCHOLOGICAL EFFECTS OF CORPORAL PUNISHMENT UPON CHILDREN

Psychological and scientific data has repeatedly held that physical corporal punishment of children by parents or caretakers has deleterious effects upon children both in childhood and later in teenage and adult years.[4] The psychological literature, particularly within the trauma body of work, has persistently and consistently signaled that violence begets more violence; violence in the home can lead to a child becoming a violent teenager or adult, or a victim of interpersonal violence later in life.[5] Governments and organizations across the globe have therefore espoused views condemning physical discipline of children in the home. Many countries have increasingly banned the practice.[6] However, many nations across the globe not only allow the practice of corporal punishment under their laws but encourage it as a form of appropriate discipline for children.

The consequences of violence in the home—of any kind—may manifest in the child in the form of anxiety disorders. These disorders include post-traumatic stress disorder (PTSD), which can include resultant mental health issues, such as depression and suicidal ideation,[7] or other consequential behaviors, such as "acting out, bedwetting and elimination disorders."[8] The psychological and social science literature is replete with indications that PTSD is commonly associated with violence or other trauma.[9]

Children who have been physically disciplined by their parents grow up with this learned behavior as the norm, and subsequently may later hit their own children.[10] Family violence in general is cyclical and intergenerational.[11] For example, a 2011 study of a county in central China, conducted by several United Nations agencies, found that men who witnessed their mothers being beaten, when they were children, were at least three times more likely to beat their own children, when compared to men who had not witnessed such violence.[12]

Certainly, it should be noted that there are critics of the conclusion that all physical discipline is damaging to children, often pointing to the fact that physical abuse and physical discipline are distinct, and discipline perhaps can even be beneficial. They view physical discipline as an appropriate way to shape or curb a child's misbehavior, whereas child abuse is a separate issue. While this may be true in the purest sense of the words, often parental discipline falls into a gray area, instead of into black and white categories of corporal punishment versus excessive or abusive corporal punishment.

This chapter takes the normative stance that any physical discipline is harmful to children, and many would argue—including the American Academy of Pediatrics (AAP), as will be explained in detail here—that physical discipline is harmful regardless of intent or excessiveness on the part of the parent.[13] Why then do a fair amount of countries and nations legalize and even espouse physical discipline instead of non-physical punishments like time-outs, taking away privileges, and the like? What factors weigh in the equation about which countries, states, and nations permit physical corporal punishment by parents and caretakers? These questions inspired our research to examine countries worldwide and their laws (or lack of laws) about physical discipline of children in the home.

COMMON LAW, STATUTES, AND LAWS

Many parenting laws reflect the norms of the particular countries where they emanate. As far back as the ancient Greeks, Hebrews, Romans and Babylonians, fathers had a proprietary interest in their children, thus allowing the sale, exchange, or even killing of their children.[14] During the Colonial era through the early 19th century, immigrants who came to the United States brought with them the tradition of corporal punishment, which was thought to be a necessary means of restraint to correct sinful or immoral behavior.[15] Even during the Enlightenment period, when parents were advised to be loving and tender with their children, they were to command strict obedience at an early age.[16] It was not until later in the 19th century that young Western settlers began to abandon the harsh rule of parental supremacy.[17] Yet, in many parts of the globe, parental supremacy still reigns.[18]

In certain cultures, corporal punishment is not viewed as detrimental but rather as a tool to aid in child development.[19] In other segments of society, where parents are concerned about raising children in a society that often condemns those of a different nationality, race, and class, children need to be reared to follow rules in order to protect themselves from harm by the government or law enforcement.[20] Thus, strict discipline in the home is seen as enabling children to flourish in society.[21] Furthermore, in some regions, parents are seen as having an actual duty to discipline their children even if harshly.[22] Still other countries have entirely outlawed physical discipline against children in the home, such as in Sweden, Norway, New Zealand, Honduras, Brazil, and Portugal.[23] For various reasons, some countries are further behind than others in their progress on children's rights.

In many countries, there is variance even within the same nation's borders. This is most apparent within the United States, because there are 50 individual states and no overarching federal Supreme Court precedent pertaining exclusively to child corporal punishment in the home. State laws govern what type and to what extent physical corporal punishment is allowed, and also when the discipline is too excessive and deemed to be child abuse and/or child neglect. As can be expected, these definitions vary in many ways within the nation.[24]

Ultimately, state laws governing each of the 50 U.S. states dictate the severity, the extent, the method, and the permissibility of various forms of parental discipline.[25] No real uniformity exists across the 50 states about what types of corporal punishment are allowed, tolerated, or punished. Significantly, however, in 2019, the AAP published an updated statement hardening their stance and shifting their approach relating to parental discipline.[26] The policy statement condemns corporal punishment as an effective means of parental discipline. In its 2019 policy statement, the AAP defines corporal punishment as "non-injurious, open-handed hitting with the intention of modifying child behavior."[27] The AAP cites evidence to suggest that corporal punishment is not an effective strategy for disciplining children, and it cites research that demonstrates a correlational relationship between children who are disciplined with corporal punishment and those who later on develop behavioral problems and aggressive and depressive symptoms.[28] Due to an increase in research on this topic, pediatricians are more confident stating that parents should refrain from hitting and verbally insulting their children and instead set behavioral expectations and practice positive reinforcement of good behavior. Whether this unprecedented statement condemning corporal punishment from a national group of pediatricians will have any effect upon the laws of any particular state remains to be seen, but it certainly is a normative and possibly a transformative shift in American societal views, which is one example of changing global norms on the topic.[29]

The Impact of the CRC

One source of guidance across all countries on the topic of child corporal punishment emerges from an international human-rights treaty mentioned in the introduction of this chapter. Specifically, the CRC, the most widely ratified human-rights treaty in the world,[30] offers some guidance on a whole range of legal issues and rights pertaining to children. When a country signs but does not ratify a treaty—as is the case of the United States with respect to the CRC—that country is still bound not to contravene the treaty's object or purposes.[31] Thus, to some extent, the CRC retains force and legitimacy even in the United States.

As a whole, the CRC conveys humanitarian, economic, social, cultural, political and legal rights to the individual child, thereby allowing children's rights to parallel those of adults.[32] The CRC challenged the use of corporal punishment, labeling the practice as a violation of children's dignity and a form of violence against children. Article 19 guarantees that children are protected from physical and mental violence.

Despite the progressive provisions contained in the CRC, many would argue that enforcement is weak. Although 194 countries ratified the agreement,[33] corporal punishment in homes most certainly still exists across the globe.[34]

THE INTERDISCIPLINARY RESEARCH TEAM AND THE DATA SET EXAMINING CORPORAL PUNISHMENT IN THE HOME IN EVERY COUNTRY

In the fall of 2017, the Interdisciplinary Research Team met to define goals for the study. Several law students collected information on the changing legal status of corporal punishment by assessing reports from two existing sources: (1) reports on every state and territory from the Global Initiative to End All Corporal Punishment of Children[35] and (2) country reports from the UN Committee on the Rights of the Child.[36] These sources were examined to determine the status and original date of legal bans on corporal punishment in the home, inter alia, in 192 countries from 1970 to 2016.

As a party to the CRC, each country is required to submit an initial report and subsequent periodic reports to the United Nations, detailing a variety of things.[37] Parties to the CRC are required to take steps to eliminate the corporal punishment of children and report on any progress or challenges. As such, the researchers examined reports submitted to the United Nations, looking specifically for any discussion on societal norms regarding corporal punishment and attempts to modify beliefs and behaviors surrounding corporal punishment.

Researchers additionally reviewed all reports submitted to the United Nations' Committee on the Rights of the Child, searching for terms including "corporal punishment," "discipline," "hit," "slap," and "spank," and reviewed all sections that addressed the disciplining of children in the home. Each report was then coded based on the depth of reporting on corporal punishment of children. The designation of "0" was assigned to reports that did not make any mention of corporal punishment in their self-reports. The designation of "1" was assigned to reports that made some mention of corporal punishment but did not provide detail on the rates of corporal punishment nor steps that have been taken to prevent corporal punishment. Finally, the designation of "2" was assigned to reports that provided detail on the occurrence of corporal punishment and the steps taken to prevent corporal punishment. We noted several interesting trends, which are explained below.

SOCIAL NORMS THEORY, RE-NORMING, AND NORM CASCADES

One trend that we noticed is that the norms surrounding physical discipline in a country started to affect nearby countries. For example, as we explain below, when Sweden issued zero tolerance for physical discipline, many of the Scandinavian countries followed soon thereafter. One way to interpret the trend is to look at a country's norms. Norms are the rules and expectations of behavior within a specific culture.[38] Looking to the norms within a specific culture can shed light on what behavior is deemed acceptable and customary within that culture.[39] If a society wishes to change the frequency of a particular behavior, it would work to change its set of norms to reflect that the behavior is no longer deemed acceptable. The law, and what is permissible behavior under the law, can serve as a normalizing force in society, defining what will and will not be acceptable as the norm.[40] When utilizing social norms theory to decrease negative behavior, we see success in many types of behavior, such as increasing community safety, decreasing drunk driving, and stigmatizing domestic violence.[41] In this chapter, we apply norms to corporal punishment of children by caretakers and parents in the home.

Norm cascades, coined by law professor Cass Sunstein, are part of social norms theory and focus upon considerable transformations within social norms.[42] The norms focus upon certain behavior and deem it appropriate, which has been shown to "promote pro-social behavior." The most recent example of a norm cascade has been the #MeToo movement, which has served to alter societal perception of the minimizing and normalization of sexual assault.[43] Professor Sunstein explains[44] that "norm cascades occur when societies are presented with rapid shifts toward new norms."[45] Finnemore and Sikkink explain how the term is used in their arena:

> Norm influence may be understood as a three-stage process. . . . The first stage is "norm emergence"; the second stage involves broad norm acceptance, which we term, following Cass Sunstein, "norm cascade"; and the third stage involves internalization. The first two stages are divided by a threshold or "tipping" point, at which a critical mass of relevant state actors adopt the norm.[46]

We are using specifically the theoretical framework of norm cascades to explain how Scandinavian countries and other parts of Europe followed Sweden's lead over a period of years. We also suggest in our conclusion, that potentially another pertinent norm cascade could be started in other countries, if desired, or even intra-country.

Another somewhat related concept to norm cascades is the idea of "re-norming," which came about in the context of research into group dynamics and team building.[47] One way to describe re-norming is as a process by which "new ideas are implemented," and members within the group adjust to these new ideas.[48] Again, when we look at the broader body of literature on social norms research, the theory examines individuals and their perceptions of how others in society behave.[49] The theory is often utilized in the context of reducing negative behavior or at least reducing the normalization of such behavior, such as with drunk driving, sexual assault, or narcotics use.

Some research examining re-norming in the context of domestic violence can be instructive here. For example, when the World Bank studied 100 countries and their domestic violence laws, it looked at how the laws affected societal views and acceptance of such violence.[50] It was noted that in 1995, only 13 of 100 countries had laws outlawing domestic violence.[51] "By 2013, that number had increased to seventy-six out of 100 countries."[52] A World Bank report found that in countries that had enacted anti-domestic violence legislation, women's acceptance of spousal abuse became lower than in other countries where domestic violence was still permitted by law.[53]

Ultimately, in this chapter, we studied if this pattern emerged in the case of corporal punishment against children in the home. One thing we note is that the phenomenon of re-norming to decrease toxic norms is most effective if started during early childhood, and is later reinforced with law and education.[54] In the next sections, we apply these theoretical frameworks to the countries we studied in our data set.

TRENDS IN OUR RESEARCH

In researching the raw data, as well as the self-reporting CRC reports from around the globe, we found various patterns and trends. Prior to 1979, no country had formally banned the use of corporal punishment in the home. Following ratification of the CRC, the number of countries with home bans against the practice accelerated. More than 10 countries had banned corporal punishment by 2000, more than 30 countries by 2010, and more than 50 countries by 2016 (the most recent year in our data). Interestingly, countries with English legal origin and common law countries were much less likely to ban physical discipline in the school setting,[55] while countries with higher levels of female political empowerment—that is, more female representation in formal political positions and stronger property rights for women—acted more quickly to ban corporal punishment against students in schools.[56]

In general terms, Sweden has long been a frontrunner in the world on children's rights. As pertinent here, Sweden was the first country in the world to abolish child corporal punishment in all settings. Using any physical discipline on children was officially outlawed in 1979.[57] The goals of the ban were

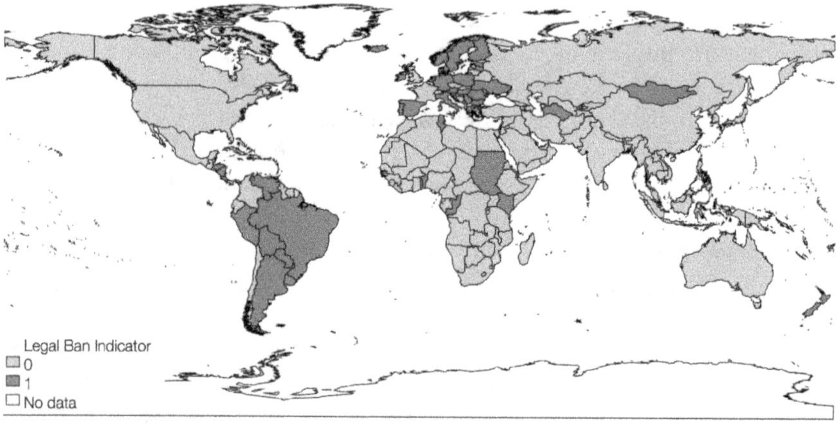

Figure 9.1 Status of Legality of Corporal Punishment at Home by Country in 2016.
Source: Figure created by Lucy Sorensen.

to: (1) reduce public support for corporal punishment; (2) encourage earlier identification of children at risk for physical abuse; and (3) facilitate earlier, more supportive intervention.[58] Data shows that these objectives had been met with a decrease in support for corporal punishment since 1965, from 53% to 11%, and thus a decline in the use of corporal punishment.[59]

Then, an interesting trend was seen when many of the neighboring European countries Sweden followed suit. In nearby countries, Sweden's norms arguably started a norm cascade that trended toward a societal shift in favor of new norms over the course of several years.[60] While the cascade was not rapid in the true sense of the word, we still see over a period of years the domino effect of countries falling in line with new norms of neighboring countries. Once Sweden banned corporal punishment in 1979, corporal punishment was banned in Finland in 1983, followed by Norway in 1987, then it began to reach the European mainland as early as 1989 in Austria.[61]

Moreover, the ban on violence has changed attitudes among the population as a whole.[62] For example, in Sweden, rates of corporal punishment against children have fallen to below 3%.[63] Similarly in Finland, a study revealed that attitudes toward corporal punishment have become much more negative as opposed to in 1981, when 47% of Finland's adult population believed corporal punishment to be acceptable.[64]

Norm changing can be a slow process. For instance, in a survey of German parents in 2012, "four out of ten parents admit[ted] to smacking their children on the bottom and ten percent [admitted to slapping] their children across the face."[65] Many of the parents surveyed showed remorse for their actions and blame these on a "knee-jerk reaction."[66] Germany is continuing to work through the lengthy process of overcoming what was once the norm for their society and child-rearing into a society that recognizes the dangers of corporal punishment on their children.[67]

We then more deeply examined the country of Ethiopia. Ethiopia has also taken proactive steps toward changing the norms.[68] As of 2013, the Family Code of 2000 has been revised to eliminate the right of parents to administer "light bodily punishments on children."[69] After identifying a need for extending broader education of its citizens, the Ethiopian government has worked to implement widespread education programs.[70] The government cites the public's lack of awareness about alternative forms of child discipline and lack of awareness about the rights of children in Ethiopian homes.[71] The hope of the government is that with the implementation of preventive measures that challenge the traditional attitudes of people toward children, the use of corporal punishment will decrease.[72]

In its CRC self-report to the United Nations, Ethiopia reported that the increased broadcasting of programs about domestic relations from the media is playing a significant role in sparking a dialogue about child discipline.[73] The Ethiopian government has also taken steps to collaborate with other countries to develop awareness campaigns and increase children's rights.

In addition to Sweden and Ethiopia, there are other examples of countries trying to raise public awareness about corporal punishment, described in more detail in our fuller article published by William and Mary Law School.[74]

CONCLUSION

Research on implementation and enforcement of the law awaits. For now, the groundwork can be paved for increasing awareness in various communities, that then may translate to the changing of norms and acceptance of child corporal punishment as a proper form of discipline. For countries that share our normative argument against child corporal punishment in the home, the theories of social norms and re-norming can be utilized to create norm cascades and tipping points on a global level inter-country or intra-country, as needed. And ultimately, it is our hope that this will provide a safer environment for our world's children.

NOTES

1. This chapter is an abridged version of a longer law review article published and with permission by William and Mary Law School at the following citation: *Corporal Punishment, Social Norms and Norm Cascades: Examining Cross-National Laws and Trends in Homes Across the Globe,* 26 WM. & MARY J. RACE, GENDER, SOC. JUST. 483–524 (2020).

2. *See* Sir William Blackstone, Commentaries on the Laws of England in Four Books 453 (George Sharswood, vol. 1, 1753) ("The legal power of a father-for a mother, as such, is entitled to no power, but only to reverence and respect; the power of a father, I say, over the persons of his children ceases at the age of twenty-one [. . .] Yet, till that age arrives, this empire of the father continues even after his death; for he may by his will appoint a guardian to his children."); *see* Sarah Abramowicz, *English Child Custody Law, 1660–1839: The Origins of Judicial Intervention in Paternal Custody*, 99, no. 5 Colum. L. Rev. 1344–92 (June 1999) (discussing how mothers had no enforceable rights to custody over the father or the father's appointed guardian); *see* Dara Purvis, *The Origin of Parental Rights: Labor, Intent, and Fathers*, 41 Fla. St. U. L. Rev. 645–96 (2014) (explaining how children were viewed as property, specifically of the father, in 10th-century England).

3. *See* Convention on the Rights of the Child, art. 11, Nov. 20, 1989, 1577 U.N.T.S. 3.

4. *See, e.g.*, Elizabeth T. Gershoff et al., *The Strength of the Causal Evidence Against Physical Punishment of Children and Its Implications for Parents, Psychologists, and Policymakers*, 73, no. 5 Am. Psychol. 626–638 (2018), https://psycnet.apa.org/doi/10.1037/amp0000327

5. Terra Pingley, The Impact of Witnessing Domestic Violence on Children: A Systematic Review 11 (May 2017) (unpublished Master of Social Work Clinical Research Paper) (on file with St. Catherine University School of Social Work), https://sophia.stkate.edu/cgi/viewcontent.cgi?article=1779&context=msw_papers ("Social learning theory explains that children exposed to parental violence are more likely to experience violence themselves, and go on to violent acts towards others."); *see* Gregory Routt & Lily Anderson, *Adolescent Violence towards Parents*, 20 J. Aggression, Maltreatment & Trauma 1, 11 (2011), http://www.courts.ca.gov/documents/BTB_XXII_II_3.pdf ("Instrumental violence is evident when violence is modeled by a parent at home and a child learns a lesson that aggressive behavior is a way to get what he or she wants (Jaffe, Wolfe, & Wilson, 1990)."); *see* The Body Shop International & United Nations Children's Fund, *Behind Closed Doors: The Impact of Domestic Violence on Children*, UNICEF (2009), https://www.unicef.org/protection/files/BehindClosedDoors.pdf

6. Lucy Sorensen, Victor Asal, Charmaine Willis, Melissa Breger, *Paddling the Pupils: The Legality (or Not) of Corporal Punishment in Schools* (2019) (unpublished manuscript) (on file with author), https://ssrn.com/abstract=3429160

7. Robert D. Sege, MD, PhD, FAAP & Benjamin S. Siegel, MD, FAAP, *Effective Discipline to Raise Healthy Children*, 142 Pediatrics 1 (2018). at 1161; Jessica Koolick et al., *PTSD Symptoms in Young Children Exposed to Intimate Partner Violence in Four Ethno-racial Groups*, 9 J. Child & Adolescent Trauma 97, 97 (2016) (explaining that previous research has consistently found children exposed to intimate partner violence have internalizing problems such as depression, anxiety, and symptoms of PTSD).

8. Sege, supra note 7 at 1163; Jill Astbury et al., *The Impact of Domestic Violence on Individuals*, 173, no. 8 Med. J. Austl. 427–31 (2000) (stating that some of the psychological consequences of childhood violence include bedwetting and running away).

9. Breger, *supra* note 24, at 1161. (Melissa L. Breger, *Healing Sex-Trafficked Children: A Domestic Family Law Approach to an International Epidemic*, 118, no. 3 W. VA. L. REV. 1131–80, April 2016).

10. Didi Kristen Tatlow, *China's Harsh Child Discipline, Through the Lens of Domestic Violence*, N.Y.TIMES (Mar. 9, 2016), https://www.nytimes.com/2016/03/10/world/asia/china -corporal-punishment-education-discipline.html [http://perma.cc/58F3-N9TR]

11. Didi Kristen Tatlow, *China's Harsh Child Discipline, Through the Lens of Domestic Violence*, N.Y.TIMES (Mar. 9, 2016), https://www.nytimes.com/2016/03/10/world/asia/china -corporal-punishment-education-discipline.html [http://perma.cc/58F3-N9TR]

12. Didi Kristen Tatlow, *China's Harsh Child Discipline, Through the Lens of Domestic Violence*, N.Y.TIMES (Mar. 9, 2016), https://www.nytimes.com/2016/03/10/world/asia/china -corporal-punishment-education-discipline.html [http://perma.cc/58F3-N9TR]

13. *See* Donald E. Greydanus M.D. et al., *Corporal Punishment in Schools: Position Paper of the Society for Adolescent Medicine*, 32, no. 5 J. ADOLESCENT HEALTH 385–93 (May 2003) ("Advocates of corporal punishment note that it should be proportioned out in limited doses, based on the offense and without attempt to physically harm."); *see* David Orentlicher, *Spanking and Other Corporal Punishment of Children by Parents: Undervaluing Children, Overvaluing Pain*, 38 HOUS. L. REV. 147–85 (1998) ("There are several potential harms from corporal punishment. The most obvious risk is that of physical injury to the child.").

14. Leonard P. Edwards, *Corporal Punishment and Legal System*, 36 SANTA CLARA L. REV. 983, 986–87 (1995–1996).

15. See Leonard P. Edwards, *Corporal Punishment and Legal System*, 36 SANTA CLARA L. REV. 983, 986–87 (1995–1996).

16. Leonard P. Edwards, *Corporal Punishment and Legal System*, 36 SANTA CLARA L. REV. 983, 989 (1995–1996).

17. Leonard P. Edwards, *Corporal Punishment and Legal System*, 36 SANTA CLARA L. REV. 983, 989 (1995–1996); see Elliott West, Growing Up With The Country: Childhood On The Far Western Frontier, 158–59 (1989).

18. Leonard P. Edwards, *Corporal Punishment and Legal System*, 36 SANTA CLARA L. REV. 983, 989 (1995–1996).

19. *See* Sorensen, *supra* note 6, at 11.

20. *See* Carla Murphy, *Parenting While Black: Toya Graham on Violence, Fear and Freddie Gray*, SLICE (Aug. 11, 2015 9:43am), https://talkingpointsmemo.com/theslice/parenting-while-black-toya-graham-baltimore-freddie-gray ("There was a time when Black children were the best behaved children in the world [and that was a time] when our mothers [hit us] like Toya Graham."); *see* Karen Valby, *The Realities of Raising a Kid of a Different Race*, TIME, https://time.com/the-realities-of-raising-a-kid-of-a-different-race/ (discussing how raising a Black child includes teaching them how to survive in modern society); *see* Janell Ross, *Black Parents Take Their Kids to School on How to Deal with Police*, WASH. POST (Jan. 3, 2017), https://www.washingtonpost.com/national/black-parents-take-their-kids-to-school-on-how-to-deal-with

-police/2017/01/03/86129c1c-c6be-11e6-bf4b-2c064d32a4bf_story.html?noredirect=on&utm_term=.4a8b7e36b7f0

21. One study shows many United States adults think it is acceptable and even necessary at times to spank a child, but these findings varied demographically with the highest approval in the American South, among the Black community, Conservative Protestants, and persons with lower socioeconomic status and education. *See* Catherina A. Taylor et al., *Perceived Social Norms, Expectations, and Attitudes Toward Corporal Punishment Among an Urban Community Sample of Parents*, 88 J. U. Health 254–69 (2011); *see* Ta-Nehisi Coates, *Race, Parenting and Punishment*, Atlantic (Jan. 22, 2010), https://www.theatlantic.com/entertainment/archive/2010/01/race-parenting-and-punishment/34005/?utm_source=atl&utm_medium=email&utm_campaign=share (discussing how Black people who commit transgressions are subject to a higher price, thus, Black parents punish more frequently and often harsher than parents of other cultures).

22. This chapter also does not delve into issues of what happens to a family when corporal punishment laws are enforced, such as the removal of children from parents as part of the general child welfare system. Thus, the chapter does not address the related issue of class-and race-based implicit biases and decision-making that are implicated in the American child welfare system; these are researched and noted extensively in already existing literature. *See generally*, Dorothy Roberts, Shattered Bonds: The Color of Child Welfare (2003); *see also*, Martin Guggenheim, What's Wrong with Children's Rights (2007).

23. Jacqueline Howard, *These Are the Countries Where Spanking Is Illegal*, CNN (Mar. 12, 2018), https://www.cnn.com/2018/03/12/health/spanking-laws-parenting-without-borders-intl/index.html. Sixty countries, states, and territories have fully prohibited using corporal punishment against children at home, including: Albania, Andorra, Argentina, Aruba, Austria, Benin, Bolivia, Brazil, Bulgaria, Cape Verde, Congo, Costa Rica, Croatia, Curaçao, Cyprus, Denmark, Estonia, Faroe Islands, Finland, Germany, Greece, Greenland, Honduras, Hungary, Iceland, Ireland, Israel, Kenya, Latvia, Liechtenstein, Lithuania, Luxembourg, Malta, Mongolia, Montenegro, Netherlands, New Zealand, Nicaragua, Norway, Paraguay, Peru, Pitcairn Islands, Poland, Portugal, Moldova, Romania, San Marino, Slovenia, South Sudan, Spain, St. Maarten, Svalbard, Jan Mayen, Sweden, Macedonia, Togo, Tunisia, Turkmenistan, Ukraine, Uruguay, and Venezuela.

24. In an effort to distinguish between corporal punishment and abuse, Elisabeth Gershoff looks to various statutory defintions in the United States noting that some states require that the discipline is "appropriate" or "moderate," "necessary" or with "nondeadly force"; Pate, Matthew, and Laurie Gould. *Corporal Punishment Around the World* (Santa Barbara: Praeger Books, 2012), 61.

25. As explained earlier, some states, such as New York, will allow limited forms of parental discipline, but any action that moves beyond the tolerated and culturally acceptable norms of discipline in the state is named "excessive corporal punishment"—and is governed by the laws of child neglect (N.Y Penal Law § 35.10).

26. See Robert D. Sege, MD, PhD, FAAP & Benjamin S. Siegel, MD, FAAP, *Effective Discipline to Raise Healthy Children*, 142 Pediatrics 1 (2018); *see*

Jacqueline Howard, *Pediatrcians Strengthen Stance Against Spanking Kids*, CNN (Nov. 18, 2018), https://www.cnn.com/2018/11/05/health/spanking-children-healthy-discipline-study. The American Association for Pediatricians came forward with its first public admonishment of physical discipline against children.

27. Jacqueline Howard, *Pediatricians Strengthen Stance Against Spanking Kids*, CNN (Nov. 18, 2018), https://www.cnn.com/2018/11/05/health/spanking-children-healthy-discipline-study

28. AAP. See also Pate & Gould, Corporal Punishment Around the World, (2012, Praeger Books) page xxi (citing a range of psychological effects of child corporal punishment later in the child's life, such as bullying, low school achievement, higher school dropout rates). See also Susan M. Turner, title, at page 84, Something To Cry About: An Argument against Corporal Punishment of children in Canada, by Susan M. Turner.

29. The AAP even goes one step further to declare that non-physical discipline, such as verbal degradation and verbally abusive behavior, constitutes inappropriate parental discipline for children. Notably, the AAP indicated that "verbal abuse" is not appropriate as discipline either.

30. Convention on the Rights of the Child, G.A. Res. 25, U.N. GAOR, 44th Sess.61st plen. mtg., Annex, U.N. Doc. A/44/25 (1989); Maria Grahn-Farley, *International Child Rights at Home and Abroad: A Symposium on the UN Convention on the Rights of the Child: I. Foreword: Crossing Borders*, 30, no. 4 CAP. U. L. REV. 657 (2002); UN lauds Somalia as country ratifies landmark children's rights treaty, UN NEWS (Jan. 20, 2015) https://news.un.org/en/story/2015/01/488692-un-lauds-somalia-country-ratifies-landmark-childrens-rights-treaty

31. *See* Melissa L. Breger, *Against the Dilution of a Child's Voice in Court*, 20 IND. INT'L & COMP. L. REV. 175, 178 (2010).

32. *See, e.g.*, Maria Grahn-Farley, *International Child Rights at Home and Abroad: A Symposium on the UN Convention on the Rights of the Child: Foreword: Crossing Borders*, 30, no. 4 CAP. U.L. REV. 657, 659–661 (2002); Howard Davidson, *A Model Child Protection Legal Reform Instrument: The Convention On The Rights Of The Child And Its Consistency With United States Law*, 5, no. 2 GEO. J. FIGHTING POVERTY 185–200 (1998).

33. Human Rights Watch. Accessed 10/13/2021 at https://www.hrw.org/news/2014/11/17/25th-anniversary-convention-rights-child

34. Lucy Sorensen, Victor Asal, Charmaine Willis, Melissa Breger, *Paddling the Pupils: The Legality (or Not) of Corporal Punishment in Schools* (2019) (unpublished manuscript) (on file with author), https://ssrn.com/abstract=3429160

35. The Global Initiative to End All Corporal Punishment (last visited October 31, 2018), https://endcorporalpunishment.org/

36. *See* Committee on the Rights of the Child, UNITED NATIONS HUMAN RIGHTS OFFICE OF THE HIGH COMMISSONER, https://www.ohchr.org/EN/HRBodies/CRC/Pages/CRCIndex.aspx (last visited July 23, 2019).

37. *See* Convention on the Rights of the Child, UNITED NATIONS TREATY COLLECTION, https://treaties.un.org/Pages/ViewDetails.aspx?src=IND&mtdsg_no=IV-11&chapter=4&lang=en (last visited July 29, 2019).

38. Melissa Breger, *Reforming by Renorming: How the Legal System Has the Potential to Change a Toxic Culture of Domestic Violence*, 44, no. 2 NOTRE DAME J. LEGIS. 171, 173 (April 2018).

39. Melissa Breger, *Reforming by Renorming: How the Legal System Has the Potential to Change a Toxic Culture of Domestic Violence*, 44, no. 2 NOTRE DAME J. LEGIS. 171, 173 (April 2018).

40. Melissa Breger, *Reforming by Renorming: How the Legal System Has the Potential to Change a Toxic Culture of Domestic Violence*, 44, no. 2 NOTRE DAME J. OF LEGIS. 171, 173 (April 2018) (internal references omitted).

41. *Id.* For example, the lessons from re-norming have been particularly successful in combating drunk driving. When there was a marked decrease of drunk driving fatalities, research indicated that it was not due to increased penalties, but rather changes in the social stigma associated with drunk driving. Groups such as Mothers Against Drunk Driving enlisted not only the law as their ally but society as a whole to re-norm behavior in order to reform behavior. By changing societal acceptance of driving while inebriated, through media and education, friends and family members everywhere became the key deterrent by re-norming safe and acceptable behavior.

42. *See* Cass R. Sunstein, *Social Norms and Social Roles*, 96 COLUM. L. REV. 903, 909 (1996).

43. *See* Joan. C. Williams et al., *What's Reasonable Now? Sexual Harassment Law After the Norm Cascade*, 2019 MICH. ST. L. REV. 139, 142 (2019). #MeToo began in 2017 with Alyssa Milano's tweet to highlight the number of women who have faced sexual harassment. She included the hashtag "#MeToo" in solidarity with other women who faced similar forms of harassment. The hashtag went viral, and encouraged many other women to share their stories. In the late 1990s, only 34% of Americans thought sexual harassment was a serious problem. By late 2017, following the #MeToo Twitter trend, approximately 75% of Americans believed sexual harassment and assault were very important issues for America.

44. CASS R. SUNSTEIN, FREE MARKETS AND SOCIAL JUSTICE (1999).

45. *Id.* at 38.

46. Martha Finnemore & Kathryn Sikkink, *International Norm Dynamics and Political Change*, 52, no. 4 INT'L. ORG. 887, 895 (Autumn 1998).

47. Melissa L. Breger, *Reforming by Re-Norming: How the Legal System Has the Potential to Change a Toxic Culture of Domestic Violence*, 44, no. 2 NOTRE DAME J. LEGIS. 171, 188 (April 2018).

48. Melissa L. Breger, *Reforming by Re-Norming: How the Legal System Has the Potential to Change a Toxic Culture of Domestic Violence*, 44, no. 2 NOTRE DAME J. LEGIS. 171, 188 (April 2018); Matt Grant, *Organizational Change: Thinking It Through* (2014), https://www.slideshare.net/humansnotrobots/organisational-change-thinking-it-through

49. *See generally* Daniel M. Kahan, *Gentle Nudges v. Hard Shoves: Solving the Sticky Norms Problem*, 67, no. 3 U. CHI. L. REV. 607–45 (Summer 2000).

50. Melissa Breger, *Reforming by Renorming: How the Legal System Has the Potential to Change a Toxic Culture of Domestic Violence*, 44, no. 2 NOTRE DAME J. LEGIS 171, 191 (April 2018).

51. Melissa Breger, *Reforming by Renorming: How the Legal System Has the Potential to Change a Toxic Culture of Domestic Violence*, 44, no. 2 NOTRE DAME J. LEGIS 171, 192 (April 2018).

52. Melissa Breger, *Reforming by Renorming: How the Legal System Has the Potential to Change a Toxic Culture of Domestic Violence*, 44, no. 2 NOTRE DAME J. LEGIS 171, 192 (April 2018).

53. See Nurith Aizenman, *Alarming Number of Women Think Spousal Abuse is Sometimes Ok*, NPR (Mar. 18, 2015, 12:16 PM), https://www.npr.org/sections/goat-sandsoda/20 15/03/18/392860281/alarming-number-of-women-think-spousal-abuse-i s-sometimes-ok [http://perma.cc/HK5V-39E3]

54. Melissa Breger, *Reforming by Renorming: How the Legal System Has the Potential to Change a Toxic Culture of Domestic Violence*, 44, no. 2 NOTRE DAME J. LEGIS. 171, 189 (April 2018).

55. Lucy Sorensen et al., Paddling the Pupils: The Legality (or Not) of Corporal Punishment in Schools 12, 22 (Aug. 2, 2019) (unpublished manuscript) (available at https:// ssrn.com/abstract=3429160), supra at note 6.

56. Lucy Sorensen et al., Paddling the Pupils: The Legality (or Not) of Corporal Punishment in Schools 12, 17, 22–23 (Aug. 2, 2019) (unpublished manuscript) (available at https:// ssrn.com/abstract=3429160), supra at note 6.

57. Corporal punishment of children in Sweden, GLOBAL INITIATIVE TO END ALL CORPORAL PUNISHMENT OF CHILDREN, https://endcorporalpunishment.org/reports-on -every-state-and-territory/sweden/ (last updated February 2020). Pate and Gould book on pages 64–65.

58. Joan E. Durrant, *Evaluating the Success of Sweden's Corporal Punishment Ban*, 23, no. 5 CHILD ABUSE & NEGLECT 435, 444 (May 1999).

59. *Id.* (After the repeal of the Criminal Code defense in Sweden, one-half of the Swedish population believed that corporal punishment was necessary in child-rearing in 1965, by 1981, that decreased by 50%, and by 1994, the percentage of the population that supported corporal punishment even in its mildest form had decreased further); *see* Save the Children Sweden, *Never Violence—Thirty Years on from Sweden's Abolition of Corporal Punishment*, GOV'T. OFF. SWED. 17 (2009), https://www.government.se/contentassets/6bfb214c582448b6ace4d32978361577/never-violence---thirty-years-on-from-swedens-abolition-of-corporal-punishment (showing that the positive attitudes toward and use of physical punishment in Sweden has been on a steady decline since the 1960s, with the percentage of positive attitudes in the 2000s being under 10% and the use just above 10%).; see also Pate and Gould book on page 67 (Rates of child maltreatment hospitals have declined by one-sixth).

60. Cass R. Sunstein, *Social Norms and Social Roles*, 96 COLUM. L. REV. 903, 912 (1996).

61. Corporal punishment of children in Finland, GLOBAL INITIATIVE TO END ALL CORPORAL PUNISHMENT OF CHILDREN, https://endcorporalpunishment.org/reports-on -every-state-and-territory/finland/ (last updated June 2020); Corporal punishment of children in Norway, GLOBAL INITIATIVE TO END ALL CORPORAL PUNISHMENT OF CHILDREN, https://endcorporalpunishment.org/reports-on-every-state-and-territory/ norway/ (last updated June 2019); Corporal punishment of children in Latvia, GLOBAL

Initiative to End All Corporal Punishment of Children, https://endcorporalpunishment.org/reports-on-every-state-and-territory/latvia/ (last updated June 2020).

62. *See* generally, *The Positive Impact of Prohibition of Corporal Punishment on Children's Lives: Messages from Research*, Global Initiative to End All corporal Punishment, http://endcorporalpunishment.org/wp-content/uploads/research/Summary-of-research-impact-of-prohibition.pdf (June 2015) (summarizing research that shows reductions in the approval and use of corporal punishment in some countries which have reformed their laws to prohibit all corporal punishment of children); *see* Jennifer E. Lansford et al., *Change Over Time in Parents' Beliefs About and Reported Use of corporal Punishment in Eight Countries With and Without Legal Bans*, 71 Child Abuse & Neglect 44–55 (2018), https://www.ncbi.nlm.nih.gov/pmc/articles/PMC5407940/pdf/nihms828426.pdf

63. Consideration of Reports Submitted by States Parties Under Article 44 of the Convention, U.N. Doc. CRC/C/SWE/5 at 32.

64. Consideration of Reports Submitted by States Parties Under Article 44 of the Convention, U.N. Doc. CRC/C/FIN/4 at 50.

65. Kay-Alexander Scholz, Nearly Half of German Parents Hit Their Children, DEUTSCHE WELLE (Mar. 13, 2012), https://www.dw.com/en/nearly-half-of-german-parents -hit-their-children/a-15806121 [https://perma.cc/R3FX-Z9LB]

66. Kay-Alexander Scholz, Nearly Half of German Parents Hit Their Children, DEUTSCHE WELLE (Mar. 13, 2012), https://www.dw.com/en/nearly-half-of-german-parents -hit-their-children/a-15806121 [https://perma.cc/R3FX-Z9LB]

67. *See* Kay-Alexander Scholz, Nearly Half of German Parents Hit Their Children, DEUTSCHE WELLE (Mar. 13, 2012), https://www.dw.com/en/nearly-half-of-german-parents -hit-their-children/a-15806121 [https://perma.cc/R3FX-Z9LB]

68. Consideration of Reports Submitted by States Parties Under Article 44 of the Convention, U.N. Doc. CRC/C/ETH/4-5 at 21.

69. Consideration of Reports Submitted by States Parties Under Article 44 of the Convention, U.N. Doc. CRC/C/ETH/4-5 at 21.

70. Consideration of Reports Submitted by States Parties Under Article 44 of the Convention, U.N. Doc. CRC/C/ETH/4-5 at 21.

71. Consideration of Reports Submitted by States Parties Under Article 44 of the Convention, U.N. Doc. CRC/C/ETH/4-5 at 21.

72. Consideration of Reports Submitted by States Parties Under Article 44 of the Convention, U.N. Doc. CRC/C/ETH/4-5 at 28.

73. Consideration of Reports Submitted by States Parties Under Article 44 of the Convention, U.N. Doc. CRC/C/ETH/4-5 at 28.

74. Supra at note 1, *Corporal Punishment, Social Norms and Norm Cascades: Examining Cross-National Laws and Trends in Homes Across the Globe.*

Chapter 10

Structural Violence as a Driver of Interpersonal Violence against Children

Missed Connections in the Convention on the Rights of the Child and English Law

Jessica Lynn Corsi[1]

INTRODUCTION

While the exact causal pathways are a matter of debate, it is generally agreed that poverty can drive violence, including violence against children (VAC). The law is an important tool for addressing both poverty and violence, but law rarely addresses the connections between the two. Instead, the law regarding VAC often focuses on interpersonal violence and families. Using a law-in-context approach that situates law in broader social, economic, and political contexts,[2] this chapter considers evidence from several social sciences alongside a doctrinal legal approach. It proposes a new framework—the Rights-Poverty-Violence framework—that highlights the challenges facing legal approaches to VAC. This framework could enhance law's efficacy in addressing VAC by bridging disconnects regarding what drives or contributes to VAC and how law responds to VAC. While recognizing the complexity of identifying causal pathways as to what drives violence and/or poverty, and the multiple challenges law faces in incorporating theories from other disciplines, ultimately it concludes that a stronger relationship between law and evidence from the social sciences could enhance law's ability to respond to VAC.

Presently, the world is experiencing a global outbreak of a novel coronavirus resulting in a disease known as COVID-19.[3] This public health crisis has numerous negative effects, two of which include an increase in the number of children living in poverty,[4] and an increase in the rates of VAC.[5] Structural violence (defined later in the chapter) such as poverty and direct violence such as VAC are linked.[6] Data reveals links between poverty and VAC,[7] with Maternowska and Fry calling poverty a "driver" of VAC,[8] and noting that economic shocks, job changes, and poverty contribute to VAC in the home.[9] In the UK, as globally, the pandemic-related spike in VAC is linked in part to the concomitant economic crisis and the financial insecurity of children's caregivers.[10] While data collection during a pandemic is complex, as are understandings of what causes violence, the hypothesis that COVID-19 is driving increased VAC parallels evidence from previous pandemics.[11] Furthermore, the connections between poverty and VAC exist beyond times of crisis and impact children even in the best of times.

This chapter proceeds as follows. Section II defines key terms such as violence, children, and poverty, situating these terms in its Rights-Poverty-Violence framework. Section III explicates the links between structural and interpersonal VAC, articulating how Maternowska et al.'s model regarding drivers of VAC can be used to scrutinize law. While poverty is not the only structural driver of VAC—for example, gender inequity plays a large role in driving VAC—it is one that deserves more attention, especially given the law's relative silence on the connection. As the UK is a party to the Convention on the Rights of the Child (CRC), Section IV assesses the CRC's approach to poverty as a driver of VAC. Section V analyzes the current legal regime for child protection in England, examining the extent to which they acknowledge the role of poverty regarding VAC. Section VI concludes that child protection and poverty alleviation remain disconnected in law, outlining several implications of this. This chapter concludes that while updating the law to reflect the evidence base that poverty drives VAC could be a complicated endeavor, failing to do so undermines law's capacity to alleviate such violence.

KEY TERMS AND THE RIGHTS-POVERTY-VIOLENCE FRAMEWORK

Social Sciences Data/Evidence

This chapter employs the term social sciences data or evidence throughout. It does so with some caveats. First, there is no one "social science," but rather multiple disciplines, and dispute and contestation within and between them. Second, like knowledge in any discipline, knowledge in the social sciences is not politically neutral and can reproduce power structures that facilitate violence and poverty. Third, it is useful to bear in mind that there is "a fundamental difference between 'social sciences in law' and 'law as a social science.'"[12] This chapter speaks of the former, meaning drawing on findings from the social sciences to inform the content and practice of the law. The chapter advocates the considered use of rigorous social science findings to achieve law reforms aimed at reducing both poverty and VAC.

Interpersonal Violence

The World Health Organization (WHO) defines interpersonal violence as "violence between individuals," such as family violence inclusive of child maltreatment.[13] This chapter addresses structural violence as a driver of interpersonal VAC, with the interpersonal violence focused on violence enacted by parents/guardians against children in their homes. This violence can go by many names, including assault, wounding, grievous bodily harm, abuse, ill-treatment, failure to protect, abandonment, cruelty, and neglect.[14] Regarding "what counts" as violence, this chapter adopts the position of the CRC Committee, which stated that "all forms of violence against children, however light, are unacceptable. . . . Frequency, severity of harm and intent to harm are not prerequisites for the definitions of violence."[15]

Structural Violence

The concept "structural violence" is associated with Johan Galtung. His 1969 article *Violence, Peace, and Peace Research* defined structural violence as violence that can harm or kill a person but is not perpetrated by an actor.[16] Rather, the violence is built into a system based on unequal distribution and unequal power to make distribution decisions.[17] An important part of Galtung's definition is that the harm resulting from structural violence is avoidable.[18] While Galtung's concept of structural violence has been critiqued as ignoring individuals and their intentions,[19] the Rights-Poverty-Violence framework developed in this chapter recognizes that what Galtung names as structural violence, such as poverty, is not an inevitability, but a result of choices made by individuals in power. Similarly, legal responses to both child poverty and VAC are made by powerful individuals. Thus, there is agency and intention driving both child poverty and VAC. The distinction is that individual action drives poverty, which then in turn can drive interpersonal VAC; the poverty is a mediating driver in a complex web of interaction.

Although alternative descriptions such as inequality or social injustice could be employed,[20] these concepts obscure the depth of harm caused and the actual violence done to the body, as well as the links between poverty and physical violence. The phrase structural violence refocuses attention on the link to bodily harm. Additionally, it draws attention to the policy and legal choices that are made that result in poverty and could therefore contribute to driving these harms.

Children

Both the CRC and England's Children Act 1989 define children as anyone under the age of 18.[21]

Poverty

There is no fixed definition of poverty. Measurements vary considerably and the methodological choices behind these measurements are contested and political. Poverty can be measured as absolute, such as the extreme international poverty rate for persons living on less than $1.90 USD/day referenced by the UN and World Bank (WB).[22] In the UK, absolute poverty is measured as "absolute low income," which is a relative measurement versus an absolute measurement, defined as "equivalised income . . . below 60 per cent of the 2010/11 median income adjusted for inflation."[23] The UK government's "relative low income" measurement for households defines relative poverty as having "equivalised income . . . below 60 per cent of median income."[24] The UK may be changing its measure of poverty in the near future.[25]

Beyond income, the UN measures poverty in terms of capability and basic needs: "Poverty entails more than the lack of income and productive resources to ensure sustainable livelihoods. Its manifestations include hunger and malnutrition, limited access to education and other basic services, social discrimination and exclusion, as well as the lack of participation in decision-making."[26]

The UN's definition of poverty aligns with the human-rights corpus in which the CRC sits,[27] and the Rights-Poverty-Violence framework. The CRC focuses on the rights of a child to foster her capabilities, whether through freedom of expression,[28] freedom of religion and conscience,[29] access to media and books,[30] attaining the highest standard of health,[31] or by achieving a "standard of living adequate for the child's physical, mental, spiritual, moral and social development."[32] Poverty measurements that focus solely on income fail to capture the impact that poverty has on human development[33] and human rights.[34]

To date, the UK has not adopted a rights-based approach to poverty. England's Child Poverty Act of 2010 committed the government to eradicating child poverty using the absolute and relative low-income measures, as well as terms such as persistent poverty and combined low-income and material deprivation, to measure child poverty.[35] As of 2014, there was a focus on the government addressing the root causes of child poverty.[36] The Child Poverty Act was abolished by the 2016 Welfare Reform and Work Act, which removes both the commitment to end poverty and the previous measurements of child poverty; it refocused government action to reporting on children living in workless households and child educational attainment levels.[37]

This chapter is critical of the UK's approach to measuring and legally addressing poverty, as poverty and having a low income are not always equivalent.[38] The chapter employs alternative measurements and approaches, such as the UN Special Rapporteur on Extreme Poverty's measurements of poverty in the UK. The Rapporteur employed data from the Social Metrics Commission (SMC), an independent research body whose approach is more aligned with international standards than the current UK approach.[39] The SMC measurement addresses issues such as disability and uses a more comprehensive measurement of income relative to other factors such as debt, assets, and costs to determine total resources available.[40] Given this, in the English legal context, focusing on deprivation rather than poverty may be more useful for alleviating VAC.

The Rights-Poverty-Violence Framework

This chapter takes a rights-based approach to poverty and violence.[41] This approach facilitates an inquiry into the relationship between poverty and VAC, because it moves beyond assessing poverty as a number to analyzing poverty's harmful effects on human development. A rights-based approach to poverty aligns with the socio-ecological model of VAC employed in this chapter and discussed in the next section. Both the socio-ecological model and a rights-based approach capture complexity, overlapping forces, and the intersectional nature of both child poverty and VAC. This framework is illustrated in figure 10.1. The figure grossly oversimplifies the complex relationships between rights, poverty, and violence. It is offered as a jumping-off point for conceptualization.

At the bottom of the triangle, the thin arrow flowing from violence to poverty illustrates that violence can cause or exacerbate poverty. The larger arrow flowing from poverty to violence conveys the more pronounced relationship between poverty as a driver of violence. From the top of the triangle, rights connect to both violence and poverty as a tool that can help alleviate these phenomena. This chapter proposes that rights regimes can do so by addressing the connections between violence and poverty. The law can contribute to alleviating VAC by enshrining a child's right to be free from both poverty and violence and recognizing the connections between poverty and VAC.

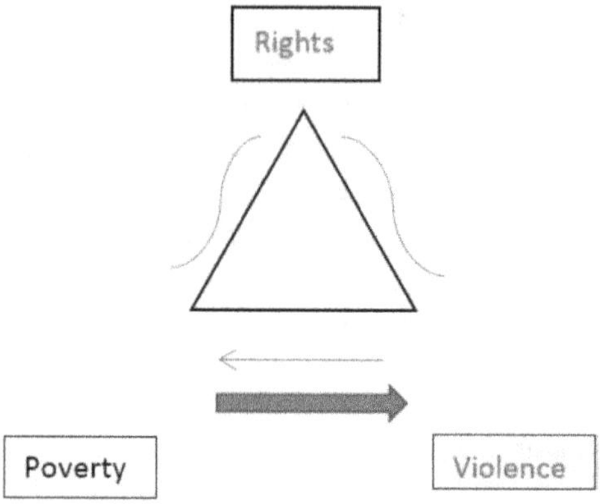

Figure 10.1 The Rights-Poverty-Violence Framework. *Source:* Dr. Jessica Lynn Corsi.

Associations between Structural and Interpersonal VAC

This chapter draws on the Maternowska socio-ecological model of VAC via its Rights-Poverty-Violence framework. This socio-ecological model links structural and interpersonal "domains," capturing the complex interplay between various forces that shape VAC.[42] Starting with the question, "What drives violence affecting children and what can be done about it?"[43] and acknowledging that "we are still discovering what drives violence,"[44] Maternowska et al. [hereinafter Maternowska] identified poverty as one of several key "drivers" of VAC.[45] They define drivers as "the institutional and structural levels that create the conditions in which violence is more or less likely to occur."[46] This is not to say that violence cannot also drive poverty,[47] or to overlook that violence and poverty may share common causes.[48] Similarly, this is not to ignore other institutional and structural drivers, such as gender inequity,[49] or culture.[50] The evidence gathered by Maternowska regarding poverty as a driver of VAC is compelling, underrepresented in law, and worth exploring further.

The multi-year, multi-country study was methodologically rigorous, drew on data from diverse settings, and leveraged the expertise of governments, practitioners, and researchers. Across the four countries of varying income levels and economic structures (Italy, Peru, Vietnam, Zimbabwe), they identified "family stress including poverty and unemployment" and a family's finances as interpersonal risk factors for VAC.[51] In their model, structural refers to "the macro-level political, economic and social policy environments."[52] In this sense, it aligns with the concept of structural violence. Interpersonal is defined as the "immediate context of violence and situational interactions between individuals involving household, family or intimate or acquaintance relationships."[53] All of these domains are overlapping and dynamic, as represented by Maternowska's child-centered socio-ecological graphic below.

The Maternowska model communicates the complexity of the various forces that cause violence.[54] Maternowska created this model in part because of overemphasis on individual and relational factors without reflection on structural drivers.[55] Without a model capturing the dynamic interplay of overlapping domains, violence prevention efforts are "fractured" and therefore less effective.[56] This can lead to "dealing with violence primarily as a series of separate incidents, failing to recognize its deep social and economic roots."[57] The Maternowska model is designed to be used by policymakers and move the discussion of structural drivers of VAC outside of academia and into national ownership.[58] The next two sections extend the Maternowska model and the Galtung triangle to develop a theory regarding how the CRC and English law could or should address the connections between child poverty and VAC.

THE CRC AND THE RIGHTS-POVERTY-VIOLENCE FRAMEWORK

It is useful to begin with an inquiry into the CRC before analyzing English law. Because the UK is a States Party, the CRC's obligations should shape UK legislative choices.[59] Even if they don't have this effect in practice, the CRC's requirements remain a lens through which to assess whether or not the UK is fulfilling its legal commitments to children. There are limitations to the CRC's approach to both poverty and violence that could be a product

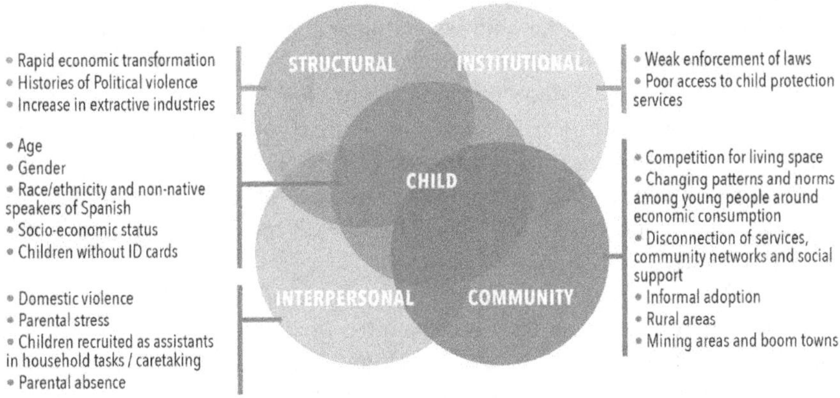

Figure 10.2 The Socio-Ecological Model of Violence against Children. *Source:* M. Catherine Maternowska and Alina Potts, 2017.

of States Parties understanding of these issues and/or political will to address these issues. Assessing this could shed light on municipal practice and possibility. Because the CRC aims to influence domestic law, shortcomings in the CRC's content and the Committee's interpretation of it could be mirrored in domestic approaches.

Beyond legal hierarchies, as figure 10.1 conveys, there are important conceptual connections between rights, poverty, and violence that are at least partially captured in the CRC and that could prove fruitful as a framework for legally addressing VAC. Figure 10.1 is not a model of the CRC but a proposal for how the law can improve its efforts to conceptualize and address VAC. The CRC does not explicitly recognize a right to be free from poverty or use the word poverty. There are several articles where the right to be free from poverty can be read in.[60] Article 27(1) instructs "States Parties [to] recognize the right of every child to a standard of living adequate for the child's physical, mental, spiritual, moral and social development." The CRC Committee recognized the "harmful impact of poverty on . . . [child] development, health, and education."[61] This does not erase that key aspects of Article 27 remain debated or undefined, such as the precise meaning of "adequate" or "development." Still, because there is a "close correlation between living in poverty and being denied an adequate standard of living,"[62] and because the Committee has explicitly named poverty in its commentary interpreting this and related articles, it is reasonable to conclude that the CRC could provide legal protections against child poverty, providing a legal basis for the Rights-Poverty-Violence framework.

In contrast to the approach to poverty seen in 27(1) and echoed in other CRC articles,[63] the remaining sections of Article 27 align with the UK approach to poverty as a household income issue. Article 27(2) emphasizes that "the parent(s) or others responsible for the child have the primary responsibility to secure, within their abilities and financial capacities, the conditions of living necessary for the child's development." This moves the focus away from structural forces to the household level. The attention on the household remains even with Article 27(3)'s instruction to States Parties that they "shall take appropriate measures to assist parents and others responsible for the child to implement this right and shall in case of need provide material assistance and support programs, particularly with regard to nutrition, clothing and housing."

Article 27's emphasis on a parent or guardian's primary responsibility for the child is part of a thread that runs from the preamble of the CRC through other articles, including 5, 9, 10, 11, 18, 21, and 23.[64] The CRC's weighting of the family echoes the unique status afforded to family units in other human-rights treaties.[65] Despite this special focus on the family, the distinction between primary and sole responsibility is important, and indicates "a collaborative model" in which primary caregivers are not "required to completely exhaust all their physical, emotional, and financial capacities in taking measures to secure the conditions necessary for the child's development before a state's obligation to assist them under paragraph 3 is invoked."[66] The CRC places great weight on the role of the state in assisting parents/guardians to fulfill their duties.[67] The CRC Committee has not limited the role of the state in providing adequate living conditions to children via parental assistance.[68] A state's obligation under the CRC to "fulfil the minimum core obligation for social, economic and cultural rights"[69] must go beyond a household model to focus on the needs of the child. States are instructed to prevent families from living in poverty.

Under the CRC, a child's needs include the right to be free from violence. Article 19 obligates states to take all appropriate measures, including legislative or judicial, to protect children from all forms of violence, including when the child is in the care of parents/guardians. Article 19 does not mention poverty, and the text of the CRC does not link poverty or structural drivers to VAC. However, the Committee's General Comment No. 13 on "The right of the child to freedom from all forms of violence" connects violence prevention to poverty prevention. It lists "poverty reduction strategies, including financial and social support to families at risk" as an example of "social policy measures to reduce risk and prevent violence against children."[70] It also states that specific forms of violence such as abandonment or neglect are frequently driven by poverty,[71] and recalls the need for "Poverty Reduction Strategy Papers and sector-wide approaches to development to include a strong focus on children's rights" regarding state obligations to protect children from violence.[72] Like the Maternowska model of VAC, it recognizes "family risk factors such as poverty, unemployment, discrimination and marginalization"[73] and instructs states to mainstream poverty alleviation "across the measures (legislative, administrative, social, and educational) and stages of intervention (from prevention to recovery and reintegration)."[74] The Rights-Poverty-Violence framework could facilitate these connections via legislation that utilizes the model.

Thus, General Comment No. 13 makes clear that there is a connection between poverty and VAC and that states are obligated to "mainstream" this connection "across" the measures they put in place to address VAC. This includes legal approaches to VAC. While the recognition of the connection between poverty and VAC within the CRC does not extend to the level noted in the Maternowska model or the Rights-Poverty-Violence Framework, it provides a legal obligation that should be mirrored in States Parties' VAC laws and policies. It is against this obligation and the Rights-Poverty-Violence framework that the next section analyzes English law.

ENGLISH LAW REGARDING VAC VIS-À-VIS THE RIGHTS-POVERTY-VIOLENCE FRAMEWORK

The English legal approach to VAC fails to incorporate rights or links between VAC and child poverty. There are several English laws addressing VAC, yet in very few instances do these laws address poverty. For example, English law criminalizes many forms of VAC, such as assaulting or wounding a child, allowing or causing serious physical harm to a child, or neglecting a child.[75] However, the structure of criminal law limits the consideration of background forces, because it focuses on the voluntary acts or omissions of individuals and the results of that individual's action(s) or omissions.[76] Causal considerations concern only the relationship between a perpetrator's actions or omissions and the harm suffered. When crimes include a contextual element, they do so as part of the elements of the crime, not to understand drivers of the crime.

When English criminal law considers material deprivation, which is related to although not the same as poverty, it does so in the perpetrator/victim framework without reference to wider societal structures. For example, regarding neglect, Section 1(2) of the Children and Young Persons Act 1933 holds a "parent or personal legally liable to maintain a child" accountable for neglect if s/he/they "fails to provide adequate food, clothing, medical aid or lodging for the child or having been unable to provide the above failed to take steps to procure it to be provided." Thus, material deprivation is considered within the framework of VAC, but the focus is on the acts/omissions and responsibility of legal guardians, not on structural drivers that can lead to such deprivation. Rather than look at structures that drive these harms of child deprivation, this law as written has the potential to criminalize guardians for being poor. Given its role in addressing the most serious harms in society, criminal law remains an essential part of addressing the harms of VAC. Yet, because of criminal law's focus on individuals rather than structure, it would take a reconceptualization of criminal law—perhaps in this particular case if not as a field—to link it to the Rights-Poverty-Violence framework.

Beyond crime, there are English laws that take a broader view of preventing and addressing VAC. These are generally classed as laws concerning child protection or child safeguarding, which empower the state to intervene if a child's parents or guardians are harming them or not protecting them from harm.[77] For example, Part V of the Children Act 1989 concerns protecting children from serious harm and allows emergency protection orders, the removal of the child in emergency situations, and investigations into the situation of the child by local authorities. Part 2 of the Children's Act 2004 elaborates upon the mechanisms, bodies, and persons in charge of safeguarding the welfare of children, and states that local authorities should be acting to "improv[e] the well-being of children in the authority's area" with well-being to include "physical and mental health and emotional well-being; protection from harm and neglect; education, training and recreation; the contribution made by them to society; [and] social and economic well-being."[78] Such Acts make provisions for the economic well-being and where necessary state provision of material aid to certain children, recognizing material needs in a manner similar to a rights-based approach to poverty.[79] However, they do not link poverty and violence beyond what was examined previously regarding English criminal law, wherein a parent or legal guardian's act or omission causing material deprivation can amount to VAC. Within English child-protection law, poverty, particularly on the macro-level, is not acknowledged as a driver of VAC.

Statutory guidance on how to implement English child-safeguarding laws employ an interpersonal and institutional (social work, police) rather than a structural focus. This means that the policy supporting legal implementation also fails to connect violence and poverty. The current guidance, Working Together to Safeguard Children 2018, applies to "all organizations and agencies who have functions relating to children. Specifically, this guidance applies to all local authorities, clinical commissioning groups, police" and "should be complied with unless exceptional circumstances arise."[80] The guidance frequently employs terms for specific types of violence like abuse, neglect, and exploitation, or references specific forms of violence like trafficking. At no point does it connect poverty and VAC. The word "violence" is almost never mentioned. In a few instances, the guidance reviews statutory requirements for children in need including children facing violence;[81] advice for health-care workers regarding addressing domestic violence;[82] and definitions of sexual abuse.[83] The 2010 and 2011 Munro Reports on child protection go a bit further toward a socio-legal approach. These reports include recourse to contextual (economic, social, political) factors and knowledge from other disciplines, recognize the complexities surrounding VAC, use systems analysis, stress early intervention, and comment on poverty as a risk factor.[84] However, the Reports' focus remains primarily on the institution of social work and the individuals with social work oversight, rather than on structure. Furthermore, they reference poverty without making any connection to violence. In short, England's policy approach to VAC evidences little to no recognition of poverty as a driver of VAC.

England's legal approach to child poverty similarly omits reference to violence, and at present, even to poverty as such. The Child Poverty Act 2010 began as a government commitment to "eradicate" child poverty by 2020.[85] The Act set the government four targets concerning the alleviation of relative, absolute, and persistent poverty, as well as "combined low income and material deprivation."[86] The overarching goal was to ensure children did not suffer "socio-economic disadvantage," a framing not dissimilar to a rights-based approach. This Act was focused on poverty and not on its additional implications. The subsequent Child Poverty Strategy 2014–2017 briefly mentioned abuse as a risk factor for poor children growing up to be poor adults,[87] but no further connection between poverty and violence was made.

With a change to a Conservative government, the Child Poverty Act 2010 was abolished by the Welfare and Work Reform Act 2016. The Welfare and Work Reform Act removed the focus on poverty, replacing it with measurements of children living in workless households and child educational attainment.[88] The Child Poverty Act was renamed The Life Chances Act 2010,[89] reflecting its new emphasis on household-level measurements and the abolition of macro-level targets. In short, there is no longer English law that directly addresses poverty. The current law's overemphasis on parental responsibility undermines the CRC's collaborative approach and "abandon['s] parents" in favor of a "minimalist state."[90]

Concomitantly and in line with the shrinking of government intervention, funding from the central government to the local authorities in charge of child safeguarding decreased by billions of pounds between 2010 and 2020.[91] This leaves local authorities already struggling to assist families in need of support[92] substantially less resourced for services designed to address child deprivation and VAC. If local authorities cannot provide for parents, parents in turn are less able to provide for their children, and this does not bode well for VAC. In England, the VAC and child poverty approaches are not only siloed, they are encumbered by legislative hurdles. It may be the case that legislating poverty alleviation could be beneficial to reducing VAC in England. Political will to address both poverty and the connections between poverty and VAC will be necessary to use budgets for such aims.

CONCLUSION

In both the text of the CRC and in English law, the child protection and the poverty alleviation fields are disconnected. Neither legal authority adequately incorporates the evidence base showing poverty as a driver of VAC. The CRC Committee's interpretation of VAC as linked to poverty and requiring state-level poverty alleviation is an important step in connecting the two phenomena but is not reflected in English law. There is silence at the highest levels, with authority figures such as the Children's Commissioner for England abstaining from recommending that the law address the connection.[93] Controversies over the evidence base could exacerbate this, including challenges in proving that poverty causes violence.[94] The social sciences do not offer definitive proof, and lawmakers may find it difficult to legislate on the basis of this uncertainty.[95] Integrating evidence from different disciplines can be a challenge.[96] Politics play a role, as both the demonization of the poor and the emphasis on individual responsibility versus structure that drives poverty continue.[97] Notwithstanding the many reasons for the divide, by not addressing poverty, the law perpetuates poverty and inequality; the same laws that seek to address VAC can reproduce it.

These deficiencies are not unique to the law's approach to poverty as a structural driver, but rather, represent law's limits generally speaking. Given this, it is prudent to ask whether or not the law can hope to address structural violence such as poverty. It may be that the law is not the best tool for this problem. Efforts to achieve "legal empowerment for the poor" have been critiqued as ignoring structural tensions and power relations,[98] and for overlooking that economic models are both contested and sites of contestation.[99] There is a weak track record of the law addressing such issues comprehensively. This raises the question of the extent to which the law can hope to capture context and structure, and what would be needed to achieve this in a legal text. For example, the preamble of treaties establish context, but as this chapter states regarding the CRC, the broader picture is often lost in the articles. In the English legal context, Acts of Parliament are substantially distinct from more contextualized treaties. Law reform that aligns with data from social sciences research could create significant legal changes in both substance and form. It is not clear whether legal change at this level is desired or possible.

There are many barriers to achieving legal recognition of poverty as a driver of VAC. And yet, even if the law *cannot* adequately address poverty in order to address violence, it *should* address poverty to address violence. What is meant by this perhaps paradoxical statement is that while the law is an imperfect tool, because of the significance of law in the structure of both municipal and international order, its failure to address the drivers of interpersonal violence is a gap that can be understood as a driver itself. Given the evidence base, law's ability to take the problem seriously requires a reimagining of its capacity to address the drivers behind the immediate causes. It is hoped that the Rights-Poverty-Violence Framework might contribute in some way to this reimagining. Without this or a similar framework, the law cannot adequately address child poverty, VAC, or their connection. The result is children suffering where they need not.

This framework or related law-in-context approaches could help, because a closer relationship between law reform and relevant data from social sciences research could inform changes to both the structure and content of the law. This could foster innovative solutions to the problems of child poverty and VAC. It is indisputable, for example, that there is an important relationship between poverty and violence, even if the exact causal mechanisms of this relationship are not fully understood or agreed upon. Stronger links between legal drafting and scientific and scholarly data could expand the law's capacity to reflect the lived experience of children and others experiencing violence. It must also be accompanied by a willingness to break with tradition regarding how the law has approached VAC in the past. Hopefully, the need to end VAC will compel effective legal innovation.

NOTES

1. The author gratefully acknowledges the comments of Alexandria Innes and Riikka Kotanen on earlier drafts; editorial feedback from Melissa Breger; helpful discussions with Kirrily Pells that assisted in shaping the chapter; the British Academy for providing a forum to workshop this chapter; the many useful comments received from participants at this British Academy workshop; and a seed grant from the British Academy that inspired, among other things, development of this chapter.

2. See e.g. Stephen Bottomley and Simon Bronitt, eds., *Law in Context* (Federation Press, 2012).

3. Shunqing Xu and Yuanyuan Li, "Beware of the second wave of COVID-19," *The Lancet*, 395, no. 10233 (April 25, 2020): 1321–1322.

4. UNICEF data, "Child poverty and COVID-19," (June 2020), https://data.unicef.org/topic/child-poverty/covid-19/

5. E.g. Amiya Bhatia, Camilla Fabbri, Ilan Cerna-Turoff, Clare Tanton, Louise Knight, Ellen Turner, Michelle Lokot, Shelley Lees, Ben Cislaghi, Amber Peterman, Alessandra Guedes, and Karen Devries, "COVID-19 response measures and violence against children," *Bulletin of the World Health Organization* 98, no. 9 (2020): 583–583A. doi: 10.2471/BLT.20.263467; World Health Organization, "Addressing violence against children, women, and older people during the Covid-19 pandemic: Key actions," (June 18, 2020). https://www.who.int/publications-detail-redirect/WHO-2019-nCoV-Violence_actions-2020.1

6. Johan Galtung and Tord Höivik, "Structural and direct violence: A note on operationalization," *Journal of Peace Research* 8, no. 1 (March 1, 1971): 73–76; United Nations Children's Fund, "Structural violence against children in southeast Asia," UNICEF, Kathmandu (2018), https://www.unicef.org/rosa/sites/unicef.org.rosa/files/2018-08/SVACS%20report%28web%29August%202.pdf; Steven Lee, "Is poverty violence?" in *Institutional Violence*, eds. Dean Curtin and Robert Litke (Amsterdam/Atlanta: Rodopi, 1999): 5–12.

7. See e.g. Paul Bywaters, Lisa Bunting, Gavin Davidson, Jennifer Hanratty, Will Mason, Claire McCartan and Nicole Steils, "The relationship between poverty, child abuse and neglect: an evidence review," *Joseph Rowntree Foundation* (March 2016), https://www.researchgate.net/profile/Jennifer_Hanratty/publication/295812966_The_relationship_between_poverty_child_abuse_and_neglect_an_evidence_review/links/58208f7c08ae40da2cb4ede7/The-relationship-between-poverty-child-abuse-and-neglect-an-evidence-review.pdf; Bill Gillham, Gary Tanner, Bill Cheyne, Isobel Freeman, Martin Rooney, and Allan Lambie, "Unemployment rates, single parent density, and indices of child poverty: Their relationship to different

categories of child abuse and neglect," *Child Abuse & Neglect*, 22, no. 2 (February 1998): 79–90.

8. M. Catherine Maternowska and Deborah Fry, "The multi-country study on the drivers of violence affecting children: An overview," *Vulnerable Children and Youth Studies*, 13, sup1 (2018): 12–25.

9. M. Catherine Maternowska, Alina Potts, and Deborah Fry, *The Multi-country Study on the Drivers of Violence Affecting Children. A Cross-country Snapshot of Findings* (Florence: UNICEF Office of Research - Innocenti, 2016), 3, 6. Poverty is thought to be a driver of many types of violence in addition to VAC; see e.g. Robert D. Crutchfield and Tim Wadsworth, "Poverty and Violence," in *International Handbook of Violence Research*, eds. Wilhelm Heitmeyer and John Hagan (Springer, 2005), 67–82.

10. See e.g. Eleni Romanou and Emma Belton, *Isolated and Struggling: Social Isolation and the Risk of Child Maltreatment, in Lockdown and Beyond* (London: NSPCC, June 2020), https://learning.nspcc.org.uk/media/2246/isolated-and-struggling-social-isolation-risk-child-maltreatment-lockdown-and-beyond.pdf; UNICEF, "Child protection and COVID-19," (April 2020), https://data.unicef.org/topic/child-protection/covid-19/

11. E.g. Bhatia et al, "COVID-19," 583–583A; Lucy Cluver, Jamie M. Lachman, Lorraine Sherr, Inge Wessels, Etienne Krug, Sabine Rakotomalala, Stephen Blight et al, "Parenting in a time of Covid-19," *Lancet: Correspondence* 395, no. 10231 (April 11, 2020): E64. doi: 10.1016/S0140-6736(20)30736-4

12. Marc Galanter, "The future of law and social sciences research," *North Carolina Law Review*, 52, no. 5 (1974): 1065.

13. World Health Organization, Violence Prevention Alliance, Definition and typology of violence, https://www.who.int/violenceprevention/approach/definition/en/

14. E.g. in the English context, see Offences Against Persons Act 1861, ss 47, 20, and 18 Section 5 of the Domestic Violence, Crime and Victims Act 2004; Children and Young Persons Act 1933.

15. Committee on the Rights of the Child, "General Comment No. 13 (2011): The right of the child to freedom from all forms of violence," CRC/C/GC/13, (April 18, 2011), para 17, https://www2.ohchr.org/english/bodies/crc/docs/CRC.C.GC.13_en.pdf

16. Johan Galtung, "Violence, peace, and peace research," *Journal of Peace Research*, 6, no. 3 (1969), 171.

17. Galtung, "Violence, peace, and peace research," 172.

18. Ibid, 168–169.

19. Sylvia Walby, Jude Towers, Susan Balderston, Consuelo Corradi, Brian Francis, Markku Heiskanen, Karin Helweg-Larsen, Lut Mergaert, Philippa Olive, Emma Kelly, Heidi Stöckl and Sofia Strid, *The Concept and Measurement of Violence Against Women and Men*, (Policy Press Bristol University, 2017), 35.

20. Galtung, "Violence, peace, and peace research," 171.

21. The United Nations, 1989, "Convention on the rights of the child (CRC)" *Treaty Series* 1577 (November): 3, Article 1; Children Act 1989, s 105(1).

22. Resolution adopted by the General Assembly on September 25, 2015: Transforming our world: the 2030 Agenda for Sustainable Development, A/RES/70/1, October 21, 2015, Goal 1. Extreme poverty/the international poverty line was measured as $1.25/day in goal 1.1 in 2015, but was updated to $1.90/day; see Francisco Ferreira, Dean Mitchell Jolliffe, and Espen Beer Prydz, "The international poverty line has just been raised to $1.90 a day, but global poverty is basically unchanged. How is that even possible?", *World Bank Blogs,* October 4, 2015, https://blogs.worldbank.org/developmenttalk/international-poverty-line-has-just-been-raised-190-day-global-poverty-basically-unchanged-how-even

23. Department for Work & Pensions, "Households below average income: An analysis of the UK income distribution: 1994/95-2018/1," (March 26, 2020,) https://assets.publishing.service.gov.uk/government/uploads/system/uploads/attachment_data/file/875261/households-below-average-income-1994-1995-2018-2019.pdf, 2

24. Ibid.

25. Department for Work and Pensions. "Development of a new measure of poverty: statistical notice," (May 17, 2019), https://www.gov.uk/government/statistics/development-of-a-new-measure-of-poverty-statistical-notice

26. United Nations, What is poverty?, https://www.un.org/en/sections/issues-depth/poverty/

27. Asbjørn Eide, *A Commentary on the United Nations Convention on the Rights of the Child, Article 27: The Right to an Adequate Standard of Living* (3rd edn., Martinus Nijhoff 2007).

28. CRC, Article 13.

29. CRC, Article 14.

30. Ibid, Article 17.

31. Ibid, Article 24.

32. Ibid, Article 27.

33. Rod Hick, "The capability approach: insights for a new poverty focus," *Journal of Social Policy*, 41, no. 2 (2012): 291–308.

34. Polly Izard, *Poverty and Human Rights: Sen's 'Capability Perspective' Explored* (Oxford University Press, 2006).

35. Steven Kennedy, Child Poverty Act 2010: a short guide, SN/SP/5585, (July 4, 2014), 1–15. https://researchbriefings.files.parliament.uk/documents/SN05585/SN05585.pdf

36. Department for Education, "Child Poverty Strategy 2014-17," (June 26, 2014), https://assets.publishing.service.gov.uk/government/uploads/system/uploads/attachment_data/file/324103/Child_poverty_strategy.pdf

37. Welfare Reform and Work Act 2016.

38. Gerry Redmond, "Child poverty and child rights: Edging towards a definition," *Journal of Children and Poverty*, 14, no. 1 (2008): 63–82.

39. Report of the Special Rapporteur on extreme poverty and human rights, "Visit to the United Kingdom of Great Britain and Northern Ireland," A/HRC/41/39/Add.1 (April 23, 2019) footnote 3.

40. Social Metrics Commission, "A new measure of poverty for the UK, The final report of the Social Metrics Commission," (September 2018), https://socialmetricscommission.org.uk/MEASURING-POVERTY-FULL_REPORT.pdf, 7.

41. On the connection between poverty and child rights, see e.g. Aoife Nolan and Kirrily Pells, "Children's economic and social rights and child poverty: The state of play," *International Journal of Children's Rights*, 28, no. 1 (2020): 111–132; Rosalind Dixon and Martha C. Nussbaum, "Children's rights and a capabilities approach: The question of special priority," *Cornell Law Review*, 97, no. 3 (March 2012), 549–594.

42. Maternowska and Fry, "The multi-country study on the drivers," 12–25.

43. Ibid, 16.

44. Ibid, 18.

45. Maternowska, Potts, and Fry, Deborah, "A cross-country snapshot," 2; see also Kirrily Pells and Martin Woodhead, "Changing children's lives: Risks and opportunities," Young Lives, Department for International Development, University of Oxford, (2014), https://www.younglives.org.uk/content/changing-childrens-lives-risks-and-opportunities

46. Maternowska Fry (2018) "The multi-country study on the drivers," 13.

47. See e.g. Eldin Fahmy, Emma Williamson, and Christina Pantazis, "Evidence and policy review: Domestic violence and poverty," *Joseph Rowntree Foundation* (2016): 4 https://research-information.bris.ac.uk/ws/portalfiles/portal/80376377/JRF_DV_POVERTY_REPORT_FINAL_COPY_.pdf; Sam Staley, *Drug Policy and the Decline of American Cities* (New Brunswick: Transaction Publishers, 1992).

48. See e.g. Crutchfield, Robert D. Crutchfield, "Labor stratification and violent crime," *Social Forces*, 68, no. 2 (December 1989): 489–512; Emilie Anderson Allen and Darrel J. Steffensmeier, "Youth underemployment, and property crime: Differential effects of job availability and job quality on juvenile and young adult arrest rates," *American Sociological Review*, 54, no. 1 (February 1989): 107–123.

49. Maternowska and Fry, "The multi-country study on the drivers," 15.

50. World Health Organization, Changing cultural and social norms supportive of violent behaviour (2009), https://www.who.int/violence_injury_prevention/violence/norms.pdf

51. Maternowska, Potts, and Fry, "A cross-country snapshot of findings," 3.

52. Ibid, 2.

53. Ibid.

54. Maternowska and Fry, "The multi-country study on the drivers of violence," 20.

55. Ibid, 13.

56. Know Violence in Childhood Learning Initiative. "Ending violence in childhood." (2017). http://www.knowviolenceinchildhood.org/publication/flagship-report, 65

57. Ibid.

58. Maternowska and Fry, "The multi-country study on the drivers," 15.

59. Article 4 states that "States Parties shall undertake all appropriate legislative, administrative, and other measures for the implementation of the rights recognized in the present Convention. With regard to economic, social and cultural rights, States Parties shall undertake such measures to the maximum extent of their available resources and, where needed, within the framework of international co-operation."

See Children Act 2004, 2A, re: the need for the Children's Commissioner established by the Act to have regard to the CRC.

60. Mark Henaghan Ruth Ballantyne, "Child poverty in New England: A contravention of articles 6 and 27 of the convention on the rights of the child 1989," *Stellenbosch Law Review,* 26 (2015): 380–398.

61. Aoife Nolan, "Art.27 the right to a standard of living adequate for the child's development," in *The UN Convention on the Rights of the Child: A Commentary,* ed. John Torbin (Oxford University Press, 2019), 1034, citing CO Norway, CRC/C/MNG/CO/3-4 para 47; CO Tajikistan, CRC/C/TJK/CO/2 para 59, CO Pakistan, CRC/C/PAK/CO/4 para 77; CO Djibouti, CRC/C/DJI/CO/2 para 61.

62. Aoife Nolan, "Art.27," 1032; See also Aoife Nolan, "Poverty and Child Rights," in *Oxford Handbook of Children's Rights*, eds. Jonathan Todres and Shani M. King (Oxford University Press, 2019).

63. I.e. the "development" of the child is mentioned 13 times in preamble and articles of the CRC; Arts. 5 and 14 also mention the "evolving capacities" of the child; and there is an emphasis throughout on the attainment of ESCR rights that align with a capacities approach.

64. See e.g. Olga A. Khazova, "International Children's Rights Law: Child and the Family," in *International Human Rights of Children*, eds. Ursula Kilkelly and Ton Liefaard (Springer, 2019), 161–186.

65. Universal Declaration of Human Rights GA Res 217A (III) UN Doc A/810 (10 December 1948) art 16(3); International Covenant on Economic Social and Cultural Rights (adopted December 16, 1966, entered into force January 3, 1976) 993 UNTS 3 art 10(1); International Covenant on Civil and Political Rights (adopted December 16, 1966, entered into force March 23, 1976) 999 UNTS 171 art 23(1); European Social Charter (adopted October 18, 1961, entered into force February 26, 1965) 529 UNTS 89 art 16 (Council of Europe); American Convention on Human Rights (adopted November 22, 1969, entered into force July 18, 1978) 1144 UNTS 123 art 17(1); African Charter on Human and Peoples' Rights (adopted June 27, 1981, entered into force October 21, 1986) 1520 UNTS 217 art 18(1); African Charter on the Rights and Welfare of the Child (adopted July 11, 1990, entered into force November 29, 1999) CAB/LEG/24.9/49 art 18(1).

66. Aoife Nolan, "Art.27," 1042.

67. John Tobin and Florence Seow, "Art.18 parental responsibilities and state assistance," in *The UN Convention on the Rights of the Child: A Commentary*, ed. John Torbin (Oxford University Press, 2019).

68. CRC Committee, "General Comment No 21 (2017): Children in street situations," (17 June 2017) CRC/GC/C/21 ('CRC GC 21') para 49.

69. Ibid.

70. CRC Committee, "General Comment 13," para 43(a)(iv).

71. Ibid, para 20(e), footnote 7; para 72(e), footnote 26.

72. Ibid, para 74, fn 27.

73. Ibid, 18 April 2011, para 72(f).

74. Ibid, 18 April 2011, para 72.

75. Laws concerning the criminal liability of adult (and in some cases, 16 and 17 year old) perpetrators of VAC include the following: the Offences Against Persons Act 1861 (ss 47, 20, and 18), which criminalizes causing actual bodily harm, wounding, or grievous bodily harm; Section 5 of the Domestic Violence, Crime and Victims Act 2004, which criminalizes causing or allowing the death or serious physical harm of a child; and Section 1(1) of the Children and Young Persons Act 1933, which creates liability for a person aged 16 or older responsible for a child, who causes or directly "assaults, ill-treats . . . neglects, abandons or exposes" a child "in a manner likely to cause him unnecessary suffering or injury to health (whether the suffering or injury is of a physical or a psychological nature)." Not all VAC is criminalized; see the defense of "lawful chastisement," Children Act 2004, s58.

76. See e.g. Jeremy Horder, *Ashworth's Principles of Criminal Law*, 8th ed. (Oxford University Press, 2016), 101–130; A. P. Simester, J. R. Spencer, F. Stark, G. R. Sullivan, and G. Virgo, *Simester and Sullivan's Criminal Law: Theory and Doctrine*, 6th ed. (Hart Publishing, 2016), 89–128.

77. See e.g. Jonathan Herring, "Chapter 11: Child protection," in *Family Law*, 7th ed. (Pearson, 2015).

78. Children Act 2004, s10(2).

79. E.g. Children Act 1989 s17; Children and Families Act 2014, Part 3.

80. Department for Education, "Working Together to Safeguard Children: A guide to inter-agency working to safeguard and promote the welfare of children," (July 2018), https://assets.publishing.service.gov.uk/government/uploads/system/uploads/attachment_data/file/942454/Working_together_to_safeguard_children_inter_agency_guidance.pdf, 4.

81. Ibid, 20.

82. Ibid, 40.

83. Ibid, 103.

84. Eileen Munro, "The Munro review of child protection part one: A systems analysis." (2010); Eileen Munro, "The Munro review of child protection: Final report, A child-centred system," (2011).

85. Steven Kennedy, "Child Poverty Act," 1.

86. Ibid, 5.

87. Department for Education, "Child Poverty Strategy," 98.

88. Life Chances Act 2010, Section A1A.

89. Welfare Reform and Work Act 2016, ss. 7(12), 36(2)(d).

90. Aoife Nolan, "Art.27," 1042.

91. Local Government Association, "Local government funding: Moving the conversation on" (3 July 2018).

92. Judith Masson, "The state as parent: The reluctant parent? The problems of parents of last resort." *Journal of Law and Society*, 35, no. 1 (March 2008): 52–74.

93. The work of the Commissioner does not situate poverty as a driver of violence; see e.g. Children's Commissioner for England, "Annual Report and Accounts 2019-20" (July 16, 2020), as one example of the household focus regarding risk factors for VAC.

94. Joseph F. Donnermeyer, "What's place got to do with it? Explaining violence in a rural context," in *The Routledge International Handbook of Violence Studies*, eds. Walter S. DeKeseredy, Callie Marie Rennison, and Amanda K. Hall-Sanchez (Routledge, 2018), 95–120; Robert D. Crutchfield and Tim Wadsworth, "Poverty and violence," in *International Handbook of Violence Research*, eds. Wilhelm Heitmeyer and John Hagan (Springer, 2005), 67–82.

95. See e.g. Laura Robertson and Karen Broadhurst, "Introducing social science evidence in family court decision-making and adjudication: Evidence from England and Wales," *International Journal of Law, Policy and The Family*, 33, no. 2 (June 2019): 181–203; Murray Levine, Leah Wallach, David I. Levine, and Deborah Goldfarb, "An illustration of the intersection of social science and the law: The legal rights of adolescents to make medical decisions," *Hastings Women's Law Journal*, 30, no. 2 (2019): 241–260; Richard A. Warshak, "Social science and children's best interests in relocation cases: 'Burgess' revisited," *Family Law Quarterly*, 34, no. 1 (Spring 2000): 83–113; Zoe Rathus, "'The research says . . .': perceptions on the use of social science research in the family law system," *Federal Law Review,* 46, no. 1 (2018): 85–111; Irwin Sandler, Michael Saini, Marsha Kline Pruett, Joanne L Pedro-Carroll, Janet R Johnston, Amy Holtzworth-Munroe, and Robert E Emery, "Convenient and inconvenient truths in family law: Preventing scholar-advocacy bias in the use of social science research for public policy," *Family Court Review*, 54, no. 2 (2016): 150–166.

96. See e.g. Brenda Hale, "Should judges be socio-legal scholars?" *Socio-legal Studies Association 2013 Conference* (March 26, 2013.) https://www.supremecourt.uk/docs/speech-130326.pdf; Association of Family and Conciliation Courts, "Guidelines for the Use of Social Science Research in Family Law," (2018), 1, https://www.afccnet.org/Portals/0/AFCC%20Guidelines%20for%20the%20Use%20of%20Social%20Science%20Research%20in%20Family%20Law.pdf?ver=2020-03-30-092936-097

97. See e.g. Tracy Shildrick, "Lessons from Grenfell: Poverty propaganda, stigma and class power," *The Sociological Review*, 66, no. 4 (2018): 783–798; Gill Valentine and Catherine Harris, "Strivers vs Skivers: Class prejudice and the demonisation of dependency in everyday life," *Geoforum*, 53 (May 2014): 84–92.

98. Willem Assies, "Legal empowerment of the poor: with a little help from their friends?" *The Journal of Peasant Studies*, 36, no. 4 (October 2009): 909–924.

99. Ben Cousins, "Capitalism obscured: the limits of law and rights-based approaches to poverty reduction and development," *The Journal of Peasant Studies*, 36, no. 4 (October 2009): 893–908.

Chapter 11

Children's Voices in Family Law Proceedings in Australia, the United Kingdom, New Zealand, and Canada

Michelle Fernando

INTRODUCTION

Children have a right to express their views in family law decision-making and have those views taken into account. They must be given opportunities to be heard. These rights are enshrined in Article 12 of the United Nations Convention on the Rights of the Child (UNCRC), which recognizes that children have the capacity to be active participants in decisions that affect their lives.

Children's views are routinely taken into account when making decisions for parenting arrangements that are in their "best interests." Nevertheless, children continue to report that they are dissatisfied with their level of participation and are unconvinced that their views are properly considered.[1] This could be because the methods by which children's views are ascertained and reported to decision-makers disregard children's autonomy in favor of "protecting" them from litigation. For example, children are rarely given an opportunity to have their views advocated by a lawyer or to meet with a judge, and almost never appear as a party or a witness.[2]

This chapter compares the laws, practices and attitudes relating to children's participation in contested family law (custody) proceedings in Australia, England and Wales, Scotland, New Zealand, and the Canadian province of Ontario. The discussion is limited to court proceedings after parental separation, and does not extend to child protection proceedings or pre-court processes such as mediation. Examining the main methods of hearing from children; expert reports, legal representation and judicial meetings with children, I explore the variations in each jurisdiction, and how these methods work to promote, or stifle, children's right to be heard.

I observe that despite, at times, significant efforts to improve the way children's voices are ascertained and heard, children still feel voiceless. I explore the role judges may play in influencing a social norm that children are autonomous beings whose rights must be respected.

WHY SHOULD WE LISTEN TO CHILDREN?

The UNCRC reflected a new understanding that children are the subject of rights, rather than mere recipients of adult protection, and that those rights demand that they are entitled to be heard.[3] Every country in the world has ratified the UNCRC, except for the United States, which has signed but not ratified it. Even then, as argued by Breger, "the [UN]CRC retains force and legitimacy even in the United States."[4]

Each ratifying country has undertaken to take all appropriate measures to implement the rights it contains (art 4). Several rights in the UNCRC have been or were already enshrined in various domestic laws of the countries discussed. Even where those rights do not have the force of law, it is widely accepted that a ratified international convention is to be used as an aid in interpreting domestic law.

The UNCRC grants a wide range of rights to children in ratifying countries. Significantly for this discussion, it includes the rights in art 3.1 and art 12. Article 3.1 states, "In all actions concerning children . . . the best interests of the child shall be a primary consideration."

Article 12 states:

1. States Parties shall assure to the child who is capable of forming his or her own views the right to express those views freely in all matters affecting the child, the views of the child being given due weight in accordance with the age and maturity of the child.
2. For this purpose, the child shall in particular be provided the opportunity to be heard in any judicial and administrative proceedings affecting the child, either directly, or through a representative or an appropriate body, in a manner consistent with the procedural rules of national law.

The UN Committee on the Rights of the Child issued guidance on the interpretation of art 12. It decreed that children involved in judicial and administrative proceedings must be informed in a "child friendly manner" about their right to be heard, how they can be heard, and other aspects of the proceedings.[5] Expressing a view is a choice for children and not an obligation, and children are entitled to choose not to exercise their right to be heard.[6]

The Committee also clarified that children must be given the choice of whether their views are heard directly, or indirectly through a "representative or appropriate body." Children must receive information and be made aware of the possible consequences of each. The Committee recommended that, wherever possible, children must be given the opportunity to be directly heard in proceedings.[7]

It is important that we listen to what children have to say in family law proceedings because their views are part of, and help to inform us about, their best interests. Furthermore, being involved in decision-making may have benefits for children. Children have important insights into their lives and are able to impart unique knowledge, including proposing solutions.[8] Children who feel that they have participated effectively in decision-making processes may have better psychological and physical outcomes.[9] Being involved in decision-making processes may weigh more importantly than the result in determining a child's feelings of justice.[10]

Through the UNCRC, we recognize that children have a right to have a say in decisions that affect them and have their views taken into account. The discussion then turns to how, and to what extent, that right is respected and implemented in different countries. Unfortunately, the prevalent view is that, despite the UNCRC, "children have often remained absent from the decision-making process following parental separation."[11]

LEGISLATIVE RECOGNITION OF CHILDREN'S VIEWS

These jurisdictions have been chosen for comparison because of similarities in culture, legal systems, and general approach to contested disputes involving children. All employ an adversarial mode of trial for family law matters. All hold the welfare or best interests of the child as the paramount consideration in family law decision-making[12] and compel the court to take into account any views expressed by children who are the subject of proceedings.

For example, section 60CC(3)(a) of the Australian Family Law Act 1975 states that in determining what is in a child's best interests, the court must consider "any views expressed by the child and any factors (such as the child's maturity or level of understanding) that the court thinks are relevant to the weight it should give to the child's views." In this respect these jurisdictions comply with the requirement in art 12.1 of the UNCRC that children's views be given "due weight."

However, only New Zealand and Scotland have legislated children's right to be given opportunities to express their views.[13] For example, Section 6 of the New Zealand Care of Children Act 2004 states that the child must be given "reasonable opportunities to express views on matters affecting the child." In the other jurisdictions discussed, a court could be challenged on the basis that a child's views have not been properly considered or given weight. However, in Australia at least, there is no legislative obligation to seek the child's views or to give them opportunities to be heard.[14]

HOW CHILDREN ARE HEARD IN FAMILY LAW PROCEEDINGS

This chapter focuses on three common methods of hearing from children, and variations as found in the different jurisdictions. These three methods are reports from child-welfare experts who have spoken with children about their views, legal representation of children's views or best interests, and meetings between judges and children. It is also common for parents and others to present evidence of what children have said to them, but this is given little weight due to its lack of probative value and reliability.[15]

Australia

Aside from accounts from parents, the most common method of ascertaining children's views in family law proceedings in Australia is through a report from a family consultant, called a "family report." A family consultant is a psychologist or social worker who speaks with the children and each parent and may observe their interactions. The report must include the views of the child[16] and the family consultant's recommendations about the care arrangements they consider to be in the child's best interests.[17] Where a case involves complex issues, such as allegations of child abuse or mental health problems, the parties or the court may appoint a specialized "single expert witness" to provide a report.[18] Due to the expertise of report writers, reports are generally highly regarded and are given significant weight. The court's final decision is generally consistent with the recommendations in the report.[19]

In a fewer number of cases, the court appoints an Independent Children's Lawyer (ICL) to represent the best interests of the child. The broad rule is that the court will appoint an ICL where it considers the child's interests require representation.[20] This would include cases involving allegations of child abuse, where there is high conflict between the parents or where a child appears alienated from a parent.[21] This means that in cases where the issues are considered to be relatively straightforward, an ICL is unlikely to be appointed.

An ICL is a "best interests" representative, meaning that the lawyer is required to form an independent view about the best interests of the child and act accordingly.[22] They are not the child's legal representative and are not obliged to act on any instructions from the child.[23] Where the child's views do not accord with what the ICL believes to be in their best interests, the ICL must submit that it is not in the child's best interests that the child's views be followed.[24] Many children feel marginalized by "best interests" advocacy, which contradicts their understanding that a lawyer should advocate for their wishes and not their best interests.[25] An ICL is not obliged to meet with a child, but the lawyer must ensure that any views expressed by the child are conveyed to the court.[26] In practice, the ICL discharges this duty by ensuring that the child's views have been included in the family report.[27]

There are guidelines to inform ICLs and others about their role.[28] The guidelines encourage ICLs to meet with children in all cases, unless the child is under school age, or there are significant practical limitations or in "exceptional circumstances."[29] Despite the guidelines, there is significant variation in whether ICLs meet with children and how they see their role.[30] A recent study found that ICLs perceived their role in facilitating a child's participation as less important than their roles in evidence gathering and assisting to manage the litigation.[31] The same study found that lack of meaningful direct contact between ICLs and children made parents and children concerned about ICLs' capacity to understand and advocate for children's best interests.[32] The Australian Law Reform Commission has recommended that the Family Law Act be amended to require ICLs to comply with the guidelines, including the expectation that ICLs meet with children.[33]

It is very uncommon for Australian judges to meet with children, and there are only a handful of cases, unreported and reported, which describe that a meeting took place. In a survey I conducted of all Australian family law judicial officers in 2010, 86% of respondents indicated that they had never met with a child in proceedings for the purpose of ascertaining the child's views.[34] On the rare occasions when judicial meetings have occurred, this has most often happened in closed court or judges' chambers and in the presence of a family consultant who reports back to the parties on what occurred.

Australian judges are generally reluctant to meet with children. Many believe that meetings may yield useful evidence of children's views and give judges greater understanding of the needs and best interests of individual children.[35] Yet, most are concerned that judges lack the skills or training to meet with children and interpret their views.[36] Australian judges are also concerned that parents may attempt to manipulate or pressure their children.[37] However, most are confident that, if they did meet with children, they would ensure that principles of due process are maintained.[38]

Despite Australia's reference to the UNCRC in the "objects" of children's proceedings,[39] Australia is not compliant with Article 12. Children are not given a right to participate in family law proceedings, and there is no obligation to ensure that a child has had the opportunity to express his or her views. Children's views are mediated through representatives, experts, or witnesses. Children are given no say over how their views are presented, and no opportunity to challenge the evidence if they believe they have been misrepresented.

England and Wales

England and Wales are similar to Australia in that evidence of children's views is commonly provided in a report from a child welfare expert from the Children and Family Court Advisory and Support Service (CAFCASS),[40] who will put forward a position that the officer believes is in the best interests of the child, which might not accord with the child's views.[41] The court may order that the child be made party to the proceedings but this is exceptional.[42]

It is recognized in both case law and practice that a judge may exercise discretion to meet with a child;[43] however, this is rare and has traditionally been discouraged.[44] Guidelines for Judges Meeting Children became effective in April 2010,[45] and emphasize that the primary purpose of a meeting between a judge and a child is to benefit the child, and not to gather evidence, which is the responsibility of the CAFCASS officer.[46]

Scotland

In Scotland, children's views can be heard through several methods including a report from a welfare expert or curator ad litem, written communication from the child to the court, a meeting with a judge, and the appointment of a lawyer who is directly instructed by the child.[47] However, research suggests that only a minority of children have their views considered.[48]

While not routine, a court may instruct a child welfare expert to provide a report, which can include a request to ascertain a child's views.[49] Otherwise, a curator ad litem (usually a lawyer) may be appointed to protect the child's interests and may also be asked to ascertain the child's views.[50] The curator ad litem will write a report containing their factual observations.[51] The curator must have spoken with the child but can present the child's views according to their discretion.[52] Recent research found that judges rely significantly on these reports, despite the fact that they may only partially relay children's views.[53] Furthermore, "neither [the child welfare expert, nor the curator ad litem] has a responsibility to advocate for the child nor to support the child in stating her views, directly to the court."[54]

Methods by which children's views may be directly heard are through a completed Form F9, a judicial meeting with a child, or a child being represented by a lawyer. When an application is made in family law proceedings, the judge may order that the child be served with a copy of the application (called intimation). The child will then receive a Form F9 requesting their views. The form comprises a letter addressed to the child informing the child about their right to tell the sheriff (judge) about their views, by completing a "What I Think" form. Children are also informed that they can seek help from a lawyer or from designated child law organizations.[55]

The use of a judicial meeting to ascertain the child's views has been specifically mentioned with approval in Scottish case law.[56] Interestingly, in interviews with 20 Scottish judges in 2002–2004 the majority said that they would be willing to speak with a child if the child so requested, and none said that they would never speak with a child.[57] Fiona Raitt observed that, even where Scottish judges have expressed apprehension about their skill and ability to speak with children, they are often committed to finding a solution.[58] This is very different from Australia, where judges are reluctant to speak with children and feel restrained by their perceived lack of training.

Canada (Ontario)

In Ontario, a court may make an order requesting the appointment of the Office of the Children's Lawyer (OCL) as the child's litigation guardian.[59] The OCL is a publicly funded office which represents children's legal interests.[60] The OCL has responsibility for determining whether and what kind of assistance will be provided.[61] Due to budgetary constraints the OCL declines services in about one-third of cases where a court has requested its involvement, which is "a major concern to family justice professionals and parents."[62]

If appointed by the OCL, a clinical investigator (usually a social worker) will ascertain and report on the child's views, and offer an opinion about how the child's views relate to their best interests.[63] While this report is funded by the OCL, a court may also order a private assessment by a psychologist or psychiatrist[64] which must be paid for by one or both of the parties.[65]

Ontario has "the largest and oldest program in Canada of child representation in family relationship cases."[66] Case law has affirmed that, unlike the role of the ICL in Australia, the child's lawyer is a direct representative and not a "best interests" advocate.[67] The OCL has confirmed that if the views expressed by a child are strong, consistent and independent, the child's lawyer will advocate those views. If the child's lawyer wishes to take a position contrary to the child's views, they must have cogent reasons and the OCL may not approve that stance.[68]

Ontario judges have discretion to speak with children.[69] In 2009, Canadian researchers Rachel Birnbaum and Nicholas Bala interviewed 30 judges in Ontario about their views on speaking with children. Most expressed a real reluctance to meet with children,[70] and only six had ever spoken with a child in a private family law matter.[71] As in Australia, Canadian judges expressed concern that meeting with children would encourage parents to attempt to influence their children, and that judges may lack skills and training to conduct the task properly. Canadian judges were also concerned with issues of due process, such as if a child wished their views to remain confidential, or the prospect of the judge themselves becoming a witness.[72] These issues did not appear to trouble Australian judges.[73]

The OCL recently added Voice of the Child Reports (VCRs) to its suite of services for family cases. A lawyer or mental health professional, retained solely for the purposes of preparing the report, interviews the child and presents the child's perspectives and views on the issues in dispute. The reports can include the interviewer's opinion about the strength and consistency of the child's views, but more often they simply provide a summary of the child's statements with no evaluation or commentary. VCRs provide less information than a clinical investigator's report, and "offer less opportunity for children to directly influence outcomes than if they were represented by counsel."[74] They are also much less expensive than either of these options and, because of this, are becoming more common.[75]

Children have reported that they are pleased with VCRs as a way of communicating their views to the court and to their parents.[76] A significant feature is that many interviewers offer children an opportunity to exclude matters they discuss from the final report.[77] This removes the criticism from children that their views have been "filtered" by a third party without the child knowing how their views have been presented. However, it is still an indirect method of hearing from children and "may not be as empowering as meeting directly with the judge."[78] Furthermore, Birnbaum warns that "there must also be an awareness of the intrinsic limitations of [VCRs] as they may not reveal the true views and preferences of children who are subject to parental pressure or manipulation, or whose views may be changing."[79]

New Zealand

The views of children in New Zealand are most commonly heard through a lawyer for the child, who, after recent reforms, now represents both the child's views and best interests. Less commonly, but more often than in the other jurisdictions discussed, New Zealand judges meet with children to listen to their views.

In New Zealand there has always been a reluctance to order expert reports in family law cases, particularly for the purposes of ascertaining a child's views.[80] The 2014 Family Justice Reforms (2014 reforms)[81] aimed to further limit reports by raising the legislative threshold for ordering a report from "necessary" to "essential," and a report may only be ordered if it will not result in undue delay.[82] The legislation confirms that a report must not be used solely or primarily to ascertain the child's views.[83] This position is vastly different from Australia and England and Wales, where expert reports are likely to be the primary means of ascertaining children's views and there is nothing prohibiting a court from ordering a report for this sole purpose.

The 2014 reforms also changed the threshold for appointment of a lawyer for the child and clarified the lawyer's role. Previously, lawyers for children were appointed in every case that was likely to proceed to a hearing, unless the appointment would serve "no useful purpose." This threshold was elevated to appointment only if the court has concerns for the child's safety or well-being and considers the appointment necessary.[84] There were concerns that the elevated threshold represented a retreat in the recognition of children's rights, but a recent review found that the change hasn't resulted in a decrease in the number of lawyers for children appointed.[85]

Unlike in Australia, a lawyer for the child is not strictly a "best interests" advocate. The lawyer must "provide independent representation and advice to the child in a manner that the lawyer considers promotes the welfare and best interests of the child."[86] They must ensure that any views expressed by the child to the lawyer are put before the court.[87] Another key change in the 2014 reforms was to make it clear that the lawyer for the child can present the child's views and promote their welfare and best interests at the same time. Previously, if the child's views did not accord with what the lawyer believed was in their best interests, the lawyer would invite the court to appoint a "counsel to assist" to represent the child's best interests. Now, in most cases, lawyers must manage both aspects of the role.[88]

A lawyer for the child is statutorily obligated to meet with a child to find out his or her views. The only exception is if, because of exceptional circumstances, a judge directs that it is inappropriate for the lawyer to meet with the child.[89] This is different from Australia, where it is well-known that ICLs do not always meet with children. Aside from presenting the child's views, the lawyer for the child must explain to the child the content of any expert report,[90] ensure that any parenting orders made are explained in a manner and language that the child will understand,[91] act as conduit between the judge and the child in relation to any request for a judicial meeting,[92] and usually attend any meeting between the child and the judge.[93] These varied tasks demonstrate that the role played by the lawyer for the child is larger in scope than that of the ICL in Australia and suggest a closer and more ongoing relationship between lawyer and child.

Despite this important role, a review of the 2014 reforms found that children's voices are still not sufficiently heard or advocated for. The main criticisms are that children are not kept informed about the progress of court proceedings, and lawyers may not have the appropriate knowledge and skills to effectively advocate for children. Lawyers also have inconsistent practices in how they approach their role.[94] Nevertheless, the review considered that the 2014 reforms are working well and do not require amendment. It found the elevated threshold for appointment of lawyers for children "achieves an appropriate balance between upholding children's right to participate in decisions concerning them while ensuring resources are targeted to cases where those resources are needed."[95] Furthermore, the clarification of the dual role of advocate and best interests representative "suitably limits the exposure of children to court-appointed professionals."[96]

In stark contrast to Australia and England and Wales, New Zealand has a "long unbroken history of judicial interviewing."[97] A study of judges conducted by Nicola Taylor and John Caldwell found that most New Zealand Family Court judges "were enthusiastic in their encouragement of judicial meetings and highlighted the benefit for them, the child and the decision-making process."[98] New Zealand case authority has stated that where a child wishes to speak with the judge and has firm views and/or sufficient maturity, the judge should exercise his or her discretion to speak with the child.[99] The value of a judicial meeting to ascertain the wishes of children has been endorsed in numerous cases.[100] However, authority also confirms that the decision to meet with a child remains a matter for the individual discretion of the trial judge.[101]

Judges interviewed by Taylor and Caldwell emphasized that, in their minds, the purpose of a judicial meeting with a child was not to elicit the child's views, but to honor the legislative requirement that children have "reasonable opportunities to express views." Judges see meetings with children as allowing children a forum to express their views directly, and an opportunity to reassure the child that the judge is the decision-maker and to explain the process. Several judges regarded the meeting as a "meet and greet" only.[102] While it is important for a child to have opportunities to express their views, meet the decision-maker and have processes explained, the fact that judges do not see meetings with children as an opportunity to elicit their views may conflict with children's beliefs about the purpose of the meeting, leading to further dissatisfaction.

DISCUSSION

It is clear that each of the jurisdictions discussed has a suite of methods available to ascertain the views of children and adduce them into evidence. To that extent, children are arguably given an "opportunity to be heard" in compliance with art 12.2 of the UNCRC. However, studies with children consistently show that despite these "opportunities," many children do not feel that they have been listened to, or that their views have been properly taken into account. Children have expressed dissatisfaction with the ways their views have been ascertained or presented.[103]

Children have reported that they are not happy about a process which relies on questioning by a third party who filters and interprets what the child has said,[104] which is always the case when children's views are presented through an expert report. Children are not given a say in how their views are presented, nor any opportunity to challenge the contents of the report if they believe they have been misrepresented. Children have expressed greater satisfaction with VCRs in Ontario, because their views may be presented without commentary or evaluation, and the child may have some say about what is included in the report.[105] However, it is still an indirect method of making children's voices heard.

The "best interests" model of legal representation is arguably not an adequate way of ensuring children's participation, because lawyers prioritize their other roles of evidence gathering and litigation management over facilitating children's participation.[106] Many lawyers do not even meet with children or take any steps to present the child's views to the court.

Meetings with judges allow children to present their views directly to the decision-maker, and children have viewed that method positively, saying that children should have the opportunity to talk with a judge if they wish to.[107] However, even in jurisdictions where judicial meetings with children are common, this is an entirely discretionary exercise and is dependent upon court officers communicating a child's request to meet with a judge, and a judge being willing to meet with a child. This may not occur if judges feel that they lack the skills and training to speak with children, or if they feel prohibited because of concerns about parental manipulation or due process.

Furthermore, judges who meet with children are motivated by a desire to allow children to express their views and meet the decision-maker, rather than as a forensic exercise to ascertain the child's views. If judges' reasons for meeting with children are different from children's expectations, the practice of judicial meetings with children may not be able to be reconciled with children's participation rights.[108]

Given these limitations, it may be that a direct model of legal representation, where lawyers are instructed by children and must represent their views, is the best way to ensure that a child's voice is heard and that their views are taken seriously.[109] However, even then, children's views are mediated by a lawyer, who may not have the appropriate knowledge and skills to effectively advocate for children and whose approach may not be consistent with best-practice standards.[110]

This accords with a recent Australian study where some children reported that, even where direct engagement with court officers occurred, the nature of the professional enquiry and interaction insufficiently acknowledged the children's experiences and needs in the context of their parents' separation.[111] The study suggested that the experiences of many children engaging with the family law system led to disappointment when they identified a failure by professionals to genuinely listen to and value their views and experiences.[112]

When asked, children routinely report that they want to have more of a say in the decisions that affect them. Despite sometimes significant changes in policy and practice to promote children's right to be heard, children's voices continue to be excluded. Alan Prout wrote, "The promise to be heard is taken seriously by children and the failure to see it through creates disappointment and even cynicism about democratic values."[113] Many attribute the lack of involvement of children in family law decision-making to perceptions and assumptions of professionals and parents about children's capacity and competency, and concerns about vulnerability to manipulation and distress that participation will cause.[114] However, research suggests that "steps taken to shield children and young people from their parents' litigation, while benevolent in their intention, may be associated with the experience of harm on the part of children and young people where their agency and capacity to participate in decision making affecting them is not acknowledged and accommodated."[115]

CONCLUSION: THE ROLE OF JUDGES IN INFLUENCING SOCIAL NORMS

It is interesting to consider how the manner in which children's views are treated and described in cases may influence the perception of children's agency. In general, family law cases make clear that the child's views are just one consideration, among many others, that are relevant in making a decision that is in the child's best interests. There is generally no specific acknowledgment of the child's right to be heard or to have a say in decisions that affect them. In *Rewriting Children's Judgments*, the authors wrote:

> Judgments at all levels and across all jurisdictions routinely pursue limited, often distinctly disempowering approaches to children's rights. Many judgments fail to engage with children's rights issues, confining their adjudication to a factual review of the available evidence rather than a more nuanced understanding of how that evidence might be interpreted in the light of established children's rights norms and research intelligence. [116]

Two cases from Australia's highest court illustrate this phenomenon. Both cases centered around the views of older children and (in one case) a lack of legal representation. In both, the High Court treated the ascertainment of children's views as no more than a forensic exercise relevant for the judicial process and there was no acknowledgment of the child's right to express their views or be given the opportunity to be heard.[117] This can be contrasted with judgments that expressly recognize children's rights to participate in decisions that affect them, which are much smaller in number. For example, in *BJG v. DLG*, Martinson J noted that "all children in Canada have legal rights to be heard in all matters affecting them. . . . Decisions should not be made without ensuring that those legal rights have been considered."[118]

An increase in judgments written from a child's rights perspective may influence a greater prioritization of children's rights and acknowledgment of their right to be heard and participate. The visibility of human-rights norms in judicial decision-making "is acknowledged as a litmus test against which their effective implementation can be assessed."[119] This concept is explored in depth by Tobin who acknowledges judges' ability to influence and promote human-rights norms but also discusses some of the barriers that must be overcome to facilitate a substantive rights approach.[120]

Children continue to be silenced in the making of decisions that perhaps affect their lives the most. It falls to judges to influence the norm about how we view children and their voices in proceedings by demonstrating respect for children's rights in judgments and treating children as autonomous social participants in the conduct of proceedings. This is particularly important in family law proceedings, which center on the best interests of children and should not prioritize the interests of parents.

NOTES

1. Rachel Carson et al., *Children and Young People in Separated Families: Family Law System Experiences and Needs* (Melbourne: Australian Institute of Family Studies, 2018); Megan J. Gollop, A.B. Smith and Nicola J. Taylor, "Children's Involvement in Custody and Access Arrangements after Parental Separation," *Child and Family Law Quarterly* 12 (2000).

2. Nicholas Bala and Rachel Birnbaum, "Rethinking the Role of Lawyers for Children: Child Representation in Canadian Family Relationship Cases," *Cahiers de Droit* 59, no. 4 (February 2018): 787–829; Fiona Morrison et al., *Children's Participation in Family Actions: Probing Compliance with Children's Rights Research Report* (Scottish Government, 2020), 63.

3. Gerison Lansdown, *Promoting Children's Participation in Democratic Decision-Making* (Florence: UNICEF, 2001), 1.

4. Melissa Breger, "Against the Dilution of a Child's Voice in Court," *Indiana International and Comparative Law Review* 20, no. 2 (2010): 178.

5. United Nations Committee on the Rights of the Child, *Day of General Discussion on the Right of the Child to be Heard* (United Nations, 2006), [40], https://www.ohchr.org/Documents/HRBodies/CRC/Discussions/Recommendations/Recommendations2006.doc

6. United Nations Committee on the Rights of the Child, *General Comment No 12: The Right of the Child to be Heard*, CRC/C/GC/12 (United Nations, 2009), [16], https://www2.ohchr.org/english/bodies/crc/docs/AdvanceVersions/CRC-C-GC-12.pdf

7. Ibid., [35], [41].

8. Carol Smart, Amanda Wade and Bren Neale, "Objects of Concern: Children and Divorce," *Child and Family Law Quarterly* 11, no. 4 (1999): 366.

9. Australian Law Reform Commission and Human Rights and Equal Opportunities Commission (ALRC and HREOC), *Seen and Heard: Priority for Children in the Legal Process*, ALRC Report 84 (Sydney: Commonwealth of Australia, 1997): [13.55]; Joan Kelly, "Legal and Educational Interventions for Families in Residence and Contact Disputes," *Australian Journal of Family Law* 15, no. 2 (2001): 113.

10. Breger, "Against the Dilution of a Child's Voice," 193.

11. Rachel Birnbaum and Nicholas Bala, "Views of the Child Reports: The Ontario Pilot Project," *International Journal of Law, Policy and the Family* 31, no. 3 (December 2017): 344–362.

12. *Family Law Act 1975* (Cth) (FLA) s60CA; *Care of Children Act 2004* (NZ) (COCA) s4(1); *Children (Scotland) Act 1995* s11(7)(a); *Children Act 1989* (UK) s1(1); *Divorce Act* RSC 1985, c3, 2nd Supp (Can) s16(8).

13. COCA s6; *Children (Scotland) Act 1995* s11(7).

14. *Bondelmonte v. Bondelmonte* (2017) 341 ALR 179, [43]-[44].

15. *Reynolds v. Renolds* (1973) 1 ALR 318, 325 (Mason J); Bala and Birnbaum, "Rethinking the Role of Lawyers for Children," 796.

16. FLA s62G(3A).

17. Patrick Parkinson and Judy Cashmore, *The Voice of a Child in Family Law Disputes* (New York: Oxford University Press, 2008), 47.

18. *Family Law Rules 2004* (Cth) div 15.5.2.

19. ALRC and HREOC, *Seen and Heard*, [16.36].

20. FLA s68L(2).

21. *Re K* (1994) 17 Fam LR 537, 555.

22. FLA s68LA(2).

23. FLA s68LA(4).

24. *In the Marriage of Wotherspoon and Cooper* (1981) 7 Fam LR 71, 76.

25. ALRC and HREOC, *Seen and Heard*, [13.56]–[13.57].

26. FLA s68LA(5)(b).

27. Rae Kaspiew et al., *Independent Children's Lawyers Study: Final Report*, 2nd ed. (Canberra: Australian Institute of Family Studies, 2014), 37.

28. Family Law Courts, *Guidelines for Independent Children's Lawyers* (2013). http://www.familycourt.gov.au/wps/wcm/connect/fcoaweb/about/policies-and-procedures/guidelines-independent-childrens-lawyer

29. Ibid., [6.2].

30. Kaspiew et al., *Independent Children's Lawyers*, Chapter 3.

31. Ibid., 29.

32. Ibid., Executive Summary.

33. Australian Law Reform Commission (ALRC), *Family Law for the Future: An Inquiry into the Family Law System Final Report*, ALRC Report no. 135 (Brisbane: Commonwealth of Australia, 2019), [12.9].

34. Michelle Fernando, "What Do Australian Family Law Judges Think About Meeting with Children?" *Australian Journal of Family Law* 26, no. 1 (2012): 53.

35. Ibid., 64–65.

36. Ibid., 65–66.

37. Ibid., 67.

38. Ibid., 70.

39. FLA s60B(4).

40. *Children Act* 1989, c. 41, s7 (UK).

41. Baroness Hale of Richmond, "Children's Participation in Family Law Decision Making: Lessons from Abroad," *Australian Journal of Family Law* 20, no. 2 (2006): 125.

42. Morrison et al., *Children's Participation in Family Actions*, [6.4.4].

43. *Re M (A Minor) (Justices' Discretion)* [1993] 2 FLR 706 (Booth J).

44. Ibid., *B v. B (Minors)* [1994] 2 FLR 489 (Wall J).

45. Family Justice Council, *Guidelines for Judges Meeting Children who are Subject to Family Proceedings* (2010), http://www.fnf.org.uk/downloads/Guidelines_for_Judges_Meeting_Children.pdf

46. Ibid., Preamble, [5].

47. Fiona Raitt, "Judicial Discretion and Methods of Ascertaining the Views of a Child," *Child and Family Law Quarterly* 16, no. 2 (2004): 155.

48. Morrison et al., *Children's Participation in Family Actions*, 30.

49. *Shields v. Shields* [2002] SCLR 334.

50. Morrison et al, *Children's Participation in Family Actions*, 29.

51. Raitt, "Judicial Discretion," 155.

52. *Shields v. Shields* [2002] SCLR 334, [11].

53. Morrison et al., *Children's Participation in Family Actions*, 30.

54. Ibid., 29.

55. https://www.scotcourts.gov.uk/rules-and-practice/forms/sheriff-court-forms/ordinary-cause-forms, accessed 21 May 2020.

56. *Shields v. Shields* [2002] SCLR 334.

57. Fiona Raitt, "Hearing Children in Family Law Proceedings: Can Judges Make a Difference?" *Child and Family Law Quarterly* 19 (2007): 204, 209.

58. Ibid.

59. *Courts of Justice Act* R.S.O. 1990, c. C43, s89(3) (Ontario).

60. Office of the Children's Lawyer, https://www.ontario.ca/page/office-childrens-lawyer

61. Ibid.

62. Bala and Birnbaum, "Rethinking the Role of Lawyers for Children," 808.

63. Ibid., 798.

64. *Children's Law Reform Act* R.S.O. 1990, c. C12, s30.

65. Barbara Fidler and Rachel Birnbaum, "Child Custody Disputes: Private and Public Assessments," *Canadian Family Law Quarterly* 25, no. 2 (2006): 139.

66. Bala and Birnbaum, "Rethinking the Role of Lawyers for Children," 820.

67. *Strobridge v. Strobridge* (1992) 10 OR (3d) 540, 540.

68. Personal communication between Katherine Kavassalis, Legal Director, Personal Rights, Office of the Children's Lawyer, and the author dated September 15, 2021.

69. *Children's Law Reform Act* R.S.O. 1990, c. C12, s64.

70. Rachel Birnbaum and Nicholas Bala, "Judicial Interviews with Children in Custody and Access Cases: Comparing Experiences in Ontario and Ohio," *International Journal of Law, Policy and the Family* 24, no. 3 (October 2010): 300–337.

71. Ibid., 317.

72. Ibid., 320.

73. Fernando, "What Do Australian Family Law Judges Think About Meeting with Children?"

74. Birnbaum and Bala, "Views of the Child Reports," 346.

75. Bala and Birnbaum, "Rethinking the Role of Lawyers for Children," 798.

76. Birnbaum and Bala, "Views of the Child Reports," 349.

77. Ibid., 346.

78. Ibid.

79. Rachel Birnbaum, "Views of the Child Reports: Hearing Directly from Children Involved in Post-Separation Disputes," *Social Inclusion* 5, no. 3 (2017): 152.

80. *K v. K* [2005] NZFLR 28 [92].

81. *Care of Children Amendment Act (No 2) 2013* (NZ).

82. COCA s133(3) and (6).

83. COCA s133(6)(e).

84. COCA s7.

85. *Te Korowai Ture ā-Whānau: Final Report of the Independent Panel Examining the 2014 Family Justice Reforms* (Wellington: Ministry of Justice, 2019), 78, https://www.justice.govt.nz/assets/Documents/Publications/family-justice-reforms-final-report-independent-panel.pdf

86. See New Zealand Law Society, Family Law Section, *Lawyer for the Child Best Practice Guidelines* (2015), [5.1], https://www.justice.govt.nz/assets/Documents/Publications/fc-fls-best-practice-guidelines.pdf

87. Ibid., [5.2].

88. Ibid., [5.6].

89. *Family Court Act 1980* (NZ), s9B(2), (3).

90. Unless the lawyer considers that to do so would be contrary to the child's welfare and best interests (COCA s134(5)).

91. COCA, s55(4).

92. New Zealand Law Society, *Best Practice Guidelines*, [10].

93. https://www.justice.govt.nz/family/about/lawyer-for-child/

94. *Te Korowai Ture ā-Whānau*, 86.

95. Ibid., 87.

96. Ibid.

97. John Caldwell, "Judicial Interviews of Children: Some Legal Background," *New Zealand Family Law Journal* 5, no. 9 (2007): 216.

98. Nicola Taylor and John Caldwell, "Judicial Meetings with Children: Documenting Practice within the New Zealand Family Court," *New Zealand Law Review* 2013, no. 3 (2013): 462.

99. *Brown v. Argyll* [2006] NZFLR 705, [48] (Priestly J).

100. *LJG v. RTP [Child Abduction]* [2006] NZFLR 589, [88] (O'Dwyer J); *Knight v Finn* [2003] NZFLR 38, [27] (Neal J).

101. *Brown v. Argyll* [2006] NZFLR 705, [47] (Priestly J); *M v Y* [1994] 1 NZLR 527, [527] (Hardie Boys J).

102. Taylor and Caldwell, "Judicial Meetings with Children," 456–457.

103. *Te Korowai Ture ā-Whānau*; Morrison et al., *Children's Participation in Family Actions*; Carson et al., *Children and Young People*.

104. See Parkinson and Cashmore, *The Voice of a Child in Family Law Disputes,* 149; Liz Trinder, "Competing Constructions of Childhood: Children's Rights and Children's Wishes in Divorce," *Journal of Social Welfare and Family Law* 19, no. 3 (1997): 300; Bren Neale and Carol Smart, *Agents or Dependents?: Struggling to Listen to Children in Family Law and Family Research*, Working Paper 3 (Centre for Research on Family, Kinship and Childhood, University of Leeds, 1998).

105. Birnbaum and Bala, "Views of the Child Reports," 346.

106. Kaspiew et al., *Independent Children's Lawyers*, [2.3.3].

107. Patrick Parkinson, Judy Cashmore and Judi Single, "Parents' and Children's Views on Talking to Judges in Parenting Disputes in Australia," *International Journal of Law, Policy and the Family* 21, no. 1 (2007): 89; Dale Bagshaw et al., "The Effect of Family Violence on Post-Separation Parenting Arrangements: The Experiences and Views of Children and Adults from Families Who Separated Post-1995 and Post-2006," *Family Matters* 86 (March 2011): 49–61; Rachel Birnbaum, Nicholas Bala and Francine Cyr, "Children's Experiences with Family Justice Professionals in Ontario and Ohio," *International Journal of Law, Policy and the Family* 25, no. 3 (December 2011): 398.

108. Morrison et al., *Children's Participation in Family Actions*, 69.

109. Linda Elrod, "Client-Directed Lawyers for Children: It is the 'Right' Thing to Do," *Pace Law Review* 27, no. 4 (2007); Breger, "Against the Dilution of a Child's Voice."

110. *Te Korowai Ture ā-Whānau*, 86.

111. Carson et al., *Children and Young People*, 46.

112. Ibid., 92.

113. Alan Prout, "Participation, Policy and the Changing Conditions of Childhood," in *Hearing the Voices of Children: Social Policy for a New Century*, ed. Christine Hallett and Alan Prout (London: Routledge, 2003), 21.

114. Nicola Taylor, Pauline Tapp and Mark Henaghan, "Respecting Children's Participation in Family Law Proceedings," *International Journal of Children's Rights* 15, no. 1 (2007): 61.

115. Carson et al., *Children and Young People*, 93.

116. Helen Stalford, Kathryn Hollingsworth and Stephen Gilmore, "Introducing Children's Rights Judgments," in *Rewriting Children's Judgments: From Academic Vision to New Practice*, ed. Stalford, Hollingsworth and Gilmore (Oxford: Hart Publishing, 2017), 6.

117. *RCB as Litigation Guardian of EKV, CEV, CIV and LRV v. Hon Justice Colin James Forrest* (2012) 247 CLR 304; *Bondelmonte v. Bondelmonte* (2016) 341 ALR 179.

118. *BJG v. DLG*, 2010 YKSC 44 [2]. Other examples include *LEG v AG*, 2002 BCSC 1455; *Michel v. Graydon*, 2020 SCC 24 (Martin J); *Director-General, Department of Community Services v. De Lewinski* (1996) FLC 92-674 (Nicholson CJ); *N v. N* (2000) FLC 93-059 (Mullane J); *Re D (a child) (abduction: custody rights)* [2007] 1 AC 619 (Baroness Hale).

119. Helen Stalford and Kathryn Hollingsworth, "Judging Children's Rights: Tendencies, Tensions, Constraints and Opportunities," in Stalford, Hollingsworth and Gilmore, *Rewriting Children's Judgments*, 21.

120. John Tobin, "Judging the Judges: Are they Adopting the Rights Approach to Matters Involving Children?" *Melbourne University Law Review* 33, no. 2 (2009).

Chapter 12

Educational Norms as They Relate to Disabled Children across the Globe

Mark Henaghan

REALITY AND DEFINITION

Internationally agreed-upon norms for the education of disabled children are found in the 1989 United Nations Convention on the Rights of the Child (CRC) and the 2006 Convention on the Rights of Persons with Disabilities (CRPD).[1] These norms set the bar for countries across the globe to meet, depending on their resources.

The reality is that an estimated 80% of children with disabilities live in low-income countries with the least financial resources.[2] The number of children with disabilities across the globe is difficult to estimate as there is less formal recording of children with disabilities in countries that have the least resources.[3] One estimation of the number of children across the globe with disabilities is that there are some 150 million,[4] and given this estimate was made some 15 years ago, there are probably quite a lot more in 2021, the year this chapter was written.

John Lawrence has estimated that "around 40 million . . . of the 115 million children currently out of school have disabilities, most of which are often neither visible nor simply diagnosed."[5] There is a difference in enrollment rates depending on whether the impairment is physical, where children are more likely to attend school, or intellectual or sensory, where they are less likely to attend. For example, in Rwanda, only 300 of an estimated 10,000 deaf children were enrolled in primary and secondary schools.[6]

Educational norms for children with disabilities are not only grounded in the wide and disparate range of resources that different countries have, they are also grounded in how they are interpreted and seen.

There are two distinct models of disability. One is called the "traditional" or "medical" model, where those with disabilities are seen primarily as disabled because of their individual traits.[7] The emphasis in this model is placed on curing and restoring the individual to normality.[8] In the 1970s and 1980s, the medical model was challenged by those with disabilities on the basis that it curbed their "autonomy, independence and dignity."[9] What emerged was the social model of disability, which positions disability "as a structural and social problem wherein people are fundamentally disabled by society."[10] The way so-called "disability" is seen determines how it is responded to.

In 2006, the UN Committee on the Rights of the Child (CRC Committee) produced a general comment on disability which provides a guide on how to implement the rights of children with disabilities.[11] The Committee made it clear as to what approach should be taken by states when implementing the rights of children with disabilities by saying: "The barrier is not the disability itself but rather a combination of social, cultural, attitudinal and physical obstacles which children with disabilities encounter in their daily lives."[12] The Committee has adopted the CRPD definition of disability by recognizing that disability is an "evolving concept," which is a consequence of "the interaction between persons with impairments and attitudinal and environmental barriers."[13]

Article 1 of the CRPD defines disability in an open-ended, inclusive way, as: "persons with disabilities include those who have long-term physical, mental, intellectual or sensory impairments which in interaction with various barriers may hinder their full and effective participation in society on an equal basis with others." This is the definition of disability that this chapter is based on and against which the educational norms for disabled children will be evaluated.

The theme of this chapter is that, while it is important to have norms that set the targets that states must meet, it is even more crucial to be eternally vigilant in how these norms are being interpreted and implemented if disabled children are to receive equal opportunities to education as other children. On the global scale, states which have resources to remove barriers that inhibit the educational opportunities for so-called "disabled children" should pool their resources to provide support for states that lack the resources to provide equality of opportunity for their disabled children. Only then will the global norms for the education of disabled children have the impact which they aspire to.

INTERNATIONAL NORMS ON THE EDUCATION OF DISABLED CHILDREN

As Lundy and O'Lynn point out, the right to education has long been an established feature of international human-rights law.[14] The right to education was included in the 1948 Universal Declaration of Human Rights and then expanded in the 1966 International Covenant on Economic, Social and Cultural Rights. Lundy and O'Lynn recognize that because the right to education retains "continuous and ready endorsement by state parties [it] is indicative of the fact that it is one of most widely recognized rights of children: there are few governments who do not see themselves as bound to provide education as a matter of entitlement."[15]

At the heart of the international norms on the education of disabled children is their right to fully and equally enjoy all the human rights and fundamental rights and freedom that everyone has.[16] As the right to education is long established as a fundamental human right, it is particularly important that disabled children have access to education. As Enoch Chilemba points out, the CRC is the first global human-rights treaty to explicitly list disability in its general anti-discrimination provisions.[17] Along with non-discrimination, the CRC Committee has highlighted the best interest of the child, the child's survival and development, and the child's participation as the four cardinal principles for the implementation of the CRC.[18] Those norms will be used to test the implementation of the international right to education, to which disabled children are entitled.

The key international norms that are specific to education are availability and accessibility of education; equal opportunity to education; inclusive education at all levels; reasonable accommodation of the individual's requirements; support required for persons with disabilities within the general education system to facilitate their effective education; and effective individualized support measures provided in environments that maximize academic and social development, consistent with the goal of full inclusion.[19]

In order for these important norms to become realities for children with disabilities, the CRC Committee recommended a number of specific actions. These range from collecting data on the status of children with disabilities and how they are progressing to using the data to develop comprehensive national policies to ensure the needs of children with disabilities are being addressed.[20]

For the policies to work, the CRC Committee requires prejudices and beliefs that foster discrimination against disabled children be counteracted; legislative measures that redress the structural and social inequalities that children with disabilities have to face; adequate resources; development of knowledge and skills in appropriately qualified teachers who can meet the needs of children with disabilities; ensuring support for the carers of children with disabilities; and including consultation with the children with disabilities and their families.[21]

It is crucial that the voices of children with disabilities are heard in relation to all aspects of their education if they are to be truly empowered and feel fully included in their societies. The CRC Committee recommended strongly that "children with disabilities be heard in all procedures affecting them and that their views be respected in accordance with their evolving capacities."[22] Bronagh Byrne identifies three reasons why children with disabilities have had their participatory rights severely curbed: "[a] belief that they have no views to express; an assumption that their interests and lives will always be articulated by adult caretakers; and concern that their views will be too expensive or difficult."[23]

Hultman and others conducted research with social workers through seven focus-group interviews with 35 municipal social workers from communities in different parts of Sweden in order to gain a deeper understanding of Swedish social workers' experience of disabled children's participation.[24] The goal of the study was to discover the ways the social workers' knowledge about impairment and disability, combined with their legal understanding and local context, influenced children's participation in formal meetings and decision-making. What the study found was that the participation of disabled children was illusory. In the words of the authors of the study: "[i]n elusive participation, the dimensions of power asymmetries between and discrepancy among policy, practice and legislation; norms and perceptions of normality; judgement of children's abilities and conflicting perspectives and needs interact with each other. Combined, these dimensions contribute to positioning disabled children in subordinate positions."[25]

An example from the study as to how disabled children were put in a subordinate position is that where parents and children had conflicting needs and wishes, the social workers took a "needs-based approach" (reflecting the best interests principle) to justify young children's lack of influence, based on the assumption "that young children lack the ability to make decisions on personal matters."[26] The authors of the study concluded that the social workers needed to reflect on and critically evaluate their personal values and social norms that affect their understanding of disabled children.[27] They conclude that the social workers "need to shift their focus from assessing whether disabled children can participate to considering how best to enable their participation . . . [in order to] to shift the balance of power and increase their recognition of diversity and children's own perspectives."[28]

The grundnorm for this chapter is that, at the center of the educational norms for disabled children, is the need for disabled children to participate in the provision of their education.[29] All the other norms, such as dignity, self-development, inclusiveness, and accommodation of needs must be based on the perspectives and experiences of the disabled child. Otherwise, it becomes tokenism and will inevitably fail.

The Special Rapporteur on the Right to Education in its report on the right to education of persons with disabilities placed a strong emphasis on the need for radical structural and cultural change and value shifts if the system is to be truly inclusive and enable individual differences.[30] The Special Rapporteur said: "the system that excludes cannot be the same system that includes or promises to include" and continued that "so-called 'integrated education' . . . [gives] rise to separation based on the subjective effects of 'being included'."[31]

The next section of this chapter will critically evaluate the policies and legislation of a number of countries on the degree to which the education rights of disabled children are based on the experiences and participation of disabled children.

POLICIES FOR THE EDUCATION OF DISABLED CHILDREN FROM AROUND THE GLOBE—THE RHETORIC

The policies and legislation on the education of disabled children in New Zealand, Australia, the United Kingdom, the United States, and Canada are the focus of this part of the chapter.

There are some key commonalities among countries on the education right of disabled children. All have a strong emphasis on there being no discrimination against children with a disability when it comes to education.[32] No discrimination is primarily expressed by a consistent policy of inclusion of children with disabilities in so-called "mainstream" education.

All the countries recognize the need to adapt the conditions within their education system to meet the needs of children with disabilities. This is done in different ways.

In New Zealand, this is done via a New Zealand Disability Strategy.[33] This is primarily focused on achieving outcomes for those with a disability, such as social skills, resilience, determination, confidence, belonging, identity, and a full life beyond school. This is to be achieved by providing funding to modify schools, employ teacher aides, and provide technology and equipment that enable learning for those with disabilities. There is also the provision of special schools and special classes for those with more severe disabilities.

In Australia, it is done through the Disability Standards for Education 2005, where one of the key obligations is to make "reasonable" adjustments.[34] This is not the same as adjustments that meet the needs of particular pupils with a disability. The term "reasonable" is an objective criterion that can have limits placed on it due to, for example, financial limitations. The Standards do not require changes if they would impose unjustifiable hardship on the education provider.

The UK uses the same criteria of "reasonable" adjustments in the goal of achieving equality for the education of disabled children.[35]

In the United States, the Individuals with Disabilities Education Act 1990, which is federal law, starts with an Individual Education Program, which requires accommodation and modification for the needs of the individual child.[36] This is further explained by the principle of the least restrictive environment for disabled children in their education. The least restrictive environment means the environment most like that of typical children in which the child with a disability can succeed academically. This is because of a strong emphasis on the integration of disabled children, which has the potential to limit their ability to learn if the external conditions are not sufficiently adapted to their needs.

When it comes to the core norm of obtaining the views and listening to the educational experiences of those with disabilities, there is a different approach and a complete lack of detail in how it is to be done. New Zealand in its Disability Strategy 2016–2026 says that disabled people are to be consulted and actively involved in the development and implementation of legislation and policy.[37] There is no detail on how this is to happen and how frequently it is to occur. Nor is there any indication of how the disabled children who will be consulted are to be chosen and what "actively involved" and "consultation" mean. It is not the same as listening to the views and perspectives of individual disabled children who are living their educational experiences, which may or may not be working for them.

Australia, in its Disability Standards of Education 2005, places an obligation on the state to consult in order to understand the impact of a student's disability and to determine whether any adjustments or changes are needed to assist the student. It does not say who the consultation is to be with, how it is to be done or the degree to which the views and experiences of the disabled child will be taken into account.

Standard 10 of the Equality Act 2010 in the UK sets out the requirements of accessibility for disabled pupils, which requires the local authority to develop a strategy to increase the extent to which disabled pupils can participate in the school's curriculum, and each school must prepare an accessibility plan to execute the strategy. In preparing the plan, the school must "take account" of the pupils' disabilities and any preferences expressed by them or their parents. The plan can be inspected by an inspector, but there does not appear to be any clear mechanism for checking with the views and experiences of disabled pupils. It appears to be a bureaucratic paper check that the plan is in place.

The Special Educational Needs and Disability Code of Practice: 0 to 25 years in the UK provides statutory guidance for organizations that work with and support children and young people who have special educational needs or disabilities.[38] The Code explains the duties of local authorities, health bodies, schools, and colleges to provide for those with special educational needs under Part 3 of the Children and Families Act 2014 (UK). One of the principles of the Code is to take into account the views of children, young people and their families and enable them and their parents to participate in decision-making.[39] There is very little guidance in the Code of Practice for how best to provide the appropriate conditions for children to express their views and experiences. The emphasis is on how it is a requirement to ensure that they are involved and actively supported in contributing to their needs assessment. When it comes to support, all the Code says is that it must be the support "necessary" to enable them to participate, which includes information on their rights and entitlements.[40]

As Laura Lundy has eloquently argued, there is much more to enabling children to express their views and experiences than just providing information that they have the right to do it.[41] First, children must be given a safe and inclusive space to express their views safely. Second, they must be given appropriate information to facilitate the expression of their views. They must be given the information they need to form a view, and they must know that they do not have to take part. Third, children's views must be communicated to a person who has the responsibility to listen to them. Finally, it is important to ensure that the child's views are taken seriously and acted upon where appropriate.

In the United States, one pillar of the Individuals with Disabilities Education Act 1990 is parent and teacher participation. This is about a good family-professional partnership where parents and teachers work together to determine the best ways of working with and providing information for a student. The pillar says that parents should be able to provide valuable input about their child for their placement and educational goals. There is no mention of obtaining the views and experiences of the child. The United States is not a signatory to the CRC, which may explain why there is no emphasis on the expression of Article 12 of the Convention (the child's right to express views) in legislation and policy.

RESEARCH OUTCOMES OF DISABLED CHILDREN IN EDUCATION—THE REALITIES

A 2006 survey of Disability and Education in New Zealand gives a picture of the limitations that children with disabilities face in education.[42] Of 33,200 disabled children in the 5–14 age range, 46% of their parents/caregivers reported that their child had been "limited" in some way at school because of disability.[43] The higher the need for support, the more likely the child suffered some kind of limitation. For example, 70% of children with high support needs were reported to suffer limitations, compared to 22% with low support needs.[44]

The limitations varied according to the type of disability. For example, 61% of children who used technical aids were the most likely to have participated in sports and the playing of games with others restricted at school. By way of comparison, the largest proportion of children with disabilities who found it difficult to make friends were those who had a psychological or psychiatric disability (56%).[45]

A third of all the groups of disabled children, including those who used technical aids, those who had a psychological, psychiatric, or intellectual disability, and those who had a speaking disability, were more likely to experience limitations when going on school outings or camps.

The most likely children with disabilities to change schools were those with psychological and psychiatric conditions (38%) and those with intellectual disability (36%). Changing schools is very disruptive for school education.[46] The end result is that 36% of the 15–24-year-old disabled young people at the time of the survey, who were also disabled while in formal education or training, had no educational qualification—as compared with the 19% of non-disabled young people aged 15–24 who had no educational qualification.[47]

Julie Alesech and Shoba Nayar point out that central to the success of a disabled child to so-called mainstream education is the facilitation of their acceptance and belonging within the school setting.[48] Yet, as they go on to say, there is a dearth of literature in New Zealand and internationally that directly addressed this issue. Their study addressed the question: "How do New Zealand school settings help or hinder a sense of acceptance and belonging in children identified as having special education needs?"[49] Six case studies were set up in schools in the Auckland region (New Zealand's most populous city) to represent a typical sample of New Zealand students, classrooms, and schools. The study used a thematic analysis of interview data collected from the child, parent, guardian, teacher and other professionals working with the child's school, as well as classroom observation and document review.

An earlier study by Richard Rose and Michael Shevlin based on 120 semi-structured interviews with disabled children found that having the support of teachers and other staff were important to the children's sense of acceptance within the school environment.[50] As Abraham Maslow pointed out in his work, feeling that one is accepted and belongs is a very basic human need essential for human growth and development.[51] As Alesech and Nayar point out: "Children with disability are at risk of not experiencing a sense of acceptance and belonging, which is detrimental to their social, academic, health and psychological outcomes."[52]

In their study, Alesech and Nayar used five pillars as the basis for children feeling a sense of acceptance and belonging at school.[53] First, attitude includes the significance of creating a positive, accepting culture for children with special needs. Second, an individualized approach recognizes that each child is unique and needs a program that targets their individual needs. The third pillar is having teachers who are knowledgeable about how to teach children who have learning, social, and/or behavioral difficulty and who are prepared to gain an in-depth knowledge (social, emotional, medical, and family) about that child. The fourth pillar is effective teaching and learning techniques in the classroom. The keys are to enable each child's success by encouragement and incentives, such as rewards when things are done well, and engaging children through the use of fun activities, such as art, music, drama and dance, as well as physical activity, such as swimming, soccer, and netball.

The final pillar is the adherence to education law, which is described as a "vital factor in the inclusion of children who have special needs in New Zealand school settings and a fundamental human right."[54] Alesech and Nayar give an example from their study of a boy being told by the school to be kept at home during the cross-country and the Christmas concert, which made the boy and his mother feel "rejected, isolated and not accepted by the school."[55] This clearly infringes the boy's rights in Section 8 of the Education Act 1989 to have the same rights to enroll and receive education as children who do not have special education needs.

Alesech and Nayar conclude that there is a gap between the theory of law and practice in schools in New Zealand.[56] The gaps are caused mainly by inadequate financial investment, limited professional development, lack of educational resources and support. Alesech and Nayar place a strong emphasis on the inclusion of "the voices of children who have special education needs in decision-making processes so that their needs are effectively catered for."[57] They conclude that the five pillars need "constant review" to ensure that they meet the needs of each individual child.[58]

Carol Hamilton also reinforces the reality that there is a gap between intention and implementation.[59] She finds that well-intentioned pronouncements are not always accompanied by the resources necessary to see goals for inclusion become embedded practices in all New Zealand schools. Hamilton writes about the recent mooting in New Zealand of a risk-monitoring predictive model to target individual students at risk of educational failure. The four predictive at-risk categories that were proposed are abuse of the child or their siblings, whether a parent has been to prison, whether the family has a history of welfare dependency, and whether the child's mother has any educational qualification. While such predictive models may be well-intentioned, they run the risk of losing the individual child's needs, which are particularly important for disabled children.

Kerry Purdue in her study of children with disabilities in early childhood education found that despite nondiscriminatory and inclusive policies in the early childhood sector, "some children with disabilities and their families experience exclusionary and discriminatory early childhood settings and struggle to access quality education" where they are readily excluded.[60] The main reasons for the barriers to inclusion found by Purdue were, first, the view that children with disabilities are so significantly different that their educational needs can only be met by special education experts.[61] The issue is seen as one which resides in the child, not the environment. Second, some of the early childhood centers had policies that deterred the inclusion of children with disabilities. These policies include not having to enroll children with disabilities, delaying entry of children with disabilities on the basis that they were not ready to accommodate them, and parents being asked to pay for additional support for their child to attend. All such policies breach the law of equal rights to education with other children. Third, when teachers lacked understanding of the law to include children in the curriculum, they limited the children's involvement and excluded them from involvement.[62] Finally, some centers did make the efforts necessary to have the resources that the children needed to enhance their learning.

The picture is much the same in Australia, where the Australian Human Rights Commission carried out a study entitled: "Access to education for students with a disability: Barriers and difficulties."[63] The study found a long list of discriminatory practices against children with disabilities in the Australian education system. It found, among other things, inconsistency between education providers in how they accommodated the children, insufficient disability support funding, insufficient technological aids and other devices, curriculum adaptation and curriculum needs not addressed, lack of teacher training and support and integration aide training and negative and resistant attitude of teachers and principals and discrimination, social isolation, teasing, bullying or harassment by nondisabled students.

Sadly, the same story recurs in the UK. Chrissie Rogers—whose paper is based on the experiences of British parents who have children with "special education needs" within mainstream education—notices that actual "inclusion" is not necessarily occurring in practice.[64] Rogers identifies a tension between a desire to embrace difference based on "equal rights" (the inclusive goal) and putting the main emphasis on educational performance where the focus is a highly structured testing and examination culture, which leaves very little if any room for differences (the performance goal). The culture of the league tabling of schools trumps the inclusion of children with disabilities. Rogers finds that the hopes and expectations of children with disabilities are challenged repeatedly. The result is that "children with difficulties that include 'anti-social' behavior appear to have a significant chance of exclusion from mainstream school," and the quieter children with disabilities, while they are not excluded from school, "may experience ridicule, or at best low self-esteem."[65]

Rogers identifies that while children with disabilities are "included" in mainstream education, they are excluded at three different levels.[66] They are excluded practically by often being removed from the class into an individual teaching unit. They are excluded intellectually because they often cannot access the curriculum in the same way their peers do. They are also excluded emotionally because it is difficult for them to become part of friendship groups and social networks.

Helena Towle in her report *Disability and Inclusion in Canadian Education* begins by saying that, "compared to adults without disabilities, adults with disabilities in Canada have lower levels of education, higher rates of unemployment and lower household incomes in addition to challenge accessing affordable housing, health care, and transportation."[67] The report recommends, among other things, that teachers are provided with more resources and support, and that there is major support provided to students with disabilities and their families, both inside and outside the classroom.

The theme of failing to adapt the environment to the individual's needs of the child with a learning disability keeps recurring. The education system in different countries has an image of itself that blocks its ability to be able to adapt its teaching and assessment methods to the needs of individual children to bring the best out in them and give them the sense of belonging and achievement needed to fully develop their capacity for learning. There is no excuse for this in the countries discussed, in that not only are they falling well short of their legislative aspirations and the international norms on children with disabilities, but they have the financial resources necessary to make the necessary changes and adaptation.

The situation is even worse for children with disabilities in countries where there are less resources. In Cambodia, for example, a large number of children have been disabled by landmines and through becoming combat victims.[68] This led to the National Education Strategies Plan for 2006–2015, formulating a national policy and strategies for disabled children, the 2008 Education Law, and the 2009 Protection and Promotion of Rights of Disabled Persons Law making specific reference to children with disabilities, stating that disabled learners have the same rights as able learners and have separate special rights. The statutes are described by Maya Kalyanpur as "top-down responses to international imperatives."[69] The reality found by Kalyanpur is that "the Ministry of Education [in Cambodia] would prefer to focus on . . . 'low-cost, high-impact children,' or those who could avail of an educational system with minimal government intervention."[70] This means that the majority of children with disabilities in Cambodia are out of school, and those who are at school were in regular classrooms without adequate support.[71]

Nidhi Singal shows a similar situation exists in India, where the lives of children with disabilities are found to be marked by poverty and marginalization from mainstream social processes.[72] This is because little is provided for by the state for children with disabilities, apart from few government scholarships.

In South Africa, it is estimated up to 70% of children of school age with disabilities are out of school, and those who attend schools are mostly in separate "special" schools for learners with disabilities.[73] The main barriers to inclusive education for children with disabilities in South Africa are the "general lack of support and resources, as well as the prevailing negative attitudes towards disability."[74]

Alison Croft asked the question of whether a survey of childhood disability prevalence is a necessary and feasible place to start when extending education for disabled children in low-and middle-income countries, who are at risk of becoming poor with it.[75] The question is based on the premise that education is thought to have the potential to contribute to breaking the connection between disability and poverty but exacerbates poverty where it excludes disabled people. Croft concludes "that the most pragmatic and ethical way forward is to make the most of knowledge we already have to develop and continue learning from [the] existing [state of affairs]."[76]

MAKING NORMS ON THE RIGHTS OF DISABLED CHILDREN TO EDUCATION A REALITY

Disabled children and their families are often in disadvantaged, vulnerable, and powerless situations. They often lack the resources necessary to take action to ensure the norms for their children become acted upon and implemented.

Lisa Waddington and Carly Toepke advocate for strategic litigation to accomplish change.[77] The idea is not just to win the individual case, but to use the case to promote compliance with the obligations found in international conventions such as the CRC and CRPD.

For example, in *Moore v. British Columbia (Education)*, Jeffrey Moore's parents brought a complaint to the British Columbia Human Rights Commission, arguing that their child, diagnosed with dyslexia, was not provided with adequate schooling options.[78] The Supreme Court of Canada ruled in favor of the Moore family by requiring school districts to promote individual programs for children with disabilities based on appropriate assessment of the individual child.

The European Court of Human Rights in *Horvárth v. Hungary* found that placing Roma children in a school that was segregated was a violation of their right to education and their right not to be discriminated against.[79] The Court found that placing the Roma children in segregated special schools "might have compounded [the childrens'] difficulties and compromised their subsequent personal development, instead of helping them integrate into ordinary schools and develop the skills that would facilitate life among the majority population."[80] The same reasoning can be applied to children with disabilities.

The Canadian Courts have been consistent in finding in favor of schools being tailored to meet the individual needs of disabled children. For example, the Ontario Court of Appeal found in *Wynberg v. Ontario* that schools cannot use a "one-size fits all" approach for children who need individualized accommodation.[81] The only way for educational authorities to not make accommodations for children with disabilities is for them to show that the accommodation would create a "deleterious effect" (for example, infringing on the rights of other students) that would outweigh the benefits of accommodation.[82]

By way of comparison, the United States Court of Appeals (7th Circuit) in *Board of Education v. Ross* placed the burden of proof on the student with a disability to prove that being educated in mainstream with the use of reasonable accommodation would be satisfactory.[83] This cuts against the idea that including children in mainstream schools with appropriate support and accommodation is presumed to be beneficial for children with disabilities by requiring them to prove it.

Unless there are lawyers prepared to take action on behalf of children with disability and their families, or unless it is possible for the children and their families to form class actions, litigation is most likely to be well beyond the means of those who most need support from the legal system. The unequal resources that plague legal systems become particularly stark when it comes to disabled children and their families.[84]

The only way implementation of policies that benefit the education of disabled children will become widespread is when a Minister and Ministry of Education make it a priority and provide financial resources for the training of specialist teachers and give those teachers the recognition that they deserve, as well as to adapt the curriculum and the classroom. For this to happen, champions must lobby the Minister with the voices of disabled children and their families to ensure their needs are heard and given priority.

CONCLUSION

International norms on the education of children with disabilities provide the framework and the values which set the scene for better education for children with disabilities. The centerpiece of the framework of norms is to listen to, take seriously and act on the voices and experiences of children with disabilities and their families. The research that has been done has shown where the gaps are and what needs to be done to improve the educational outcomes of children with disabilities. At the heart of the matter is the need for an attitude that will not rest until every disabled child gets an education that truly meets their needs and enables them to achieve their full potential.

NOTES

1. Thank you very much to Christian Poland for his invaluable editing.

2. World Health Organization, *Disability, Including Prevention, Management and Rehabilitation*, 1.

3. UNICEF, *Right of Children with Disabilities to Education*, 3.

4. UNICEF, *State of the World's Children 2006*, 28.

5. Lawrence, *Right to Education for Persons with Disabilities*, 7. It is estimated that 90% of children with disabilities in developing countries attend school.

6. Karangwa and Kobusingye, *Consultation Report on Education of the Deaf in Rwanda*, 7 (cited in World Health Organization, *World Report on Disability*, 207).

7. Byrne, "Art. 23 Children with Disabilities," 862.

8. Oliver, *The Politics of Disablement*; Oliver, "Re-defining Disability: A Challenge to Research"; Marks, *Disability*; and Oliver, "The Social Model of Disability: Thirty Years On."

9. Byrne, "Art. 23 Children with Disabilities," 862.

10. Byrne, "Art. 23 Children with Disabilities," 862. For further analysis of the model, see Oliver, *The Politics of Disablement*; and Finkelstein, *Attitudes and Disabled People: Issues for Discussion.* For extensions of the social model, see Corker and Shakespeare, *Disability/Postmodernity*; and Shakespeare, *Disability Rights and Wrongs Revisited.*

11. CRC Committee, *General Comment No. 9*, para. 6.

12. CRC Committee, *General Comment No. 9*, para. 5.

13. CRPD, preamble para. 5.

14. Lundy and O'Lynn, "The Education Rights of Children," 260.

15. Lundy and O'Lynn, "The Education Rights of Children," 260. See also UNCESCR, *General Comment No. 14.*

16. CRC, art. 2; and CRPD, art. 7.

17. Chilemba, "International Law on the Rights of Children with Disabilities," 364.

18. CRC Committee, *General Comment No. 5*, para. 12. See also Kilkelly, "Disability and Children"; and CRC, art. 3, 6, 12.

19. CRC, art. 28; and CRPD, art. 24.

20. CRC Committee, *General Comment No. 9*, para. 19. An example of such a study and collection of data is the AIHW, *Children with Disabilities in Australia.* See also CRC Committee, *Nepal* (2005), para. 60(a); and CRC Committee, *Nigeria*, para. 46.

21. See, for example, CRC Committee, *Phillippines*, para. 55; CRC Committee, *Nepal* (2005), para. 59(c); CRC Committee, *Greece*, para. 51(a); CRC Committee,

Nepal (2016), para. 47(c); CRC Committee, *France*, para. 58(d); CRC Committee, *Samoa*, para. 41(f); CRC Committee, *Ireland*, para. 48(c); CRC Committee, *Viet Nam*, para. 55(c); CRC Committee, *Democratic People's Republic of Korea*, para. 36(f); CRC Committee, *Pakistan*, para. 50; CRC Committee, *General Comment No. 9*, para. 32. The need for and importance of consultation is in CRPD, art. 4(3). It has also been emphasized by UNCESCR, *General Comment No. 5*, para. 14. See also Gerison Lansdown, *See Me, Hear Me*.

22. CRC Committee, *General Comment No. 9*, para. 32.
23. Byrne, "Art. 23 Children with Disabilities," 868.
24. Hultman et al., "Elusive Participation."
25. Hultman et al., "Elusive Participation," 45, 47.
26. Hultman et al., "Elusive Participation," 47.
27. Hultman et al., "Elusive Participation," 46.
28. Hultman et al., "Elusive Participation," 47.
29. The grundnorm (fundamental norm) is a concept in Hans Kelsens' *Pure Theory of Law*. It denotes the basic underlying norm of a legal system.
30. Human Rights Council, *Right to Education of Persons with Disabilities*.
31. Human Rights Council, *Right to Education of Persons with Disabilities*, para. 50.
32. Education Act 1989, s 8 (NZ); Disability Discrimination Act 1992 (Cth), s 22 (Austl.); Equality Act 2010, s 85 (UK); Individuals with Disabilities Education Act 1990 (USA). In Canada, there is no special education provision, special education services are designed by each province. The primary focus is on mainstreaming students.
33. Office for Disability Issues, *New Zealand Disability Strategy*.
34. "Students with disability," Australian Government Department of Education, Skills and Employment, last modified December 17, 2020, https://www.dese.gov.au/swd/
35. Equality Act 2010, s 88 (UK).
36. Described by the US Supreme Court in *Honig v. Doe*, 484 U.S. 305 (1988), 311 as "the centerpiece of the statute's education delivery system for disabled children."
37. Office for Disability Issues, *New Zealand Disability Strategy*, 23.
38. Department for Education and Department of Health (UK), *Special Educational Needs and Disability Code of Practice*.
39. As required by Children and Families Act 2014, s 19 (UK).
40. Department for Education and Department of Health (UK), *Special Educational Needs and Disability Code of Practice*, para. 1.9.
41. Lundy, "'Voice' Is Not Enough."
42. Statistics New Zealand, *Disability and Education in New Zealand in 2006*.
43. Statistics New Zealand, *Disability and Education in New Zealand in 2006*, 3.
44. Statistics New Zealand, *Disability and Education in New Zealand in 2006*, 19.
45. Statistics New Zealand, *Disability and Education in New Zealand in 2006*, 18.
46. Statistics New Zealand, *Disability and Education in New Zealand in 2006*, 18.
47. Statistics New Zealand, *Disability and Education in New Zealand in 2006*, 22.
48. Alesech and Nayar, "Acceptance and Belonging in New Zealand."
49. Alesech and Nayar, "Acceptance and Belonging in New Zealand," 85.

50. Rose and Shevlin, "A Sense of Belonging."

51. See Maslow's "Hierarchy of Needs" in Maslow, *A Theory of Human Motivation.*

52. Alesech and Nayar, "Acceptance and Belonging in New Zealand," 90.

53. Alesech and Nayar, "Acceptance and Belonging in New Zealand," 94–102.

54. Alesech and Nayar, "Acceptance and Belonging in New Zealand," 101 (citations omitted).

55. Alesech and Nayar, "Acceptance and Belonging in New Zealand," 102.

56. Alesech and Nayar, "Acceptance and Belonging in New Zealand," 106.

57. Alesech and Nayar, "Acceptance and Belonging in New Zealand," 104.

58. Alesech and Nayar, "Acceptance and Belonging in New Zealand," 106.

59. Hamilton, "Children with Disabilities in New Zealand Schools."

60. Purdue, "Barriers." See also MacArthur, "Tensions and Conflicts"; and Macartney, "Disabled by the Discourse."

61. Purdue, "Barriers," 133.

62. Purdue, "Barriers," 137.

63. "Access to Education for Students with a Disability," Australian Human Rights Commission, 1996, https://humanrights.gov.au/our-work/access-education-students-disability-barriers-and-difficulties

64. Rogers, "Experiencing an 'Inclusive' Education."

65. Rogers, "Experiencing an 'Inclusive' Education," 62.

66. Rogers, "Experiencing an 'Inclusive' Education," 59.

67. Towle, *Disability and Inclusion in Canadian Education.*

68. Kalyanpur, "Paradigm and Paradox."

69. Kalyanpur, "Paradigm and Paradox," 1058.

70. Kalyanpur, "Paradigm and Paradox," 1058.

71. Kalyanpur, "Paradigm and Paradox," 1063.

72. Singal, *Education of Children with Disabilities in India.*

73. Donohue and Bornman, "The Challenges of Realising Inclusive Education in South Africa."

74. Donohue and Bornman, "The Challenges of Realising Inclusive Education in South Africa," 4.

75. Croft, "Promoting Access to Education for Disabled Children in Low-Income Countries."

76. Croft, "Promoting Access to Education for Disabled Children in Low-Income Countries," 233.

77. Waddington and Toepke, *Moving Towards Inclusive Education as a Human Right.*

78. *Moore v. British Columbia (Education)*, 2012 SCC 61, [2012] 3 SCR 360.

79. *Horváth v. Hungary*, (2013) 57 EHRR 31 (ECHR).

80. *Horváth v. Hungary*, para. 127.

81. *Wynberg v. Ontario*, (2006) 82 OR (3d) 561 (ONCA), para. 140–141.

82. *Wynberg v. Ontario*, para. 186.

83. *Board of Education of Township High School District No. 211 v. Ross*, 486 F. 3d 267 (7th Cir 2007).

84. See McBarnet. "Law, Policy, and Legal Avoidance."

Part IV

CULTURE

COMPARING THE NORMS, THEMES, AND LEGAL STRUCTURES OF FAMILY LAW ACROSS THE GLOBE

Chapter 13

Children's Right to Know Their Genetic Origins? A Comparative Analysis of Approaches to Donor Linking

Fiona Kelly

INTRODUCTION

Over the past two decades, a growing number of donor-conceived people from across the globe have asserted the right to know their genetic origins, including the identity of their sperm and/or egg donor. Advocates for reform have argued that maintaining donor anonymity interferes with identity development and may harm the psychological well-being and physical health of donor-conceived children. In more recent years, donor-conceived adults have been joined by a number of scholars who have framed access to identifying information as a human-rights issue, arguing that while releasing information necessarily involves the balancing of competing rights, and thus demands close attention to issues of proportionality, the rights of the child must prevail.[1] Finally, parents[2] who used donated gametes to conceive ("recipient parents"), as well as some donors,[3] have also expressed support for change. Though the overall global trend in recent years has been toward ending anonymity, approaches to the release of identifying information to donor-conceived people— referred to as "donor linking"—vary dramatically. Through a review of domestic regulation across Europe, North America, and Australasia, three general approaches to donor linking have been identified: (1) the "prospective approach" where donor anonymity is prospectively abolished by law and children conceived after the date of legislative enactment have access to their donor's identifying information when they reach a certain age; (2) the "self-regulation" approach where responsibility for decision-making around anonymity and donor linking is left to the discretion of the fertility industry and their customers; and (3) the "retrospective approach" where donor anonymity is retrospectively abolished by law, enabling all donor-conceived people, whenever they were conceived, to access their donor's identifying information. This chapter explores the three approaches to donor linking and the differing social and legal norms that underlie them. It is argued that the different approaches to donor linking reflect, at least in part, the particular legal, historical, and cultural norms of each jurisdiction, suggesting that a uniform approach to the issue may be difficult.

While the regulation of donor linking may not be understood as falling within the traditional parameters of family law, the concept requires one to grapple with many of the more contentious themes of modern family law: definitions of kinship and the process of kin-making, recognition of non-normative families, and the relative significance of genetic and social ties to defining family and parentage. How donor linking should be understood in the context of these debates is difficult to pin down, in part because these trends themselves are often contradictory. For example, Susan Boyd has highlighted the conflicting nature of (Canadian) parentage trends, noting that at the same time that many jurisdictions have amended their family laws to recognize lesbian and gay families and non-biological parents by giving legal weight to preconception intention, there has been a simultaneous emphasis on the significance of bio-genetic ties in parenting disputes between heterosexual couples, and genetic paternity in particular.[4] Donor linking laws are another example of these contradictory trends. Donor linking could be understood as emblematic of a new era in family law whereby who counts as kin is an open, empirical question that may yield multiple and sometimes contradictory answers. As a growing number of jurisdictions extend legal recognition to a range of non-normative families, such as families created by same-sex couples, the domain of kinship has grown. As Hertz and Nelson argue, relationships created through donor linking—whether with other families who use the same donor, between donor siblings raised in different homes, or between donors and their multiple donor offspring—are examples of some of these new forms of kinship.[5] However, donor linking could also be understood as an example of the reification of fatherhood as a genetic relationship alone, especially now that genetic ties can be definitively proven through DNA. Donor-linking laws, which are sometimes portrayed as reuniting donor-conceived children with their "real" father, resonate with arguments made by fathers' rights activists across a number of jurisdictions, which tend to treat fatherhood as the product of a genetic tie, rather than a relationship of care and responsibility.[6] Thus, while donor-linking laws may be seen as existing on the fringe of mainstream family law, they are inextricably linked to broader family law norms.

The chapter begins by providing a brief overview of the arguments typically made for and against donor-linking laws. It then considers how lawmakers across several jurisdictions have responded to the demand for reform, and the ways in which decision-making has been shaped by the cultural and legal norms of each jurisdiction. The chapter concludes by considering whether the emergence of various informal methods for identifying donors, such as online voluntary registers, social media searches, and direct-to-consumer genetic testing, has effectively already ended anonymity, raising questions about the relevance of law in the future.

JUSTIFICATIONS FOR ENDING OR MAINTAINING ANONYMITY

Over the past two decades, a growing number of donor-conceived people have advocated for an end to donor anonymity through legal regulation. Advocates from within the donor conception community tend to frame ending anonymity as a moral issue that requires an ethical response. Their arguments focus on the psychological impact of anonymity on donor-conceived people and appeal to notions of fairness, equality, and good ethical practice. Those who oppose reform, or who express caution about the circumstances in which information is released, tend to focus on the privacy rights of donors, as well as the impact on the fertility industry and its future customers if all donors are required to be known.

Three lines of reasoning are commonly drawn on to support the shift from anonymity to an open disclosure model. These arguments have been made in a variety of contexts across multiple jurisdictions, including before domestic courts, law reform bodies, and government inquiries, as well as within academic literature. The first and most common argument is that by denying donor-conceived people access to information about their genetic origins they are being denied important information about their identity, and that the withholding of this information interferes with their identity development and can cause psychological distress.[7] Knowledge of one's genetic origins is increasingly understood in Western society as imperative to the development of personal identity and positive psychological well-being. As Hertz and Nelson note, "we are at a particular moment in history where public opinion leans towards the belief that genes are determinants of looks, behaviour and personality."[8] Origins information is therefore understood to have "a 'constitutive' character,"[9] where knowledge of one's genetic origins is believed to provide a deeper or "complete" understanding of oneself.[10] This belief can intensify when donor-conceived people feel different from the family in which they were raised, often because they have different physical characteristics, talents, or personality traits.[11] Knowing the identity of their donor is therefore regarded as the means by which to reveal the "truth" of their own identity.

Underlying the argument that origins information is key to identity formation is the notion that genes *themselves* create kinship.[12] Though not a universal position within the donor-conception community, some donor-conceived people report that they perceive their donor relatives, particularly their donor siblings, as family even in circumstances where they have not yet been identified.[13] Thus, ending anonymity and enabling access to information about donor relatives gives donor-conceived people the opportunity to actualize the kinship relationships they perceive to exist based on genetic connection alone.

While arguments around the significance of donor information to identity formation have been framed as an ethical or moral issue in most jurisdictions, in others it has been suggested that access to this knowledge constitutes a human right.[14] It has been argued that there is a positive "right to know," grounded in constitutional law, anti-discrimination legislation, or international human-rights law, depending on the jurisdiction. However, only Germany, through a series of constitutional decisions over two decades, has accepted that its citizens have a "right to know" their genetic ancestry.[15] Others, such as the province of British Columbia, Canada, have rejected the existence of a "right to know," holding that access to information about one's biological origins is not so "fundamental" that it warrants constitutionally protected status.[16]

The second argument made by donor-conceived people in favor of reform is that anonymity denies them access to their medical history, which may be important to the health and well-being of themselves and their own children. Concerns raised by donor offspring about their lack of access to potentially relevant family medical information fall into two categories. The first relates to being unable to respond to general requests for information, such as routine family history questioning from a doctor.[17] The second relates to the risk of a donor-conceived child inheriting a significant genetic condition from the donor.[18] In such a case, the donor-conceived person may miss the opportunity to participate in early screening, be at higher risk of misdiagnosis, or experience delayed diagnosis or treatment when compared with a person who has access to their family medical history.

Finally, donor-conceived people argue that maintaining donor anonymity places them at risk of entering into a consanguineous relationship with a donor sibling or other donor relative. While such an assertion may initially seem far-fetched, there are a number of reported cases of donor siblings coming in contact with each other inadvertently,[19] particularly when the children are being raised within tight-knit communities, such as those created by single mothers by choice or lesbian mothers.[20] The issue is exacerbated by the fact that in some jurisdictions there are no laws limiting the number of offspring a donor can produce or a requirement that births even be reported to the gamete bank.[21]

While arguments against ending donor anonymity have been more muted, they are relatively consistent across jurisdictions. The first series of arguments focus on the ways in which ending anonymity would be in breach of various domestic laws. For example, those who oppose ending anonymity consistently argue that reform would violate privacy laws, which are in some cases constitutionally enshrined, particularly if the reform had retrospective application. The strength of this argument varies from jurisdiction to jurisdiction depending on the strength of the relevant privacy laws. It is notable that the one jurisdiction that has introduced a retrospective linking law where donor information can be released without the donor's consent—the state of Victoria, Australia—has relatively weak privacy laws and no constitutionally protected right to privacy. In contrast, in Canada, where there is a constitutionally protected right of privacy, a retrospective law that provided unfettered retrospective access to adoption records in the province of Ontario[22] was struck down as unconstitutional by the Ontario Superior Court within a week of coming into force on the basis that adoptees and birth parents "have a reasonable expectation of privacy under the Charter."[23]

The second argument against ending anonymity focuses on the negative impact of reform on the fertility industry and its future customers.[24] It is argued that ending anonymity would lead to a donor shortage and potentially the collapse of the industry. This would, in turn, harm people who rely on donated sperm and eggs to build their families, increase the likelihood of fertility tourism to countries without regulation, many of which are in the developing world, and result in an expansion of the already significant underground trade in gametes.

REGULATORY RESPONSES TO DEMANDS FOR DONOR-LINKING LAWS

How arguments around reform have been received and responded to has varied in each jurisdiction depending on its legal, political, social, economic, and historical context. As noted above, an analysis of domestic regulation across Europe, North America, and Australia identified three approaches to donor linking: (1) the prospective approach; (2) self-regulation; and (3) the retrospective approach. Each approach, and the local norms that have shaped it, are discussed below.

The Prospective Approach

In countries in which a decision has been made to end donor anonymity, prospective legislation has been the most common way in which to do so. The typical approach is to introduce legislation which requires donors to consent to having their identity released to their donor offspring when the offspring reach a certain age. What this means in practice is that all children conceived *after the date of legislative enactment* have a statutory right to their donor's identity. Donor-conceived people conceived before this date, and their donors, do not experience a change in legal conditions.

Starting in the early 1980s, jurisdictions including Sweden, Austria, the United Kingdom, New Zealand, Argentina, and several states in Australia began to introduce various forms of prospective donor linking. In some cases, such as Norway, these reforms required the removal of laws that provided for donor anonymity.[25] In others, the issue had not previously attracted legal regulation. However, in almost every jurisdiction that introduced prospective linking laws, the fertility industry was either already subject to some form of legal regulation, or the linking laws formed part of a much larger regulatory package. For example, some jurisdictions had already introduced, or simultaneously introduced, limits on offspring numbers per donor, or registers which collected information about donor conception births. When donor anonymity was banned in the United Kingdom, for example, the fertility industry had already been regulated via legislation for almost 15 years.[26] Part of that regulatory system included mandated record-keeping and the gathering of non-identifying information from donors, even though this information was not available to donor offspring. In other jurisdictions, such as the Netherlands, there was a period of time before identity release was mandated when legislation gave donors the option of having their identity released to offspring if they wished.[27] These earlier legal interventions into assisted reproduction meant that when prospective linking laws were proposed, the cultural shift toward openness had already begun.

A second key feature of the jurisdictions that have introduced prospective linking laws is that the cost of assisted reproduction is subsidized by government via the country's universal healthcare system, implicating the state in assisted reproduction and its outcomes.[28] For example, in New Zealand the national health system substantially subsidizes treatment packages for in vitro fertilization and intrauterine insemination, while in the United Kingdom assisted reproduction is partially subsidized by the NHS. The argument has been made by advocates for reform that if the state is partially funding the industry there is, at the very least, a moral obligation to protect the interests of any resulting children. Providing donor-linking services has thus been treated as part of the state's obligation to the donor-conceived children it helped create.

Finally, in each jurisdiction with prospective laws, reform was preceded by considerable public discussion about whose interests should be prioritized when assisted conception is used. In a number of cases, this conversation was initiated and then facilitated by a government inquiry or committee that heard testimony from members of the donor conception community. Highlighting the often close relationship between changing family law norms and donor-linking reforms, the government inquiries were often prompted by growing public debate about assisted reproduction generally. It was common for the terms of reference to also include questions such as whether access to assisted reproduction should be limited to married heterosexual couples, if and how lesbian and gay parents should be recognized, how to protect women from reproductive exploitation, and the legalization of surrogacy. For example, in Finland, donor-linking laws were part of a much broader reform package that also provided single women and same-sex couples with access to assisted reproduction services for the first time.[29] Similarly, in Ireland, linking laws were part of an Act that also included parentage provisions that extended rights to same-sex couples who used assisted reproduction to build their families.[30] Donor-linking laws in prospective jurisdictions can thus be understood as part of a larger policy discussion and reform agenda around the changing nature of the modern family. Governments were already being called on to respond to new family norms and donor-linking laws were treated as a component of this larger, progressive, package of reform.

In conclusion, the countries that have introduced prospective linking laws tend to be those where government already regulated the fertility industry to some degree, at least partially subsidized treatment, and where linking laws were easily located within a narrative of progressive family law reform. The introduction of donor-linking laws was not without controversy in these jurisdictions, but previous state involvement in the industry meant that the regulation of assisted reproduction was already a generally accepted norm. The introduction of prospective donor-linking laws was typically presented as part of a narrative of progress, where the availability of linking became the next step in government engagement with, and regulation of, the industry.

The Self-Regulation Approach

The jurisdictions where there are no donor-linking laws—the "self-regulation" jurisdictions—are notable for the relative absence of government involvement in their fertility industry. While these jurisdictions are not identical in their characteristics, they tend to share some common features. In most cases, they not only lack donor-linking laws, but also have little regulation of assisted reproduction beyond health-related requirements around the testing and appropriate use of gametes. Assisted reproduction treatment also tends to be privately funded. In contrast to the prospective approach jurisdictions, the industry in self-regulation jurisdictions is entirely market-driven and customer-focused, where the customer is the individual receiving treatment. Anti-regulatory sentiment within the industry in these jurisdictions is often high.

The United States embraces a self-regulation model, creating a situation where the fertility industry experiences almost no oversight. Decisions around information release are treated as a matter of donor "choice" and access to donor information is a service to be purchased by recipient parents. While it is common for donor-conceived adults and support groups, such as the Donor Sibling Registry,[31] to lobby government to intervene in the industry, it has been able to resist all incursions. The only industry oversight in the United States comes from the American Society for Reproductive Medicine (ASRM), an industry group which has actively lobbied against legislation. The Ethics Committee of the ASRM has recommended the indefinite retention of gamete donation records and encourage clinics to have an information-sharing policy.[32] However, many American clinics do not adhere to the guidelines, creating a wide variation across clinics in relation to both record-keeping and information exchange.[33]

The countries where self-regulation is favored are often ones in which reproduction is itself a contentious issue, making governments reluctant to engage with the topic. For example, in the United States, state governments may be wary of regulating the fertility industry due to the political nature of reproduction in the United States in general, as well as public disagreement about who should have access to assisted reproduction services. In other countries, such as Greece and Spain, the lack of regulation around donor linking is tolerated at least in part due to the ongoing social stigma around infertility and donor conception, which is often reinforced by traditional and religious beliefs about the family.[34] Stigma is particularly pervasive around male infertility, making linking with sperm donors especially repugnant. A self-regulation approach to donor linking in these countries allows governments to avoid participation in public debates about controversial issues.

While self-regulation jurisdictions might not have donor-linking legislation, donor linking may still occur. However, it is the market that determines what services are available. In the United States, for example, where there is demand from sperm and egg bank customers, and a willingness to pay a premium price,[35] gametes from "willing to be known" donors can be purchased. Similarly, in Denmark, where anonymity is still permitted and donor linking is not facilitated by law, sperm banks now offer both anonymous and "ID-release" donors, with the latter costing substantially more. Whether these choice-based programs meet the needs of donor offspring is largely unknown as few have reached the requisite age to request their donor's identity. Several

American sperm banks, such as Xytex (xyConnects) and the Seattle Sperm Bank (SSB Connects), also provide web linking services that enable parents of donor-conceived children, as well as adult offspring, to register their interest in contact. If parents, donor siblings, and/or the donor (xyConnects only) wish to make contact, he or she can join the service and information can be exchanged. However, beyond offering the online service, the sperm bank plays no role in information exchange or the management of any relationships that develop.

Self-regulation jurisdictions are typically those where governments are reluctant to engage with reproduction and provide no financial support for industry users. Decisions about donor linking are thus market-driven. It is clear, however, that some portion of the "market" in these countries wants donor-linking services. Thus, while these jurisdictions lack any legal support for donor linking, the practice still occurs. However, because of the lack of formal oversight, availability is dependent on the individual sperm bank and typically comes at a premium price.

The Retrospective Approach

The final response to calls for donor-linking laws is the retrospective approach which involves the introduction of legislation that enables all donor-conceived people, whenever they were conceived, to access their sperm and/or egg donor's identity. In effect, retrospective legislation provides donor-conceived people with the identifying information of donors who donated under conditions of anonymity. The retrospective approach was adopted in Switzerland[36] in 2001 and in the state of Victoria, Australia[37] in 2015. However, because of the destruction of historical records in Switzerland, the law has had little practical impact.[38] In contrast, in Victoria, hundreds of donor-conceived people who were conceived using anonymous donor sperm in the 1960s to 1980s, have been able to access their donor's identity.[39]

Given the distinctiveness of the Victorian approach, it is worth exploring the jurisdiction's legal and social evolution in detail. Victoria has always been at the forefront of both the development of assisted reproduction technologies—Victorian doctors were among the pioneers of the technology of in vitro fertilization (IVF)—as well as the legal regulation of the industry. This history and, in particular, the high level of state government involvement in the industry as far back as the early 1980s, arguably paved the way for the introduction of the state's retrospective laws. The debate about how assisted reproduction should be regulated in Victoria began in 1982 when the state government established the Committee to Consider the Social and Legal Issues Arising from In Vitro Fertilization. The Committee published two reports, with the second considering the ethical use of donated gametes.[40]

While the Committee supported the use of donated gametes in Victoria, it emphasized the importance of honesty and integrity in the process, taking the view that donor-conceived offspring had a right to non-identifying information about their donor. Drawing on the Committee's findings, in 1984 Victoria became the second jurisdiction in the world to enact legislation regulating donor conception and in vitro fertilization. A key feature of the *Infertility (Medical Procedures) Act* 1984 (Vic), which came into force in 1988, was a Central Register which served as a repository for information about parties engaged in donor conception. The Act mandated that identifying information about donors, recipients, and children conceived through donor conception be recorded in the Register. Once they reached adulthood, children could access information about their donor(s) if their donor consented.

The existence of the Central Register dating back to 1988 has meant that, unlike most jurisdictions, Victoria has fairly comprehensive donor records, making retrospective donor linking possible. There is also evidence that the work of the Committee and the legislation that followed prompted cultural change within the industry in Victoria, with some clinics reporting that they started recruiting only donors who were willing to be known as early as 1984.[41] Clinicians suspected that the legislation was a precursor to ending anonymity and they wanted to prepare their donors for that possibility. As a result, many of the men who donated sperm in Victoria in the 1980s were open to being known to their donor offspring,[42] making the introduction of retrospective donor-linking laws almost 40 years later less confronting than it might be in jurisdictions where anonymity had always been the industry norm.

Ten years after Victoria introduced the Central Register and mandated record-keeping for all donor-conception births, the *Infertility Treatment Act* 1995 (Vic) abolished donor anonymity altogether. From 1998 onward, all Victorian donors were required to consent at the time they donated to having their identity released to offspring when the children turned 18. If a donor-conceived adult wished to learn the identity of their donor they could apply to the Central Register and the information would be supplied as of right. However, those conceived between 1988 and 1998 could still only access their donor's identity with consent, and those conceived prior to 1988 had no information rights at all. The latter group could apply to Victoria's Voluntary Register, where donors, donor-conceived adults, and recipient parents could lodge their details and indicate their openness to contact. However, outreach to donors was not possible under the Voluntary Register which meant that many donors were unaware their offspring were looking for them.

The path to retrospective legislation in Victoria began in 2010 when the Victorian Parliamentary Law Reform Committee (the LRC) conducted an inquiry into access by donor-conceived people to information about their donors.[43] A growing number of donor-conceived Victorians had begun speaking publicly about their dissatisfaction with the legal status quo and, in particular, the differential treatment of donor-conceived people depending on when they were conceived. It was argued that if donor-conceived people had a right to know their genetic heritage, as was frequently stated about the 1998 legislation, then that right should apply no matter the date of conception.

At its public hearings, the LRC heard from a wide range of stakeholders, including fertility doctors, parents of donor-conceived children, donors, academics, and representatives of government agencies. However, it was the testimony of donor-conceived adults that captured the Committee's imagination and drove the recommendations for reform. Many spoke of the considerable distress experienced as a result of not knowing their donor's identity, characterizing the absence of kinship knowledge as a lack of agency over their own origins and past.[44] The Committee also heard from ten donors, six of whom supported retrospective access to pre-1988 information for donor-conceived adults.

Most submissions to the LRC supported the view that the law's primary concern should be the interests and well-being of donor-conceived children. In its report, the LRC noted that Victoria's existing legislation, as well as the federal National Health and Medical Research Council *Ethical Guidelines on the Use of Assisted Reproductive in Clinical Practice and Research* (2017), state that the welfare of donor-conceived children be regarded as "paramount."[45] It was therefore the conclusion of the LRC that where there was conflict between the rights of donors and those of donor-conceived people, the rights of the latter should prevail. By denying information rights to those conceived prior to 1988, Victorian law placed the "burden of suffering" on the donor-conceived person, which was in violation of the paramountcy principle.[46] As the Committee explained, it was difficult "to reconcile how the welfare and interests of a donor-conceived person can be in law both paramount *and* subordinate to donor anonymity, as is currently the case."[47] It was thus concluded that wherever such a conflict arose in the legislative framework, it was necessary to amend it in favor of the donor-conceived.

The LRC delivered its final report in March 2012. It recommended that the Victorian government introduce legislation to allow all donor-conceived people to obtain identifying information about their donors, irrespective of whether donors had been assured of anonymity when they donated. However, to balance the right of donor-conceived people to know their genetic origins with the privacy rights of donors, it was recommended that pre-1988 donors be given the option of filing a "contact veto," which would enable them to refuse contact with donor offspring to whom they have been identified, or to specify the type of contact with which they are comfortable.

Within 18 months of the LRC's report, the *Assisted Reproductive Treatment Further Amendment Act* was passed. The Act differed from the LRC's recommendations on one key issue. Instead of providing those conceived prior to 1988 with an unfettered right to access their donor's identity, it permitted access only if the donor consented. However, when the government changed in 2016, the consent provision was removed and replaced with the contact preference system originally recommended by the LRC. The new law came into effect on March 1, 2017, prompting an immediate surge in applications from donor-conceived adults for information.[48] As noted above, unlike many jurisdictions, a significant number of Victoria's historical donor records are still available and in good condition, making donor linking straightforward in most cases.[49]

The Victorian approach to donor linking is unique and is likely the product of the imposition, and gradual cultural acceptance, of legal regulation from the very early days of the fertility industry in the state. The clinical response to the initial legislation meant that donors were acclimated to the idea of being known to their donor offspring from the early 1980s, which arguably reduced the degree of opposition to retrospectives laws 40 years later. Since the introduction of the retrospective legislation, more than half of the pre-1998 donors contacted about an application have agreed to some form of contact, suggesting a reasonable level of acceptance of the law among donors.[50] This unique historical context makes Victoria somewhat of an outlier in the field of donor linking. However, it suggests that countries that have introduced prospective laws over the past two decades may find an eventual transition to retrospective laws less contentious.

CONCLUSION

While the overall regulatory trend globally is toward increasing the availability of information to donor-conceived people, the various responses to donor linking discussed in this chapter highlight the significant role each jurisdiction's historical, legal, social, and economic norms play in the approach taken. Most notably, the greater the level of government involvement in the fertility industry in general, whether via legal regulation or financial subsidies for treatment, the more likely it is for donor-linking laws to have been passed. In contrast, in countries where self-regulation prevails, government has had minimal involvement with the fertility industry and financial support for individuals undergoing treatment is generally not available.

However, as noted above, the absence of donor-linking laws does not mean linking is not occurring. In jurisdictions where donor linking is not formally available, donor-conceived adults, recipient parents and even donors frequently engage in donor linking using informal methods, such as online voluntary registers, social media searches, and direct-to-consumer genetic testing.[51] The frequency of these activities in many jurisdictions suggests that norms within the donor conception community are changing at a faster pace than the law. Some scholars have argued that the growing availability of informal linking practices, and DNA testing in particular, have effectively already ended donor anonymity.[52] This raises questions about the relevance of law to donor linking in the future. In jurisdictions where donor linking is not supported by law, or where its availability is limited to certain individuals, donor-conceived people may withdraw from the legal sphere, choosing to pursue linking through informal means instead. The distinctions between the three approaches identified in this chapter may ultimately become less important as members of the donor conception community take matters into their own hands.

NOTES

1. Sonia Allan, "Access to Information About Donors by Donor-Conceived Individuals: A Human Rights Analysis," *Journal of Law and Medicine* 20, no. 3 (2013): 655; Lucy Frith, "Beneath the Rhetoric: The Role of Rights in the Practice of Non-anonymous Gamete Donation," *Bioethics* 15 (October 2001): 473.

2. Tabitha Freeman, Vasanti Jadva, Wendy Kramer, and Susan Golombok, "Gamete Donation: Parents' Experiences of Searching for their Child's Donor Siblings and Donor," *Human Reproduction* 24, no. 3 (March 2009): 505.

3. Marilyn Crawshaw, Eric Blyth and Ken Daniels, "Past Semen Donors' views about the use of a Voluntary Contact Register." *Reproductive Biomedicine Online*, 14, no. 4 (2007): 411; Ken Daniels, Eric Blyth, Marilyn Crawshaw, and Ruth Curson, "Short Communication: Previous Semen Donors and Their Views Regarding the Sharing of Information with Offspring," *Human Reproduction* 20, no. 6 (June 2005): 1670.

4. Susan Boyd, "Gendering Legal Parenthood: Bio-Genetic Ties, Intentionality and Responsibility," *Windsor Yearbook of Access to Justice* 25 (2007): 63–94.

5. Rosanna Hertz and Margaret Nelson, *Random Families: Genetic Strangers, Sperm Donor Siblings and the Creation of New Kin* (New York: Oxford University Press, 2019).

6. See, e.g., Fiona Kelly, "Producing Paternity: The Role of Legal Fatherhood in Maintaining the Traditional Family." *Canadian Journal of Women and the Law* 21 (2009): 315; Richard Collier and Sally Sheldon, "Fathers' Rights, Fatherhood and Law Reform," in *Fathers' Rights Activism and Law Reform in Comparative Perspective*, ed. Richard Collier and Sally Sheldon (Portland: Hart Publishing, 2006), 1 at 15.

7. See, e.g., Marilyn Crawshaw, Ken Daniels, Damian Adams, Kate Bourne, J.A.P van Hooff, Wendy Kramer, Lauri Pasch, and Petra Thorn, "Emerging Models for Facilitating Contact Between People Genetically Related Through Donor Conception:

A Preliminary Analysis and Discussion," *Reproductive Biomedicine & Society Online* 1, no. 2 (December 2015): 70; Eric Blyth, Marilyn Crawshaw, Lucy Frith, and Caroline Jones, "Donor-Conceived People's Views and Experiences of Their Genetic Origins: A Critical Analysis of the Research Evidence," *Journal of Law & Medicine* 19, no. 4 (2012): 769; Vasanti Jadva, Tabitha Freeman, Wendy Kramer, and Susan Golombok, "Experiences of Offspring Searching for and Contacting Their Donor Siblings and Donor," *Reproductive BioMedicine Online* 20, no. 4 (April 2010): 523.

8. Hertz, "Random Families," 5.

9. Leah Gilman and Petra Nordqvist, "Organizing Openness: How UK Policy Defines the Significance of Information and Information Sharing About Gamete Donation," *International Journal of Law, Policy and the Family* 32, no. 3 (December 2018): 316–33.

10. Maren Klotz, *(K)Information: Gamete Donation and Kinship Knowledge in Germany and Britain* (Frankfurt: Campus Verlag, 2014).

11. Fiona Kelly, Deborah Dempsey, Jennifer Power, Kate Bourne, Karin Hammarberg and Louise Johnson, "From Stranger to Family or Something in Between: Donor Linking in an Era of Retrospective Access to Anonymous Sperm Donor Records in Victoria, Australia," *International Journal of Law, Policy and the Family* 33, no. 3 (2019): 277, 286.

12. Hertz, "Random Families," 5.

13. Kelly, "From Stranger to Family."

14. Allan, "Access to information"; Frith, "Beneath the Rhetoric"; John Tobin, "Donor-Conceived Individuals and Access to Information About Their Genetic Origins: The Relevance and Role of Rights," *Journal of Law and Medicine* 19 (2012): 742–57; Richard Chisholm, "Information Rights and Donor Conception: Lessons from Adoption?," *Journal of Law and Medicine* 19 (2012): 722.

15. In a 1989 decision about the information rights of an individual who had been born out of wedlock, Germany's Constitutional Court held that Germans have the right to know their genetic identity (BVerfGE (1989) *German Constitutional Court 31.01.1989. Kenntnis der eigenen Abstammung*. BVerfGE 79, 256). In a 2013 decision known as *Sarah P*, which was specifically about donor-conceived people, a regional appeals court ruled that the right of a child to know their origins is more important than the right of a doctor to assure that a sperm donor remains anonymous. Then in 2015, the German Supreme Court further held that all children have a right of access to information under Articles 1(1) and 2(1) of the German Constitution, regardless of age, trumping any right the donor might have to privacy (BGH, Urteil vom 28. January 2015 – XII ZR 201/13).

16. *Pratten v. British Columbia (Attorney General)*, 2012 BCCA 480 at 50.

17. Kelly, "From Stranger to Family"; Sonia Allan, "Donor Conception, Secrecy and the Search for Information," *Journal of Law & Medicine* 19, no. 4 (2012): 637.

18. Sonia Allan, *Donor Conception and the Search for Information: From Secrecy and Anonymity to Openness* (New York: Routledge, 2017), 38–42.

19. Fiona Kelly and Deborah Dempsey, "Experiences and Motives of Australian Single Mothers by Choice Who Make Early Contact with their Child's Donor Relatives," *Medical Law Review* 24 (2016): 571, 582, 588; Stu Marvel, "Tony Danza

is My Sperm Donor? Queer Kinship and the Impact of Canadian Regulations Around Sperm Donation," *Canadian Journal of Women & the Law* 25 no. 3 (2013): 221, 232.

20. Marvel, "Tony Danza," 233.

21. An American Society of Reproductive Medicine survey of more than 5,000 sperm bank found that 35–40% of respondents had not or did not plan to report their pregnancy to the sperm bank. Michelle Ottey and S Seitz, "Trends in Donor Sperm Purchasing, Disclosure of Donor Origins to Off- spring, and the Effects of Sexual Orientation and Relationship Status on Choice of Donor Category: A Three Year Study," *Supplement Fertility and Sterility* 96, no. 3 (2011): S268.

22. *Adoption Information Disclosure Act* (2005).

23. *Cheskes v. Ontario (Attorney General)* (2007) 87 O.R. (3d) 581.

24. See, e.g., Guido Pennings, "How to Kill Gamete Donation: Retrospective Legislation and Donor Anonymity," *Human Reproduction* 27 no. 10 (2012): 2881–2885.

25. Bioteknologiloven av 1994 (Act on Biotechnology 1994).

26. *Human Fertilisation and Embryology Act 1990* (UK).

27. Between 1990 and 2004, Dutch donors could choose to be anonymous or known. From June 2004, all donors were legally required to be known to offspring who reached a certain age.

28. Patrick Prag and Melinda Mills, "Assisted Reproductive Technology in Europe: Usage and Regulation in the Context of Cross-Border Reproductive Care," in *Childlessness in Europe: Contexts, Causes and Consequences*, eds. Michaela Kreyenfeld and Dirk Konietzk (Cham, Switzerland: SpringerOpen, 2017), 289.

29. Allan, "Donor Conception and the Search for Information" at 121.

30. *Children and Family Relationships Act* 2015, Act No. 9 of 2015, s 5(1).

31. The Donor Sibling Registry is a US-based, not-for-profit online registry where donor-conceived people, donors, and parents can add their details and look for matches.

32. American Society for Reproductive Medicine, "Informing Offspring of Their Conception by Gamete or Embryo Donation: A Committee Opinion Ethics Committee of the American Society for Reproductive Medicine," *Fertility Sterility* 100, no. 1 (March 2013): 45.

33. Allan, "Donor Conception and the Search for Information," 145.

34. Allan, "Donor Conception and the Search for Information," 183.

35. Allan notes that the purchase of sperm from American donors who are "willing to be known" can be up to $120 more per straw than the sperm of an anonymous donor. Allan "Donor Conception and the Search for Information," 151.

36. *Federal Act on Medically Assisted Procreation* of 18 December 1998.

37. *Assisted Reproductive Treatment (Amendment) Act* 2015 (Vic).

38. Allan, "Donor Conception and the Search for Information," 139.

39. Victorian Assisted Reproductive Treatment Authority (VARTA), Annual Reports, 2017/18; 2018/19. Available at: https://www.varta.org.au/resources/page/annual-reports

40. The Committee to Consider the Social, Ethical and Legal Issues Arising from In Vitro Fertilization (Victoria), *Report on Donor Gametes in IVF* (August 1983).

41. Fiona Kelly & Deborah Dempsey, *The History of Donor Conception Records in Victoria*, Victorian Assisted Reproductive Treatment Authority, Melbourne, 2018, 14 and 21.

42. A study conducted by the Victorian Assisted Reproductive Treatment Authority with 41 previously anonymous donors prior to the retrospective legislation being introduced found that just under half of the donors interviewed supported the retrospective release of identifying information to donor offspring. Victorian Assisted Reproductive Treatment Authority, "Consultation with donors who donated gametes in Victoria, Australia before 1998: Access by donor-conceived people to information about donors," May 2013.

43. Parliament of Victoria, Law Reform Committee, *Inquiry into Access by Donor-conceived People to Information about Donors: Report of the Law Reform Committee*, Melbourne, 2012.

44. Parliament of Victoria, *Inquiry into Access*, 39–41.

45. National Health and Medical Research Council, *Ethical Guidelines on the Use of Assisted Reproductive in Clinical Practice and Research*, Australia (2017).

46. Parliament of Victoria, *Inquiry into Access*, 74.

47. Parliament of Victoria, *Inquiry into Access*, 74.

48. Victorian Assisted Reproductive Treatment Authority, Annual Reports, 2017/18; 2018/19. Available at: https://www.varta.org.au/resources/page/annual-reports

49. Kelly, "History of Donor Conception Records."

50. Victorian Assisted Reproductive Treatment Authority, Annual Reports, 2018/19, 16.

51. Deborah Dempsey and Fiona Kelly, "Transnational Third-Party Assisted Conception: Pursuing the Desire for 'origins' Information in the Internet Era," in *Babies for Sale? Transactional Surrogacy Human Rights and the Politics of Reproduction*, ed. Miranda Davies (London: Zed Books, 2017), 204–18.

52. Joyce Harper, Debbie Kennett, and Dan Reisel, "The End of Donor Anonymity: How Genetic Testing is Likely to Drive Anonymous Gamete Donation out of Business," *Human Reproduction* 31, no. 6 (June 2016): 1135.

Chapter 14

Transgender Family Rights Issues and Concerns

A Comparative Legal Analysis of Asia and Europe

Yeshwant Naik

INTRODUCTION

The legal status of trans persons concerning gender change and gender markers will be examined in this chapter, alongside their rights to marriage, divorce, adoption, and custody. Family law, judicial approach, and jurisprudence with regard to trans persons will also be analyzed. This comparative analysis of trans family rights in Asia and the European Union (EU) is important because it highlights the shared social and legal attitudes toward trans people in the East and West. Hong Kong and Singapore have referred to judgments made by the British court, especially concerning the marriage of trans persons. After a detailed analysis of the development of the law in the UK, the trial judge held that *Corbett v. Corbett* was good law in Hong Kong.[1] The term "trans" is used here to refer to those who have changed their gender to male or female either with or without sex-reassignment surgery. "Gender change" is used here to refer to the administrative procedures and laws concerning the competency and limits of trans and gender-diverse people to change their sex (with or without sex-reassignment surgery). Changing a "gender marker" means to change one's gender identity on official documents to male or female or other. It should also be noted that some jurisdictions separate sex (biological differences between males and females) from gender (the male or female role in society), whereas others use them interchangeably.

Many Asian jurisdictions allow gender change, but gender markers are subject to restrictions (administrative, medical, psychological, etc.). Gender change is allowed in the EU, but gender markers are subject to restrictions.

Few jurisdictions allow self-declared gender identity as legally sufficient. Social exclusion and discrimination against trans people exist across countries. Advocacy, judicial competence, and literacy in trans issues are poor and as a result judges have erred while deciding cases, and lawmakers have their own understanding of trans persons. The majority perceive gender as binary, male and female, and lack knowledge of gender transformation.[2]

The landmark judgments of EU courts affect mindsets. Asian court verdicts are usually on the domestic or national level; some Japanese local courts have delivered decisions in favor of trans people. Such decisions are mostly on a case-by-case basis. Hence, the situation of trans persons in Asia and Europe is similar, except for the positive attitude shown by the EU Courts. On the national or domestic level, the situation is similar in most jurisdictions. Some countries are tolerant, and few maintain silence on transgender issues.

LEGAL RECOGNITION IN ASIA

Legal recognition of post-transition name and gender is fundamental for trans persons; physical safety is protected if identity documentations reflect changed names and genders. Name and gender changes on one document such as a driver's license are often not recognized for purposes like marriage. Most countries require a law or regulation to authorize the amendments.[3] Some disallow amended birth certificates, and others insist on a court order. Most require surgery. Some require proof that the surgery took place from a medical practitioner, psychologist, or screening committee. Rules and statutes differ across countries. Name and gender changes on identity documentation are usually looked at suspiciously, especially to reduce fraud,[4] and involve lengthy bureaucratic processes. To avoid this time-consuming process, a court order recognizing the legal name and gender change or an amended birth certificate can help provide quick relief. Many Asian countries lack written rules or laws about gender change, and the procedural requirements concerning the change of name and gender vary.[5]

An understanding of the differences in legal status across countries provides a comprehensive view. The comparative legal analysis presented here, which relies on analytical and law-in-context research methods, is limited to Southeast Asia, Southwest Asia, and South Asia. Although the general judicial stance on trans rights is progressive, the legal status of changing name and gender has been restrictive.

In Thailand, trans persons can legally change their name after undergoing a sex-change operation, but male-to-female trans government employees are not allowed to wear female uniforms at work and are still expected to perform military service. Cases of discrimination and inequality are common, for example, even after undergoing sex-reassignment surgery, hospitals refuse to allow trans women to stay in the women's ward.[6]

Singapore allows trans people to change their gender on documents such as passports and identity cards, but not on birth certificates.[7] Indonesia allows them to change their legal gender on official documents after undergoing sex-reassignment surgery and after receiving a judge's approval.[8] The situation is similar in Vietnam. On November 24, 2015, Vietnam passed a landmark law by a vote of 282-84 that enshrined rights for transgender people who have undergone sex-reassignment surgery. The legislation allows those who have undergone sex reassignment to register under their preferred sex. However, for the law to be fully enforced, a further bill, the "Law on Gender Affirmation" needs to be passed.[9]

In Hong Kong, legal gender can be changed on documents such as identity cards and passports, but not on birth certificates; to change one's birth certificate, sex-reassignment surgery is required.[10] In 2019, three trans persons identifying as male were not allowed to change their gender on their identity cards. Justice Thomas Au Hing-Cheung ruled against the three applicants, "a complete sex change would be the only 'workable way' for the local government to determine a person's gender. Although the trio, all born female, identify as men, and have had their breasts removed and undergone hormone therapy, they all still have their uterus and ovaries."[11]

In Japan, change of legal gender has been allowed since 2003, but only after undergoing sex-reassignment surgery and sterilization.[12] The Act on Special Cases in Handling Gender for People with Gender Identity Disorder 2004 states at least two competent medical practitioners must approve of the change of gender, and the application must be approved by the Family Court. The gender change is recorded in the Family Register subject to the following requirements: an applicant must be at least 20 years of age; unmarried at the time of application; have no minor children;[13] have no gonads, or the gonads are permanently dysfunctional; and have genitalia like that of the other sex. The conditions that one must have no minor children and must have genitalia with the appearance of that of the other sex appear to be draconian and have come under severe criticism; these stringent conditions cause many trans people to suffer from shame and discrimination.[14]

In Taiwan, legal gender can be changed after sex-reassignment surgery; there are few cases of recognition of legal gender.[15] In 2018, the Taiwanese government announced plans to introduce a third gender option on documents such as passports and identification cards.[16]

South Korea allows trans persons to change their legal gender with a court decision subject to strict requirements: gender-affirming surgery, sterilization, being at least 19 years of age and unmarried. South Korea's national health insurance does not cover gender-affirming care.[17] Trans persons who have not undergone the legal gender reassignment recognition process have to serve in the military under their sex assigned at birth; without surgery, they are considered male.[18] They can be exempted if diagnosed with severe gender identity disorder.

Mongolia has no affirmative law, namely, no specific law disallowing them to change the gender marker on documents. The Law on Civil Registration states that the sex on documentation can be changed based on relevant medical records.[19]

In the People's Republic of China (PRC) there are few cases of recognition of legal gender.[20] Chinese law allows name changes, but disallows the freedom to determine gender markers on documentation; sex-reassignment surgery is required. A certificate of gender authentication must be obtained, which is issued by a hospital authorized to conduct such surgeries, along with verification of the certificate from the office of a notary public or a judicial accreditation body. Trans persons must show that their workplace or educational institution approves of the gender transition. The same applies when a trans person undergoes gender-affirming surgery outside the country or province.[21] The Shanxi government implemented draconian guidelines to restrict gender reassignment surgery: one must apply to the police before surgery; live openly as that gender for at least the last three years; not have a criminal record; be at least 20 years of age; have gone through considerable therapy; married persons should have consent from their partners; and they must tell their immediate family about their plans for surgery.[22]

In these jurisdictions, administrative or bureaucratic procedures are mandatory; the self-identification of gender is not legally recognized. Courts have delivered landmark judgments on trans identity and rights, but the implementation of laws by the state has been sporadic and ineffective. While courts have become involved in adjudicating trans rights issues over the last few decades, lawmakers have failed to establish clear standards.

In 2013, hijras, who are eunuchs, intersex, asexual or transgender people in the Indian subcontinent, were recognized as a third gender by the Government of Bangladesh.[23] There is, however, no clarity regarding who may qualify as hijra, nor any policy guidelines for individuals intending to legally change their gender on official documents. Hijras have been subjected to medical check-ups and publicly stripped naked, [24] leading to extreme violations of human rights. The implementation of a rights-based procedure for their recognition is still awaited.

A 2007 ruling by the Supreme Court of Nepal decriminalized homosexuality. It recognized a third gender category and directed the government to create a committee for the legalization of same-sex marriage. It recognized the criteria for identifying gender as based on self-identification.[25] The government started issuing citizenship with an "Other" ("O") option for trans people, but there is no provision allowing trans females to have an "F" marker or trans males to have an "M" marker. They can open bank accounts, own property, register for the university, and vote as a "third gender."[26] But the implementation of this ruling has been weak in communities due to the insensitive legal structure and bureaucracy.

In India, The Transgender Persons (Protection of Rights) Act, 2019, was passed on November 26, 2019.[27] It confers the right to choose to be identified as a man, woman, or transgender, regardless of sex-reassignment surgery and hormonal therapy. But this Act fails to fulfill provisions of the 2014 Supreme Court of India verdict in *National Legal Services Authority v. Union of India*.[28] It imposes a restriction that a revised certificate should be obtained to change gender, and the District Magistrate should examine the "correctness" of the medical certificate issued by a Medical Superintendent or Chief Medical Officer. This requirement is a direct violation of the NALSA judgment, which recognizes the right to self-identification of gender without the interference of a medical certificate or surgery. Another major defect of the Act is that it fails to provide any reservation in education or employment to trans people,[29] which is another violation of the NALSA judgment. The Act is opposed on many counts, it fails to safeguard and recognize the fundamental freedoms and human rights assured to trans people by the NALSA judgment, thereby providing grounds for discrimination that might cover a range of other violations.

To give effect to the judgment at the state level, trans welfare boards have been set up in some states. Policies and directives have been issued to protect trans people. Some policies provide access to free sex-reassignment surgery, financial aid for sex-reassignment surgery, free housing, citizenship documents, admissions to educational institutions, scholarships for higher education, and the formation of self-help groups; they also provide alternative sources of income, pension schemes, skill development for employment, financial aid to parents of trans people, separate toilets in public places, shelter and sanitation for the homeless, and issuance of self-identification identity cards.[30] But the implementation is ineffective because some states have withdrawn from its schemes "due to inconsistencies, money bouncing back to the government and lack of initiative in the state's performance budget for the Board."[31]

The situation in Sri Lanka is similar. Legal name and gender change are possible. To undergo sex-reassignment surgery, a psychiatrist must be consulted; the doctor decides whether the patient should have the procedure. On receipt of an official letter, the patient is then able to begin hormone therapy.[32] Trans persons are given an amended birth certificate mentioning their previous gender and the history of their transition. With no new birth certificate, though, trans persons are discriminated against in terms of education, housing, and employment.[33] Trans persons report repeated harassment and mistreatment by police. Despite the significant drop in the number of arrests of gender nonconforming and other LGBTI people—from 1,755 in 2008 to 472 in 2014—there is still continued criminalization of sexual activity between members of the same sex and many are arrested for gender nonconformity.[34]

In 2009, the Supreme Court of Pakistan allowed trans people to undergo sex-reassignment surgery. It ruled that they were entitled to the equal benefit and protection of the law, and directed the government to protect them from discrimination, violence, and harassment.[35] In 2010, it ordered the full recognition of the trans community, including the provision of free medical and educational facilities, microcredit schemes, and job quotas for trans people in every government department.[36] In 2017, the Lahore High Court ordered the government to include trans people in the national census.[37] Considering the judicial stance and interests of the trans community, the Government of Pakistan has introduced the following legislations: the Right to Change Legal Gender, 2009; Equal Citizens, 2009; and the Rights of the Transgender Person/Protection of Rights Act, 2018. This legislation provides for protection against discrimination and harassment, right to inherit, property rights, health, education, employment, right to vote, and right to hold public office.

Gender change recognition is not possible in Bhutan, Maldives, Myanmar, Brunei, or the Philippines (with exceptions only). In West Asia, Iran and Kyrgyzstan allow access to legal gender recognition only after sex-reassignment surgery.[38]

In Asia, self-identification of gender is only recognized by the Supreme Court of Nepal and India, although its enforcement lacks political will. Sex-reassignment surgery is a precondition for name and gender change in most jurisdictions.[39] Trans people find that these restrictions infringe on their liberty to determine their own gender. Due to risks and high expenses, many do not wish to undergo sex-reassignment surgery. None of the countries provide healthcare facilities to trans people. By disallowing name or gender change, or providing a history on reissued birth certificates, trans status is denied and discrimination in education, health, and employment increases.

Legal change of name and gender is important if trans people are to obtain an amended birth certificate, without which entering a legally recognized relationship, or civil union, is not possible. Marriage forms the foundation for many other legal rights: parental, property, inheritance, immigration, divorce, and custodial. Issues pertaining to the validity or equivalence of pre- and post-transition marriages are still unclear in Asia. Some courts have decided such issues on a case-by-case basis. Courts have mostly interpreted and validated marriage as a union between a man and woman. The analysis below shows how the law, courts, and politics interpret trans marriage.

MARRIAGE AND DIVORCE

In Singapore, the Women's Charter was amended in 1996 to allow a trans person (who has legally changed his or her gender) to legally marry any person of the opposite sex. It maintains the general rule that same-sex marriage is void.[40] A valid marriage constitutes the union of a man and woman; marriage between persons who are not male and female at the time of marriage is void.[41] The law only recognizes trans persons as being of their post-operative sex for the purposes of marriage in its narrow sense,[42] it does not recognize their post-operative sex.[43] The gender on the National Registration Identity Card is considered the prima facie evidence of the sex of the holder.[44] Technically, since same-sex sexual activity is illegal among men, sexual activity between a male and a post-operative male-to-female transsexual would be illegal.[45] Other areas of law consider trans persons to be their pre-operative gender.[46]

In July 2019, a proposal to regulate sex changes for trans individuals was presented to the Thai National Assembly. The bill should allow persons to change their gender on documents after sex-reassignment surgery. It also covers name changes, marriage rights, and military conscription.[47] In Indonesia, trans people can marry after sex-reassignment surgery after receiving a government-issued identity card declaring their new gender.[48]

Marriage in Hong Kong is a Christian or civil union. Procreation is important and non-consummation is a ground to nullify. "Woman" doesn't yet include "post-operative male-to-female transsexual,"[49] but the judiciary has considered expanding it;[50] and it advised the legislature to draft specific legislation to consider different aspects of laws pertaining to trans persons.[51] Although Taiwan and China allow trans people to marry, there is no specific legislation to that effect.[52]

Taiwan was the first Asian nation to perform same-sex marriages. Same-sex marriage became legal on May 24, 2019, but same-sex couples are only allowed to adopt a child genetically related to one of them. Amendments to this new legislation, especially concerning transnational marriages and assisted reproduction, are still in the making.[53]

It is interesting how trans people end legal marriages in China. In the response to inquiries about the termination of a marriage following the sex change of one of the parties, the Ministry of Civil Affairs General Office Letter No. 127 reads:

> When one party to a marriage undergoes a sex change and completes procedures to change the gender marker on their legal identification to the opposite sex, the originally registered marriage is still lawful and has effect, and a party to the marriage cannot merely declare the marriage void. If no disputes over

> asset division between the parties exists, marriage registration authorities may process a formal divorce with the agreement of the parties.[54]

Trans persons and their partners may receive full marriage and adoption rights only when they are in a legal, heterosexual marriage; to be in such a marriage requires sex-reassignment surgery and legal gender recognition.[55] In contrast, Article 24 of the Japanese Constitution and Articles 731–737 of the Japanese Civil Code restrict marriage to one man and one woman. Same-sex marriage is illegal. Per Article 3 of the Law Concerning Special Cases in Handling Gender for People with Gender Identity Disorder,[56] a trans person cannot remain married to their existing partner after sex-reassignment surgery. This condition operates as a violation of the right "to found a family" under Article 23 of the Japanese Constitution.[57]

In South Korea, trans people can marry, but only after legal gender change recognition. There are no positive laws approving same-sex marriage, nor are there laws restricting trans or cisgender persons from marrying a person of the same gender. The law is silent on adoption by trans people.[58]

The Mongolian Constitution defines marriage as an institution between man and woman.[59] Same-sex marriage and adoption are barred. The Criminal Code of Mongolia is undergoing a major legal reform process that intends to criminalize hate crimes, rape against a person of any sex, and perpetrators of domestic violence, which includes "partners" and even those who live in family relations. The draft doesn't reference sexual orientation or gender identity.[60]

Judicial activism in Nepal has provided relief to the LGBT community. In 2013, the Supreme Court of Nepal sent a strong indication in support of same-sex marriage.[61] It observed:

> Individuals can decide as to choose their ways of living either separately or in partnership together with homosexuals or heterosexuals—with or without solemnizing marriage. Although in the prevailing laws and tradition "marriage" denotes legal bond between heterosexuals—male and female; the legal provisions on the homosexual relations are either inadequate or mute by now.[62]

In the Nepal Constitution, same-sex marriage and the protection of sexual minorities were to be established, but negotiations to that effect have failed.[63] The Nepali Civil Code, which came into effect in August 2018, does not address same-sex marriage but defines marriage as being between opposite sexes.[64]

Same-sex and transgender marriage is not recognized in Sri Lanka. Family laws refer only to "male" and "female" as the two parties of a marriage.[65] In Pakistan, many trans people face legal barriers to relationships, marriage, parenting, health care, housing, and other government benefits. A district screening committee grants gender-change certificates; the likelihood of discrimination cannot be overlooked.[66] The certificate is important since it assures marriage and adoption inheritance rights to trans people. The legal reforms do not guarantee social inclusion. Violence and discrimination persist.[67] Quoting the NALSA judgment,[68] which recognizes the right of trans persons to marry and the self-identification of gender, the Madras High Court of the Tamil Nadu State ruled that "bride" under the Hindu Marriage Act, 1955, includes trans women. It directed authorities to register a marriage between a man and a trans woman and the state of Tamil Nadu to ban sex-selective surgeries on intersex infants.[69] The judge stated:

> When the right of the transgender persons to marry has been upheld by the apex court, in the very nature of things, they cannot be kept out of the purview of the Hindu Marriage Act [. . .] the Hon'ble Supreme Court held that Article 14 of the Constitution of India which affirms that the State shall not deny to "any person" equality before the law or the equal protection of the laws within the territory of India would also apply to transgenders.[70]

Countries that do not recognize trans marriage also prohibit same-sex marriage, except for Taiwan, which recognizes same-sex marriage but not trans marriage. Most countries lack policies or precedents on pre- or post-transition marriage. Post-transition marriages have been invalidated by courts because marriage between same-sex couples is prohibited in their respective countries because homosexuality is criminalized or gay marriage lacks legal recognition. All countries insist on medical or surgical transition. Gender transitioning is presumed to be done for the purpose of getting married heterosexually. Many jurisdictions allow trans persons to change their name and gender on their birth certificate but do not recognize the same for the purpose of marriage. There are no provisions to protect unmarried trans partners.

No country expressly prohibits trans people from becoming legal parents, but the laws pertaining to parentage and adoption are silent on whether a trans person can become an adoptive or biological parent. Most countries have no specific provisions, but trans people wishing to adopt might encounter informal discrimination.[71] Trans parents in Japan are at risk of losing their parental rights since they cannot remain married to their partner post-transition. Laws concerning female-to-male trans people, surrogacy, artificial insemination, and parentage are largely unsettled.[72]

Provisions are unclear pertaining to the dissolution of a marriage with a spouse who is undergoing or has undergone gender transition: whether gender transition is a ground for divorce; the impact of gender transition on marriage; and whether such a marriage leads to annulment or declaration of invalidity, as well as the impact on the annulment or declaration of child custody, visitation, maintenance claims, property and liability distribution. Because judges (in only a few jurisdictions) assess such matters on a case-by-case basis, bias, misunderstanding, and prejudice influences decisions. Asia is not progressive in terms of trans rights; discrimination, social exclusion, and inequality endure.[73]

LEGAL RECOGNITION IN EUROPE

Most European countries, in contrast, have provisions for the legal change of name and gender. The European Court of Human Rights (ECHR) has been influential in the making of gender recognition laws. The landmark verdict *Goodwin v. United Kingdom* uplifted the provisions enlisted in the European Convention for the Protection of Human Rights and Fundamental Freedoms and recognized gender change.[74] There are still many countries in Europe where gender change is unrecognized.

Gender change is possible with prohibitive requirements in Azerbaijan, Andorra, Armenia, Belarus, Bosnia and Herzegovina, Croatia, Cyprus, Czech Republic, Former Yugoslav Republic of Macedonia, Estonia, Georgia, Latvia, Lithuania, Moldova, Montenegro, Russia, Slovakia, Slovenia, Serbia, Turkey, and Ukraine.[75] Depending on local rules and laws, gender can be changed without legal support. Hungary,[76] Kosovo, Liechtenstein, and Monaco do not recognize gender change.[77] Bulgaria, Italy, Luxembourg, Netherlands, Poland, Romania, Switzerland[78] require a final court order and medical or psychological expert opinion. Swiss courts do not require surgical intervention or sterilization to grant gender recognition. Dissolution of marriage is not a condition for granting gender recognition in Switzerland.[79]

In Bulgaria and Hungary, gender reassignment means the dissolution of marriage.[80] With too many strict regressive restrictions, gender recognition laws in most countries are merely a paper tiger. Psychological and physical examinations, as well as the presentation of certification by a medical institution or practitioner, are prerequisites for gender change.

In Finland and Sweden, the applicant wishing to change gender must be single; if married or living in a registered partnership, the partner's consent is required. The applicant must provide proof of sterilization or infertility.[81] In *Hämäläinen v. Finland*, the ECHR held that a Finnish rule requiring married applicants to convert their relationship to a registered partnership prior to obtaining recognition was compatible with the right to private and family life under Article 8 ECHR.[82]

In Germany, trans citizens are unable to conceive children and undergo surgical intervention.[83] Belgium insists on reports from a psychiatrist and surgeon.[84] In Iceland, it is necessary to receive diagnosis and treatment by a qualified team of the medical institution, followed by confirmation from the expert committee.[85] In Portugal and Spain, one must submit a report of a diagnosis of gender identity disorder that has been prepared by a multidisciplinary team of clinical sexologists or a certificate by a doctor or clinical psychologist, respectively.[86]

The UK[87] passed the Gender Recognition Act in 2004. A medical report is required for gender recognition. In the case of married or partnered applicants, dissolution of the marriage is required before gender change is recognized. In Poland, a married person must divorce before the new gender is officially recognized.[88] In Austria and Luxemburg, the constitutional court allowed a transsexual woman the right to change her sex while remaining married to her wife. The German Constitutional Court held that a forced divorce would amount to a breach of Articles 7 and 9 of the Charter of Fundamental Rights (Respect for private and family life and Right to marry and "right to found" a family).[89]

In France, Denmark, Norway, Austria, Sweden, and Ireland, gender can be changed without medical treatment or surgery or proof of sterilization. Minors can apply for gender change with the consent from parents or guardians.[90] Luxembourg has a bill under parliamentary consideration extending the right to apply to change a child's gender marker.[91]

Self-declaration of gender is allowed in Denmark and Malta;[92] in Ireland, self-declaration only applies to binary choices. A minor's application must be filed by a parent or guardian. Denmark and Malta have extended recognition rights to non-binary persons and minors. Ireland has passed a bill to extend recognition rights to non-binary persons and minors, and the Federal Ministry of Family Affairs in Germany recently recommended the inclusion of non-binary persons and minors.[93] Germany even extended legal gender recognition to stateless persons, refugee residents in Germany, or to those who are from a country that does not have a law of this nature and hold an unlimited right of residence or a permanent resident permit.[94] A third gender option is now available in Germany, Malta, and Austria.[95]

Portugal, Belgium, Spain, and Luxembourg have proposals to allow legal gender recognition based on self-declaration of the trans person.[96] Norway's law is the most progressive: minors aged 16 to 18 can apply for gender recognition; minors aged 6 to 16 can apply when supported by a parent or guardian; and minors under 6 can apply at a parent's request with input from the child if they are capable.[97] The autonomous region of Andalusia is progressive concerning gender recognition. The Andalusian Parliament passed a separate law on trans status in 2014. Self-declaration is enough; medical documentation is not necessary and the applicant's privacy is protected.[98]

Greece passed the Law on Legal Recognition of Gender Identity in October 2017. It bars medical requirements, including sterilization, for persons aged

17 and over. The law requires applicants to be unmarried. Gender recognition is available to minors aged 15 to 17, but is subject to certification from psychological and medical commissions. Gender change is not available to persons under 15.[99]

Still, provisions for legal gender recognition in many countries are lacking. Not all countries provide gender recognition for minors. Non-binary identities are not recognized, not even in the European countries allowing the self-declaration of gender identity. The legislature of European countries should draft effective gender recognition laws that consider human rights protection and the European Convention for the Protection of Human Rights and Fundamental Freedoms. Individual country legislatures should remove medical and unnecessary administrative requirements restricting easy access to gender recognition; the interests of minor applicants and non-binary gender identities are important. The ECHR has recognized the right of trans people to marry, but they might have to prove infertility or undergo gender reassignment surgery first. Alternatively, they may be required to divorce before their gender identity can be legally recognized.

TRANSGENDER FAMILY RIGHTS

Initial challenges to British law by the ECHR began with *Corbett v. Corbett* (1970); the court nullified post-transition marriage since the transgender spouse's birth sex was immutable for the purpose of marriage and same-sex couples were prohibited from marrying.[100] A similar decision was delivered in *Rees v. The United Kingdom.* The applicant was born and registered as a female, but later received treatment to live as a male. He complained that the UK failed to amend his birth certificate. He alleged a violation of privacy and right to marry. Rejecting his plea, the court observed that:

> the right to marry guaranteed by Article 12 (art. 12) refers to the traditional marriage between persons of opposite biological sex. [. . .] Article 12 is mainly concerned to protect marriage as the basis of the family.[101]

The ECHR responded positively in *Cossey v. The United Kingdom* which involved a male-to-female transsexual who had undergone full gender-reassignment surgery and wished to marry. The commission, which examined the case to determine its eligibility for hearing by the full court, considered the *Rees* judgment but did not agree on its emphasis on procreation. By majority votes the commission held that there was a violation of Article 12 and observed:

> It is certified by a medical expert that the applicant is anatomically no longer of male sex. She has been living after the gender reassignment surgery as a woman and is socially accepted as such. In these circumstances it cannot, in the Commission's opinion, be maintained that for the purposes of Article 12 the applicant still has to be considered as being of male sex. The applicant must therefore have the right to conclude a marriage [. . .] with the man she has chosen to be her husband.[102]

Nevertheless, the court disagreed with the commission and held that there was no violation of Article 8 or 12 and maintained that there was still a lack of activism for the provision of trans marriage rights in the European States.

In *Sheffield and Horsham v. the United Kingdom* Government (1998), the ECHR held that a nation can refuse to re-register people after sex-assignment surgery and that prohibiting postoperative transsexuals to marry does not amount to a human rights violation. However, the court was critical of the UK's failure to take necessary steps in this direction, as "there is increased social acceptance to trans-sexualism and an increased recognition of the problems which post-operative transsexual people encounter."[103] By this time, Germany, the Netherlands, Denmark, Sweden, and Belgium had already recognized trans people as members of the opposite sex.[104] The issue originating in *Corbett v. Corbett*, whether adults with no legal or biological ties can establish family life, was addressed before the ECHR in some detail in *X, Y & Z v. UK*[105]:

> The Court found no violation of Article 8 [right to respect for private and family life] of the ECHR. The Court observed that there is no common European standard with regard to the granting of parental rights to transsexuals, and since the law appears to be in a transitional stage, the respondent State must be afforded a wide margin of appreciation; therefore the United Kingdom law which does not recognize relationship between X and Z has not violated their right to respect for family life. Based on the finding on Article 8, it was not necessary to examine Article 14 [prohibition of discrimination].

The ECHR recognized the de facto family ties of a transgender male and his partner. However, in recognizing the couple's family life, it effectively viewed the applicants as an opposite-sex couple. In doing so, it extended the meaning of family life beyond marriage and blood relations.[106] *P v. S and Cornwall County Council*[107] is another landmark case of the European Court of Justice (ECJ) extending the scope of sex equality to discrimination against transgender people. It held that "the Equal Treatment Directive was an expression of a fundamental principle of equality and that the Directive precluded dismissal for a reason related to gender reassignment."

In a landmark judgment in 2002, *Christine Goodwin v. UK* and *I v. UK Government,*[108] the ECHR held that "prohibiting post-transition marriage violates the European Convention for the Protection of Human Rights and Fundamental Freedoms[;]" it recognized the transgender plaintiff's post-transition sex as her marital sex, thereby reversing the ruling in Corbett, which held that birth sex was immutable.[109] During this time, the House of Lords in *Bellinger v. Bellinger* [2003] UKHL 21, remarked that the:

> recognition of a change of gender for the purposes of marriage would require some certainty regarding the point at which the change takes place. This point is not easily ascertainable. At what point would it be consistent with public policy to recognise that a person should be treated for all purposes, including marriage, as a person of the opposite sex to that which he or she was correctly assigned at birth? This is a question for Parliament, not the courts.[110]

In this case, the parties participated in a marriage ceremony, but Mrs. B had previously undergone gender reassignment surgery. Section 11(c) of the 1973 Act required a marriage to be between a male and a female. It was argued that the section was incompatible.

In response, the British government passed the Gender Recognition Act 2004 (GRA), changing the legal standard for recognition of preferred gender and marriage rights for trans people. It treats trans people as belonging to the new gender for all legal purposes, including family relationships, marriage, employment, welfare benefits, and health and social care. Shortly afterward, in *KB v. NHS Pensions Agency & the Secretary of State for Health*, the ECJ acknowledged the unmarried partner of a transgender man as his "de facto wife" for the purpose of survivor pension benefits.[111]

Although the ECHR recognizes the right of trans people to marry, many states still require proof of infertility or of undergoing gender reassignment surgery as a precondition for marriage. At times, trans people have had to separate from their spouses before receiving legal recognition of their gender identity. Concerning parentage and child custody rights, the notion of traditional family dominates. In *X, Y & Z v. UK*, the ECHR said it was unclear whether it would be in a child's best interests to have her trans father recognized as her lawful parent.

Like Asia, the specific legal provisions in Europe are unsettled pertaining to female-to-male trans persons and surrogacy and artificial insemination. The provisions pertaining to parentage, divorce, the dissolution of pre- and post-transition marriage, the impact of annulment or declaration on child custody, visitation, maintenance claims, and property and liability distribution are also unclear.

CONCLUSION

In conclusion, trans people suffer discrimination, social exclusion, deprivation of rights, and loss of freedom in almost every part of the world, although the level of discrimination varies from country to country. The Yogyakarta Principles, a set of principles on the application of international human-rights law in relation to sexual orientation and gender identity, should be adopted into national laws across countries to protect trans rights.[112] The Principles affirm binding international legal standards with which all states must comply. They promise a different future in which all people are born free and equal in dignity and rights.

It is the responsibility of countries to protect trans people from violence, harassment, and discrimination. If countries suppress the freedoms of trans persons, discrimination, harassment, and violence will continue. Over the years, trans people have internalized freedom and there were several instances in which they internalized rights and claimed rights. The judiciary and the state have merely acted as intermediaries toward achieving freedoms and rights. Constitutionality and rights occur even before a court case, and this is evident in the trans rights movement. The culture of constitutionality is crucial to lives regardless of gender. This culture of constitutionality is expanding and growing around the world. And this is inspiring.

NOTES

1. Patrick Jiang, "Legislating for Transgender People: A Comparative Study of the Change of Legal Gender in Hongkong, Singapore, Japan and the United Kingdom," *Hong Kong Journal of Legal Studies* 7 (2013): 42, 47.
2. Thekla Morgenroth, et al., "Defending the Sex/Gender Binary: The Role of Gender Identification and Need for Closure," *Social Psychological and Personality Science* 12 (2020): 194855062093718. doi: 10.1177/1948550620937188
3. Jennifer L. Levi and Elizabeth E. Monnin-Browder, *Transgender Family Law* (Indiana: AuthorHouse, 2012), 19.
4. Ibid., 17.
5. Ibid., 16–17.
6. Rik Glauert, "Transgender Activists in Thailand Propose Law to Protect Their Rights," *Gay Star News*, July 29, 2019, https://www.gaystarnews.com/article/transgender-activists-in-thailand-propose-law-to-protect-their-rights/#gs.sftbhg
7. Sylvia Tan, "Being Gay (Lesbian or Transgender) in Singapore," *Focus* 65 (2011), https://www.hurights.or.jp/archives/focus/section2/2011/09/being-gay-lesbian-or-transgender-in-singapore.html

8. Indonesia at Melbourne, "Sex or Gender? Aming's Challenge," *Coconuts Jakarta*, June 24, 2016, https://coconuts.co/jakarta/features/sex-or-gender-amings-challenge/

9. Sen Nguyen, "LGBT Rights: Vietnam Recognises Transgender People, But There's a Flaw in Its Law," *This Week in Asia*, June 21, 2019, https://www.scmp.com/week-asia/society/article/3015423/lgbt-rights-vietnam-recognises-transgender-people-theres-flaw-its; "Vietnam: Positive Step for Transgender Rights," *Human Rights Watch*, November 30, 2015, https://www.hrw.org/news/2015/11/30/vietnam-positive-step-transgender-rights

10. Violet Law, "Hong Kong Court Denies Male Status to 3 Transgender Men," *AP News*, February 1, 2019, https://apnews.com/6128011e768f49e28118f0c9646c5e54

11. Chris Lau, "Transgender Trio Fail in Legal Bid to Be Listed as Male on Hong Kong ID Card," *South China Morning Post*, February 1, 2019, https://www.scmp.com/news/hong-kong/law-and-crime/article/2184662/transgender-men-fail-legal-bid-be-listed-male-hong-kong

12. Jiang, "Legislating for Transgender People," 54–56.

13. Ibid., 55.

14. Ibid., 56.

15. Ibid., 33.

16. Beh Lih Yi, "Taiwan Mulls Third Gender Option on Passports, IDs," *Reuters*, January 16, 2018, https://www.reuters.com/article/taiwan-lgbt/taiwan-mulls-third-gender-option-on-passports-ids-idUSL8N1O61JZ

17. Horim Yi, Winston Luhur, and Taylor N.T. Brown, "Public Opinion of Transgender Rights in South Korea," *Williams Institute*, December 2019, https://williamsinstitute.law.ucla.edu/wp-content/uploads/South-Korea-English-Dec-2019.pdf

18. Ibid.

19. Article 20(1) of the Law on Civil Registration, see *Being LGBT in Asia: Mongolia Country Report. A Participatory Review and Analysis of the Legal and Social Environment for Lesbian, Gay, Bisexual and Transgender (LGBT) Persons and Civil Society*, UNDP, USAID (2014), 19–20. https://www.undp.org/content/dam/rbap/docs/Research%20&%20Publications/hiv_aids/rbap-hhd-2014-blia-mongolia-country-report.pdf

20. Jiang, "Legislating for Transgender People," 33.

21. "Legal Gender Recognition in China: A Legal and Policy Review," UNDP, August 5, 2018, 21–23, https://www.cn.undp.org/content/china/en/home/library/democratic_governance/legal-gender-recognition-in-china--a-legal-and-policy-review-.html

22. Nancy Sun, "Shanxi Permits Transgender Persons to Change Gender Information," *All-China Women's Federation*, January 9, 2014, http://www.womenofchina.cn/html/womenofchina/report/168827-1.htm

23. Adnan Hossain, "The Paradox of Recognition: *hijra*, Third Gender and Sexual Rights in Bangladesh," *Culture, Health & Sexuality* 19, no. 12 (2017): 1418. doi: 10.1080/13691058.2017.1317831

24. "'I Want to Live With My Head Held High': Abuses in Bangladesh's Legal Recognition of Hijras," *Human Rights Watch*, December 23, 2016, https://www.hrw.org/report/2016/12/23/i-want-live-my-head-held-high/abuses-bangladeshs-legal-recognition-hijras

25. *Sunil Babu Pant and Others v. Government of Nepal and Others*, Writ No. 917 of the year 2064 BS (2007 AD).

26. Michael Bochenek and Kyle Knight, "Establishing a Third Gender Category in Nepal: Process and Prognosis," *Emory International Law Review* 26, no. 1 (2012): 11–41.

27. It was introduced in the Lok Sabha on July 19, 2019 and passed on August 5, 2019. In November 2019, it was debated in the Rajya Sabha and was subsequently passed on November 26, 2019.

28. *National Legal Services Authority v. Union of India,* WP (Civil) No. 400 of 2012, https://www.refworld.org/cases,IND_SC,5356279d4.html (accessed on February 20, 2020).

29. Ajita Banerjie, "Why India's Transgender People Are Protesting Against a Bill that Claims to Protect Their Rights," Scroll.in, November 26, 2019, https://scroll.in/article/944882/why-indias-transgender-people-are-protesting-against-a-bill-that-claims-to-protect-their-rights

30. TK Devasia, "Why Kerala's Free Sex-Change Surgeries Will Offer a New Lifeline for the Transgender Community," Scroll.in, March 19, 2016, https://scroll.in/article/804496/why-keralas-free-sex-change-surgeries-will-offer-a-new-lifeline-for-the-transgender-community; Ashwani Sharma, "Himachal Pradesh to bring transgenders under social security net," *The Indian Express*, September 7, 2016, https://indianexpress.com/article/india/india-news-india/himachal-pradesh-to-bring-transgenders-under-social-security-net-3018937/

31. Divya Kartikeyan, "Tamil Nadu, Once a Pioneering State for Welfare of Transgenders, Now Shuns the Third Gender," Firstpost, May 25, 2017, https://www.firstpost.com/india/tamil-nadu-once-a-pioneering-state-for-welfare-of-transgenders-now-shuns-the-third-gender-3476538.html

32. Anukshi Jayasinha, "What It Means To Be Transgender In Sri Lanka," Roarmedia, October 5, 2016, https://roar.media/english/life/reports/means-transgender-sri-lanka/

33. Ibid.

34. "All Five Fingers Are Not the Same," 2.

35. "SC Orders Equal Benefits for Transvestites," *Dawn*, July 15, 2009, https://www.dawn.com/news/879507

36. "Don't We Count? Transgender Pakistanis Feel Sidelined by Census," *Pakistan Today*, October 7, 2017, https://www.pakistantoday.com.pk/2017/10/07/dont-we-count-transgender-pakistanis-feel-sidelined-by-census/

37. Waqar Mustafa, "Pakistan Counts Transgender People in National Census for First Time," *Reuters*, January 9, 2017, https://www.reuters.com/article/us-pakistan-transgender-census/pakistan-counts-transgender-people-in-national-census-for-first-time-idUSKBN14T1XK

38. Zhan Chiam, Sandra Duffy, and Matilda González Gil, *Trans Legal Mapping Report: Recognition Before the Law* (Geneva: ILGA, 2017).

39. See generally: UNDP and Asia Pacific Transgender Network, Legal Gender Recognition: A Multi-Country Legal and Policy Review in Asia (UNDP and Asia Pacific Transgender Network 2017), https://www.asia-pacific.undp.org/content/rbap/en/home/library/democratic_governance/hiv_aids/legal-gender-recognition--a-multi-country-legal-and-policy-revie.html

40. Jiang, "Legislating for Transgender People," 48–50.

41. *Lim Ying v. Hiok Kian Ming Eric* (1992) 1 SLR 184.

42. Jiang, "Legislating for Transgender People," 50.

43. See, e.g., Tan Cheng Han, "Transsexuals and the Law of Marriage in Singapore: Lim Ying v. Hiol Kian Ming Eric," *Singapore Journal of Legal Studies* (December 1991): 509–16 .

44. Jiang, "Legislating for Transgender People," 50.

45. Ibid., 51.

46. Ibid., 52.

47. Nancy Sun, "Shanxi Permits Transgender Persons to Change Gender Information."

48. Indonesia at Melbourne, "Sex or Gender? Aming's Challenge."

49. Jiang, "Legislating for Transgender People," 49–52.

50. Ibid., 53.

51. Ibid., 57.

52. Ibid., 33.

53. Yeh Su-ping, Ku Chuan, Liu Shih-yi, and Evelyn Kao, "Draft Gay Marriage Bill to be Further Amended: Justice Ministry," *Focus Taiwan*, February 21, 2019, https://focustaiwan.tw/politics/201902210017. See, "Taiwan's Cabinet Passes Same-Sex Marriage Bill," *Taiwan Today*, February 22, 2019, https://www.taiwantoday.tw/news.php?unit=2,6,10,15,18&post=150370

54. "Legal Gender Recognition in China: A Legal and Policy Review," 48.

55. Ibid., 48.

56. Law No. 111 of 2003: Law Concerning Special Cases in Handling Gender for People with Gender Identity Disorder.

57. "JAPAN: Human Rights Violation against Lesbian, Gay, Bisexual and Transgender Persons, A Shadow Report," April 2012 (accessed on February 18, 2020), https://ilga.org/wp-content/uploads/2016/02/Shadow-Report-.pdf

58. Horim Yi, "Public Opinion of Transgender Rights in South Korea," 1–2.

59. See Article 16, Constitution of Mongolia.

60. A revised draft of the criminal code was submitted to the Parliament in April 2014; see *Being LGBT in Asia: Mongolia Country Report*, 19–20.

61. *Rajani Shah v. National Women Commission et al.*, Supreme Court of Nepal, April 11, 2013, Writ No. 069-WH-0030; see Kyle Knight and Kellea Miller, *Bridges to Justice: Case Study of LGBTI Rights in Nepal*, Astraea Lesbian Foundation for Justice, 2015.

62. *Rajani Shah v. National Women Commission et.al*, Supreme Court of Nepal, April 11, 2013, Writ No. 069-WH-0030.

63. John Narayan Parajuli, "Nepal enters crisis mode as constitution talks fail," *BBC*, May 28, 2012, https://www.bbc.com/news/world-asia-18234114

64. Sunil Babu Pant, "Marriage Provision Under New Civil Code of Is Unconstitutional," *Panichan*, August 23, 2018, https://pahichan.com/marriage-provision-under-new-civil-code-of-is-unconstitutional/

65. Marriages are registered under the Marriage Registration Ordinance, Kandyan Marriage and Divorce Act, or the Muslim Marriage and Divorce Act.

66. Ayesha Umar, "Assessing Social Inclusion through Transgender Legal Reforms in Pakistan," forthcoming, October 7, 2018, https://papers.ssrn.com/sol3/papers.cfm?abstract_id=3433495 (accessed on February 19, 2020).

67. Umar, "Assessing Social Inclusion through Transgender Legal Reforms in Pakistan."

68. *National Legal Services Authority v. Union of India* ,WP (Civil) No 400 of 2012, https://www.refworld.org/cases,IND_SC,5356279d4.html (accessed on February 20, 2020).

69. *Arunkumar v. The Inspector General of Registration,* W.P. (MD) No. 4125 of 2019 and W.M.P. (MD) No. 3220 of 2019. https://indiankanoon.org/doc/188806075/ (accessed on February 20, 2020).

70. *Arunkumar v. The Inspector General Of Registration,* W.P. (MD) No. 4125 of 2019 and W.M.P. (MD) No. 3220 of 2019. https://indiankanoon.org/doc /188806075/ (accessed on February 20, 2020).

71. Levi, *Transgender Family Law*, 73.

72. Ibid., 71.

73. John Garry, "What We Can Learn from Countries with Progressive Transgender Rights," May 7, 2020, https://matadornetwork.com/read/countries-progressive-transgender-rights/ (accessed on May 21, 2020).

74. *Christine Goodwin v. UK*, App. No. 28957/95, 35 Eur. H.R. Rep. 18 (2002).

75. Chiam, *Trans Legal Mapping Report*, 27–30, 32–34, 36–39, 41–42, 80.

76. Applications for gender change have been suspended while new legislation is being drafted.

77. Chiam, *Trans Legal Mapping Report*, 34, 36, 38. A case currently before the European Court of Human Rights, *Rana v. Hungary* (40888/17), taken by an Iranian refugee resident in Hungary, challenges the lack of procedure for legal gender recognition in Hungary for persons born overseas; see Chiam, *Trans Legal Mapping Report*, 66.

78. Ibid., 29, 36–37, 39–41, 44.

79. Ibid., 82.

80. Cristina Castagnoli, *Transgender Persons' Rights in the EU Member States*, (Brussels: European Parliament, 2010), 9.

81. Chiam, *Trans Legal Mapping Report*, 32.

82. *Hämäläinen v. Finland*, (2015) 1 FCR 379, 88 and 89.

83. Castagnoli, *Transgender Persons' Rights in the EU Member States*, 22.

84. Ibid., 19.

85. Chiam, *Trans Legal Mapping Report*, 63.

86. Ibid., 73, 78.

87. Castagnoli, *Transgender Persons' Rights in the EU Member States*, 8.

88. Ibid., 9.

89. Ibid., 9.

90. Chiam, *Trans Legal Mapping Report*, 27, 31, 33, 35, 39, 43.

91. Ibid., 46.

92. Ibid., 38.

93. Ibid., 46.

94. Ibid., 59.

95. Marjolein van den Brink and Peter Dunne, *Trans and Intersex Equality Rights in Europe—A Comparative Analysis* (Luxembourg: Publications Office of the European Union, 2018), https://ec.europa.eu/info/sites/info/files/trans_and_intersex_equality_rights.pdf

96. Chiam, *Trans Legal Mapping Report*, 45.

97. Ibid., 25.

98. Ibid., 42.

99. Ibid., 60.

100. *Corbett v. Corbett* (1970) 2 All ER 33.

101. *Rees v. The United Kingdom*, ECHR (9532/81, (1987) 9 EHRR 56, Para 49 and 50.

102. *Cossey v. The United Kingdom*, ECHR (10843/84, (1990), Para 45 and 46.

103. *Sheffield and Horsham v. the United Kingdom*, App. No. 22985/93, 23390/94 (ECtHR, 30 July 1998).

104. Stephen Whittle, "Sensible Policy, Excellent Practice: Challenging the 'Common Sense' of Legal Recognition for Transsexual People," forthcoming, http://e-space.mmu.ac.uk/617329/12/Sensible%20Policy%20v8-final-sw%20(2).pdf (accessed on February 26, 2020).

105. *X, Y and Z v. United Kingdom,* App. No. 21830/93, 24 Eur. H.R. Rep. 143 (1997), https://www.globalhealthrights.org/health-topics/health-care-and-health-services/x-y-z-v-united-kingdom/ (accessed on February 25, 2020).

106. Loveday Hodson, *Different Families Same Rights? Lesbian, Gay, Bisexual and Transgender Families under International Human Rights Law* (ILGA-Europe, 2007), 26, https://www.ilga-europe.org/resources/ilga-europe-reports-and-other-materials/different-families-same-rights-lgbt-families-under

107. *P v. S and Cornwall County Council* (1996) ECR I-2143 (C-13/94), See https://eur-lex.europa.eu/legal-content/EN/TXT/?uri=CELEX:61994CJ0013 (accessed on February 26, 2020).

108. *Christine Goodwin v. UK* and *I v. UK Government*, 35 Eur. H.R. Rep.18, https://hudoc.echr.coe.int/eng#{"itemid":["001-60596"] (accessed on February 25, 2020). See Levi, *Transgender Family Law,* 46 and Whittle, "Sensible Policy, Excellent Practice."

109. Levi, *Transgender Family Law,* 46.

110. Para 18.

111. *KB v. NHS Pensions Agency & the Secretary of State for Health*, [2004] ECJ102, See Whittle, "Sensible Policy, Excellent Practice."

112. *The Yogyakarta Principles* is a document about human rights in the areas of sexual orientation and gender identity; see https://www.ishr.ch/news/yogyakarta-principles-application-human-rights-law-relation-sexual-orientation-and-gender (accessed on February 28, 2020).

Chapter 15

The Place of Normative Pluralism in Family Laws

Family and Marital Union in Ethiopia

Sileshi Bedasie Hirko

NORMATIVE PLURALISM: INTRODUCTION

Ethiopia's Historical Past and Present Context

Located in the Horn of Africa, Ethiopia—the second-most populous state in the continent—is composed of several nations, nationalities, and peoples. Given its predominant agrarian economic activities, the largest portion of Ethiopia's population resides in the rural areas. Dating back to its inception as an imperial state in the 1880s,[1] the modern Ethiopia constitutes over 80 nations, nationalities, and peoples. Owing to their primordial existence, most of the nations, nationalities, and peoples are endowed with their own rich cultures, languages, and distinct traditions of governance. Despite these rich and diverse but neglected backgrounds, Ethiopia's possible emergence of sociocultural pluralism was rather cabined within its deep-rooted and assimilative system of an imperial state centralization.[2] In particular, an overarching reason for the constrained normative space is attributed to the country's disputed project of modern state formation and the consequent imperial centralization.[3]

Subdued and subjected to a violent imperial policy of assimilation,[4] Ethiopia's multinational constituents—the nations, nationalities, and peoples—were thus conflated into a stifling unitarian regime dismantled in 1991. In effect, the repressive imperial regime had led to the emergence of a dominant sociocultural tradition. Rooted in an embedded and subtle ethnocentrism of the major ruling group, the hegemonic sociocultural dominance served to entrench and permeate the imperial system of centralization. Outliving the imperial era itself, the once-built sociocultural dominance continued far too long to constrain or foreclose the space required for the diverse and more robust local norms to flourish and shape the state's normative regimes. In fact, Ethiopia's imperial foundation was rather antithetical to the existing diversities and their manifestations. In consequence, relevant local societal norms were left no room to thrive and inform national policy and legal regimes.

Nonetheless, Ethiopia's recent transition from its age-old and stifling unitarianism to the current multinational federalism has changed the old status quo. Indeed, it has made imperative for the country to open up the normative spaces and acknowledge the hitherto suppressed diverse local norms. Evident in this regard is the proliferation of the whole gamut of laws at federal and state levels. Yet, there still remain the deep-rooted legacies of Ethiopia's monolithic and imperial past that continue lurking beneath the country's sociocultural and legal traditions. As such, the insidious legacies of the repressive past tend to undermine a progressive accommodation of the normative diversities essential for a flourishing multinational legal pluralism.

NORMATIVE PLURALISM IN ETHIOPIA: AN OVERVIEW IN A CONTEXT

As indicated above, the re-emergence and development of normative pluralism in modern Ethiopia are integral to its recent multinational constitution. Indeed, Ethiopia's official adoption of multinational federalism as a mode of governance in 1995 marked a historic phenomenon to usher in a new era for the constitutional recognition of the rights of nations, nationalities, and peoples without discrimination. Although its practical implementation is still far from full realization, the recognition of multinationalism and the consequent normative pluralism have been a milestone for the new multinational Ethiopia. Affirming the onset of the long-awaited recognition of multinational egalitarianism, the preamble to the Federal Democratic Republic of Ethiopia's (FDRE) Constitution refers to *the nations, nationalities, and peoples* of Ethiopia as sovereigns that have agreed to build a political and economic community based upon the core principles of a democratic federalism.[5] The recognition of Ethiopia's long-suppressed multinationalism has thus resulted in the revival of a normative pluralism. In particular, a legal pluralism has become the peculiar feature of Ethiopia's multinational federalism.[6]

In its broadest sense, a legal pluralism is defined as "state of affairs, for any social field, in which behavior pursuant to more than one legal order occurs."[7] In its narrow and legalistic sense, a legal pluralism refers to the existence and operation of several legal orders within a jurisdiction. It is in this sense that Ethiopia's multinational federalism has led to a legal pluralism that stems from the constitutional mandates of legislative and judicial organs established at federal and state levels. For instance, several laws operate in Ethiopia to regulate, inter alia, family matters.

From eleven regional states, seven regional states have thus far enacted their own family laws. In an apparent overlap with its regional counterpart, the Federal Family Code of 2000 (Revised Family Code) was enacted and has been in operation to regulate family matters within Addis Ababa (aka *Finfinne*, in *Afan Oromo*) and Dire Dawa. In the existing federal setup, both chartered cities are still integral to the region of their location despite the facade of their administrative separation. Hence, there might exist a shared normative space and an overlap in the jurisdictions for the application of relevant family laws.

In this chapter, a loose notion of normative pluralism is used to indicate the existence of several legal and social norms that shape a gamut of vital matters the various family laws govern in Ethiopia. For the purpose of this chapter, "normative pluralism" is understood to encompass diverse legal, societal, and human-rights norms.[8] Hence, it is inclusive of a legal pluralism. Cognizant of their amorphous conflation, the term "societal practices" denotes a blend of customs, and established social and religious practices with a significant bearing upon family matters. In addition to the formal legal norms that remain central to this chapter, the discussions might thus draw upon informal local norms depending upon their relevance and significance.

NOTION, SOURCES, AND ATTRIBUTES OF FAMILY

Notion and Normative Underpinnings of Family

As a matter of common parlance, family remains a vital societal institution.[9] Indeed, it is the founding source and pillar of a society. While there appears to be a consensus on the cardinal significance of family, its notion, scope, and attributes are often disputed. The lack of consensus is imputed to the diverse views on the notions, natures, kinds, and functions of family. In turn, the notions, sources and features of family are both shaped by, and stem from, the underpinning normative pluralism. Furthermore, various philosophical and interdisciplinary perspectives inform family and all its multifaceted attributes. As regards the theoretical justifications undergirding the notions, natures, and attributes of family, scholars in the field point out three major theories: contract-based, community-based, and rights-based theories.[10]

In Ethiopia, a blend of the theories underpins the notions and attributes of family. For instance, the contract-based theories regard the family as a contractual association that originates from the volition of individuals.[11] In so doing, the theories underscore the freedoms of spouses to regulate their family relationships, subject to the interests and well-being of their children.[12] As a result, spouses have the freedoms to use contractual or private ordering to regulate their personal and pecuniary relations upon conclusion, during the continuance, and dissolution, of their marriage.[13]

Given the freedoms of the spouses and the consequent variance, Minnow and Stanley underline the potential roles of contractual ordering to promote pluralism and diversities in family lives.[14] As the authors point out, contracts are not effective enough to guarantee enhanced freedoms. For instance, the varying economic and social conditions of the spouses might constitute impediments that undermine an effective and balanced bargaining power.

In contrast to a legal regulation, a contractual regulation might thus fail to ensure an equitable distribution of marital properties.[15] Antagonistic to public regulation as a state's interference, the approach tends to promote an excessive individualism.[16] In particular, the contractual ordering is critiqued for its neglect of vital public interests in the regulation of family relationships.[17] In an attempt to strike a balance between individual and public interests, the rights-based theories seek to ensure "equal freedom and opportunity for everyone in society."[18] While noting the pertinent public interests and their implications, the rights-based theories justify the extension of individual rights or freedoms to family matters.[19]

To this end, the rights-based approaches "require public articulation of the kinds of freedoms that deserve protection and the qualities of human dignity that warrant social support."[20] Rights-based theories are thus useful to underscore the respect for, and protection of, certain individual freedoms as vital social values.[21] Nevertheless, the theories are critiqued for lacking "a rich understanding of relationships, including their preconditions, their responsibilities, and their consequences."[22]

According to community-based theorists, families are "expressions of personal and social relationships larger than individuals."[23] For these communitarian theorists, families are "not simply private associations but also . . . crucial institutions that help compose civil society and the polity."[24] Emphasizing the significant roles of social norms or values of the community to define and inform the notions of family,[25] the communitarians justify the state's reasonable interference to regulate family matters.[26] In effect, the theorists reject the contractarians' view that "leaves family definition and responsibilities to the private ordering of individuals."[27]

Nevertheless, the community-based theories that emphasize shared moral values and standards are not immune to criticisms. In particular, the theories are critiqued for being prescriptive and lacking enough room to accommodate the pluralism and diversities that the contract-based and rights-based theories offer.[28]

The variance in the notions of family, and the debates on family law and policy "reflect the complexity of human aspirations" to enjoy, inter alia, freedom, equality, and interrelationship.[29] No single set of theories suffices to inform the notions, natures, and attributes of family. Although one might dominate the other, each set of theories has its own merits and demerits. For instance, contract-based theories are valued for fostering individual freedoms and contractual pluralism. Nonetheless, the theories not only neglect public interests or social values, but also "fail to protect individuals against oppressive bargains and ongoing patterns of social inequality."[30]

In the same vein, the community-based theories are useful to underscore the public nature of family institution and the roles of societal values. Yet, the theories might "invite disputes" over the kinds of families and moral values the society should approve with a consequent constraint upon individual freedoms.[31] Critiqued for its emphasis of individual freedoms, the rights-based theories attempt to "promote pluralism while also putting forward as societal values certain basic freedoms guaranteed to each individual."[32] According to Minnow & Shanely, "enriching rights-based theories with strong attention to relationships and their pre-conditions—holds more promise for family law than other approaches."[33]

In Ethiopia, the notions and functions of family hold a central place in the country's diverse societies. Although its notion can be gathered from various legal provisions, there exists no single definition of family under Ethiopian law. In terms of its components, there are various kinds of family in Ethiopia. Inclusive of close relatives and a nuclear family, an extended family is quite dominant. In particular, it is common to find blended or extended families throughout the countrysides. However, the family laws primarily regulate a nuclear family that comprises spouses and their children. In order to ban a marriage between relatives and create grounds for maintenance, the legal regulation however encompasses an extended family. Despite the variance in degrees, the above-mentioned theories underpin the notion and attributes of family. A combination of the theories shapes various family matters ranging from the nature, forms, conclusion, effects, and dissolution of marriage. Likewise, the theories inform the notions of filiation, parental rights, adoption, and family support.

For instance, art.34 of the FDRE Constitution regards family as "the natural and fundamental unit of society." In the same vein, art.18(1) of the African Charter states that "[the] family shall be the natural unit and basis of society" the state has the duty to protect.[34] To this effect, the Constitution underscores the need for legal protection of family both by society and the state.[35] Furthermore, enshrining similar wordings in its preamble, the Revised Family Code affirms the protection of the family as its guiding principle and objective.[36] As Elshtain correctly notes, "the family is a prerequisite for any form of social life."[37] As such, a "particular ideal of the family is imperative to create a more humane society."[38]

Given the age-old socioeconomic contexts in Ethiopia, the community-based theories embedded in shared social values and norms are predominant to shape the notion and attributes of family. In a testament to these realities, the FDRE Constitution recognizes the roles of customary and religious practices in the celebration of marriage and in the adjudication of marital disputes.[39] As required under art.17(3) of the African Charter, Ethiopia is bound to promote and protect moral and traditional values a community recognizes. In particular, art.18 (2) of the African Charter requires member states to assist the family as "the custodian of morals and traditional values recognized by the community."

Hence, the community-based notion of the family is accorded a legal recognition and protection. In addition to reflecting the central tenets of the rights-based and community-based theories, the FDRE Constitution and the Revised Family Code also acknowledge the freedoms of the spouses to conclude a valid marriage based upon their full and free consent.[40] Besides a consensual divorce upon court's approval,[41] the family law recognizes the primacy of a valid marriage contract to regulate pecuniary relations.[42] Furthermore, the constitutional recognition of the spouses' individual freedoms upon conclusion, during the continuance, and dissolution, of marriage reflects the views of both the rights-based and contractual theorists. In a nutshell, the family laws in Ethiopia draw on a blend of the major approaches highlighted above.

Sources of Family Relationship

Regardless of the underpinning theories, family gives rise to relations that entail legal effects. In Ethiopia, family relationships arise from both biological and non-biological relations. In general, the sources of family relationships with a legal recognition are marriage, nonmarital (irregular) union, and adoption.[43] A natural bond of family relationship stems from a biological filiation that in turn arises from a birth within or outside wedlock.[44] In this sense, children born in the marital and nonmarital unions are deemed to be born in a wedlock.[45] For a child born outside wedlock, a bond of paternal filiation can be established through a valid acknowledgment[46] and a judicial declaration.[47] In contrast, an adoptive filiation arises from an agreement and creates an artificial bond of family relation with similar legal effects.[48] Intended to establish sustainable family bonds, an adoptive filiation is thus a contractual or non-biological source of family relationships.

There are strong societal norms that justify adoption as a source of family relationship. Pre-dating a legal recognition, adoption (called *guddifecha* in *Afan Oromo*) has been practiced among Oromo people for centuries before the practice expanded to other peoples in Ethiopia.[49] In a deviance from this deep-rooted societal practice, the legal regulation under the Revised Family Code requires the judicial approval of the adoption for the filiation to produce legal effects.[50] In contrast, the Oromia Family Code takes an exceptional approach to embrace an adoption made according to the custom of the community.[51] In so doing, it reflects the underpinning societal norms to recognize unwritten adoption as a legitimate source of family relationship.

Inclusive of filiation that occurs in the unions, marriage and nonmarital unions generate both biological and non-biological family relationships.[52] For instance, the biological parent-child relationship is created between the parents and the children born in the marriage. In the same vein, a similar bond of consanguinities originates from an irregular union—a relation analogous to marriage in Ethiopia. In spite of its source, the biological family relationship exists both in the direct (ascendant-descendant) and in the collateral lines. In contrast to the unlimited bond of relationship in the direct line, the collateral blood relationship accorded a legal recognition is limited to the seventh generation.

Given the strong traditions of family bonds in Ethiopia, this legal recognition is believed to reflect both religious and social norms in the country. For instance, it has been an age-old societal tradition among Oromo people to count and recognize kinship ties extending to seventh generation. This recognition pre-dates the religious ground that carries a similar justification inherited from the Judeo-Christian traditions. In Ethiopia, several regional family laws maintain the seventh degree of relationship.

In contrast, the Revised Family Code has departed from the religious and societal norms. For a legal prohibition of a marriage among relatives, obligation of maintenance and power of guardianship, the Code's recognition of blood relationship in the collateral line is limited to brothers, sisters, uncle/niece, and aunt/nephew.[53] For the non-biological aspects, the marital relationship between spouses creates bond of affinities between a spouse and the close relatives of his/her spouse.[54] For instance, the family relationship arising from marriage extends up to third degree or generation in the collateral line. In a significant departure from the Civil Code of 1960 and other regional family laws, the collateral affinities under Revised Family Code are limited to a woman and her brother-in-law as well as a man and his sister-in-law.[55] Despite the societal norms that tend to blur the distinction, the bond of affinities attached to a marriage is not applicable for a nonmarital union.[56]

Nature and Attributes of Family

As noted above, family has multiple dimensions. Embedded in the contractual, communitarian and rights-based theories as well as their combinations, the nature and attributes of family can be understood as a private, public, and holistic institution. As a distinct institution, each aspect of the institution entails both common and distinct attributes. The regulation of the attributes warrants the respective roles of spouses, state, and the community. Despite its characterization, the institution has social, legal, and economic dimensions and attributes.

Family as a Private Institution

Considered natural and indissoluble, family is regarded as a private association or institution made up of a heterosexual couple and their children.[57] Given this private dimension of the family, both contract-and-rights-based theorists emphasize the individual roles of the family members.[58] As a private institution, various personal matters in the private realm of the family such as sexual and reproductive issues are best regulated through a regime of private ordering.[59] Indeed, the proponents of private ordering—advocating for maximum individual freedoms—question the legitimacy of state's interference with the contractual freedoms of the spouses.[60]

In so doing, this family dimension underscores the dominance of individuals' freedoms and privacy over their domestic relations. Left to a contractual model for the spouses to regulate their intimate personal matters, the private nature of the family is accorded a legal recognition. Cognizant of this private dimension, various human-rights instruments guarantee the respect for, and protection of, the individual freedoms essential for private lives.

Furthermore, embedded in the national law and societal norms, the dimension is evident from both marital and quasi-marital relations. For instance, the law recognizes spouses' contractual freedoms for the conclusion of marriage,[61] regulation of personal relations such as a joint determination of common residence,[62] separation agreement,[63] and contractual regulation of personal properties.[64] In the same vein, the spouses are entitled to conclude an agreement for a consensual divorce,[65] and conditions of divorce, subject to court's approval.[66] Nonetheless, a matter as private as having normal sexual relation is prescribed for the spouses to observe unless the relation poses a serious risk to their health.[67] Perhaps, the obligation tends to be quite intrusive into the couple's private affairs. Yet obligating spouses to consummate a marriage implies, and stems from, the latter's purpose of promoting procreation.

Family as a Public Institution

Although spouses' joint decisions are crucial, both the state and the society retain legitimate interests in the family relations. As explained above, a number of legal regimes such as human rights, constitutional, and family laws recognize and protect family as the fundamental basis of a society. In effect, family is not a mere private association but also a public institution with significant public interest and policy implications. Hence, not all matters left to the will and whims of the spouses as personal matters of private lives are insulated from state's interference. As reflected in its regulation of marital and quasi-marital issues, the state's reasonable interference via policies and laws is directed toward "channeling behavior and resolution of disputes."[68] In relation to marriage and its effects, the state both prescribes the substance of the relationship and acts as an ultimate arbiter of disputes arising thereof.[69] Other than those private matters reserved for private ordering, the law thus regulates several matters of compelling public concerns.

As embodiments of societal values intended to advance public interests, the public policies underpinning the legal regulation can be made in the form of prescriptive directives or legitimate restrictions on the spouses' freedom of contract.[70] Justified to protect and promote public values embedded in the family as a public institution, the roles of states are reflected through policies and laws. Incorporated into the laws or accorded a legal recognition, social and religious norms are also used to complement the public regulation of the family. For instance, public policy requires compliance with the conditions of a valid marriage (e.g., prohibition of child, bigamous and incestuous marriages). Likewise, mandatory personal relations (e.g., mutual respect, cohabitation, consummation, and fidelity) are deemed major family matters of public regulation.

Furthermore, the mandatory and presumptive regime of common property, court's jurisdiction over petition and conditions of divorce, child support, judicial declaration of paternal filiation, limited grounds of disowning, court's approval of adoption, and the obligation of maintenance are all intended to protect and advance the public interests involved in the family relations. In addition to the private and public legal regimes, religious and social norms are also vital and, in most cases, even more effective than the legal regimes. For instance, their effective roles are evident in condemning coercive or forced, bigamous, and incestuous marriages/adulterous relation, uncontrolled divorce, and abandonment/abusive treatment of children.

As indicated in the *African Protocol on the Rights of Women*, spouses have the joint duties to safeguard the interests of the family, protect and educate their children.[71] In the same vein, the *African Charter* requires all individuals to respect and promote the harmonious development of the family.[72] Offering children an enabling environment for their well-being, family institution proves instrumental to promote the best interest of the children.[73] Given the public dimension of the institution, public laws such as criminal laws criminalize underage, coercive, bigamous and incestuous marriages as well as child neglect and abortion.[74] Likewise, tort law holds third parties liable for inciting conjugal desertion and violation of laws regulating family matters.[75]

In short, legal regulation and protection of the family are justified as a matter of public policy that promotes family's public interest. To this end, both family members and third parties bear duties. In addition to the legal reforms made to ensure gender equalities and enhanced individual freedoms, a set of existing age-old societal norms underscores the need for a stronger family as a public institution.

Family as a Holistic Institution

Arising from both marital and recognized quasi-marital unions, family is a vital institution with both private and public attributes. As explained above, both individual members and the public at large have stakes in the unions that form the basis of the family. Given the importance of essential individual freedoms and the public interests, and the interdependence between both dimensions, family can be better viewed as a holistic institution. As the basic unit of a multidimensional and complex society, a holistic nature of family is manifest in its legal, social and economic attributes.

In other words, the legal, social, and economic considerations involved in the institution both affirm its holistic dimensions and necessitate an accommodation of a normative pluralism for its appropriate regulation. As such, a holistic family institution requires balancing the interests of the individual members, the state, and the society at large. In mediating the competing theoretical views, an emerging relational rights approach deems family as an inextricable blend of private and public institution shaped by social policy and state action.[76]

In this sense, family is thus understood as a holistic public institution with both private and public attributes. Indeed, the holistic nature of the family is recognized both in the legal regimes and societal norms in Ethiopia. As such, not only the individual members but also both the state and the society are required to protect the family and promote the values it enshrines. In Africa, "family is considered as the custodian of morals and traditional values recognized by the community."[77] Given its public nature, the state is responsible to protect the family as a public institution while its private aspect is subject to a private ordering. In effect, the plurality of legal and non-legal norms has played significant roles in determining the attributes of family as a holistic institution.

FORMATION OF MARITAL UNION

In Ethiopia, there are both marital and non/quasi-marital unions that are accorded a legal protection. A marital union arises from a valid marriage, while the quasi-marital relation stems from an irregular/informal union—an equivalent term for a common law marriage in other countries. Although protecting and promoting a lawful marital union is the central objective of the family laws, a nonmarital (irregular) union, as a matter of an age-old practice, is thus given a limited legal recognition. In fact, the legal regulation of a nonmarital union dates back to the 1960s. Nonetheless, a better protection of its legal effects has been ensured over the recent decades.

Despite the variance in the central objective of the laws and their degrees of protection, both marital and nonmarital unions are the two conjugal unions regulated in Ethiopia. Culminated in reforming the existing family laws, the turn of the millennium marked a period of significant developments in the conclusion, dissolution, and legal effects of a valid marriage. Distinct from the preferred valid marriage, an irregular union has been offered a modest legal protection in the country.

Notion and Attributes of Marriage

Notion of Marriage

Given the rapid developments with an emphasis on individual freedoms, the traditional notion of marriage as a fundamental and essential institution appears to be changing in the West. As a result, marriage is considered to be a principal matter of private ordering shielded against interference from the state and the public at large. In contrast, marriage is still a fundamental institution with strong public concerns addressed or safeguarded through legal and societal regulation in Ethiopia. In particular, Ethiopia's ratification of several human-rights instruments, and their incorporation into the national constitution have introduced more freedoms and gender equalities.

For instance, the FDRE Constitution requires conclusion of a valid marriage upon the "free and full consent" of the spouses.[78] Furthermore, both men and women have equal rights in a marital union.[79] In addition to its recognition of the roles of religious and societal norms,[80] the Constitution extends to a valid marriage the legal protection stipulated for the family as the fundamental unit of society.[81] In reaffirming the constitutional guarantee, the Revised Family Code underscores spouses' freedoms and gender equalities in a marriage during its conclusion, continuance, and dissolution.[82] In other words, the freedoms and equal treatment of the spouses in a marital union span from its creation to its undesired termination.

In relation to the notion of marriage, it is important to note that neither the FDRE Constitution nor the Revised Family Code does provide for a definition of marriage. An exception in this regard is the Amhara Family Code (AFC) that stipulates a definition of marriage. As per Article 11 of the Code, marriage is defined as "a relationship whereby a man and a woman, having attained majority, officially establish out of their own free will and consent with an intention to sustainable [*sic*] live together united in law, or a legal institution structured as a result of this relationship thereto." From this definition, one can note certain basic attributes of a valid marriage embedded in the Constitution and the relevant legal provisions of the Revised Family Code.

Attributes of Marriage

Considered a blend of both relational contract and civil status,[83] a valid marriage is an important institution that constitutes the primary source and organic unit of the family. In other words, as implied in the above-mentioned definition, marriage is considered a contractual, legal, and societal relation or institution. As a legal relation, a valid marriage engenders enforceable legal effects consisting of rights and duties. In general, most of the major attributes elaborated above are relevant to the notion and attributes of a valid marriage. Despite the current trends in other jurisdictions, marriage was once known as a heterosexual, monogamous, and permanent marital union.[84] In Africa, the traditional attributes of a valid marriage still remain dominant and functional.

In Ethiopia, the heterosexual, monogamous, contractual, public, and permanent or long-lasting attributes of a valid marriage embedded in the ratified regional human-rights instruments are recognized in the FDRE Constitution and the family laws. For instance, the heterosexual and monogamous attributes of a valid marriage are evident from the constitutional and legal provisions that refer to marriage as a contractual relation between *a man* and *a woman*.[85] Indeed, both same-sex and bigamous marriages are prohibited, and further criminalized as serious offenses against public morals.[86] In the event bigamies are given a due legal recognition, the criminal law however acknowledges an exception for a bigamous marriage concluded on the grounds of established religious and customary practices.

Enshrined in the family laws, the need for an official solemnization of a marriage, the substantive regulation of its conditions and effects, and the limited grounds for its dissolution reflect the long-lasting, and public attributes of a valid marriage. Evidencing an entrenched sociological aspect of marriage in Ethiopia, this set of attributes has strong implications for public welfare. As these attributes are often ingrained in, and derived from, deep-rooted religious and societal practices, the religious and social norms condemn a nonmarital sexual affair as a deliberate abuse of marital relation. In so doing, the norms reinforce and complement the legal duties imposed upon the spouses to safeguard a valid marriage while discouraging unlawful intimate unions. In sum, the existing legal, religious, and social norms underpin the attributes and notion of marriage both as a contractual and as a societal institution that deserves a due protection in Ethiopia.

Nonessential Conditions of a Valid Marriage

As mentioned above, the formation of a valid marriage as a basic societal institution is subject to legal regulation. To this end, the family law regime provides for conditions of a valid marriage. Based on their legal effects, the conditions required for the conclusion of a valid marriage can be categorized into essential and nonessential conditions. As opposed to the essential conditions of a valid marriage, the nonobservance of nonessential conditions does not render the marriage invalid. Yet, the nonessential conditions are significant to distinguish a valid marriage from nonmarital relations. Furthermore, they are useful to evidence the conclusion of the marriage. It is thus important to discuss the nonessential and essential conditions of a valid marriage. It is also worth noting that most conditions derive from societal norms.

Forms of a Valid Marriage

For conclusion of a valid marriage, one of the nonessential conditions is the form or mode of the marriage. Recognized in both federal and regional family laws, there are three forms of a valid heterosexual and monogamous marriage. In its usage of the terms, "forms of marriage," the law refers to the modes of celebration of the marriage. According to its mode of celebration, the form of the marriage is considered civil, religious, and customary.[87] Introduced since 1960, a civil marriage is a marriage concluded before an officer of civil status in accordance with the procedures prescribed by the law.[88] For a civil marriage, the formalities of celebration are stipulated under Article 25 of the Revised Family Code. As per the law, a civil marriage "shall be deemed to be concluded before an officer of civil status when a man and a woman have appeared before an officer of civil status for the purpose of concluding marriage and the officer of civil status has accepted their respective consent."[89] Common in the cities, a civil mode of celebration is regulated by the law.

In contrast, a religious form of marriage occurs when the intending spouses celebrate their marriage according to the prescribed religious acts or rites of the religion of both spouses, or one of them.[90] In so doing, the law leaves the procedures of celebration to be determined according to the preferred religious practices.[91] As a result, this entails a normative pluralism given the diverse religious procedures prescribed by different religions.[92] For the customary mode of celebration, the conclusion of a valid marriage takes place between a man and a woman in accordance with the custom of the community both or one of the spouses belongs to, or the community at the place of their residence.[93] That is, the observance of the ceremonial procedures the custom prescribes marks the official celebration of the marriage.[94]

Given the diverse nations and nationalities with their respective customs and cultures, the procedures the customs dictate might vary from one nation to the other or from one place to another. In both religious and customary modes, the procedures are manifestations of the beliefs, values, and practices underpinning the concerned religions and customs. In contrast to the civil marriage, the remaining modes of celebration are more common in the rural than in the urban areas. Although the form of a marriage is important to mark an official solemnization of the marriage, the nonobservance of the formalities does not constitute a ground for annulment of the marriage.[95]

Despite the legislative silence, the significance of the form or mode of celebration lies both in marking the conclusion and proof of marriage.[96] For instance, its importance for proof of marriage is recognized in a regional family law.[97] Furthermore, celebration of a marriage in one of the forms is also instrumental to distinguish a valid marriage from an irregular union.[98] In addition to the above modes of celebration, the Revised Family Code also recognizes marriage celebrated abroad in accordance with the form prescribed at the place of its celebration. Nonetheless, the marriage and its mode shall not contravene public morals in Ethiopia.[99] For instance, a same-sex marriage recognized abroad becomes invalid for contravening public morals.[100] In its reach and effect, the issue of public morals thus surpasses the mere mode of celebration and serves as a normative standard to determine the substantive content of the marriage itself.

Registration of Marriage

Once a valid marriage is concluded in one of the forms, a competent officer of civil status is required to undertake the formal registration of the marriage.[101] While the registration of a civil marriage occurs upon its celebration,[102] the registration for other modes of marriage is made upon the request of the spouses or the initiative of the officer of civil status.[103] Although the institutional infrastructure for marriage registration is put in place in the major cities, a countrywide registration is far from immediate realization.

In effect, a marriage certificate that is expected to be issued upon registration is often missing despite its importance for various legal purposes such as proof of the marriage.[104] In spite of its practical and legal significance, the registration or otherwise of a valid marriage does not however determine both the valid nature and legal effects of the marriage. Instead, a valid marriage shall produce a legal effect upon the date of its conclusion irrespective of its non-registration.[105] In this sense, the requirement of marriage registration is thus considered one of the nonessential conditions of a valid marriage.

Essential Conditions of a Valid Marriage

For a marriage to be valid, there are certain essential conditions that must be observed. In this regard, both the FDRE Constitution and the family laws prescribe for the intending spouses' to observe the conditions. As mentioned above, most essential conditions derive their normative forces from both religious and social norms. A major point of distinction, the violations of the essential conditions result in the invalidation or dissolution of the marriage.[106] Included in the required essential conditions are free consent, marriageable age, and observance of legal impediments. Due to the legal impediments, both bigamous and incestuous (between close relatives) marriages are prohibited. In the same vein, existing bonds of consanguinities (blood ties) and affinities (marital ties) constitute absolute legal impediments against conclusion of a valid marriage.

Free and Full Consent

Central to the contractual dimension of a valid marriage, free and full consent is one of the essential conditions. The condition is grounded both in the FDRE Constitution and human-rights instruments.[107] As such, the requirement of free and full consent underscores the freedoms of the spouses to decide on matters of their private lives without coercion.[108] For the marriage to be valid, the consent shall be free from acts or conducts of violence.[109] The consent is deemed to be vitiated when it is given under duress. Duress vitiates the consent when one is forced to assent in order to protect oneself or one's ascendants, descendants, or a close relative against a serious and an imminent danger or threat of danger.[110] The condition of free consent is important to prevent the conclusion of a forced marriage. Nevertheless, the practice of forced marriage is justified in some rural areas as a matter of societal practice. As opposed to the Civil Code, the Revised Family Code does not require the consent of the parents to confirm the mutual consent of the intending spouses. In fact, this is one of the areas that bear the transformative influence of human-rights norms.

For a free and full consent, the consent must also be free from a fundamental error. The marriage is invalid if the consent is deemed to be vitiated due to a fundamental error.[111] As per art.13 (3) of the Revised Family Code, the fundamental error includes errors on the personal identities of the spouses, their incurable or hereditary state of health, bodily confirmation for required consummation, and homosexual behavior. Although the list of fundamental error is illustrative, it is worth noting that not all errors are deemed fundamental to vitiate the consent. Hence, a marriage concluded under duress or due to a fundamental error is subject to annulment for want of free and full consent.[112] Furthermore, both acts of violence (e.g., abduction) and fraud constitute punishable crimes under the Criminal Code.[113] Yet, an action for annulment of such an invalid marriage is time-bound, the lapse of which entails consequent validation.

Marriageable Age

Attaining marriageable age is another essential condition required for a valid marriage. Given the need for the spouses to be mature for a sustainable marital union and in order to prevent child marriage, a valid marriage shall be concluded between spouses at or above 18 years of age.[114] As a minimum marriageable age, the threshold concurs with the majority age required for juridical acts under the national law.[115] An exception to the rule is a dispensation to be requested from the Office of Attorney General for a maximum period of two years. For the exception to operate, there should be a serious cause to justify the dispensation.[116]

Under art.581(1) of the Civil Code, the marriageable age was 15 for women and 18 for men. In consonance with relevant human-rights norms,[117] the removal of disparities in the age threshold and its role for the prevention of child marriage are among areas of new developments. Despite the marriageable age set at 18, there are still wide practices of child marriage in different rural parts of Ethiopia. For instance, over 1,000 child marriages were concluded in the Amhara region within a period of four months in 2020.[118] Justified as matter of societal practices in the region, the incident shows the glaring gap between the law and the societal practices.

The marriage concluded below the age of 18 and without the required dispensation shall be considered invalid and subject to dissolution, unless the minor attains the required age at the time of application for dissolution.[119] Furthermore, the Criminal Code prohibits a child marriage.[120] It is also a crime to have a sexual relation with a minor outside or in a child marriage.[121] Nonetheless, the marriage acquires a subsequent validation after the minor attains the marriageable age.

Grounds of Impediments

Subject to time limit, the issues of vitiated consent and under-marriageable age are considered grounds of relative impediments. In contrast, the conclusion of bigamous and incestuous marriages constitute absolute grounds of legal impediments. That is, the grounds of invalidation and their legal effects do not disappear with the passage of time. In relation to bigamies, the sole exception to the absolute grounds of impediment is the dissolution of a prior marriage. In effect, this entails a subsequent validation of the bigamous marriage and its conversion into a consequent monogamous marriage.[122] In principle, as provided under art.11 of the Revised Family Code, a person is prohibited from concluding a second marriage before the dissolution of the preceding marriage.

Construed to exclude a bigamous marriage,[123] the FDRE Constitution offers a heterosexual and monogamous marriage a legal protection as a basic unit of the family. In line with the constitutional provisions, both the family laws and the Criminal Code are explicit in their prohibition of a bigamous marriage in Ethiopia. Absent a religious justification with a due legal recognition of the exception,[124] a bigamous marriage remains invalid and is thus subject to annulment.[125] Save the Harari Family Code,[126] all the existing family laws do not recognize the exception contemplated in the Criminal Code. Given the existence of religious and societal practices that somehow tolerate a bigamous marriage in some rural parts of Ethiopia, there exist disparities between the legal norms and the practices. Perhaps, it takes time for the legal and human-rights norms to take root and transform the practices toward reinforcing the constitutional protection accorded to a monogamous marriage.

As noted above, the prohibition of a marriage between consanguinities or affinities constitutes another ground of absolute impediments. For an impediment of an incestuous marriage, persons with blood ties within the recognized degrees are not allowed to conclude a valid marriage. Likewise, persons sharing marital ties arising from a marital union are also prohibited from concluding a valid marriage. While the relationships of blood or marital ties in the direct line are not subject to specific degrees or limits,[127] there is a variance in the degree of impediments stemming from the relationships in the collateral line.

For instance, the Oromia Family Code prohibits the conclusion of a valid marriage between relatives within seventh degree of generations. In contrast, the prohibition under the Revised Family Code is limited to a marriage between a man and his sister or aunt, or a woman and her brother or uncle.[128] Due to affinities, a marriage between a man and his sister-in-law, or a wife and her brother-in-law is prohibited under the law. In both Oromia and Tigray Family Codes, this prohibition extends further up to a third degree of generations.[129] In effect, there exist disparities on the degrees of family relationships due to the variances among different family codes in Ethiopia.

Despite the discrepancies, an invalid marriage concluded in violation of the impediments arising from consanguinities or affinities entails the dissolution of the marriage upon the application of an interested person or the public prosecutor.[130] As long as the marriage remains intact, the legal impediments operate to constitute absolute grounds of annulment. That is, their invalidating effects are not time-bound. Furthermore, the acts are proscribed as punishable crimes. In addition to the legal norms, both religious and societal norms underpin the legal impediments. In this regard, the Revised Family Code is often critiqued, among others, for falling short of reflecting the deep-rooted societal norms. In contrast, the Oromia Family Code, with its extensive prohibition, somehow goes further to embrace the existing religious and social norms.

Outside the gap between the legal and societal norms, there still exists a potential intrastate conflict of laws among the Revised Family Code and other regional family laws. For example, a marriage between cousins is valid in areas within the material jurisdiction of the Revised Family Code. Yet, the same marriage becomes invalid for being a proscribed incestuous marriage in the Oromia region. Complicating the consequences of the disparities, a single Criminal Code operates throughout Ethiopia to prohibit an incestuous marriage. Given the inevitable inter-regional mobilities of the spouses, a conflict of laws arises from the criminal enforcement of the impediments within a region or across regions. Absent rules of conflict of laws in Ethiopia, the disparities not only promote forum shopping but also undermine a uniform criminal enforcement of the laws.

In sum, the various essential conditions required for a valid marriage are free and full consent, minimum marriageable age, and observance of legal impediments against bigamous and incestuous marriages. In addition to the legal prescriptions, the societal norms also support a compliance with the essential conditions. Indeed, most of the conditions that are considered legal requirements are grounded in societal or religious practices. As their invalidating effect is subject to a limited duration, the nonobservance of conditions of free consent and marriageable age might be considered relative impediments. In contrast, the legal impediments related to consanguinities, affinities, and bigamies are not subject to time limits. Grounded in strong public policy and societal norms, the legal impediments operate to constitute absolute grounds for the invalidation or dissolution of the marriage.

It is worth mentioning that the Revised Family Code treats an invalid marriage concluded in violations of the essential conditions as a voidable marriage.[131] Hence, the marriage produces the same legal effects of a valid marriage until its invalidation. Yet, this is not a uniform legal approach. For instance, the Oromia Family Code deviates from this approach. The Code recognizes the legal effects of an invalid marriage as long as an established practice of equity justifies the recognition.[132] With regard to filiation as a legal effect of a marriage, all family laws make no distinction between a valid and an invalid marriage.

CONCLUSION

Operating in a multinational state with its own federal structure, Ethiopia's pluralist normative regimes are constituted of international human-rights norms, constitutions, federal and regional/local laws, societal and religious norms. Integral to the broader context of the existing multinational federalism, the operation and interaction of this normative pluralism have shaped the development of family laws in Ethiopia. In both federal and regional state laws, the existing normative regimes underpin several family matters ranging from the notion, attributes, and nature of the family to the essential conditions for the conclusion of a valid marriage. While a blend of theories undergirds the holistic nature of the family and its attributes, various international and regional human-rights provisions underline the duties of the state and the society to protect family as the fundamental unit of the society. In addition to integrating the human-rights instruments, the FDRE Constitution affirms the guarantees for the protection of the family and the equal marital rights of the spouses in a monogamous and heterosexual marriage.

Furthermore, various human-rights norms have informed the conditions of a valid marriage such as free and full consent, and minimum marriageable age. In the same vein, both societal and religious norms have a significant influence in shaping the notion of family, the nature of marriage and the conditions for its conclusion. In Ethiopia, the influence of the socio-religious norms is more manifest in their abhorrence of incestuous, bigamous, and forced/fraudulent marriages. In terms of integrating human rights and societal norms to inform family matters, there is still a need for an adequate accommodation of the normative pluralism. For those norms embraced, there exists a tension among the relevant norms. Absent reasonable degree of harmonization, the pluralism might entail undesirable incoherencies in the family law regimes across regional states. Given their universal nature, an exception to the normative disparities is the uniform application of the integrated human-rights norms.

NOTES

1. See generally Bonnie K. Holcomb & Sisai Ibssa, *The Invention of Ethiopia: The Making of a Dependent Colonial State in Northeast Africa* (Trenton: Red Sea Press, 1990).

2. Christophe Van der Beken, "Ethiopia: From Centralized Monarch to A Federal Republic," *Afrika Focus* 20, no. 1(2007): 13–48; Christopher Clapham, "Centralization and Local Response in Southern Ethiopia," *African Affairs* 74, no. 294 (Jan. 1975): 72–81.

3. See Christopher Clapham, "Ethnicity and the National Question in Ethiopia," in *Conflict and Place in the Horn of Africa: Federalism and Its Alternatives*, eds. Peter Woodward & Murray Forsyth (Brookfield: Dartmouth Publishing, 1994), 37.

4. Beken, *supra* note 2; Clapham, *supra* note 2.

5. The Constitution of Federal Democratic Republic of Ethiopia (FDRE), Constitution Proc No.1/1995, Preamble & art.8.

6. See Alemayehu Fentaw, "Legal Pluralism: Its Promises and Pitfalls for Ethiopia," *Jimma University Journal of Law* 1, no.1 (October 2007): 35–66.

7. John Griffiths, "What is Legal Pluralism?" *Journal of Legal Pluralism and Unofficial Law* 24, no. 24 (1986): 1–56.

8. See generally William Twining, "Normative and Legal Pluralism: A Global Perspective," *Duke Journal of Comparative and International Law* 20 (2010): 473–517.

9. Michael S. Wald, "Introduction," University *of Michigan Law Reform* 18, no. 4 (1985): 799.

10. Martha Minnow & Mary Lyndon Shanley, "Relational Rights and Responsibilities: Revisioning the Family in Liberal Political Theory and Law," *Hypatia* 11, no. 1 (1996): 5.

11. Ibid., 5 & 9.

12. Ibid. Gary S. Becker, *A Treatise on the Family* (Cambridge: Harvard University Press, 1991), 135–154 & 179–200; Carol Weisbrod, "The Way We Live Now: A Discussion of Contracts and Domestic Relations," *Utah Law Review* 2 (1994): 777.

13. Minnow & Shanley, "Relational Rights," 9. Marjorie Maguire Shultz, "Contractual Ordering of Marriage: A New Model for State Policy," *California Law Review* 70, no. 2 (1982): 204.

14. Minnow & Shanley, "Relational Rights," 9.

15. Ibid., 11.

16. Ibid., 9–10; Lenore Weitzman, "Marriage Contracts," *California Law Review* 62, no. 4 (1974): 1275.

17. Minnow & Shanley, "Relational Rights," 12.

18. Ibid., 5; Margaret J. Radin, "Market Inalienability," *Harvard Law Review* 100, no. 8 (1987): 1849.

19. Minnow & Shanley, "Relational Rights," 17.

20. Ibid., 20.

21. Ibid.

22. Ibid.

23. Ibid., 13. Milton C. Regan, *Family Law and the Pursuit of Intimacy* (New York: New York University Press, 1993), 42 & 125.

24. Minnow & Shanley, "Relational Rights," 13. For some of theorists, traditional sources are important to articulate the content of social norms and form of relationships the community endorses. Ibid.

25. Ibid.,13; Mary Ann Glendon, *Rights Talk: The Impoverishment of Political Discourse* (Cambridge: Harvard University Press, 1991); Jean B. Elshtain et al., "A Communitarian Position on the Family," *National Civic Review* (Winter 1993): 25–35; Elshtain, "Accepting Limits," *Commonweal* 18, no. 20 (November 22, 1991): 685–686.

26. Minnow & Shanley, "Relational Rights," 13. William Galston, *Liberal Purposes: Goods, Virtues, and Diversity in the Liberal State* (Cambridge: Cambridge University Press, 1991), 14.

27. Minnow & Shanley, "Relational Rights," 13.

28. Ibid., 16. Due to their coercive authoritative decisions, "community-based theorists may exacerbate social and political divisions along religious and cultural lines." Ibid.

29. Ibid., 9.

30. Ibid., 17 & 20.

31. Ibid., 16 & 20.

32. Ibid., 17.

33. Ibid., 20.

34. African Charter on Human and Peoples' Rights, adopted June 27, 1981, OAU Doc. CAB/LEG/67/3 rev.5, 21 I.L.M.58 (1982), entered into force Oct. 21, 1986. International Covenant on Economic, social and Cultural Rights, adopted Dec. 16, 1966, entered into force Jan.3, 1976, art.10(1)[ICESCR]; The African Charter on the Rights and Welfare of the Child, adopted on July 11, 1990, entered into force Nov. 29, 1999, art.18[ACRWC]. Universal Declaration of Human Rights, adopted on Dec.10, 1948, art.16(3)[UDHR].

35. FDRE Constitution, art.34(3).

36. Revised Family Code Proc. No.213/2000, Preamble, para 1. Oromia Family Code Proc. No.83/2004, Preamble, para 1; The Amhara National Regional Family Code Proc. No. 79/2003, Preamble, para.1.

37. Jean Bethke Elshtain, "Feminism, Family and Community," in *Feminism and Community*, eds. Penny Weiss & Marilyn Friedman (Philadelphia: Temple University Press, 1995), 268.

38. Ibid.

39. FDRE Constitution, art.34(4 & 5).

40. FDRE Constitution, art.34(2); Revised Family Code, Preamble, para 2 & art.6. Oromia Family Code, Preamble, para. 2 & art.25(1). ICESCR, art.10(1); African Charter, art.18(3); Protocol to the African Charter on human and Peoples' Rights on the Rights of Women in Africa, adopted on July 11, 2003, entered into force on November 25, 2005, art.6(a)[African Protocol on the Rights of Women]. UDHR, art.16(2).

41. Revised Family Code, arts. 76(a), 77(1) & 80. Oromia Family Code, arts. 99–100.

42. Revised Family Code, arts.42, 60, 80(2–3) & 85(1).

43. See Oromia Family Code, arts.1–8; Revised Family Code, arts.8–10, 104, 125 & 180–181.

44. Revised Family Code, arts.124–125.

45. Ibid, arts.126 & 130.

46. Ibid, arts.131–142.

47. Ibid, arts.143–145.

48. Oromia Family Code, arts.180–181.

49. John H. Beckstrom, "Adoption in Ethiopia Ten Years after the Civil Code," *Journal of African Law* 16, no. 2 (1972): 145–168.

50. Revised Family Code, arts.180–181 & 194; Amhara Family Code, arts.191–192 & 205; Oromia Family Code, arts.198, 207 & 212.

51. Oromia Family Code, art.197. This provision uses "or" to join adoption according to custom and adoption based on agreement.

52. Ibid, art.2.

53. Revised Family Code, arts.8, 210(3)(d) & 225. For the purpose of maintenance, the relationship is limited to brothers and sisters.

54. Ibid, art.9.

55. Ibid, art.9(2).

56. Ibid, art.100(1).

57. Minnow & Shanley, "Relational Rights," 5 & 6. Although the notion of marriage is stretched to include same-sex marriage elsewhere, heterosexual marriage alone is protected in Ethiopia. Same-sex marriage is prohibited under Ethiopian laws.

58. Ibid.

59. Ibid., 7. Shultz, "Contractual," 204.

60. Weitzman, "Marriage Contracts," 1257. Wietzman states that "there is a serious question as to whether the state has any legitimate interest interfering with contracts regarding non-commercial sexual relations between consenting adults." Ibid.

61. FDRE Constitution, art.34(1); Revised Family Code, Preamble, para 2 & art.6; Oromia Family Code, art.25(1).

62. Revised Family Code, art.54.

63. Ibid, art.55.

64. Ibid, art.42. As stated under art.42(1) of the Code, "the spouses may, before or on the date of their marriage, regulate by a contract the pecuniary effects of their marriage."

65. Ibid, art.77.

66. Ibid, art.80(2 & 3) and 83(1).

67. Ibid, art.53(2).

68. Shultz, "Contractual," 211–212. Melvin Aron Eisenberg, "Private Ordering Through Negotiation: Dispute Settlement and Rule-making," *Harvard Law Review* 89, no. 4 (February 1976): 637.

69. Shultz, "Contractual," 212.

70. Ibid., 212 & 214.

71. African Protocol on the Rights of Women, art.6(i). ICESCR, art.10(1).

72. African Charter, arts.27 & 29(1). As stated under art.27 of the Charter, "every individual shall have duties towards his family and society."

73. CRC, art.20(1).

74. Criminal Code, arts.545 (abortion), art.582 (coercion), art.587 (abduction), art.646 (fraud), art.648 (early marriage), art.650 (bigamy), art.652 (adultery) and art.654–655 (incest).

75. Civil Code of 1960, arts.2035 & 2050. In addition to parent's breach of their duty to educate and supervise their children, a forceful or illegal interference with a lawful custody of a child is also a tortious act that entitles the custodian to claim damages. Ibid at arts.2052 & 2111.

76. Minnow & Shanley, "Relational Rights," 5 & 6.

77. African Charter, art.18(2).

78. FDRE Constitution, art.34(1 & 3).

79. Ibid, art.34(1).

80. Ibid, art.34(4 & 5).

81. Ibid, art.34.

82. Revised Family Code, Preamble, para 2; FDRE Constitution, art.34(1) & 35(2).

83. See Janet Halley, "Behind the Law of Marriage (I): From Status/Contract to the Marriage System," *UNBOUND* 6, no. 1 (2010): 2 & 12–19. Despite the debate

of dichotomization, marriage is neither status nor contract, but a status plus elements of contract. Ibid., 2. In Ethiopia, its nature as a status is more dominant. Elizabeth S. Scott & Robert E.Scott. "Marriage as Relational Contract," *Virginia Law Review* 84, no. 7(1998): 1225–1334.

84. Shultz, "Contractual," 230. In the past, marriage in other jurisdictions such as the USA was heterosexual, monogamous, and permanent. Ibid. John Witte, "The Nature of Family, The Family of Nature: The Surprising Liberal Defense of the Traditional Family in the Enlightenment," *Emory Law Journal* 64 (2015): 591, 593.

85. FDRE Constitution, art.34(1 & 2); Revised Family Code, arts.1–4.

86. Revised Family Code, arts.5 & Criminal Code Proc No.414/2004, art.650 (bigamy), arts.629–632 (homosexual) & 647(unlawful marriage).

87. Revised Family Code, arts.1–4. Oromia Family Code, arts.19–23; Amhara Family Code, arts.12–16.

88. Revised Family Code, arts.1(1) & (2).

89. Ibid, art.2.

90. Ibid, art.3.

91. Ibid, art.26.

92. Sileshi B. Hirko, "A Post-Divorce Cohabitation Never Equals a Remarriage in Ethiopia: A Case Comment," *Haramaya Law Review* 3, no. 1 (2014): 80.

93. Revised Family Code, art.4; Oromia Family Code, art.22.

94. Revised Family Code, art.27; Hirko, "Post-Divorce Cohabitation," 81.

95. Revised Family Code, art.39.

96. Hirko, "Post-Divorce Cohabitation," 80–82 & 85.

97. Ibid at 82 & 84–85. The Southern Nations, Nationalities and People's Regional State (SNNPRs) Family Code, Proc. No. 75/2004, art.108.

98. Hirko, "Post-Divorce Cohabitation," 82–83.

99. Revised Family Code, art.5.

100. *Explanatory Notes on the Revised Family Code 2000* at 3. Revised Family Code, arts.5 & 13(3)(d).

101. Revised Family Code, art.28. Registration of Vital Events and National Identity Card Proclamation No. 760/2012, arts.6(20)(a) & 30–33.

102. Revised Family Code, art.25(5 & 6).

103. Ibid, art.29.

104. Ibid, art.28(2) & 29(1). From among several details, the particulars of the record of marriage and the certificate include date, place, and form of a marriage. Ibid, art.30.

105. Ibid, art.28(3). As the provision states: "any marriage shall have effect from the date of its conclusion."

106. Ibid, arts.31–39.

107. FDRE Constitution, art.34(2); UDHR, art.16(3); ICESCR, art.10(1); African Charter, art.18(3), African Protocol on Right of Women, art.6(a).

108. See Egon Schwelb, "Marriage and Human Rights," *The American Journal of Comparative Law* 12, no. 3 (1963): 351–354.

109. Revised Family Code, art.6 & 14 (1).

110. Ibid, art.14(2).

111. Ibid, art.13(1).

112. Ibid, arts.13(1), 14(1), 35 (1) & 36(1).

113. Criminal Code, arts.587 (abduction) & 646 (fraud or deception in marriage).

114. Revised Family Code, art.7(1).

115. Ibid, arts.215 & 310(a). A minor is a person under majority age and the minor becomes major when he attains 18 years of age.

116. Ibid, art.7(2).

117. For instance, art.16(1) of the UDHR requires the conclusion of a marriage between men and women of *full age* (emphasis added). African Protocol on the Rights of Women, art.6(b)["the minimum age of marriage for women shall be 18 years"].

118. As reported in May 2020, "more than 500 girls have been rescued from child marriage in northern Ethiopia since schools were shut due to the new coronavirus." Emeline Wuilbercq, "Hundreds of Children Weddings Thwarted in Ethiopia as Coronavirus Locks Girls out of Schools," *Reuters*, May 14, 2020.

119. Revised Family Code, art.31.

120. Criminal Code, art.648.

121. Ibid., arts.626–627.

122. Ibid, art.33(2); Oromia Family Code, art.50(2).

123. Sileshi Bedasie Hirko, "The Disputed Constitutionality of the Precedential Practice of the Federal Supreme Court and Its Implications for Oromia Family Law: The Case of Bigamous Marriage in Ethiopia," *Journal of African Law,* 63, no. 2 (2019): 195–197.

124. Criminal Code, art.651.

125. Revised Family Code, art.33(1); Oromia Family Code, art.50(1).

126. Hirko, "Constitutionality of the Precedential Practice," 196. Harari Regional State Family Code, Proc. No.80/2008, art.11(2). The Code recognizes the conclusion of a bigamous marriage justified on a religious ground.

127. Revised Family Code, art.8(1) & 9(1).

128. Ibid, art.8(2).

129. Oromia Family Code, art.28(2); Tigray Family Code, art.4.

130. Revised Family Code, art.32.

131. See RFC, art.85; Hirko, "Constitutionality of the Precedential Practice," 197; Mehari Redai, *Some Points for Understanding the Revised Family Law,* Vol. 1, 2nd ed. (Addis Ababa: Commercial Printing Press, 2010), 43.

132. Oromia Family Code, art.123. See generally Sileshi Bedasie Hirko, "The Liquidation of Pecuniary Effects of Bigamous Marriage in Ethiopia: A Critical Review of the Precedents of the Federal Supreme Court and Rule of Equity under the Oromia Regional Family Code," *International Journal of Law, Policy and the Family* 30, no. 1 (April 2016): 32–49.

Chapter 16

Imperfect Families

Preserving Family Unity and Communities in South Africa and the United States

Deseriee Kennedy

INTRODUCTION

Policies regarding family preservation and child welfare differ across the globe. While most nations profess to act in a child's best interests, there are significant variations in how countries implement that principle. There is little agreement about what it means to work in a child's best interest when determining "neglect," or when a parent is responsible for failing to provide for a child's basic needs like food, housing, and clothing, particularly for the poor. Decisions about whether to remove a child from a parent's custody, place them into state care, and terminate parental rights are difficult ones that raise complicated issues involving competing interests. These decisions juxtapose parental rights and responsibilities, the state's obligations, and a child's right to live in a safe and nurturing environment. When these issues arise, economic resources, race, racism, class, classism, gender, and sexism often intersect. The interlocking stresses of poverty, racism, substance abuse, and parental involvement with the criminal justice system apply pressures on families that can trigger state intervention in a family on the grounds of child neglect. However, reliance on family separation as a means of resolving cases of neglect may be ineffective in helping resolve the underlying issues that precipitated state involvement and may do significant harm to children and their families. Interventionist and punitive child welfare policies intersect with poverty and a criminal justice system that disproportionately punishes the poor and people of color, splitting families apart.[1]

Child welfare policies, poverty, and a racially biased criminal justice system reinforce each other to control families that live on society's margins.

Poverty can increase the risk of involvement with child welfare agencies since interlocking conditions related to poverty may increase rates of child maltreatment and may also expose families to allegations of neglect. Substance abuse and mental health challenges can exacerbate poverty conditions, increasing the likelihood of state intervention in families through child welfare and criminal institutions. The disproportionate mass incarceration of people of color contributes to the child welfare system's family separation problem. Professor Dorothy Roberts has stated that "the child welfare system in the nation's largest cities . . . is basically an apartheid institution."[2] The magnitude of the crisis and the collateral impact on children in the United States warrants an analysis of whether United States' policy would benefit from comparing approaches to policies in other countries. Shared democratic ideals coupled with a history of racial hierarchies and discrimination suggest that South Africa's child welfare policies may provide an apt comparison.[3] Such a comparison provides an opportunity to caution against child welfare and criminal justice policies that rely on child removal and fail to respect family unity.

South Africa's recognition of the Convention on the Rights of the Child (CRC) contrasts with the United States' continued refusal to ratify the treaty and this difference is reflected in child welfare policy. The comparison of the disparate approaches to supporting families in the United States and South Africa makes clear that recognizing children's rights and adopting international treaties alone without committing significant resources to needy communities and parents will do little to protect children and their families. Both countries' unequal provision of resources results in disparities in child welfare and state intervention in families based on economic wealth and race.

COMPOUNDED DEPRIVATIONS AND THE INTERSECTION OF CHILD WELFARE AND MASS INCARCERATION

The United States is one of the wealthiest countries in the world. Still, smaller and smaller percentages of the population share their economic resources as wealth inequality grows in ways that reify racial and economic stratification. While one in seven Americans is poor, blacks and Hispanics are twice as likely to live in poverty than whites. Despite the country's great wealth, more than 14% of its children live in poverty, and 71% are children of color. The individual poverty felt by these children is heightened by living in segregated and poor communities. Many live in communities that experience "compounded deprivations." They often face under- and unemployment, housing insecurity, high crime rates, and criminal justice interventions, underperforming schools and other barriers, and solutions lie not in individual approaches but in holistic interventions by making durable investments in poor, black, and Hispanic neighborhoods.

The role of the government in safeguarding the well-being of American children is deeply contested. States cannot neatly draw dividing lines between parental rights, state responsibility, and child welfare, and outlining such borders is the most problematic in dealing with the nations' poor. On the one hand, the United States recognizes that parents have constitutional rights to the care and custody of their children.[4] However, under *parens patriae*, states may intervene in families when necessary to protect the child from abuse or neglect. Federal law defines abuse and neglect as "any recent act or failure to act on the part of a parent or caregiver that results in death, serious physical or emotional harm, sexual abuse, or exploitation, or an act or failure to act that presents an imminent risk of serious harm."[5] However, the acts or omissions that constitute neglect warranting state intervention are primarily left to individual states.[6] The term "neglect" permits subjective determinations by the state about a parent's ability to adequately provide food, clothing, shelter, or supervision.[7] All too often, conditions of living in poverty are conflated with child neglect, resulting in greater involvement with the child welfare system for the poor.[8] In so doing, American child welfare policies traditionally focused primarily on parental responsibility and separation as distinguished from family support and preservation.[9] Child welfare systems have also disproportionately policed and targeted black and brown communities. Many states relied on child removal to control communities of color seeking to advance civil rights.[10] For example, in the civil rights era of the late 1950s and 1960s, southern states relied on a combination of cutting government financial support for children and draconian morality laws to penalize black mothers and to remove or threaten to remove their children.[11] Similarly, "Indian boarding schools" created by the military in the 1870s as a campaign to "extinguish" tribal nations continued to separate Native American children from their parents until the 1970s.[12] Even today, blacks, Latinos, and Native Americans continue to be disproportionately drawn into the child-welfare and foster-care systems, spend more time in foster care than white children and have worse outcomes.[13] Thus, the approach to child welfare followed in the United States has been subject to significant criticism regarding the apparent biases that result in children of color being disproportionately represented among children in state care.[14]

There are typically more than 400,000 children in state-maintained foster care, at any given time, with most due to claims of neglect. Nearly half of those children are placed with nonrelatives.

The stated goal for only about half of these children is family reunification, resulting in rising parental terminations.[15] Federal legislation has played a significant role in accelerating child removal. The 1997 Adoption and Safe Families Act (ASFA) provides financial incentives to states to increase children's adoptions out of foster care.[16] Furthermore, ASFA mandates that state child-welfare agencies move to terminate parental rights to free children up for adoption when a child has been in state care for 15 out of the last 22 months unless one of the narrow exceptions provided in the statute applies.[17] The most common exceptions are a compelling reason that terminating the relationship is not in the child's best interest or that the state has failed to make "reasonable efforts" to reunite the family.[18] However, the statute does not define the level of "effort" required by the states to reunify families. The "efforts" required can consist of a case or reunification plan mandating that the parent admit to the alleged wrongdoing, engage in parenting classes, drug and alcohol abuse treatment, mental health counseling, secure housing, obtain employment, and other requirements set by the caseworker.[19] The impact of the ASFA incentivized states to terminate parental rights and more quickly. As a result, the federal government devoted more funds to foster care and adoption than family preservation.[20] This led to harsh results for low-income families and families of color.[21] The current substance abuse and opioid crises and the over-reliance on incarceration as a solution to drug use and related crimes has also contributed to increases in foster-care numbers and parental terminations.[22] Since substance abuse affects brain function and behavior, recovery is a "long-term process" that "frequently requires multiple episodes of treatment" that "attends to multiple needs of the individual."[23] Thus, the ASFA legislative time frames proved to be particularly unrealistic for families suffering from a range of traumas related to racial discrimination, poverty, family violence, mental health challenges, substance abuse, and other traumas.[24]

Recently, there have been legislative efforts in the United States to prioritize family preservation in child welfare policies to protect children. A recent shift in federal funding is designed to support family preservation. The Family First Prevention Services Act (FFPSA or "Family First"), enacted in 2018, provides funding to prevent entry into foster care.[25] It allows funds that previously could only be used for foster care to be used for prevention services to enable children to stay with their parents or relatives.[26] The states can use federal funds to provide mental health and substance abuse prevention, treatment, and parenting classes.[27] States may also use federal money to pay for some of the parents' attorneys' costs in child-welfare legal proceedings.[28] The Act recognizes the harm of family separation and removing children from their families and communities but fails to provide sufficient protection.[29] Additionally, the 12-month time frame in the FFPSA may be too short to allow families to address the range of the issues they may be facing. Although a step in the right direction, the legislative change focuses too narrowly on child welfare without addressing the other institutional structures related to findings of neglect, such as poverty, substance abuse, and intimate partner violence.[30] Nor does the change sufficiently move from an adversarial, crisis-based approach to child welfare to a "primary prevention" approach that invests in communities as a means of avoiding unnecessary intervention in families.[31]

The United States child welfare model focuses more on protecting children from their parents than on prioritizing addressing poverty-related conditions and preserving family ties whenever possible. This approach underestimates the importance of families and communities to child well-being.[32] This rights-based approach may not serve child-welfare principles and has historically negatively impacted low-income families and families of color disproportionately.[33] Child welfare policies rooted in helping children by protecting them from their families ignore the varied institutional, structural, and systemic issues affecting child welfare.[34] This approach is not only adversarial but marginalizing.[35] Approaching child welfare from this perspective raises the question of what it means to act in a child's best interest if the remedy is family separation. It ignores the view that a "child's 'best interests' cannot, in many instances, be distinguished from the interests and rights of the child's family and community."[36]

Child welfare and criminal justice policies intersect to create a perfect storm of family disruption.[37] The reliance on prison to respond to social problems directly impacts children and families. More than 10 million people are in prison worldwide, with the female imprisonment rate growing substantially more rapidly than for men.[38] With an incarceration rate of 698 per 100,000 inhabitants, the United States houses more than 2.2 million prisoners, an imprisonment rate that dwarfs that of most other industrialized nations.[39] Most of those in prison are parents of minor children, and the rising rates of incarcerated women mean more mothers are in prison than ever before.[40] As a result, millions of children worldwide are affected by a state's response to a parent's criminal acts. United States policies have resulted in 1 in 12 children with a parent in prison. More than 5.7 million American children have experienced parental incarceration at some point in their lives.[41] Current child-welfare policies have proven inadequate in dealing with these challenges.[42] The population of incarcerated families presents a critical juncture at which the failures of a series of policies and systems intersect to increase the potential for adverse effects on children.[43] Large-scale incarceration schemes directly affect families and the problem's scale is unprecedented and it establishes that treating family law separately from criminal law is impractical. The two systems should develop an appreciation for the intersection of child welfare and criminal justice.[44]

Data analysis of prison populations reveals that prisons' overuse falls most heavily on people of color and the poor.[45] African Americans and Latinos are disproportionately represented among those in jail and prison.[46] People of color comprise 67% of the prison population, while only 37% of the general population.[47] The result in the United States is that one out of every three black and one out of every six Latino men in America will spend time in prison.[48] African American women are imprisoned at twice the rate of white women, and Latina women are incarcerated at 1.3 times the rate of white women.[49] The rise in incarceration rates among blacks and Latinos is mainly attributable to the drug wars, the racially disparate application of law and policy, and the punitive approach to drug use and poverty.[50] Most women are jailed for nonviolent drug, property, or public-order offenses.[51] And most sentences result from plea bargains, in which the defendant pleads guilty in exchange for leniency and does not receive a trial.[52] Black and Latino children are disproportionately affected by these outcomes.[53] Black children are more than seven and a half times more likely, and Latino children are more than two and a half times more likely than white children to have an incarcerated parent.[54] Estimates show that 1 out of every 10 black children has an incarcerated parent. Families are directly impacted by criminal justice policies in which the average length of a prison sentence is longer than the ASFA timeline (2.6 years for state and more than 11 years for a federal conviction) and prosecutors rely on plea bargains to convict defendants without trial.[55] As Dorothy Roberts noted in, *Shattered Bonds*, "A major cause of family disruption is the high incarceration rate among young Black fathers and a growing number of Black mothers."[56]

In some communities, adults are incarcerated at such high rates that many children are left without one or both parents to care for them.[57] Imprisoning a parent can entangle a family with a state child-welfare system that is ostensibly designed to protect them but can frequently lead to the termination of parental rights and permanent disruption of families.[58] Neighborhoods with the highest incarceration rates frequently deal with a host of social and economic ills.[59] These communities are often dealing with high rates of poverty, unemployment, violence, and racial segregation. Many who live in these communities experience a cycle of imprisonment and release, which can break up families, destabilize neighborhoods, and disrupt social networks that support the community's children. Children separated from a parent due to foster care or parental incarceration deal with multiple issues, including the trauma of physical separation and the stigma and trauma associated with having a family member caught in the carceral state.[60] A range of studies show that these children have worse effects, including economic privation, housing instability, behavior problems, and lower school performance.[61] Although evidence shows a child's life improved by separating them from an abusive or violent parent, most children are involved with the state due to neglect, not abuse charges. These children suffer from the loss of a flawed but caring parent.[62]

Child welfare and criminal justice policies that do not consider how the systems interlock to impact families devalue families in communities of color.[63] In contrast, post-apartheid South Africa has taken steps to place families at the center of child welfare considerations.

POST-APARTHEID SOUTH AFRICA AND THE INCARCERATION, CHILDREN, AND FAMILIES

The United States and South Africa share a history of racism and a myth of white racial superiority that plays a role in economic and structural inequities, policy, and legislation involving children and families.[64] The ongoing racial disparities in socioeconomic status, educational opportunities, and criminal justice make South Africa, with its apartheid past, a fitting comparison for U.S. child welfare policies. The South African apartheid-era government warehoused black and brown bodies, including children, as part of a system of white supremacy.[65] Apartheid laws created conditions that forced separation between parents and children, and children played a significant role in ending formal systems of racial oppression.[66] Modern South Africa embraces the concept of children's rights in principle and has developed a more family-centric approach to children and family preservation than in the United States. Although the country continues to face challenges in implementing these policies and addressing poverty, the focus on family preservation and child well-being is instructive.

There is a sense that the country's ratification of international agreements on children's rights was a critical inflection point in developing South African child welfare policies.[67] South Africa ratified the Universal Declaration of Human Rights, the International Covenant on Civil and Political Rights, and the United Nations Convention on the Rights of the Child (CRC).[68] Preserving family unity is a cornerstone of the Universal Declaration of Human Rights. It states that "the family is the natural and fundamental group unit of society and is entitled to protection."[69] The declaration represents the truism that family units are central to societies' continuation and children's socialization. Although the language in the declaration is merely aspirational, the principle of the importance of the family unit is echoed in the International Covenant on Civil and Political Rights, which provides that the state must protect the family as "the natural and fundamental group unit of society" (ICCPR). The CRC further establishes that the child's best interests should be a primary consideration in all actions concerning children and sets the government as a safety net for, and not the primary caretaker, of children. The CRC highlights that a child has a right to be heard on issues pertaining to them.[70] South Africa also ratified the African Charter on the Rights and Welfare of Children.[71] The

African Charter acknowledges the "reciprocal and multilateral" nature of the relationship between the family and the child.[72]

South Africa's adoption of international conventions on prisoners' treatment has also affected its criminal justice policies about parents and their children. The country's adoption of the United Nations Rules on the Treatment of Women Prisoners and Non-Custodial Measures for Women Offenders (the "Bangkok Rules") recognizes parents' importance to families. For example, the Bangkok Rules prefer noncustodial sentences for pregnant women and women with dependent children and allow for caretaking responsibilities for children and other family members to be a factor in determining an appropriate sentence.[73] The Bangkok Rules incorporate provisions of the United Nations Standard Minimum Rules for Non-Custodial Measures (Tokyo Rules), stipulating that prison should be used as a last resort.[74] The Bangkok Rules require courts to be responsible for what happens to the children, and parents should be sent to prisons as close to their homes as possible.[75] Under the Bangkok Rules, mothers must be given information about caretaker options, the long-term consequences of their choices, and how they can keep in contact with their children. Parents who are to be incarcerated must be permitted to make arrangements for their children's care, even if it delays taking them into custody.[76] The Bangkok Rules also advises a registration process for all prisoners, including recording the names, ages, location, and custody information about their children.[77] The Bangkok and Tokyo Rules encourage the development of diversionary and sentencing alternatives and restorative justice.[78] Therapeutic interventions are particularly crucial for women offenders since many have experienced domestic violence, sexual abuse, and mental health issues.[79]

There are apparent differences in the development of constitutional rights in South Africa, making their approach to child neglect and family preservation illuminating. South Africa incorporated many of these central international principles into its constitutional documents, and international law is binding or persuasive authority in South Africa.[80] Additionally, the 1996 South African Constitution was developed through a more inclusive process than the U.S. Constitution and deals explicitly with the rights of families, children, and culture in ways that differ markedly from the United States.[81] The country's Constitution provides greater protection to children than many other countries.[82] Its Constitution makes central the child's best interest in all decisions concerning them. It provides that their "best interests are of paramount importance in every matter" concerning them.[83] The South African Bill of Rights recognizes children's right to "family care or parental care, or to appropriate alternative care."[84] Furthermore, it provides that children have the right to "have a legal practitioner assigned to the child by the state, and at state expense, in civil proceedings affecting the child."[85] South African children have the right to be heard, and the nation requires international law to be respected when making decisions involving them and their care.[86]

The Children's Act, Constitution, and other child-focused legislation in South Africa influence a child welfare practice that is trending toward increased recognition of the role of poverty and other social ills in child welfare.[87] South Africa refocuses the conversation about child welfare from parental responsibility to a community-development approach focused on preventative services, which is "responsive to the 'voice of the children'" and the family, where "family" is broadly defined.[88] "The right to 'family care' includes the right to be cared for by the extended family" as well as unrelated people with whom the child has a relationship.[89] The Children's Act takes a broad view of individuals who may be a child's caregiver. It allows for parents to confer rights on any person interested in the care and well-being of a child.[90] The Children's Act focus is on the child's well-being first and parental rights and biology second.[91] In determining a child's "best interests," the Children's Act requires the child's views and wishes be considered.[92] A conciliatory approach or mediation is preferred over adversarial or confrontational approaches to resolve disputes concerning families.[93]

Child welfare practices in South Africa try to be sensitive to different cultural practices. It is common for children to live apart from their parents and relatives in South Africa, and child-headed households are not uncommon.[94] Most South African children who are not living with their parents live instead with grandparents or relatives.[95] These children are not considered abandoned, and parents continue to support and regularly see their children.[96] Child removal and the use of foster care is not the primary solution to child welfare concerns. Of the 19.7 million children in South Africa, it is estimated that fewer than 5% of the total child population is not living with relatives.[97] Children placed into foster care in South Africa are considered "in need of care and protection," as outlined in Section 150(1) of the Children's Act.[98] It is believed that there are more than 400,000 South African children in foster care at any given time.[99] However, similar to the United States, the overwhelming majority of the children available for adoption are black.[100] South African children end up in the system, mainly due to poverty, violence, and gender inequality.[101] Yet, the focus on mandatory reporting provisions under South African law is on deliberate or willful neglect. "The removal of a child from his or her parents or caregivers is an extreme measure."[102] When social workers remove children, the action is subject to immediate review by the courts.[103]

Although critical of South Africa's child welfare system's ability to live up to its goals, Schmid describes the modern child welfare system as based on principles focused more on family unity.[104] This post-apartheid "Developmental Social Welfare" approach recognizes the value of social investments to improve quality of life, promote social justice and equity, as well social inclusion, and partnerships with communities in developing policy.[105] According to Schmid, "the primary method of intervention is that of community development."[106] This approach prioritizes early intervention, and the focus is on the family, not parental responsibility alone.[107] South African child welfare law includes a state obligation to support families and their parents by providing paid parenting leaves, early childhood development services, social assistance grants, and prevention and early intervention programs.[108] However, the promise of providing resources for families in South Africa is limited by the country's economic realities of high crime rates and poverty levels.

South African case law highlights the intersection between child welfare and the criminal justice system. Current incarceration rates in South Africa are below that of the United States. However, crime continues to be a significant problem in the country.[109] The incarcerated in South Africa tend to face poverty, deprivation, and trauma to their families.[110] Like in the United States, most women in South African prisons are mothers, and these women are predominately black or "Colored."[111] Research suggests that formerly incarcerated parents and their families face many of the same challenges in South Africa as in the United States. Researchers have found that the incarceration of a parent is an essential indicator of intergenerational crime. Returning prisoners face difficulty re-establishing themselves into society, finding jobs, and locating services to help them sustain their families.[112] However, given the concern about parental incarceration's impact on child well-being, protections under South African law permit sentencing courts to consider parenthood in meting out sentences.

The South African Constitutional Court recognized children's right to a relationship with their parents and the importance of family integrity.[113] In *S v. M*, the Constitutional Court reversed the four-year sentence of a single parent finding that the South Africa Constitution required courts to consider the interests of the children of convicted parents when sentencing them to serve time in prison. Recognizing the children's need for their parent's presence in the home, the court ultimately suspended their custodial sentence and imposed house arrest and community service. A later case found that alternative sentencing is not always required if another parent can care for the children but agreed that courts should weigh the effect of a custodial sentence on the child before sentencing a parent.[114]

South African laws and policies protect the legal rights of children and families. However, persistently high poverty rates have limited the country's ability to implement the changes in meaningful ways that would improve childhood outcomes. The nation's wealth inequality results in poor and migrant children seeing worse impacts and more significant state intervention.

The economic disparities in South Africa have led to an inability to achieve the promise of children and family rights embedded in the nation's laws. Like in the United States, economic inequality, unemployment, and disparate access to South African services disproportionately affect blacks. Comparing the two nations suggests that the adoption of children's rights legislation alone is insufficient to improve prospects of the most vulnerable children and communities. Formal recognition of children's right to a connection to their families without economic investment in poor communities and communities of color will do little to reduce child poverty or state intervention in families. Economic justice that focuses on eliminating racial, gender, and economic disparities is vital to ensuring child welfare and family stability. An interventionist approach that removes children from one family and substitutes it with another more economically secure family is not a viable solution to the compounded deprivations wrought by racial and economic injustice.

CONCLUSION

Economic inequalities, regressive child welfare, and criminal justice policies unfairly impact black and brown communities. Child welfare and criminal justice laws and policies must make children's best interests part of the calculus in dealing with their parents. Progressive child welfare policies cannot divorce the child's needs from that of the family and their community. A holistic approach to caring for children and ensuring their well-being must include providing support for families, preserving family unity whenever possible, and providing social support to their community. In her article addressing the South Africa child welfare system, Schmid states what is required is a "family-centered, community-based promotion of child and family well-being" that addresses the systemic issues that families in crisis face.[115] It is essential to attend to poverty's "compounded deprivations": joblessness, housing insecurity, poor health, substance abuse, underperforming schools, institutional divestment, and harsh criminal justice sanctions and their collateral consequences that fall disproportionality on black and brown communities in restorative ways.[116] Keeping children in their neighborhoods allows families to strengthen and repair relationships and foster family reunification.[117] South Africa's embrace, at least in principle, of the importance of family preservation to a child's well-being may provide a valuable model for reforming the United States' child welfare and criminal justice policies.

That said, children's rights policies without racial and economic justice are unlikely to result in securing child well-being and family stability. The most important tenets of the CRC may be those that neither the United States nor South Africa has effectuated in law or principle. Article 18 of the

CRC provides that states "render appropriate assistance to parents and legal guardians in the performance of their child-rearing responsibilities and shall ensure the development of institutions, facilities, and services for the care of children." Article 27 goes further to "recognize the right of every child to a standard of living adequate for the child's physical, spiritual, moral, and social development" and that states, "shall take appropriate measures to assist parents . . . to implement this right and shall in case of need provide material assistance . . . particularly with regard to nutrition, clothing, and housing." The comparison of U.S. and South African child welfare policies clarifies that without sufficient economic support for children, their families, and communities, children will always be vulnerable to neglect, abuse, and excessive state intervention.

NOTES

1. Dorothy E. Roberts, "Prison, Foster Care, and the Systemic Punishment of Black Mothers," *University of California Law Review,* 59 (August 2012): 1476, https://www.uclalawreview.org/pdf/59-6-2.pdf

2. Dorothy E. Roberts, "Child Welfare and Civil Rights," *University of Illinois Law Review* 2003 (December 2020): 172, https://illinoislawreview.org/print/volume-2003-issue-1/child-welfare-and-civil-rights/

3. Barbara Bennett Woodhouse, "Recognizing Children's Rights Lessons From South Africa," S.P.G. Human Rights., ABA., 26 (1999): 15; Barbara Bennett Woodhouse, "The Constitutionalization of Children's Rights: Incorporating Emerging Human Rights into Constitutional Doctrine," *University of Pennsylvania Journal of Constitutional Law* 2 (1999): 3, https://scholarship.law.upenn.edu/jcl/vol2/iss1/1

4. Meyer v. Nebraska, 262 U.S. 390 (1923); *Pierce v. Society of Sisters*, 268 U.S. 510 (1925).

5. Child Abuse Prevention and Treatment Act, Pub. L. No. 111-320, 42 U.S.C. § 5101 (2010).

6. "Definitions of Child Abuse and Neglect—Child Welfare Information Gateway," Child Welfare Information Gateway, accessed October 29, 2020, https://www.childwelfare.gov/topics/systemwide/laws-policies/statutes/define/

7. Tanya Cooper, "Racial Bias in American Foster Care: The National Debate," *Marquette Law Review* 97, no. 2 (2013): 227, http://scholarship.law.marquette.edu/mulr/vol97/iss2/3.; Stephanie Ledesma, "The Vanishing of the African-American Family: 'Reasonable Efforts' and Its Connection to the Disproportionality of the Child Welfare System," *Charleston Law Review* 9, no. 1 (2014): 58.

8. Dorothy E. Roberts, *Shattered Bonds The Color of Welfare* (New York: Basics Civitas Books, 2002), pp. 26, 33; Cooper, "Racial Bias," 227–228.

9. Jeanette Schmid, "Responding to the South Africa Child Welfare Crisis," 23 *Canadian Social Work Review*, 23, no. 1/2 (2006): 111–127, https://www.jstor.org/stable/41669848.; Michelle Burrell, "What Can the Child Welfare System Learn

in the Wake of the Floyd Decision?: A Comparison of Stop-and-Frisk Policing and Child Welfare Investigations," *City University of New York Law Review* 22, no. 1 (Winter 2019): 124–47.

10. Laura Briggs, *Taking Children. A History of American Terror* (Berkeley: University of California Press, 2020), 32, 46, 103, and 128.

11. Briggs, *Taking Children*, 33–37.

12. Briggs, *Taking Children*, 50.

13. Cooper, "Racial Bias," 217, 240; Briggs, *Taking Children*; Shanta Trivedi, "The Harm of Child Removal," *New York University Review of Law & Social Change,* 43 (February 2019): 523, 536–537. doi: 10.2139/ssrn.3341033; "Racial Disproportionality and Disparity in Child Welfare," *Child Welfare Information Gateway*, 2016, https://www.childwelfare.gov/pubpdfs/racial_disproportionality.pdf

14. Schmid, "Responding to the South Africa," 113; Roberts, *Shattered Bonds*, 26; Jina Lee, Zenobia Bell, and Mae Ackerman-Brimberg, "Implicit Bias in the Child Welfare, Education and Mental Health Systems," n.d., *National Center for Youth Law,* accessed October 30, 2020, https://youthlaw.org/publication/implicit-bias-in-the-child-welfare-education-and-mental-health-systems/

15. "The AFCARS Report" U.S. Department of Health & Human Services, Administration for Children & Families, Administration on Children, Youth and Families, Children's Bureau, Adoption and Foster Care Analysis and Reporting System, 2019, https://www.acf.hhs.gov/sites/default/files/cb/afcarsreport27.pdf

16. Adoption and Safe Families Act of 1997, Pub. L. No. 105-89, 111 Stat. 2115 (1997) (codified in scattered sections of Title 42 of the United States Code); Deseriee Kennedy, "Children, Parents & the State: The Construction of A New Family Ideology," *Berkeley Journal of Gender, Law & Justice* 26 (2011): 78, https://ssrn.com/abstract=2359718

17. Kennedy, "Children, Parents & the State," 104–105; Roberts, *Shattered Bonds*, 110.

18. ASFA 42 U.S.C. § 671(a)(15)(B)(i) (2020).

19. Roberts, *Shattered Bonds*, 81–82; Sylvia A. Harvey, "How a Trip to Prison Cost Kenneth Clark His Right to Be a Parent." The Nation, www.thenation.com. July 20, 2020, https://www.thenation.com/article/society/prison-parents-children-asfa.; Burrell, "What Can the Child Welfare System Learn," 134–135, 139.

20. Fabiola Villalpando, "Family First Prevention Services Act: An Overhaul of National Child Welfare Policies," *Children Legal Rights Journal* 39, no. 3 (2019): 283–284, https://lawecommons.luc.edu/clrj/vol39/iss3/5

21. Roberts, *Shattered Bonds*, 109.

22. Nina Williams-Mbengue, "Family First: Federal Child Welfare Law," National Conference of State Legislatures. 27, no. 24 (2019): 1–2, www.ncsl.org. https://www.ncsl.org/research/human-services/family-first-implementing-landmark-federal-child-welfare-law.aspx.; Villalpando, "Family First," 283.

23. "Principles of Effective Treatment," National Institute on Drug Abuse, September 18, 2020, https://www.drugabuse.gov/publications/principles-drug-addiction-treatment-research-based-guide-third-edition/principles-effective-treatment; Villalpando, "Family First," 283.

24. Kennedy, "Children, Parents & the State," 106.

25. The Family First Prevention Services Act of 2018, Pub. L. 115–123, Bipartisan Budget Act of 2018, Title VII, section 50702. (codified as amended in scattered sections of 42 U.S.C.) ("FFPSA"); Villalpando, "Family First," 283.

26. FFPSA, Sect. 50702.

27. FFPSA, Sect. 50702.

28. Social Security Act § 474(a)(3); "45 C.F.R. § 1356.60, Fiscal Requirements (Title IV-E)," LII / Legal Information Institute, accessed October 30, 2020, https://www.law.cornell.edu/cfr/text/45/1356.60; U.S. Department of Health & Human Services Office of the Administration for Children & Families, Children's Bureau, *Child Welfare Policy Manual*, Part 8.1, Title IV-E, Administrative Functions/Costs, Questions #20, 30–32 (January 7, 2019), https://www.acf.hhs.gov/cwpm/public_html/programs/cb/laws_policies/laws/cwpm/policy_dsp_pf.jsp?id=8

29. Villalpando, "Family First," 284.

30. Villalpando, "Family First," 285.

31. Jeannette Schmid, "Trends in South African Child Welfare from 2001-2010," *CSDA Research Report*. (Johannesburg: Centre for Social Development in Africa, University of Johannesburg, 2012), 1–15.

32. Jeanette Schmid, "Responding to the South African Child Welfare Crisis," *Canadian Social Work Review/Revue Canadienne de Service Social* 23, no. 1/2 (2006): 111–127, https://www.jstor.org/stable/41669848

33. Schmid, "Responding to the South African," 133; Burrell, "What Can the Child Welfare System Learn," 124, 134.

34. Schmid, "Responding to the South African," 118; Roberts, "Prison, Foster Care," 1499.

35. Schmid, "Responding to the South African."

36. Schmid, "Responding to the South African," 120.

37. Roberts, "Prison, Foster Care"; Roberts, *Shattered Bonds*, 200–202.

38. Roy Walmsley, "World Prison Population List (11th ed.)," *Institute for Criminal Policy Research*, 2015. https://www.prisonstudies.org/sites/default/files/resources/downloads/world_prison_population_list_11th_edition_0.pdf; "Fact Sheet: Incarcerated Women and Girls," *The Sentencing Project*, June 6, 2019, https://www.sentencingproject.org/publications/incarcerated-women-and-girls/

39. Michelle Alexander, *The New Jim Crow* (New York: The New Press, 2020), p. 7; Walmsley, "World Prison Population."

40. John Gramlich, "Black Imprisonment Rate in the U.S. Has Fallen by a Third since 2006," Pew Research Center, May 6, 2020, https://www.pewresearch.org/fact-tank/2020/05/06/share-of-black-white-hispanic-americans-in-prison-2018-vs-2006/

41. Kara Gotsch, "Families and Mass Incarceration," The Sentencing Project, April 24, 2018, https://www.sentencingproject.org/publications/6148/

42. Samuel V. Schoonmaker, "Criminal Law or Family Law: The Overlapping Issues," *Family Law Quarterly*, 44, no. 2 (Summer 2010): 155–167, https://www.jstor.org/stable/25740740

43. Roberts, *Shattered Bonds*, 200.

44. Jessica Jacobson, Catherine Heard, and Helen Fair, "Prison, Evidence of Its Use and Over-use from Around the World," *Institute for Criminal Policy Research*, London (2017): 2, https://www.prisonstudies.org/sites/default/files/resources/downloads/global_imprisonment_web2c.pdf; National Research Council, *The Growth of Incarceration in the United States, Exploring Causes and Consequences* (Washington, DC: The National Academies Press, 2014), 260, doi: 10.17226/18613; Chesa Boudin, "Children of Incarcerated Parents: The Child's Constitutional Right to the Family Relationship," *Journal of Criminal Law & Criminology, Forthcoming* 101, no. 1 (2011): 77, 83, 115; Roberts, "Prison, Foster Care," 1499.

45. Jacobson, "Prison, Evidence," vii.

46. Gramlich, "Black Imprisonment Rate."

47. Gotsch, "Families and Mass Incarceration."

48. Gotsch, "Families and Mass Incarceration."

49. Gotsch, "Families and Mass Incarceration."

50. Alexander, *The New Jim Crow*, 8, 243.

51. Lauren E Glaze, Laura M Maruschak, and BJS Statisticians, "Bureau of Justice Statistics Special Report Parents in Prison and Their Minor Children," *Bureau of Justice Statistics Special Report,* March 30, 2010, https://www.bjs.gov/content/pub/pdf/pptmc.pdf

52. Alexander, *The New Jim Crow*, 109.

53. Alexander, *The New Jim Crow*.

54. Glaze, Parents in Prison.

55. *The Growth of Incarceration in the United States*, 283, 289; Mary W. Byrne, Lorie Goshin, and Barbara Blanchard-Lewis, "Maternal Separations During the Reentry Years for 100 Infants Raised in a Prison Nursery," *Family Court Review* 50, no. 1 (January 2012): 77–90. doi: 10.1111/j.1744-1617.2011.01430.x

56. Roberts, *Shattered Bonds*, 200.

57. Roberts, "Prison, Foster Care."

58. Kennedy, "Children, Parents & the State"; Deseriee Kennedy, "The Good Mother": Mothering, Feminism, and Incarceration," *William & Mary Journal of Women & the Law* 18, no. 2 (2012): 161, 172–190, https://scholarship.law.wm.edu/wmjowl/vol18/iss2/2; Roberts, "Prison, Foster Care," 1491–1492.

59. Roberts, "Prison, Foster Care," 1480–1481.

60. Roberts, *Shattered Bonds*, 202; Cooper, "Racial Bias," 218; Trivedi, "The Harm of Child Removal," 527, 540, 542, 544, 549, 550.

61. *The Growth of Incarceration in the United States*, 279.

62. *The Growth of Incarceration in the United States*, 262.

63. Danielle Kaeble and BJS Statistician, "Time Served in State Prison, 2016," *Bureau of Justice Statistics* (November 2018), https://www.bjs.gov/content/pub/pdf/tssp16.pdf; Villalpando, "Family First," 285; "Fact Sheet: Incarcerated Women and Girls."

64. Roberts, *Shattered Bonds*; Alexander, *The New Jim Crow*; Warren Binford, "The Constitutionalization of Children's Rights in South Africa," *New York Law School Law Review* 60, (2015/2016): 356–360.

65. Binford, "The Constitutionalization of Children's Rights in South Africa," 341–342.

66. Binford, "The Constitutionalization of Children's Rights in South Africa," 342–343; Woodhouse, "The Constitutionalization of Children's Rights," 37–38; "Inaugural Speech, Pretoria [Mandela]- 5/10/94." 2019. University of Pennsylvania—African Studies Center, May 11, 1994, https://www.africa.upenn.edu/Articles_Gen/Inaugural_Speech_17984.html

67. Schmid, "Trends in South African Child Welfare," 10.

68. Tshepo L. Mosikatsana, "Children's Rights and Family Autonomy in the South African Context: A Comment on Children's Rights Under the Final Constitution," *Michigan Journal of Race & Law* 3, no. 2 (1998): 344; Convention on the Rights of the Child, G.A. Res. 25, U.N. GAOR, 44th Sess., U.N. Doc. A/736 (1989).

69. The United Nations. 1948. *Universal Declaration of Human Rights*, Article 16.3, 1948.

70. *The Growth of Incarceration in the United States*, 283, 289; Byrne, "Maternal Separations," 78.

71. Binford, "The Constitutionalization of Children's Rights in South Africa," 339–340.

72. Binford, "The Constitutionalization of Children's Rights in South Africa," 341.

73. U.N. General Assembly, "United Nations Rules for the Treatment of Women Prisoners and Non-Custodial Measures for Women Offenders (the Bangkok Rules): note / by the Secretariat," United Nations, (October 2010), https://www.refworld.org/docid/4dcbb0ae2.html

74. *The Bangkok Rules*, Rules 57, 58; U.N. General Assembly, "United Nations Standard Minimum Rules for Non-Custodial Measures (The Tokyo Rules): Resolution/Adopted by the General Assembly," United Nations (April 1991), https://www.refworld.org/docid/3b00f22117.html

75. *The Bangkok Rules*, Rules 64, 4.

76. *The Bangkok Rules*, Rules 2.

77. *The Bangkok Rules*, Rules 3.

78. *The Bangkok Rules*, Rules 57, 58, 60.

79. *The Bangkok Rules*, Rules 60.

80. Katharine Hall, Linda Richter, Zitha Mokomane, and Lori Lake. 2018. "Children, Families and the State Collaboration and Contestation," *Children's Institute, University of Cape Town* (November 2018): 48, http://childrencount.uct.ac.za/uploads/publications/South%20African%20Child%20Gauge%202018_Children%20Families%20and%20the%20State.pdf

81. Woodhouse, "The Constitutionalization of Children's Rights," 4.

82. Binford, "The Constitutionalization of Children's Rights in South Africa," 344.

83. Binford, "The Constitutionalization of Children's Rights in South Africa," 344–345, 355; Constitution of the Republic of South Africa, 1996, section 28.

84. South Africa Constitution, section 28.

85. South Africa Constitution, section 28.

86. Binford, "The Constitutionalization of Children's Rights in South Africa," 344–345.

87. Schmid, "Trends in South African Child Welfare," 8.

88. Ozah, Karabo, and Ann Skelton. "Legal Perspectives: Children, Families and the State," *South African Child Gauge* (2018): 46–60, http://www.ci.uct.ac.za/sites/default/files/image_tool/images/367/Child_Gauge/South_African_Child_Gauge_2018/Chapters/legal%20perspectives%20-%20children%2C%20families%20and%20the%20state.pdf; Schmid, "Trends in South African Child Welfare," 6–7.

89. Tshepo, "Children's Rights," 375; Karabo Ozah, and Ann Skelton, "Legal Perspectives," 49, http://www.ci.uct.ac.za/sites/default/files/image_tool/images/367/Child_Gauge/South_African_Child_Gauge_2018/Chapters/legal%20perspectives%20-%20children%2C%20families%20and%20the%20state.pdf

90. Hall, "Children, Families," 55.

91. Ozah, "Legal Perspectives," 50.

92. Ozah, "Legal Perspectives," 57; *South Africa: Act No. 38 of 2005, Children's Act* (South Africa) (2006), section 10, https://www.refworld.org/docid/46b82aa62.html (accessed October 30, 2020).

93. Hall, "Children, Families," 56–57; Ozah, "Legal Perspectives," 56.

94. Katharine Hall and Winnie Sambu, "Demography of South Africa's Children," *Children's Institute, University of Cape Town* (2019), http://www.ci.uct.ac.za/sites/default/files/image_tool/images/367/Child_Gauge/South_African_Child_Gauge_2019/CC/CC2019%20-%20Demography%20of%20South%20Africa%E2%80%99s%20children.pdf

95. Deirdre Blackie, *Sad, Bad and Mad: Exploring Child Abandonment in South Africa* (Master's diss., University of the Witwatersrand, Faculty of Humanities, May 2014), 7, https://www.researchgate.net/publication/276171687_Sad_Bad_Mad_Exploring_Child_Abandonment_in_South_Africa

96. Hall, "Demography."

97. Hall, "Demography."

98. Children's Act, section 38.

99. Candice Fortune, *An Overview of the Foster Care Crisis in South Africa and its Effect on the Best Interests of the Child Principle: A Socioeconomic Perspective* (Master's diss., Faculty of Law at the University of the Western Cape, 2016), 14, https://core.ac.uk/download/pdf/84690625.pdf

100. Dee Blackie, consultant to the National Adoption Coalition South Africa, "Fact Sheet on Child Abandonment Research in South Africa," *National Adoption Coalition* (May 20, 2014), https://bettercarenetwork.org/sites/default/files/Fact%20Sheet%20Research%20on%20Child%20Abandonment%20in%20South%20Africa.pdf

101. Dee, "Fact Sheet."

102. Ozah and Skelton, "Legal Perspectives," 56.

103. Ozah, "Legal Perspectives," 58–59; Children's Act, section 110; "C and Others v Department of Health and Social Development, Gauteng and Others (CCT 55/11) [2012] ZACC 1; 2012 (2) SA 208 (CC); 2012 (4) BCLR 329 (CC) (11 January 2012)," SAFLII, accessed October 30, 2020, http://www.saflii.org/za/cases/ZACC/2012/1.html

104. Schmid, "Responding to the South African."

105. Schmid, "Responding to the South African," 116.

106. Schmid, "Responding to the South African," 116.

107. Schmid, "Responding to the South African," 116.

108. Ozah, "Legal Perspectives," 61.

109. Michael N. Khwela, "A Need to Re-integrate Prisoners to the Community: A Case of Polokwane Medium B Prison, South Africa," *Athens Journal of Social Sciences* 1, no. 2 (2014): 145–156. doi: 10.30958/ajss.1-2-5

110. Khwela, "A Need to Re-integrate," 146, 149.

111. William Luyt, "Imprisoned Mothers in South African Prisons with Children Outside of the Institution," *European Journal of Crime Criminal Law and Criminal Justice* 16, no. 3 (2008): 299–223, 311, 315, https://www.researchgate.net/publication/240679345_Imprisoned_Mothers_in_South_African_Prisons_with_Children_Outside_of_the_Institution

112. Lukas Muntingh and Johan Naude, "Community Safety, Offender Re-Entry and Local Government Community Safety, Offender Re-Entry and Local Government," *Network on Reducing Re-offending* (2012), http://repository.uwc.ac.za/bitstream/handle/10566/5093/Community_safety_offernder_re-entry_and_local_government.pdf?sequence=1&isAllowed=y

113. "S v M (CCT 53/06) [2007] ZACC 18; 2008 (3) SA 232 (CC); 2007 (12) BCLR 1312 (CC) (26 September 2007)," SAFLII, http://www.saflii.org/za/cases/ZACC/2007/18.html

114. "S v S and Another (CCT147/18) [2019] ZACC 22; 2019 (8) BCLR 989 (CC); 2019 (6) SA 1 (CC) (27 June 2019)," 2019. SAFLII, accessed October 30, 2020. http://www.saflii.org/za/cases/ZACC/2019/22.html

115. Schmid, "Responding to the South African," 119–120.

116. Kristin L. Perkins and Robert J. Sampson, "Compounded Deprivation in the Transition to Adulthood: The Intersection of Racial and Economic Inequality Among Chicagoans, 1995–2013," *The Russell Sage Foundation Journal of the Social Sciences* 1, no. 1 (2015): 35–54, http://www.jstor.com/stable/10.7758/rsf.2015.1.1.03; Robert Sampson, "Move Up or Out? Confronting Compounded Deprivation," *N.Y.U. Furman Center, The Dream Revisited,* (July 2015), https://furmancenter.org/research/iri/essay/move-up-or-out-confronting-compounded-deprivation

117. "Community Based Care Mechanisms," Better Care Network, accessed October 30, 2020, https://bettercarenetwork.org/library/the-continuum-of-care/community-based-care-mechanisms

Conclusion

Melissa L. Breger

One of the key themes of this book is the evolution of family law over time. After reading this compilation of 16 informative chapters, one feels incentivized to learn even more about the future trajectory and landscape of family law. The family is such a fascinating subject of study. How the law examines the subject of the family is equally intriguing.

In an attempt to summarize all of the insightful points offered within these chapters, the old adage "so much food for thought" comes to mind. *Merriam-Webster* dictionary tells us that "food for thought" is a noun-phrase meaning "something that should be thought about or considered carefully." Grammarist.com tells us that this idiom has been around since the 1800s and means, "something worth thinking about, something worth mulling over, something that should be pondered in order to obtain the full understanding of the idea." Yet in this context, I am also contemplating this concept even more literally. The ideas in this book can be sustenance for one's mind, yet inevitably nourish one's curiosity about the future. As I edited this book, my mind was simultaneously sated and hungry to discover more. Ultimately, this process has been such a satisfying journey—so much so, that I have envisioned the creation of another volume in the near future.

It has been remarkable to learn about the family from its very cellular level all the way through to its theoretical levels. Again, taking this quite literally, we learned from chapter 13 in part IV about the origins of the gamete (at the cellular level) after having learned through part I about the theoretical underpinnings of family formation through intimate partnerships around the globe. Then in parts II and III, we delved into parenting children and some of the practical realities of the law regulating such. It has been eye-opening to examine how society and the law both regulate the familial unit, yet also defer to the privacy of the familial unit itself. Looking at these issues through the various lenses of countries around the globe, the four parts of the book contribute a rich, varied, and invaluable perspective to the current dialogue of family law.

One of the overarching goals of the book is to look beyond current boundaries and explore how extremely broad and expansive the study of family law can be. The book explores the differences and commonalities in the conceptualization and legal treatment of families throughout different legal traditions. The collection offers various analyses about how different countries across the globe shape family law.

Family law changes as society itself changes. Although the law is often criticized as being too slow to align with modern times, it does eventually mesh with the current norms. Arguably, societal norms take on an importance in family law with greater frequency than in many other areas of law. This is perhaps due to the high volume of family law disputes and cases, perhaps because the concept of family is steeped in all of our lives and society in some fashion, or perhaps because of the sensitive and intricate nature and significance of laws and family. Thus, as described in the Introduction, the underlying theme of the chapters was rooted in the concepts of social norms. This common theoretical thread was woven through the chapters demonstrating how the law reflects normative attitudes, and how social norms impact the law. Family laws are created to reflect new norms, and new norms influence family law legislation and court rulings.

In the initial book proposal, I set out to explore several fundamental questions, such as: What is a family? What does it mean to be a parent? How can we see children as autonomous beings, yet keep their vulnerability safe? How does culture inform family law, and how does family law inform culture? What do the norms of a society tell us about the law, and what does the law tell us about the norms of a society?

While the authors of these chapters have endeavored to answer many of these questions directly, they concurrently asked other questions to allow readers to create their own assessments. The authors in this book approach these questions from different lived realities and different spaces, yet we all share a collective curiosity for further inquiry into family law. For as nourished and sated as one may be after having read the wise words in this book, one may still thirst to learn even more about one of the most important aspects of human life: the family. Whether analyzing a family of 2 or analyzing a family of 20, family law needs to address each and every kind of family indeed. Our research and our quest for knowledge must continue to provide even deeper and wider perspectives on the evolving field of family law.

Bibliography

A v A [2012] EWHC 2219 (Fam).

Abd al-Karîm Lafgun. *Nawâzil Qusantina.* Oran, 2018.

Abramowicz, Sarah. "English Child Custody Law, 1660–1839: The Origins of Judicial Intervention in Paternal Custody." *Columbia Law Review* 99, no. 5 (June 1999): 1344–1392.

Adams, Michele A. "Framing Contests in Child Custody Disputes: Parental Alienation Syndrome, Child Abuse, Gender, and Fathers' Rights." *Family Law Quarterly* 40, no. 2 (Summer 2016): 315–338.

Addo, Fenaba, and Sharon Sassler. "Financial Arrangements and Relationship Quality in Low-Income Couples." *Family Relationships* 59, no. 4 (October 2010): 408–423.

Adoption and Safe Families Act of 1997, Pub. L. No. 105-89, 111 Stat. 2115 (1997).

African Charter on Human and Peoples' Rights (Adopted 27 June 1981, Entered into Force 21 October 1986) 1520 UNTS 217.

African Charter on the Rights and Welfare of the Child (Adopted 11 July 1990, Entered into Force 29 November 1999) CAB/LEG/24.9/49.

Aizenman, Nurith. "Alarming Number of Women Think Spousal Abuse is Sometimes Ok." NPR, March 18, 2015, 12:16 PM. https://www.npr.org/sections/goatsandsoda/2015/03/18/392860281/alarming-number-of-women-think-spousal-abuse-is-sometimes-ok; http://perma.cc/HK5V-39E3

Akerlof, George, Janet Yellen, and Michael Katz. "An Analysis of Out-of-Wedlock Childbearing in the United States." *The Quarterly Journal of Economics* 111, no. 2 (May 1996): 277–317.

Akhtar, Rajnaara. "Unregistered Muslim Marriages in the UK, Examining Normative Influences Shaping Choice of Legal Protection." In *Personal Autonomy in Plural Societies, A Principle and its Paradoxes*, edited by Marie-Claire Foblets, Michele Graziadei, and Alison Dundes Renteln, 140–155. Oxfordshire, UK: Taylor and Francis, 2018.

Akhtar, Rajnaara C., Rebecca Probert, and Annelies Moors. "Informal Muslim Marriages: Regulations and Contestations." *Oxford Journal of Law and Religion* 7, no. 3 (October 2018): 367–375.

Alber, Erdemute. "'The Real Parents are the Foster Parents:' Social Parenthood Among the Baatombu in Northern Benin." In *Cross-Cultural Approaches to Adoption*, 33–47. Oxfordshire: Routledge Press, 2004.

Alberta Government. "Resolution Services: Spousal/Partner Support." January 2017. https://www.alberta.ca/assets/documents/rcas-general-information-spousal-and-partner-support.pdf

Alef is for Abba. https://www.facebook.com/zedekhevraati (accessed 12 March 2020).

Alesech, Julie, and Shoba Nayar. "Acceptance and Belonging in New Zealand: Understanding Inclusion for Children With Special Education Needs." *International Journal of Whole Schooling* 16, no. 1 (2020): 84–116.

Alexander, Michelle. *The New Jim Crow*. New York: The New Press, 2020.

Alhaji Mohamed v Knott [1969] 1 QB 1.

Al-Kharshi. *Sharh Mukhtasar Khalîl*. Le Caire, 1899.

Alkiviadou, Natalie. "Hate Speech on Social Media Networks: Towards a Regulatory Framework?" *Information and Communications Technology Law* 28, no. 1 (2018): 19–35. DOI: 10.1080/13600834.2018.1494417

Allan, Sonia. "Access to Information About Donors by Donor-Conceived Individuals: A Human Rights Analysis." *Journal of Law and Medicine* 20, no. 3 (2013): 655–670.

Allan, Sonia. *Donor Conception and the Search for Information: From Secrecy and Anonymity to Openness*. New York: Routledge, 2017.

Allan, Sonia. "Donor Conception, Secrecy and the Search for Information." *Journal of Law & Medicine* 19, no. 4 (2012): 631–650.

Allen, Emilie Anderson, and Darrel J. Steffensmeier. "Youth Underemployment, and Property Crime: Differential Effects of Job Availability and Job Quality on Juvenile and Young Adult Arrest Rates." *American Sociological Review* 54, no. 1 (February 1989): 107–123.

"Al-Madjalla al-Qadâ'iyya (Ministry of Justice)." *Algiers*.

Al-Saedy v Musawi (Presumption of Marriage) [2010] EWHC 3293 (Fam).

American Convention on Human Rights (Adopted 22 November 1969, Entered into Force 18 July 1978) 1144 UNTS 123.

American Law Institute. *Principles of the Law of Family Dissolution: Analysis and Recommendations*. American Law Institute, 2000.

American Society for Reproductive Medicine. "Informing Offspring of Their Conception by Gamete or Embryo Donation: A Committee Opinion Ethics Committee of the American Society for Reproductive Medicine." *Fertility Sterility* 100, no. 1 (March 2013): 45–49.

Anderson, Astrid. "Adoption and Belonging in Wogeo, Papua New Guinea." In *Cross-Cultural Approaches to Adoption*, 111–126. Oxfordshire: Routledge Press, 2004.

Antognini, Albertina. "Nonmarital Contracts." *Stanford Law Review* 73, no. 1 (January 2021): 67–154.

Antognini, Albertina. "The Law of Nonmarriage." *Boston College Law Review* 58, no. 1 (January 2017): 1–63.

Appell, Annette R. "Blending Families Through Adoption: Implications for Collaborative Adoption Law and Practice." *Boston University Law Review* 75, no. 4 (1995): 997–1062.

Appell, Annette R. "Reflections on the Movement Toward a More Child-Centered Adoption." *Western New England Law Review* 32, no. 1 (May 2010): 1–32.

Appell, Annette R. "The Endurance of Biological Connection: Heteronormativity, Same-Sex Parenting and the Lessons of Adoption." *Brigham Young University Journal of Public Law* 22, no. 2 (2008): 289–325.

Apt (Otherwise Magnus) v Apt [1948] P 83.

Arnett, Dugan. 2019. "With Dad's Support, One Teen is Playing 'Fortnite' Instead of Going to High School." The Boston Globe, July 6, 2019. https://www.bostonglobe.com/metro/2019/07/06/father-son-all-teen-bid-for-esports-stardom/EhZCdGUDYouhT2DEkilhCL/story.html

ASFA. 42 U.S.C. § 671(a)(15)(B)(i) (2020).

Assies, Willem. "Legal Empowerment of the Poor: With a Little Help From Their Friends?" *The Journal of Peasant Studies* 36, no. 4 (October 2009): 909–924.

Association of Family and Conciliation Courts. "Guidelines for the Use of Social Science Research in Family Law." 2018. https://www.afccnet.org/Portals/0/AFCC%20Guidelines%20for%20the%20Use%20of%20Social%20Science%20Research%20in%20Family%20Law.pdf?ver=2020-03-30 092936-097

Astbury, Jill, Judy Atkinson, Janet Duke, Patricia Easteal, Susan E. Kurrle, Paul R. Tait, and Jane Turner. "The Impact of Domestic Violence on Individuals." *Medical Journal of Australia* 173, no. 8 (2000): 427–431.

Atkin, William R. "'De Facto Relationships' in New Zealand—A Largely Unified Law." *Family Law Quarterly* 50, no. 2 (Summer 2016): 303–325.

Attorney General v Akhter [2020] EWCA Civ 122.

Australian Bureau of Statistics. "Marriages and Divorces." Australia. 2018. Accessed November 27, 2019 https://www.abs.gov.au/statistics/people/people-and-communities/marriages-and-divorces-australia/latest-release.

Australian Institute of Health and Welfare (AIHW). "Children with Disabilities in Australia." (DIS 38). Canberra: Australian Institute of Health and Welfare (AIHW), 2004.

Australian Law Reform Commission. "Family Law for the Future: An Inquiry into the Family Law System Final Report." ALRC Report No. 135. Brisbane: Commonwealth of Australia, 2019.

Australian Law Reform Commission and Human Rights and Equal Opportunities Commission. "Seen and Heard: Priority for Children in the Legal Process." ALRC Report No. 84. Sydney: Commonwealth of Australia, 1997.

Awuku v. Secretary of State for the Home Department [2017] EWCA Civ 178.

B v B (Minors) [1994] 2 FLR 489.

Baade, Björnstjern. "Fake News and International Law." *The European Journal of International Law* 29, no. 4 (2018): 1357–1376. DOI: 10.1093/ejil/chy071 2019.

Backe-Hansen, Elizabeth, Ingrid Højer, Yvonne Sjöblom, and Jan Storø. "Out of Home Care in Norway and Sweden—Similar and Different." *Psychosocial Intervention* 22 (December 2013): 193–202.

Baden, A. "'Do You Know Your *Real* Parents?' And Other Adoption Microaggressions." *Adoption Quarterly* 19, no. 1 (February 2016): 1–25.

Baden, Amanda, Doug Shadel, Ron Morgan, Ebony E. White, Elliotte S. Harrington, Nicole Christian, and Todd A. Bates. "Delaying Adoption Disclosure: A Survey of Late Discovery Adoptees." *Journal of Family Issues* 40, no. 9 (2019): 1154–1180.

Badruddin, Hj Ibrahim, and Azizah Mohd. "The Child's Right to Maintenance: The Extent of the Family's Responsibilities in Islamic Law and According to the Family Law Provisions of Muslim Countries." *Arab Law Quarterly* 25, no. 4 (January 2011): 401–422.

Baer, Janine M. *Growing in the Dark: Adoption Secrecy and Its Consequences.* Xlibris Corp, 2004.

Bagshaw, Dale, Thea Brown, Sarah Wendt, Alan Campbell, Elspeth McInnes, Beth Tinning, Becky Batagol, Adiva Sifris, Danielle Tyson, Joanne Baker, and Paula Fernandez Arias. "The Effect of Family Violence on Post-Separation Parenting Arrangements: The Experiences and Views of Children and Adults from Families Who Separated Post-1995 and Post-2006." *Family Matters* 86 (March 2011): 49–61.

Bala, Nicholas, and Rachel Birnbaum. "Rethinking the Role of Lawyers for Children: Child Representation in Canadian Family Relationship Cases." *Cahiers de Droit* 59, no. 4 (February 2018): 787–829.

Bala, Nicholas, Rachel Birnbaum, Karine Poitras, Michael Saini, Francine Cyr, and Shawna LeClair. "Shared Parenting in Canada: Increasing Use But Continued Controversy." *Family Court Review: An Interdisciplinary Journal* (Special Issue: International Demographics of Joint Custody) 55, no. 4 (October 2017): 513–530. DOI: 10.1111/fcre.12301

Bamforth, Nicholas. "The Benefits of Marriage in All But Name? Same-Sex Couples and the Civil Partnership Act 2004." *Child and Family Law Quarterly* 19, no. 2 (June 2007): 133–160.

Banerjie, Ajita. "Why India's Transgender People Are Protesting Against a Bill That Claims to Protect Their Rights." Scroll.in, November 26, 2019. https://scroll.in/article/944882/why-indias-transgender-people-are-protesting-against-a-bill-that-claims-to-protect-their-rights

Bano, Samia. "An Exploratory Study of Sharīʿah Councils in England With Respect to Family Law." October 2012. https://www.reading.ac.uk/web/files/law/An_exploratory_study_of_Shariah_councils_in_England_with_respect_to_family_law_.pdf

Barkan, Noam. "Not Surrendering." *Yedeot Aharonot*, 14 January 2018. https://www.yediot.co.il/articles/0,7340,L-5070955,00.html [Hebrew].

Barker, Nicola. *Not the Marrying Kind: A Feminist Critique of Same-Sex Marriage.* Basingstoke: Palgrave Macmillan, 2012.

Barlow, Anne, and Janet Smithson. "Legal Assumptions, Cohabitants' Talk and the Rocky Road to Reform." *Child and Family Law Quarterly* 22, no. 3 (September 2010): 328–350.

Bartholet, Elizabeth. "Homeschooling: Parent Rights Absolutism vs. Child Rights to Education & Protection." *Arizona Law Review* 62, no. 1 (2020): 1–80.

Bartholet, Elizabeth, Rachel Coleman, James Dwyer, Milton Gaither, and Frank E. Vandervort. "No Need for Bullying in the Debate on Homeschooling." The Imprint, 26 May 2020. https://imprintnews.org/child-welfare-2/no-need-bullying-in-debate-homeschooling/43876

Becker, Gary. *A Treatise on the Family.* Cambridge: Harvard University Press, 1991.

Beckstrom, John H. "Adoption in Ethiopia Ten Years After the Civil Code." *Journal of African Law* 16, no. 2 (1972): 145–168.

Beken, Christophe Van der. "Ethiopia: From Centralized Monarch to a Federal Republic." *Afrika Focus* 20, no. 1 (2007): 13–48.

Ben Issaschar, Yaacon. "The Holocaust of the Divorced Fathers: 150 Are Killed Every Year." *News1: First Class*, 4 December 2011. http://www.news1.co.il/Archive/003-D-66620-00.html. [Hebrew].

Benmelha, Al-Ghawti. *Qânûn al-usra 'alâ daw' al-fiqh wa-l qadâ'*. Alger, 2015.

Bernardi, Laura, and Dimitri Mortelmans. "Advances in Research on Shared Physical Custody by Interdisciplinary Approaches." In *Shared Physical Custody*, edited by Laura Bernardi and Dimitri Mortelmans, 5–21. Cham, Switzerland: Springer, 2021.

Berry, Marianne. "Adoptive Parents' Perceptions of, and Comfort With, Open Adoption." *Child Welfare* 72, no. 3 (May 1993): 231–253.

Better Care Network. "Community Based Care Mechanisms." https://bettercarenetwork.org/library/the-continuum-of-care/community-based-care-mechanisms (accessed 30 October 2020).

Bhatia, Amiya, Camilla Fabbri, Ilan Cerna-Turoff, Clare Tanton, Louise Knight, Ellen Turner, Michelle Lokot, Shelley Lees, Ben Cislaghi, Amber Peterman, Alessandra Guedes, and Karen Devries. "COVID-19 Response Measures and Violence Against Children." *Bulletin of the World Health Organization* 98, no. 9 (2020): 583–583A. DOI: 10.2471/BLT.20.263467.

Binford, Warren. "The Constitutionalization of Children's Rights in South Africa." *New York Law School Law Review* 60 (2015/2016): 333–363.

Bingham, John. "Mass Polygamy in UK Muslim Community – Claim." The Telegraph, December 10, 2014. https://www.telegraph.co.uk/news/religion/11284421/Mass-polygamy-in-UK-Muslim-community-claim.html

Bird, Gloria W., Rick Peterson, and Stephanie H. Miller. "Factors Associated with Distress Among Support-Seeking Adoptive Parents." *Family Relations* 51, no. 3 (July 2002): 215–220.

Birnbaum, Rachel. "Hearing the Voices of Lawyers and Clinical Investigators Who Represent Children in Child Custody and Access Disputes." *Canadian Family Law Quarterly* 24, no. 3 (2005): 281–303.

Birnbaum, Rachel. "Views of the Child Reports: Hearing Directly From Children Involved in Post-Separation Disputes." *Social Inclusion* 5, no. 3 (2017): 148–154.

Birnbaum, Rachel, and Nicholas Bala. "Judicial Interviews With Children in Custody and Access Cases: Comparing Experiences in Ontario and Ohio." *International Journal of Law, Policy and the Family* 24, no. 3 (October 2010): 300–337.

Birnbaum, Rachel, and Nicholas Bala. "Views of the Child Reports: The Ontario Pilot Project." *International Journal of Law, Policy and the Family* 31, no. 3 (December 2017): 344–362.

Birnbaum, Rachel, Nicholas Bala, and Francine Cyr. "Children's Experiences With Family Justice Professionals in Ontario and Ohio." *International Journal of Law, Policy and the Family* 25, no. 3 (December 2011): 398–422.

Bitiukova, Natalija, Judit Bayer, Petra Bard, Judit Szakacs, Alberto Alemanno, and Erik Uszkiewicz. *Disinformation and Propaganda: Impact on the Functioning of the Rule of Law in the EU and its Member States*. European Parliament's

Policy Department for Citizens' Rights and Constitutional Affairs, 2018. http://www.europarl.europa.eu/RegData/etudes/STUD/2019/608864/IPOL_STU(2019)608864_EN.pdf

Blackie, Deirdre. "Fact Sheet on Child Abandonment Research in South Africa." National Adoption Coalition, May 20, 2014. https://bettercarenetwork.org/sites/default/files/Fact%20Sheet%20Research%20on%20Child%20Abandonment%20in%20South%20Africa.pdf

Blackie, Deirdre. "Sad, Bad and Mad: Exploring Child Abandonment in South Africa." Master's Dissertation, University of the Witwatersrand, Faculty of Humanities, 2014.

Blumenthal v. Brewer, 69 N.E.3d 834 (Ill. 2016).

Blyth, Eric, Marilyn Crawshaw, Lucy Frith, and Caroline Jones. "Donor-Conceived People's Views and Experiences of Their Genetic Origins: A Critical Analysis of the Research Evidence." *Journal of Law & Medicine* 19, no. 4 (2012): 769–789.

Bochenek, Michael, and Kyle Knight. "Establishing a Third Gender Category in Nepal: Process and Prognosis." *Emory International Law Review* 26, no. 1 (2012): 11–41.

Bondelmonte v Bondelmonte (2017) 341 ALR 179.

Bontems, Claude. *Le droit musulman algérien à l'époque coloniale. De l'invention à la codification.* Genève, 2014.

Borrmans, Maurice. *Statut personnel et famille au Maghreb de 1940 à nos jours.* Paris: La Haye, 1977.

Bottomley, Stephen, and Simon Bronitt. *Law in Context.* Sydney: Federation Press, 2012.

Boubakeur, Hamza. *Le Coran, traduction et commentaire en français.* Alger, 1994.

Boudin, Chesa. "Children of Incarcerated Parents: The Child's Constitutional Right to the Family Relationship." *Journal of Criminal Law & Criminology* 101, no. 1 (2011): 77–118.

Bowman, Cynthia. "Social Science and Legal Policy: The Case of Heterosexual Cohabitation." *Cornell Journal of Law and Family Studies* 9, no. 1 (2007): 1–52.

Boyd, Susan B. "Autonomy for Mothers? Relational Theory and Parenting Apart." *Feminist Legal Studies* 18, no. 2 (August 2010): 137–158. DOI: 10.1007/s10691-010-9152-3

Boyd, Susan B. "Backlash Against Feminism: Canadian Custody and Access Reform Debates of the Late 20th Century." *CJWL* 16, no. 2 (2004): 255–290.

Boyd, Susan B. "Demonizing Mothers: Fathers' Rights Discourses in Child Custody Law Reform Processes." *Journal of the Motherhood Initiative for Research and Community Involvement* 6, no. 1 (2004): 52–74.

Boyd, Susan B. "Gendering Legal Parenthood: Bio-Genetic Ties, Intentionality and Responsibility." *Windsor Yearbook of Access to Justice* 25 (2007): 63–94.

Breger, Melissa. "Against the Dilution of a Child's Voice in Court." *Indiana International and Comparative Law Review* 20, no. 2 (2010): 175–194.

Breger, Melissa. "Healing Sex-Trafficked Children: A Domestic Family Law Approach to an International Epidemic." *West Virginia Law Review* 118, no. 3 (April 2016): 1131–1180.

Breger, Melissa. "Reforming by Re-Norming: How the Legal System Has the Potential to Change a Toxic Culture of Domestic Violence." *Notre Dame Journal of Legislation* 44, no. 2 (April 2018): 170–200.

Breger, Melissa, Lucy Sorensen, Victor Asal, and Charmaine Willis. "Corporal Punishment, Social Norms and Norm Cascades: Examining Cross-National Laws and Trends in Homes Across the Globe." *William & Mary Journal of Race, Gender, and Social Justice* 26 (2020): 483–524. https://papers.ssrn.com/sol3/papers.cfm?abstract_id=3413969

Briggs, Laura. *Taking Children: A History of American Terror*. Berkeley: University of California Press, 2020.

Brink, Marjolein van den, and Peter Dunne. *Trans and Intersex Equality Rights in Europe: A Comparative Analysis*. Luxembourg: Publications Office of the European Union, 2018. https://ec.europa.eu/info/sites/info/files/trans_and_intersex_equality_rights.pdf

Brodzinsky, David M. "Adjustment to Adoption: A Psychosocial Perspective." *Clinical Psychology Review* 7, no. 1 (1987): 25–47.

Brodzinsky, David M. "A Stress and Coping Model of Adoption Adjustment." In *The Psychology of Adoption*, 3–24. Oxford: Oxford University Press, 1990.

Brodzinsky, David M. "Family Structural Openness and Communication Openness as Predictors in the Adjustment of Adopted Children." *Adoption Quarterly* 9, no. 4 (2006): 1–18.

Brodzinsky, David M. "Long-Term Outcomes in Adoption." *Future of Children* 3, no. 1 (2003): 153–166.

Brodzinsky, David M., Leslie M. Singer, and Anne Braff. "Children's Understanding of Adoption." *Child Development* 55, no. 3 (June 1984): 869–878.

Brodzinsky, David M., and Marshall D. Schechter. *The Psychology of Adoption*. Oxford: Oxford University Press, 1990.

Brodzinsky, David M., Marshall D. Schecter, and Robin Marantz Henig. *Being Adopted: The Lifelong Search for Self*. New York, NY: Anchor Books, 1992.

Brown, Alan. *What is The Family of Law?: The Influence of the Nuclear Family*. Oxford: Hart Publishing, 2019.

Brown, Susan. *Families in America*. Berkeley: University of California Press, 2017.

Brown v Argyll [2006] NZFLR 705.

Büchler, Andrea. "Islamic Family Law in Europe? From Dichotomies to Discourse—Or: Beyond Cultural and Religious Identity in Family Law." *International Journal of Law in Context* 8, no. 2 (2012): 196–210.

Buchler, Andrea, and Eveline S. Kayasseh. "Fostering and Adoption in Islamic Law – Under Consideration of the Laws of Morocco, Egypt, and the United Arab Emirates." *Electronic Journal of Islamic & Middle Eastern Law* 6 (2018): 31–55.

Buck, Trevor. *International Child Law*, 2nd ed. London: Routledge, 2011.

Bukhari, Muhammad ibn Ismail. *Sahih Bukhari*. Karachi Karkhanah-I Tijarat-I Kutub, 1996.

Bukhari Sahîh (sans date ni lieu d'édition).

Bulletin judiciaire de l'Algérie. Published Before 1962. Algiers.

Burnell, George M., and Mary A. Norfleet. "Women Who Place Their Infants Up for Adoption: A Pilot Study." *Patient Counseling & Health Education* 1, no. 4 (1979): 169–172.

Burrell, Michelle. "What Can the Child Welfare System Learn in the Wake of the Floyd Decision?: A Comparison of Stop-and-Frisk Policing and Child Welfare Investigations." *City University of New York Law Review* 22, no. 1 (Winter 2019): 124–147.

Byrne, Bronagh. "Art. 23 Children With Disabilities." In *The UN Convention on the Rights of the Child: A Commentary*, edited by John Tobin, 856–901. Oxford: Oxford Commentaries on International Law, 2019.

Byrne, Mary W., Lorie Goshin, and Barbara Blanchard-Lewis. "Maternal Separations During the Reentry Years for 100 Infants Raised in a Prison Nursery." *Family Court Review* 50, no. 1 (January 2012): 77–90. DOI: 10.1111/j.1744-1617.2011.01430.x

Bywaters, Paul, Lisa Bunting, Gavin Davidson, Jennifer Hanratty, Will Mason, Claire McCartan, and Nicole Steils. "The Relationship Between Poverty, Child Abuse and Neglect: An Evidence Review." *Joseph Rowntree Foundation*, March 2016. https://www.researchgate.net/profile/Jennifer_Hanratty/publication/295812966_The_relationship_between_poverty_child_abuse_and_neglect_an_evidence_review/links/58208f7c08ae40da2cb4ede7/The-relationship-between-poverty-child-abuse-and-neglect-an-evidence-review.pdf

C and Others v. Department of Health and Social Development, Gauteng and Others (CCT 55/11) [2012] ZACC 1; 2012 (2) SA 208 (CC).

CAA 4575/00 Row v. Dow 323 (2001) (Israel).

Cadoz, François. *Droit musulman. Examen critique de la traduction qu'a faite M. Perron du livre de Khalil.* impr. de E. Monniot, Paris: Bar-sur-Aube, 1870.

Cahn, Naomi. "Birthing Relationships." *Wisconsin Women's Law Journal* 17, no. 2 (2002): 163–198.

Cahn, Naomi. "Perfect Substitutes or the Real Thing?" *Duke Law Journal* 52, no. 6 (2003): 1077–1166.

Cahn, Naomi, and June Carbone. "Parents, Babies and More Parents." *Chicago-Kent Law Review* 92, no. 1 (July 2017): 9–53.

Cahn, Naomi, and June Carbone. *Red Families v. Blue Families: Legal Polarization and the Creation of Culture*. New York: Oxford University Press, 2010.

Caldwell, John. "Judicial Interviews of Children: Some Legal Background." *New Zealand Family Law Journal* 5, no. 9 (2007): 215–226.

California Family Code §§ 297, 297.5, 7601, 8617 (2014).

Canadian Legal FAQs. "Adult Interdependent Relationships." https://www.law-faqs.org/alberta-faqs/family-law/adult-interdependent-relationships/ (accessed 8 July 2020).

Capacity and Guardianship Law (1962). (Israel).

Carbone, June, and Naomi Cahn. "Blackstonian Marriage, Gender, and Cohabitation." *Arizona State Law Journal* 51, no. 4 (December 2019): 1247–1283.

Carbone, June, and Naomi Cahn. "Nonmarriage." *Maryland Law Review* 76, no. 1 (2016): 55–121.

Carbone, June, and Naomi Cahn. "The Triple System of Family Law." *Michigan State Law Review* 2013: 1185–1229.

Care of Children Act 2004 (NZ).

Care of Children Amendment Act (No. 2) 2013 (NZ).

Carp, E. Wayne. *Adoption Politics: Bastard Nation & Ballot Initiative*. Lawrence: University of Kansas Press, 2004.

Carp, E. Wayne. *Family Matters: Secrecy and Disclosure in the History of Adoption*. Cambridge, MA: Harvard University Press, 1998.

Carson, Rachel, Edward Dunstan, Jessie Dunstan, and Dinika Roopani. *Children and Young People in Separated Families: Family Law System Experiences and Needs*. Melbourne: Australian Institute of Family Studies, 2018.

Casey, Dame Louise. "A Review into Opportunity and Integration." December 2016. https://assets.publishing.service.gov.uk/government/uploads/system/uploads/attachment_data/file/575973/The_Casey_Review_Report.pdf

Castagnoli, Cristina. *Transgender Persons' Rights in the EU Member States*. Brussels: European Parliament, 2010.

Chambers, Claire. *Against Marriage: An Egalitarian Defence of the Marriage-Free State*. Oxford: Oxford University Press, 2017.

Charnay, Jean-Paul. "Le rôle du juge français dans l'élaboration du droit musulman algérien." *Revue internationale de droit compare* 15, no. 4 (1963): 705–721.

Chaudhary, Kaiser. *Pakistani Marriages and the Private International Laws of Germany and England*. Nijmegen: Wolf Legal Publishers, 2014.

Cherlin, Andrew. "Between Poor and Prosperous: Do the Family Patterns of Moderately-Educated Americans Deserve a Closer Look?" In *Social Class and Changing in an Unequal America*, edited by Marcia J. Carlson and Paula England, 68–84. Stanford: Stanford University Press, 2011.

Cherlin, Andrew. *Labor's Love Lost: The Rise and Fall of the Working Class Family in America*. New York: Russell Sage Foundation, 2014.

Cherlin, Andrew. *The Marriage-Go-Round: The State of Marriage and the Family in America Today*. New York: Vintage Books, 2010.

Chiam, Zhan, Sandra Duffy, and Matilda González Gil. *Trans Legal Mapping Report: Recognition Before the Law*. Geneva: ILGA, 2017.

Child Abuse Prevention and Treatment Act, Pub. L. No. 111-320, 42 U.S.C. § 5101 (2010).

Child Welfare Information Gateway. "Definitions of Child Abuse and Neglect: Child Welfare Information Gateway." https://www.childwelfare.gov/topics/systemwide/laws-policies/statutes/define/ (accessed 29 October 2020).

Child Welfare Information Gateway. *Postadoption Contact Agreements Between Birth and Adoptive Families*. Washington, DC: U.S. Department of Health and Human Services, Children's Bureau, 2019.

Child Welfare Information Gateway. "Racial Disproportionality and Disparity in Child Welfare." 2016. https://www.childwelfare.gov/pubpdfs/racial_disproportionality.pdf

Child Welfare Information Gateway. *Searching for Birth Relatives*. Washington, DC: U.S. Department of Health and Human Services, Children's Bureau, 2018.

Children Act 1995 (Scotland).

Children and Families Act 2014.

Children and Young Persons Act 1933.

Children's Act 1989 (UK).

Children's Act, Section 110, 2004 (UK).

Children's Commissioner for England. "Annual Report and Accounts 2019–20." July 16, 2020. https://www.childrenscommissioner.gov.uk/wp-content/uploads/2020/07/occ-annual-report-and-accounts-2019-20.pdf

Children's Defense Fund, Child Trends, American Bar Association Center on Children and the Law, Case Family Programs, Child Focus, and Generations United. "Making It Work: Using the Guardianship Assistance Program (GAP) to Close the Permanency Gap for Children in Foster Care." 2012.

Children's Law Reform Act R.S.O. 1990, c. C12.

Chilemba, Enoch M. "International Law on the Rights of Children with Disabilities." In *International Human Rights of Children*, edited by Ursula Kilkelly and Ton Liefaard, 359–387. Singapore: Springer Nature, 2019. DOI: 10.1007/978-981-10-4184-6_19

Chisholm, Richard. "Information Rights and Donor Conception: Lessons From Adoption?" *Journal of Law and Medicine* 19, no. 4 (2012): 722–741.

Chodroff, Carol N. "Children's Need for Safe Housing." *Children's Legal Rights Journal* 24, no. 1 (2012): 2–7.

Christian, Cinda L., Ruth G. McRoy, Harold D. Grotevant, and Chalandra M. Bryant. "Grief Resolution of Birthmothers in Confidential, Time-Limited Mediated, Ongoing Mediated, and Fully Disclosed Adoptions." *Adoption Quarterly* 1, no. 2 (December 1997): 35–58.

Civil Unions & Domestic Partnership Statutes. "National Conference of State Legislatures." http://www.ncsl.org/research/human-services/civil-unions-and-domestic-partnership-statutes.aspx (last updated 10 March 2020).

Clapham, Christopher. "Centralization and Local Response in Southern Ethiopia." *African Affairs* 74, no. 294 (January 1975): 72–81.

Clapham, Christopher. "Ethnicity and the National Question in Ethiopia." In *Conflict and Place in the Horn of Africa: Federalism and Its Alternatives*, edited by Peter Woodward and Murray Forsyth. Brookfield: Dartmouth Publishing, 1994.

Clapton, Gary. *Birth Fathers and Their Adoption Experiences.* London: Jessica Kingsley Publishers, 2008.

Cluver, Lucy, Jamie M. Lachman, Lorraine Sherr, Inge Wessels, Etienne Krug, Sabine Rakotomalala, and Stephen Blight, et al. Ward, Jennifer Doubt, and Kerida McDonald. "Parenting in a Time of Covid-19." *Lancet: Correspondence* 395, no. 10231 (April 11, 2020): E64. DOI: 10.1016/S0140-6736(20)30736-4

Coalition for Responsible Home Education. "An Issue Brief: At-Risk Homeschooled Children" 2017. https://www.responsiblehomeschooling.org/wp-content/uploads/2017/05/CRHE-At-Risk-Children-Brief.pdf

Coates, Ta-Nehisi. "Race, Parenting and Punishment." Atlantic, 22 January 2010. https://www.theatlantic.com/entertainment/archive/2010/01/race-parenting-and-punishment/34005/?utm_source=atl&utm_medium=email&utm_campaign=share

Cohen, Noga. “The Discourse About False Accusations Covers Women’s Hatred.” *Haaretz*, 16 April 2016. https://www.haaretz.co.il/blogs/nogacohen/BLOG-1.2909463. [Hebrew].

Collier, Richard, and Sally Sheldon, eds. *Fathers’ Rights Activism and Legal Reform in Comparative Perspective*. Oxford and Portland: Hart Publications, 2006.

Collins, Lawrence, A. V. Dicey, and J. H. C. Morris. *Dicey, Morris, and Collins on the Conflict of Laws*, 15th ed. London: Sweet & Maxwell, 2018.

Collins v. Wassell, 323 P.3d 1216, 1225–26 (Haw. 2014).

Colo. Rev. Stat. Ann. §§ 14.2—117, 15-22-101; 15-22-112.

Committee on the Rights of the Child (CRC Committee). “Concluding Observations on the Combined Second to Fourth Periodic Reports of Samoa (CRC/C/WSM/CO/2-4).” 12 July 2016.

Committee on the Rights of the Child (CRC Committee). “Concluding Observations on the Combined Third and Fourth Periodic Reports of Ireland (CRC/C/IRL/CO/3-4).” 1 March 2016.

Committee on the Rights of the Child (CRC Committee). “Concluding Observations on the Combined Third to Fifth Periodic Reports of Nepal (CRC/C/NPL/CO/3-5).” 8 July 2016.

Committee on the Rights of the Child (CRC Committee). “Concluding Observations on the Fifth Periodic Report of France (CRC/C/FRA/CO/5).” 23 February 2016.

Committee on the Rights of the Child (CRC Committee). “Concluding Observations on the Fifth Periodic Report of the Democratic People’s Republic of Korea (CRC/C/PRK/CO/5).” 23 October 2017.

Committee on the Rights of the Child (CRC Committee). “Consideration of Reports Submitted by States Parties Under Article 44 of the Convention—Concluding Observations: Greece (CRC/C/GRC/CO/2-3).” 13 August 2012.

Committee on the Rights of the Child (CRC Committee). “Consideration of Reports Submitted by States Parties Under Article 44 of the Convention – Concluding Observations: Nepal (CRC/C/15/Add.261).” 21 September 2005.

Committee on the Rights of the Child (CRC Committee). “Consideration of Reports Submitted by States Parties Under Article 44 of the Convention—Concluding Observations: Nigeria (CRC/C/15/Add.257).” 13 April 2005.

Committee on the Rights of the Child (CRC Committee). “Consideration of Reports Submitted by States Parties Under Article 44 of the Convention—Concluding Observations: Pakistan (CRC/C/15/Add.217).” 27 October 2003.

Committee on the Rights of the Child (CRC Committee). “Consideration of Reports Submitted by States Parties Under Article 44 of the Convention—Concluding Observations: Philippines (CRC/C/15/Add.259).” 21 September 2005.

Committee on the Rights of the Child (CRC Committee). “Consideration of Reports Submitted by States Parties Under Article 44 of the Convention—Concluding Observations: Viet Nam (CRC/C/VNM/CO/3-4).” 22 August 2012.

Committee on the Rights of the Child (CRC Committee). “General Comment No. 5: General Measures of Implementation of the Convention on the Rights of the Child (CRC/C/GC/5).” 27 November 2003.

Committee on the Rights of the Child (CRC Committee). "General Comment No. 9: The Rights of Children With Disabilities (CRC/C/GC/9)." 27 February 2007.

Committee on the Rights of the Child. "General Comment No. 13 (2011): The Right of the Child to Freedom From All Forms of Violence (CRC/C/GC/13)." 18 April 2011, para. 17. https://www2.ohchr.org/english/bodies/crc/docs/CRC.C.GC.13_en.pdf

Committee on the Rights of the Child. "United Nations Human Rights Office of the High Commissioner." https://www.ohchr.org/EN/HRBodies/CRC/Pages/CRCIndex.aspx (last visited 23 July 2019).

Committee to Consider the Social. "Ethical and Legal Issues Arising from In Vitro Fertilization (Victoria), Report on Donor Gametes in IVF (August 1983)."

Consideration of Reports Submitted by States Parties Under Article 44 of the Convention, U.N. Doc. CRC/C/SWE/5.

Consideration of Reports Submitted by States Parties Under Article 44 of the Convention, U.N. Doc. CRC/C/ETH/4-5.

Consulate General of France in New York, Civil Union (PACS) (2013). https://newyork.consulfrance.org/Civil-Union-PACS

Convention on the Rights of Persons with Disabilities (CRPD), 30 March 2007, 2515 U.N.T.S. 3.

Convention on the Rights of the Child (CRC), 20 November 1989, 1577 U.N.T.S. 3.

Convention on the Rights of the Child, G.A. Res. 25, U.N. GAOR, 44th Sess.61st plen. mtg., Annex, U.N. Doc. A/44/25 (1989).

Convention on the Rights of the Child, G.A. Res. 25, U.N. GAOR, 44th Sess., U.N. Doc. A/736 (1989).

Cook, Kay, and Kristin Natalier. "Gender and Evidence in Family Law Reform: A Case Study of Quantification and Anecdote in Framing and Legitimising the 'Problems' With Child Support in Australia." *Feminist Legal Studies* 24, no. 2 (July 2016): 147–167. DOI: 10.1007/s10691-016-9317-9

Cook, Kay, and Kristin Natalier. "The Gendered Framing of Australia's Child Support Reforms." *International Journal of Law, Policy and the Family* 27, no. 1 (April 2013): 28–50. DOI: 10.1093/lawfam/ebs013

Cooper, Tanya. "Racial Bias in American Foster Care: The National Debate." *Marquette Law Review* 97, no. 2 (Winter 2013): 215–277. http://scholarship.law.marquette.edu/mulr/vol97/iss2/3

Copen, Casey, Kimberly Daniels, and William Mosher. "First Premarital Cohabitation in the United States: 2006–2010 National Survey of Family Growth." *Nat'l Health Statistics Report* (April 2013): 1–15. http://www.cdc.gov/nchs/data/nhsr/nhsr064.pdf

Cordle, Cynthia E. "Open Adoption: The Need for Legislative Action." *Virginia Journal of Social Policy & Law* 2, no. 2 (1995): 275–306.

Corker, Mairian, and Tom Shakespeare. *Disability/Postmodernity: Embodying Disability Theory*. New York: Continuum, 2002.

Corporal Punishment of Children in Finland. "Global Initiative to End All Corporal Punishment of Children." https://endcorporalpunishment.org/reports-on-every-state-and-territory/finland/ (last updated June 2020).

Corporal Punishment of Children in Latvia. "Global Initiative to End All Corporal Punishment of Children." https://endcorporalpunishment.org/reports-on-every-state-and-territory/latvia/ (last updated June 2020).

Corporal Punishment of Children in Norway. "Global Initiative to End All Corporal Punishment of Children." https://endcorporalpunishment.org/reports-on-every-state-and-territory/norway/ (last updated June 2019).

Corporal Punishment of Children in Sweden. "Global Initiative to End All Corporal Punishment of Children." https://endcorporalpunishment.org/reports-on-every-state-and-territory/sweden/ (last updated February 2020).

Coston, Bethany M., and Michael Kimmel. "White Men as the New Victims: Reverse Discrimination Cases and the Men's Rights Movement." *Nevada Law Journal* 13, no. 2 (2013): 386.

Cousins, Ben. "Capitalism Obscured: The Limits of Law and Rights-Based Approaches to Poverty Reduction and Development." *The Journal of Peasant Studies* 36, no. 4 (October 2009): 893–908.

Crawshaw, Marilyn, Ken Daniels, Damian Adams, Kate Bourne, J. A. P. van Hooff, Wendy Kramer, Lauri Pasch, and Petra Thorn. "Emerging Models for Facilitating Contact Between People Genetically Related Through Donor Conception: A Preliminary Analysis and Discussion." *Reproductive Biomedicine & Society Online* 1, no. 2 (December 2015): 71–80.

CRC Committee. "General Comment No. 21 (2017): Children in Street Situations (CRC/GC/C/21)." 17 June 2017.

Cretney, Stephen. *Family Law in tTwentieth Century: A History*. Oxford: Oxford University Press, 2003.

Cretney, Stephen. *Same Sex Relationships: From 'Odious Crime' to 'Gay Marriage.'* Oxford: Oxford University Press, 2006.

Croft, Alison. "Promoting Access to Education for Disabled Children in Low-Income Countries: Do We Need to Know How Many Disabled Children There Are?" *International Journal of Educational Development* 33, no. 3 (May 2013): 233–243.

Crutchfield, Robert D. "Labor Stratification and Violent Crime." *Social Forces* 68, no. 2 (December 1989): 489–512.

Crutchfield, Robert D., and Tim Wadsworth. "Poverty and Violence." In *International Handbook of Violence Research*, edited by Wilhelm Heitmeyer and John Hagan, 67–82. The Netherlands: Springer, 2005.

D is for Dad. https://www.facebook.com/zedekhevraati (accessed 15 December 2019).

DA 1125/99 K.Z v. D.L 5 (2000) (Israel).

Dagan, Buzaglo Noga, and Yael Hasson. *Gender Wage Gap in Israel: 2020*. Tel Aviv, Israel: Adva Center, 2020. https://adva.org/wp-content/uploads/2020/03/Gender-Gaps-2020.pdf. [Hebrew].

Dagan, Hanoch, and Daphna Hacker. "The Doctrine of Specific Shared Ownership Toward the Fourth Act in HCJ 4602/13." *Law Studies* 32, no. 1 (2019): 519–544. [Hebrew].

Dailey, Anne C., and Laura A. Rosenbury. "The New Law of the Child." *The Yale Law Journal* 127, no. 6 (April 2018): 1448–1537.

Daniels, Ken, Eric Blyth, Marilyn Crawshaw, and Ruth Curson. "Short Communication: Previous Semen Donors and Their Views Regarding the Sharing of Information With Offspring." *Human Reproduction* 20, no. 6 (June 2005): 1670–1675.

Daniluk, Judith C., and Joss Hurtig-Mitchell. "Themes of Hope and Healing: Infertile Couples' Experiences of Adoption." *Journal of Counseling & Development* 81, no. 4 (2003): 389–399.

Darom, Naomi. "Divorce in Israel: The Dark Side of the Custody Battles." *Haaretz*, 9 September 2014. https://www.haaretz.co.il/magazine/.premium-1.2436824. [Hebrew].

Davidson, Howard. "A Model Child Protection Legal Reform Instrument: The Convention on The Rights of the Child and its Consistency With United States Law." *Georgetown Journal on Poverty Law and Policy* 5, no. 2 (1998): 185–200.

Dawn M. v. Michael M., 55 Misc. 3d 865 (N.Y. Sup. Ct. 2017).

D.C. Code Ann. §§32-701; 32-710.

DCR (Reshon Letzion) 207/09 N.M, N.H, N.l, N.Y v. N.M (2009) (Israel).

del Valle, Jorge F., and Amaia Bravo. "Current Trends, Figures and Challenges in Out of Home Child Care: An International Comparative Analysis." *Psychosocial Intervention* 22 (2013): 251.

Dempsey, Deborah, and Fiona Kelly. "Transnational Third-Party Assisted Conception: Pursuing the Desire for 'Origins' Information in the Internet Era." In *Babies for Sale? Transactional Surrogacy Human Rights and the Politics of Reproduction*, edited by Miranda Davies, 204–218. London: Zed Books, 2017.

Department for Culture, Media and Sport. *Civil Partnership Review (England and Wales): A Consultation*. London: Department for Culture, Media and Sport, June 26, 2014.

Department for Education. "Child Poverty Strategy 2014–17." 26 June 2014. https://assets.publishing.service.gov.uk/government/uploads/system/uploads/attachment_data/file/324103/Child_poverty_strategy.pdf

Department for Education. "Working Together to Safeguard Children: A Guide to Inter-Agency Working to Safeguard and Promote the Welfare of Children." July 2018. https://assets.publishing.service.gov.uk/government/uploads/system/uploads/attachment_data/file/942454/Working_together_to_safeguard_children_inter_agency_guidance.pdf

Department for Education and Department of Health (UK). "Special Educational Needs and Disability Code of Practice: 0 to 25 Years – Statutory Guidance for Organisations Which Work With and Support Children and Young People Who Have Special Educational Needs or Disabilities." January 2015. https://assets.publishing.service.gov.uk/government/uploads/system/uploads/attachment_data/file/398815/SEND_Code_of_Practice_January_2015.pdf

Department of Trade and Industry. *Civil Partnership: A Framework for the Legal Recognition of Same-Sex Couples*. London: Department of Trade and Industry, 2003.

Department for Work and Pensions. "Development of a New Measure of Poverty: Statistical Notice." May 17, 2019. https://www.gov.uk/government/statistics/development-of-a-new-measure-of-poverty-statistical-notice

Department for Work and Pensions. “Households Below Average Income: An Analysis of the UK Income Distribution: 1994/95–2018/19.” 26 March 2020. https://assets.publishing.service.gov.uk/government/uploads/system/uploads/attachment_data/file/875261/households-below-average-income-1994-1995-2018-2019.pdf

de Schutter, Olivier, and Kees Waaldijk. “Major Legal Consequences of Marriage, Cohabitation and Registered Partnership for Different-Sex and Same-Sex Partners in Belgium.” In *More or Less Together: Levels of Legal Consequences of Marriage, Cohabitation and Registered Partnership for Different-Sex and Same-Sex Partners. A Comparative Study of Nine European Countries*, edited by Kees Waaldijk. Leiden University, December 2005. https://openaccess.leidenuniv.nl/handle/1887/12585

DeShaney v. Winnebago County Department of Social Services, 489 U.S. 189 (1989).

Devasia, T. K. “Why Kerala’s Free Sex-Change Surgeries Will Offer a New Lifeline for the Transgender Community.” Scroll.in, March 19, 2016. https://scroll.in/article/804496/why-keralas-free-sex-change-surgeries-will-offer-a-new-lifeline-for-the-transgender-community

Deykin, Eva Y., Patricia Patti, and Jon Ryan. “Fathers of Adopted Children: A Study of the Impact of Child Surrender on Birthfathers.” *American Journal of Orthopsychiatry* 58, no. 2 (1988): 240–248.

Diduck, Alison. “Family Law and Family Responsibility.” *In Responsibility, Law and the Family*, edited by Jo Bridgeman, Heather Keating, and Craig Lind. Aldershot: Ashgate Publishing Limited, 2013.

Director-General, Department of Community Services v De Lewinski (1996) FLC 92-674.

“Dividing Property Between Unmarried Partners.” Alberta.ca. Accessed 8 July 2020 www.alberta.ca/dividing-property-between-unmarried-partners.aspx.

Divorce Act RSC 1985, c3, 2nd Supp.

Dixon, Rosalind, and Martha C. Nussbaum. “Children’s Rights and a Capabilities Approach: The Question of Special Priority.” *Cornell Law Review* 97, no. 3 (March 2012): 549–594.

Doek, Jaap E. “What Does the Children’s Convention Require?” *Emory International Law Review* 20, no. 1 (2006): 199–208.

Doherty, Amy L. “Foster Care and Adoption: A Look at Open Adoption.” *Journal of Contemporary Legal Issues* 11, no. 1 (1997): 591–596.

Domestic Violence, Crime and Victims Act (2004).

Donnermeyer, Joseph F. “What’s Place Got to Do With It? Explaining Violence in a Rural Context.” In *The Routledge International Handbook of Violence Studies*, edited by Walter S. DeKeseredy, Callie Marie Rennison, and Amanda K. Hall-Sanchez, 95–120. London: Routledge, 2018.

Donohue, Dana, and Juan Bornman. “The Challenges of Realising Inclusive Education in South Africa.” *South African Journal of Education* 34, no. 2 (2014): 1–14.

Douglas, Gillian, Norman Doe, Sophie Gilliat-Ray, Russell Sandberg, and Asma Khan. “Social Cohesion and Civil Law: Marriage, Divorce and Religious Courts.”

June 2011. http://orca.cf.ac.uk/10788/1/Social%20Cohesion%20and%20Civil%20Law%20Full%20Report.pdf

Dragiewicz, Molly. *Equality With a Vengenace: Men's Right Groups, Battered Women, and Antifeminist Backlash.* Boston: Northeastern University Press, 2011.

Dragiewicz, Molly. "Patriarchy Reasserted: Fathers' Rights and Anti-VAWA Activism." *Feminist Criminology* 3, no. 2 (April 2008): 121–144.

Dukali v. Lamrani [2012] EWHC 1748 (Fam).

Dulout, Fernand. *Traité de droit musulman et algérien modern.* Alger, 1947.

Durrant, Joan E. "Evaluating the Success of Sweden's Corporal Punishment Ban." *Child Abuse & Neglect* 23, no. 5 (May 1999): 435–448.

Dwyer, James G. "First Parents: Reconceptualizing Newborn Adoption." *Capital University Law Review* 37, no. 2 (2008): 293–320.

Dwyer, James G. *The Oxford Handbook of Children and the Law*. Oxford: Oxford University Press, 2020.

Dwyer, James G., and Shawn F. Peters. *Homeschooling: The History and Philosophy of a Controversial Practice*. Chicago: University of Chicago Press, 2019.

Ebrahim, Zofeen T. "Don't We Count? Transgender Pakistanis Feel Sidelined by Census." *Pakistan Today*, October 7, 2017. https://www.pakistantoday.com.pk/2017/10/07/dontwe-count-transgender-pakistanis-feel-sidelined-by-census/

Edwards, Leonard P. "Corporal Punishment and the Legal System." *The Santa Clara Law Review* 36 (1995–1996): 983–1023.

Eichner, Maxine. *The Free-Market Family: How the Market Crushed the American Dream (And How It Can Be Restored).* Oxford: Oxford Scholarship Online, 2020.

Eide, Asbjørn. *A Commentary on the United Nations Convention on the Rights of the Child, Article 27: The Right to an Adequate Standard of Living*, 3rd ed. Martinus Nijhoff, 2007.

Eisenberg, Melvin Aron. "Private Ordering Through Negotiation: Dispute Settlement and Rulemaking." *Harvard Law Review* 89, no. 4 (February 1976): 637–681.

El Gamal v. Al-Maktoum [2011] EWHC B27 (Fam).

Electronic Journal of Islamic and Middle Eastern Law (EJIMEL) 7 (2019). http://www.ejimel.uzh.ch

Eli, Daniel. "Divorced Men Are Committing Suicide and the Feminist Inquisition is Celebrating." Men and Fathers (Blog Posting on File With Author).

Elrod, Linda. "Client-Directed Lawyers for Children: It is the 'Right' Thing to Do." *Pace Law Review* 27, no. 4 (2007): 869–920.

Elshtain, Jean B. "A Communitarian Position on the Family." *National Civic Review* (Winter 1993): 25–35.

Elshtain, Jean B. "Accepting Limits." *Commonweal* 18, no. 20 (November 22, 1991): 685–686.

Elshtain, Jean B. "Feminism, Family and Community." In *Feminism and Community*, edited by Penny Weiss and Marilyn Friedman. Philadelphia: Temple University Press, 1995.

"Equal Parenting Equals Child Interest." Accessed March 12, 2020 https://bit.ly/37oFzUr.

"Equal Parenting: For Equal Parenting After Divorce." https://www.facebook.com/parental.equality.israel1/ (accessed 12 March 2020).

European Social Charter (Adopted 18 October 1961, Entered into Force 26 February 1965) 529 UNTS 89 Art 16 (Council of Europe).

"Fact Sheet: Incarcerated Women and Girls." The Sentencing Project, June 6, 2019. https://www.sentencingproject.org/publications/incarcerated-women-and-girls/

Fahmy, Eldin, Emma Williamson, and Christina Pantazis. "Evidence and Policy Review: Domestic Violence and Poverty." *Joseph Rowntree Foundation*, 2016. https://research-information.bris.ac.uk/ws/portalfiles/portal/80376377/JRF_DV_POVERTY_REPORT_FINAL_COPY_.pdf

Faludi, Susan. *Backlash: The Undeclared War Against American Women.* New York: Doubleday, 1992.

Family Amendment (Maintenance) Law, 1959. (Israel).

Family First Prevention Services Act of 2018, Pub. L. 115-123, Bipartisan Budget Act of 2018, Title VII, section 50702. (Codified as Amended in Scattered Sections of 42 U.S.C.).

Family Law Act 1975 (Cth).

Family Law Courts. "Guidelines for Independent Children's Lawyers." 2013. http://www.familycourt.gov.au/wps/wcm/connect/fcoaweb/about/policies-and-procedures/guidelines-independent-childrens-lawyer

Family Property Act Sec. 7 (2020). http://www.qp.alberta.ca/documents/Acts/F04P7.pdf. (Canada).

FAR 1858-14 Roe v. Doe (2014) (Israel).

FAR 2433/04 G.T v. D.T (2005) (Israel).

FAR 5750/03 Ohana v. Ohana (2003) (Israel).

FAR 919/15 Row v. Dow (2017) (Israel).

FC (Jerusalem) 1886/04 A.L, R.L, B.L, S.L, v. D.L (2006).

FC (Reshon Letzion) 37671/09 S.M v. A.M (2009) (Israel).

FC 28951/09 (Reshon Letzion) A.G.G, M.G, A.G v. T.G (2010) (Israel).

Fentaw, Alemayehu. "Legal Pluralism: Its Promises and Pitfalls for Ethiopia." *Jimma University Journal of Law* 1, no. 1 (October 2007): 35–66.

Fenwick, Helen, and Andy Hayward. "Rejecting Asymmetry of Access to Formal Relationship Statuses for Same – And Different-Sex Couples at Strasbourg and Domestically." *European Human Rights Law Review*, no. 6 (December 2017): 544–563.

Fernando, Michelle. "What Do Australian Family Law Judges Think About Meeting with Children?" *Australian Journal of Family Law* 26, no. 1 (2012): 51–77.

Ferreira, Francisco, Dean Mitchell Jolliffe, and Espen Beer Prydz. "The International Poverty Line Has Just Been Raised to $1.90 a Day, But Global Poverty is Basically Unchanged. How is That Even Possible?" *World Bank Blogs*, October 4, 2015. https://blogs.worldbank.org/developmenttalk/international-poverty-line-has-just-been-raised-190-day-global-poverty-basically-unchanged-how-even

Fidler, Barbara, and Rachel Birnbaum. "Child Custody Disputes: Private and Public Assessments." *Canadian Family Law Quarterly* 25, no. 2 (2006): 137–167.

Fineman, Martha Albertson. "Why Marriage?" *Virginia Journal of Social Policy and the Law* 9, no. 1 (2001): 239–271.

Finkelstein, Victor. *Attitudes and Disabled People: Issues for Discussion*. New York: World Rehabilitation Fund, 1980.

Finnemore, Martha, and Kathryn Sikkink. "International Norm Dynamics and Political Change." *International Organization* 52, no. 4 (Autumn 1998): 887–917.

Fitzsimmons v. Mini Coach of Boston, Inc., 799 N.E.2d 1256, 1257 (Mass. 2003).

Flood, Michael. "'Fathers' Rights' and the Defense of Paternal Authority in Australia." *Violence Against Women* 16, no. 3 (2010): 328–347.

Forteau, Mathias. "L'ordre public 'transnational' ou 'réellement international': l'ordre public international face à l'enchevêtrement croissant du droit international privé et du droit international public." *Journal du droit international* (2011).

Fortune, Candice. "An Overview of the Foster Care Crisis in South Africa and Its Effect on the Best Interests of the Child Principle: A Socioeconomic Perspective." Master's Dissertation, Faculty of Law at the University of the Western Cape, 2016.

Fostering Connections to Success and Increasing Adoptions Act of 2008, Pub. L. 110-351 (2008).

Française Service-Public. "Pacs: en Mairie à Partir du 1er Novembre 2017." 16 May 2017. https://www.servicepublic.fr/particuliers/actualites/A11143

Francoz-Terminal, Laurence. "Registered Partnerships in France." In *The Future of Registered Partnerships – Family Recognition Beyond Marriage?*, edited by Jens M. Scherpe and Andy Hayward, 153–184. Cambridge: Intersentia, 2017.

Franzina, Pietro. "Some Remarks on the Relevance of Article 8 of the ECHR to the Recognition of Family Status Judicially Created Abroad." *Diritti Umani e Diritto Internazionale* 5, no. 3 (2011): 609–616.

Freeman, Michael. "The New Birth Right? Identity and the Child of Reproduction Revolution." *International Journal of Children's Rights* 4, no. 3 (1996): 273–297.

Freeman, Tabitha, Vasanti Jadva, Wendy Kramer, and Susan Golombok. "Gamete Donation: Parents' Experiences of Searching for Their Child's Donor Siblings and Donor." *Human Reproduction* 24, no. 3 (March 2009): 505–516.

Fregier, Casimir. *De la législation algérienne. Sa codification, sa révision, sa reformation.* Sétif, 1862.

"French Cohabiting Unmarried Couples Are 'More Equal.'" The Connexion, November 24, 2017. https://www.connexionfrance.com/French-news/French-cohabiting-unmarried-couples-are-more-equal

Frith, Lucy. "Beneath the Rhetoric: The Role of Rights in the Practice of Non-Anonymous Gamete Donation." *Bioethics* 15 (October 2001): 473–484.

Fulchiron, Hugues. "Le mariage est-il soluble dans le partenariat (et réciproquement)?" In *Mélanges en l'honneur de Jean Hauser*. LexisNexis/Dalloz, 2012.

Gaddie, Leigh. "Open Adoption." *Journal of the American Academy of Matrimonial Lawyers* 22, no. 2 (2009): 499–516.

Gager, Kristin Elizabeth. *Blood Ties and Fictive Ties: Adoption and Family Life in Early Modern France*. Princeton, NJ: Princeton University Press, 1996.

Gaither, Milton. *The Wiley Handbook of Home Education*. Hoboken: Wiley-Blackwell, 2016.

Galanter, Marc. "The Future of Law and Social Sciences Research." *North Carolina Law Review* 52, no. 5 (1974): 1065.

Galston, William. *Liberal Purposes: Goods, Virtues, and Diversity in the Liberal State*. Cambridge: Cambridge University Press, 1991.

Galtung, Johan. "Violence, Peace, and Peace Research." *Journal of Peace Research* 6, no. 3 (1969): 167–191.

Galtung, Johan, and Tord Höivik. "Structural and Direct Violence: A Note on Operationalization." *Journal of Peace Research* 8, no. 1 (March 1, 1971): 73–76.

Garrison, Marsha. "Nonmarital Cohabitation: Social Revolution and Legal Regulation." *Family Law Quarterly* 42, no. 3 (Fall 2008): 309–331.

Ge, Xiaojia, Misaki N. Natsuaki, David M. Martin, Leslie D. Leve, Jenae M. Neiderhiser, Daniel S. Shaw, Georgette Villareal, Laura Scaramella, John B. Reid, and David Ross. "Bridging the Divide: Openness in Adoption and Postadoption Psychosocial Adjustment Among Birth and Adoptive Parents." *Journal of Family Psychology* 22, no. 4 (2008): 529–540.

Gershoff, E. T., G. S. Goodman, C. L. Miller-Perrin, G. W. Holden, Y. Jackson, and A. E. Kazdin. "The Strength of the Causal Evidence Against Physical Punishment of Children and Its Implications for Parents, Psychologists, and Policymakers." *American Psychologist* 73, no. 5 (2018): 626–638. DOI: 10.1037/amp0000327

Gilbert, Neil. "A Comparative Study of Child Welfare Systems: Abstract Orientations and Concrete Results." *Children and Youth Services Review* 34, no. 3 (March 2012): 532– 536.

Gilbert, Neil, Nigel Parton, and Marik Skivenes. "Introduction." In *Child Protection Systems: International Trends and Orientations*, edited by Neil Gilbert, Nigel Parton, and Marik Skivenes, 2011.

Gillham, Bill, Gary Tanner, Bill Cheyne, Isobel Freeman, Martin Rooney, and Allan Lambie. "Unemployment Rates, Single Parent Density, and Indices of Child Poverty: Their Relationship to Different Categories of Child Abuse and Neglect." *Child Abuse & Neglect* 22, no. 2 (February 1998): 79–90.

Gilman, Leah, and Petra Nordqvist. "Organizing Openness: How UK Policy Defines the Significance of Information and Information Sharing About Gamete Donation." *International Journal of Law, Policy and the Family* 32, no. 3 (December 2018): 316–333.

Glass, Jennifer, and Philip Levchak. "Red States, Blue States, and Divorce: Understanding the Impact of Conservative Protestantism on Regional Variation in Divorce Rates." *American Journal of Sociology* 119, no. 4 (January 2014): 1002–1046. DOI: 10.1086/674703.

Glauert, Rik. "Transgender Activists in Thailand Propose Law to Protect Their Rights." Gay Star News, July 29, 2019. https://www.gaystarnews.com/article/transgender-activists-in-thailand-propose-law-to-protect-their-rights/#gs.sftbhg

Glaze, Lauren E., Laura M. Maruschak, and B. J. S. Statisticians. "Bureau of Justice Statistics Special Report Parents in Prison and Their Minor Children." *Bureau of Justice Statistics Special Report*, March 30, 2010. https://www.bjs.gov/content/pub/pdf/pptmc.pdf

Glendon, Mary Ann. *Rights Talk: The Impoverishment of Political Discourse.* Cambridge: Harvard University Press, 1991.

Godin, Frédéric. *De l'application du droit musulman en Algérie.* Alger, 1900.

Godsoe, Cynthia. "Adopting the Gay Family." *Tulane Law Review* 90, no. 2 (2015): 311–372.

Godsoe, Cynthia. "The Permanency Puzzle." *Michigan State Law Review* 2013 (2013): 1113–1136.

Goldstein, Dana. "Are Civics Lessons a Constitutional Right? This Student is Suing for Them." NY Times, November 28, 2018. https://www.nytimes.com/2018/11/28/us/civics-rhode-island-schools.html?smtyp=cur&smid=tw-nytimes

Gollop, J. Megan, A. B. Smith, and Nicola J. Taylor. "Children's Involvement in Custody and Access Arrangements After Parental Separation." *Child and Family Law Quarterly* 12, no. 4 (2000): 383–400.

Golub, Andrew, and Megan Reid. "Cohabitation and Repartnering Among Low-Income Black Mothers." *Journal of Black Sexuality and Relationships* 1, no. 3 (Winter 2015): 57–74. DOI: 10.1353/bsr.2015.0006

Gotsch, Kara. "Families and Mass Incarceration." The Sentencing Project, April 24, 2018. https://www.sentencingproject.org/publications/6148/

Government Equalities Office, Implementing Opposite-Sex Civil Partnerships: Next Steps, July 2019.

Governmental Committee on Aspects of Parental Responsibility Upon Divorce (The Shnit Committee), Interim Report, 2008. [Hebrew].

Governmental Committee on Aspects of Parental Responsibility Upon Divorce (The Shnit Committee), Final Report, 2011. [Hebrew].

Governmental Committee on Child Support (The Shifman Committee) Final Report, 2012. [Hebrew].

Graf, Nikki. "Key Findings on Marriage and Cohabitation in the U.S." Pew Research Center, November 6, 2019. https://pewrsr.ch/2NnfuOJ

Graham, George. "Whangai Tamariki: The Custom Pertaining to the Adoption of Children in Accordance With Ancient Maori Custom." *Journal of Polynesian Society* 57, no. 3 (1948): 268–278.

Grahn-Farley, Maria. "International Child Rights at Home and Abroad: A Symposium on the UN Convention on the Rights of the Child: I. Foreword: Crossing Borders." *The Capital University Law Review* 30, no. 4 (2002): 657–710.

Gramlich, John. "Black Imprisonment Rate in the U.S. Has Fallen by a Third Since 2006." Pew Research Center, May 6, 2020. https://www.pewresearch.org/fact-tank/2020/05/06/share-of-black-white-hispanic-americans-in-prison-2018-vs-2006/

Grant, Matt. "Organizational Change: Thinking It Through." 2014. https://www.slideshare.net/humansnotrobots/organisational-change-thinking-it-through

Graycar, Reg. "Family Law Reform in Australia, or Frozen Chooks Revisited Again?" *Theoretical Inquiries in Law* 13, no. 1 (2012): 241–269.

Greydanus, Donald E., M. D., Helen D. Pratt, Richard C. Spates, Anne E. Blake-Dreher, Marissa A. Greydanus-Gearhart, and Dilip R. Patel. "Corporal Punishment in Schools: Position Paper of the Society for Adolescent Medicine." *Journal of Adolescent Health* 32, no. 5 (May 2003): 385–393.

Griffiths, John. "What is Legal Pluralism?" *Journal of Legal Pluralism and Unofficial Law* 24, no. 24 (1986): 1–56.

Grotevant, Harold D., and Ruth G. McRoy. *Openness in Adoption: Exploring Family Connections.* Thousand Oaks, CA: Sage Publications, 1998.

Guggenheim, Martin. *What's Wrong With Children's Rights*. Massachusetts: Harvard University Press, 2007.

Gupta-Kagan, Josh. "Non-Exclusive Adoption and Child Welfare." *Alabama Law Review* 66, no. 4 (2015): 715–765.

Gupta-Kagan, Josh. "The New Permanency." *U.C. Davis Journal of Juvenile Law & Policy* 19, no. 1 (Winter 2015): 1–83.

Gutfeld, Arnon, and Yoram Rabin. 2017. "Homeschooling in the U.S. and Its Lesson for Israel." *Israel Yearbook on Human Rights* 47 (October 2017): 175–220.

Guzzo, Karen. "Trends in Cohabitation Outcomes: Compositional Changes and Engagement Among Never-Married Young Adults." *Journal of Marriage and Family* 76, no. 4 (August 2014): 826–842. https://www.ncbi.nlm.nih.gov/pmc/articles/PMC4712741/

Hacker, Daphna. "Children's Exclusion From Divorce Proceedings." *College of Management Law Review* 22 (2006): 63–72. [Hebrew].

Hacker, Daphna. "Divorced Israeli Men's Abuse of Transnational Human Rights Law." *Canadian Journal of Women and the Law* 28, no. 1 (April 2016): 91–115.

Hacker, Daphna. "Legal Activism in Family Law." ICON-S-Il (Blog), 1 May 2018. https://bit.ly/39rQ9Mx

Hacker, Daphna. "Men's Groups as a New Challenge to the Israeli Feminist Movement: Lessons From the Ongoing Gender War Over the Tender Years Presumption." *Israel Studies* 18, no. 3 (2013): 29–40.

Hacker, Daphna. *Parenthood in the Law: Behind the Scene of Custody and Visitation Upon Divorce*. Tel Aviv: Hakibbutz Hameuchad Publishing House Ltd, 2008. [Hebrew].

Hacker, Daphna. "Religious Tribunals in Democratic States: Lessons from the Israeli Rabbinical Courts." *Journal of Law and Religion* 27, no. 1 (2012): 59–81.

Hacker, Daphna, and Michal Frenkel. "Active Parenthood and Employment Equal Opportunities: The Need to Change the Characteristics of the Labor Force." *Labor, Society and Law* 11 (2005): 275–303. [Hebrew].

Hacker, Daphna, and Ronen Shamir. "Concepts of Motherhood, Fatherhood and Family in Israeli Courts: A Case Study." *Israeli Sociology* 5, no. 2 (2003): 311–340. [Hebrew].

Hacker, Daphna, and Ruth Halperin Kaddari. "The Ruling Rules in Custody Disputers: On the Dangers of the Parental Sameness Illusion in a Gendered Reality." *Mishpat and Mimshal* 15, no. 1–2 (2013): 91–170. [Hebrew].

Hacklay, Ziona, Nehama Goldberger, and Miriam Aburaba. *Suicide in Israel.* Ministry of Health, 2017.

Hadad, Eliezer. "On the Status of Women in Rabbinical Courts." *The Israeli Democracy Institute*, 2013. https://en.idi.org.il/publications/6859

Hale, Baroness Brenda. "Children's Participation in Family Law Decision Making: Lessons from Abroad." *Australian Journal of Family Law* 20, no. 2 (2006): 119–126.

Hale, Brenda. "Homosexual Rights." *Child and Family Law Quarterly* 16, no. 2 (June 2004): 125–134.

Hale, Brenda. "Should Judges Be Socio-Legal Scholars?" Socio-legal Studies Association 2013 Conference, March 26, 2013. https://www.supremecourt.uk/docs/speech-130326.pdf

Haley, Alex. *Roots*. New York, NY: Doubleday, 1976.

Hall, Katharine, Linda Richter, Zitha Mokomane, and Lori Lake. "Children, Families and the State Collaboration and Contestation." *Children's Institute*, University of Cape Town, November 2018. http://childrencount.uct.ac.za/uploads/publications/South%20African%20Child%20Gauge%202018_Children%20Families%20and%20the%20State.pdf

Hall, Katharine, and Winnie Sambu. "Demography of South Africa's Children." *Children's Institute*, University of Cape Town, 2019. http://www.ci.uct.ac.za/sites/default/files/image_tool/images/367/Child_Gauge/South_African_Child_Gauge_2019/CC/CC2019%20-%20Demography%20of%20South%20Africa%E2%80%99s%20children.pdf

Halley, Janet. "Behind the Law of Marriage(I): From Status/Contract to the Marriage System." *Unbound* 6, no. 1 (2010): 1–58.

Halperin-Kaddari, Ruth. *Women in Israel: A State of Their Own*. Philadelphia: University of Pennsylvania Press, 2004.

Halperin-Kaddari, Ruth, and Adi Blotner. "Mysticism." *Lawyer: Israel Bar Association Journal* 19 (April 2013): 112–115. [Hebrew].

Halperin-Kaddari, Ruth, Keren Horovitz, and Shay Zilberberg. "The Chaos in Child Support Judgements." *Law and Business Journal* (IDC Law Review) 19, no. 3 (December 2016): 1235–1269. [Hebrew].

Hamden, Ben, and Uthman Khodja. *Aperçu historique et statistique sur la Régence d'Alger*. Paris, 1833.

Hamilton, Carol. "Children with Disabilities in New Zealand Schools." In *Moving Towards Inclusive Education*, 19–37. Leiden, The Netherlands: Brill, 2020. DOI: 10.1163/9789004432789_002

Han, Tan Cheng. "Transsexuals and the Law of Marriage in Singapore: Lim Ying v. Hiol Kian Ming Eric." *Singapore Journal of Legal Studies* (December 1991): 509–516.

Hanoteau et Letourneux. *La Kabylie et les coutumes kabyles*. Paris: Hanoteau et Letourneux, 1868.

Hardin, Mark. "Child Protection Cases in a Unified Family Court." *Family Law Quarterly* 32, no. 1 (Spring 1998): 147–199.

Harding, Rosie. "'Dogs Are "Registered," People Shouldn't Be': Legal Consciousness and Lesbian and Gay Rights." *Social and Legal Studies* 15, no. 4 (December 2006): 511–533.

Harper, Joyce, Debbie Kennett, and Dan Reisel. "The End of Donor Anonymity: How Genetic Testing is Likely to Drive Anonymous Gamete Donation out of Business." *Human Reproduction* 31, no. 6 (June 2016): 1135–1140.

Hartman, Ann, and Joan Laird. "Family Treatment After Adoption: Common Themes." In *The Psychology of Adoption*, 221–239. Oxford: Oxford University Press, 1990.

Harvey, Sylvia A. "How a Trip to Prison Cost Kenneth Clark His Right to Be a Parent." The Nation, July 20, 2020. https://www.thenation.com/article/society/prison-parents-children-asfa

Hawaii Department of Health. "About Reciprocal Beneficiary Relationships." http://health.hawaii.gov/vitalrecords/about-reciprocal-beneficiary-relationships/#register (accessed 13 October 2017).

Hawaii Rev. Stat. Ann. §§ 560:2-102-402, 572B-1 et seq, 572C-1 to C-7.

Hayward, Andy. "Equal Civil Partnerships, Discrimination and the Indulgence of Time." *Modern Law Review* 82, no. 5 (September 2019): 922–935.

Hayward, Andy. "Same-Sex Registered Partnerships – A Right to be Recognised?" *Cambridge Law Journal* 75, no. 1 (January 2016): 27–30.

Hayward, Andy. "The Steinfeld Effect: Equal Civil Partnerships and the Construction of the Cohabitant." *Child and Family Law Quarterly* 31, no. 4 (December 2019): 283–302.

Henaghan, Mark, and Ruth Ballantyne. "Child Poverty in New England: A Contravention of Articles 6 and 27 of the Convention on the Rights of the Child 1989." *Stellenbosch Law Review* 26 (2015): 380–398.

Henney, Susan M., Ruth G. McRoy, Susan Ayers-Lopez, and Harold D. Grotevant. "The Impact of Openness on Adoption Agency Practices: A Longitudinal Perspective." *Adoption Quarterly* 6, no. 3 (2003): 31–51.

Herring, Jonathan. "Chapter 11: Child Protection." In *Family Law*, 7th ed. Harlow, England: Pearson, 2015.

Hertz, Rosanna, and Margaret Nelson. *Random Families: Genetic Strangers, Sperm Donor Siblings and the Creation of New Kin.* New York: Oxford University Press, 2019.

Hick, Rod. "The Capability Approach: Insights for a New Poverty Focus." *Journal of Social Policy* 41, no. 2 (2012): 291–308.

Hirko, Sileshi B. "A Post-Divorce Cohabitation Never Equals a Remarriage in Ethiopia: A Case Comment." *Haramaya Law Review* 3, no. 1 (2014): 77–109.

Hirko, Sileshi B. "The Disputed Constitutionality of the Precedential Practice of the Federal Supreme Court and Its Implications for Oromia Family Law: The Case of Bigamous Marriage in Ethiopia." *Journal of African Law* 63, no. 2 (2019): 193–223.

Hirko, Sileshi B. "The Liquidation of Pecuniary Effects of Bigamous Marriage in Ethiopia: A Critical Review of the Precedents of the Federal Supreme Court and Rule of Equity Under the Oromia Regional Family Code." *International Journal of Law, Policy and the Family* 30, no. 1 (April 2016): 32–49.

HM Government. *Equal Marriage: The Government's Response*. London: HM Government, 2012.

Hodson, Loveday. "Different Families Same Rights? Lesbian, Gay, Bisexual and Transgender Families under International Human Rights Law." *ILGA-Europe*, 2007. https://www.ilga-europe.org/resources/ilga-europe-reports-and-other-materials/different-families-same-rights-lgbt-families-under

Holcomb, Bonnie K., and Sisai Ibssa. *The Invention of Ethiopia: The Making of a Dependent Colonial State in Northeast Africa*. Trenton: Red Sea Press, 1990.

Holtan, Amy, Bjørn Helge Handegård, Renee Thørnblad, and Svein Arild Vis. "Placement Disruption in Long-Term Kinship and Nonkinship Foster Care." *Children & Youth Services Review* 35, no. 7 (July 2013): 1087–1094.

Holtan, Amy, John Andreas Ronning, Bjørn Helge Handegård, and Andre Sourander. "A Comparison of Mental Health Problems in Kinship and Nonkinship Foster Care." *European Journal of Child and Adolescent Psychiatry* 14, no. 4 (July 2005): 200–207.

Holtan, Amy, and Renee Thørnblad. "Kinship Foster Parenting; Gender, Class and Labour-Force Participation." *European Journal of Social Work* 12 (2009): 465.

Home Office. "Family Policy: Partners, Divorce and Dissolution." May 2019. https://assets.publishing.service.gov.uk/government/uploads/system/uploads/attachment_data/file/835362/Partner_divorce_and_dissolution_guidance_v.1.0ext.pdf

Home Office. "The Independent Review into the Application of Sharia Law in England and Wales Presented to Parliament by the Secretary of State for the Home Department by Command of Her Majesty." February 2018. https://assets.publishing.service.gov.uk/government/uploads/system/uploads/attachment_data/file/678478/6.4152_HO_CPFG_Report_into_Sharia_Law_in_the_UK_WEB.pdf

Horder, Jeremy. *Ashworth's Principles of Criminal Law*, 8th ed. Oxford: Oxford University Press, 2016.

Horstman, Haley K., Colleen W. Colaner, and Christine E. Rittenour. "Contributing Factors of Adult Adoptees' Identity Work and Self-Esteem: Family Communication Patterns and Adoption-Specific Communication." *Journal of Family Communication* 16, no. 3 (2016): 263–276.

Hossain, Adnan. "The Paradox of Recognition: Hijra, Third Gender and Sexual Rights in Bangladesh." *Culture, Health & Sexuality* 19, no. 12 (2017). DOI: 10.1080/13691058.2017.1317831

Howard, Jacqueline. "Pediatricians Strengthen Stance Against Spanking Kids." CNN, November 18, 2018. https://www.cnn.com/2018/11/05/health/spanking-children-healthy-discipline-study

Howard, Jacqueline. "These Are the Countries Where Spanking is Illegal." CNN, March 12, 2018. https://www.cnn.com/2018/03/12/health/spanking-laws-parenting-without-borders-intl/index.html

Howe, R. Brian, and Katherine Covell. "Child Poverty in Canada and the Rights of the Child." *Human Rights Quarterly* 25, no. 4 (November 2003): 1067–1087.

HSLDA. "Our Mission." September 18, 2019. Accessed 22 September 2020 https://hslda.org/post/our-mission.

https://shared-parenting.co.il/ (accessed 12 March 2020).

Hultman, Lill, Ulla Forinder, Ann-Marie Öhrvall, Pernilla Pergert, and Kerstin Fugl-Meyer. "Elusive Participation – Social Workers' Experience of the Participation of Children With Disabilities in LSS Assessments." *Scandinavian Journal of Disability Research* 21, no. 1 (2019): 38–48. DOI: 10.16993/sjdr.558

Human Rights Council. "The Right to Education of Persons With Disabilities: Report of the Special Rapporteur on the Right to Education." *Venor Muñoz* (UN Doc A/HRC/4/29), 19 February 2007.

Human Rights Watch. Accessed 13 December 2021 https://www.hrw.org/news/2014/11/17/25th-anniversary-convention-rights-child.

Human Rights Watch. "'I Want to Live With My Head Held High': Abuses in Bangladesh's Legal Recognition of Hijras." December 23, 2016. https://www.hrw.org/report/2016/12/23/i-want-live-my-head-held-high/abuses-bangladeshs-legal-recognition-hijras

Huseman, Jessica. "Small Group Goes to Great Lengths to Block Homeschooling Regulation." ProPublica, August 27, 2015. https://www.propublica.org/article/small-group-goes-great-lengths-to-block-homeschooling-regulation

Ibn al-Hammam. *Shar Fath al-Qadîr.* Beirut, 2003.

Ibn Djuzayy. *al-Qawânîn al-fiqhiyya fî talkhîs madhab al-Mâlikiya.* Beyrouth, 2013.

Ibn Rushd. *Bidâyat al- Mujtahid wa nihâyat al-muqtasid.* Beirut, 1988.

Ill. Comp. Stat. Ann. 750-75/1.

In the Marriage of Wotherspoon and Cooper (1981) 7 Fam LR 71.

Inhorn, Marcia C. "'He Won't Be My Son': Middle Eastern Muslim Men's Discourses of Adoption and Gamete Donation." *Medical Anthropology Quarterly* 20, no. 1 (March 2006): 94–120.

International Covenant on Civil and Political Rights (Adopted 16 December 1966, Entered into Force 23 March 1976) 999 UNTS 171.

International Covenant on Economic Social and Cultural Rights (Adopted 16 December 1966, Entered into Force 3 January 1976) 993 UNTS 3.

Islamic Law Blog. "Symposium: On 'The Independent Review into the Application of Sharia Law in England and Wales' by the UK Home Office." https://islamiclaw.blog/2018/03/19/symposium-on-the-independent-review-into-the-application-of-sharia-law-in-england-and-wales-by-the-uk-home-office/

Israeli Central Bureau of Statistics. "Employed Persons Usually Working Part-Time, by Reason for Part-Time Work, Population Group and Sex." August 2018. https://old.cbs.gov.il/reader/shnaton/templ_shnaton.html?num_tab=st12_21&CYear=2018. [Hebrew].

Israeli Central Bureau of Statistics Media Release. "Data Collection for the International Women's Day." March 2019. https://www.cbs.gov.il/he/mediarelease/DocLib/2019/075/11_19_075b.pdf

Israeli Central Bureau of Statistics Media Release. "Religion and Self-Definition of Extent of Religiosity: Selected Data From the Society in Israel Report, No. 10." June 2018. http://www.cbs.gov.il/he/mediarelease/DocLib/2018/195/32_18_195b.pdf. [Hebrew].

Israeli Parliament. *Protocol of the Joint Committee of the Rights of the Child and the Committee of the Advancement of Women's Status* (7 February 2012): 28–29. [Hebrew].

Izard, Polly. *Poverty and Human Rights: Sen's 'Capability Perspective' Explored.* Oxford: Oxford University Press, 2006.

Jackson, Layla, and Kathryn O'Sullivan. "Muslim Marriage (Non)-Recognition: Implications and Possible Solutions." *Journal of Social Welfare and Family Law* 39, no. 1 (February 2017): 22–41.

Jacobson, Jessica, Catherine Heard, and Helen Fair. *Prison, Evidence of Its Use and Over-Use From Around the World*. London: Institute for Criminal Policy Research, 2017. https://www.prisonstudies.org/sites/default/files/resources/downloads/global_imprisonment_web2c.pdf

Jadva, Vasanti, Tabitha Freeman, Wendy Kramer, and Susan Golombok. "Experiences of Offspring Searching for and Contacting Their Donor Siblings and Donor." *Reproductive BioMedicine Online* 20, no. 4 (April 2010): 523–532.

"JAPAN: Human Rights Violation Against Lesbian, Gay, Bisexual and Transgender Persons A Shadow Report." April 2012. Accessed 18 February 2020 https://ilga.org/wp-content/uploads/2016/02/Shadow-Report-.pdf.

Jayasinha, Anukshi. "What It Means to be Transgender in Sri Lanka." Roarmedia, October 5, 2016. https://roar.media/english/life/reports/means-transgender-sri-lanka/

Jeckman, Ladani Orit. "Legal Activism in Israeli Family Law." MA Thesis, Tel Aviv University, Israel, 2020.

Jeffreys, Sheila. "The Need to Abolish Marriage." *Feminism & Psychology* 14, no. 2 (May 2004): 327–331.

Jiang, Patrick. "Legislating for Transgender People: A Comparative Study of the Change of Legal Gender in Hongkong, Singapore, Japan and the United Kingdom." *Hong Kong Journal of Legal Studies* 7 (2013): 31–74.

Johansen v. Norway, 23 Eur. Ct. H.R. 33, 44 (1996).

Johnson, Louise, Kate Bourne, Karen Hammarberg, Maggie Kirkman, Jane Rosamond, and Woodward Fisher. "Consultation With Donors Who Donated Gametes in Victoria, Australia Before 1998: Access by Donor-Conceived People to Information About Donors." *Victorian Assisted Reproductive Treatment Authority*, May 2013.

Johnson, Suzanne M., and Elizabeth O'Connor. *The Gay Baby Boom: The Psychology of Gay Parenthood*. New York, NY: New York University Press, 2002.

Joslin, Courtney. "Marital Status Discrimination 2.0." *Boston University Law Review* 95, no. 3 (May 2015): 805–831.

Jowett, Adam, and Elizabeth Peel. "'A Question of Equality and Choice': Same-Sex Couples' Attitudes Towards Civil Partnership After the Introduction of Same-Sex Marriage." *Psychology and Sexuality* 8, nos. 1–2 (April 2017): 69–80.

Joyce, Kathryn. "The Homeschool Apostates." The American Prospect, February 10, 2014. https://prospect.org/civil-rights/homeschool-apostates-d2/

Judge, Sharon. "The Impact of Early Institutionalization on Child and Family Outcomes." *Adoption Quarterly* 7, no. 3 (2004): 31–48.

Juffer, Femmie. "Children's Awareness of Adoption and Their Problem Behavior in Families With 7-Year-Old Internationally Adopted Children." *Adoption Quarterly* 9, nos. 2–3 (2006): 1–22.

K v A [EWHC] 3850 (Fam).

K v K [2005] NZFLR 28.

Kaeble, Danielle, and B. J. S. Statistician. "Time Served in State Prison, 2016." *Bureau of Justice Statistics*, November 2018. https://www.bjs.gov/content/pub/pdf/tssp16.pdf

Kahan, Daniel M. "Gentle Nudges vs. Hard Shoves: Solving the Sticky Norms Problem." *University of Chicago Law Review* 67, no. 3 (Summer 2000): 607–645.

Kalmuss, Debra, Pearila B. Namerow, and Ursula Bauer. "Short-Term Consequences of Parenting Versus Adoption Among Young Unmarried Women." *Journal of Marriage and the Family* 54, no. 1 (February 1992): 80–90.

Kalyanpur, Maya. "Paradigm and Paradox: Education for All and the Inclusion of Children With Disabilities in Cambodia." *International Journal of Inclusive Education* 15, no. 10 (2011): 1053–1071.

Kaplan, Amit. *Invisible Work: Work Time and Gender Information and Policy Principles.* Jerusalem: The Van Leer Jerusalem Institute, 2012. [Hebrew].

Kaplan, Amit, and Anat Herbst. "Stratified Patterns of Divorce: Earnings, Education, and Gender." *Demographic Research* 32 (2015): 949–982.

Karangwa, Evariste, and Mary Kobusingye. *Consultation Report on Education of the Deaf in Rwanda.* Rwanda: Rwandan Ministry of Education, 2007.

Kartikeyan, Divya. "Tamil Nadu, Once a Pioneering State for Welfare of Transgenders, Now Shuns the Third Gender." Firstpost, May 25, 2017. https://www.firstpost.com/india/tamil-nadu-once-a-pioneering-state-for-welfare-of-transgenders-now-shuns-the-third-gender-3476538.html

Kaspiew, Rae, Rachel Carson, Sharnee Moore, John De Maio, Julie Deblaquiere, and Briony Horsfall. *Independent Children's Lawyers Study: Final Report*, 2nd ed. Canberra: Australian Institute of Family Studies, 2014.

Kaye, Miranda, and Julia Tolmie. "Discoursing Dads: The Rhetorical Devices of Fathers' Rights Groups." *Melbourne University Law Review* 22, no. 1 (1998): 162–194.

Kazia, Amanda. "4 Myths About Common-Law Relationships." *CBC News*, 20 March 2013. http://www.cbc.ca/news/canada/4-myths-about-common-law-relationships-1.1315129

Kelly, Fiona, and Deborah Dempsey. "Experiences and Motives of Australian Single Mothers by Choice Who Make Early Contact With Their Child's Donor Relatives." *Medical Law Review* 24, no. 4 (2016): 571–590.

Kelly, Fiona, and Deborah Dempsey. *The History of Donor Conception Records in Victoria.* Melbourne: Victorian Assisted Reproductive Treatment Authority, 2018.

Kelly, Fiona, Deborah Dempsey, Jennifer Power, Kate Bourne, Karin Hammarberg, and Louise Johnson. "From Stranger to Family or Something in Between: Donor Linking in an Era of Retrospective Access to Anonymous Sperm Donor Records in Victoria, Australia." *International Journal of Law, Policy and the Family* 33, no. 3 (2019): 277–297.

Kelly, Joan. "Legal and Educational Interventions for Families in Residence and Contact Disputes." *Australian Journal of Family Law* 15, no. 2 (2001): 92–113.

Kennedy, Deseriee. "Children, Parents & the State: The Construction of a New Family Ideology." *Berkeley Journal of Gender, Law & Justice* 26 (2011): 78–138. https://ssrn.com/abstract=2359718

Kennedy, Deseriee. "'The Good Mother:' Mothering, Feminism, and Incarceration." *William & Mary Journal of Women & the Law* 18, no. 2 (2012): 161–200. https://scholarship.law.wm.edu/wmjowl/vol18/iss2/2

Kennedy, Steven. "Child Poverty Act 2010: A Short Guide." *SN/SP/5585* (4 July 2014): 1–15. https://researchbriefings.files.parliament.uk/documents/SN05585/SN05585.pdf

Khalil Ibn Ishaq. *Mukhtasar fi-l fiqh al Imâm Mâlik.* Alger, 2012.

Khalil ibn Ishaq al-Jund and Tahir Ahmad Zawi. *Mukhtasar Khalil.* Al-Qahirah: Dar Ihya-Kutub al Arabiyah, 1980.

Khazova, Olga A. "International Children's Rights Law: Child and the Family." In *International Human Rights of Children*, edited by Ursula Kilkelly and Ton Liefaard, 161–186. New York: Springer, 2019.

Khwela, Michael N. "A Need to Re-Integrate Prisoners to the Community: A Case of Polokwane Medium B Prison, South Africa." *Athens Journal of Social Sciences* 1, no. 2 (2014): 145–56. DOI: 10.30958/ajss.1-2-5

Kilkelly, Ursula. "Disability and Children: The Convention on the Rights of the Child." In *Human Rights and Disability: The Current Use and Future Potential of United Nations Human Rights Instruments in the Context of Disability*, edited by Gerard Quinn and Theresia Degener, 191–227. New York and Geneva: United Nations, 2002.

Kilkelly, Ursula. "Using the Convention of the Rights of the Child in Law and Policy: Two Ways to Improve Compliance." In *The Human Rights of Children: From Vision to Implementation*, 179–197. UK: Ashgate Publishing Limited, 2011.

Kim, Ji Hyun, Scott Oliver, and Margaret Ryznar. "The Rise of PACS: A New Type of Commitment From the City of Love." *Washburn Law Journal* 56, no. 1 (Winter 2017): 69–92.

Klein David O., and Joshua R. Wueller. "Fake News: A Legal Perspective." *Journal of Internet Law* 20, no. 10 (2017): 1–13.

Klotz, Maren. *(K)Information: Gamete Donation and Kinship Knowledge in Germany and Britain.* Frankfurt: Campus Verlag, 2014.

Knight, Kyle, and Kellea Miller. *Bridges to Justice: Case Study of LGBTI Rights in Nepal.* Astraea Lesbian Foundation for Justice, 2015.

Knight v Finn [2003] NZFLR 38.

Know Violence in Childhood Learning Initiative. "Ending Violence in Childhood." 2017. http://www.knowviolenceinchildhood.org/publication/flagship-report

Knox, Barbara L., Suzanne P. Starling, Kenneth W. Feldman, Nancy D. Kellogg, Lori D. Frasier, and Suzanna L. Tiapula. "Child Torture as a Form of Child Abuse." *Journal of Child and Adolescent Trauma* 7, no. 1 (2014): 37–49.

Koolick, Jessica, Maria M. Galano, Andrew Grogan-Kaylor, Hannah Clark, Nora Montalvo-Liendo, and Sandra A. Graham-Bermann. "PTSD Symptoms in Young Children Exposed to Intimate Partner Violence in Four Ethno-Racial Groups." *Journal of Child & Adolescent Trauma* 9 (2016): 97–107.

Kunzman, Robert, and Milton Gaither. "Homeschooling: An Updated Comprehensive Survey of the Research." *Other Education: The Journal of Educational Alternatives* 9, no. 1 (2020): 253–336.

Kutty, Faisal. "Islamic Law and Adoptions." In *The Intercountry Adoption Debate: Dialogues Across Disciplines*, 526–564. Newcastle Upon Tyne: Cambridge Scholars Press, 2015.

Lamidi, Esther. "Are Cohabiting Unions Lasting Longer? Two Decades of Change in the Duration of Cohabitation (1980–2004)." 2015. http://paa2015.princeton.edu/papers/153280.

Lansdown, Gerison. *Promoting Children's Participation in Democratic Decision-Making*. Florence: UNICEF, 2001.

Lansdown, Gerison. *See Me, Hear Me: A Guide to Using the UN Convention on the Rights of Persons With Disabilities to Promote the Rights of Children*. London: Save the Children, 2009.

Lansford, Jennifer E., Claudia Cappa, Diane L. Putnick, Marc H. Bornstein, Kirby Deater-Deckard, and Robert H. Bradley. "Change Over Time in Parents' Beliefs About and Reported Use of Corporal Punishment in Eight Countries With and Without Legal Bans." *Child Abuse & Neglect* 71 (2018): 44–55. https://www.ncbi.nlm.nih.gov/pmc/articles/PMC5407940/pdf/nihms828426.pdf

Lapp, Amber. "How Class Influences Pregnancy Ambivalence." *Institute for Family Studies*, 27 April 2015. http://family-studies.org/how-class-influences-pregnancy-ambivalence/

Lassiter v. Department of Social Services, 452 U.S. 18 (1981).

Lau, Chris. "Transgender Trio Fail in Legal Bid to be Listed as Male on Hong Kong ID Card." *South China Morning Post*, 1 February 2019. https://www.scmp.com/news/hong-kong/law-and-crime/article/2184662/transgender-men-fail-legal-bid-be-listed-male-hong-kong

Law, Violet. "Hong Kong Court Denies Male Status to 3 Transgender Men." *AP News*, February 1, 2019. https://apnews.com/6128011e768f49e28118f0c9646c5e54

Lawrence, John. *The Right to Education for Persons with Disabilities: Towards Inclusion*. Paris: UNESCO, 2004.

Lazer, David M. J., Matthew Baum, Yochai Benkler, Adam Berinsky, Kelly Greenhill, Filippo Menczer, and Miriam Metzger, et al. "The Science of Fake News: Addressing Fake News Requires a Multidisciplinary Effort." *Science* 359, no. 6380 (March 2018): 1094–1096. DOI: 10.1126/science.aao2998

Leblic, Isabelle. "From French Polynesia to France: The Legacy of Fa'a'amu Traditional Adoption in 'International' Adoption." *Anthropologica* 56, no. 2 (2014): 449–462.

Leckey, Robert. "Cohabitation, Law Reform, and the Litigants." *International Journal of Law, Policy, and the Family* 31, no. 2 (August 2017): 131–146.

Ledesma, Stephanie. "The Vanishing of the African-American Family: 'Reasonable Efforts' and Its Connection to the Disproportionality of the Child Welfare System." *Charleston Law Review* 9, no. 1 (2014): 29–73.

Lee, Jina, Zenobia Bell, and Mae Ackerman-Brimberg. "Implicit Bias in the Child Welfare, Education and Mental Health Systems." *National Center for Youth Law*, n.d. https://youthlaw.org/publication/implicit-bias-in-the-child-welfare-education-and-mental-health-systems/ (accessed 30 October 2020).

Lee, Steven. "Is Poverty Violence?" In *Institutional Violence*, edited by Dean Curtin and Robert Litke, 5–12. Amsterdam/Atlanta: Rodopi, 1999.

LEG v AG, 2002 BCSC 1455.

"Legal Gender Recognition in China: A Legal and Policy Review." *UNDP*, 5 August 2018.

Levi, Jennifer L., and Elizabeth E. Monnin-Browder. *Transgender Family Law*. Indiana: AuthorHouse, 2012.

Levine, Murray, Leah Wallach, David I. Levine, and Deborah Goldfarb. "An Illustration of the Intersection of Social Science and the Law: The Legal Rights of Adolescents to Make Medical Decisions." *Hastings Women's Law Journal* 30, no. 2 (2019): 241–260.

Lichter, Daniel, Sharon Sassler, and Richard Turner. "Cohabitation, Post-Conception Unions, and the Rise in Nonmarital Fertility." *Social Science Research* 47 (2014): 134–147.

Life Chances Act 2010.

Lifshitz, Anat, and Shahar Lifshitz. "Support of Children Aged 6 to 15 Following FAR 5750/03." *Bar-Ilan Law Studies* 32 (2020): 545–633. [Hebrew].

Lind, Craig. "Sexuality and Same-Sex Relationships in Law." In *Sexually Repositioned: Diversity and the Law*, edited by Belinda Brooks-Gordon, Lorraine Gelsthorpe, Martin Johnson, and Andrew Bainham, 109–130. Oxford: Hart Publishing, 2004.

LJG v RTP [Child Abduction] [2006] NZFLR 589.

Local Government Association. "Local Government Funding: Moving the Conversation On." July 2018. https://www.local.gov.uk/moving-the-conversation-on/funding

Lubienski, Christopher, Tiffany Puckett, and T. Jameson Brewer. 2013. "Does Homeschooling "Work"? A Critique of the Empirical Claims and Agenda of Advocacy Organizations." *Peabody Journal of Education* 88, no. 3 (2013): 378–392.

Lund-Andersen, Ingrid. "The Danish Registered Partnership Act, 1989: Has the Act Meant a Change in Attitudes?" In *Legal Recognition of Same-Sex Partnerships: A Study of National, European and International Law*, edited by Robert Wintemute and Mads Andenaes, 417–426. Oxford: Hart Publishing, 2001.

Lundy, Laura. "'Voice' is Not Enough: Conceptualising Article 12 of the United Nations Convention on the Rights of the Child." *British Educational Research Journal* 33, no. 6 (December 2007): 927–942. http://www.jstor.org/stable/30032800

Lundy, Laura, and Patricia O'Lynn. "The Education Rights of Children." In *International Human Rights of Children*, edited by Ursula Kilkelly and Ton Liefaard, 259–276. Singapore: Springer Nature, 2019. DOI: 10.1007/978-981-10-4184-6_11

Luyt, William. "Imprisoned Mothers in South African Prisons With Children Outside of the Institution." *European Journal of Crime Criminal Law and Criminal Justice* 16, no. 3 (2008): 89–114. https://www.researchgate.net/publication/240679345_Imprisoned_Mothers_in_South_African_Prisons_with_Children_Outside_of_the_Institution

M v Y [1994] 1 NZLR 527.

Maan, Yaara. *The Right to Active Fatherhood: Recommendations for Changing the Maternity Leave Policy in Israel*. Tel Aviv, Israel: The Israel Women's Network, February 2018. [Hebrew].

MacArthur, Jude. "Chapter 10: Tensions and Conflicts: Experiences in Parent and Professional Worlds." In *Counterpoints 270 (2004) Volume Entitled "Ideology and the Politics of (In)Exclusion,"* 166–182. http://www.jstor.org/stable/42978592

Macartney, Bernadette. "Disabled by the Discourse: Some Impacts of Normalising Mechanisms in Education and Society on the Lives of Disabled Children and Their Families." *New Zealand Research in Early Childhood Education* 11 (2008): 33–50.

Macfarlane, Julie. "Understanding Trends in American Muslim Divorce and Marriage: A Discussion Guide for Families and Communities." *ISPU*. 2012. https://www.ispu.org/wp-content/uploads/2016/08/ISPU-Report_Marriage-II_Macfarlane_WEB.pdf

Maine Rev. Stat. § 1891(5) (2016).

Mainemer, Henry, Lorraine Gilman, and Elinor Ames. "Parenting Stress in Families Adopting Children From Romanian Orphanages." *Journal of Family Issues* 19, no. 2 (1998): 164–180.

Mangold, Susan Vivian. "Extending Non-Exclusive Parenting and the Right to Protection for Older Foster Children: Creating Third Options in Permanency Planning." *The Buffalo Law Review* 48 (2000): 835–879.

Manning, Wendy, and Bart Stykes. "Twenty-Five Years of Change in Cohabitation in the U.S., 1987–2013." *National Center for Family and Marriage Research Family Profile FP-15-01*, 2015.

Maravel, Alexandra. "The U.N. Convention on the Rights of the Child and the Hague Conference on Private International Law: The Dynamics of Children's Rights Through Legal Strata." *Transnational Law & Contemporary Problems* 6, no. 2 (1996): 309–328.

Marks, Deborah. *Disability: Controversial Debates and Psychosocial Perspectives*. London: Routledge, 1999.

Marr, Elisha. "U.S. Transracial Adoption Trends in the 21st Century." *Adoption Quarterly* 20, no. 3 (2017): 222–251.

Martin, Claude, and Irene Théry. "The PACS and Marriage and Cohabitation in France." *International Journal of Law, Policy and the Family* 15, no. 1 (April 2001): 135–158.

Marvel, Stu. "Tony Danza is My Sperm Donor? Queer Kinship and the Impact of Canadian Regulations Around Sperm Donation." *Canadian Journal of Women & the Law* 25, no. 2 (2013): 221–248.

Marvin v. Marvin, 557 P.2d 106 (Cal. 1976).

Mary Green and Ajad Farhat v Malta, no. 38797/07, ECHR 2010.

Masci, David, and Claire Gecewicz. "Share of Married Adults Varies Widely Across U.S. Religious Groups." *Pew Research Center*, 19 March 2018. http://pewrsr.ch/2u8PzCP

Mashhour, Amira. "Islamic Law and Gender Equality – Could There be a Common Ground?: A Study of Divorce and Polygamy in Sharia Law and Contemporary Legislation in Tunisia and Egypt." *Human Rights Quarterly* 27, no. 2 (2005): 562–596.

Maslow, Abraham. "A Theory of Human Motivation." *Psychological Review* 50, no. 4 (1943): 370–396. DOI: 10.1037/h0054346.

Mass. Gen. Laws, ch. 209A, § 1 (2019).

Masson, Judith. "The State as Parent: The Reluctant Parent? The Problems of Parents of Last Resort." *Journal of Law and Society* 35, no. 1 (March 2008): 52–74.

Maternowska, M. Catherine, Alina Potts, and Deborah Fry. *The Multi-Country Study on the Drivers of Violence Affecting Children. A Cross-Country Snapshot of Findings*. Florence: UNICEF Office of Research – Innocenti, 2016.

Maternowska, M. Catherine, and Deborah Fry. "The Multi-Country Study on the Drivers of Violence Affecting Children: An Overview." *Vulnerable Children and Youth Studies* 13, Suppl 1 (2018): 12–25.

Matsumura, Kaiponanea. "Choosing Marriage." *U.C. Davis Law Review* 50, no. 5 (June 2017): 1999–2066.

Matter of David S. v. Samantha G. 59 Misc. 3d 960 (N.Y. Fam. Ct. 2018).

Matter of Munson and Beal, 146 A.3d 153, 158 (N.H. 2016).

Matter of Tomeka N.H. v. Jesus R., 183 A.D.3d 106 (N.Y. Sup. Ct. App. Div. 2020).

Mazeh, Yoav. "False Allegation of Sexual Abuse and Domestic Violence." March 2016. https://bit.ly/367rURB. [Hebrew].

McBarnet, Doreen. "Law, Policy, and Legal Avoidance: Can Law Effectively Implement Egalitarian Policies?" *Journal of Law and Society* 15, no. 1 (Spring 1988): 113–121.

McCarthy, Frankie. "Cohabitation: Lessons From North of the Border?" *Child and Family Law Quarterly* 23, no. 3 (September 2011): 277–301.

McGinn, Michael F. "Developmental Challenges for Adoptees Across the Life Cycle." In *Handbook of Adoption: Implications of Researchers, Practitioners and Families*, 61–76. Thousand Oaks, CA: Sage Publications, 2007.

McGlone, Katalina, Linda Santos, Rowena Fong, Charles Mueller, and Lynne Kazama. "Psychological Stress in Adoptive Parents of Special-Needs Children." *Child Welfare* 81, no. 2 (2002): 151–171.

McLaughlin, Steven D., Susan Pearce, Diane L. Manninen, and Linda D. Winges. "To Parent or Relinquish: Consequences for Adolescent Mothers." *Social Work* 33, no. 4 (1988): 320–324.

McQuiggan, Meghan, and Mahi Megra. *Parent and Family Involvement in Education: Results From the National Household Education Surveys Program of 2016*. Washington, D.C.: U.S. Department of Education, 2017.

McRoy, Ruth G., Harold D. Grotevant, Susan Ayers-Lopez, and Susan M. Henney. "Open Adoptions: Longitudinal Outcomes for the Adoption Triad." In *Handbook of Adoption: Implications of Researchers, Practitioners and Families*, 175–189. Thousand Oaks, CA: Sage Publications, 2007.

Mee, John. "Cohabitation Law Reform in Ireland." *Child and Family Law Quarterly* 23, no. 3 (September 2011): 323–343.

Menzies, Robert. "Virtual Backlash: Representations of Men's 'Rights' and Feminist 'Wrongs' in Cyberspace." In *Reaction and Resistance: Feminism, Law, and Social Change*, edited by Dorothy E. Chunn, Susan B. Boyd, and Hester Lessard, 65–97. Vancouver: UBC Press, 2007.

Meyer, Daniel R., Judi Bartfeld, Irwin Garfinkel, and Patricia Brown. "Child Support Reform: Lessons From Wisconsin." *Family Relations* 45, no. 1 (January 1996): 11–18.

Meyer v. Nebraska, 262 U.S. 390 (1923).

Mignot, Jean-Francois. "'Simple' Adoption in France: Revival of an Old Institution (1804–2007)." *Revue Francaise de Sociologie* 56 (2015): 525–560.

Milberger v. KBHL, LLC, 486 F. Supp. 2d 1156, 1160–65 (D. Haw. 2007).

Miles, Joanna, Fran Wasoff, and Enid Mordaunt. "Cohabitation: Lessons From Research North of the Border?" *Child and Family Law Quarterly* 23, no. 3 (September 2011): 302–322.

Mineo, Liz. "A Warning on Homeschooling." *The Harvard Gazette*, 15 May 2020. https://news.harvard.edu/gazette/story/2020/05/law-school-professor-says-there-may-be-a-dark-side-of-homeschooling/

Minn. Stat. Ann. § 513.075.

Minow, Martha, and Mary Lyndon Shanley. "Relational Rights and Responsibilities: Revisioning the Family in Liberal Political Theory and Law." *Hypatia* 11, no. 1 (1996): 4–29.

Moi, Toril. "'I Am Not a Feminist, But . . .': How Feminism Became the F-Word." *PMLA* 121, no. 5 (October 2006): 1735–1741.

Monk, Daniel. "Home Education: A Human Right?" In *International Perspectives on Home Education: Do We Still Need Schools?*, edited by Paula Rothermel, 166–178. London: Palgrave Macmillan, 2015.

Monnickendam-Givon, Jiska, and Rada Haisesi. "Data on Suicide Rates Among Adults According to Familial Status." *Research and Information Center, Israeli Parliament*, 22 May 2017.

Mont. Code Ann. § 40-1-403.

Morand, Marcel. *Etudes de droit musulman algérien.* Alger, 1910.

Morand, Marcel. *Introduction à l'étude du droit musulman algérien.* Alger, 1921.

Morrison, Fiona, E. Kay, M. Tisdall, Judith Warburton, Alison Reid, and Fiona Jones. "Children's Participation in Family Actions: Probing Compliance with Children's Rights Research Report." *Scottish Government*, 2020.

Mosikatsana, Tshepo L. "Children's Rights and Family Autonomy in the South African Context: A Comment on Children's Rights Under the Final Constitution." *Michigan Journal of Race & Law* 3, no. 2 (1998): 341–393.

Muñoz Díaz v. Spain, no. 49151/07, ECHR 2009.

Munro, Eileen. "The Munro Review of Child Protection Part One: A Systems Analysis." *Department for Education*, 2010.

Munro, Eileen. "The Munro Review of Child Protection: Final Report, a Child-Centered System." *Department for Education*, 2011.

Muntingh, Lukas, and Johan Naude. "Community Safety, Offender Re-Entry and Local Government Community Safety, Offender Re-Entry and Local Government." *Network on Reducing Re-Offending*, 2012. http://repository.uwc.ac.za/bitstream/handle/10566/5093/Community_safety_offernder_re-entry_and_local_government.pdf?sequence=1&isAllowed=y

Murphy, Carla. "Parenting While Black: Toya Graham on Violence, Fear and Freddie Gray." *Slice*, 11 August 2015. https://talkingpointsmemo.com/theslice/parenting-while-black-toya-graham-baltimore-freddie-gray

Mustafa, Waqar. "Pakistan Counts Transgender People in National Census for First Time." *Reuters*, 9 January 2017. https://www.reuters.com/article/us-pakistan-transgender-census/pakistan-counts-transgender-people-in-national-census-for-first-time-idUSKBN14T1XK

Na v MSK [2018] EWFC 54.

Naama Lanski. "Dad's Voice." *Israel Hayom*, 10 June 2016. https://www.israelhayom.co.il/article/388213. [Hebrew].

Nashrat al-Qudât (Ministry of Justice), Algiers.

National Center for Lesbian Rights. "Marriage, Domestic Partnerships, and Civil Unions: Same-Sex Couples Within the United States." 2017. http://www.nclrights.org/wp-content/uploads/2013/07/Relationship_Recognition.pdf

National Education Association. *2020–2021 NEA Resolutions*. Washington, D. C.: National Education Association, 2020. https://www.nea.org/sites/default/files/2020-09/NEA%20Resolutions_2020-2021.pdf

National Institute on Drug Abuse. "Principles of Effective Treatment." https://www.drugabuse.gov/publications/principles-drug-addiction-treatment-research-based-guide-third-edition/principles-effective-treatment (last accessed 18 September 2020).

National Research Council. *The Growth of Incarceration in the United States, Exploring Causes and Consequences*. Washington, D.C.: The National Academies Press, vol. 260, 2014. DOI: 10.17226/18613.

Natnaela, Berkley. *Women Receiving Child Support From the National Insurance Institute of Israel-2017*. Jerusalem: The National Insurance Institute of Israel, 2018. https://www.btl.gov.il/Publications/survey/Pages/seker_297.aspx. [Hebrew].

Neale, Bren, and Carol Smart. "Agents or Dependents?: Struggling to Listen to Children in Family Law and Family Research." Working Paper 3. Centre for Research on Family, Kinship and Childhood, University of Leeds, 1998.

Neriya Ben-Shahar, Rivka. "To Be the Wife of a Talmid Hacham [Torah Scholar]: How Ultra-Orthodox Women Perceive the Socio-Economic Reality of the 'Learners' Society.'" *The Study of the Ultra-Orthodox Society* 2 (2015): 169–192. [Hebrew].

New Zealand Law Society, Family Law Section. "Lawyer for the Child Best Practice Guidelines." 2015. https://www.justice.govt.nz/assets/Documents/Publications/fc-fls-best-practice-guidelines.pdf

Nguyen, Sen. "LGBT Rights: Vietnam Recognizes Transgender People, But There's a Flaw in Its Law." *This Week in Asia*, 21 June 2019. https://www.scmp.com/week-asia/society/article/3015423/lgbt-rights-vietnam-recognises-transgender-people-theres-flaw-its

N.H. Rev. Stat. Ann. § 457:39.

Nielsen, Linda. "Family Rights and the Registered Partnership in Denmark." *International Journal of Family Law* 4, no. 3 (1990): 297–307.

N.J. Div. of Youth & Fam. Servs. v. P.P., 852 A.2d 1093 (N.J. 2004).

N.J. Stat. Ann. § 25:1-5(h).

N.J. Stat. Ann. §§ 37:1-28; 37:1-36, Invalidated by Garden State Equal. v. Dow, 79 A.3d 1036 (N.J. 2013).

Nolan, Aoife. "Art.27 The Right to a Standard of Living Adequate for the Child's Development." In *The UN Convention on the Rights of the Child: A Commentary*, edited by John Torbin, 1021–1055. Oxford: Oxford University Press, 2019.

Nolan, Aoife. "Poverty and Child Rights." In *Oxford Handbook of Children's Rights*, edited by Jonathan Todres and Shani M. King. Oxford: Oxford University Press, 2019.

Nolan, Aoife, and Kirrily Pells. "Children's Economic and Social Rights and Child Poverty: The State of Play." *International Journal of Children's Rights* 28, no. 1 (2020): 111–132.

Norrie, Kenneth McK. "Marriage is for Heterosexuals – May the Rest of Us be Saved From It." *Child and Family Law Quarterly* 12, no. 4 (December 2000): 363–369.

Norwegian Child Welfare Act §§ 4-20, 4-20a, 4-21.

N v N (2000) FLC 93-059.

Obergefell v. Hodges, 576 U.S. 644, 135 S Ct 2584 (2015).

Offences Against Persons Act 1861.

Office for Disability Issues. "Te Tarī Mō Ngā Take Hauātanga." In *New Zealand Disability Strategy 2016–2026*. Wellington: Ministry of Social Development, 2016.

Office for National Statistics. "Families and Households in the UK." 15 November 2019. https://www.ons.gov.uk/releases/familiesandhouseholdsintheuk2019

Ohlsson-Wijk, Sofi. "Sweden's Marriage Revival: An Analysis of the New-Millennium Switch From Long-Term Decline to Increasing Popularity." *Population Studies* 65, no. 2 (2011): 183–200. www.jstor.org/stable/23056741

Olatunji, Michael Olalekan. "Contemporary Homeschooling and the Issue of Racism: The Case of South Africa." In *The Wiley Handbook of Home Education*, edited by Milton Gaither, 494–516. Hoboken: Wiley-Blackwell, 2016.

Oliver, Michael. "Re-Defining Disability: A Challenge to Research." In *Disabling Barriers, Enabling Environments*, edited by John Swain. London: SAGE Publications, 1993.

Oliver, Michael. *The Politics of Disablement: A Sociological Approach*. London: Macmillan Education, 1990.

Oliver, Michael. "The Social Model of Disability: Thirty Years On." *Disability and Society* 28, no. 7 (2013): 1024–1026. DOI: 10.1080/09687599.2013.818773

Orentlicher, David. "Spanking and Other Corporal Punishment of Children by Parents: Undervaluing Children, Overvaluing Pain." *The Houston Law Review* 38 (1998): 147–185.

Ozah, Karabo, and Ann Skelton. "Legal Perspectives: Children, Families and the State." *South African Child Gauge* (2018): 46–60. http://www.ci.uct.ac.za/sites/default/files/image_tool/images/367/Child_Gauge/South_African_Child_Gauge_2018/Chapters/legal%20perspectives%20-%20children%2C%20families%20and%20the%20state.pdf

Palacios, Jesus, and Yolanda Sanchez-Sandoval. "Stress in Parents of Adopted Children." *International Journal of Behavioral Development* 30, no. 6 (2006): 481–487.

Pant, Sunil Babu. "Marriage Provision Under New Civil Code of is Unconstitutional." *Panichan*, 23 August 2018. https://pahichan.com/marriage-provision-under-new-civil-code-of-is-unconstitutional/

Pappas, Stephanie. "Genetic Testing and Family Secrets." *Monitor on Psychology* 49 (2018): 44. https://www.apa.org/monitor/2018/06/cover-genetic-testing

Parajuli, John Narayan. "Nepal Enters Crisis Mode as Constitution Talks Fail." *BBC*, 28 May 2012. https://www.bbc.com/news/world-asia-18234114

Parental Alienation Syndrome. "Equal Parenting Equals Child Interest." https://shared-parenting.co.il/parental-alienation/ (accessed 3 January 2020).

ParentalRights.org. "About ParentalRights.org." n.d. https://parentalrights.org/about/ (accessed 22 September 2020).

"Parental Rights: Protecting Children by Empowering Parents." https://parentalrights.org/ (accessed 22 September 2020).

Parkinson, Patrick. "Family Property Division and the Principle of Judicial Restraint." *UNSW Law Journal* 41, no. 2 (June 2018): 380–400.

Parkinson, Patrick, Jude Cashmore, and Judi Single. "Parents' and Children's Views on Talking to Judges in Parenting Disputes in Australia." *International Journal of Law, Policy and the Family* 21, no. 1 (2007): 84–107.

Parkinson, Patrick, and Judy Cashmore. *The Voice of a Child in Family Law Disputes*. New York: Oxford University Press, 2008.

Parliament of Victoria. "Inquiry into Access by Donor Conceived People to Information About Donors: Report of the Law Reform Committee" *Melbourne: Law Reform Committee*, 2012.

Partridge, Penny C. "The Particular Challenges of Being Adopted." *Smith College Studies in Social Work* 61, no. 2 (1991): 197–208.

Pate, Matthew, and Laurie Gould. *Corporal Punishment Around the World*. Santa Barbara: Praeger Books, 2012.

Patten, Eliza. "The Subordination of Subsidized Guardianship in Child Welfare Proceedings." *N.Y.U. Review of Law and Social Change* 29 (2004): 237–276.

Pells, Kirrily, and Martin Woodhead. "Changing Children's Lives: Risks and Opportunities." *Young Lives*, Department for International Development, University of Oxford, 2014. https://www.younglives.org.uk/content/changing-childrens-lives-risks-and-opportunities

Pennings, Guido. "How to Kill Gamete Donation: Retrospective Legislation and Donor Anonymity." *Human Reproduction* 27, no. 10 (2012): 2881–2885.

Perelli-Harris, Brienna. "Universal or Unique? Understanding Differences in Partnership Experiences Across Europe." In *Unequal Family Lives: Causes and Consequences in Europe and the Americas*, edited by Naomi R. Cahn, June Carbone, Laurie F. DeRose, and W. Bradford Wilcox, 83–104. Cambridge: Cambridge University Press, July 2018. https://www.cambridge.org/core/books/unequal-family-lives/universal-or-unique-understanding-diversity-in-partnership-experiences-across-europe/AC49D5C35AA804D96E095B0CD93195C9/core-reader

Perelli-Harris, Brienna, and Mark Lyons-Amos. "Changes in Partnership Patterns Across the Life Course: An Examination of 14 Countries in Europe and the United States." *Demographic Research*, 2015. https://www.demographic-research.org/volumes/vol33/6

Perelli-Harris, Brienna, and Mark Lyons-Amos. "Partnership Patterns in the United States and Across Europe: The Role of Education and Country Context." *Social Forces* 95, no. 1 (September 2016): 251–282. DOI: 10.1093/sf/sow054

Perkins, Kristin L., and Robert J. Sampson. "Compounded Deprivation in the Transition to Adulthood: The Intersection of Racial and Economic Inequality

Among Chicagoans, 1995–2013." *The Russell Sage Foundation Journal of The Social Sciences* 1, no. 1 (2015): 35–54. DOI: 10.7758/rsf.2015.1.1.03

Pierce v. Society of Sisters, 268 U.S. 510 (1925).

Pingley, Terra. "The Impact of Witnessing Domestic Violence on Children: A Systematic Review." 11, May 2017. Unpublished Master of Social Work Clinical Research Paper (On File With St. Catherine University School of Social Work). https://sophia.stkate.edu/cgi/viewcontent.cgi?article=1779&context=msw_papers

Pösö, Tarja, Marit Skivenes, and Anne-Dorthe Hestbæk. "Child Protection Systems Within the Danish, Finnish and Norwegian Welfare States—Time for a Child Centric Approach?" *European Journal of Social Work* 17 (2013): 475–490.

Prag, Patrick, and Melinda Mills. "Assisted Reproductive Technology in Europe: Usage and Regulation in the Context of Cross-Border Reproductive Care." In *Childlessness in Europe: Contexts, Causes and Consequences*, edited by Michaela Kreyenfeld and Dirk Konietzk, 289. Cham, Switzerland: SpringerOpen, 2017.

Prout, Alan. "Participation, Policy and the Changing Conditions of Childhood." In *Hearing the Voices of Children: Social Policy for a New Century*, edited by Christine Hallett and Alan Prout, 11–15. London: Routledge, 2003.

Purdue, Kerry. "Barriers to and Facilitators of Inclusion for Children With Disabilities in Early Childhood Education." *Contemporary Issues in Early Childhood* 10, no. 2 (June 2009): 133–143. DOI: 10.2304/ciec.2009.10.2.133

Purvis, Dara. "The Origin of Parental Rights: Labor, Intent, and Fathers." *Florida State University Law Review* 41 (2014): 645–696.

Putnam-Hornstein, Emily. "Report of Maltreatment as a Risk Factor for Injury Death: A Prospective Birth Cohort Study." *Child Maltreatment* 16, no. 3 (2011): 163–174.

Pylkkänen, Anu. "Substitute Children and Adoption in Finnish Legal History." *Scandinavian Journal of History* 20 (1995): 129–140.

R. v Immigration Appeal Tribunal Ex parte. Jan [1995] Imm AR 440.

Racketeer Influenced and Corrupt Organizations Act (RICO), 18 U.S.C., Chapter 96, §1961–1968.

Radin, Margaret J. "Market Inalienability." *Harvard Law Review* 100, no. 8 (1987): 1849–1937.

Raitt, Fiona. "Judicial Discretion and Methods of Ascertaining the Views of a Child." *Child and Family Law Quarterly* 16, no. 2 (2004): 151–164.

Ramsey, Sarah H., and Daan Braveman. "'Let Them Starve': Government's Obligation to Children in Poverty." *Temple Law Review* 68, no. 1 (1995): 1607–1648.

Rathus, Zoe. "'The Research Says . . .': Perceptions on the Use of Social Science Research in the Family Law System'." *Federal Law Review* 46, no. 1 (2018): 85–111.

Rault, Wilfried, and Krystyna Horko. "The Intimate Orientations of the First 'PACS' Couples in France." *Population* (English Edition, 2002) 66, no. 2 (April–June 2011): 303–331. http://www.jstor.com/stable/41488603

RCB as Litigation Guardian of EKV, CEV, CIV and LRV v Hon Justice Colin James Forrest (2012) 247 CLR 304.

Re D (a Child) (Abduction: Custody Rights) [2007] 1 AC 619.

Re K (1994) 17 Fam LR 537.

Re M (A Minor) (Justices' Discretion) [1993] 2 FLR 706.

Rebell, Michael A. *Courts and Kids: Pursuing Educational Equity Through the State Courts*. Chicago: University of Chicago Press, 2013.

Rebell, Michael A. *Flunking Democracy: Schools, Courts, and Civic Participation*. Chicago: University of Chicago Press, 2018.

Rebell, Michael A. "The Right to Education in the American State Courts." In *The Future of Economic and Social Rights*, edited by Katharine G. Young, 137–157. Cambridge: Cambridge University Press, 2019.

Redmond, Gerry. "Child Poverty and Child Rights: Edging Towards a Definition." *Journal of Children and Poverty* 14, no. 1 (2008): 63–82.

Regan, Milton C. *Family Law and the Pursuit of Intimacy*. New York: New York University Press, 1993.

Report of the Israeli NGOs for Fathers' Rights by the Coalition for the Children and Family, www.ccfisrael.org, to the 47th Session of the Committee on Economic, Social, and Cultural Rights (to be held on November 14–December 2, 2011) Regarding Implementation of the International Covenant on Economic, Social and Cultural Rights – ICESCR in Israel. http://ccfisrael.org/wp-content/uploads/2011/07/CCFISRAEL-REPORT-TO-UN-7-7-2011.pdf

Report of the Special Rapporteur on Extreme Poverty and Human Rights. "Visit to the United Kingdom of Great Britain and Northern Ireland." *A/HRC/41/39/Add.1*, 23 April 2019.

Resolution Adopted by the General Assembly on 25 September 2015. "Transforming Our World: The 2030 Agenda for Sustainable Development." *A/RES/70/1*, 21 October 2015, Goal 1.

Revue algérienne des sciences juridiques, économiques et politiques, Faculté de Droit de l'Université d'Alger (Published Since 1962).

Revue algérienne, tunisienne et marocaine de législation et de jurisprudence, Faculté de Droit de l'Université d'Alger (Published Before 1962).

Reynolds v Renolds (1973) 1 ALR 318.

Rhoades, Helen. "Yearning for the Law: Fathers' Groups and Family Law Reform in Australia." In *Fathers' Rights Activism and Legal Reform in Comparative Perspective*, edited by Richard Collier and Sally Sheldon. Oxford and Portland: Hart Publications, 2006.

Riche, Bouteldja. "Hanoteau et Letourneux: Les avatars de la traduction/interprétation juridique." *Revue al-Mutardjim, Université d'Oran* 5, no. 2 (2005): 215–224.

Riley, Nancy E., and Krista E. Van Vleet. *Making Families Through Adoption*. Thousand Oaks, CA: Sage Publications, 2012.

Roberts, Dorothy E. "Child Welfare and Civil Rights." *University of Illinois Law Review* 2003 (December 2020): 171–182. https://illinoislawreview.org/print/volume-2003-issue-1/child-welfare-and-civil-rights

Roberts, Dorothy E. "Prison, Foster Care, and the Systemic Punishment of Black Mothers." *University of California Law Review* 59 (August 2012): 1476–1499. https://www.uclalawreview.org/pdf/59-6-2.pdf

Roberts, Dorothy E. *Shattered Bonds: The Color of Child Welfare.* New York: Basic Books, 2002.

Robertson, Laura, and Karen Broadhurst. "Introducing Social Science Evidence in Family Court Decision-Making and Adjudication: Evidence From England and Wales." *International Journal of Law, Policy and the Family* 33, no. 2 (June 2019): 181–203.

Roby, Jini L., and Stephanie Matsumura. "If I Give You My Child, Aren't We Family? A Study of Birthmothers Participating in Marshall Islands–U.S. Adoptions." *Adoption Quarterly* 5, no. 4 (2002): 7–31.

Rogers, Chrissie. "Experiencing an 'Inclusive' Education: Parents and Their Children With 'Special Educational Needs.'" *British Journal of Sociology of Education* 28, no. 1 (2007): 55–68. http://www.jstor.org/stable/30036184

Rolock, Nancy. "Post-Permanency Continuity: What Happens After Adoption and Guardianship From Foster Care?" *Journal of Public Child Welfare* 9 (2015): 153–173.

Romanou, Eleni, and Emma Belton. *Isolated and Struggling: Social Isolation and the Risk of Child Maltreatment, in Lockdown and Beyond.* London: NSPCC, June 2020. https://learning.nspcc.org.uk/media/2246/isolated-and-struggling-social-isolation-risk-child-maltreatment-lockdown-and-beyond.pdf.

Rose, Richard, and Michael Shevlin. "A Sense of Belonging: Childrens' Views of Acceptance in 'Inclusive' Mainstream Schools." *International Journal of Whole Schooling* 13, no. 1 (2017): 65–80.

Rosen, Leora N., Molly Dragiewicz, and Jennifer C. Gibbs. "Fathers' Rights Groups: Demographic Correlates and Impact on Custody Policy." *Violence Against Women* 15, no. 5 (May 2009): 513–531.

Rosenberg, Elinor B. *The Adoption Life Cycle: The Children and Their Families Through the Years.* New York: The Free Press, 1992.

Rosevear, Evan, Ran Hirschl, and Courtney Jung. "Justiciable and Aspirational Economic and Social Rights in National Constitutions." In *The Future of Economic and Social Rights*, edited by Katharine G. Young, 37–65. Cambridge: Cambridge University Press, 2019.

Ross, Janell. "Black Parents Take Their Kids to School on How to Deal With Police." *The Washington Post*, 3 January 2017. https://www.washingtonpost.com/national/black-parents-take-their-kids-to-school-on-how-to-deal-with-police/2017/01/03/86129c1c-c6be-11e6-bf4b-2c064d32a4bf_story.html?noredirect=on&utm_term=.4a8b7e36b7f0

Rothermel, Paula. *International Perspectives on Home Education: Do We Still Need Schools?* London: Palgrave Macmillan, 2015.

Roussier, Jules. "L'application du Chra' au Maghreb en 1959." In *Die Welt*, 1959, no. ½.

Roussier-Theaux. "Jules, La neutralisation du droit de djebr." In *Revue Africaine*, Alger, 1938.

Routt, Gregory, and Lily Anderson. "Adolescent Violence Towards Parents." *Journal of Aggression, Maltreatment & Trauma* 20 (2011): 1–11. http://www.courts.ca.gov/documents/BTB_XXII_II_3.pdf

Rutten, Susan. "Protection of Spouses in Informal Marriages by Human Rights." *Utrecht Law Review* 6, no. 2 (2010): 77–92.

Ryznar, Margaret, and Anna Stępień-Sporek. "Cohabitation Worldwide Today." *Georgia State University Law Review* 35, no. 2 (Winter 2019): 299–328.

Sampson, Robert. "Move Up or Out? Confronting Compounded Deprivation." *N.Y.U. Furman Center, The Dream Revisited*. July 2015. https://furmancenter.org/research/iri/essay/move-up-or-out-confronting-compounded-deprivation

"S v M (CCT 53/06) [2007] ZACC 18; 2008 (3) SA 232 (CC); 2007 (12) BCLR 1312 (CC) (26 September 2007)." SAFLII. http://www.saflii.org/za/cases/ZACC/2007/18.html (South Africa).

"S v S and Another (CCT147/18) [2019] ZACC 22; 2019 (8) BCLR 989 (CC); 2019 (6) SA 1 (CC) (27 June 2019)." SAFLII. 2019. http://www.saflii.org/za/cases/ZACC/2019/22.html (South Africa) (accessed 30 October 2020).

Samuels, Elizabeth J. "Surrender and Subordination: Birth Mothers and Adoption Law Reform." *Michigan Journal of Gender & Law* 20, no. 1 (2013): 33–82.

Samuels, Elizabeth J. "The Idea of Adoption: An Inquiry into the History of Adult Adoptee Access to Birth Records." *Rutgers Law Review* 53, no. 2 (2001): 367–436.

Sandler, Irwin, Michael Saini, Marsha Kline Pruett, Joanne L. Pedro-Carroll, Janet R. Johnston, Amy Holtzworth-Munroe, and Robert E. Emery. "Convenient and Inconvenient Truths in Family Law: Preventing Scholar-Advocacy Bias in the Use of Social Science Research for Public Policy." *Family Court Review* 54, no. 2 (2016): 150–166.

Santosky v. Kramer, 455 U.S. 745 (1982).

Saslow, Eli. *Rising Out of Hatred: The Awakening of a Former White Nationalist*. New York City: Doubleday, 2018.

Sassler, Sharon, and Amanda Miller. "Class Differences in Cohabitation Processes." *Family Relationships* 60 (2011): 163–177.

Sassler, Sharon, and Daniel Lichter. "Cohabitation and Marriage: Complexity and Diversity in Union-Formation Patterns." *Journal of Marriage and Family* 82 (2020). DOI: 10.1111/jomf.12617

Save the Children Sweden, Never Violence – Thirty Years on from Sweden's Abolition of Corporal Punishment, Gov't. Off. Swed. 17 (2009). https://www.government.se/contentassets/6bfb214c582448b6ace4d32978361577/never-violence---thirty-years-on-from-swedens-abolition-of-corporal-punishment

Sayare, Scott, and Maïa de la Baume. "In France, Civil Unions Gain Favor Over Marriage." *New York Times*, 15 December 2010. https://www.nytimes.com/2010/12/16/world/europe/16france.html

Schalk and Kopf v. Austria, no. 30141/04, ECHR 2010.

Scherpe, Jens M. "The Past, Present and Future of Civil Partnerships." In *The Future of Registered Partnerships – Family Recognition Beyond Marriage?*, edited by Jens M. Scherpe and Andy Hayward, 561–587. Cambridge: Intersentia, 2017.

Scherpe, Jens M., and Andy Hayward. *The Future of Registered Partnerships – Family Recognition Beyond Marriage?* Cambridge: Intersentia, 2017.

Scherpe, Jens M., and Brian Sloan. "Contractualisation of Family Law in England & Wales: Autonomy vs Judicial Discretion." In *Contractualisation of Family Law – Global Perspectives*, edited by Frederik Swennen, 165–191. Springer, 2015.

Schmid, Jeanette. "Responding to the South African Child Welfare Crisis." *Canadian Social Work Review/Revue Canadienne de Service Social* 23, no. ½ (2006): 111–127. https://www.jstor.org/stable/41669848

Schmid, Jeannette. *Trends in South African Child Welfare From 2001–2010*. CSDA Research Report. Johannesburg: Centre for Social Development in Africa, University of Johannesburg, 2012.

Schneider, Carl. "The Channelling Function in Family Law." *Hofstra Law Review* 20 (Spring, 1992): 495–532.

Scholz, Kay-Alexander. "Nearly Half of German Parents Hit Their Children." *Deutsche Welle*, 13 March 2012. https://www.dw.com/en/nearly-half-of-german-parents -hit-their-children/a-15806121; https://perma.cc/R3FX-Z9LB

Schoonmaker, Samuel V. "Criminal Law or Family Law: The Overlapping Issues." *Family Law Quarterly* 44, no. 2 (Summer 2010): 155–167. https://www.jstor.org/stable/25740740

Schwartz, Laura J. "Models for Parenthood in Adoption Law: The French Conception." *Vanderbilt Journal of Transnational Law* 28, no. 5 (1995): 1069–1120.

Schwelb, Egon. "Marriage and Human Rights." *The American Journal of Comparative Law* 12, no. 3 (1963): 337–383.

"SC Orders Equal Benefits for Transvestites." *Dawn*, 15 July 2009. https://www.dawn.com/news/879507.

Scott, Elizabeth S., and Robert E. Emery. "Gender Politics and Child Custody: The Puzzling Persistence of the Best-Interests Standard." *Law and Contemporary Problems* 77 (2014): 69–108.

Scott, Elizabeth S., and Robert E. Scott. "Marriage as Relational Contract." *Virginia Law Review* 84, no. 7 (1998): 1225–1334.

Sege, Robert D., and Benjamin S. Seigel. "Effective Discipline to Raise Healthy Children." *Pediatrics* 1 (2018): 142.

Şerife Yiğit v. Turkey, No. 3976/05, ECHR 2009.

Seymore, Malinda L. "Sixteen and Pregnant: Minors' Consent in Abortion and Adoption." *Yale Journal of Law & Feminism* 25, no. 1 (2013): 99–158.

Seymore, Malinda L. "Ethical Lawyering in Adoption: Centering the Child in Adoption Law." *Adoption Quarterly* 24, no. 1 (2020): 48–68.

Seymore, Malinda L. "Openness in International Adoption." *Columbia Human Rights Law Review* 46, no. 3 (2015): 163–226.

Shagroon v Sharbatly [2012] EWCA Civ 1507.

Shah, Prakash. "Attitudes to Polygamy in English Law." *International and Comparative Law Quarterly* 52, no. 2 (2003): 369–400.

Shah, Prakash. "Inconvenient Marriages, or What Happens When Ethnic Minorities Marry Trans-Jurisdictionally." *Utrecht Law Review* 6, no. 2 (2010): 17–32.

Shakespeare, Tom. *Disability Rights and Wrongs Revisited*, 2nd ed. New York: Routledge, 2014.

"Shared Custody." Eleanor Leibovitch Law Firm. https://bit.ly/2V6RWlj (accessed 30 December 2019).

Shared Parenting. "Parental Alienation Syndrome—Whether a Syndrome or Not—Is Destructive to the Whole Family System." https://shared-parenting.co.il/wp-content/uploads/2014/03/רדמס-תינור.pdf (accessed 3 January 2020).

"Shared Parenting Equals Children's Interests." https://shared-parenting.co.il/joint-custody/ (accessed 15 December 2019).

Sharma, Ashwani. "Himachal Pradesh to Bring Transgenders Under Social Security Net." *The Indian Express*, 7 September 2016. https://indianexpress.com/article/india/india-news-india/himachal-pradesh-to-bring-transgenders-under-social-security-net-3018937/

Shava, Menashe. "Maintenance of Minor Children in Jewish Law and in Positive Law." (part 1 & 2) *Tel Aviv Law Review* 7, nos. 2 & 3 (1979–1980): 316–344, 583–617. [Hebrew].

Shields v Shields [2002] SCLR 334.

Shildrick, Tracy. "Lessons From Grenfell: Poverty Propaganda, Stigma and Class Power." *The Sociological Review* 66, no. 4 (2018): 783–798.

Shochetman Eliav. "Women's Status in Marriage and Divorce Law." In *Women's Status in Israeli Law and Society*, edited by Frances Raday, Carmel Shalev, and Michal Liban-Kobi, 380–436. Jerusalem: Shocken, 1995. [Hebrew].

Shúilleabháin, Máire Ní. "Overseas Marriage and Divorce in Islamic Form: A Critical Perspective on the Development of Irish Private International Law." In *Minority Religions Under Irish Law Islam in National and International Context*, edited by Kathryn O' Sullivan, 131–156. Boston: Brill, 2019.

Shulman, Jeffrey. "50-State Survey: Home School Regulations: Notification, Certification, Curriculum and Assessment Requirements." Unpublished Manuscript, on File With Author, 2018.

Shulman, Jeffrey. "Private School Regulation: Individual Rights and Educational Responsibilities." In *The Oxford Handbook of Children and the Law*, edited by James Dwyer, 701–732. Oxford: Oxford University Press, 2020.

Shulman, Jeffrey. *The Constitutional Parent: Rights, Responsibilities, and the Enfranchisement of the Child.* New Haven: Yale University Press, 2014.

Shultz, Marjorie Maguire. "Contractual Ordering of Marriage: A New Model for State Policy." *California Law Review* 70, no. 2 (1982): 204–334.

Siegel, Deborah H. "Open Adoption of Infants: Adoptive Parents' Feelings Seven Years Later." *Social Work* 48, no. 3 (2003): 409–419.

Siegel, Deborah H., and Susan Livingston Smith. *Openness in Adoption: From Secrecy and Stigma to Knowledge and Connections.* Evan B. Donaldson Adoption Institute, 2012.

Simester, A. P., J. R. Spencer, F. Stark, G. R. Sullivan, and Graham Virgo. *Simester and Sullivan's Criminal Law: Theory and Doctrine*, 6th ed. Oxford: Hart Publishing, 2016.

Singal, Nidhi. *Education of Children With Disabilities in India* (2010/ED/EFA/MRT/PI/21). Cambridge: United Nations Educational, Scientific and Cultural Organization, 2009.

Sir William Blackstone. *Commentaries on the Laws of England in Four Books*. George Sharswood 1, 1753.
Skivenes, Marit, and June Thoburn. "Pathways to Permanence in England and Norway: A Critical Analysis of Documents and Data." *Children & Youth Services Review* 67 (2016): 152–160.
Skivenes, Marit, and Øyvind Samnøy Tefre. "Adoption in the Child Welfare System – A Cross-Country Analysis of Child Welfare Workers' Recommendations for or Against Adoption." *Children & Youth Services Review* 34 (2012): 2220–2228.
Smart, Carol, Amanda Wade, and Bren Neale. "Objects of Concern: Children and Divorce." *Child and Family Law Quarterly* 11, no. 4 (1999): 365–376.
Smart, Carol, and Selma Sevenhuijsen, eds. *Child Custody and the Politics of Gender*. London: Routledge, 1989.
Smith, Carole, and Janette Logan. *After Adoption: Direct Contact and Relationships*. London: Routledge, 2004.
Smith, Daniel W., and David M. Brodzinsky. "Stress and Coping in Adopted Children: A Developmental Study." *Journal of Clinical Child Psychology* 23, no. 1 (1994): 91–99.
Smyth Bruce M., Jennifer E. McIntosh, Robert E. Emery, and Shelby L. Higgs Howarth. "Shared-Time Parenting: Evaluating the Evidence of Risks and Benefits to Children." In *Parenting Plan Evaluations: Applied Research for the Family Court*, edited by Lesley Drozd, Michael Saini, and Nancy Olesen, 118–169. Oxford: Oxford University Press, 2016.
Soares, Joana, Sara Ralha, Maria Barbosa-Ducharne, and Jesus Palacios. "Adoption-Related Gains, Losses and Difficulties: The Adopted Child's Perspective." *Child & Adolescent Social Work Journal* 36, no. 3 (2019): 259–268.
Social Metrics Commission. "A New Measure of Poverty for the UK, The Final Report of the Social Metrics Commission." September 2018. https://socialmetricscommission.org.uk/MEASURING-POVERTY-FULL_REPORT.pdf
Social Security Act § 474(a)(3); "45 C.F.R. § 1356.60, Fiscal Requirements (Title IV-E)." LII/Legal Information Institute. https://www.law.cornell.edu/cfr/text/45/1356.60 (accessed 30 October 2020).
"Some Preliminary Data on Homeschool Child Fatalities—Homeschooling's Invisible Children." 2016. https://hsinvisiblechildren.org/commentary/some-preliminary-data-on-homeschool-child-fatalities/ (accessed 22 September 2020).
Sorensen, Lucy, Charmaine Willis, Victor Asal, and Melissa L. Breger. "Paddling the Pupils: The Legality (or Not) of Corporal Punishment in Schools 12, 22. 2 August 2019. (unpublished manuscript). https:// ssrn.com/abstract=3429160 (accessed 22 September 2020).
South Africa: Act No. 38 of 2005, Children's Act (South Africa), (2006), Section 10. https://www.refworld.org/docid/46b82aa62.html (accessed 30 October 2020).
Spector Dana. "Men in A Trap." *Yediot Aharonot*, 27 January 2012. [Hebrew].
Staley, Sam. *Drug Policy and the Decline of American Cities*. New Brunswick: Transaction Publishers, 1992.
Stalford, Helen, and Kathryn Hollingsworth. "Judging Children's Rights: Tendencies, Tensions, Constraints and Opportunities." In *Rewriting Children's Judgments:*

From Academic Vision to New Practice, edited by Helen Stalford, Kathryn Hollingsworth, and Stephen Gilmore, 17–52. Oxford: Hart Publishing, 2017.

Stalford, Helen, Kathryn Hollingsworth, and Stephen Gilmore. "Introducing Children's Rights Judgments." In *Rewriting Children's Judgments: From Academic Vision to New Practice*, edited by Helen Stalford, Kathryn Hollingsworth, and Stephen Gilmore, 3–16. Oxford: Hart Publishing, 2017.

Starr, Sonja and Lea Brilmayer. "Family Separation as a Violation of International Law." *Berkeley Journal of International Law* 21, no. 2 (2003): 213–287.

State of Connecticut Office of the Child Advocate. *Examining Connecticut's Safety Net for Children Withdrawn From School for the Purpose of Homeschooling—Supplemental Investigation to OCA's December 12 2017 Report Regarding the Death of Matthew Tirado*. Hartford: State of Connecticut Office of Governmental Accountability, 2018.

Statistics Canada. "Portrait of Families and Living Arrangements in Canada—Families, Households and Marital Status." *2011 Census of Population*. September 2012. https://www12.statcan.gc.ca/census-recensement/2011/as-sa/98-312-x/98-312-x2011001-eng.pdfStatistics New Zealand. "Disability and Education in New Zealand in 2006." *Wellington*, November 2008. https://web.archive.org/web/20190203012336/http://archive.stats.govt.nz/~/media/statistics/browse-categories/health/disabilities/disability-education-nz-2006/dae-nz.pdf

Statistisk sentralbyrå [Statistics Norway]: Adoptions. https://www.ssb.no/en/adopsjon.Steinbach, Anja, Lara Augustijn, and Gerrit Corkadi. "Joint Physical Custody and Adolescents' Life Satisfaction in 37 North American and European Countries." *Family Processes* (2020): 1–17. DOI: 10.1111/famp.12536

Strobridge v Strobridge (1992) 10 OR (3d) 540.

Sun, Nancy. "Shanxi Permits Transgender Persons to Change Gender Information." *All-China Women's Federation*, 9 January 2014. http://www.womenofchina.cn/html/womenofchina/report/168827-1.htm

Sunstein, Cass R. *Free Markets and Social Justice*. Oxford: Oxford University Press, 1999.

Sunstein, Cass R. "Social Norms and Social Roles." *Columbia Law Review* 96 (1996): 903–968.

Su-ping, Yeh, Ku Chuan, Liu Shih-yi, and Evelyn Kao. "Draft Gay Marriage Bill to be Further Amended: Justice Ministry." *Focus Taiwan*, 21 February 2019. https://focustaiwan.tw/politics/201902210017

Sutton, Jeffrey. *51 Imperfect Solutions: States and the Making of American Constitutional Law*. Oxford: Oxford University Press, 2018.

Sweden Children and Parents Code, Chapter 6, § 8.

Swennen, Frederik. "Un-Coupling Family Law: The Legal Recognition and Protection of Adult Unions Outside of Conjugal Coupledom." *Feminist Legal Studies* 28, no. 1 (March 2020): 39–60.

Sykes, Margaret. "Adoption With Contact: A Study of Adoptive Parents and the Impact of Continuing Contact With Families of Origin." *Adoption & Fostering* 24, no. 4 (2000): 20–32.

"Taiwan's Cabinet Passes Same-Sex Marriage Bill." *Taiwan Today*, 22 February 2019. https://www.taiwantoday.tw/news.php?unit=2,6,10,15,18&post=150370

Taylor, Catherine A., Lauren Hamvas, Janet Rice, Denise L. Newman, and William DeJong. "Perceived Social Norms, Expectations, and Attitudes Toward Corporal Punishment Among an Urban Community Sample of Parents." *Journal of uHealth* 88 (2011): 254–269.

Taylor, Nicola, and John Caldwell. "Judicial Meetings With Children: Documenting Practice Within the New Zealand Family Court." *New Zealand Law Review* 2013, no. 3 (2013): 445–464.

Taylor, Nicola, Pauline Tapp, and Mark Henaghan. "Respecting Children's Participation in Family Law Proceedings." *International Journal of Children's Rights* 15, no. 1 (2007): 61–82.

Tan, Sylvia. "Being Gay (Lesbian or Transgender) in Singapore." *Focus* 65 (2011). https://www.hurights.or.jp/archives/focus/section2/2011/09/being-gay-lesbian-or-transgender-in-singapore.html

Tatlow, Didi Kristen. "China's Harsh Child Discipline, Through the Lens of Domestic Violence." *New York Times*, 9 March 2016. https://www.nytimes.com/2016/03/10/world/asia/china -corporal-punishment-education-discipline.html; http://perma.cc/58F3-N9TR

Te Korowai Ture ā-Whānau. *Final Report of the Independent Panel Examining the 2014 Family Justice Reforms*. Wellington: Ministry of Justice, 2019. https://www.justice.govt.nz/assets/Documents/Publications/family-justice-reforms-final-report-independent-panel.pdf

"Tender Years Doctrine Discussion, KMs Receive Threats." *Radio103*, 12 December 2013. https://103fm.maariv.co.il/programs/Media.aspx?ZrqvnVq=FMGGEH&c41t4nzVQ=EIK&fbclid=IwAR0hcuSLwyhLgzq-_NFgw7X_hRoWOAJ62yAE8VZ0QiN8uEhA-CfUvo-CpRk. [Hebrew].

Testa, Mark F. "New Permanency Strategies for Children in Foster Care." In *Child Welfare Research: Advances for Practice and Policy*, edited by Duncan Lindsey and Aron Shlonsky, 108. New York: Oxford University Press, 2008.

Testa, Mark F. "The Quality of Permanence—Lasting or Binding? Subsidized Guardianship and Kinship Foster Care as Alternatives to Adoption." *Virginia Journal of Social Policy and Law* 12 (2005): 499.

Testa, Mark F., and Jennifer Miller. "Evolution of Private Guardianship as a Child Welfare Resource." In *Child Welfare for the 21st Century: A Handbook of Practices, Policies, and Programs*, edited by Gerald P. Mallon and Meg McCartt Hess, 405. New York: Columbia University Press, 2005.

Tex. Bus. & Com. Code Ann. § 26.01(b)(3).

Tex. Fam. Code Ann. § 2.401 (West 2005), Invalidated by Ranolls v. Dewling, 223 F. Supp. 3d 613, 623.

The Bangkok Rules, Rules 57, 58; U.N. General Assembly. "United Nations Standard Minimum Rules for Non-Custodial Measures (The Tokyo Rules): Resolution/ Adopted by the General Assembly." *United Nations*, April 1991. https://www.refworld.org/docid/3b00f22117.html

The Body Shop International and United Nations Children's Fund. *Behind Closed Doors: The Impact of Domestic Violence on Children*. UNICEF, 2009. https://www.unicef.org/protection/files/BehindClosedDoors.pdf

The Coalition for Children and Family in Israel. http://ccfisrael.org/israel_fathers_rights_news/; http://ccfisrael.org/ (accessed 15 December 2019).

"The Global Initiative to End All Corporal Punishment." https://endcorporalpunishment.org/ (last visited 31 October 2018).

"The Parental Rights Amendment—Parental Rights." https://parentalrights.org/amendment/ (accessed 22 September 2020).

"The Positive Impact of Prohibition of Corporal Punishment on Children's Lives: Messages From Research." *Global Initiative to End All Corporal Punishment*, June 2015. http://endcorporalpunishment.org/wp-content/uploads/research/Summary-of-research-impact-of-prohibition.pdf

The Ruth and Emanuel Rackman Center for the Advancement of Women's Status. "The Ruling in DAR 919/15 Roe v. Doe: Presentation and Analysis." September 2017. https://bit.ly/2FceQhZ. [Hebrew].

The Torture Victims Protection Act (TVPA), Pub. L. 102-256, 106 Stat. 73 (1992).

The United Nations. *Universal Declaration of Human Rights*, Article 16.3, 1948.

Tibon, Yair. "Every Son That is Born You Must Throw Into the Nile." *News1: First Class*, 15 April 2008. http://www.news1.co.il/Archive/003-D-29038-00.html. [Hebrew].

Tobin, Brian. "Marriage Equality in Australia and Ireland: Separate Jurisdictions, Similar Politics." *Australian Journal of Family Law* 32, no. 3 (September 2019): 294–312.

Tobin, Brian. "The Regulation of Cohabitation in Ireland: Achieving Equilibrium Between Protection and Paternalism?" *Journal of Social Welfare and Family Law* 35, no. 3 (June 2013): 279–289.

Tobin, John. "Donor-Conceived Individuals and Access to Information About Their Genetic Origins: The Relevance and Role of Rights." *Journal of Law and Medicine* 19, no. 4 (2012): 742–757.

Tobin, John. "Judging the Judges: Are They Adopting the Rights Approach to Matters Involving Children?" *Melbourne University Law Review* 33, no. 2 (2009): 579–625.

Tobin, John, and Florence Seow. "Art.18 Parental Responsibilities and State Assistance." In *The UN Convention on the Rights of the Child: A Commentary*, edited by John Torbin. Oxford: Oxford University Press, 2019.

Tomer, Zarhin. "Family Judges Complain of Growing Threats From Parents." *Haaretz*, 29 August 2012. https://www.haaretz.co.il/news/law/1.1811594. [Hebrew].

Towle, Helena. *Disability and Inclusion in Canadian Education: Policy, Procedure, and Practice*. Canada: Canadian Centre for Policy Alternatives, 8 July 2015.

Trinder, Liz. "Competing Constructions of Childhood: Children's Rights and Children's Wishes in Divorce." *Journal of Social Welfare and Family Law* 19, no. 3 (1997): 291–305.

Turner, Susan M. *Something to Cry About: An Argument Against Corporal Punishment of Children in Canada*. Ontario: Wilfrid Laurier University Press, 2002.

Twining, William. "Normative and Legal Pluralism: A Global Perspective." *Duke Journal of Comparative and International Law* 20 (2010): 473–517.

Tzameret, Hagar, Naomi Chazan, Hanna Herzog, Yulia Basin, Ronna Brayer-Garb, and Hadass Ben Eliyahu. *Gender Index 2018: Gendered Inequality in Israel.* Jerusalem, Israel: The Van Leer Jerusalem Institute, 2018. https://bit.ly/2IS4k1e (accessed 12 March 2020). [Hebrew].

Tzimoki, Tova. "A History: Recently a Female Qadi Appointed in the Sharia Court." *Ynet*, 25 April 2017. https://www.ynet.co.il/articles/0,7340,L-4953581,00.html. [Hebrew].

Umar, Ayesha. "Assessing Social Inclusion Through Transgender Legal Reforms in Pakistan." Forthcoming, 7 October 2018. https://papers.ssrn.com/sol3/papers.cfm?abstract_id=3433495 (accessed 19 February 2020).

UNDP and USAID. "Being LGBT in Asia: Mongolia Country Report: A Participatory Review and Analysis of the Legal and Social Environment for Lesbian, Gay, Bisexual and Transgender (LGBT) Persons and Civil Society." Bangkok. 2014. https://www.undp.org/content/dam/rbap/docs/Research%20&%20Publications/hiv_aids/rbap-hhd-2014-blia-mongolia-country-report.pdf

U.N. General Assembly. "United Nations Rules for the Treatment of Women Prisoners and Non-Custodial Measures for Women Offenders (the Bangkok Rules): Note/By the Secretariat." United Nations. October 2010. https://www.refworld.org/docid/4dcbb0ae2.html

UNICEF. "Child Poverty and COVID-19." June 2020. https://data.unicef.org/topic/child-poverty/covid-19/

UNICEF. "Child Protection and COVID-19." April 2020. https://data.unicef.org/topic/child-protection/covid-19/

UNICEF. "The Right of Children With Disabilities to Education: A Rights-Based Approach to Inclusive Education." Switzerland. 2012.

UNICEF. *The State of the World's Children 2006: Excluded and Invisible*. New York: UNICEF, 2005.

Unif. Marriage and Divorce Act § 209 (Unif. Law Comm'n 1973).

United Nations. "Convention on Consent to Marriage, Minimum Age for Marriage and Registration of Marriages." November 1962.

United Nations. "What is Poverty?" https://www.un.org/en/sections/issues-depth/poverty/

United Nations Children's Fund. *Structural Violence Against Children in Southeast Asia.* Kathmandu: UNICEF, 2018. https://www.unicef.org/rosa/sites/unicef.org.rosa/files/2018-08/SVACS%20report%28web%29August%202.pdf

United Nations Committee on Economic, Social and Cultural Rights (UNCESCR). "CESCR General Comment No. 5: Persons with Disabilities (E/1995/22)." 9 December 1994.

United Nations Committee on Economic, Social and Cultural Rights (UNCESCR). "CESCR General Comment No. 14: The Right to the Highest Attainable Standard of Health (Art.12) (E/C.12/2000/4)." 11 August 2020.

United Nations Committee on the Rights of the Child. *Day of General Discussion on the Right of the Child to be Heard.* United Nations, 2006. https://www

.ohchr.org/Documents/HRBodies/CRC/Discussions/Recommendations/Recommendations2006.doc

United Nations Committee on the Rights of the Child. *General Comment No 12: The Right of the Child to be Heard. CRC/C/GC/12*. United Nations, 2009. https://www2.ohchr.org/english/bodies/crc/docs/AdvanceVersions/CRC-C-GC-12.pdf

United Nations General Assembly. *United Nations Convention on the Rights of the Child, United Nations Treaty Series* (Vol. 1577, p. 3). New York City: United Nations Treaty Collection, 20 November 1989.

United Nations International Covenant on Civil and Political Rights. *United Nations Treaty Series* (Vol. 999, p. 171 and Vol. 1057, p. 407). New York City: United Nations Treaty Collection, 16 December 1966.

United Nations International Covenant on Economic, Social and Cultural Rights. *United Nations Treaty Series* (Vol. 993, p. 3). New York City: United Nations Treaty Collection, 16 December 1966.

United States v. Carolene Products Company. 1938. 304 U.S. 144 (United States Supreme Court).

Universal Declaration of Human Rights GA Res 217A (III) UN Doc A/810 (10 December 1948).

University of Pennsylvania—African Studies Center, May 11, 1994. "Inaugural Speech, Pretoria [Mandela]." https://www.africa.upenn.edu/Articles_Gen/Inaugural_Speech_17984.html

U.S. Department of Health and Human Services, Office of the Administration for Children & Families, Administration on Children, Youth and Families, Children's Bureau. "Age at Adoption Finalization: October 1, 2010 to September 30, 2011." 2011. https://www.acf.hhs.gov/sites/default/files/cb/final_age2011.pdf

U.S. Department of Health & Human Services, Office of the Administration for Children & Families, Administration on Children, Youth and Families, Children's Bureau. "Foster Care Statistics 2017." 2019. https://www.childwelfare.gov/pubPDFs/foster.pdf

U.S. Department of Health & Human Services, Office of the Administration for Children & Families, Administration on Children, Youth and Families, Children's Bureau. "Synthesis of Findings: Subsidized Guardianship Child Welfare Waiver Demonstrations." 2011. http://www.acf.hhs.gov/sites/default/files/cb/subsidized_0.pdf

U.S. Department of Health & Human Services, Office of the Administration for Children & Families, Children's Bureau. "The AFCARS Report: Interim FY 2003 Estimates as of June 2006." 2006. https://www.acf.hhs.gov/sites/default/files/cb/afcarsreport26.pdf

U.S. Department of Health & Human Services, Office of the Administration for Children & Families, Children's Bureau. "The AFCARS Report: Preliminary FY 2018 Estimates as of August 22, 2019 – No. 26." 2019. https://www.acf.hhs.gov/sites/default/files/cb/afcarsreport26.pdf

U.S. Department of Health & Human Services, Office of the Administration for Children & Families, Children's Bureau. "Trends in Foster Care and Adoption FY

2009-FY 2018." 2019. https://www.acf.hhs.gov/sites/default/files/cb/trends_fostercare_adoption_09thru18.pdf

Utah Code Ann. § 30-1-4.5.

Utley, Tom. "A Straight Couple Whining Because They Can't Have a Civil Partnership? Give Me Strength!" *The Daily Mail*, 5 December 2014.

Valby, Karen. "The Realities of Raising a Kid of a Different Race." *Time*. https://time.com/the-realities-of-raising-a-kid-of-a-different-race/

Valentine, Gill, and Catherine Harris. "Strivers vs Skivers: Class prejudice and the Demonisation of Dependency in Everyday Life." *Geoforum* 53 (May 2014): 84–92.

Van Gysel, Alain-Charles. "La cohabitation légale: quo vadis?" *Revue trimestrielle de droit familial* (May 2015): 9–40.

Van Leer Jerusalem Institute. "Gender Inequalities in Employment, Gender Index 2018: Gendered Inequality in Israel." https://bit.ly/2Fcz3o0 (accessed 12 March 2020). [Hebrew].

VanOrman, Alicia, and Paola Scommegna. "Understanding the Dynamics of Family Change in the United States." July 2016. http://www.prb.org/pdf16/prb-population-bulletin-71.1-complex-families-2016.pdf

Verdier, Pierre. "'Limited Adoption' in France." *Adoption & Fostering* 12, no. 1 (1988): 41–44.

"Victorian Assisted Reproductive Treatment Authority, Annual Reports, 2017/18." https://www.varta.org.au/resources/page/annual-reports

"Victorian Assisted Reproductive Treatment Authority, Annual Reports, 2018/19." https://www.varta.org.au/resources/page/annual-reports

"Vietnam: Positive Step for Transgender Rights." *Human Rights Watch*, 30 November 2015. https://www.hrw.org/news/2015/11/30/vietnam-positive-step-transgender-rights

Villalpando, Fabiola. "Family First Prevention Services Act: An Overhaul of National Child Welfare Policies." *Children Legal Rights Journal* 39, no. 3 (2019): 283–286. https://lawecommons.luc.edu/clrj/vol39/iss3/5

Vite, Sylvain, and Herve Boechat. *A Commentary on the United States Convention on the Rights of the Child: Article 21 Adoption*. Boston: Martinus Nijhoff Publishers, 2008.

Vora, Vishal. "The Continuing Muslim Marriage Conundrum: The Law of England and Wales on Religious Marriage and Non-Marriage in the United Kingdom." *Journal of Muslim Minority Affairs* 40, no. 1 (2020): 148–162.

Waaldijk, Kees. "Others May Follow: The Introduction of Marriage Quasi-Marriage, and Semi-Marriage for Same-Sex Couples in European Countries." *New England Law Review* 38, no. 3 (2003–2004): 569–590.

Waaldijk, Kees. "Small Change: How the Road to Same-Sex Marriage Got Paved in the Netherlands." In *Legal Recognition of Same-Sex Partnerships: A Study of National, European and International Law*, edited by Robert Wintemute and Mads Andenaes, 437–464. Oxford: Hart Publishing, 2001.

Waddington, Lisa, and Carly Toepke. "Moving Towards Inclusive Education as a Human Right: An Analysis of International Legal Obligations to Implement

Inclusive Education in Law and Policy." University of Maastricht Faculty of Law Working Papers, 2014.

Waggoner, Lawrence. "Marriage Is on the Decline and Cohabitation Is on the Rise: At What Point, If Ever, Should Unmarried Partners Acquire Marital Rights?" *Family Law Quarterly* 50, no. 2 (Summer 2016): 215–246.

Wahba al-Zahili. *al-Fiqh al-islamî wa adillatuhu*. Damascus, 1984.

Walby, Sylvia, Jude Towers, Susan Balderston, Consuelo Corradi, Brian Francis, Markku Heiskanen, Karin Helweg-Larsen, Lut Mergaert, Philippa Olive, Emma Kelly, Heidi Stöckl, and Sofia Strid. *The Concept and Measurement of Violence Against Women and Men*. Bristol: Policy Press, Bristol University, 2017.

Wald, Michael S. "Introduction." *University of Michigan Law Reform* 18, no. 4 (1985): 799–804.

Walmsley, Roy. *World Prison Population List*, 11th ed. Institute for Criminal Policy Research, 2015. https://www.prisonstudies.org/sites/default/files/resources/downloads/world_prison_population_list_11th_edition_0.pdf

Warshak, Richard A. "Social Science and Children's Best Interests in Relocation Cases: "Burgess" Revisited." *Family Law Quarterly* 34, no. 1 (Spring 2000): 83–113.

Weinreb, Alex, Dov Chernichovsky, and Aviv Brill. "Israel's Exceptional Fertility." In *State of the Nation Report 2018, Taub Center for Social Policy Studies in Israel*, December 2018. http://taubcenter.org.il/wp-content/files_mf/exceptionalfertility-eng.pdf

Weisbrod, Carol. "The Way We Live Now: A Discussion of Contracts and Domestic Relations." *Utah Law Review* 2 (1994): 777–815.

Weisskopf v Jewish Agency for Israel, Inc., No 12-6844 (SDNY 2013) (On File With Author).

Weitzman, Lenore. "Marriage Contracts." *California Law Review* 62, no. 4 (1974): 1169–1258.

Weitzman Lenore J. *The Divorce Revolution: The Unexpected Social and Economic Consequences for Women and Children in America*. New York: Free Press, 1987.

Welfare Reform and Work Act 2016.

West, Elliott. *Growing Up with the Country: Childhood on the Far Western Frontier*. New Mexico: University of New Mexico Press, 1989.

West, Robin. "Religious Rights as Protected Wrongs: The Case of Homeschooling." (Unpublished Manuscript, On File With Author), 2013.

"What is Joint Custody?" *Rotenberg Law Firm*. https://rotenberglaw.co.il/What-Is-Joint-Custody? (accessed 30 December 2019).

Whittle, Stephen. "Sensible Policy, Excellent Practice: Challenging the 'Common Sense' of Legal Recognition for Transsexual People." Forthcoming. http://e-space.mmu.ac.uk/617329/12/Sensible%20Policy%20v8-final-sw%20(2).pdf (accessed 26 February 2020).

Wierzbicki, Michael. "Psychological Adjustment of Adoptees: A Meta-Analysis." *Journal of Clinical Child Psychology* 22, no. 4 (1993): 447–454.

Wilcox, Bradford, and Nicholas Wolfinger . *Soul Mates: Religion, Sex, Love, and Marriage Among African Americans and Latinos*. New York: Oxford University Press, 2016.

Wiley, Mary O., and Amanda Baden. "Birth Parents in Adoption: Research, Practice, and Counseling Psychology." *The Counseling Psychologist* 33, no. 1 (2005): 13–50.

Wilkinson, Sue, and Celia Kitzinger. "In Support of Equal Marriage: Why Civil Partnership Is Not Enough." *Psychology of Women Review* 8, no. 1 (Spring 2006): 54–57.

Willems, Geoffrey. "Registered Partnerships in Belgium." In *The Future of Registered Partnerships—Family Recognition Beyond Marriage?*, edited by Jens M. Scherpe and Andy Hayward, 381–408. Cambridge: Intersentia, 2017.

Williams, Joan C., Jodi Short, Margot Brooks, Hilary Hardcastle, Tiffanie Ellis, and Rayna Saron. "What's Reasonable Now? Sexual Harassment Law After the Norm Cascade, 2019." *Michigan State Law Review* 139 (2019): 139–224.

Williams-Mbengue, Nina. "Family First: Federal Child Welfare Law." *National Conference of State Legislatures* 27, no. 24 (2019): 1–2. www.ncsl.org; https://www.ncsl.org/research/human-services/family-first-implementing-landmark-federal-child-welfare-law.aspx

Wilson, William. *When Work Disappears: The World of the New Urban Poor.* New York: Vintage Books, 1996.

Winkler, Robin, and Margaret Van Keppel. *Relinquishing Mothers in Adoption: Their Long-Term Adjustment.* Melbourne, Australia: Institute of Family Studies, 1984.

Wisso, Therese, and Helena Johansson. "Transferring Custody From Birth Parents to Foster Parents—An Ambiguous Matter." *Journal of Social Welfare and Family Law* 40 (2018): 321–339.

Witte, John. "The Nature of Family, the Family of Nature: The Surprising Liberal Defense of the Traditional Family in the Enlightenment." *Emory Law Journal* 64 (2015): 591–676.

Wolfgram, Susan M. "Openness in Adoption: What We Know So Far – A Critical Review of the Literature." *Social Work* 53, no. 2 (2008): 133–142.

Woodhouse, Barbara B. "Recognizing Children's Rights Lessons From South Africa." *S.P.G. Human Rights* 26, no. 2 (Spring 1999): 15–18.

Woodhouse, Barbara Bennett. "The Constitutionalization of Children's Rights: Incorporating Emerging Human Rights into Constitutional Doctrine." *University of Pennsylvania Journal of Constitutional Law* 2, no. 1 (December 1999): 1–52. https://scholarship.law.upenn.edu/jcl/vol2/iss1/1

World Bank. "Women, Business and the Law 2019: A Decade of Reform." 2019. https://openknowledge.worldbank.org/bitstream/handle/10986/31327/WBL2019.pdf?sequence=4&isAllowed=y

World Health Organization. "Addressing Violence Against Children, Women and Older People During the Covid-19 Pandemic: Key Actions." 18 June 2020. https://www.who.int/publications-detail-redirect/WHO-2019-nCoV-Violence_actions-2020.1

World Health Organization. "Changing Cultural and Social Norms Supportive of Violent Behavior." 2009. https://www.who.int/violence_injury_prevention/violence/norms.pdf

World Health Organization. "Disability, Including Prevention, Management and Rehabilitation (WHA 58.23)." 25 May 2005.

World Health Organization. "Violence Prevention Alliance, Definition and Typology of Violence." https://www.who.int/violenceprevention/approach/definition/en/

World Health Organization. "World Report on Disability." 2011.

Xu, Shunqing, and Yuanyuan Li. "Beware of the Second Wave of COVID-19." *The Lancet* 395, no. 10233 (25 April 2020): 1321–1322.

Yi, Beh Lih. "Taiwan Mulls Third Gender Option on Passports, IDs." *Reuters*, 16 January 2018. https://www.reuters.com/article/taiwan-lgbt/taiwan-mulls-third-gender-option-on-passports-ids-idUSL8N1O61JZ

Yi, Horim, Winston Luhur, and Taylor N. T. Brown. "Public Opinion of Transgender Rights in South Korea." *Williams Institute*, December 2019. https://williamsinstitute.law.ucla.edu/wp-content/uploads/South-Korea-English-Dec-2019.pdf

Young, Katharine G. *The Future of Economic and Social Rights*. Cambridge: Cambridge University Press, 2019.

Yulius, Hendri, and Indonesia at Melbourne. "Sex or Gender? Aming's Challenge." *Coconuts Jakarta*, 24 June 2016. https://coconuts.co/jakarta/features/sex-or-gender-amings-challenge/

Zackin, Emily J. *Looking for Rights in All the Wrong Places: Why State Constitutions Contain America's Positive Rights*. Princeton: Princeton University Press, 2013.

Z. H. and R. H. v. Switzerland, no. 60119/12, ECHR 2015.

Zill, Nicholas. "The Changing Face of Adoption in the United States." *Institute of Family Studies (Blog)*, 8 August 2017. https://ifstudies.org/blog/the-changing-face-of-adoption-in-the-united-states

"2012 (4) BCLR 329 (CC) (11 January 2012)." SAFLII. http://www.saflii.org/za/cases/ZACC/2012/1.html (South Africa) (accessed 30 October 2020).

"2016 Census, Statistics Canada." August 2017. https://www150.statcan.gc.ca/n1/daily-quotidien/170802/dq170802a-eng.html

42 U.S.C. §§ 671, 673, 675.

Index

About the Contributors

Victor Asal is the director of the Center for Policy Research and a professor of political science in Rockefeller College at the University at Albany, State University of New York. His research focuses on non-state actor violence and the causes of political discrimination particularly related to ethnicity, sexuality, and gender. He has been involved in research projects funded by the Defense Advanced Research Projects Agency, Defense Threat Reduction Agency, Department of Homeland Security, National Science Foundation, and Office of Naval Research.

Elizabeth Bartholet is the Morris Wasserstein Professor of Law (Emeritus) and founding Faculty Director of the Child Advocacy Program at Harvard Law School. She has specialized in civil rights and family law, particularly child welfare, adoption, and reproductive technology. Her recent publications explore a variety of family law topics including child welfare, child rights, and education.

Melissa L. Breger is the President William McKinley Distinguished Professor of Law at Albany Law School. She has been teaching at the law school level for more than 20 years, having started teaching at her alma mater, the University of Michigan Law School. Before teaching, she dedicated her career to helping women, families, and children in New York City. She has published numerous book chapters and law review articles relating to family law, and is a coauthor of the New York Domestic Violence Law treatise, published by Thomson-Reuters-West. She currently teaches Evidence, Family Law, Constitutional Criminal Procedure, Gender and the Law, and Juvenile Law.

Naomi Cahn is the Justice Anthony M. Kennedy Distinguished Professor of Law, Nancy L. Buc '69 Research Professor in Democracy and Equity, and director, Family Law Center, University of Virginia School of Law. She is an expert in family law, trusts and estates, feminist jurisprudence, reproductive technology, and aging and the law. Prior to joining the University of Virginia faculty in 2020, she taught at George Washington Law School, where she twice served as associate dean. With Professor Carbone, she is the coauthor of numerous articles and books. She has also served as the reporter for the Uniform Law Commission Drafting Committee on developing a uniform act on the rights of cohabitants.

June Carbone is the Robina Chair of Law, Science and Technology at the University of Minnesota Law School. She received her JD from the Yale Law School, and her AB from the Woodrow Wilson School of Public and International Affairs at Princeton University. She has written *From Partners to Parents: The Second Revolution in Family Law* (2000), the third, fourth, and fifth editions of *Family Law* with Leslie Harris and the late Lee Teitelbaum (2005, 2009, 2014), *Red Families v. Blue Families* (2010); *Marriage Markets: How Inequality is Remaking the American Family* (2014), both with Naomi Cahn.

Jessica Lynn Corsi is a law lecturer at City, University of London's Law School and the Centre for Violence and Society. Her work takes both a doctrinal and interdisciplinary approach and concerns how law can prevent or eliminate violence and foster equality. She holds a PhD in law and an LLM in public international law from Cambridge University, a JD from Harvard Law School, and a BSFS from Georgetown University's School of Foreign Service. Her forthcoming monograph, *Legality and the Doctrine of Sources in the Creation of International Criminal Law: Rape and other Sexual Crimes*, will be published by Cambridge University Press in 2022.

Michelle Fernando is a senior lecturer in law at the University of South Australia. Her research focuses on how children's voices are heard and represented in family law disputes involving domestic matters and international child abduction. Her recent work ranges from children's objections in Hague Child Abduction Convention proceedings to the applicability of Australian de facto relationship laws to people in nontraditional relationships. She is a coauthor of the 10th edition of the monograph, *Family Law in Australia* (LexisNexis).

Daphna Hacker is a full professor at the Law Faculty and Faculty of Humanities at Tel Aviv University. She is currently heading the NCJW

Women and Gender Studies Program. Her socio-legal research focuses on the intersection of law, families and gender and provides empirical as well as normative insights in relation to singlehood and gender, post-divorce parental arrangements, inheritance conflicts, filial piety toward elder parents, and transnational families. She has published numerous articles in leading legal and socio-legal journals and is the author of three books. Her latest, published by Cambridge University Press in 2017, is titled *Legalized Families in the Era of Bordered Globalization*, and won the best book award by the Law & Society Association.

Andy Hayward is an associate professor at Durham Law School, Durham University, United Kingdom. His research explores from both domestic and comparative law perspectives the legal regulation of adult relationships, in particular, marriage, civil partnership, and cohabitation. He has published widely on the evolution of civil partnerships and with Professor Jens Scherpe, he co-edited *The Future of Registered Partnerships: Family Recognition beyond Marriage?* (Intersentia, 2017).

Mark Henaghan is a professor of law at the University of Auckland in New Zealand, a Barrister and Solicitor of the High Court of New Zealand, and an associate member of the International Academy of Family Lawyers. He is an elected Fellow of the Royal Society of New Zealand for his contribution to the Humanities. He is chairman of the Donald Beasley Institute which specializes in research with people who have disabilities. He focuses on children's rights, relationship property, assisted human reproduction, domestic violence, and child abuse. He has authored more than 150 books and articles on family law.

Sileshi Bedasie Hirko is a Queen Elizabeth II Diamond Jubilee Advanced Scholar and a Post-Doctoral Fellow affiliated with University of Ottawa and Open African Innovation Research Organization (Open AIR) in Canada. For several years, he had worked as an assistant professor at Haramaya University in Ethiopia. His recent book titled *Rethinking Copyright for Sustainable Human Development* explores the complementarities between copyright and higher education in the context of access to knowledge. He has taught family law, and his research interests range from intellectual property and international trade law to human development.

Josh Gupta-Kagan is a professor of law at the University of South Carolina School of Law, where he specializes in legal issues affecting children and families, especially child protection and juvenile justice issues and teaches the Juvenile Justice Clinic and Parents, Children, and the State. Previously, he practiced at the Children's Law Center, a legal services organization in Washington, DC devoted to a wide range of children's legal issues. His scholarship has appeared in the *Stanford Law Review*, *University of Chicago Law Review*, *Fordham Law Review*, and *Journal of Empirical Legal Studies*, among other law journals. He received his bachelor's degree from Yale College and his JD from the New York University School of Law, where he was a Root-Tilden-Kern Public Interest Scholar.

Fiona Kelly is the dean of La Trobe University Law School, Melbourne, Australia. Her research often combines family law and health law, with a particular focus on the legal regulation of assisted reproduction. She has published in a variety of journals on topics including the judicial treatment of donor-conceived families and autonomous motherhood.

Deseriee Kennedy is a professor of law at Touro Law Center. Previously, she was a tenured member of the faculty at the University of Tennessee College of Law. She teaches civil procedure, family law, domestic violence, public health law, and racism and the law. Her scholarship involves the intersection of family law, criminal justice, poverty, and race. She has published numerous book chapters and law review articles, and is a coauthor of a treatise on New York Domestic Violence Law which is updated yearly and published by Thomson-Reuters-West. A former Freedman Fellow at Temple Law School, she has a BA from Lehigh University and a JD from Harvard Law School.

Nahas Mahieddin is a research member of the Research Laboratory on the Rights of the Child and the Family in Algeria. He was previously faculty of Law and Political Science where he taught legal studies at the University of Oran 2, and former director of the Children's Rights Laboratory. He was also the former director of the Institute of Law and Administrative Sciences, and the Center for Research and Information in Social and Human Sciences at the University of Oran Es Sénia.

Yeshwant Naik is a senior researcher at the Faculty of Law, Westfälische Wilhelms-Universität Münster, Germany. Previously, he was an assistant professor of law at GR Kare College in Goa, India. He holds an LLM from Goa University and a PhD in law from the Westfälische Wilhelms-Universität Münster. After being awarded a fellowship by the Fritz Thyssen Stiftung in 2018, his research came to focus upon discrimination among gay men. His most recent monograph was published by Springer in 2021. He has also published in the fields of comparative and constitutional law and human rights with a focus on LGBTIQ+ rights.

Malinda L. Seymore is a professor of law at Texas A&M University School of Law. Her areas of expertise include adoption, criminal law, criminal procedure, and evidence. She teaches classes on her areas of interest as well as a women and the law course. Her most recent articles dive into adoption, abortion, and fatherhood.

Lucy Sorensen is an assistant professor of Public Administration and Policy in the Rockefeller College of Public Affairs and Policy at University at Albany, State University of New York. Her research focuses on the intersection of education policy, human development, and social inequality. She received her PhD in public policy and MA in economics from Duke University and her BA in economics and East Asian studies from Yale University.

Michael Wells-Greco, solicitor, is an assistant professor in private international law and family law in Europe at Maastricht University and a consultant lawyer to the Permanent Bureau of the Hague Conference on Private International Law. His interests include family law and European Union law, and the protection of the child in international law. His recent research includes a piece on children and inter-country surrogacy arrangements.

Charmaine N. Willis is a PhD candidate in political science at the University at Albany, State University of New York, with specializations in comparative politics and international relations. She graduated with a Master of Arts in International Affairs from American University's School of International Service in 2011 and interned for the US-Korea Institute at Johns Hopkins University while living in Washington, DC. She specializes in East Asian politics, with a focus on the Korean Peninsula, Japan, and the Philippines. Substantively, she researches civil society, social movements, terrorism, and international security. She is also an adjunct professor at the University of Maine.

www.ingramcontent.com/pod-product-compliance
Lightning Source LLC
LaVergne TN
LVHW011701200926
848484LV00004B/1020
* 9 7 8 1 7 9 3 6 1 8 3 5 1 *